CONFLICT IN
NICARAGUA

Other Books by Jiri Valenta

Soviet Intervention in Czechoslovakia, 1968: Anatomy of a Decision (Baltimore: Johns Hopkins University Press, 1979).

Eurocommunism between East and West, coedited with V. Aspaturian and D. Burke (Bloomington: Indiana University Press, 1980).

Soviet Decisionmaking for National Security, coedited with W. Potter (London: Allen & Unwin, 1984).

Grenada and Soviet/Cuban Policy: Crisis and the US/OECS Intervention, coedited with Herbert Ellison (Boulder, Colorado: Westview Press, 1985).

Other Books by Esperanza Durán

Latin America and the World Recession, an edited volume (Cambridge: Cambridge University Press, 1985).

European Interests in Latin America (London: Routledge and Kegan Paul for The Royal Institute of International Affairs, 1985).

Guerra y Revolución. Las grandes potencias y México, 1914−1918 (Mexico, D.F.: El Colegio de Mexico, 1985).

CONFLICT IN
NICARAGUA

A Multidimensional Perspective

Edited by

Jiri Valenta
University of Miami

Esperanza Durán
Royal Institute of International Affairs

Boston
Allen & Unwin
London • Sydney • Wellington

Allen & Unwin, Inc.
8 Winchester Place, Winchester, MA 01890, USA

The U.S. Company of
Unwin Hyman, Ltd

P.O. Box 18, Park Lane, Hemel Hempstead, Herts HP2 4TE, UK
40 Museum Street, London WC1A 1LU, UK
37/39 Queen Elizabeth Street, London SE1 2QB, UK

Allen & Unwin Australia Pty Ltd
8 Napier Street, North Sydney, NSW 2060, Australia

Allen & Unwin (New Zealand) Ltd, in association with
Port Nicholson Press Ltd
Private Bag, Wellington, New Zealand

Library of Congress Cataloging-in-Publication Data

Conflict in Nicaragua.

  Bibliography: p.
  Includes index.
  1. Nicaragua—Politics and government—1979–
2. Frente Sandinista de Liberación Nacional. 3. Geo-
politics—Nicaragua. I. Valenta, Jiri. II. Durán,
Esperanza, 1949–
F1528.C656   1987   972.85′053   87-1108
ISBN 0–04–497033–1 (alk. paper)
ISBN 0–04–497034–X (pbk. : alk. paper)

British Library Cataloguing in Publication Data

Conflict in Nicaragua : a multidimensional
  perspective.
  1. Nicaragua—Politics and government—
  1979–
I. Valenta, Jiri   II. Duran, Esperanza
972.85′053   F1528
    ISBN 0–04–497033–1
    ISBN 0–04–497034–X Pbk

Contents

Foreword

The issue of Nicaragua arouses political passions, those that we see expressed almost daily in the newspapers of Europe, Latin America, and the United States. Few issues are more divisive within the politics of certain countries, and the evolution of the Nicaraguan drama threatens to drive a wedge between countries that are friends, allies, and partners. Although the facets of the problem are diverse and complicated, they are more often expressed in slogans and rhetoric than by dispassionate analysis.

In an effort to promote a rational, constructive dialogue on Nicaragua, the Royal Institute of International Affairs and the Institute of Soviet and East European Studies of the Graduate School of International Studies of the University of Miami held a three-day seminar in London in April 1986. Participants included scholars, government officials, and journalists from European and American countries ranging from Finland to Argentina.

This volume contains the papers presented. The viewpoints represent those who favor a negotiated settlement through the Contadora process, those who espouse the policies of the Reagan administration, and those who analyze the different tendencies of the Nicaraguan democratic opposition-in-exile. One participant from Managua presents a paper representing the views of the Sandinistas. (Members of the Sandinista government were invited to the seminar but chose not to attend, presumably for fear of legitimizing the exiled opposition.)

Of all the international conferences yet held on this topic, this one may go on record as having been the most thorough exploration of the issues without pointless polemics. For this achievement, great credit is due to Dr.

Esperanza Durán of the Royal Institute in London and Professor Jiri Valenta, Director of the Institute of Soviet and East European Studies of the Graduate School of International Studies, University of Miami.

Thanks to their efforts in drawing up and managing a sound program, the seminar participants left the conference with a far better appreciation of the problem—and of one another's viewpoints. That is as much as any international conference can accomplish.

Since the conference, a number of important events have occurred. The U.S. Congress has approved the controversial $100 million aid package to the *contras*. The latter, meanwhile, have reconciled important differences among themselves and now present a more united front to the outside world. The Socialist International, at its June 1986 meeting in the Lima, Peru, admitted members of the Bloque Opositor del Sur (Southern Opposition Front) as observers over the objections of the Sandinista government leaders, who were also observers. The Nicaraguan government has shut down the last opposition newspaper, the prestigious *La Prensa*, and has blocked two key members of the Catholic hierarchy from returning to Nicaragua, actions denounced by the Pope during his June 1986 visit to Colombia. Meanwhile, the Contadora peace efforts remain at an impasse. All these events show a deteriorating situation, making negotiated settlement increasingly remote. They also justify the foresight of the organizers of the conference.

The generosity of the sponsors who made the conference possible have enabled us to share its proceedings with a larger audience. The struggle of forces within and outside Nicaragua engages all the issues of democracy, development, human rights, and national interests that concern the Western democracies. We hope that our academic institutions have contributed to a rational debate of these issues.

AMBLER H. MOSS, JR.

Dean, Graduate School of
International Studies
University of Miami and
former U.S. Ambassador to
Panama (1978–82)

Preface

This, we believe, is a different book on Nicaragua—different not only because it examines the Nicaraguan conflict in the most comprehensive fashion at national, regional, and international levels, but also because the contributors were brought together to foster a dialogue encompassing all points of view regarding the crisis, a dialogue that one observer described as including "different participants in the civil war of Nicaragua."[1] Moreover, the book contains several key documents indispensable to an understanding of the Nicaraguan conflict, above all the full text in English of the 1977 "General Political–Military Platform of the FSLN."

The contributors to the volume surely do not represent a single point of view; nor were they held to a rigid frame of reference. With a free rein to express their own judgments, they were invited to share their ideas as authoritative analysts or actors in the evolving Nicaraguan drama. Their only common starting point was an invitation to consider the Nicaraguan conflict through a number of questions that had been raised in an article by Jiri and Virginia Valenta in *Problems of Communism* (September–October 1985).

Conflict in Nicaragua provides a unique forum, perhaps the only one so far, for an open and balanced discussion of all points of view on the Nicaraguan crisis. One clash of competing opinions comes at the very

---

1. Martii Haikio's report, "A Carrot on a Stick Offered Nicaragua," *Uusi Suomi* (Helsinki, Finland), May 9, 1986.

beginning—between the introduction by U.S. Ambassador Harry Shlaudeman and the immediately following comment by Francisco Villagrán Kramer, a Central American and former vice-president of Guatemala. Shlaudeman reflects the perspective of a chief negotiator in U.S.–Nicaraguan talks between 1984 and 1985, and above all the frustrations of U.S. diplomats in their attempts to find a political solution to the crisis; Villagrán Kramer, though agreeing with Shlaudeman that there is still no consensus among key players about a solution to the crisis, nevertheless appeals for a continuation of the negotiation process among Nicaragua, other Latin American countries, and the United States as the only way to prevent escalation of the conflict.

The book includes chapters by key players in the Nicaraguan opposition, especially Arturo J. Cruz of the United Nicaraguan Opposition (UNO) and Alfredo César of the Southern Opposition Front (BOS), all of whom have impeccable democratic credentials. Repeated efforts to get high-level representation of the FLSN point of view on all aspects of the conflict were frustrated. However, the commentary of Francisco López, head of Nicaragua's Institute of Economic and Social Research in Managua, does elucidate very well the official FSLN position on the origins and consequences of the Nicaraguan conflict. Indeed, López's presence at the London conference, which furnished the papers for this volume, and his eagerness to write a contributing chapter were interpreted by one respected observer as "a willingness for dialogue on the part of Managua."[2]

Finally, the volume contains several documents which are indispensable supplements to Part I and Part II (the roots and internal dimensions of the conflict): the FSLN Program of 1969; the FSLN Platform of 1977; and the Nicaraguan Constitution, drafted in 1986. Also included are documents very relevant to understanding the regional and international dimensions of the conflict (Parts III and IV): the Contadora Act on Peace and Cooperation in Central America of 1986 and a report on a meeting of a secret regional caucus of the Socialist International (SI).

The most significant document published in this book is the 1977 FSLN Platform, a crucial guide to understanding Sandinista policies. To the best knowledge of the editors, this is the first time that the full English text of the platform has appeared in a scholarly volume. Ironically, the platform is not well known among Western scholars and even some leaders of the Nicaraguan democratic opposition. The original Spanish version was virtually unknown even among some U.S. Government analysts as late as 1985. The platform came into the hands of this writer via Ambassador Álvaro Taboada Terán, a former president of the Nicaraguan Christian Socialist Party, an active participant in the anti-Somoza struggle, former FSLN

---

2. Jaime Arias's report in *La Vanguardia* (Barcelona, Spain), May 4, 1986.

ambassador to Ecuador (1980–1982), and currently a Research Associate of the Institute for Soviet and East European Studies (ISEES) at the Graduate School of International Studies (GSIS), the University of Miami. Thanks to him, this document, now part of the ISEES collection, is available to a wider audience of interested scholars and analysts.

Organization

The book is divided into five sections. Part I offers concepts of the Nicaraguan conflict and examines the various interpretations of its origins. Part II treats the internal dimensions of the crisis, questions concerning the regime's legitimacy, and the evolution of FSLN ideological posture and authoritarian structures. Part III deals with the regional aspects of the crisis: FSLN revolutionary interventionism in Central America and the negotiations process between the FSLN regime and neighboring governments in Latin America under the auspices of the Contadora process. Part IV is devoted primarily to the international aspects of the crisis, in particular Soviet, Cuban, and Western European perceptions and policies toward Nicaragua. Part V offers a synthesis of viewpoints and conclusions based on the exchange of ideas presented in the foregoing chapters.

The first chapter, by Jiri and Virginia Valenta, conceptualizes the revolutionary process in Nicaragua by assessing the transformation of the FSLN into a Leninist vanguard party, analyzing Nicaragua's "socialist transformation" socioeconomically and comparing the phenomenon with that in other Leninist or Leninist-oriented regimes. It also provides an overview of the FSLN relationship with the USSR, Cuba, and other communist countries. The Sandinistas have accepted Leninist organizational theory as the leading guide of their movement, and the FSLN has developed strong ideological and military ties with the Soviet Union and Cuba. The "socialist transformation" of Nicaragua continues to proceed very slowly, nevertheless, as the FSLN apparently seeks to avoid for now the excesses of Stalinism. The Valentas conclude that Nicaragua has not yet become a full-fledged Leninist regime but that it clearly is heading in that direction.

The Valenta chapter stimulated commentary by the leader of the Nicaraguan democratic opposition, Arturo J. Cruz, who agrees that the present conflict is rooted in the ongoing Leninization of Nicaragua with the help of Soviet and Cuban advisors. Cruz's conclusions are challenged by FSLN official Francisco López, who argues that regional socioeconomic factors, rather than the Leninist orientation of the FSLN and its support for regional revolution, are at the root of the Nicaraguan problem and that of Central America as a whole. López also sees the Nicaraguan revolution as having strong historical roots, in particular the traditionally alleged hegemonic designs of the United States, which, he argues, have conditioned, if not determined, the ongoing conflict, and, most recently, U.S. "low-intensity warfare strategy" in Nicaragua aimed at undermining the Contadora process. López disagrees with the Valentas' setting the Nicaraguan revolution within the East–West context. In his view, the revolution is exclusively internal; his government has not exported revolution, he insists, nor is it interested in superpower rivalry.

Former FSLN Ambassador to Ecuador Álvaro Taboada argues in his commentary that the present conflict in Nicaragua was mainly determined by long-existing FSLN strategic goals. Practical decisions for achieving these goals were formulated in 1979–1981, when the basic coercive instruments of power were created and institutionalized by the FSLN National Directorate. During that early period, he writes, the hopes and possibilities for eventual democracy were dashed as the repressive power structure of the Sandinista state became clearly Leninist, permitting only a collaborationist position on the part of those in government. Alfredo César, echoing Taboada's views, argues in his brief commentary that the FSLN was pursuing a regressive, internal course while seeking an external *modus vivendi* with the United States, much as Cuba had done earlier. Only effective and multiple pressures by Western democratic forces can reverse this course, according to César.

The two chapters in Part II deal in detail with issues of Nicaraguan internal politics. Professor Margaret Crahan explores the issues of FSLN legitimacy, dissent, human rights, and church/state relations. While critical of the FSLN's human rights policies, Crahan concludes that the Nicaraguan government is legitimate, irrespective of its ideology. In her view, the Nicaraguan government satisfies three important criteria for legitimacy: (1) widespread diplomatic recognition, (2) effective control of the national territory and population, and (3) maintenance of public stability (law and order). Although the government has been defective in meeting two other criteria, fulfillment of international treaty obligations and ensuring respect for the full spectrum of its citizens' human rights, she argues, under present international law the FSLN government is legitimate.

Mr. Arturo Cruz Sequeira, differing at least by implication with some of Crahan's conclusions, insists that the FSLN has so far not learned from its own experience. There exists a huge gap in Nicaragua, Cruz argues, between FSLN ideological dogma and objective Nicaraguan reality. The FSLN underestimated the strength of the *petite bourgeosie* and the traditional values of Nicaraguan society. The academic argument about legitimacy, he insists, cannot hide the fact that the Leninist authoritarian state and its machinery are becoming well entrenched in Managua.

In Part III, Mark Falcoff examines the evolution of FSLN revolutionary interventionism in Central America. The FSLN revolutionary agenda and policies for Central America and the growing Nicaraguan army upset the region's equilibrium; this is a view shared by most Central American leaders. Falcoff, echoing U.S. negotiator Ambassador Shlaudeman, argues that the FSLN does not negotiate in good faith. Contadora was a fragile body held together loosely by an agreement on what should *not* happen, but it had no consensus on common aims. Thus the Contadora process is, in Falcoff's view, not likely to lead to the restoration of regional equilibrium but to a "Central American Yalta."

Dr. Esperanza Durán disagrees, at least implicitly, with some of Falcoff's conclusions about the Contadora process. The motivation of the Contadora principals was not opposition against the United States, she writes. True, the Contadora negotiations ran into a dead end in 1986, but, she insists, the Contadora process is not necessarily finished. It can be revived and remains, in Durán's view, the best vehicle for solving the regional conflict. To revive the process, a new strategy is called for that would include important actors who have not yet participated in the negotiating process. The Contadora negotiations have not focused enough on U.S. regional interests and participation in the conflict, and have almost completely ignored the Nicaraguan opposition groups. For the negotiating process to succeed, argues Durán, the United States must form part of it, and the views of the democratic elements of the resistance must be aired. Nevertheless, Durán argues that the confrontation is essentially one between the United States (the Nicaraguan opposition by its side) and the Sandinista government (supported by the USSR and Cuba) more than one between the Sandinista government and its Central American neighbors.

The focus of the chapter by Professor Vernon Aspaturian is the significance of Nicaragua in Soviet and Cuban strategic calculations and actual Soviet and Cuban policies. Echoing Valenta's view, Aspaturian maintains that there are important similarities between the Leninization process in some East-Central European countries in the late 1940s and the process of socialist transformation in Nicaragua in the 1980s. Though a small country, Nicaragua is not negligible in the Soviet calculus; indeed, its geopolitical location is highly significant. In Aspaturian's estimate, the Soviets would not provide effective military assistance in case of a U.S. invasion of Nicaragua. However, the relationship with Moscow is used effectively by Managua to deter the United States from taking such action.

Minister of State for Intra-German Affairs Ottfried Hennig, of the German Federal Republic, examines the West European relationship with Central America in general and with Nicaragua in particular. He connects Western Europe's increased interest in Central America to fears about the development of a new "Vietnam" quagmire. From a self-interest standpoint, the West European nations cannot be indifferent to the dangers of a conflagration spreading from Nicaragua to the whole of Central America or to the prospects of a strong political–military involvement by the United States in Central America. Thus a coordinated U.S./West European policy should prevent the spreading of the Nicaraguan conflict and its exploitation by the USSR and Cuba. The West European nations, in Hennig's view, should do more to help solve Central American problems and at a minimum not obstruct U.S. policy.

President Reagan's National Security advisor Raymond Burghardt argues in his commentary that the key problem in resolving the Nicaraguan conflict has been the FSLN's obstinance during the bilateral and multilateral negotiations with other Latin American nations and the United States between 1984 and 1985. Reflecting on his own experience as Ambassador Shlaudeman's deputy in U.S.–Nicaraguan negotiations, Burghardt points out that the FSLN's continuous refusal to accept the mechanisms to verify security measures proposed by its Central American neighbors and Nicaragua's insistence on preconditions have been the major factors blocking future negotiations. Agreeing by implication with Durán's argument, Burghardt suggests that the United States would renew bilateral talks if the Sandinistas agreed to negotiate with the democratic opposition inside and outside the country.

The concluding chapter by Jiri Valenta is an attempt to synthesize the previous discussions. The essay certainly does not reflect unanimity of opinion among the contributors but rather the exchanges among the basic schools of thought represented. The various interpretations of the historical roots of the Nicaraguan conflict notwithstanding, the FSLN internal and regional policies have led to an intensification of the crisis. There appears to be a growing consensus about the undemocratic, authoritarian nature of the FSLN regime, although there is still disagreement about FSLN legitimacy and the way to resolve the crisis. On the latter point, there seems to be increasing agreement that neither political accommodation with the present FSLN regime (unacceptable without FSLN concessions on the issue of the democratic Nicaraguan opposition) nor its overthrow by military intervention is an acceptable U.S. policy option. The best alternative available to U.S. policymakers at the time of writing is the continuing application of broad, multiple pressures on the FSLN to force its internal accommodation with the democratic opposition and its abandonment of its revolutionary regional strategy. This option, however, would require a close cooperation of the various branches of the Nicaraguan democratic opposition by the exclusion of Somocista elements, as well as better coordination of long-term policies (including funding) and the commitment to them by the United States. These efforts would need to be supplemented by other measures such as thorough democratization of the resistance forces, effective public diplomacy, and determined efforts by a credible U.S. administration to make Soviet–Cuban security ties with Nicaragua prohibitive.

JIRI VALENTA

Acknowledgments

It was our hope and purpose in organizing the conference at Chatham House in London, England, April 28—May 1, 1986, which gave rise to the present volume, to bring together a broad and balanced range of views to engage in frank and honest analysis of the Nicaraguan conflict. We secured only limited, although very distinguished, official Nicaraguan representation in the person of Dr. Francisco López, Director of the Institute of Economic and Social Studies (INIES) in Managua, whose contribution was most valuable. It was also extremely useful and worthwhile to have had a broad and high-powered group of participants from the Nicaraguan opposition as well as participants from Latin America, the United States, and Europe who engaged in often virulent and always open debate. Frankness and honesty were never lost.

We wish to acknowledge our intellectual debt to Virginia Valenta, who helped to design and organize the project. Her own understanding of Latin American culture, as well as her research and editorial contributions, and above all her encouragement and support, were indispensable. Next, we want to acknowledge our gratitude to a former Nicaraguan ambassador to Ecuador and now a Research Associate in the Institute for Soviet and East European Studies (ISEES) of the University of Miami, Álvaro Taboada Terán, whose dedication to this project was admirable, and to Dr. Sonia Sluzar and Professor Margaret Crahan.

We would also like to acknowledge the support of the dean of the Graduate School of International Studies, former Ambassador to Panama, Ambler H. Moss, Jr., Admiral Sir James Eberle, Director of the Royal

Institute of International Affairs, Royal Institute Director of Studies William Wallace, and the staff both at the Royal Institute of International Affairs and at the Graduate School of International Studies (GSIS) for their helpful support in this enterprise. Lastly we would like to gratefully acknowledge the dedicated assistance of John Cunningham, research assistant at the Institute for Soviet and East European Studies of GSIS.

Finally, we are pleased to acknowledge the generous support, with no strings attached, of several institutions: the Institute for Soviet and East European Studies at the Graduate School of International Studies of the University of Miami, the Royal Institute of International Affairs, the Olin Foundation, the Heritage Foundation, and the United States Information Agency.

ESPERANZA DURÁN   JIRI VALENTA

Introduction

I offer here a few thoughts and pose a few questions based on 2 years of experience with Central American negotiations. In Chapter 12, my colleague Ray Burghardt of the National Security Council discusses more specifically the views and policy of the United States. This book deals with the Nicaraguan phenomenon at three levels: internal, regional, and geopolitical. That framework seems logical to me if we bear in mind that the problem is both regional—that is, an issue engaging all of Latin America—and subregional, or very much a Central American problem. The two are quite different. Concern in Argentina, for example, centers on how the crisis in Central America will affect the shape of that country's internal politics. But the concern in El Salvador is considerably more immediate and pressing; there the problem is one of life or death for a young and hard-pressed democracy.

There is another aspect this book does not treat explicitly: Nicaragua as an issue in U.S. politics. As Mark Falcoff points out in Chapter 8, the debate in our country over Nicaragua is to a considerable degree a debate over much more than Central America. It involves the past, particularly Vietnam, and the future role of our country in the continuing struggle for peace and freedom in the world.

The terms of the debate in the United States, Latin America, and Europe tend to focus us on what we think is a false dichotomy between support for armed resistance to the Sandinista regime and negotiations. There can be no quarrel about the desirability of a negotiated settlement. But we believe that negotiations, to be successful, must be accompanied by effective pressure.

And as far as I see, only the armed resistance applies effective pressure. President Reagan's adversaries generally call for renunciation of the use of force and what they invariably characterize as "serious negotiations." But it is not at all clear what is meant by "serious negotiations." After all, negotiations have been going on for a long time now. The Contadora Process is almost $3\frac{1}{2}$ years old; we have had the experience of the Manzanillo talks—nine sessions of direct discussions between the U.S. and Nicaraguan governments—most of them 2 days in length. Mr. Burghardt and I have traveled about 250,000 miles over the last 2 years in pursuit of what we thought were serious negotiations. To decide whether we have been deceiving ourselves, it would first seem necessary to determine what it is negotiations are supposed to produce—what the parties can reasonably expect to obtain and what they think they must obtain.

If one has listened to the various debates in and out of our Congress, one might well have come away thinking that, despite the emotion and acrimony on display, there is a general consensus, at least in Washington, on what U.S. policy toward Nicaragua should seek to achieve. Most of those rising against the president's policy appear to agree with the president, for example, that the goals of that policy should include democratization in Nicaragua, an end to the military—security ties between Nicaragua and the Soviet Union, a reduction in Nicaraguan arms and troop levels, and the cessation of Sandinista support for subversion.

The argument, then, has so far been more about means than goals. But if there is a rough consensus in Washington on objectives, at least a consensus in terms of what is said publicly, then it becomes particularly important for those who dispute the means being employed to try to answer the question of what negotiations can reasonably be expected to produce under varying conditions—with or without pressure, with what kind of pressure, and the like. That would seem to be a sensible context in which to discuss the issue. My own view is that the administration's diplomatic or negotiating record can be judged inadequate or nonserious only if one thinks the four announced objectives of the president's policy are mistaken. Put another way, that means saying, up front, that one is willing to settle for less, how much less, and with what consequences. Those who disagree with our objectives, as well as our means, as some of the contributors to this volume presumably do, should still be clear on what they expect negotiations to produce and to what extent the results would meet the requirements for peace and security of those affected by the crisis in Central America, including the United States. That in turn calls for a close look at the negotiating record—a record that in my experience gets very little attention from those who contest the administration's policy.

In remarks about negotiations, it seems to me that the first questions are who should negotiate and what should they negotiate about. The bill on aid to the Nicaraguan resistance our Senate recently passed called for the establishment of a congressional commission to monitor no less than five separate sets of putative negotiations: the Contadora process, negotiations among the Central Americans themselves, bilateral U.S.–Nicaraguan talks, negotiations between the Sandinistas and the armed and unarmed resistance, and dealings between Duarte and the FMLN. That is a lot of negotiating parties.

Contadora alone now involves 13 governments directly and others, including my own, indirectly. We still believe Contadora is the correct forum. The issues in Central America are tightly interlocked. A comprehensive agreement is therefore required. The Contadora process in its Document of Objectives has defined the terms of such an agreement in what we believe are entirely satisfactory terms. The natural tendency when the process is frustrated, as it has been for a number of months now, is to look for partial, bilateral solutions, as in the ongoing negotiations between Costa Rica and Nicaragua on their border problems. Given the close interrelationship of the issues, we have to ask what effect partial agreements would have on the chances for an overall settlement. I think it would not be a positive effect. In any case, for our part we are highly adverse to the substitution of cosmetics for substance. Central America is littered with the bones of dead and useless treaties, rhetorical exercises that produced more troubles than remedies.

Although attempts to promote partial, bilateral agreements threaten the Contadora process, there is a role for negotiations outside the Contadora format. The Contadora Document of Objectives itself calls for national reconciliation where internal conflicts exist. By necessity that would mean a negotiated internal settlement in Nicaragua—one that would assure the democratic liberties Contadora also calls for. I find one of the more striking aspects of the Sandinistas' policy their vehement rejection of what they call "symmetry." What that means, in this curious formulation of theirs, is that President Duarte must negotiate a settlement with the FMLN if there is to be peace in El Salvador; but that in the case of Nicaragua, internal negotiations are neither required nor possible.

A number of Central American leaders I have talked to would like to find a way to negotiate an overall settlement among the five themselves, without leaving it to outsiders to propose solutions. The Central American chiefs of state met at the mountain town of Esquipulas in May 1986. Perhaps this will lead to a new regional approach. But we must remember that all previous efforts to promote direct negotiations among the five have failed. They have failed quite simply because the Sandinistas have not been willing to negotiate seriously with their neighbors.

As for Nicaraguan–U.S. bilateral negotiations, the Nicaraguan government keeps saying it wants to negotiate with what Comandante Borge delicately calls "the monster" and Foreign Minister D'Escoto calls "the master of the dogs." But I ask, what are we supposed to negotiate? If the Sandinistas continue to refuse to negotiate regional issues within Contadora, as they have since June 1985, and if they refuse to discuss the Contadora drafts with us, as they did at Manzanillo, and if they reject any talks with the armed resistance, what is there for the U.S. and Nicaraguan governments to talk about? One answer might be that there is the question of U.S. respect for, and adherence to, a regional agreement, if one were concluded. We have said repeatedly, most recently in a letter to the Congress by my successor, that as a matter of policy we will support and abide by a comprehensive, verifiable, and simultaneous implementation of the Contadora Document of Objectives as long as the Sandinistas are complying. Anyone who knows our political system knows that that would have to be the case regardless. No negotiation—no separate protocol—is required for the purpose. That was a point I kept trying to explain to Vice-Minister Tinoco at Manzanillo.

One illustration of what I am talking about when I urge a close look at the negotiating record is the issue of limitations on arms and troop levels in the area. The three Contadora draft treaties, or *actas*, tabled so far all provide for negotiations on such limits after signature. There are surely few among us who would not advocate an end to the military buildup and reductions in military levels in Central America. Contadora's strongest advocates, at least in the United States, often point to what they call demilitarization as a particularly significant objective of the process. Yet it is not at all clear to me, from what I know of the negotiating record, that the Nicaraguan government has ever been willing to commit itself to the concept of a reduction of military levels or to the goal of a reasonable military equilibrium in Central America. In fact, remarks Father D'Escoto made to the press on his return from the last meeting in Panama appeared to indicate the contrary—that Nicaragua would not give up its military buildup whatever the United States might do about support for the *contras*. Perhaps the minister did not mean to give that impression, and perhaps there is something on the negotiating record I am not aware of. But it is difficult to ignore the fact that a heavy degree of militarization as a means of social mobilization and control has been a key component of the Cuban model. And it is the Cuban model the Sandinistas are clearly following.

Related to this issue is a problem Contadora has grappled with from the begining, but not very successfully. That is the problem of simultaneity. Contadora's second draft *acta*—the September 7, 1984, draft that Nicaragua professed to accept—illustrates the issue. In an unusual but not entirely unreasonable approach, the Contadora group has sought to have key provisions of the treaty they seek to fashion come into force on signature rather than awaiting ratification. In Latin America, as in the United States, ratification can be an uncertain process. There are all too many instances in Latin American history of important agreements signed but never ratified. The September 7 draft would have accomplished two major Sandinista objectives on signature: end of support and safe haven for the armed Nicaraguan resistance and a flat prohibition on international military maneuvers in Central America. But the draft would have left dangling for later and most uncertain negotiation the issue of arms and troop limits.

The latest Contadora version of an overall agreement establishes complicated procedures under which commitments would again come into force on signature, but this time for most part only provisionally. If negotiations did not succeed—and I fear they might not—all commitments would lapse except those on cutting off outside aid to irregular/insurrectional forces. The result would be to leave us exactly where we are, except that the Nicaraguan armed resistance would be deprived of outside aid while the Sandinistas would have undertaken an unverifiable commitment to end support for subversion in neighboring countries. (Such commitments are obviously self-enforcing in democracies. They are no such thing in totalitarian states.) The appropriate remedy would be to provide for negotiation of all the security issues prior to signature. The fact that the governments of the Contadora group do not propose it suggests to me that they are as dubious, given the Nicaraguan position, about the prospects for successful negotiations on military levels, under present conditions, as I am.

Finally, there is a broader question that has preoccupied me since I first became entangled in these issues. That has to do with the internationalism, in the Marxist–Leninist sense, of the *Frente Sandinista*. It really seems to me the central issue. I remember at one point during the Manzanillo talks I received a press note quoting Nora Astorga, in Ethiopia of all places, as pledging *Sandinismo* to "international proletarian solidarity." I said to Vice-Minister Tinoco that the phrase had a very clear and ominous meaning for me, one that called into question the utility of the talks we were conducting. Tinoco responded to the effect that perhaps I did not understand what was meant. I am afraid that I did understand, all too well. At another point in the talks the Nicaraguan delegation volunteered to us that a commitment they were offering, under certain conditions with respect to the nonuse of their territory for the support of insurgencies in neighboring countries, would not extend to their right to admit onto their territory, as they might choose, citizens of other Central American nations. We had not raised the need for such a denial, and the volunteered statement seemed to be intended to convey a message. I suspect the message was that we could not expect the Sandinistas to concede the principle of revolutionary solidarity in the form of continuing political support and safe haven for Central America's fellow revolutionaries. The import of that for the long term and for the reliability of any agreement not subject to rigorous verification is obvious.

Mark Falcoff discusses the *Frente's* internationalism in greater detail in Chapter 8. In particular he refers to David Nolan's monograph on the ideology of Sandinismo. Certainly I come away from reading the record Nolan lays out—and the one Jiri and Virginia Valenta present in their excellent piece—with the sense that along with Fidel Castro, the leaders of *Sandinismo* believe that the duty of the revolutionary is to make the revolution—and to make it wherever and whenever he can. That has led some of us to the conclusion that democratization in Nicaragua is every bit as much a security issue as it is a political and moral issue. If, however, the rhetoric of *Sandinismo* is not to be taken seriously, it is important we understand why—why we can safely ignore the programs and pronouncements of a quarter of a century, from Carlos Fonseca on.

HARRY W. SHLAUDEMAN

U.S. Ambassador to Brazil,
former U.S. special envoy
for Central America
(1984–1986)

A Comment on the Crisis in Central America

The events in Nicaragua that culminated in the downfall of the Somoza dynasty and the collapse of the National Guard after the Sandinista triumph in 1979 paved the way for profound and fundamental changes in that country. A few months later, armed confrontations exploded in El Salvador and Guatemala. Though these incidents, like the events in Nicaragua, had been taking shape for a decade, by 1980 the focus of the crisis widened as external actors appeared, some directly and others backstage.

More recently Honduras has found itself drawn into the turmoil. There the conflicts in bordering zones with Nicaragua (as well as the conflicts of Nicaragua with Costa Rica) are much less reflective of a spillover effect from the Nicaraguan revolution than of the active presence of Nicaraguans and other nationals—counterrevolutionaries better known as *contras*—and the support they receive, under the banner of "freedom fighters," from abroad. Moreover, insurgency and counterinsurgency generate within each country in Central America, or between neighboring countries, different kinds of tensions, thereby making it clear that the crisis, notwithstanding insistence to the contrary, is not necessarily concentrated in Nicaragua or El Salvador. Thus it is pertinent to clarify the regional dimension and the international implications of the crisis from a Central American perspective.

The perspective that countries outside the area have of the geopolitical space also influences the Central American outlook. The United States places the region in a broad geostrategic context. Hence, the concept of the Caribbean Basin, and the fact that the United States dispatches its land, air, and sea forces with a frequency it feels is necessary to its objectives. The

Soviet Union, in turn, makes its presence felt in a restrained manner at the diplomatic level in Costa Rica and Panama, whereas in Nicaragua it exercises its right to support, assist, and cooperate with the Sandinistas, without going so far as to give the impression that it wishes to confront the United States in Central America.

The ideological content of the Central American crisis is not ignored by the South American countries. It is perceived that the radical forces of the right in Central America look to the current U.S. government as their ally and protector; and believe that it is up to that government to solve the fundamental problems of the region. In their view the source of regional conflict can be found in Nicaragua, not in El Salvador or Guatemala. Right-wing forces in the region perceive that a return to the status quo prevailing before 1979 is the most desirable course. In order to reestablish it, the United States is called on to preserve stability and facilitate a return to "controllable models."

For sectors of the radicalized left, "North American imperialism" stifles the course of national and popular revolutions. Therefore, the presence of the Soviet Union and Cuba in Nicaragua, although it introduces risk factors, serves nevertheless as a counterweight to the U.S. influence (a belief also not unknown to the Soviet Union).

Since the dissolution in 1838 of the Federation of United Provinces of Central America, reestablishment of the Federation has been an aspiration of the region's political leadership (although less on the part of Costa Rica than the other countries). Active communication between political parties and movements, ideological solidarities, and increasing economic links have created a pattern of relations. Thus, in Central America, intervention by one government in the internal affairs of another, or support for political factions seeking to overthrow a government, have not been considered gross violations of the rule of law, provided no external power sponsors such activity.

The most important effort in the current century was the establishment of the Central America Common Market and a limited customs union in the late 1950s. These in turn increased links between the countries and created strong social and cultural interrelations. An important practice developed whereby the nonrecognition of a government did not restrict its participation in the different institutional mechanisms—among them, the Councils of Ministers and Vice-Ministers of Economy, Finance, Agriculture, and Health and of the governors of the Central Banks. Even with a break in diplomatic relations, there has remained enough flexibility to permit normal intercourse between countries, as was true in Honduras and El Salvador during the 1970s. Consequently, interdependence is a fact that is not overlooked by governments; not least because it is considered that the countries of the region, separately, are no longer viable in an increasingly interdependent world. The region's unity is imperative if it is to contribute to some sort of area development and the welfare of the Central American people. Disruptions in relations, links, and common objectives serve no regional or national purpose other than to preserve underdevelopment.

These factors have led to the functional implementation of a two-track policy: On the one hand, governments have had openly to voice their ideological discrepancies, mainly in regard to Nicaragua's *Sandinismo*; but on the other hand they have had to show, in different degrees, their acceptance or reluctance to support U.S. concerns and actions in the region. This has been especially true as their financial dependence on the United States has become greater.

This two-track policy has been followed mainly as a result of apprehensions about the expansion of *Sandinismo* in the region. At the same time, in order to prevent Nicaragua's drifting away from the region's legitimate interests, governments have had to strike a delicate balance between the interests and pressures of the United States as a hegemonic power in the region and the interests of the other countries concerned. In one area of policy, external relations, the Central American countries opened up the initiatives of the Contadora group. At the same time, however, another area of policy, the intraregional economic area, has been kept as domestically pure as possible, in the hope of avoiding external interference. For many Central Americans, it is important, if not vital, that the region manage itself without providing other countries (Mexico, Venezuela, and Cuba in particular) with more leverage than they already have through the actions of Contadora.

A review of the facts allows a better understanding of the effects of the two-track policy. While the Contadora process advances, and successive drafts and modifications are carefully analyzed, open criticism of regional governments, mainly Nicaragua, has been evident. This has created the impression in countries outside the region that existing differences among the Central American countries are profound and practically unsolvable. The fact that one country, Honduras, allows its territory to be used by the *contra* factions as a base for incursions against Nicaragua, while drums of war are heard in the vicinity, gives the impression of hostile neighbors between whom normal relations do not exist.

Since 1980, however, the five governments of Central America have held successive meetings to ensure the survival of the Common Market and even have signed, in late 1984, a new external tariff treaty. Nicaragua is one of the signatories. Together with Panama, the five Central American countries agreed—first in San José, Costa Rica, in September 1984 and then in Luxembourg in November 1985—to establish a common framework for cooperation with the European Community and its member countries. This agreement established the basic rule that no country should be excluded from the benefits of such economic and political cooperation. Also, in 1985 the Youth Peace Olympics were held in Guatemala with the participation of all the countries of the region. Nicaragua's vice-president presided over his country's delegation. Furthermore, the presence of various heads of state at the inaugurations of other elected presidents—as was the case of Presidents Daniel Ortega, Napoleón Duarte, and José Azcona at the inauguration of Vinicio Cerezo—provided limited but useful contacts at the executive level and the opportunity to program other meetings. Among these meetings, the one that took place in Esquipulas in May 1986 (see Glossary) is a perfect example of the importance of these contacts.

The most recent contacts at the highest level have also afforded the Nicaraguan government an opportunity to become aware of the fact that not all the issues raised by the U.S. government are strictly U.S. apprehensions or misgivings; they are shared by other Central American governments. Nicaragua, on its part, has been able to give evidence that it is willing to abide by common rules set up by consensus, but not by U.S. imposition. This perspective is understood and shared by democratic political sectors in the region, although not by the radical right (e.g., Republican National Alliance (ARENA) in El Salvador, National Liberation Movement (MLN) in Guatemala, and important sectors of the Nicaraguan *contras*). Nicaragua has also stressed the point that *Sandinismo* does not see itself excluded from Central America and is therefore willing to engage in fruitful negotiations. This is Nicaragua's position, provided that no restrictions are imposed on its internal structure and its revolutionary course, whose aim is to establish a more just society with a dual or mixed economy, nonalignment, and sufficient capacity to defend itself from external aggression. Nicaragua has then agreed to the constitution of the Central American parliament, whose members are to be elected in free, democratic popular elections.

Basic questions remain to be clarified. Will the U.S. administration accept a Contadora Act negotiated by Central American governments as testimony of an agreement that should also be respected by third parties? Is there a possibility that the United States would adhere to its basic stipulations by way of a protocol, or will the U.S. government consider the Act insufficient? These basic questions, like those concerning the attitudes of the Soviet Union, fall outside the domain of the region's governments.

To understand the U.S. government's reservations and apprehensions, Central American governments and responsible ideological sectors must bear in mind what Cuba has represented, strategically and psychologically, for the United States. In other words, they must understand the fear that a "second Cuba" could occur in the hemisphere. It is this context within which the United States places Nicaragua, and which helps explain the revival of the "domino theory." The problem thus lies in the parameters set by the "first Cuba." These were determined in 1962 by means of an informal agreement between the United States and the Soviet Union, which Cuba reluctantly accepted. Basically, they consisted of the removal of missiles by the Soviet Union, and its commitment that no offensive weapons that could endanger the United States would be installed on Cuban territory. On its part, the United States agreed to respect Cuban territorial integrity and its right to self-determination. Since then, global and regional plans for action and the defense of North America take into consideration "what to do in Cuba."

The factors surrounding the Cuban case are not present in the case of Nicaragua. First, Nicaragua recognizes that it would not be in its interest (or that of other Central American countries, with whom it has to coexist in order to ensure its future economic viability) to accommodate permanent Soviet or Cuban military installations. Second, such actions would destroy all possibility of an eventual compromise with the United States, as well as the negotiations of Contadora, which are important for Nicaragua. Finally, the Soviet Union, strategically and technologically, does not require military installations in a Central American country. If those reasons are known to the United States, and the Cuban case is not about to be repeated, the question arises: what other elements obstruct U.S. acceptance of the Contadora principles and proposals, and why are there problems in bilateral relations between the United States and Nicaragua?

The most objective reply can be found in the frequency with which President Reagan and other spokesmen of his administration refer to Nicaragua when appealing to the U.S. Congress to back their policies in the region. These references trouble Central Americans because they have complicated the course of negotiations sponsored by Contadora. In 1985 President Reagan made frequent formal and informal declarations stating that it is not only the ideology and internal structure of Nicaragua's government that concern the United States but also the nature of its relations with the Soviet Union and Cuba. His support for the *contras* reveals that Nicaragua has progressively become an external issue as well as a domestic political one. Nevertheless, the president has persisted in the basic approach made on April 4, 1985, when he proposed internal negotiations between all *contra* factions and the Sandinistas, with the Catholic Church playing the role of mediator—an approach consistently rejected by Nicaragua. This has been coupled with an appeal to Congress to consent to aid the *contras* without preconditions.

One can add that the Contadora effort has concentrated more on the level of conflict among Central American governments—some of which lack the full power of decision—and less on the conflict between those governments and the ideological sectors within their respective nations. This concern also figures in the United Nations mandate to the group. For instance, Contadora has not been able to pursue the extraordinary efforts of President Napoleón Duarte and the Salvadoran guerrillas, arising out of the meeting in La Palma in 1984. Likewise, the opening of a framework for negotiations in Guatemala and Nicaragua has stumbled on strong resistance from the governments in those two countries, some of which is understandable, but which might be placed in a different perspective in light of, for example, the recent experience of government-guerrilla negotiations in Colombia.

From a Latin American perspective, the conclusion is, then, not only structural but functional. That is, the regional dimension of the crisis does not allow it to be settled by a return to the models of 1907, 1923, or 1954, when inter-Central American treaties were signed in Washington, or on board North American warships, or matters were solved with armed intervention. And this is true because, paraphrasing Simón Bolívar, for too long Central Americans have sown in the sea, and in so doing, they have lacerated the land and its best men. Today, they do not sow but they face combat on firm ground. It is time to turn our eyes in the direction of human beings, and their dignity as such, and offer one sole option: peace without repression, development without oppression.

FRANCISCO VILLAGRÁN KRAMER
Former vice-president
of Guatemala

NICARAGUA
CENTRAL AMERICA
AND
THE CARIBBEAN

UNITED STATES

GULF OF MEXICO

BAHAMA ISLANDS

ATLANTIC OCEAN

CUBA

MEXICO

BELIZE

HONDURAS

GUATEMALA
EL SALVADOR

HAITI
JAMAICA
DOMINICAN
REPUBLIC
PUERTO
RICO

LESSER

ANTILLES

CARIBBEAN SEA

NICARAGUA

PACIFIC OCEAN

COSTA
RICA

PANAMA

GRENADA
TRINIDAD & TOBAGO

VENEZUELA

UNIVERSITY OF MIAMI
CARTOGRAPHIC LABORATORY
JEB 86

COLOMBIA

Kilometers
0   300   600

NICARAGUA

DEPARTMENTS AND CAPITAL CITIES

——— International Boundary	★ National Capital
——— Department Boundary	• Internal Administrative Capital

• PART ONE •
Roots of the Crisis

• CHAPTER ONE •

The FSLN in Power

Jiri Valenta and
Virginia Valenta

The Sandinista National Liberation Front (FSLN) toppled the regime of Nicaraguan dicatator Anastasio Somoza Debayle in 1979. Yet even today the FSLN—its road to power, its political complexion and orientation, and its objectives—remains the subject of heated debate. Some still argue that the Sandinista regime is a nationalistic, nonaligned, although radical, Third World government. Others emphasize the Marxist–Leninist overtones characterizing its seizure and consolidation of power, its foreign relations, and its efforts to introduce socialism to Nicaraguan society. The topic is of more than academic interest, for the Sandinistas' increasingly repressive rule has engendered domestic opposition as well as external involvement in the affairs of Nicaragua both by those who support and by those who oppose the regime. This raises fears that the conflict may intensify and spill over into neighboring countries.

In attempting to fathom the nature of the Sandinista regime, we address the following questions: What factors brought about the FSLN insurgency? How did the Front conceive of itself, and what specific road did it follow to victory? To what extent has the FSLN become a Leninist-oriented party? What instruments of control does the FSLN have at its disposal, and how are they employed in dealing with opposition to the regime? What is the nature of relations between Sandinista Nicaragua and the USSR, Cuba, and other communist states? What are the major objectives of the Sandinista program, and what policies has the FSLN employed in efforts to transform Nicaraguan society? In considering these questions, we have drawn from a wide range of FSLN publications and documents, and materials from elsewhere in Central America, from Cuba, and from the Soviet Union; from documents seized in Grenada in autumn of 1983; and from interviews with leaders of the Nicaraguan opposition as well as current and former FSLN members.

The Revolutionary Environment

Nicaragua's geography, history, and socioeconomic conditions all have provided a rich medium for guerrilla warfare. The most significant geographic feature bearing on Nicaragua's history is its close proximity to the United States. Policymakers in the United States traditionally have considered Nicaragua strategically important and therefore have been inclined to intervene, directly and indirectly, in Nicaraguan affairs to protect perceived strategic interests. One concern was the possibility that a foreign power other than the United States might build a trans-isthmus canal on Nicaraguan rather than Panamanian territory. American interventionism has given rise to a certain degree of "Yankeephobia," tempered by feelings of considerable attraction between the two people. Within Nicaragua, the lightly populated northeastern mountains have been the customary place of refuge for guerrilla bands, whether the nationalist forces of General Augusto César Sandino in the late 1920s or the FSLN in the 1960s and 1970s. Sandino's Army for the Defense of National Sovereignty, recruited mainly from the Nicaraguan peasantry but bolstered by volunteers from elsewhere in Latin America, conducted guerrilla operations from 1927 to 1933 against the U.S. Marines, whose return to Nicaragua in 1927 followed similar Marine interventions in that country dating back to 1909.

Despite a subsequent recasting of his image by the FSLN, Sandino was neither a Leninist nor a Marxist nor a socialist; nor was he a pro-Soviet "antiimperialist." Principally, Sandino wanted to expel the U.S. Marines; after they left Nicaragua in 1933, he actually made peace with the Nicaraguan government. True, the Comintern attempted to exploit Sandino's struggle and bring him into the communist fold through his private secretary, Augustín Farabundo Martí, founder of El Salvador's Communist party. But Sandino broke all Comintern connections in 1930 and dismissed Martí from his staff, a "betrayal" denounced by the Comintern.[1]

---

1. Before his execution in 1932, Martí himself stated that Sandino "was unwilling to embrace the communist program that I stood for. He had raised only the flag of independence, of emancipation, while my aim was social revolt." Quoted in Blanca Luz, *Contra la corriente* [Against the Current] (Santiago, 1936), as cited in Stephen Clissold, ed., *Soviet Relations with Latin America, 1918–1968: Documentary Survey* (London: Oxford University Press, 1970), p.

Nevertheless, the FSLN leadership later revived and refurbished the image of Sandino, making him the embodiment of their "antiimperialist" revolution. The FSLN's founding father, Carlos Fonseca, and FSLN leaders such as Sergio Ramírez rescued Sandino's writings from oblivion, and Ernesto Cardenal embellished the Sandino myth with the poem *"Hora O"* ("Zero Hour"), which recounts Sandino's death in 1934 at the hands of Anastasio ("Tacho") Somoza's National Guard. Fonseca, who was also an FSLN historian, blended the image of antiimperialist, revolutionary Sandinism with the legacy of the famous Nicaraguan poet Rubén Darío, whose words appear on the back cover of the FSLN platform of 1977[2] (see Appendix A).

If geography and the Sandino legend gave form and enthusiasm to the FSLN insurgency, socioeconomic underdevelopment and political repression were its major catalysts. From Spanish colonial masters, the country inherited a rigid class stratification. An authoritarian political culture in which democratic traditions never had an opportunity to take root was maintained, first, by a privileged minority consisting of export-oriented land owners and, from 1927 on, by the National Guard under the control of the Somoza family. The conservative hierarchy of the Catholic Church constituted yet another pillar of authoritarianism in nominally democratic Nicaragua.

The oppressive rule of the Somoza dynasty established conditions favorable to revolution, as did, to a lesser extent, Nicaragua's subservient client relationship with the United States. All three Somozas were adept at cultivating U.S. support and were eager to play the role of U.S. proxies abroad, even during the Korean and Vietnam wars, when Washington declined their offers of help. During his lifetime, the first Anastasio Somoza ("Tacho") ruled Nicaragua through a National Guard whose corruption he encouraged; by coopting the ruling Liberal party, friendly businessmen, and landlords; and by skillfully manipulating domestic opposition. He was succeeded by his son Luis, who presided over a relatively peaceful Nicaragua in the 1950s and 1960s, when modernization and economic growth were the basis for an expanding middle class.

15; see also Robert J. Alexander, *Communism in Latin America* (New Brunswick, N.J.: Rutgers University Press, 1957), pp. 377–78. For a recent, more positive Soviet assessment of Sandino, see *Latinskaya Amerika: entsiklopedicheskiy spravochnik* [Latin America: Encyclopedic Handbook] (Moscow: Izdatelstvo "Sovetskaya Entsiklopediya," 1982), part. 2, p. 420.

2. See Carlos Fonseca, *Sandino–Guerrillero Proletario* [Sandino–Proletarian Guerrilla] (Managua: Colección Juan de Dios Muñoz, 1980); Sergio Ramírez, ed., *El Pensamiento Vivo de Sandino* [The Living Thought of Sandino], 6th ed. (San José, Costa Rica: Editorial Universitaria Centroamericana [EDUCA], 1974); Ernesto Cardenal, *Antología* (Managua: Editorial Nueva Nicaragua, 1983), pp. 57–75; and Humberto Ortega's analysis in *Cuba Socialista* (Havana), September–October 1984, pp. 34–47.

The dynasty began to disintegrate in the 1970s under Luis's brother and successor, Anastasio ("Tachito") Somoza, a graduate of the U.S. Military Academy at West Point. As Régis Debray observes, "The [Sandinist] Front's best ally . . . was Somoza himself."[3] Corrupt like his predecessors, Tachito lacked their adeptness in political manipulation. This was evident in his handling of the aftermath of the Christmas earthquake of 1972, which killed 10,000 Nicaraguans. Relief funds were shamelessly misused, while downtown Managua lay in shambles. Somoza's continued exploitation of the Nicaraguan economy for his personal benefit, his contrived reelection in 1974, and his blatant disregard for the people's basic social needs further undermined the regime's legitimacy, antagonized a majority of the population, and sowed the seeds of revolution.

The Road to Power

After the FSLN's 1979 victory, it was fashionable in the United States and Western Europe to view the revolutionaries as nationalists or, at worst, confused socialist radicals. Careful examination of the evidence suggests, however, that from its founding, the FSLN has been led by dedicated, Leninist-oriented revolutionaries with long-standing ties to the Cuban and (to a lesser degree) Soviet Communist parties. Although the Front experienced various ups and downs, including near-extermination in the early 1970s, it eventually surmounted existing factional struggles and reemerged as a Leninist-oriented "vanguard," that is, an elitist organization under a largely unified command operating according to the vertical ruling principles of Leninist democratic centralism. Willing to form alliances with a diversity of anti-Somoza elements, the pragmatic FSLN consistently exploited Somoza's errors and, with international support (particularly from Soviet-backed Cuba), succeeded in transforming its fledgling guerrilla struggle into a successful popular insurgency.

Somoza, too, misjudged the FSLN and its leadership. To him, it "all began" in 1963, when the FSLN stepped up its activities in the northeastern mountains of Nicaragua.[4] Yet an organized Leninist party in Nicaragua actually dates back to June 1944 when the Nicaraguan Socialist party (Partido Socialista Nicaragüense—PSN) was formed. In deference to Stalin's wartime strategy of a united front, the PSN supported the Somoza regime,

3. Régis Debray, "Nicaragua: Radical Moderation, "*Le Monde Diplomatique* (Paris), September 1979, pp. 6–9. For more discussion of the Somoza era, see Thomas W. Walker, *Nicaragua: The Land of Sandino* (Boulder, Colo.: Westview, 1982).

4. As told to Jack Cox in *Nicaragua Betrayed* (Boston: Western Islands, 1980), p. 23.

partnered as it was with the United States in the antifascist alliance.[5] Carlos Fonseca, a co-founder of the Sandinistas, was at that time active in Nicaragua's Socialist Youth, the PSN's student arm. In addition, both Fonseca and his friend Tomás Borge were exposed to Marxist works in Guatemala during the tenure of leftist Jácobo Arbenz (1953–1954), and they organized a communist group among university students in the Nicaraguan city of León. Fonseca formally joined the PSN in 1955. Both men, as they later recounted, were unhappy with the weak and conservative PSN leaders,[6] who still regarded Sandino as a petty bourgeois nationalist, although there is no evidence of open criticism by Borge or Fonseca of the Soviet foreign policy line that informed PSN positions. On the contrary, Fonseca assented to the Soviet line when, under the auspices of the PSN, he attended the Sixth World Youth Festival in Moscow in 1957. He remained in the USSR four months after the festival had adjourned. (Borge was incarcerated in Nicaragua at this time.) After his Russian sojourn, Fonseca revealed his pro-Soviet views in *A Nicaraguan in Moscow*, which naively describes the USSR as a state with a free press and total freedom of religion.[7]

The success of the 1959 Cuban revolution seemed to validate and strengthen the Fonseca–Borge criticism of the nonviolent strategy of the PSN. In June 1959, Fonseca was joined by dozens of Nicaraguans and Cubans in an effort to organize armed struggle in Nicaragua's central region, close to Honduras. Although this effort failed, both Fonseca and Borge afterward visited Cuba. Fidel Castro and Ernesto ("Che") Guevara encouraged them to return to Nicaragua in 1960 in order to organize a guerrilla struggle modeled on Fidel's July 26 Movement. The PSN publicly disclosed Fonseca's would-be secret return, however, an action that led to his arrest and expulsion from the country.[8]

By now thoroughly disenchanted with the "pacifist line" of the PSN, or what they termed the "old Marxist sector,"[9] Fonseca, Borge, and Silvio

---

5. On Stalin's orders, this policy was articulated in the Americas by the general secretary of the U.S. Communist party, Earl Browder. See Carlos Fonseca, "Nicaragua: Zero Hour" and editorial comments on this item in *Sandinistas Speak* (New York: Pathfinder Press, 1982), p. 31. This essay originally appeared in *Tricontinental* (Havana), no. 14, 1969.

6. See a 1970 interview with Fonseca published in *Bohemia* (Havana), November 16, 1979, pp.50–55. See also Tomás Borge, *El Axioma de la Esperanza* [The Axiom of Hope] (Bilbao: Editorial Desclee De Brouwer, 1984), p. 20–21.

7. *Un Nicaragüense en Moscú* [A Nicaraguan in Moscow] (Managua: Publicaciones de Unidad, 1958).

8. David Nolan, *The Ideology of the Sandinistas and the Nicaraguan Revolution* (Coral Gables: Institute of Interamerican Studies, University of Miami, 1984), p. 23. Incidentally, there has never been a public denunciation of Fonseca or Borge by the USSR.

9. See Fonseca, "Nicaragua: Zero Hour," pp. 31–34.

Mayorga, another friend and former PSN activist, met in Tegucigalpa, Honduras, in 1961 to create a guerrilla organization modeled on Castro—Guevara lines. Originally, the organization was simply the National Liberation Front (FLN); the Sandinista label was added in 1962. Not all the early FSLN members were communists or even Marxists; for example, Rigoberto Cruz and Colonel Santos López, both survivors of Sandino's army, were included not for their ideology but for their knowledge of guerrilla tactics. Reduced to a few dozen members in the struggle with the National Guard during the Río Coco (1963) and Pancasán (1967) campaigns, the Front remained throughout the 1960s a small force without mass support. Like Guevara in his last Bolivian campaign of 1967, the FSLN discovered how difficult it is for middle-class, university-educated men to gain the support of peasants in a highly stratified social environment. In the mid-1960s, the Front attracted primarily students, including Daniel and Humberto Ortega, sons of a veteran of Sandino's army.

Faced with the meager results of their romantic revolutionary efforts, FSLN leaders began to look for a more realistic strategy. Fonseca, in particular, called for "a clearly Marxist—Leninist ideology."[10] As for tactics, by 1969 the movement had developed a new program—"a very important qualitative leap," as Humberto Ortega would later call it—based on the concept of *Guerra Popular Prolongada* or GPP (Prolonged Popular War), which foresaw and supported a protracted rural insurgency similar to the long guerrilla wars that preceded the victories of revolutionaries in China and Vietnam. The main strategic objectives of the FSLN were a military takeover and the establishment of "a revolutionary government based on a worker—peasant alliance." The new government would "eliminate foreign policy submission to Yankee imperialism" and "support authentic unity with the fraternal peoples of Central America" by coordinating "the efforts to achieve national liberation" in the region.[11] (See Appendix B.)

To strengthen discipline, the FSLN leaders, who now clearly saw themselves as a "vanguard organization," established in 1969 a National Directorate (*Dirección Nacional*, or DN) to lead the movement. Fonseca, who had spent some time in the USSR and Cuba, became secretary general of the DN. Other members included Borge, who had been trained to be a commander at a Cuban military school (probably between 1968 and 1970); Henry Ruiz, who studied for 2 years at Moscow's Patrice Lumumba University and trained in the Middle East with the Palestine Liberation Organiza-

10. Ibid., p. 34.
11. The FSLN program of 1969 was published in *Tricontinental*, no. 17 (March—April 1970): pp. 61–68; it is reprinted in *Sandinistas Speak*, pp. 13–22. See Appendix B, pp. 321–29. Humberto Ortega's comments on the 1969 program are from *Cuba Socialista*, pp. 34–47.

tion (PLO); and Humberto Ortega, who also had received instruction in Cuba. [12]

Although the official Soviet line on armed struggle in Latin America did not change until 1979–1980,[13] there is at least indirect evidence that the Soviet leadership approved of Fonseca's drive to overcome ideological vacillations in the early 1960s. In spite of Soviet–Cuban differences over tactics in the 1960s and 1970s, the KGB probably assisted in efforts to train, finance, and arm the FSLN with the help of Cuban intermediaries.[14]

The nearly total destruction of the FSLN at the hands of the National Guard in 1975 discredited the GPP line within the FSLN and strengthened the position of a different faction, the *Tendencia Proletaria* (TP—Proletarian Tendency). Led by Jaime Wheelock (today a member of the DN and minister of agricultural development and agrarian reform) and Luis Carrión (currently vice-minister of interior), this faction advocated a shift from the focus on Asian-style revolution in rural areas of the central region to a more orthodox focus on ideological indoctrination of the proletarian masses in the cities of the Pacific lowlands. The TP leaders argued that the FSLN's struggle ought to be conditioned by objective historical forces such as the level of economic development, and that the more class-conscious proletariat should be in the vanguard. Fonseca and Borge, with the latter leading the attack, condemned Wheelock and Carrión as "petit-bourgeois" and expelled them from the FSLN in October 1975 in the classic spirit of Leninist "democratic centralism." [15] Despite their expulsion, the TP leaders began

12. On Ruíz, see *New York Times*, March 28, 1984; on the training of Borge and Ortega, see Nolan, *Ideology of the Sandinistas*, pp. 139 and 148, and authors' interviews in Nicaragua. Fonseca also visited the People's Republic of China in the 1960s. This fact was revealed only after the FSLN established diplomatic relations with the PRC. See *El Nuevo Diario* (Managua), April 18, 1986, p. 10.

13. A subsequent positive Soviet appraisal of the FSLN's 1969 program appears in *Latinskaya Amerika*, pt. 2, p.420. However, content analysis of open Soviet literature on the Nicaraguan situation prior to 1979 indicates extraordinary caution, perhaps out of uncertainty over the staying power of the Sandinistas. For further discussion, see Jiri Valenta, "The USSR, Cuba, and the Crisis in Central America,"*Orbis* (Philadelphia), Fall 1981, pp. 715–746.

14. Edén Pastora, a former FSLN guerrilla hero, disclosed in a 1985 interview that as a Sandinista leader he had received aid from "the KGB through Fidel Castro." See *La Prensa* (Panama City), March 16, 1985, p. 1.

15. For Wheelock's views, see his *Raíces Indígenas de la Lucha Anticolonialista en Nicaragua* [Indigenous Roots of the Anticolonialist Struggle in Nicaragua] (Mexico City: Siglo Veintiuno, 1974), a work apparently drafted during his study in East Germany; and *Imperialismo y Dictadura: Crisis de Una Formación Social* [Imperialism and Dictatorship: Crisis of a Social Formation] (Mexico City: Siglo Veintiuno, 1975). See also Jaime Wheelock and Luís Carrión, *Apuntes Sobre el Desarrollo Económico y Social de Nicaragua* [Notes on the Economic and Social Development of Nicaragua] (Managua: Secretaría Nacional de Propaganda y Educación Política del FSLN, 1980). On the TP expulsions, see Nolan, *Ideology of the Sandinistas*, pp. 57–58.

to build an anti-Somoza organization among the urban masses, a successful effort that helped lay the groundwork for the final FSLN offensive in the cities in 1979.

A third faction, the *Tendencia Insurreccional* (Insurrectional Tendency) or *Tendencia Tercerista* (Third Way Tendency), participated in the 1975 DN internal debate. Led by Humberto Ortega (today a member of the DN and minister of defense) and supported by Ortega's brother, Daniel, and an old Mexican friend, Victor Tirado López, the TT was in some respects the most Leninist group of all. Its leaders believed that socioeconomic and political conditions in Nicaragua were ripe for a rapid, popularly based anti-Somoza insurgency, to be led by an elite vanguard (the FSLN) struggling primarily, but not exlusively, in the cities. Like Lenin, they believed that a determined vanguard could influence objective historical conditions for revolution. The FSLN, and the *terceristas* in particular, had received a boost from the spectacular seizure of 30 government hostages in December 1974, in exchange for whom the Sandinistas obtained the release of FSLN prisoners (including Daniel Ortega), a $1 million ransom, and the opportunity to broadcast their revolutionary message over Nicaragua's public media.

The *terceristas* promoted the idea of an anti-Somoza coalition that was to include not only workers and peasants but also elements of the middle class, particularly the intelligentsia, students, and the petite bourgeoisie. Talk of a broad societal coalition appealed to many Nicaraguans, and to outside observers—all of whom failed to see the transitory nature of the proposed alliance. Western observers tended to view the *terceristas* as a moderate faction inspired by social democratic and Christian democratic ideas, a view strengthened when Edén Pastora, a legendary guerrilla commander who happened to be a former member of the Conservative party, moved to the forefront of the Sandinista struggle, leading the seizure of the National Palace in August 1978. This interpretation prompted various groups, especially Western social democrats, to support the *terceristas* in the late 1970s and early 1980s in the hope that the FSLN as a whole would follow a moderate, social democratic line.

For all their wrangling, the diverse FSLN elements between 1976 and 1979 did not stop sharing a perception of the common enemy and somehow managed to maintain a productive division of labor. Régis Debray describes this synergistic relationship: ". . . it is in contradicting each other, and sometimes violently, that the tendencies have ended up complementing one another. The divisions of the Sandinista Front have played out as multiplication, increasing each time its capacity for initiatives instead of diminishing it." [16]

16. Debray, "Nicaragua," pp. 6–9.

Somoza's imposition of martial law in 1975 and the ensuing repressions (during which Fonseca was killed and Borge captured) unwittingly helped the TT. In May 1977 the *terceristas* took control of the "beheaded" National Directorate and adopted a new FSLN platform, authored mainly by Humberto Ortega and entitled "General Political Military Platform of the FSLN for the Triumph of the Popular Sandinista Revolution." (For the platform text, see Appendix A.) This program is even more Leninist and less Marxist than the initial FSLN program of 1969. The later document displays quotes from the poet Rubén Darío and references to the legacy of Sandino. In this new document the Sandinistas' struggle also is viewed as a continuation of the historical revolutionary process "toward socialism" initiated by the "glorious October revolution" in Russia. Sandino's war against the "Yankee interventionists" of the 1920s is described by the program as a Nicaraguan "Holy War," to be compared with the Soviet war against the Nazis.

The Leninist vanguard of the FSLN, not the Marxist proletariat, was to guide the revolutionary process. The FSLN "Marxist-Leninist organization" was to become "an iron-hard Leninist party," as the platform clearly states. Moveover, in the words of Lenin quoted in the FSLN platform, pragmatism rather than doctrinal rigidity was to be the norm: "Today the tragedy lies in our routine, in our doctrinairism, in the inherent immobility of intellectualism, in the senile fear of all initiative." [17] (See Appendix A.)

The platform goal was to establish "a revolutionary, popular democratic government" (*un Gobierno Revolucionario Democrático-Popular*) evocative of the popular democratic stage of government through which the East European communist states passed briefly in the post–World War II period. Nevertheless, as the platform explains, economic conditions in Nicaragua differed from those in Europe in the 1940s and would not allow "the immediate establishment of socialism." Specifically, "strategic and tactical factors do not permit the open establishment of socialism in this phase." But the revolutionary process would "sooner or later [lead] to socialism." There should be no mistake about the FSLN's final objectives: "The popular democratic phase should be for the Sandinista cause a means for consolidating its revolutionary position and organizing the masses, so that the process moves unequivocally toward socialism." The platform stated: "Our

---

17. *See Plataforma General Político–Militar del FSLN Para el Triunfo de la Revolución Popular Sandinista* [The FSLN's General Political–Military Platform for the Triumph of the Sandinista Popular Revolution], Appendix A, pp. 291–93, 309, 317. We are indebted to Álvaro Taboada for making available a copy of the Spanish version of this document. The Soviets now consider the publication of the platform to have been a significant act. See *Latinskaya America*, part 2, p. 420.

destination is socialism, a historically concrete mode of production"; the FSLN's cause is "the sacred and historical cause of Marx, Engels, Lenin, and Sandino."

As to tactics, the Front was to enter into "tactical and temporary" alliances with the Nicaraguan masses while preserving the "political hegemony" of the FSLN, and to "create a mass struggle without enlarging FSLN" ranks. The movement was to utilize classic Leninist organizational principles: "conscious political discipline . . . the application of democratic centralism . . . the rational division of labor and collegial responsibility . . . revolutionary criticism and self-criticism," and "obedience to the superior organs of the vanguard . . . rejecting any factional or divisive manifestation." [18]

Sandinista efforts to broaden the anti-Somoza alliance got a boost from Pastora's spectacular August 1978 attack on the National Palace. This raid resulted in the seizure of over 1500 prominent hostages and their ransoming for $500,000, the release of FSLN prisoners (including Borge), and another chance to air FSLN views on the public media. As the commandos (and the released prisoners) were driven through Managua to the airport, they were cheered by many Nicaraguans, suggesting even then that Somoza's days were numbered.

Somoza's response to the FSLN over the next 2 years was inconsistent and ultimately advantageous to the Sandinistas. A policy of limited democratization afforded the guerrillas and their supporters greater freedom of movement and association than they had earlier known, while the murder of Pedro Joaquín Chamorro Cardenal, editor of the respected Nicaraguan newspaper *La Prensa*, helped broaden the anti-Somoza opposition, which was now joined by a number of businessmen and professionals. By 1978, when the FSLN launched broad-based offensives in several major cities, the anti-Somoza struggle had become a virtual civil war. In this effort, the FSLN has admitted to drawing on the experience of "the boldness of the Cubans," as well as the "experience of the Bolshevik revolution regarding the modes of regular military fighting and especially the political firmness that is necessary to maintain the war." [19]

Several external factors also contributed to the FSLN victory. From the United States, the Carter administration's reluctance to back Somoza undermined the power of the regime, which had relied heavily on Somoza's supposedly special ties with Washington. Furthermore, beginning in 1978, the FSLN received war materiel from Cuba, as well as from Venezuela and

18. Appendix A, pp. 302–303, 309–310, 315.
19. See interview with Humberto Ortega in *Granma* (Havana), August 21, 1979, p. 6, and in *Sandinistas Speak*, p. 77.

Panama, and from private sources in the United States. In addition, Sandinista guerrillas were given sanctuary in neighboring Costa Rica and Honduras. Humberto Ortega has acknowledged that the flow of arms and the FSLN's ability to organize a broadcasting system to guide the insurgents played key roles in the final campaign. Probably more important was Fidel Castro's insistence on FSLN unity (as a condition for continued aid). This led to unification of the Sandinista factions under the nine-man National Directorate, consisting of three representatives from each faction, and the unification of all guerrilla units under a single command. Achieved between December 1978 and March 1979, this Cuban-sponsored unification of command and control was a decisive factor in the final victorious offensive against Somoza.[20]

Consolidating Power

The Sandinista movement that came to power in the summer of 1979 was a more experienced and pragmatic group than the romantic July 26th Movement that took over Cuba in 1959. And, unlike in Cuba, decision making has tended to be collective rather than the preserve of a charismatic leader. Nevertheless, one figure stands out above the rest: Tomás Borge is the oldest, most experienced, and most individualistic leader in the DN. Some even believe that the ambitious Borge could emerge as supreme leader.[21] More self-effacing but equally powerful is Humberto Ortega, the FSLN's chief strategist, minister of defense, and coordinator of the Defense and Security Commission.

The intent to transform the FSLN guerrilla organization into a Leninist revolutionary party has been apparent from the outset. As Borge put it in 1980, the plan was to fashion the FSLN into "a revolutionary party organized and guided by scientific priniciples . . . a realistic, flexible party [in-

20. *Sandinistas Speak*, pp. 82–83. Ortega, however, downplayed the Cuban factor in the unification of the FSLN command. On Castro's role in this development, see Nolan, *Ideology of the Sandinistas*, pp. 97–98.

21. Whenever National Directorate members attend a political function together, Borge arrives first; and if a chair is symbolically left empty to evoke the memory of Carlos Fonseca, Borge takes his place next to it. See interviews with Borge in *Caretas* (Lima), May 22, 1983, pp. 26–32, 38, and *Excélsior* (Mexico City), June 4, 1984, pp. 1A, 20A, 21A, and 38A. Borge is quite publicity conscious. In a visit to Borge's office, we obtained numerous publications of his speeches in both English and Spanish, which was not the case with other key FSLN leaders, such as Humberto Ortega. In these publications Borge continually stresses his close relationship with FSLN founding father Fonseca. Content analysis of speeches of the Ortega brothers suggests that they downplay Borge's role as Fonseca's closest comrade-in-arms and as a founding father of the FSLN.

spired by] the principles of internationalism." Elsewhere he refers to the FSLN as "the vanguard of the party, [and] without the party there is no revolution."[22] More recently he explained candidly, "I believe that it would be frivolous, and even dishonest, to say that no one here talks of Marxism—Leninism . . . I believe we are Marxists."[23]

The Nicaraguan president, Daniel Ortega, tends to be more guarded in interviews with Western media, at least when speaking about his personal views. When asked if he is a Marxist, he usually replies: "We are Sandinistas [with] a Christian upbringing [who are familiar] with both Christ and Marx."[24] In a speech to the PSN (secretly transcribed), however, DN member and FSLN political commission coordinator Bayardo Arce confirmed the intent of the FSLN to move toward a single-party Leninist system and to maintain its *"strategic ties* with the USSR and the socialist community."[25] (Insistence on the maintenance of strategic ties with the USSR and other communist countries is hardly consistent with Nicaragua's official non-aligned posture.)

To strengthen the party, the FSLN National Directorate has carried out important organizational changes. These include the creation of a National Secretariat and three DN commissions—Political, Defense and Security, and State. The Political Commission operates as the executive body of the DN when the DN is not in session and oversees the other two commissions. Below these commissions are a number of functional departments dealing with various aspects of domestic and foreign policy and the economy.[26] From a recent visit to the FSLN Secretariat, the authors can confirm the establishment of a number of departments and sections comparable to Soviet, East European, and Cuban prototypes (e.g., departments of propaganda, political education, and international relations). The Secretariat's section for North America is quite accessible, but sections dealing with

22. Speech by Borge, "The Time Has Come To Organize the Revolutionary Party," reported in *Barricada* (Managua), September 16, 1980, p.2, and interview in *Juventud Rebelde* (Havana), October 28, 1980, p. 3.

23. Interview with Borge during a visit to Madrid, in *Le Monde Diplomatique* (Mexico City ed.), September 1984, pp. 32—33.

24. Interview on Baden-Baden Südwestfunk Television Network, July 12, 1984, trans. Foreign Broadcast Information Service, *Daily Report: Latin America* (Washington, D.C.), July 20, 1984, pp. P. 13—19. Hereinafter cited as *FBIS—LAM*.

25. See "Comandante Bayardo Arce Contends that Marxism—Leninism and the One Party System are Going To Be Introduced," *La Vanguardia* (Barcelona), July 31, 1984, pp. 3, 8, 9 [emphasis added].

26. Interview with ND member Comandante Carlos Núñez, "The Watchword Is Organization, Organization and More Organization," *Barricada*, December 11, 1979, p. 4; see also, "The Task of Mobilizing the Masses Requires a Solid and Well-Structured Vanguard," ibid., September 16, 1980.

security, the military, and FSLN relations with other Leninist or Leninist-oriented regimes are surrounded by tight security.

These institutional arrangements have not eliminated policy disagreements. For example, with regard to the Catholic opposition, Borge and his GPP faction in State Security favor direct operations to discredit the Church, while the *terceristas* view such steps as unnecessary.[27] The FSLN leadership has also apparently been divided over how to handle Pastora's "treacherous" activities abroad, with the Ortega brothers reportedly favoring a reconciliation through Cuban mediators and Borge allegedly ordering and planning the assassination attempt on Pastora in 1984.[28] The *tercerista* Ramírez, a member of the junta (prior to January 1985) but not of the DN, is considered to be the most moderate of the FSLN leaders. Said to abhor the use of violence in dealing with the opposition, he even hinted at one point in 1980 that the problem with the FSLN internally was that "we have all the power."[29]

By and large, factionalism has been contained by the continued inclusion in the National Directorate of representatives and leaders of all three major tendencies of the FSLN (see Table 1). This balance also is observed in DN commissions. The Defense and Security Commission is coordinated by Humberto Ortega from the TT but also includes Borge from the GPP and Luis Carrión from the TP (*Tendencia Proletaria*—Proletarian Tendency) This is the same Carrión once expelled from the FSLN by a committee headed by Borge; he is now deputy vice-minister of interior under his former nemesis. The Political Commission (abolished in August 1985) was coordinated by Arce of the GPP, while Humberto Ortega represented the TT. Coordinator of the State Commission, which is entrusted with carrying out the economic and social programs of the revolution, is Jaime Wheelock of the TP. Other members are Henry Ruiz of the GPP and Daniel Ortega of the TT. It is noteworthy that each commission is headed by a representative of a different FSLN tendency.

In August 1985, there was a reorganization within the National Director-

27. From authors' interviews in Nicaragua and from the transcript of an extensive *Washington Post* interview with Miguel Bolaños Hunter, a former high-level official from the F-2 department of the General Directorate of State Security, at the Heritage Foundation, Washington D.C., June 16–17, 1983, pp. 2 and 42. The authors are indebted to Bruce Weinrod of the Heritage Foundation for providing them with a copy of the transcript.

28. From interviews in Nicaragua and Costa Rica in December 1984. Daniel Ortega was quoted in *El País* (Madrid) of July 15, 1982, p. 8, as saying, "Edén fought and had his own merits, this must be acknowledged." Pastora himself reported policy disagreements between the Ortega brothers and Borge. See interview in *La Prensa* (Panama City), March 18, 1985, p. 1A.

29. Authors' interviews in Managua; and interview with Ramírez in *Svenska Dagbladet* (Stockholm), March 14, 1980, p. 7, trans. *FBIS-LAM*, April 3, 1980, pp. 138–40.

TABLE 1
National Directorate of the FSLN, July 1985

Ranked According to Real Power	Political Tendency	Bureaucratic Responsibility	Leadership Committee
Tomás Borge	Leader of the GPP	Mininster of Interior	Member of Defense and Security Commission*
Humberto Ortega	Co-leader of the TT	Minister of Defense	Coordinator of Defense and Security Commission and member of Political Commission*
Daniel Ortega	Co-leader of the TT	President of Nicaragua	Member of State Commission*
Jaime Wheelock	Leader of the TP	Minister of Agricultural Development and Agrarian Reform	Coordinator of State Commission and member of Political Commission*
Bayardo Arce	GPP		Coordinator of Political Commission¤
Henry Ruíz	GPP	Minister of Foreign Cooperation	Member of State Commission
Luis Carrión	TP	Vice-Minister of Interior	Member of Defense and Security Commission
Carlos Núñez	TP	President of National Assembly	Coordinator of Mass Organizations in FSLN Secretariat
Víctor Tirado	TT		Responsible for Trade Unions in FSLN Secretariat

*Member of the Executive Committee (the Political Commission was abolished in August 1985.)

SOURCES: "The Task of Mobilizing the Masses Requires a Solid and Well Structured Vanguard," Barricada (Managua), September 16, 1980; N. Yu. Smirnova, "The Shaping of the Party of the Nicaraguan Revolution," Voprosy istorii KPSS (Moscow), May 1984, pp. 83–95; and Grenada Documents, Log. No. PP., and FBIS-LAM, August 6, pp. 75–6.

ate. The Political Commission was replaced by an Executive Commission with Daniel Ortega as coordinator and Bayardo Arce as deputy coordinator; other members were Tomás Borge, Humberto Ortega, and Jaime Wheelock. While the new lineup ostensibly promoted Daniel Ortega, it also brought Tomás Borge into the FSLN's Executive Commission for the first time (see Table 1). The Executive Commission is perceived as an organ of implementation for the National Directorate, something akin to the Secretariat in ruling Communist parties. Also, on August 4, 1985, the FSLN announced the establishment of seven auxiliary departments to deal with general affairs, organization, agitation and propaganda, political education, international organization, finance, and studies of Sandinism.

Borge seems closest to Moscow, having garnered a credit of $50 million for the purchase of Soviet machinery and equipment during his September 1981 visit to the USSR, and having been cited positively in Soviet sources for advocating development of the FSLN along vanguard party lines. The Ortega brothers, particularly Humberto, are viewed as protégés of Fidel Castro, although they, too, frequently travel to Moscow, East Berlin, and Sofia.[30] Despite tactical differences within the DN and perhaps among their foreign sponsors, the FSLN leaders have avoided a power struggle, such as the one that occurred in Grenada. Indeed, the intervention of U.S. and Organization of East Caribbean States (OECS) forces in that island nation in October 1983 created a siege mentality in the DN, strengthening its members' resolve to tolerate one another's differences.

In the lower ranks, FSLN members are required to "obey unhesitatingly (*acatar sin vacilación alguna*) the directions of central and intermediate organizations . . . to respect organic [*sic*] discipline . . . to defend the FSLN from the attacks of its enemies [and] to belong to one of the mass organizations."[31] The new mass organizations, which include the Sandinista Workers' Central, the Rural Workers Association, the July 19th Sandinista Youth, and the Nicaraguan Women's Association, were conceived along the model of Lenin's "transmission belts," that is, as ancillary institutions used by the party to supplement other, more direct means of social control. Their function is to counter the influence of opposition groups among the

---

30. Authors' interviews in Managua. For positive Soviet appraisals of Borge's advocacy of the FSLN as a vanguard party, see I. M. Bulychev, "Successes and Problems of the Sandinist Revolution," *Latinskaya Amerika* (Moscow), 1981, pp. 26–41. Pastora in 1982 suggested that the GPP tendency (comprising Borge, Ruíz, and Arce) was closer to Moscow than to Havana. See interviews with *Veja* (São Paulo), August 11, 1982, pp. 5,6, and 8, and with *El País*, June 6, 1982, p. 8. According to Pastora, Castro cautioned the Sandinistas against accepting Soviet tanks. See *La Prensa* (San Pedro Sula), July 15, 1982, pp. 4–5.

31. Interview with Comandante Núñez.

various sectors of society. FSLN members are also urged to take an active part in agitation and propaganda.[32]

The Sandinista regime has been flexible and willing to tolerate the continued existence of various institutions of limited pluralism, such as the semilegislative Council of State (since January 1985, the National Assembly) and various small opposition parties. It does so because, in the words of Borge, the FSLN controls the instruments of "real power . . . the revolutionary organization [i.e., the party, and] the state coercive bodies—the army, the police, and the state security bodies." Borge boasts: "We can do whatever we want with the power we have. We can remove the government and replace it with another if we like." [33] Defense Minister Ortega echoes Borge's confidence: "The enemy . . . could never snatch power from us."[34]

The Ministry of Defense under Humberto Ortega commands the Sandinista Popular Army (EPS) and the Sandinista Popular Militia (MPS). The active-duty armed forces number approximately 62,000.[35] According to the Patriotic Military Service Law of October 6, 1983, all Nicaraguan males between the ages of 18 and 40 are required to serve in the active or reserve military.[36] Since 1985, many reservists have been summoned to serve in the Reserve Infantry Battalions. As in communist states, each EPS battalion appears to have, in addition to its military commander, a deputy for political work.[37] Meanwhile, the state security organizations have been able to position intelligence operators to check on the ideological purity of the Sandinista armed forces.

The MPS traces its origins to the 1978—1979 struggle in which Nicaraguan youths fought against Somoza and alongside FSLN guerrillas. After the July 1979 victory, the militia units were anxious to join regular units of the EPS. To accommodate them, and to create a potential manpower reserve, the regime institutionalized the MPS in February 1980.[38] This was a time, it

32. "Concerning Revolutionary Propaganda," originally published as an editorial in the FSLN weekly *Poder Sandinista* (Managua), no. 34, and reprinted in *Barricada*, July 6, 1980, p. 3.

33. Tomás Borge, "A Dream Becomes a Reality," *Tricontinental* (Havana), no. 118 (1980): 18—28.

34. From a speech of June 24, 1981, reported by Radio Managua, trans. *FBIS—LAM*, July 15, 1981, pp. 60—62.

35. *The Military Balance, 1984-85* (London: International Institute for Strategic Studies, 1984), p. 123.

36. Decree No. 1327, published in *El Nuevo Diario* (Managua), July 2, 1984, pp. 4—5.

37. See a report about the activities of the counterinsurgency battalion, "Choir of Angels," *Verde Olivo* (Havana), June 9, 1983, pp. 16—17.

38. "National Day of the Sandinista Popular Militia—Decree No. 313," *Barricada*, February 24, 1980, pp. 1 and 12.

should be noted, when the FSLN faced no significant internal or external threat. Today, the MPS numbers some 40,000 men.[39]

Borge's Ministry of the Interior controls the Sandinista police, the General Directorate of State Security (DGSE), the penal system, and special forces (the Pablo Úbeda Brigade) engaged in fighting the U.S.-backed anti-Sandinista guerrillas known as the *contras*. The most crucial of these departments is the DGSE, which is headed by a Soviet-trained chief appropriately named Lenin Cerna.[40] The real power within the security apparatus seems to be wielded by the Soviets; they reportedly concentrate on intelligence operations, while the Cubans oversee counterintelligence. [41]

Still another coercive instrument of the FSLN regime is the network of Sandinista Defense Committees (CDSs) modeled on Cuba's Committees for the Defense of the Revolution and commanded by Leticia Herrera, a Soviet-educated guerrilla veteran who was formerly the wife of Daniel Ortega. Created to carry out civil defense activities (protection from air bombardment by the National Guard Air Force) during the last few years of the FSLN insurgency, the CDSs have become a crucial social institution promoting socialist transformation at the grass-roots level. About 500,000 CDS members are organized in 9,000-odd units, block-by-block, in the major cities. Some units serve as intelligence networks, for surveillance of public facilities, and as patrols, working closely with the DGSE and the Sandinista police. [42] Through their control of ration cards, job recommendations, and even permits for vaccinations, the CDSs are able to monitor the population and curtail any incipient opposition.[43]

On a more informal basis, the State Security manipulates the so-called *turbas divinas* (divine mobs), which stage demonstrations, harassments, and witch-hunts; the *turbas* were responsible for ridiculing the pope during his 1983 visit. Like the New Jewel Movement (NJM) in Grenada, the FSLN in Nicaragua has ordered its security to prepare a list of its potential enemies, ranging in categories from very dangerous to potentially dangerous to less dangerous. [44] These instruments of internal control and coercion have been

39. *The Military Balance*, p. 124. This is regarded by some U.S. analysts we have talked to as an underestimate.

40. Interview with Miguel Bolaños, p. 10.

41. Ibid., p. 34.

42. Interview with the chief of the Sandinista Police, Comandante Walter Ferreti, *Moncada* (Havana), April 1984, pp. 8–11.

43. Interview with CDS Secretary General Herrera, *Barricada*, February 17, 1984, pp. 1, 7; interview with Comandante Omar Cabezas, *La Prensa* (Managua), May 8, 1981, p. 16, and May 9, 1981, p. 8; and authors' interviews in Managua.

44. Interview with Miguel Bolaños, pp. 27–28; and interviews with two former agents of the DGSE, Rigoberto Wilford and Xavier Torres, *La Nación*, July 20, 1985, pp. 1–4.

directed in various combinations against "very dangerous" elements, such as leaders of opposition parties like the Nicaraguan Democratic Movement (MDN), the Church, the press, minority Indian groups, professional associations, leaders of private trade unions such as the Nicaraguan Workers Federation's José Altamirano (who distinguished himself as a labor leader in the anti-Somoza struggle), supporters of Edén Pastora, and even radical groups such as the Trotskyite Communist party (which criticized the "moderation" of the FSLN). [45] Punishment has varied from job dismissal and denial of ration cards to arrest, preventive detention, imprisonment, and even an occasional disappearance or violent death such as occurred when the president of the Superior Council of Private Enterprise (COSEP), Jorge Salazar, was apparently murdered by Sandinista agents during his arrest for alleged anti-Sandinista activities. [46]

The regime admits to holding some 5000 persons in jail; of them, 2000 are former National Guardsmen and another 300 have been convicted of subversive activities. [47] Since 1983, trials of dissidents have been handled by special People's Anti-Somocista Tribunals. According to the Inter-American Permanent Commission on Human Rights, during 1983 an additional 1,400 Nicaraguans were being held in detention. In the same year there were at least 102 documented instances of physical abuse and torture of political dissidents. [48] Borge, who knows the real numbers, has admitted the existence of physical abuse, and Daniel Ortega implied that at least 300 Nicaraguans were murdered or were missing as of 1985. [49]

The Misura (Miskito, Sumu, and Rama) Indians on Nicaragua's Atlantic coast have suffered especially severely at the hands of the Sandinistas. Once enjoying a fair amount of self-government and freedom to pursue their Moravian Protestant faith, these members of the Miskito, Sumo (or Sumu), and Rama tribes have resisted Cuban-assisted FSLN efforts to extend the control of the central government over their activities. As a result, they have

---

45. For such criticism, the Sandinistas forced the ultraleftist newspaper *El Pueblo* to close in January 1980. From authors' interviews in Managua, December 1984.

46. "A Sandinist Coup, " *Cambio 16* (Madrid), December 1, 1980; and Shirley Christian, *Nicaragua: Revolution in the Family* (New York: Random House, 1985), pp. 181–182.

47. U.S. Department of State, *Country Reports on Human Rights Practices for 1983*, report submitted to the Committee of Foreign Affairs, U.S. House of Representatives, and the Committee on Foreign Affairs, U.S. Senate, Joint Committee Print (Washington, D.C.: Government Printing Office, February 1984), p. 636; and idem.,*Country Reports on Human Rights Practices for 1984*(Washington, D.C.: Government Printing Office, 1985), pp. 608–624; See also Edward Cody, "Nicaraguan Special Tribunals Said To Neglect Due Process," *Washington Post,* August 3, 1985, pp. 1 and 28.

48. *Country Reports on Human Rights Practices for 1983*, p. 635.

49. Ibid.; see also interview with Humberto Ortega, *Der Spiegel,* April 28, 1986, pp. 158–165.

incurred fierce repression including seizure of church properties, denial of ration cards, impressment to work on Sandinista farms, and ultimately the mass relocation of some 10,000 Miskitos from areas on the Nicaraguan-Honduran border to areas deeper inside Nicaragua. This has resulted in the flight to Honduras of some 15,000 Indians and the decision of some 5000 Indians from various tribes to take up arms against the regime in alignment with what was formerly known as the Nicaraguan Democratic Force (FDN), headed by Adolfo Calero. [50] Negotiations by the FSLN with Indian leaders to date have succeeded in fracturing the rebel leadership without addressing the serious grievances of the people.

In dealing with the Catholic Church, the Sandinistas have used a blend of coercion and more subtle means. The FSLN has expelled foreign priests for alleged counterrevolutionary activities and has assaulted Cardinal Obando y Bravo, terminating broadcasts of his celebration of Sunday Mass and banning the circulation of *La Iglesia*, the Catholic church newspaper. They also subjected his aide, Father Bismarck Carballo, to a crude attempt at public defamation and humiliation and refused him reentry into Nicaragua in June 1986 following a trip abroad. [51] The regime also has attempted to divide and destroy the Church by playing priests and nuns against the Church hierarchy. For example, the FSLN has supported the so-called popular church, which follows radical liberation theology and which has won over some segments of the population with its literacy crusade. Moreover, four "revolutionary" priests occupy high positions in the FSLN government: The former Maryknoll missionary Miguel D'Escoto Brockman is minister of foreign affairs; the former Trappist monk Ernesto Cardenal is minister of culture; his brother, Fernando, a Jesuit, serves as minister of education; and Edgardo Parrales is Nicaragua's ambassador to the Organization of American States (OAS). The Sandinistas also have tried to use religious holidays for their purposes, for example turning *La Purísima*—a week-long celebration of the Immaculate Conception of Mary, which fore-

50. Even pro-Sandinista sources admitted a disrespectful attitude among some FSLN members toward Atlantic Coast Indians. Thus we read in *El Nuevo Diario*, June 14, 1980, p. 2: "There was a tendency not to respect the customs of the Miskitos." For an excellent discussion of the issue of the Atlantic Coast Indians, see Margaret Wilde, "The East Coast of Nicaragua: Issues for Dialogue," paper written for the Board of World Mission, Moravian Church in America, June 1984.

51. In August 1982 Father Carballo was asked to meet a woman penitent (actually a prostitute, presumably procured by the secret service). When he did so, he was hit by an agent of the DGSE's F–7 department posing as the woman's husband, and was seized and stripped by a *turba* and dragged naked down the street in front of waiting television cameras and newsmen. From interview with Miguel Bolaños, pp. 30–31, and authors' interviews in Managua.

shadows Christmas and culminates on December 8—into a party-sponsored fiesta in which even the minister of the interior participated.[52]

The FSLN clearly must move slowly in attacking the church hierarchy. A poll published in the November 10, 1981, issue of Managua's *La Prensa* indicated that 80% of the population considered itself Catholic, and only 6.9% said they belonged to no religion or were atheists. Fully 38% of respondents saw Archbishop (subsequently Cardinal) Miguel Obando y Bravo as the most popular Nicaraguan, followed by Daniel Ortega with only 13.5%. Only 8% favored a strictly Marxist education in the schools, while 70.9% favored a Christian education, and 17.1% favored a blend of Christian and Marxist education. [53]

The FSLN has attempted to control and stifle the media through censorship and the creation of "party" press to compete with the independent press. Since September 1979, all Nicaraguan journalists have been required to belong to one of two Sandinista trade unions. More important, under a state of national emergency declared March 15, 1982, in response to attacks by anti-Sandinista guerrillas, radio and print media coordinators were ordered to submit all materials planned for broadcast or publication for prior censorship by the Nicaraguan Communications Media Directorate, supervised by the Ministry of Interior.[54] In 1979 and 1980, the FSLN created two new newspapers: its own organ, *Barricada*, and the pro-FSLN daily, *El Nuevo Diario*. Until summer 1986, the respected and influential *La Prensa* was able to maintain an opposition posture despite attempted insider takeovers by Sandinista trade unionists, intimidation of officials and distributors, restriction of foreign exchange needed to import paper, mob threats and other violence, and censorship.[55] The FSLN coercive system was fur-

52. Ernesto Cardenal (and perhaps others) appears to view the revolution as "efficacious charity . . . a Christian and priestly task" and to believe that he is a "Marxist who believes in God," "follows Christ," and is a "revolutionary for his kingdom." See *El Nuevo Diario*, February 22, 1983. But there is a more cynical strain in the likes of Borge, who claims he is a believer but not a Catholic and that he deeply admires Christ as a man who struggled against imperialism. See *Tiempo* (Madrid), March 7–14, 1983, pp. 60–61.

53. The article "A 'Directed' Survey and the Expected Response," appearing in *El Nuevo Diario*, November 11, 1981, pp. 1 and 10, questioned the objectivity of the survey; *La Prensa* defended its methodology in its issue of the same day.

54. "Nicaraguan Government Establishes Control of Media," communiqué of the Communications Media Directorate, March 15, 1982. (A copy was obtained by the authors in Nicaragua.)

55. The famous Chamorro family is associated with all three newspapers. Pedro Joaquín Chamorro Barrios was editor-in-chief of his late father's *La Prensa* (with a circulation of 60,000, despite the FSLN policies) until 1985, when he left for voluntary exile in Costa Rica. *Barricada* (with a circulation of 100,000) is edited by his brother Carlos, and *El Nuevo Diario* (with a circulation of 50,000) is edited by Xavier Chamorro, a brother of the late Pedro Joaquín Chamorro Cardenal. *La Prensa*, in a very objective commentary on July 4, 1980, aptly described all three newspapers as "better" than Cuba's *Granma*, which it termed "the world's most boring" newspaper.

ther strengthened in October 1985 when the National Directorate decided to suspend for a year the fundamental rights of Nicaraguan citizens.

Cutting Down the Opposition

Secure in the power assured by the coercive instruments at its disposal, the FSLN has resorted to traditional communist "salami tactics" to whittle away at the opposition's presence in two major institutions: the Junta of the Government of National Reconstruction (JGRN—since January 1985, the presidency) and the semilegislative Council of State/National Assembly. Although neither institution exercises real power comparable to that of the FSLN's National Directorate, the retention of some bourgeois elements in the ranks of both institutions has lent a degree of legitimacy and international respectability to the FSLN regime. For the FSLN instruments of power, see Figure 1.

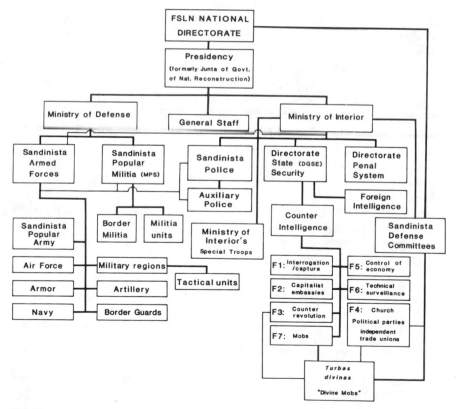

FIGURE 1.

The first five-person junta, appointed by the FSLN June 16, 1979 (before the victorious final offensive), included the well-known Sandinistas Daniel Ortega and Moisés Hassan, but also Violeta Barrios de Chamorro (widow of the former editor-in-chief of *La Prensa*), Alfonso Robelo (former chairman of COSEP and head of the MDN), and Sergio Ramírez from the FSLN-sponsored "Group of 12," since 1977 charged with projecting an image of FSLN pluralism to foreign audiences. Ramírez's role in this group was pivotal. Although he was secretly a member of the FSLN at the time, his public image as an academic of moderate persuasion helped promote the view that the junta was a genuine coalition. [56] Under increasing pressure, Chamorro, said to be suffering from poor health, and Robelo, who opposed the FSLN takeover of the Council of State and the reported nationalization of the country's banks, [57] resigned from the junta in April 1980. In an effort to maintain a pluralistic image, the FSLN appointed the Central Bank president, Arturo Cruz, a social democrat and a member of the "Group of 12," and Supreme Court Justice Rafael Córdoba Rivas as their replacements. In March 1981, however, the junta was reduced to three persons: Daniel Ortega, Ramírez (who now openly voiced his FSLN affiliation), and non-FSLN member Córdoba. Cruz, disenchanted with his figurehead status, accepted an appointment as ambassador to the United States, where he subsequently defected.

The FSLN's gradual rise to dominance over the Council of State followed a similar step-by-step approach. Established by a agreement reached at Punta Arenas, Costa Rica, in June 1979, this body was to be a pluralistic, colegislative body charged with approving or rejecting statutory changes proposed by the junta. The FSLN originally was to occupy only 13 of the 33 seats, but this agreement was disregarded even before the council's first meeting by FSLN expansion of the membership to 47—all 14 new seats going to FSLN members or FSLN supporters from the mass organizations. [58] Proceeding from Lenin's belief that communism "cannot win by the vanguard alone," the FSLN, like the East European communists in their post–World War II parliaments, formed a coalition in the Council of State, called the Patriotic Revolutionary Front, encompassing both FSLN members and a variety of representatives and fellow-travelers from the Socialist party of

---

56. Ramírez's function in this transitory, tactical government reminds one of the role of Ludvik Svoboda, who in postwar Czechoslovakia joined the short-lived government of Social Democrat Zdeněk Fierlinger as a nonparty member, only to reveal subsequently that he had been acting as a secret member of the Czechoslovak Communist party all along.

57. "I Sing, Yankee, Enemy of Mankind" ; an interview with Daniel Ortega in *Der Spiegel* (Hamburg), December 31, 1984, p. 83.

58. James D. Rudolph, ed., *Nicaragua: A Country Study* (Washington, D.C.: Government Printing Office, 1982), p. 163.

Nicaragua, the Popular Social Christian party, and the Independent Liberal party. When COSEP and MDN representatives boycotted the work of the council, the FSLN-controlled mass media, the Sandinista Defense Committees, and other Sandinista mass organizations were mobilized to stage a national rally in support of the FSLN. [59] Sandinista coercive instruments also went into action against COSEP leaders, culminating in the murder of Salazar. After mobs attacked and wrecked the MDN building in Managua in 1981, Robelo and other top leaders left Managua for voluntary exile. The Council of State was enlarged again in May 1981 with the addition of 4 members, also FSLN supporters, bringing the membership to 51. Neither the Council of State nor its successor, the National Assembly, has been allowed to challenge the authority of the true executive body, the FSLN's National Directorate.

Turning to its own ranks, the FSLN faced the touchy problem of easing out Edén Pastora, the immensely popular "Comandante Cero," who had been head of the Southern Front during the insurrection, then vice-minister of the interior, head of the Sandinista Popular Militia, and member of the FSLN's Defense and Security Commission. Wary of his popularity and ambition and distrustful of his political orientation, the leadership never appointed him to the National Directorate and soon began to accuse him of incoherence and Bonapartist ambitions. For his part, Pastora seemed disillusioned by the bureaucratization of the revolution—manifested in new uniforms, stiff manners, and stilted patterns of speech.[60] By 1981 he felt that the DN had "betrayed Sandinism . . . transforming a dictatorship of the right into one of the left," with his former comrades-in-arms (particularly Borge) becoming "new Somozas." [61] In July 1981 Pastora, unquestionably a complex and controversial personality, left Nicaragua. In 1982 he became leader of the Sandinista Revolutionary Front/Democratic Revolutionary Alliance (FRS/ARDE) guerrillas operating along the Costa Rican–Nicaraguan border.

A further effort at political consolidation came with the 1984 presidential and legislative elections. Although not entirely manipulated by the regime, the elections were not free either. As a precondition for participation, opposition parties were required to declare their support for the revolution. There were partial bans on the rights of assembly and public demonstration. Media censorship and FSLN advertisements also worked to the Sandinistas'

59. See "Combative Nation in the Streets," *Barricada*, November 13, 1980, pp. 1, 5.

60. Interviews in *El País* and *La Prensa* and *Veja* cited in note 30.

61. Ibid., Pastora was particularly critical of Borge's living in the confiscated house of a former Somoza supporter that had a parking lot for 27 cars, including Jaguars and Mercedes-Benzes. Borge subsequently moved to smaller quarters.

advantage. Moreover, some voters were led to believe that if they did not vote for the FSLN, they might lose their ration cards or even their jobs. [62] Some gatherings of the opposition parties before the election were said to have been obstructed by various pressures and sabotaged by local FSLN authorities. [63]

The most crucial aspect of the election was its lateness. By November 1984 no observer of the Nicaraguan scene—and least of all the Nicaraguan public—believed the Front was going to allow itself to lose. Moreover, participation in the elections only by the Front and a handful of small parties—three to the left of the Front and the rest splinters or factions of parties—offered the voter only a semblance of choice. Despite the limited free choice, the presidential election revealed that a significant degree of opposition to the Sandinista regime still existed in Nicaragua: The Sandinistas won 67% of the vote, the three ultra-left parties 4% and the three other principal opposition parties 29%.[64]

The FSLN leadership expected that the process of consolidating their forces would be legitimized by the adoption of a new constitution in late 1986. (For a draft of the new constitution, see Appendix C.) The draft available in the summer of 1986 does not read like the constitution of the consolidated communist regimes of the USSR and Eastern Europe adopted in the 1960s and 1970s. Instead, it reminds students of comparative communism of the East European party documents of the "popular democratic" era of the late 1940s, which were vague and offered various interpretations. The FSLN draft constitution does not clearly separate the governing party from the state or the army. Neither does the draft eliminate revolutionary institutions, such as special tribunals, or acknowledge the right of different political parties to be elected to power.

62. See interview with socialist leader Aldolfo Evertz on Radio Noticias (Managua), November 6, 1984, trans. *FBIS–LAM*, November 8, 1984, p. P ll.

63. Interestingly, this charge came not only from the "bourgeois" parties but also from the Trotskyite Communist party newspaper, *Avance* (Managua), as reported by Radio Noticias September 6, 1984, trans. *FBIS–LAM*, September 7, 1984, p. Pll.

64. The report of the Latin American Studies Association, *The Electoral Process in Nicaragua: Domestic and International Influences*, November 14, 1984, provides a good source on election results. However, the report's conclusion that the elections constituted an "impressive beginning" was challenged by Nicaraguan analysts. See Jaime Chamorro, "Electoral Farce in Numbers, Statistical Data, and Percentages," an undated Spanish-language document prepared by *La Prensa* (Managua).

The Socialist Transformation

The social and economic programs of the FSLN regime began cautiously. Once in power, the FSLN was determined to remedy socioeconomic inequities by the gradual introduction of a planned economy and redistribution of wealth to the poorer strata of society. Having learned from the mistakes of other communist nations, however, FSLN leaders decided against a precipitous disengagement from the world capitalist system. For the immediate term, they opted for a mixed economy, blending the public and private capitalist sectors. The National Directorate justified this approach by pointing out that Nicaragua had not attained the level of capitalism or developed the degree of working-class consciousness that existed in Cuba in 1959. As one Sandinista source put it, "What has taken place in Nicaragua is a Popular Revolution by workers, peasants, semi- and subproletarians, the patriotic middle class and bourgeois sectors, with a clear hegemony of the people."[65]

This is not a new concept. Lenin acknowledged that a vanguard party needed to build coalitions with peasant and bourgeois elements during the first phase of socialist transformation, and this tactic was employed both in Russia and after World War II in most of Eastern Europe. The period of cooperation lasted even longer in China—and in East Germany, whose experience Comandante Wheelock had studied firsthand.

The Sandinistas have been relatively slow to pursue their goal of nationalization and collectivization of the economy for fear of pushing domestic and foreign opposition too far. "There is no way," Wheelock observed, "that we can force the nationalization of tortilla production, that would be absurd . . . although we may have socialistic principles, we cannot resolve the transformation of our society by expropriating all the means of production." [66]

As a result of this cautious approach, three basic forms of ownership exist today in Nicaragua: (1) state ownership, the so-called People's Property Area (APP); (2) cooperatives and associations such as the Sandinista Agricultural Cooperatives (CAS); and (3) private ownership. The APP was created immediately after the 1979 revolution when the holdings of Somoza, his family, and his closest supporters were seized. The FSLN claimed that 60% of all industrial means of production belonged to the private sector as of 1984.[67] In 1985 some 61% of the farmland remained in the hands of

65. *Pensamiento Propio* (Managua), nos. 6–7 (July–August 1983): 26.
66. Ibid., p. 23.
67. *El Nuevo Diario*, January 2, 1984, p. 2.

individual producers, even though the percentage in the hands of large *latifundistas* had declined dramatically. Expropriation continued at a gradual pace until 1985, when the process appeared to be accelerated as properties belonging to opposition figures—such as Enrique Bolaños, president of COSEP—were nationalized. The amendment to the agrarian land reform in January 1986 provides for further expropriations of the land of inefficient producers or whenever the land is for public use.

The role of the central government in the planning and allocation of national resources also has gradually increased.The principal institutions involved include the Ministry of Planning, the Labor Ministry, the Institute of Social Security, the National Planning Council, and Wheelock's Ministry of Agricultural Development and Agrarian Reform. This expansion of state intervention has been accompanied by a corresponding growth in the size of the public bureaucracies. These institutions have imposed a variety of regulations and controls on the private sector and exert pressure through capital investment policies, taxation, and manipulation of credit and foreign exchange. For example, in 1983 only 24% of capital invested in industry was allotted to the private sector.[68] What were once 17 banks have been merged into 5, forming the state-operated Nicaraguan Financial Corporation. The FSLN also has established a state monopoly on foreign trade.

In the beginning, the Sandinistas' newly created Ministry of Social Welfare sought to improve the living conditions of the general populace through various public housing and school construction projects and social welfare programs. These activities indeed helped improve the quality of basic services, especially health care and housing. The FSLN also established a system of rent control, a program of urban development, and methods for controlling land and housing speculation. The first year of the revolution saw clear economic recovery and an economic growth rate of 18%.

Attempting to increase productivity, the FSLN coined slogans, which were emblazoned on huge banners and billboards, and organized popular rallies to awaken "social consciousness." In the first years, output increased in textiles, construction, and gold mining. Today, however, these radical means of mass mobilization have become unpopular with segments of the Nicaraguan populace. Economic mismanagement, bureaucratization, a mounting defense budget, and the state of emergency occasioned by the armed opposition of the so-called *contras* have led to a serious deterioration of economic conditions and living standards. In 1983 Nicaragua's economic growth stalled, and inflation reached 45%. Assessments of 1984 suggest an

68. From a confidential document cited in *La Nación Internacional* (San José), April 19–25, 1984, pp. 18–19.

even bleaker situation, with zero or negative growth and still higher rates of inflation.[69]

Arbitrary wage increases have contributed to inflationary pressures.[70] Gasoline and more essential items, such as water, toilet paper, and a host of foodstuffs, are now rationed. Nicaragua's foreign trade situation also has deteriorated. As of 1984, the country's total foreign debt was nearly $4 billion—only $1.6 billion of it inherited from the Somoza years.[71]

The FSLN's military buildup and apparent support for revolution in El Salvador led the United States to cancel its ongoing economic aid program to Nicaragua in 1981. Although aid has been forthcoming from other sources, particularly Mexico, Spain, and several communist states (see below), the latter have been unable or unwilling to provide the massive economic assistance needed to speed recovery from the damages of the insurrection. Moreover, the militarization of Nicaragua (whether to support regional revolution, as some observers contend, or to defend against *contra* opposition forces operating in border areas, as the FSLN claims) has swelled defense expenditures to an estimated 50% of the total national budget in 1985, 25% of the gross national product, and 50% of domestic production, and involves 20% of the economically active male population. These figures are from Sandinista sources.[72] This second civil war (the first being the anti-Somoza insurgency) has resulted in large losses—over $1 billion between March 1981 and October 1983; in the same period it reportedly has cost several thousand lives and has forced 100,000 people (not including the relocated Miskito Indians) to flee from communities in the northern war zone.[73]

The Sandinista regime has tried to counter worsening conditions by increasing public revenues via taxation on goods, services, sales, and imports; by establishing consumer product quotas; and by devaluing the Nicaraguan currency (córdoba) and enforcing banking regulations aimed at strict control of cash. So far, the regime has not been successful in reversing deteriorating economic trends and countering popular discontent; nor has it

---

69. Ibid. Projections for 1984–1985 are derived from authors' interviews in Nicaragua.

70. The Department of Employment and Wages of the Labor Ministry in 1984 criticized inflationary salary boosts awarded by the Institute of Social Security. See *El Nuevo Diario*, April 24, 1984, p. 9.

71. Document cited in *La Nación Internacional*, April 19–25, 1984 p. 18.

72. Marcel Niedergang in *Le Monde* (Paris), May 3, 1984, pp. 1, 5; authors' interviews in Nicaragua; and interview with Commander Henry Ruiz, Panama City Radio, March 9, 1986, trans. *FBIS–LAM*, March 12, 1986, p. 12.

73. *El Nuevo Diario*, May 22, 1984, p. 5; and document cited in *La Nación Internacional*, April 19–25, 1984, pp. 18–19.

averted the emergence of unsanctioned economic activities such as black marketeering and speculation.

Although it is faltering on the economic front, the regime has been pushing ahead with a "progressive" educational policy—including a literacy campaign—tailored to advance the socialist transformation. In workshops for middle-level teachers, the education ministry uses materials printed in Cuba and the USSR. Some of the literacy primers have been printed with the aid of Cuban experts. Even publications aimed at very young children extol the virtues not only of Sandino but also of the vanguard party, guerrilla war, the revolution, the FSLN and Carlos Fonseca, militarization, frontier guards, the armed forces, and Yankeephobia. For example, a mathematics primer teaches multiplication with illustrations of Soviet-made AK-47 rifles and hand grenades.[74] This and other primers also contain the hymn of the FSLN (composed by Tomás Borge), which children are required to memorize. Translated, one verse reads:

> *The children of Sandino*
> *Will not sell out, will not give up*
> *Let us struggle against the Yankee*
> *Enemy of all mankind.*[75]

Links with Communist Countries

As we have suggested, the Sandinista regime has close and growing ties with the Soviet Union and its allies, although public mainifestations of the relationship have been downplayed in the aftermath of the ouster of Grenada's New Jewel Movement (NJM) in 1983. As early as January 1980, a Soviet Central Committee secretary and candidate Politburo member, Boris Ponomarev, equated the Nicaraguan revolution with revolutions in Afghanistan, Ethiopia, and Angola.[76] Soviet commentary also has grouped the FSLN regime with the NJM regime under the "popular democratic" rubric, a term once used to describe the transitional stage of postwar regimes in Eastern Europe on their way to becoming

74. "Multiplication with Numbers 1 to 20. Concept," in *Matemática* [Mathematics] (Managua: Ministerio de Educacion, n.d.), p. 145. (Copy obtained by the authors in Managua.)

75. *Libro de Lectura de Primaria* (a primer), (Managua: Ministerio de Educación, n.d.), p. 140.

76. "The Inevitability of the Liberation Movement," *Kommunist* (Moscow), no. 1 (January 1980): 11–27. This formula has been repeated by other Soviet writers; see, e.g., *Pravda*, June 16, 1983.

full-fledged Leninist systems.[77] Since 1983, however, and particularly after the Grenada episode, Moscow has tended to refer to Nicaragua merely as "antiimperialist" (most likely in an attempt to lower the level of alarm in the United States), even though Nicaragua's "vanguard party" and "revolutionary liberation" struggle are still classified in the same category as the struggles of socialist-oriented vanguards in Afghanistan, Angola, and Ethiopia. Indeed, for some Soviet analysts, the Nicaraguan revolution already has made a contribution to the expansion of the "anti-imperialist democratic camp" and to the "reduction of the geopolitical area of the capitalist system."[78] Such ideological formulations carry with them increased Soviet political and moral support for given movements. Expanded ties between the Soviet bloc and Nicaragua are evident in the realms of interparty affairs, military assistance, and economic relations.

Party-to-Party Relations

In dealing with the FSLN, Moscow was dealing with a relatively small yet elitist "known quantity" that had the distinction of having come to power via a popular revolution. Although the Soviets kept a low profile vis-à-vis FSLN insurgents, the USSR recognized the Sandinista regime on the diplomatic level precisely one day after the fall of Somoza. It may be presumed that party-to-party relations were formalized during the March 1980 visit to Moscow by an FSLN delegation led by Borge, Humberto Ortega, and Henry Ruíz. Although any agreement signed then remains secret, one can speculate on a text, based on the agreement signed between the Communist party of the Soviet Union (CPSU) and Grenada's NJM in July 1982. The CPSU and the FSLN probably also agreed to establish a broad framework for party-to-party cooperation, including consultations on international matters, all-round development of state-to-state relations, and cooperation · between mass organizations in both countries.[79] The political closeness of

77. See A. Stroganov's review of A.F. Shulgovski's "Politicheskaya sistema obshchestva v Latinskoy Amerike" [The Political System of Society in Latin America], in *Latinskaya Amerika,* May 1983, p. 134.

78. B. N. Ponomarev, "Real Socialism and the Liberated Countries," *Slovo Lektora* (Moscow), March 1984, p. 14; and Yuriy Koroliov, "The Experience of the Transition Period," *America Latina* (Moscow), September 1984, pp. 43–53.

79. For the text of the CPSU–NJM agreement, see Jiri Valenta and Herbert J. Ellison, eds., *Grenada and Soviet/Cuban Policy: Crisis and the US/OECS Intervention* (Boulder, Colo.: Westview, 1985), p. 319. The FSLN has also signed party-to-party cooperation agreements with the Bulgarian and probably the East German and Czechoslovak communist parties.

the two parties is suggested by the strong pro-Soviet bias in subsequent Nicaraguan foreign policy. For example, in January 1980 the FSLN regime abstained from a United Nations vote demanding the withdrawal of Soviet forces from Afghanistan. And until December 1985 and the Sino-Soviet thaw, the FSLN leadership refused to establish diplomatic relations with the People's Republic of China.[80]

There has been increasing cooperation not only between the Nicaraguan and Soviet bloc ministries of education but also between the FSLN Institute for the Study of Sandinism and two Soviet institutions: the Latin American Institute of Social Sciences and the Institute of Marxism–Leninism of the CPSU Central Committee.[81] The Soviets established the Russian Language School now operating in Managua, donated educational material to the Marxist-Leninist Library at the National University at Leon, and together with the Bulgarians have provided donations to the FSLN newspaper *Barricada*. Since the revolution, some 2,000 Nicaraguans have received scholarships to study at universities in the USSR and other communist countries. Moreover, there are active ties between the Soviet Komsomol and the 19th of July Sandinista Youth Movement and between the Nicaraguan Peace Committee and the Peace Committee of the USSR.[82] In addition, there has been cooperation between the Soviet Society of Friendship with Nicaragua and the Nicaraguan Association of Friendship with Socialist Countries, which has helped provide scholarships for Nicaraguan students in the USSR and sponsor crippled FSLN veterans for medical treatment in Soviet cities.

A few hundred Soviet civilian advisors are in Nicaragua along with several dozen advisers from East European states. Nevertheless, the strongest communist representation is Cuban. One suspects the existence of a party-to-party agreement between the FSLN and the Cuban Communist

---

The agreement with the Bulgarian CP was signed in November 1981. See "The FSLN and the Bulgarian CP Sign an Agreement," *Barricada*, November 22, 1981, p. 12. For the comparable BCP/NJM document, see Valenta and Ellison, *Grenada*, pp. 465–467.

80. Interestingly, the FSLN-controlled Council of State turned down a motion to recognize the PRC. See José Antonio Argüello, "A No to China Is a No to a Nonaligned Nicaragua," *La Prensa* (Managua), August 20, 1980, p. 2.

81. E.g., the FSLN participated in the 14th Annual Conference of Ministers of Higher Education from Warsaw Pact countries, plus Cuba and Mongolia and "socialist-oriented" Afghanistan and Angola. See Radio Havana, September 11, 1984, trans. *FBIS-LAM*, September 13, 1984, p. Q3. For a Soviet report on the Institute for the Study of Sandinism, see E.S. Dabagyan, "Visiting among Nicaraguan Scholars," *Latinskaya Amerika*, March 1982, pp. 126–128. A council headed by Humberto Ortega reportedly supervises ideological–methodological work at the institute.

82. From authors' interviews in Nicaragua.

party (PCC). There are also close ties between the Union of Young Communists of Cuba and the 19th of July Sandinista Youth. Cuban advisers are attached to the more important FSLN departments and ministries, and hundreds of Nicaraguan youths are trained in Cuban schools. Meanwhile, many Cuban teachers (at one point 2,000 of them, but some were recalled in 1985) have been assigned to the Nicaraguan education sector, particularly the national literacy campaign, whose tactics of indoctrination are characteristically Leninist.

It is evident that the FSLN, like the NJM in Grenada, conceives of itself as a revolutionary bridge between the CPSU and PCC, on the one hand, and leftist forces in the Carribbean Basin (particularly Central America), on the other. The FSLN coordinates regional support for revolutionary movements in El Salvador (the Farabundo Martí National Liberation Front—FMLN) and in Guatemala (the Guerrilla Army of the Poor—EGP), and for the Costa Rican revolutionary underground and other Latin American revolutionary movements. The M-19 guerrillas of Colombia and the Montoneros of Argentina are also present in Nicaragua; even the Palestine Liberation Organization and Libya have regional headquarters in Managua.[83] From its special vantage point, the FSLN helps organize meetings of communist parties throughout Latin America and the Caribbean. As captured Grenada documents illustrate, the FSLN and NJM both participated in the work of a secret regional caucus of leftist parties in January 1983 (see Appendix E). Additionally, Nicaragua supplied 2000 uniforms to the Grenadian armed forces prior to 1983 and had agreed to train some Grenadian teachers.[84]

Fraternal Military Assistance

The Soviet Union and other communist states have discreetly but steadily increased their military and intelligence support for the Sandinistas. To be sure, during the insurrection it was Cuba that supplied weapons to the FSLN and helped it obtain weapons on international markets. Also, some 50 Cuban security advisers were among the Sandinista forces that captured Managua in July 1979. But subsequently the FSLN has received much more military aid. It is reasonable to assume that the first agreement for substantial arms transfers from the Soviet Union was signed during the visit by

83. Interview with Miguel Bolaños, p. 36. Close ties with the M-19 guerrillas and their role in supporting the M-19 prior to the attack on the Palace of Justice in Colombia in December 1985 were denied by the FSLN leaders. However, M-19 leaders do travel with Nicaraguan diplomatic passports while maintaining offices in Managua. See *Star and Herald* (Panama City), December 30, 1985, pp. 1–6.
84. Valenta and Ellison, *Grenada*, p. 485.

FSLN officials to Moscow, East Berlin, and Prague in March 1980. The initiation of arms transfers was confirmed publicly only at the July 1980 celebration of the revolution's anniversary in Managua, where the EPS displayed 18 ZPU light antiaircraft guns, 6 SA-7 surface-to-air missile launchers, and 100 RPG-7 antitank weapons of Soviet make plus 96 W-50 trucks from East Germany.[85]

As was true in Grenada, the first Soviet bloc arms transfers arrived well before the 1980 election of Ronald Reagan as president of the United States. Subsequently, as U.S.–Nicaraguan relations deteriorated over the issue of FSLN aid to the guerrillas in El Salvador, the communist states' shipments of military supplies to Managua increased. By summer 1981 the first T-54 and T-55 tanks had arrived on Algerian ships. On a second visit to Moscow, in November 1981, Humberto Ortega met with Soviet Defense Minister Dimitriy Ustinov and Chief of the General Staff Nikolay Ogarkov, and presumably signed a new arms agreement. In 1983, as the anti-FSLN insurgency intensified, communist arms transfers (now on Soviet bloc ships) increased, totaling some 20,000 tons of materiel (double the amounts for 1981 and 1982). In addition to dozens of tanks, there were other weapons specifically suited to counterinsurgency operations: 25 to 30 armored personnel carriers and several MI-8 helicopters.[86]

Moscow soon added An-26 transport planes, jeeps, field ambulances, and thousands more AK-47 rifles to the Nicaraguan arsenal. There were also reports of some 80 MiG fighters being held in Cuba for future delivery. Other sources stated that dozens of Nicaraguan pilots were completing training in Bulgaria, that others were going to Cuba for further study, and that the FSLN was acquiring several L-39 military trainers from Czechoslovakia to train Nicaraguan fighter pilots.[87] By late 1984 Nicaragua had more than 100 Soviet T-54 and T-55 medium tanks, over 20 light amphibious PT-76 tanks, 120 armored vehicles, more than 1000 military trucks, 120 antiaircraft missiles, 120 antiaircraft guns, and 700 shoulder-fired surface-to-air missiles.[88] (Despite the preponderance of Soviet bloc nations among those providing military assistance, Nicaragua prior to 1983 also received aid from Algeria and France.)

Again repeating their conduct in Grenada, the Soviets and Cubans are assisting in construction projects with immediate or potential military and

85. Rudolph, *Nicaragua*, p. 213.

86. From interview with Miguel Bolaños, p. 35; see also Peter Clement, "Moscow and Nicaragua: Cultivating a New Client?" *Comparative Strategy* (New York), no. 1 (1985).

87. From authors' interviews in Nicaragua.

88. Ibid., and *New York Times*, November 7, 1984.

intelligence application. Cubans, using Soviet equipment, are helping to build a military airport in Punta Huete and upgrade facilities at Puerto Cabezas, Estelí, La Rosita, and Bluefields. Meanwhile, the Soviets and Nicaraguans are conducting joint oceanographic research in the Atlantic and Pacific. Moscow was going to donate drydock and fishing-boat repair facilities at the Pacific port of San Juan del Sur, although the project is currently on hold. Cuban construction workers are building a new $80 million deepwater port at El Bluff on the Caribbean coast, financed largely by the Soviet-dominated Council for Economic Mutual Assistance (CEMA). Borge described the new port as "undoubtedly a strategically important project" that would provide Nicaragua with access to European markets without having to use the Panama Canal.[89] Again, as was true in Grenada, the Soviets are helping to build a satellite communication earth station. (Perhaps not coincidentally, the president of the Soviet–Nicaraguan Friendship Society, Vasiliy Shamshin, is also the Soviet communication minister.)

Sources in the United States and the Caribbean estimate that 3,000 Cuban military and security advisers are in Nicaragua today, although Daniel Ortega admits to only 800.[90] Between 1983 and March 1986, the group of Cuban military advisers in Nicaragua was headed by the Cuban deputy minister of defense, General Arnaldo Ochoa, who played a prominent role in Cuban military operations in Angola and Ethiopia in the 1970s. The Cuban military advisers wear uniforms indistinguishable from those of the Nicaraguans. Cuban security advisers occupy important positions in the Nicaraguan secret police. In addition, there are some 100 Soviet military–security advisers, 25 Bulgarians, 40–50 East Germans, and some 25 PLO specialists. There are also Libyan personnel and members of the Spanish Basque separatist organization ETA.[91]

It should be remembered that before 1979 many of the FSLN guerrillas—including Borge and Humberto Ortega—were trained in Cuban guerrilla schools and camps and that Ruiz, secret police chief Cerna, and CDS chief Herrera studied in the USSR. This pattern continues; dozens of Nicaraguan

89. Radio Sandino (Managua), July 4, 1985, trans. *FBIS–LAM*, July 10, 1985, p. P 10.

90. Ortega is cited by *EFE* (Madrid), March 12, 1985, trans. *FBIS-LAM*, March 13, 1985, p. P2. The deputy minister of foreign affairs of Cuba, Jorge Bolaños, has claimed that there were only 200 Cuban military advisers in Nicaragua. See *Barbados Advocate* (Bridgetown), November 9, 1984, p. 4.

91. Interview with Miguel Bolaños, pp. 16 and 33; see also *Cambio 16*, October 3, 1983, p. 29; and Tegucigalpa Cadena Audio Video, September 4, 1984, trans. *FBIS–LAM*, September 5, 1984, p. P18. Ochoa was identified as head of the group of Cuban military advisers shortly before his departure in March 1986. Ochoa was replaced by Brigadier General López; see *Barricada*, March 12, 1986, p. 8.

security personnel are trained in 2-year and shorter courses in Cuba and in 3-year or 1-year security courses in the USSR.[92]

There appears to be a rough division of labor among the communist states that give security assistance to Nicaragua—a pattern also observed in Soviet bloc dealings with such "socialist-oriented" countries as Angola, Ethiopia, South Yemen, and (formerly) Grenada. The Soviets seem to be responsible for overall coordination, whereas the Cubans provide manpower and serve as military and counterintelligence advisers; the East Germans provide trucks, police specialists, and highly qualified communication technicians and advisers to the party apparatus; the Bulgarians help to train special troops and aid in the processing of information in security matters; and the Czechoslovakians provide weapons, explosives, and ammunition.

Communist Economic Relations

Paralleling its gradual approach toward restructuring the mode of production, the FSLN government has been measured in its expansion of economic cooperation with communist states, although this is not completely of its own volition. So far, the primary objective of Soviet bloc assistance seems to be to reinforce the FSLN in political, ideological, and security aspects. Exploration of Soviet–Nicaraguan economic cooperation began in January 1980 with the visit of a high-level Soviet technical mission to Managua. Over the next 30 months a variety of trade, technical, and economic agreements were signed, and trade and economic assistance commissions were established. Between July 1979 and February 1982, for example, Soviet aid amounted only to $7.9 million compared to Cuban aid of $42.5 million. (Aid from the United States for 1979–1981 totaled $118 million.)[93] Soviet aid was highly publicized, however, as, for example, when the Soviets shipped 20,000 tons of grain to Nicaragua in 1981.

In late 1982 the Soviet Union stepped up its economic assistance to the Sandinistas. Some $100 million worth of tractors and earth-moving equipment was donated, and in 1983 Soviet bloc economic aid amounted to $240 million (including $100 million from the USSR).[94] Initially, the United

92. Interview with Miguel Bolaños, p. 33; and interview with former counterintelligence officer Alvaro Baldizón, Mainz Television Network, May 14, 1986, trans.*FBIS-LAM*, May 16, 1986, p. 15.

93. On Soviet aid, see Edmé Domínguez's paper, "Soviet Policy toward Central America, the Caribbean, and the Members of the Contadora Group"; for U.S. aid, see *Review of Nicaragua's Commitments to the OAS* (Washington, D.C.: Government Printing Office, U.S. Department of State, Bureau of Public Affairs, July 18, 1984).

94. Clement, "Moscow and Nicaragua."

States was again much more forthcoming with credits than were the communist states, extending some $72.6 million from 1979-1980. In this period, the Soviet Union made no credits available. Cuba offered a symbolic $1 million and East Germany $82 million. In 1981 the USSR offered some $73.2 million and in 1982 another $150 million. Cuba provided $3.5 million in 1981 and $50 million in 1982 (which very likely included supplies for Cuban personnel in Nicaragua). In 1982 there was an additional $26 million from East Germany, indeterminate amounts from Czechoslovakia and Bulgaria, and, in 1981, $100 million from a noncommunist ally, Libya.[95] By June 1985 the total economic aid of communist nations to Nicaragua ("annuities," credits, and machinery, excluding goods for development projects) had reached $600 million. In 1985 alone, economic aid from communist countries came to $260 million.[96]

Soviet–Nicaraguan trade has grown significantly, with Soviet exports to Nicaragua in 1983 valued at some 42.4 million rubles against 0.1 million rubles in 1980. Nicaraguan exports to the USSR grew much more slowly over that period, from 5.5 to 9.5 million rubles.[97] Although not dramatic, Soviet–Nicaraguan trade now exceeds in volume the trade of the USSR with Mexico or Peru. A regular maritime link was established between Leningrad and the Nicaraguan port of Corinto in early 1985.

Still, Moscow is hesitant to take on another Cuba. In April 1983, Victor Volskiy, director of Moscow's Latin American Institute, noted that "it has cost us a lot to send oil to Cuba—two tankers a day for 20 years. We would not like to have to repeat that on a larger scale."[98] Nicaragua is, of course, a less populous country than Cuba, and therefore expansion of Soviet and CEMA [Council of Economic Mutual Assistance] aid to Managua cannot be excluded. Indeed, for some time in 1985, Moscow became Nicaragua's major oil supplier.[99] Other signs of increased aid from the Soviet Union and some CEMA countries were the establishment of new intergovernmental Soviet–Nicaraguan and Bulgarian–Nicaraguan commissions on coopera-

95. Domínguez, "Soviet Policy toward Central America," Table II.
96. Interview with Minister of Foreign Cooperation Henry Ruiz conducted by Madrid's EFE in Warsaw on June 27, 1985, at the conclusion of a CEMA session at which Ruiz represented Nicaragua, trans. in *FBIS-LAM* July 1, 1985, pp. P/21–22; and *Barricada*, January 16, 1986 p. 5.
97. "Soviet Foreign Trade, (January–December 1983)," *Foreign Trade* (Moscow), March 1984; and Nikki Miller and Laurence Whitehead's paper, "The Soviet Interest in Latin America: An Economic Perspective."
98. *Guardian* (London), April 28, 1983, p. 15.
99. Soviet tankers with oil for Managua were said to be sailing twice a week from Leningrad to Corinto; Radio Havana, March 5, 1985, trans. *FBIS-LAM*, March 7, 1985, p. Q/5. Delayed arrival of a Soviet tanker in the early fall of 1984 forced the FSLN to reduce fuel rations. See *Wall Street Journal*, October 2, 1984, p. 38.

tion in economics, trade, science, and technology, and Nicaraguan participation as an observer at the meetings of the CEMA. At a CEMA meeting in June 1985, Nicaragua was able to secure expanded CEMA economic cooperation with the Nicaraguan agricultural, livestock, and textile industries, plus 10,000 scholarships. At present there are 1,600 Nicaraguans studying technical subjects in CEMA countries. In 1985–1986 CEMA formed a joint commission with Nicaragua to provide extensive economic aid to that country and help preserve and ensure the survival of the FSLN regime. Minister of Foreign Cooperation Ruiz did not exclude Nicaragua's joining CEMA in 1989-1990.[100]

Conclusions

Nicaragua has not yet evolved into a full-fledged Leninist state comparable to the countries of Eastern Europe, to Cuba, or to Vietnam. Yet the FSLN regime seems headed toward becoming a dictatorship of a Leninist-oriented party. The FSLN has been engaged in a gradual, skillful process of socialist transformation at home, benefiting from earlier Soviet, East European, and Cuban experiences and the awareness that too rapid a Leninization of the country would alarm the dominant power in the region—the United States. The FSLN also continues to maintain strategic ties with the USSR and pro-Soviet communist countries and a foreign policy orientation that is hardly congruent with its official, self-proclaimed nonalignment. As the draft of the new Nicaraguan constitution suggests, the FSLN government is prepared to make tactical concessions as long as it controls the real power bases—the party, the state security, and the army—and maintains its basic foreign policy strategy. On these matters, the FSLN closely follows the Soviet and Cuban models and is unlikely to make meaningful concessions.

In terms of regional politics, the National Directorate seems prepared to follow the Bolshevik example, that is, to forgo full-scale internationalism until circumstances permit a resumption of large-scale aid to revolutionaries in the region. Meanwhile, the flow of small arms to the Salvadoran guerrillas evidently continues.[101] In the long run, as a former Sandinista told us in Managua, the FSLN revolution will need to spread throughout the region or perish. This assessment conforms to an emerging consensus in Central America that the FSLN is unwilling to give up its original (1969) commit-

100. Ruiz interview cited in note 96, and ACAN (Panama City), October 23, 1985, trans. *FBIS-LAM*, October 30, 1985, pp. 16–17.

101. *New York Times*, April 11, 1984.

ment to regionwide revolution. As noted by the Salvadoran newspaper *El Diario de Hoy* on January 24, 1985, "The consensus in the Central American region is that so long as the Sandinista Communists remain in Nicaragua, the region will continue to be a permanent focus of subversion and political unrest that will threaten neighboring countries." The same view is heard from various policymakers in Honduras, Panama, and democratic Costa Rica. This interpretation was supported by a 1985 public opinion poll taken in Central America. According to this poll, 92% of the Costa Ricans, 89% of the Hondurans, 63% of the Salvadorans, and 48% of the Guatemalans regard the FSLN regime as a threat.[102] Nicaragua's military buildup has already made the EPS a dominant factor in the immediate Central American regional military balance. Costa Rica is particularly vulnerable, having only a paramilitary police force and no regular army.

As it did in Cuba, Moscow (this time with Havana's help) has made guarded political, security, and economic commitments to the FSLN. Yet, Grenada demonstrated, and various Soviet signals suggest, that the FSLN can count on nothing more than "political" support from the USSR in the event of a direct conflict with the United States.[103] The Cubans probably would provide insufficient support in such an instance, for they lack the airlift and sealift capabilities to bring in adequate reinforcements.[104]

The FSLN contends that its opposition's insurgency owes its existence to the United States. But the issue of U.S. support for the *contras* begs a more important issue: The anti-Sandinista insurgencies are symptomatic of conditions created by most Third World Leninist-oriented regimes. In every socialist-oriented country with an elitist vanguard party (Afghanistan, Angola, Ethiopia, South Yemen, Nicaragua, and Mozambique), there is a significant resistance movement, with strong popular support, that has multiplied in response to the forced socialist transformation of the society by the ruling party. In the Nicaraguan opposition forces, estimated at 19,000 men, there are at most 3,000 former Somoza National Guardsmen; thus the vast majority of the opposition are Nicaraguans disenchanted with the Sandinista revolution, many of them former Sandinistas (including former Sandinista officials Pastora, Cruz, César, and Robelo). In the largest organization, the Democratic National Front, reportedly only 1−3% of the insurgents are former National Guard members, 19% are former Sandinistas, and the remainder are peasants from the northern part of Nicaragua.

102. *La Nación* (San José), March 2−3, 1986.

103. See Jiri Valenta's testimony before the Kissinger Commission, "Soviet Policy in Central America," *Survey* (London), Autumn−Winter 1983, pp. 287−303.

104. Interview with Cuban First Deputy Minister of Foreign Affairs José Viera, *Kyodo* (Tokyo), November 8, 1984, trans. *FBIS-LAM*, November 8, 1984, p. Q/2.

Ex-Sandinistas and disenchanted civilians also provide some of the top military leadership of the opposition guerrillas.[105]

Outside players cannot "buy into" such a large insurgency. It draws its major impetus from the FSLN military buildup, from enforced recruitment, from ideological mobilization by the elite vanguard party (with its arbitrary Leninist rules of the political game), from the economic ineptitude of the government and growing national penury, from the vigilant and often coercive control of the population, and from the blatantly pro-Soviet stance of the government (e.g., 3 days of official national mourning following the death of Soviet leader Konstantin Chernenko and the refusal for 6 years to establish diplomatic relations with China).

To some former Sandinista leaders, this approach is Leninist only and not Marxist. In the words of Pastora: "I am not afraid of Marxism . . . a philosophy that teaches you to do justice, but in accordance with the social and political conditions of each country. The screw-up comes when you apply this philosophy in the Soviet style, and in accordance with the social, political, and economic laws of the Soviet Union." For Pastora, at least, the goal is to return to true Sandinism, "Nicaraguan Sandinism, not Soviet Sandinism."[106]

In Eastern Europe numerous attempts were made in the past to make communism more pluralistic, more humane. And some or all of these attempts might have flourished but for the threat or reality of Soviet military invasion. In Nicaragua, such an evolution seems precluded by the rule of an FSLN regime that has internalized Soviet and Cuban models of repression and is intent on consolidating its real power through coercive mechanisms.

105. Interview with Arturo Cruz, Guatemala Radio, March 18, 1985, trans. *FBIS-LAM*, March 21, 1985, p. P/13; also authors' interviews in Nicaragua and Costa Rica in December 1984.

106. Interview with *La Prensa* (San Pedro Sula), July 15, 1982, p.5.

• CHAPTER TWO •

Leninism in Nicaragua

Arturo J. Cruz, Sr.

I

In assessing the progress of Leninism in Nicaragua, one must recall what has taken place there the past decade. Early in the period, the Sandinista Front of National Liberation (FSLN), by assuming the military–political vanguard of the broad coalition that overthrew Somoza, gained for itself official public power in Nicaragua. Riding on a wave of moral authority and popularity, the FSLN then took over the country, reneging on early promises of freedom and democracy.

As their popular backing has eroded, the FSLN leaders have used increasing repression. Masters of manipulation and propaganda, Nicaragua's new totalitarian state has sought to conceal abuse under a facade of feigned tolerance. In the meantime, the FSLN has further consolidated a regime that foreshadows the imposition of Leninism in Nicaragua. Dissension has translated into an armed rebellion hotly debated in international political circles.

Notwithstanding its leverage, the democratic Western world has failed to impose moral restraint on the Managua government that has continued to be the beneficiary of western political support and the recipient of its financial and technical cooperation. This has further strengthened the Sandinista position and obstructed national reconciliation. The insistent efforts of peacemeakers are, nevertheless, intensely felt today. Early initiatives that achieved little more than limited progress now enter a new, more promising phase wherein Central American governments, called to a

41

greater role, have addressed the issues more directly, although still within the context of the Contadora peace effort.

The Contadora process has the commitment of four governments (Mexico, Venezuela, Panama, Colombia)—whose national pride and diplomatic prestige are at stake. Further Latin American solidarity is lent Contadora by the governments of Argentina, Brazil, Peru, and Uruguay—the Lima group. Most recently the Central American countries themselves, whose vital interests are at stake, have come to the forefront of the negotiating process.

Contadora has avoided a further escalation of the crisis while attempting to solve it within a regional scope. The Caraballeda declaration has given reason for optimism. Nevertheless, a breakthrough can be achieved only from enhancement of the Central American role. This will guarantee an effective examination of the Nicaraguan conflict from the important standpoints of Soviet–Cuban involvement and U.S. reaction. No entity or group is more suited to assess the nature of the Sandinista regime and to determine whether the Sandinista model is the best revolutionary project option for Central America than its Central American neighbors and Common Market partners. As Central American faces Central American, it is fortunate that sophisticated statesmen such as Oscar Arias, José Azcona, Napoleón Duarte, and Vinicio Cerezo, who are true democrats, should be the interlocutors of Daniel Ortega. These men, who are steering Central America along the path of economic development and social progress, merit the free world's support, because they offer the best hope for breaking the impasse.

Despite growing recognition of their glaring contempt for freedom and their increasing totalitarianism, the Sandinistas retain considerable international support. The most significant sources of this support are the continuing solidarity of the world communist movement and, in my judgment, the pervasive opposition to U.S. intervention (as well as sheer anti-Americanism) that exists in Latin America and throughout the free world. Thus the Leninist edifice currently being erected in Nicaragua rests on two pillars: communist determination to support it and, ironically, democratic reluctance to alter it. This was illustrated during the first week of April 1986 when Spain's president Felipe González referred to the *comandantes* in a way that was intended to belittle the Reagan administration's Nicaragua policy while also giving the *comandantes* a political boost: "Whether they are Marxists or not is a question of their own purview and personal competence; what really matters is that they are the legitimately elected rulers of their own country."

It may be erroneous and self-deceiving to think that *Somocismo* is buried in oblivion. But Somoza was so morally hideous that even today the world is reluctant to admit that the Sandinistas have turned out to be just as evil. The

Nicaraguan people learned very early on that they had been betrayed by the Sandinistas, but it is far more difficult for a European, an American, or any other foreigner to realize that the Sandinista dragonslayers of 1979 are the monsters of 1986. Such worldwide indulgence explains the Sandinista Front's ability to trample on democratic values with impunity. The Sandinistas' suspension of civil rights was, by and large, censured in Latin America and Western Europe, and in the U.S. media. But this censure was short-lived and soon forgotten. In the climate of tolerance that followed, the Sandinistas dared to show disrespect toward the pope and succeeded in doing so without losing substantial backing from the Catholic bishops and leaders of other denominations in the United States and elsewhere. Furthermore, the charismatic Cardinal Miguel Obando y Bravo is routinely insulted by government officials, in Sandinista newspapers, and on television and radio networks. His Eminence is taunted by irreverent cartoonists and maverick communist priests; his printing press has been seized, his radio station has been interrupted, and his homilies have been censored; his project for the establishment of a human rights commission has been disrupted; and he is not allowed to celebrate outdoor Mass or preside over public processions.

The martyred Pedro Joaquín Chamorro Cardenal's newspaper, *La Prensa*, which suffered persecution first under Somoza, became, under the Sandinistas, a universal symbol of the endurance of the free press in the face of official abuse by a totalitarian regime. Political parties, labor unions, and business guilds have limited rights and are granted only the most narrow space for their activities.

These and other repressive conditions imposed on the Nicaraguan people reveal the dictatorial nature of the FSLN leaders, who will not share power under any circumstances. Yet the Socialist International does not consider such repression a viable reason for excluding the Sandinistas from participating as observers in its Latin American bureau meetings. For an example of the FSLN skillful manipulation of the Socialist International, see Appendix E.

The current Nicaraguan regime also raises a geopolitical problem. Unparalleled Nicaraguan militarization upsets the regional balance, and the construction of the Punta Huete airport constitutes a potential menace to hemispheric security. Sandinista acquisition of Soviet-made and Soviet-supplied MI-24 helicopters and T-55 tanks, the presence of Cuban and other communist bloc advisers, and the Sandinistas' interference in El Salvador all give rise to the perception that Fidel Castro and the Sandinistas intend to convert Central America into a Leninist enclave. On the basis of these perceptions, there are good reasons for the concern of the U.S. administration. Yet President Reagan's containment policy has been opposed, both at home and abroad. The imposition of change by the United States in Nicaragua is almost impossible because of two syndromes. First is the American Vietnam syndrome. Although Washington recognizes something must be done, in Nicaragua *Americans want neither a second Cuba nor a second Vietnam,* and this ambivalence results in inactivity.

There is also a Latin American syndrome that discourages any drastic action Washington might be prepared to take against Managua. Latin America ostensibly is opposed to U.S. intervention because of the prevailing "peer pressure:" No Latin American government would publicly approve the overthrow of a communist regime in a neighboring country by the United States, even though no Latin American country (other than Nicaragua and, possibly, Guyana and Surinam) wishes to become another Cuba.

Three other factors complicate these syndromes, giving the Sandinistas greater latitude to consolidate their power by helping to distort reality and project a mythical vision of Nicaragua to the outside world. The first is liberation theology used to showcase the revolution. Two superstar clergymen are members of the cabinet: Ernesto Cardenal is minister of culture, and Miguel d'Escoto is foreign minister. The political intention behind these appointments is to give the impression that communism and religion are revolutionary partners in Nicaragua, that the Sandinistas are not atheists.

The second factor allowing the *comandantes* to generate solidarity and sympathy abroad is the international perception of the United States' financing of the Nicaraguan resistance and providing it with logistical support. Some sectors of international opinion rely only on superficial information, which is heavily influenced by Sandinista propaganda and anti-Americanism. These sectors see U.S. aid as ruthlesss aggression against the Nicaraguan people. This is undoubtedly the most effective element favoring the Sandinistas in the image competition that has characterized this crisis. It provides them with excuses for their economic failures, their curtailment of freedoms, and their military buildup. As long as the Sandinistas are able to give the appearance of being a Central American David facing a North American Goliath, they can afford to be oppressors at home and heroes abroad.

A third factor promoting international leniency regarding the Sandinistas' totalitarian behavior is that (paradoxically) they have understood very well that they must exercise some tolerance if they are eventually to consolidate their militaristic, dictatorial system. Tokenism plays a useful part here, misleading international observers. The Sandinistas' policy is shrewd: They show some flexibility and pragmatism in the short run for the sake of gradually achieving their totalitarian objectives in the long run. Moreover, as long as the Sandinistas hold absolute power, they are able to go through certain motions, such as having elections (with enough precautions not to put their power at risk), creating conditions that permit some members of the upper class to enjoy their wealth unmolested, or allowing citizens to travel abroad. These ploys bear good fruits for the regime. The credulous often regard the dissidents' denunciations of the Sandinistas' abuses as lies. Similarly, the dissidents' claims of support for principles of freedom and democracy are regarded as reactionary exaggerations.

The factors just described explain much about the Nicaraguan phenomenon. One must take them into account to make an accurate assessment of the crisis and to explore its possible solutions. These factors influence not only the internal dimension of the revolution in Nicaragua, but the central feature of Nicaragua's predicament, its external character: international notoriety, external decision makers, and propaganda abroad.

II

The shocks produced in the socioeconomic field by the "surprise package" of measures announced in installments by the Sandinistas during the early days of the revolution were not, frankly speaking, earth shattering. There was already a prevailing consensus in favor of the economic and social reforms deemed necessary to strengthen nationalism, eliminate social injustice, and assure growth—all within a climate of fairness.

The exodus of significant human resources from Nicaragua, which crippled the country's economic viability, was not triggered by sudden nationalization or socialization of the means of production but by the fear instilled by the Sandinista commissars and block committees. There was a profound uncertainty about the future, which the regime's activities compounded. The regime was responsible for the ideological invasion of the educational system; excessive governmental intrusion in production; unfair competition among government agencies for credit, equipment, and raw materials; inefficiency within the public sector; a lack of fiscal and monetary discipline; ineptitude in the official management of food distribution; the harassment of dissidents; and the general curtailment of pluralism. The last element was demonstrated by the regime's partisan terror, its rule by force of arms, and its demagoguery.

As a result, Nicaragua no longer has a viable, self sustaining economy. It is totally dependent on foreign support to finance the gaps and deficits, which have reached critical levels. A country of 3 million people has seen its foreign debt soar from $1.6 billion in July 1979 to nearly $5 billion in only 6 1/2 years. During the same period, the national currency has depreciated to a point that has virtually deprived wage earners of their purchasing power. At the beginning of this period, the official exchange rate was 10 córdobas per U.S. dollar as opposed to the free rate of 18 córdobas. In 1986 the official exchange rate reached 70 córdobas per dollar, and the free rate, 2000 córdobas.

In the process, prices have risen in an inflationary spiral. The decline in production has drastically curtailed exports, thereby reducing the foreign exchange earnings that could have been used to pay for imports. In 1979 a low-income family spent 700 cordobas monthly on food; in 1986 that family needs 12,000 cordobas. Salaries have had only very modest adjustments. A *campesino* or a truck driver must spend his entire monthly earnings to buy a pair of shoes, a pair of trousers, and a shirt. Nicaragua, a country that used to be an exporter of basic grains, is now a land of shortages, ration cards, and exasperating queues.

One of the Sandinistas' present objectives is to search for some kind of understanding with private producers that would promote a special production effort. To that end, in an on-and-off fashion, the government has sought dialogues with producers or facilitated their access to equipment and raw materials. But no progress has been made.

What Nicaragua needs is national reconciliation. The Sandinistas do not want serious commitments of a pluralistic nature and, consequently, reconciliation has not been feasible. The Sandinistas seem to be waiting for the thousands of young boys and girls currently being trained in communist countries to return to Nicaragua. The government may then proceed to nationalize the whole economy. Even under those circumstances, however, Nicaragua would need some modus vivendi with its Central American Common Market partners, and with the United States. It would also need to implement a program designed to make possible the return to Nicaragua of some 200,000 refugees, who now constitute a major social problem for Honduras, Costa Rica, and other neighbors. If the Sandinistas behaved as Nicaraguan statesmen, they would give the country real social peace. This would facilitate the return of refugees and businessmen. Social peace must be based on pluralism, however, and the Sandinistas do not seem willing to accept this.

No matter how far the Sandinistas intend to imitate the Leninist model, the Nicaraguan case may not necessarily be a carbon copy of the Cuban experience. Since Nicaragua has land borders with Costa Rica and Honduras and is closely linked with all the Central American countries, it would probably require a hybrid model. Notwithstanding that difference, Nicaragua's external dependency would remain high, and the Soviet bloc would continue to be an important source of aid. One striking difference between Nicaragua and Cuba is that after more than 7 years of revolution, the Sandinistas have not yet declared Nicaragua a communist state.

It has already been corroborated beyond a reasonable doubt that the Sandinistas used the umbrella Frente Amplio Opositor (FAO) only tactically and only as long as necessary during the insurrectionary period. Shortly before victory, they formed a new bloc, more ideologically identified with the Sandinista Front and largely constituted by the same political organizations. These are the same Communists and Socialist parties that are now incorporated in the Sandinista-controlled National Assembly.

After victory, although it preserved a pluralistic image in the formal government, the Sandinista leadership appropriated for itself the preeminent role as vanguard and sole "depository of popular power." In order to implement that resolution, the Sandinista Front took the following steps: (1) It took full control of the state and civil society, displaying the party's symbols along with national symbols or in place of them; (2) it "sandinized" the armed forces (now the Sandinista Popular Army); (3) it appointed its top leaders to key posts in the cabinet; (4) it took control of the means of communication in the country; and (5) it created grass-roots organizations to indoctrinate and minipulate youth, labor, and *campesinos*.

These actions alienated most of the non-Sandinistas allied with the party during the revolution. Nevertheless, this was a calculated action: some non-Marxists became instant Sandinistas. In contrast, those who demanded pluralism, (who were in the majority), vigorously opposed the process of "sandinization." This was the beginning of dissent against the FSLN.

The Sandinistas are not willing to give an inch in this regard; that is what makes them totalitarians. They will not permit the existence of any institution or individual leadership that presents competition to *Sandinismo*. This totalitarian characteristic is the main obstacle to peace in Nicaragua. The Sandinistas will face confrontation until the last Nicaraguan who is unwilling to renounce his or her right to dissent and his or her belief in a democratic republic has disappeared or died. Furthermore, if the Sandinistas do not accept the need to adopt some political symmetry with their neighbors, they risk a confrontation with the whole of Central America. Cuba is an island; Guyana and Surinam are separated from their stronger and larger South American neighbors by a wall of jungle. The Sandinistas, however, will prove to be expansionists in Central America, because of its permeable borders, their ideological drive, and the reciprocal distrust they inspire.

A great deal of attention is focused on the question of human rights in Nicaragua. A number of organizations from a variety of perspectives have monitored, investigated, and championed human rights. This is a crucial battle in the war of images. The Sandinistas have benefited greatly from the prevailing impression that it is the rebel forces who must account for most of the alleged violations. The truth is that there has been a lack of objectivity on this matter. The origin of the ongoing insurgency is often ignored. It was the Sandinistas' involvement in the "final offensive" of the Salvadoran rebels against the reformist government that revealed that the "revolution without frontiers" was something more than a slogan. This was surely an important factor in the U.S. decision not to let El Salvador fall under the extreme leftist onslaught encouraged by a triumphal Sandinista Front. *(Si Nicaragua Venció, El Salvador Triunfará* means "If Nicaragua triumphed, so will El Salvador.") Thus the Nicaraguan rebels became part of a defensive wall designed to contain the Sandinistas and the FMLN.

By 1982 many Nicaraguans were willing to take up arms against their country's repressive regime. The Nicaraguan war has been violent. Many innocents have lost their lives, and abuses have been committed by both sides. They must be stopped.

The aid bill approved by the U.S. Congress in the summer of 1986 includes conditions regarding respect for human rights. The Unified Nicaraguan Opposition (UNO) has established a commission that is already functioning. The commission's main objective is to make sure that all rebel groups observe a code of conduct. Similar actions are necessary on both sides. The greatest effort should be placed on ending the war, something that can be achieved only by eliminating the causes of the war. In early March six political parties made a settlement proposal to the government. These parties were the Independent Liberal party, led by Virgilio Godoy; the Conservative party of Nicaragua; the Constitutional Liberal party; the Social Christian party; the Social Democratic party; and a faction of the Democratic Conservative party. The main points of the proposal were a cease-fire, an amnesty, the suspension of the emergency law; the revival of suspended civil rights, and a national agreement on elections.

The external democratic resistance has publicly backed this peace effort of the internal opposition. The Sandinista newspaper *Barricada*, in contrast, violently attacked the leaders of these parties, calling them traitors.

Vigilance in behalf of human rights is a worthy endeavor. The Sandinistas certainly could contribute to it by restraining their terrorist mobs, by allowing their adversaries to express their views freely, and, above all, by opening the way for the free exercise of democracy.

The Sandinistas and their international supporters argue that Cardinal Obando y Bravo is not qualified to be a mediator because he has sided against the Sandinistas. This is absurd. Obando is only being consistent in his stand against totalitarianism. He stood against the dictator Somoza and now stands against the militaristic dictatorship of the FSLN. As for the core of the problem between church and state, the Cardinal has given ample proof of being a shepherd of the people in his work on behalf of the poor. He is against Leninism as the new gospel, and he is even more opposed to replacing God with a Sandinista idol. He is also against the defiance of papal orders by Sandinista priests.

The Sandinistas have provoked this conflict because they are determined to undermine the church's authority and prevent the people, by all means, from expressing their sympathy for their natural leader; the Cardinal is the national figure with the largest popular following.

It cannot be denied that Obando was in favor of change during the insurrection against Somoza or that he was instrumental in the overthrow of the tyrant. So why don't the Sandinistas try to conduct a serious dialogue with the National Conference of Bishops rather than invent excuses with which to vent their envy of Obando's popularity and moral authority? Establishing normal relations between church and state behooves a responsible government in a Catholic nation.

In early 1986, after refusing to sign the Contadora Act in November of the preceding year, the Sandinistas announced a proposal to sign the Act on June 6 of that year, on the condition that the U.S. Congress not approve the $100 million aid package for the rebels submitted by President Reagan. This implied an apparent departure from their demand for a parallel protocol between Managua and Washington. If the Sandinistas' intentions are sincere, however, and if they truly intend to proceed with a democratization process, they should also demonstrate their willingness to initiate conversations with the internal opposition regarding the agenda of the six previously mentioned political parties. Otherwise, the Sandinistas are simply aiming at the destruction of the rebel forces.

The bill providing aid to the rebel forces, approved by the U.S. Congress in summer 1986, allows for $100 million total assistance. Thirty million dollars is earmarked for nonlethal aid, including human rights; $70 million is for military purposes, including defensive and offensive weapons and training. ($5 million each for MISURASATA and BOS). Sixty million dollars have already been released. Another $40 million will be forthcoming in February, assuming that the conditions attached to the aid are observed.

III

The Sandinistas clearly have not kept the commitment they made in 1979 to establish pluralism and democracy in Nicaragua. This should warrant a reopening of the Seventeenth Conference of Foreign Ministers of the Organization of American States (where this commitment was made). But this does not seem to be technically or politically feasible because with the advent of Contadora, it is responsible for resolving all aspects of the Central American crisis, including internal conflicts. Therefore, national reconciliation efforts are within its purview, although heretofore Contadora has placed all its emphasis on a regional solution of security matters—an agreement among governments.

Until recently, Contadora has not addressed itself to the roots of the crisis: the internal problem, which requires an agreement between the Sandinistas and the opposition. It was only at Caraballeda that the question of reconciliation was dealt with for the first time.

The stark reality is that the fight for democracy in Nicaragua rests on the shoulders of the Central American governments if the Nicaraguan internal conflict is to be resolved through the Contadora mechanism. In that connection, it is convenient for the Nicaraguan democratic resistance, on the one hand, to insist on the proposal set forth by six opposition parties in Nicaragua (for immediate talks between the FSLN and all parties on peace and reconciliation) and, on the other, to support President Napoleón Duarte's four points: (1) a three-track dialogue including Duarte−FMLN, Ortega−resistance, and Managua−Washington; (2) a summit meeting of Central American presidents and the establishment of a Central American regional mechanism; (3) the signing of the Contadora Act; and (4) an additional provision establishing that the guarantor will be the Central American Parliament, which would be responsible for supervising compliance with the agreements.

In the process of gradually consolidating its totalitarian power, the Sandinista Front deviated from the broad alliance parameters of a mixed economy, external nonalignment, and internal pluralism. As a result and as already indicated, Nicaragua's economy is in a state of collapse, and there is popular discontent. The U.S. response, as defender of the status quo in the Western Hemisphere, is to support a rebellion that promises to disrupt the Sandinistas' alignment with Moscow and Havana. The Nicaraguan resistance favors a political solution that would guarantee social peace in Nicaragua, but it adamantly opposes a cosmetic settlement. If military pressure is unavoidable, U.S. aid is essential to bridge the gap in weaponry between the government and the rebels. That would mean, not victory, but a turnaround in the fight.

The rebel forces—UNO/FDN, UNO/KISAN, and UNO/FARN, plus MISURASATA and BOS—must implement a democratic revamping of their organizations as a corollary to the U.S. president's disposition to help them fight for democ-racy. The Sandinistas are experiencing a tremendous erosion of popular support, but they have a complete network of repression at hand to prevent a national uprising. Their credibility among members of the U.S. Congress is also eroding, but the possibility that direct intervention would be approved is far away.

The Latin American countries can, if they wish, help to end this tug-of-war conflict by assuming their responsibility: Threaten the Sandinistas with isolation if they turn their backs on democracy. At any rate, *now* is the time for negotiations. But it is desirable that the conclusion reached in San José in late April 1986 by the Costa Rican, Honduran, Salvadoran, and Guatemalan vice-presidents prevail in discussions—in other words, there can be no economic development without political pluralism. Due to their geographical proximity and historical ties, Nicaragua's neighbors can perhaps see this more clearly than others who are not so near and may not fully grasp the Central American reality. Nicaragua is hostage to foreign intrusion and meddling. The best way to return it to its rightful owner—the Nicaraguan people—is through Central America.

• CHAPTER THREE •

North American Interventionism

Francisco López

The conflicts currently shaking the Central American region have roots that go back to the middle of the last century—to a dispute between England and a new imperial power, the United States. Since 1823, when President James Monroe proclaimed his doctrine of America for Americans (North Americans), the United States had geopolitical interests in the Caribbean, which the English called the *Mare Nostrum*. But the region had even greater significance: What also entered into the strategic value of the zone was the possibility of constructing an interoceanic canal there, either in Panama or in Nicaragua.

It is no coincidence that, for over a century, North Americans have taken advantage of Central American civil wars to gain power in the area. For this purpose they used the mercenaries Byron Cole and William Walker, who were defeated by united Central American armed forces in 1856. Since then, the influence of the United States in Central America has been manifested in the economic, political, and social order; in effect, they consider the region to be their fourth border. Washington has come to consider Central America as a zone of its exclusive domination.

The ongoing aim of the United States to implant its supremacy in the region has meant that U.S. leaders have no reservations about encouraging and developing dictatorial regimes based on political repression and the concentration of wealth in a few hands. The dependent and underdeveloped character of the region, its cultural backwardness, social margination, and the imposition of oligarchic and dictatorial structures have been important elements in generating the crisis that Central America is experiencing at present.

Right now, the Reagan administration is trying, with all the means at its disposal, to insert the Central American crisis into the East–West conflict, with a total misunderstanding of the economic, social, and political factors that have caused the present situation in the area.

Antecedents of the Crisis

The Central American region is unlike the rest of the countries of the Third World because of its strategic position. It is located adjacent to Mexico, the Panama Canal, and the Caribbean. This explains why first the Spaniards, and then the English were so interested in dominating the region—and why, most recently, the North Americans have been so interested. This is why Central America and the Caribbean suffered 25 military interventions between 1854 and 1930 (see p. 65).

The long chain of North American interventions in the area was mainly determined by the strategic military concepts that different North American administrations have had about Central America. The economic interests of multinational corporations have not been determining factors, because there has been a subordination of the economic interests in the region to the geopolitical interest.

Another characteristic that we could add to the Central American region is its material and social backwardness and its economic dependence. Around the end of the last century, Central America entered the world market through coffee production.

> When the commune of Paris was defeated in 1870, world capitalism made a new push, which included more than ever before marginal countries, like Central America, in the continuous production of raw materials for metropolitan industry. In this new international panorama, Central America would produce and export coffee, and, later on, bananas.[1]

Central America was to export coffee, bananas, sugar, and, at the beginning of the 1950s, cotton. Around this time, the Central American Common Market began. In spite of the variety of the exports, Central American societies became increasingly dependent, for its exports were always subject to the fluctuations of unstable international prices.

---

1. Sergio Ramírez Mercado, "Augusto César Sandino, El Pensamiento Vivo" [The Living Thought of Augusto César Sandino], *Editoral Nueva Nicaragua*, p. 35.

The dependent and underdeveloped model of Central America has generated a crisis of great proportions that renders the economy incapable of providing even minimum levels of subsistence for the majority of the population.

According to ECLA 62% of the region's population live in poverty (lacking the means to satisfy the minimum basic necessities) or in misery. Even in Costa Rica, the country with the highest per capita income of the region, approximately 300,000 people (15% of the population) survive with food rations donated by charity programs which operate through North American and European aid.[2]

Moreover, this model has negatively affected employment, health, and food supplies for the majority of the population. And, at the cultural level, illiteracy in the region in 1976 was between 40 and 60%.

Geopolitics and Crisis

"When analyzing the conflicts in Central America, we ought to take the geographic factors into account as elements of prime importance when studying international relations."[3] Although the Central American countries individually have no strategic importance, the region, including the Caribbean Basin, is adjacent to three zones of commercial and military interest for the United States: southern Mexico, the Caribbean, and the Panama Canal.

A good part of U.S. imports of oil, gas, and minerals come from Mexico, Jamaica, and Venezuela. Although these countries are not part of Central America, they are close to the Caribbean and the Central American coasts. Mexico and Venezuela together have 90% of the gas reserves of Latin America. Mexico is the second supplier of critical raw materials to the United States, after Canada, and is the principal supplier of zinc, antimony, mercury, bismuth, selenium, barium, and lead. Venezuela exports to the United States 28% of its iron.

Petroleum refineries on Caribbean islands, the increase in the tested petroleum reserves in southern Mexico, the importance of North American shipments that use the Panama Canal and the Caribbean—all these factors

2. INIES—CRIES, *Una política alternativa para Centro América y El Caribe, resumen y conclusiones del Seminario Taller realizado en el ISS de La Haya* [An Alternative Policy for Central America and the Caribbean: Summary and Conclusions of the Work Shop and Seminar Held at the ISS of the Hague], June 1983, p. 24.

3. José Miguel Insulza, "Geopolítica e intereses estratégicos en Centroamérica y El Caribe" [Geopolitics and Strategic Interests in CentralAmerica and the Caribbean]. *Polémica* 16 1984, p.25 .

make the zone take on a geopolitical importance that explains in part the crisis and military conflicts. These conflicts exist when dictatorial and authoritarian governments, with the aid of the Reagan administration, confront the people of the region, who have no other option but to take up arms in search of autodetermination and sovereignty.

Low-Intensity Warfare

In the framework of this conflict, it is necessary to point out the importance of the Kissinger Report to the Reagan administration. This report has given credence to the implementation of policies that call for the defense of "democracy" in Central America. A series of policies has been characterized by the development of active diplomacy to help the "democracies" and increase economic aid to the region, excluding Nicaragua of course, in order to confront the problems of poverty and social discontent. The policies also include national security and military aid to ensure the "peaceful development" of the area.

It should be pointed out that the Kissinger Report coincides with, and serves as a theoretical framework for, what has been called "low-intensity warfare," the practical application of which is being implemented in Central America and especially in Nicaragua. Here are some of the characteristics of the doctrine:

1. A massive military response by the United States should not be necessary.
2. There should be close coordination of the military aspect with the economic, political, diplomatic, and psychological aspects.
3. The doctrine of low-intensity warfare favors a war of economic attrition, internal and external isolation, and destabilization of political power—clearly identified in the aggression against Nicaragua.

Structural Crisis

The majority of specialists in the area claim that the Central American crisis is structural in character. First, we see a crisis that cannot simply be called political, social, or economic. And although a political crisis always produces effects in the economy, and vice versa, it is different when tensions originate in, and have their roots in, several dimensions. Second, we find a crisis that has existed for a long time. It is a prolonged crisis; although it has evolved differently in each country of the region, a common characteristic of

Central America (possibly with the exception of Costa Rica) can be defined as its structural crisis.[4]

We call the crisis *structural* to differentiate our viewpoint from those that emphasize the day-to-day happenings and explain the crisis as a result of the normal low point in the cyclic functioning of the economies, which can be overcome automatically in the short term. The scope of the word *structural* also has to do with opposing the simplistic economic characterization that puts the weight of the crisis on the econmic factor so that other variables do not come into play.[5]

It has been said that the Central American crisis is the result of an acute economic stalemate, but this statement can be proved invalid by data on economic growth available through The Economic Commission for Latin America of the United Nations (ECLA). According to ECLA, between 1950 and 1958 the annual average growth rate was 5.3%. Therefore, the causes of the crisis must be looked for, among other factors, in the unequal distribution of the benefits of this growth. In Central America the situation is the accumulated result of a model, set up more than 70 years ago, under which social variations—certain increase and diversification, increase of the middle levels of bureaucrats and professionals, expansion of the service sector, etc.—do not imply any improvement in the living conditions and work of the great majority of the population.

Similar characteristics of Central American countries in their link to the international market through agricultural exports make this a fundamental focus for such economies. The five most important products are coffee, cotton, sugar, bananas, and meat. For countries of the region, these products represent a little more than 50% of the exports. For example, in 1980, 64% of the exports of Honduras and 50.6% of the exports of Guatemala consisted of these products. This explains the dependence and vulnerability of Central American economies, which are at a disadvantage in the world market in the following ways:

1. The economies are subject to the fluctuations of international prices for their products.
2. There has been a deterioration of the terms of interchange with the industrialized countries.
3. Demand from the industrialized countries has fluctuated.
4. Tariff barriers have been imposed by the industrialized countries.[6]

---

4. Ibid.

5. Roberto López, *Crisis y Alternativas en Centroamérica* [Crisis and Alternatives in Central America] (San José, Costa Rica: Icadis), 1985, p.4.

6. Miguel Angel Martínez, *Centroamérica: Análisis de una crisis y orientaciones de una*

Making a difficult situation even worse for the Central American countries are other external economic problems that have contributed to the deterioration of the already weak Central American economies. Among them are the following:

1. The Central American Common Market has stagnated and progressively deteriorated.
2. Access to loans from international organizations has been tightened.
3. The well-known and often debated foreign debt problem has worsened. For example, the foreign debt of Central America from 1978 to 1983 annually increased an average 17.7%, which was used primarily for paying interests on debts.[7]

Nevertheless, the economic crisis in Central America does not have only external causes. Serious internal factors contribute to the crisis, of which the most important are these:

1. A decrease in the volume of traditional exports
2. A decrease in internal, especially private, investment
3. Capital flight
4. Uncontrolled inflation

It is the combination of internal and external factors that has contributed to the acceleration of the crisis and has developed the political conflicts that, since 1978, have acquired such significant military dimensions. It is important to mention that although some phenomena began to appear in 1978, it was not until later, in 1980–1981, that they became part of the political and social upheaval in the region. Therefore, the social and political crises preceded the economic crisis.[8]

The Case of Nicaragua

The essay by Arturo Cruz Sequeira in this volume suffers substantially as an objective study because of a lack of reference, seemingly intentional, to the

---

posible solución [Central America: Analysis of a Crisis and Orientation for a Possible Solution] (Madrid, España: Cuaderno de Documentación, Ministerio de Asuntos Exteriores), 1984.

7. Juan Valdez Paz, *Cuba y la Crisis Centroamericana* [Cuba and the Central American Crisis], *Cuaderno de Nuestra América—2 July–December 84* (La Habana, Cuba: Centro de Estudios de Nuestra America), p. 131.

8. López, *Crisis*, p. 16.

effects of the counterrevolutionary action that since 1982 has been affecting the Nicaraguan economy with ever greater intensity.

Since 1985, Nicaragua has been promoting what has been called a survival economy that tends to confront precisely a crisis of great proportions that affects not only our country but all countries of the region. Nicaragua is not only facing an economic crisis but is confronting a war imposed by the most powerful country of the world, the United States. It is very easy to interpret the crisis in the Nicaraguan economy and "demonstrate" the chaos in the economic leadership of the country, forgetting about the economic aggres-sion (to mention just one of its manifestations) that Nicaragua is suffering.

For example, I list below some of the economic effects of the North American aggression against Nicaragua.

1. In 1984, material damages and production losses totaled about $379.6 million, which at present prices means a little more than what was exported in 1985.
2. The cost of national defense in 1984 was one-third of the national budget. This expense took resources from social sectors such as health and education, and from productive investments.
3. The loss in production of export crops and basic grains in 1984 was $282.5 million. Almost $84 million was lost by destruction of the basic infrastructure for production, especially for exports. Also, the war is most evident in those regions of the country where the main exports are grown. This has occasioned abandonment by producers and fear on the part of workers, since the counterrevolution has a systematic campaign to destroy and assassinate agricultural producers and workers.
4. There is also the financial aggression that Nicaragua suffers from international banks as the result of pressures from the United States. Owing to these pressures, Nicaragua was not able to receive loans destined for basic infrastructure projects for development, which the International Bank for Reconstruction Development (IBRD) and the Inter-American Development Bank (IDB) had identified as of great importance for the stable development of the Nicaraguan economy.

These data reflect only a small part of the direct and indirect economic damages that the aggression of the Reagan administration is producing in Nicaragua.

It is very easy, therefore, without taking into account the aggression, to speak of the collapse of the model of economic policy of the revolution. However, and in spite of the crisis imposed on Nicaragua, the agrarian reform has continued, an increase is expected this year in the industrial sector, incentives are being given in agricultural and industrial production, and higher levels are being searched for in traditional and nontraditional exports. In the middle of an undeclared war by the major world power, this effort is possible only when there really exists an identification of the people with their government. If this were not true, if this identification and help did not exist, with the economic crisis and the defense activities that the Nicaraguan people have had to confront, the work of the counterrevolution would have been successful. The following tables indicate the economic crisis in Central America, and how, in the case of Nicaragua, in spite of the external aggression, the economy is maintained at the same or better levels in some aspects than those in the rest of the countries of the area (see Tables 3.1–3.5).

The Sociopolitical Crisis

As mentioned, the levels of poverty, margination, and political repression that the people of Central America have been subject to are the product of dictatorial regimes imposed by North American governments. The history of Central America has always been a fight between defenders of the status quo and various popular struggles, sometimes encouraged by sectors of the middle classs. A status quo depends on rigid socioeconomic structures, governed by authoritarian schemes, depending economically on other powers (especially the United States since World War II). Such structures bring with them an extreme concentration of wealth and income, and the exclusion and marginalization of the great majority.[9]

As the sociologist and political scientist Edelberto Torres Rivas has said, it is in politics where the crisis appears, develops, and is resolved. The extremely repressive character of the domination model imposed by the North Americans in Central America generated, during the 1970s, an explosion among the popular masses in the majority of Central American countries. "Capitalism, in these backward societies, becomes especially vulnerable because of the polarized character which these class conflicts adopt."[10] This popular explosion against dictatorial regimes had as a consequence the triumph of the Popular Sandinista Revolution in July 1979.

Systematic political repression, political fraud, and military coups d'état have been keynotes of regimes in the area, making impossible even reformist policies—which small sectors of the dominant classes have tried, without luck, to implement. Along this line, it is worthwhile recalling the reformist projects of Jacobo Arbenz in 1954 in Guatemala, which were smashed by

9. Ibid., p. 15.
10. Edelberto Torres Rivas, *Centroamérica—Crisis y Política Internacional* [Central America: Crisis and International Politics] (Mexico City: Editorial Siglo XXI), p.46.

TABLE 3.1
Central America: Evolution of Gross National Product per Capita

Country	Annual Growth Rate					Accumulated Variation 1980–1985[a]
	1981	1982	1983	1984	1985	
Costa Rica	− 5.0	−9.5	−0.4	3.4	−2.5	− 13.8
El Salvador	−11.0	−8.4	−3.8	−1.5	−1.4	−23.8
Guatemala	− 1.8	−6.1	−5.5	−2.4	−4.2	−18.5
Honduras	− 2.8	−4.0	−4.5	−0.8	−1.7	−13.0
Nicaragua	2.0	−4.4	1.3	−4.8	−5.9	−11.6
Latin America[b]	− 1.9	−3.7	−9.8	0.8	0.5	− 8.9

[a] Preliminary estimates.
[b] Excluding Cuba.
SOURCE: CEPAL, taken from Gross National Product. These figures correspond to the population estimates of CELADE, published in the *Boletín Demográfico Año XVIII*, 1985.

TABLE 3.2
Central America: Terms of Trade
(1979 = 100)

Country	1980	1981	1982	1983	1984	1985
Guatemala	85.0	74.8	70.1	59.2	58.8	77.8
El Salvador	85.2	74.4	75.5	70.1	70.4	68.8
Honduras	101.9	87.6	87.1	86.3	85.6	84.9
Nicaragua	98.0	92.6	83.8	72.9	77.6	77.2
Costa Rica	96.3	82.4	74.1	70.4	71.8	69.9
Central America	91.5	80.8	76.4	70.3	71.0	75.4

TABLE 3.3
Terms of Trade: Losses
(Millions of Dollars)

Country	1980	1981	1982	1983	1984	1985	Total
Guatemala	−228	−327	−359	− 446	− 474	− 276	−2110
El Salvador	−159	−204	−172	− 219	− 231	− 263	−1248
Honduras	77	−187	− 87	− 95	− 107	− 118	− 517
Nicaragua	− 9	− 37	− 66	− 116	− 86	− 85	− 399
Costa Rica	− 37	−176	−226	− 252	− 271	− 308	− 127
Latin America	−356	−931	−910	−1128	−1169	−1050	−5544

SOURCE: CEPAL (Economic Commission for Latin America); CELADE (Center for Latin American Studies of Development); BID (Inter–American Development Bank); OEA (Organization of American States); SIECA (Secretariat for Central American Economic Integration); CEMLA (Center for Latin American Monetary Studies); Business Latin American; Latin American Inforpress; author's projections. Processed from the data bank of INIES/CRIES (Nicaraguan Institute for Economic and Social Studies). The acronyms for these institutions reflect their Spanish names.

North American intervention. In Central America we find, on the one hand, a certain incapability of the bourgeoisie to make suggestions and resolve adequately the social and political effects that economic growth is producing. There seems to be a constitutional weakness in their character as leaders, and therefore they give up the search for a national consensus to back up class domination. On the other hand, there is an increasing lack of control with respect to the organization of the dominated classes, which reinforces, from this point of view, the repeated lack of leadership.[11]

We are sure that the dominant classes in the social formation of Central America are weakened because of their extraordinary dependence on North American leadership. This has made possible the creation of military dicta-

11. Ibid.

TABLE 3.4
Central America: Public and Private Investment Coefficients (millions of dollars)

	1978		1979		1980		1981		1982		1983		1984	
	Amount	%	Amount	%	Amount	%	Amount	%	Amount	%	Amount	%	Amount	%
El Salvador														
Internal Gross Investment	343.0	23.5	235.2	16.4	164.8	12.5	158.5	13.1	134.7	11.9	135.2	11.9	135.9	11.8
Private	206.1	14.1	140.7	9.8	75.8	5.8	64.5	5.3	65.5	5.8	65.7	5.8	72.9	6.3
Public	96.0	6.6	94.4	6.6	93.2	7.1	86.2	7.1	69.2	6.1	61.6	5.4	55.5	4.8
Guatemala														
Internal Gross Investment[a]	480.3	16.8	416.8	13.9	355.4	11.4	409.8	13.1	331.8	11.0	265.5	9.0	271.9	9.2
Private	329.3	11.5	288.6	9.6	223.9	7.2	202.0	6.5	196.9	6.5	150.7	5.1	164.8	5.6
Public	106.7	3.7	124.8	4.2	148.7	4.8	199.5	6.4	158.9	5.3	103.8	3.5	75.0	2.5
Honduras														
Internal Gross Investment	200.0	21.7	248.5	25.4	268.5	26.0	220.0	21.1	139.5	13.6	148.0	14.5	184.5	17.6
Private	114.0	12.4	153.5	15.7	157.5	15.3	115.0	11.0	73.0	7.1	71.0	7.0	69.5	6.6
Public	69.0	7.5	74.5	7.6	97.0	9.4	90.5	8.7	92.0	9.0	105.0	10.3	112.5	10.7
Nicaragua														
Internal Gross Investment[b]	137.0	13.1	46.0	5.9	125.0	14.6	211.0	22.6	—	—	—	—	390.1	16.6
Private	75.0	7.2	24.0	3.1	45.0	5.3	32.0	3.4	—	—	—	—	—	—
Public	62.0	5.9	22.0	2.8	80.0	9.3	179.0	19.2	—	—	—	—	—	—
Costa Rica														
Internal Gross Investment	274.8	25.8	300.2	26.9	321.3	28.5	200.0	18.2	103.8	10.4	120.7	11.9	229.7	20.7
Private	190.5	17.9	212.9	19.1	182.6	16.2	135.8	12.3	78.5	7.8	—		—	
Public	80.4	7.5	99.4	8.9	100.3	8.9	76.6	7.0	51.7	5.2	—		—	

[a] In terms of constant prices.
[b] Formation of gross fixed capital.
SOURCE: Central American Monetary Council, *Statistical Bulletin*, 1983.

Francisco López

TABLE 3.5
Central America: Unemployment Rate
(1980-1985)

Country	1980	1981	1982	1983	1984	1985
Central America	20.3	20.8	27.8	28.5	31.4	32.2
Costa Rica	8.1	9.7	14.4	10.9	12.0	12.0
El Salvador	16.2	25.0	30.0	30.0	35.0	35.0
Guatemala	31.2	34.2	38.4	41.7	42.9	45.0
Honduras	15.0	19.3	20.4	21.2	25.0	25.0
Nicaragua	18.3	15.9	18.5	17.5	21.1	22.2

SOURCES: See source note to Table 3.3

torships that, rather than serving the interests of their class, are dependent on strategic and geopolitical North American interests.

The present Central American conflict therefore has its origins and causes in the elements pointed out in this study. Where the social crisis has turned into a political crisis and a struggle against the dominant classes, it is a nationalist and antiimperialist struggle.[12]

As a product of this political struggle by the Central American people, and to the extent that the same conflict acquires extraordinary military dimensions, effects are felt in the economy, since the flight of private capital on a regional level has deepened the crisis. Guatemala, El Salvador, and Nicaragua are the countries that have suffered most from this situation. From this stems the concern, and this seems to be the general opinion of the international financial organizations, that a solution to the present political and military conflicts is the most important issue in order to resolve the regional economic crisis. That is, economic measures alone will not resolve the present conflicts. Political measures and diplomatic measures, such as Contadora, are needed to confront the crisis. Another important issue concerning resolution of the conflict is the political disposition of the United States, because that country bears a large part of the responsibility for the present crisis in Central America. Thus, while the United States lacks the will to resolve the crisis, and does not support by its actions the negotiations being developed by Contadora, the crisis will continue to get worse. Soon the United States will have to make a decision: Either send politicians and diplomats to Central America or send the marines again. In the latter case, the North Americans will be forced to remember Vietnam.

12. Martínez, *Centroamérica*, p.42.

Appendix: Historic Interventions

1854 Headed by William Walker, the filibusters land in Nicaragua, planning to annex Central America to the southern states of the United States of North America. Walker proclaims himself president and reestablishes slavery in Nicaragua. The North American Kanneys and Fabens proclaim the "independence" of San Juan del Norte, sovereign territory of Nicaragua.

1856 The United States, through the Dallas-Clarendon treaty, cedes the territory of Belice, which was not theirs to begin with, to England.

1857 A united Central American force expels William Walker.

1860 The United States, on the pretext of reestablishing order, intervenes for the first time in Panama.

1867 The United States secures its property in Nicaragua through the Dickinson-Ayón treaty, which gives the United States the right to build a canal.

1897 U. S. troops, invoking the Monroe Doctrine, land in San Juan del Norte and in Corinto in Nicaragua.

1900 The United States imposes on Nicaragua and Costa Rica the Hay—Corea treaty and the Hay—Calvo treaty, this way acquiring dominion over a canal route through the Central American isthmus.

1901 Marines land in Panama.

1903 Marines land in Puerto Cortés, Honduras.

1904 Marines land in Ancón and other sites in Panama. President Theodore Roosevelt begins his policy of the "big stick."

1905 Marines land again in Puerto Cortés, Honduras.

1909 The United States intervenes in Nicaragua to overthrow the government of José Santos Zelaya, using the "Knox" Note, an ultimatum to accept U.S. conditions.

1910 Marines land in Corinto and set up their own government.

1911 The United States lands marines in Corinto and imposes a president on Honduras and Nicaragua, obliging him (and Costa Rica) to accept consolidation of debts and new loans.

1912 Marines land again in Honduras.

1912 The United States militarily occupies Nicaragua until 1925.

1914 The United States imposes on Nicaragua the Chamorro—Bryan treaty, by which Nicaragua gives the United States absolute jurisdiction for building a canal.

1918 Marines land in Colón and in Chiriquí, Panama.

1919 Marines occupy ports in Honduras in order to intervene in the elections.

1920 Marines land in Guatemala, overthrow the government, and put an end to the new Federation of Central America, which had been established with Guatemala, Honduras, and El Salvador. The pretext is to defend the lives of North American citizens and protect the legation.

1921 Marines occupy the region of Chorrera, Panama.

1924 Marines land in Honduras and occupy several cities.

1925 Marines land in Honduras and Panama to end strikes.

1926 Marines, who had left Nicaragua for a few months, come back to occupy the country until 1933, at which time the patriots, led by Augusto César Sandino, expel them after causing them embarrassing defeats.

1930 The North American banana companies provoke border wars and coups, impose presidents, and impair the national sovereignty of Guatemala, Honduras, and Panama.

Source: *Revolucion y Desarrollo*[Revolution and Development], No. 3, 1985. Managua, Nicaragua.

• CHAPTER FOUR •

Aspects of the Evolution of Law in Sandinista Nicaragua

Alvaro Taboada Terán

Law and Ideology under *Somocismo* and *Sandinismo*

Several years have elapsed since the revolutionary triumph in Nicaragua, achieved July 19, 1979. That victory, the product of a nationwide democratic unity, soon took the name of one of the political organizations that participated in the struggle against the preceding dictatorship. In this way, the Nicaraguan revolution became the Sandinista popular revolution under the banners of the Frente Sandinista de Liberación Nacional (FSLN), which considers itself the revolutionary vanguard for the liberation of Central America. The FSLN's attitude derives from its position as a ruling armed party and from its belief in the principle of proletarian internationalism.[1]

---

1. Since its foundation in 1961, the FSLN has made proletarian internationalism one of the basic expressions of its practice and ideology. Even before that time, important would-be leaders of the organization were involved in activities of international solidarity with Leninist socialism. The adherence to proletarian internationalism by the FSLN may be seen in countless actions and documents since the 1960s. See, for example, Carlos Fonseca Amador, *Sandino, guerrillero proletario*, [Sandino, Proletarian Guerrilla], Serie Pensamiento Sandinista, No. 4, Secretaría Nacional de Propaganda y Educación Política, FSLN [National Secretariat of Propaganda and Political Education, FSLN] (Managua: Colección Juan de Dios Muñoz, July 1980), pp. 32–33; and *Un año después* [One Year After], Interviews with the National Board for National Reconstruction, Serie Entrevistas, No. 2, Dirección de Divulgación y Prensa, Junta del Gobierno de Reconstrucción Nacional (JGRN) [Directorate of Information and Press, Junta of the Goverment of National Reconstruction] (Managua: Ediciones Patria Libre,

Understandably, law and politics have become closely intertwined in Nicaragua. The characteristics of the current juridical order in that country lead us to consider it a legal system in transition. Having departed from a civil law system, it has increasingly assumed the role of an instrument for the consolidation of the FSLN's political power. This process has been juridically confusing, but it has been politically clear and effective. This may be seen in the juridical-political areas related to the evolution of the Sandinistas' power and to the rights and guarantees of Nicaraguans under the FSLN regime.

An explanation of the FSLN's disregard for a series of general principles and laws, whose spirit is vital to legal systems prevailing in the West, may be found in the FSLN's Marxist−Leninist ideological foundations and its corresponding political goals.[2] This ideology has a very simple vision of the origin, finality, and supposed future extinction of law.[3]

It is useful in the present discussion to make some brief references to the previous Nicaraguan regime. Of the Somocista political system, it must be said that despite its obvious dictatorial and largely arbitrary nature, it worked within minimal legal and ideological parameters that were formally liberal-democratic and were presented as the foundation of the regime's legitimacy. This was a weak but nonetheless real constraint on some actions by the Somoza government. The several political constitutions created

---

July 1980). Daniel Ortega declared that the Sandinista government has to make a common cause with revolutions that coincide with the Sandinista project, such as the Cuban revolution and other revolutionary processes in Asia, Africa, and Central America (see pp. 19−24). See also U.S. Department of State and U.S. Department of Defense, *La conexión Soviético−Cubana en la América Central y en el Caribe* [Soviet−Cuban connection in Central America and in the Caribbean] (Washington, D.C.: GPO, March 1985); and U.S. Department of State, *Los Sandinistas y los extremistas del Oriente Medio* [The Sandinistas and the Middle-East Extremists] (Washington, D.C.: GPO, August 1985). This paper gives a well-documented account of the FSLN's proletarian internationalist links with Middle East guerrilla organizations from the 1970s to the present.

2. Among hundreds of documents and declarations by the FSLN leaders assuring the Marxist−Leninist nature of their party, figures the *Plataforma general político−militar del FSLN para el triunfo de la revolución popular Sandinista* [General Political−Military Platform of the FSLN for the Triumph of the Popular Sandinist Revolution] (hereinafter cited as General Platform), National Directorate of the FSLN, clandestine edition (some place in Nicaragua, May 4, 1977). This is an important document that defines in 63 pages the FSLN's ideology and strategy. (See Appendix A.)

3. Among classic Marxist−Leninist works on this subject, see V. I. Lenin, *El estado y la revolución* [On the State and Revolution] (Moscow: Editorial Progreso, n.d.), pp. 274−276; Karl Marx, *Crítica al programa de Gotha* [Critique of the Gotha Program], Vol. 3, Karl Marx and Frederick Engels, *Selected Works* (Moscow: Editorial Progreso, n.d.); and E. B. Paschukanis, *La teoría general del derecho y el Marxismo* [General Theory of Law and Marxism] (Mexico City: Editorial Grijalbo, 1976), pp. 55−69.

successively during the Somoza regime tried to comply, at least formally, with the legislative techniques generally accepted in democratic countries. Every one of those constitutions was accompanied by important laws that had constitutional rank: habeas corpus, for example, and the law of appeal for cases where constitutional norms or other laws were violated by government officials.

Obviously, *Somocismo* manipulated the constitutions it created, but its dictatorial power frequently had to make concessions to laws rooted in the liberal principles on which *Somocismo* tried to base its decreasing legitimacy vis-à-vis the Nicaraguan people and the democratic governments that had relations with the dictatorship in those years. To accommodate these inner contradictions and pressures, the Somoza regime had to follow a winding path. For instance, *Somocismo* had alternately to respect and suspend freedom of information, and in 1977, for the last time, restored this freedom after a long, drastic, and arbitrary period of censorship imposed in January 1975. This move proved fatal to the dictatorship because the corruption and repression protected by the censorship were afterward systematically denounced. Subsequently, political pressure against the regime grew to unprecedented levels.

Somocismo was especially opportunistic and arbitrary regarding laws that had a political content; interference by the regime was not as marked in other legal areas. In addition to the constitution, the principal laws of the prerevolutionary structure were embodied in the following codes and laws:

1. The Civil Code of Nicaragua (1904), which replaced the Civil Code of 1871.[4] Despite modifications of specific articles, most of the 3,984 articles of the Civil Code are to this day formally obligatory. This code was usually applied well, until 1979. This fact may be explained by the coinciding interests and ideology of this Napoleonic-inspired code and the interests of the regimes that governed Nicaragua. There was respect for "autonomous will" in private economic relations and for some traditional family values, all of which had clearly inspired the Civil Code. It would be a gross legal and historical mistake to assert that the Civil Code protected only the upper classes; the code regulated patrimonial and family relations that involved most Nicaraguans.

2. The Commercial Code of Nicaragua, mandatory since September 17, 1953.[5] The same general reflections regarding the Civil Code are

---

4. *Código Civil de Nicaragua* [Civil Code of Nicaragua], (Managua: Casa Editorial Carlos Heuberger, 1931), p. 887; Articles 3981−3984, pp. 887−888 (hereinafter cited as Civil Code).

5. *Código de Comerico de Nicaragua* [Commercial Code of Nicaragua] (Managua: Tipografía Asel, 1969), p. 284.

applicable to the Commercial Code, with the exception that the latter
was directed to the business sector of the population.
3. The Penal Code, mandatory since June 3, 1974.[6]
4. The Code for Penal Procedure, mandatory since June 1879.[7]
5. The Code for Civil Procedures, mandatory since January 1, 1906.[8]
6. Economic, social, and fiscal laws. These were systematically published by the Central Bank of Nicaragua under the heading Principal Economic and Social Laws of Nicaragua.

If a degree of contradiction existed between Somocismo's dictatorial nature and its liberal principles and laws, such is not the case with the FSLN. *Sandinismo* is based on an ideology that is profoundly antijuridical and devoted to the rationalization of total power. For this reason, *Sandinismo* has been more coherently arbitrary than *Somocismo* and has imposed more strongly its political will as the only real source of justice and law, not only in political issues but also in patrimonial and personal relations that have affected the whole of the Nicaraguan population. The boundaries and guarantees of law have been totally overrun by party values and will, a phenomenon that implies legal and historical regression. Amid all these circumstances one thing is certain: Revolutionary change does not necessarily imply legal and social advancement.

Some Basic Aspects of the Evolution of Law Under *Sandinismo*

Many analyses of the Nicaraguan revolution erroneously suggest that the liberal democratic consciousness of the Nicaraguan people was exhausted by 1979, and that such ideology had to be replaced by a socialist concept. Consequently, the civil law system, or any bourgeois law, could not count on a solid social basis. For this reason, the remnants of bourgeois law had to be used to effect a slow and arduous change toward socialist or Marxist–Leninist law, which was supposedly wanted by the people.[9] These assertions are notoriously wrong.

6. *Ley del Código Penal de Nicaragua* [Penal Code of Nicaragua], *La Gaceta,* No. 96 Managua, May 3, 1974, p. 965, Article 643.

7. *Código de instruccion criminal* [Code for Penal Procedures] (Managua: Edición Oficial, 1956), p. 956, Article 643.

8. *Código de procedimientos civiles de la república de Nicaragua* [Code for Civil Procedures], 2d ed. (Managua: Edición Oficial, 1956), p. 426, Article 2144.

9. See Amalia Chamorro, *Estado y hegemonía durante el Somocismo* [State and Hegemony during Somocismo], which appears in *Economía y sociedad en la construcción del estado en Nicaragua* [The Economy and Society in the Building of the Nicaraguan State] (San José, Costa

The ideology of *Somocismo* favored liberal democracy, as stated, although it was distorted by dictatorial and dynastic ambitions. *Somocismo* was based on the ideas of liberal republicanism and a market economy, exercised under the protective shadow of a strong state that had deeply penetrated all social levels in Nicaragua. That ideology is still very strong among the Nicaraguan population. What occurred under *Somocismo* was a schism between liberal democratic ideology and a dictatorial praxis which was rejected by the people.[10] Nicaraguans did not discard the formal principles of the Somocista state, but they felt deceived by the political praxis of *Somocismo*, the very existence of which contradicted the democratic principles preached by the regime. This contradiction brought about the destruction of the dictatorship.

So real is the legitimacy of the liberal democratic ideology, preached even before the "thirty-year period" in the nineteenth century, that all the anti-Somoza movements were based on demands to remedy the regime's violations of the principles of liberal democracy and the welfare state. This assertion is also valid for the movement that triumphed on July 19, 1979. Oddly enough, the Sandinista Front for National Liberation has seen the liberal democratic ideology and its legal expression as antagonistic to its own ideological foundations. Such an attitude is understandable when one takes into account the Front's political development since its birth in 1961.

The FSLN arose from a small group of former militants of the Socialist party of Nicaragua, a Marxist–Leninist party that followed the classical line. Nicaragua was industrially backward, however, and some young members of the Socialist party, which was founded in 1944, were inclined to start the armed revolutionary struggle at once, without waiting for the prescribed social and economic transformations to occur.

Marxist–Leninist ideology has been unmistakably the theoretical and practical guide of the FSLN from its inception to the present time. Even

Rica, ICAP, 1983), pp. 244–271. Chamorro's work is based on the Gramscian concept of hegemony, but it has not penetrated to the historical roots and strength that, at all levels, liberal ideology had and still has in Nicaragua. The essay has overlooked the objectives presented to the Nicaraguan people in order to mobilize them during all the movements and coalitions against *Somocismo*, not because it was liberal or bourgeois, but because *Somocismo* was violating the principles of liberal democracy. The Nicaraguan people revolted in defense of these values. *Somocismo* lost legitimacy for the above-mentioned reason and not because of widespread socialist ideology in Nicaragua.

For a view on the movements against *Somocismo*, see García, Caracas, Carlos, et al., *Alianzas políticas de la oposición en Centro-América* [Political Alliances in the Opposition in Central America] (Guatemala: INCEP, n.d.).

10. *Un análisis jurídico-político de leyes electorales en Centro-América* [A Political and Juridical Analysis on Central American Electoral Laws] (San José, Costa Rica: CEPRO-CECA), forthcoming.

before the appearance of the Front, the would-be fathers of the FSLN had founded Marxist circles at the old University of León. As early as 1957, Carlos Fonseca Amador, who would become the most important leader among the founders of the FSLN, was invited to the Sixth Congress of the World Federation of Democratic Youth held at Kiev in the summer of 1957 and to the Sixth Youth Festival, held in Moscow a short time earlier.[11] Fonseca's book, *Un Nicaragüense en Moscú* [A Nicaraguan in Moscow] reveals a deep desire for a new and superior guide to resolve Nicaragua's problems, a desire far deeper than the search for an autochthonous solution.

Fonseca's most important contribution to the FSLN was to blend, somewhat artificially, Sandino's historical role and the Marxist–Leninist ideology that was foreign to the liberal creed of the famous Nicaraguan guerrilla leader. The only possible point of contact between Sandino and Leninism was that Sandino fought a heroic antiimperialist war, and Lenin had constructed a coherent, although historically incomplete, theory of imperialism.[12] Fonseca understood how propitious the circumstances were for the creation of a Leninist–Sandinista symbiosis (no matter how artificial it might be), thanks to the existence of a Somoza dictatorship that had its roots in U.S. intervention in Nicaragua's internal affairs. Fonseca, by mixing *Sandinismo* and Marxism–Leninism, was trying to make more palatable to Nicaraguans the "scientific doctrine of the proletariat."[13]

Marxist–Leninist orthodoxy was rapidly adopted by the FSLN. Fonseca Amador said:

> With the victory of the Cuban revolution, the rebellious Nicaraguan spirit recovered its brightness. The Marxism of Lenin, Fidel, Che and Ho-Chi-Minh was taken up by the Frente Sandinista de Liberación Nacional that has started anew the difficult road of guerrilla warfare. Since 1958, year after year it has been repeated on more than a hundred occasions that guerrilla combat will lead us to a definitive liberation.[14]

11. Carlos Fonseca, *"Un Nicaragüense en Moscú"* [A Nicaraguan in Moscow] (Managua: Secretaría Nacional de Propaganda y Educación Política del FSLN [National Secretariat of Propaganda and Political Education of the FSLN], February 1980), p. 5.

12. V. I. Lenin, *El imperialismo, fase superior del capitalismo* [Imperialism: A Higher Stage of Capitalism] (Moscow: Editorial Progreso, n.d.), pp. 189–227. Despite its shortcomings, this book has an enormous appeal for social scientists and politicians, who place a predominant emphasis on foreign factors to explain the origins of underdevelopment in many countries.

13. For a short account of Sandino's clashes with communist militants, see Hurtado González Armando, *Sandino Desconocido* [The Unknown Sandino] (San José, Costa Rica: Ediciones Populares Nicaragüenses, n.d.), pp. 15–24.

14. Fonseca, *Sandino guerrillero proletario* [Sandino, Proletarian Guerrilla], pp. 32–33.

The continuity of the FSLN's Marxism–Leninism can be easily traced from Fonseca's writings to the present day, passing through the 1962 propaganda papers "Rojo y Negro" and "Trinchera" and the May 4, 1977, FSLN General Platform, a document that explains the strategic project of the "Terceristas"[15] (see Appendix A). The Terceristas comprised the allegedly moderate branch of the FSLN, which split over disagreements on tactical issues into three branches in 1975 but reunited in March 1979.

Theory, organization, and practice have marched shoulder to shoulder in the FSLN's historical evolution. When, aided by democratic groups and organizations, the FSLN took power in Nicaragua, a great national alliance was necessary, just as the Terceristas had predicted. The alliance proposed deep economic, political, and legal changes, but not without limits: All the anti-Somoza forces (including the FSLN) stipulated a mixed economy and representative democracy as major goals for the new Nicaragua. The political agreement had national and international support, and naturally it had to be framed within a proper juridical-political structure. What were some of the most important instruments of that legal structure?

The original framework of the Nicaraguan revolution was defined by three legal–political instruments: (1) the Government Program of the National Board; (2) the Fundamental Statute of the Republic; and (3) the Statute of Rights and Guarantees for Nicaraguans. It is important to recall that, in this instance, the word *statute* does not mean a legal instrument created by a legislative branch; in Nicaragua statutes were decreed by the National Board (Junta).

In their political origin, national democratic agreement, and conceptual rank, these three legal instruments are hierarchically the highest in the revolutionary legal system to the present day. The three basic documents establish very clearly: (1) the objectives and meaning of the revolution; (2) the structure of the state; and (3) the rights and guarantees for individuals and intermediate organizations. Let us now discuss these documents.

First, the Government Program of the National Board (from here on, simply the Government Program) has its antecedents in several projects

---

15. General Platform. The General Platform explained that the FSLN struggle would be developed in three stages: (1) an insurrectional war against *Somocismo* with the cooperation of all social sectors of Nicaragua, including the bourgeoisie; (2) construction of a revolutionary democracy that would lead to decreasing political and economic pluralism and to ever-increasing control by the FSLN; and (3) the final phase of Leninist socialism. The Platform declares: "With the development of the Popular Sandinista Revolution, with the triumph over the dictatorship and the firm establishment of a revolutionary popular democratic government, our present Marxist–Leninist vanguard organization will be able to develop to the maximum its organic structure, until it becomes an iron-hard Leninist Party. . . ." (see Appendix A, p. 309).

undertaken by anti-Somoza organizations from 1978 onward. The final draft was written by Nicaraguan exiles in Costa Rica and was ratified by the National Board on the first day it took power, July 19,1979. The Government Program was divided into three areas: political, economic, and social.[16]

The program's political section states that the system must be democratic and representative. The state would be structured along a classic division of powers, but the executive would also have legislative functions; these were later increased in such a way that the role of the legislative body was greatly reduced. The legislative power was to be exercised by the Council of State, which had 33 members, representatives of all the victorious democratic forces.[17] From the beginning, however, the FSLN arbitrarily multiplied its presence within the Council of State, where it sat several of its peripheral organizations that were strictly dependent on the FSLN's National Directorate. The FSLN's total control over the Council of State was formalized by Decree 374, on April 16, 1980. This decree caused a political crisis and the end of the first National Board. The number of members of the Council of State was inflated with Sandinistas. Organizations peripheral to the FSLN, such as the Sandinista Youth, the Group of 12, the Confederation of Sandinista Workers, and the Sandinista Army increased the FSLN presence on the Council of State, which grew from 33 to 47 members.

As for the judiciary, it was to be renewed under the revolutionary state, with the Supreme Court becoming effectively the highest authority of the judiciary. It must be underlined that the Government Program expressly accepted full applicability of the human rights declarations defined in several international declarations and treaties: freedom of religion, freedom of press and speech, the right to organize political parties and civic and labor organizations, etc.

The decision to form a new national, and truly nonpartisan, army was vitally important because *any* partisan army is an obstacle to democracy, as Nicaraguan history attests.[18] In order to break the cycle of Nicaraguan submission in external affairs to foreign powers, it was a very important program goal to follow an independent and genuinely nonaligned foreign policy. In the social area, the Government Program promised, among other things, emergency measures to cope with the immediate consequences of the 1979 war, a new labor code, and autonomy for the National University. (That

16. "Programa de Gobierno," *Leyes de la República de Nicaragua, época revolucionaria* ["Government Program," *Laws of the Nicaraguan Republic, The Revolutionary Period*], Vol. 1 (Managua: Ministerio de Justicia, July–December 1979), pp. 9–35.

17. Ibid., Sec. 1.2.

18. Ibid., Sec. 1.12.

university had been autonomous since 1958.) Yet the Sandinista government soon would prohibit the workers' right to strike and would suppress the university's autonomy.

The program's economic portions included the creation of a mixed economy with a state sector, a private sector, and a joint (state and private) investment sector. During the development of the new legal order, several decrees have relied on the Government Program, taking it as one source of the revolution's legal system. This is a very important fact because it reveals the program's hierarchy. Notwithstanding its legal preeminence, the program has been violated and contradicted continually by executive decrees.

In the absence of a democratic constitution, the Government Program and the two basic statutes have a hierarchic superiority in revolutionary law for two reasons: (1) because of their political origins, that is, because of the national agreement that made possible the revolutionary victory; and (2) because of their conceptual structure, which laid the basis for the new revolutionary society. Additionally, all the legal instruments—the Government Program and the basic statutes—have incorporated international treaties that are mandatory for Nicaragua.

Second, the Fundamental Statute for the Republic takes a systematic approach to the state's structure.[19] The validity of human rights declarations, as they appear in international treaties that are obligatory for Nicaragua's government, is reiterated. The concept of a new national army, which appeared in the text of the Government Program, is reinforced. The government is legally bound, within a reasonable time, to allow popular elections for a national constituent assembly.

Third, the Statute for Rights and Guarantees concedes ample judiciary guarantees (Articles 8–16).[20] It also commands the inviolability of documents and private communication, and guarantees freedom of information and speech and the right to organize political and trade union activities.

The revolutionary model initially proposed was realistic and without messianic dreams. For certain political groups, however, the strength of ideological conceptions, the attachment to strategic goals, and the belief in a redemptory and messianic mission are driving forces that are often stronger than realism. Frequently those forces tempt them to break the commitments derived from agreements with other social and political groups.

In the present case, not only had the FSLN a well-established ideological framework that was antagonistic to any bourgeois compromise but the Sandinistas had debts, commitments, and links that dated back to the 1960s with socialist governments such as Cuba's. These were reasons enough for

19. *La Gaceta,* no. 1 (Managua), August 22, 1979.
20. *La Gaceta,* no.11, September 1979.

for the FSLN to accept, simply tactically, the initial Nicaraguan revolutionary project.[21] The FSLN's strategy and pace in breaking the original revolutionary framework may become evident after a short review of the most important laws and decrees of the Sandinista government. The remainder of this section presents a brief list of those decrees, their general content, and their objectives.

Decree 53 (September 18, 1979). The creation of the Popular Sandinista Army.[22] The existence of a partisan army becomes official. The construction of a new order can be assured by the presence of a sectarian military force. This fact destroys any reasonable hope for a democratic political order, such as the one desired by Nicaraguans when they revolted against Somoza. This decree violates Point 1.2 of the Government Program and Title 4, Articles 23–27, of the Fundamental Statute.

Far from being a fortuitous matter, Decree 53 answered the old strategic aspirations of the FSLN. This organization stated in 1977 that three pillars would support the weight of the Sandinista popular revolution: (1) the FSLN as the vanguard; (2) the popular mass fronts; and (3) "the formidable presence of the Sandinista Army."[23]

Decree 66 (September 20, 1979). The Revolutionary Oath to the Banner.[24] Patriotic symbols are officially intermingled with partisan slogans and symbols. This establishes an equation between fatherland and party.

Decree 67 (September 20, 1979). The title *Sandinista* is limited by law exclusively to those organizations that are dependent on the FSLN. This decree underlines the partisan nature of the Sandinista Army.[25]

Decree 313 (February 15, 1980). This decree creates the Sandinista Popular Militias, which are obviously partisan.

Decree 374 (April 22, 1979). This decree modifies unilaterally the composition of the Council of State, increasing from 33 to 47 the number of its members. Adding peripheral organizations and collaborationists, the FSLN controls 74% of the council's vote.

21. "The necessary *popular–democratic revolutionary phase*, to be fulfilled once the tyranny is toppled, should not lead us to capitalism, reformism, or nationalism, or any other development." *General Platform, p. 30* (see Appendix A, p. 302).

22. *La Gaceta,* no. 12, September 18, 1979. Decree dated August 22, 1979.

23. See Appendix A, p. 315.

24. *La Gaceta,* no. 14, September 20, 1979, p. 145.

25. Ibid., p. 146.

In the face of these highly questionable political maneuvers, two members of the National Board resigned: Alfonso Robelo and Violeta Chamorro. This was the end of the first National Board, although three of the original members—all Sandinistas—remained: Daniel Ortega, Moisés Hassan, and Sergio Ramírez; they gave continuity to the work of the executive's head office.

Decree 388 (May 2, 1982). This decree increases the legislative powers of the National Board, which acquires the right to veto any law from the Council of State. The council loses the right to veto any decree from the National Board.[26]

The trio of Daniel Ortega, Hassan, and Ramírez are integrated into a new board of four members: Ortega, Arturo Cruz, Rafael Córdoba, and Ramírez. Cruz resigned a few months later because of his democratic convictions, but Córdoba submitted to the Sandinista project. For this reason, he decisively contributed to the splitting of the Conservative party that had collaborated with the Somoza dictatorship and has been collaborating with the present regime.

Decree 663 (March 9, 1981). This decree reduces the National Board to three members: Ortega, Córdoba, and Ramírez. A new official function, the coordination of the National Board, is bestowed on Daniel Ortega.[27] Ortega is the key person on the board, as he is the connection between the center of power (the Sandinista party) and the state or administrative apparatus that was and is subordinated to the party. At present in Nicaragua, the real power lies in the Sandinista National Directorate.

Up to this point, the FSLN had achieved a decisive victory transforming the political and legal reality in Nicaragua from a nationalist revolutionary process to a Sandinista revolution of growing Marxist–Leninist character. The subordination of the state to the party structure, according to Leninist political praxis, had been reached by the FSLN when the above-mentioned decrees, and many others of lesser importance, were dictated and enforced.

Naturally enough, the legal and political transformations did not stop there. The state's organs and enterprises at every level were closely watched by political commissaries *(responsables políticos)* who were trustworthy members of the party, devoted informants even to the political police.[28]

26. *La Gaceta,* no. 97, May 2, 1980.
27. *La Gaceta,* no. 55, March 9, 1981.
28. Comandante Daniel Ortega, *Documento de estudio, dirección de divulgacíon y prensa de la Junta de Gobierno de Reconstrucción Nacional y Casa de Gobierno* [Document for Study] (Managua, September 1981). Daniel Ortega, during the first meeting for work with ministers, vice-ministers, and directors of different organisms of the state at the Augusto César

Additionally, the FSLN entrenched itself on a block-by-block level in cities and towns, using the Sandinista Defense Committees (CDS). These committees had administrative and political functions, and even though they are not authorized by law to exercise such functions, they are nevertheless effective because they have the support of the state and political police. For instance, four CDS directors (one for each street in the block) can exert control over 80 or more persons in a given block by means of constant watching, control of food rationing cards, and recommendations for work, driver license, passport, etc.

Having secured control of the state's key political, military, and security mechanisms, the FSLN was in a position to conduct other political changes and could slowly further economic transformations toward its long-cherished Leninist ideal.

The Sandinista revolution has marched at a slower pace in the economic field than in the political area. Because of this, some goodwilled observers and some friends of the Sandinistas have pointed out that private enterprise still exists in Nicaragua, and for this reason the FSLN cannot be Marxist-Leninist. It is much more complicated than that. There is no excuse for overlooking an elementary fact so cleverly highlighted by Antonio Gramsci: All revolutions have been political at first, and only after the conquest of power are economic changes furthered.

Simultaneously with the subordination of the legislative, military, and security mechanisms to the party, the FSLN launched an offensive on judicial and procedural guarantees, thus securing more leverage for the party, which was seeking to inculcate in the people a feeling that all their rights and guarantees came from the party, the party being the only source of law.

Understandably, not everything is arbitrary in Nicaragua, but law is increasingly ancillary to the party. There is a general resemblance between the Sandinista political-legal objectives and rhetoric, on the one hand, and the rhetoric and objectives of other Leninist regimes. They share a reliance on "popular revolutionary juridical conscience" and stress the "defense of the revolution" against sabotage, counter-revolution and public felonies, etc.[29] The field for abuses is left wide open. Evidently, a new law, far more repressive than bourgeois law, is on the rise in Sandinista Nicaragua.

Origins of the similarity of and justification for very repressive legal systems in Leninist countries must be searched for, to an important extent,

Silva Center for Conventions, Managua, August 12, 1981, highlighted the importance of political commissaries at every one of those institutions. The party was very rapidly becoming a determining force in Nicaragua.

29. These characteristics in the early stages of Soviet law are briefly exposed in the initial pages of an old work that still remains important in its field. See Harold J. Berman, *Justice in the USSR. An Interpretation of Soviet Law*(Barcelona, Spain: Editorial Ariel, 1967), pp. 43–52.

in ideological coincidences that have a direct impact on concrete situations. For instance, Lenin in *The State and Revolution* not only made a prediction about the disappearance of bourgeois law but presented a cold rationalization of political and legal repression, without the old-fashioned bourgeois guarantees: all for the sake of socialism.[30]

Armed with this ideology, the FSLN did not need much effort to create and put into effect repressive laws, many of which came long before the rupture of the national unity, the danger of growing dissent and civil war, and the confrontation with the United States.

The following are some of the most important decrees that have affected the rights and guarantees of the Nicaraguans:

Decree 5 (August 22, 1979). Law for the Support of Public Security and Order. This law creates the Special Emergency Tribunals. It establishes a precedent for the creation of political tribunals meant to judge alleged or real crimes committed before the creation of the tribunals. Decree 5 violates the fundamental guarantees that must exist in any rightful judicial process. Those guarantees include the right to be judged only by tribunals that existed previous to a fault or crime, as stated in the two Nicaraguan basic statutes and in several international conventions. The Sandinista executive created, modified, and suppressed tribunals without reference to the judiciary. Repressive decrees granted and withdrew guarantees and rights, creating a climate of fear and uncertainty.

Decree 383 (April 29, 1980). This decree authorizes the permanent applicability of Decree 5, which was initially limited to the state of emergency.

Decree 10 (August 23, 1979). Law of National Emergency. Article 3 of this law expressly violates the principle that law must not be retroactive. This is a general legal principle held as mandatory in several international treaties as well as in Nicaraguan civil law.[31]

Decree 185 (December 12, 1979). This decree creates the Special Tribunals. The administration of partisan justice is reinforced. This decree is a transgression against judiciary guarantees contained in the convention of human rights ratified by the Sandinista government just 2 months and 2 days before the publication of Decree 185.

---

30. Lenin, *El Estado y la Revolución,* pp. 359–370.
31. (Civil Code.) The code's preliminary title contains, among other rules, several general principles of law.

Decree 1233. This decree creates the Popular Anti-Somocista Tribunals. The effects of the application of political justice are increased. Persons and groups that fought against Somoza are now accused of being Somocistas because of their opposition to the FSLN. Imprisonment of up to 30 years can be imposed on "counterrevolutionaries." Besides legal repression, extralegal activities on the part of the government have been denounced by different human rights organizations in well-documented cases involving even entire communities.

If we now turn our attention to laws affecting the economic sphere, we find the very important Law of Agrarian Reform. According to Articles 27–29 of this law, the organisms for agrarian development may act as judge and party on matters pertaining to the expropriation of land, invasions promoted by Sandinista organizations, and so on. This law expressly prohibits the recourse to appeal in any land dispute involving the Ministry of Agrarian Development and Land Reform.

Certainly Nicaragua needed agrarian reform, but it is not difficult to see that the FSLN has carried out that reform with a substantial dose of demagoguery. Political purposes have prevailed over technical and responsible considerations.

Nicaragua has a low demographic density: 23 inhabitants per square kilometer. At the moment of Somoza's downfall, Nicaragua had 5 million *manzanas* of public land (each *manzana* equals 7026 square meters).[32]

During its first year, the revolutionary government confiscated more than 1.3 million *manzanas*. To these figures must be added the land of some 87,000 peasant families owning small rural properties. Thus at least 435,000 persons in the rural areas (out of 3 million, the total Nicaraguan population) had some property. Another important segment of the petite bourgeoisie, from cities and towns, owned small businesses, urban property, or rural estates.

Nicaragua is basically agricultural and until 1978 was the largest producer of grains in Central America. Some 300,000 *manzanas* of different grains were cultivated by small farmers.

Conditions were propitious for the improvement of people's lives in the new Nicaragua, freed from the Somoza regime. However, those very conditions asked for mature and realistic measures from the new government. Contrary to this, the FSLN started widespread confiscations that went far beyond illegally acquired property, and beyond the actual administrative

---

32. "Sandino ayer, Sandino hoy, Sandino siempre" [Sandino Yesterday, Sandino Today, Sandino Forever], speech by Daniel Ortega celebrating the first year of the revolution. The speech appears in *Habla la Dirección de la Vanguardia* [The Directorate of the Vanguard Speaks] (Managua: Colección Juan De Dios Muñoz, July 1981), p. 14.

capacity of the state. (That policy continues to the present day.) Small farmers were harassed. Cooperativism and titles of agrarian reform were and still are manipulated. The FSLN is looking toward the future: Growing state control is already a reality and can be seen in the large, inefficient, and bankrupt collective farms in Nicaragua.

Decree 282 (February 8, 1980). By this decree the theory and practice of procurators is canceled for agrarian cases. This law offered persons who were outside Nicaragua 30 days to defend themselves when their property was taken over by the state or in any form placed under the care of the Ministry of Agrarian Development and Land Reform. Many properties so placed were really invaded by groups mobilized by the FSLN. As Nicaragua was already at peace after July 1979, many owners decided to return, urged on by this law. While the owners were going through the legal procedures, a new decree (Decree 329 published April 3, 1985) declared that all properties that were subject to Decree 282 were officially expropriated by Decree 329, a clear demonstration of FSLN arbitrariness.

This is an example of the orientation of the Sandinista legal system. The message is clear: The will of the party is the only source of law, and the law must submit itself to the goals of the vanguard.

Among literally thousands of laws, some decrees have responded to legitimate and nationally accepted purposes of a mixed economy with a strong state presence. Such is true of laws that nationalized financial institutions and exports. Many other laws, however, have hampered the private sector of the economy. On the whole, legal regulations of the economy, and the economy itself, have been used to increase the power and control of the vanguard.

A Leninist model would hardly survive in a society that had free access to information; ideological control is a must for traditional or Leninist socialism. To concede freedom of the press would be a bourgeois folly, contrary to Marxist-Leninist philosophy and practice. Once more, the FSLN has acted in accordance with its ideological basis on the key issue of mass media regulation.

Decrees 511, 512 (March 10, 1980). These decrees are more repressive than those of the Somoza regime. Previous censorship of military, economic, and political news is made official, with severe penalties for any violations. All these laws are contrary to the Statute of Rights and Guarantees for the Nicaraguans, and to conventions and treaties on human rights.

Decree 619 (December 17, 1981). The Ministry of the Interior, which has a frightening record in the field of repression, is declared by this decree to be the authority in charge of enforcing control over the mass media. Independent means of public information are few, anyway. The state owns all television channels, most radio stations, and one of the three newspapers in the country. One of the two privately owned papers is supported by the Sandinistas and follows its orientation. The only truly independent paper, *La Prensa*, is subject to suffocating censorship. This newspaper fought Somocista dictatorship for 43 years. Other newspapers such as *El Centro-Americano* simply closed after decades of work, which included constant opposition to the Somoza regime.

By October 15, 1985, a decree officially suspended political rights and guarantees. As a rather doubtful consolation, it must be said that the rights suspended by that decree never had any real application under the FSLN government.

What have been stated are examples of FSLN legislation used to change the substance, purpose, and meaning of the initial revolutionary legal framework. Lack of space makes it impossible to bring under analysis the Law of Political Parties (Decree 1313) and the Electoral Law (March 26, 1984), which also are very important. It is clear that those laws possess no real democratic purpose because of the legal and political context that prevails in the country.

After January 1985, the National Board was succeeded by the presidency as chief of the executive branch. By decree, the presidency today has all the powers and functions that the National Board once had. This situation is to remain until a new political constitution becomes legally applicable.

During 1985, the FSLN planned a final offensive to substitute formally most of the original framework of the revolution with a popular democratic constitution written by an assembly dominated by the Sandinistas. Basic aspects of a constitutional draft were defined September 5, 1985, in "Twenty Points of the FSLN for the Constitution."[33] Through this document, the FSLN proposed, without further subterfuge, a popular democracy for Nicaragua, a revealing fact because popular democracy is not only different but contrary to representative democracy, which was a fundamental goal of the 1979 revolution.[34]

33. This project was signed by Daniel Ortega as coordinator of the executive commission of the FSLN's National Directorate. *Diario Barricada* (Managua), September 6, 1985.

34.. An elementary historical fact is that "popular democracy" was a type of political and economic organization that prevailed in Albania, Czechoslovakia, Poland, Rumania, Hungary, and East Germany immediately after World War II. Communist China was declared a popular democracy after October 1949. Vietnam is a popular democracy, and Nicaragua is well on its way to that political and economic model considered by Marxism–Leninism as a stage between a bourgeois regime and the construction of socialism, without resorting, even temporarily, to a bourgeois democracy. See E. Mascitelli, ed., *Diccionario de Términos Marxistas* (Barcelona, Spain: Grijalbo, n.d.), pp. 106–107.

A deteriorating internal situation, external political pressures, and the need to retain for a time some formal democratic traits obliged the FSLN to present a more traditional constitutional draft, which contains nonetheless a constitutional regression: the establishment of a partisan armed forces, a fact already recognized at the decree level.[35] (See Appendix C.)

Since 1979, the FSLN has answered thousands of charges about its alleged or real abuses by declaring that the revolution is the source of law. Such an answer is correct only in the sense that every revolution gives birth to a new legal order. But the FSLN declaration is a serious threat to all human and political rights when it means that the vanguard's interests are to prevail over the law. And experience has shown that this is the sense in which the FSLN understands the relationship between law and revolution. Again, a Leninist orientation, in rhetoric and practice, is clear in the Sandinista party. In contrast, and despite the facts, the FSLN insists that it is only a nationalist and democratic government, FSLN representative and researcher Francisco López explains in this book. Nevertheless, the facts and trends of the Sandinista legal system show that it is in a transitional stage from an initially democratic national process toward a totalitarian model.

Conclusion: The Sandinistas' Design and Some of Its Practical Consequences

The bitter historical relations between the United States and Nicaragua, plus the Leninist doctrine adoped in 1961 by the FSLN, make it impossible, from that party's point of view, to develop mutually respectful relations with the United States. This fact is very important but nonetheless usually neglected in one-sided interpretations of the FSLN. For this reason, it is worthwhile to recall briefly a few facts pertaining to the FSLN's relations with the United States and other countries.

The Sandinista Front, for historical and ideological reasons and because of its political commitments, did not take the olive branch that the United

35. The draft of the constitution was officially presented to the National Assembly in Managua on February 21, 1986, by the president of that assembly, Carlos Núñez. See *La Constitución, Nuestro Compromiso con el Futuro* [The Constitution, Our Commitment to the Future] (Managua: Comisión Especial Constitucional, n.d.). The draft has 10 titles, 27 chapters, and 221 articles. This constitutional project does not introduce, in general terms, any better guarantees than those included in the three basic documents of the revolution in 1979. It is obvious that in Nicaragua the power lies in the party and not in the law. For this reason, it is dubious that the draft of the constitution or the constitution itself could have any supreme authority. If the FSLN did not dare in 1979 to suggest in any of the three fundamental political and legal instruments that there would be a partisan army, it now has been clearly established in the constitutional draft (Articles 177–181) (see Appendix C). There, in the ideologized army, is where the real power of the FSLN must be found. The constitution could be amended or suppressed in the future when circumstances become more favorable for the FSLN's total consolidation.

States repeatedly presented to the new Nicaraguan government. The Carter administration gave Nicaragua $139.7 million during the initial 18 months of revolution. This was composed of $117.6 million in soft loans and $20.3 million in donations. The United States actively backed Nicaragua at the World Bank with $102.7 million. The United States acted similarly at the Inter-American Development Bank. This institution loaned Nicaragua $108.1 million. No other country helped the Nicaraguan revolution as much as the United States did during the first 18 months the FSLN was in power. From July 19, 1979, to February 22, 1982, Nicaragua received more than $1.5 billion in loans and donations, an amount equivalent to Nicaragua's GNP in 1980.[36] Most of that help came from Western countries and prevented Nicaragua's economy from collapsing.

By taking a very optimistic and dogmatic position, the FSLN miscalculated Nicaragua's structural dependence. Additionally, the Sandinistas misinterpreted Nicaragua's complex social structure and the prevailing social and political realities, which permitted wide but not unlimited action on the part of the vanguard. Beyond those limits, the FSLN would meet economic and political problems and even armed resistance. Moreover, the Sandinistas made a faulty evaluation about the degree of sensitivity regarding Nicaragua's strategic geographic position relating to other nations in the hemisphere. The Sandinista government has held, since its first day in power, a militant leaning toward the Soviet Union and Cuba, despite all the aid received from the United States and other Western countries.

Following its ideological lines, the FSLN subscribed in 1979 to a secret agreement with the Cuban army. This was learned from a speech by Minister of the Interior Tomás Borge in Bluefields in May 1980. Borge publicly identified Alfonso Robelo as the traitor who disclosed the agreement with Cuba.[37] Obviously, Nicaragua was already moving away from the nonaligned position that the United States and other Western countries were ready to accept and even encourage after the fall of Somoza. The FSLN's alignment and proletarian internationalism would have a high cost, especially in deteriorating relations with the United States and Central America—with the exception of Guatemala, which receives heavy pressure from bordering Mexico.

From personal experience during my years as a diplomat, I know that diplomatic relations with Cuba and the Soviet Union were not conducted by

36. These figures were quoted in Arturo J. Cruz and J. Velázquez, comps., *Nicaragua, regresión en la revolución* [Nicaragua: Regression of the Revolution] (San José, Costa Rica: Editorial Libro Libre, 1986).

37. "La Cultura es el Pueblo" [The Culture is the People], speech by Tomás Borge delivered at Bluefields, May 25, 1980. Speech appears in *"Habla la Dirección de la Vanguardia"* [The Directorate of the Vanguard Speaks], p. 118.

the Ministry of Foreign Affairs but by the Directorate of International Relations (DRI) of the FSLN. Relations with the two most important allies of the revolution must be handled by the vanguard. This is of great importance because it reveals (1) who the strategic allies of revolutionary Nicaragua are, according to FSLN perception, and (2) that the party and not the state is the determining force, a characteristic of Leninist parties.[38]

The FSLN's alignment with the socialist bloc is so entrenched that it surpasses Latin Americanism, a concept the FSLN has manipulated for its own ends. For example, during the Falklands/Malvinas War, there was a feeling in both Managua and Havana that an Argentinian defeat would be desirable because it would demonstrate that the Soviet Union is the true strategic ally of Latin America. Feelings within power centers in Managua contrasted with the Sandinistas' vocal support for Argentina. The inclinations and links between the FSLN and communist countries are clearly presented in the essay "The FSLN in Power" by Jiri and Virginia Valenta in this book. It is not necessary to add anything further on this topic.

Internal policies have created intense difficulties for the Sandinistas. The FSLN ran into complex contradictions in the national arena when it started to harass the urban middle class and the agrarian petite bourgeoisie. Realistically considered, these sectors of the population offered a sound foundation for the construction of a democratic and prosperous order; a Leninist view would come to the opposite conclusion. The FSLN implemented systematic harassment because it believes in what Lenin once pointed out: "Petite bourgeoisie generates petite bourgeoisie as bees generate honey."

As a result of the political conduct of the FSLN, more than 500,000 Nicaraguans have fled the country, escaping from repression and living legally or illegally abroad. This situation makes it difficult to calculate the number of émigrés, although the majority are peasants (judging from the refugee camps in Honduras and Costa Rica).

As a result of widespread mistrust of the Sandinistas and the government's ineptitude in handling the economy, Nicaragua is facing bankruptcy and unprecedented poverty. Obviously the civil war has played a role in the deterioration of the economy, but that role has been grossly exaggerated for political purposes, as have the effects of the "imperialist blockade." Nicaragua still carries on trade with the rest of the world.

Part of Nicaragua's economic and social disaster is caused by the FSLN's militarism, which goes back to 1979, before the beginning of the civil war

---

38. For a study dealing with the FSLN's structure, see Jiri and Virginia Valenta, "Sandinistas in Power," *Problems of Communism* 24 (September–October 1985): 1–28, which analyzes the FSLN's ideology and partisan structure, providing ample information on the subject and tracking the most important developments of the FSLN decisional mechanisms.

against the Sandinistas and long before the rebels received U.S. aid. Repression, exodus, civil war, international alignment, international tensions, and economic disasters are costs that the FSLN is ready to impose on Nicaragua to consolidate its political and ideological model.

The Sandinista armed forces totaled more than 119,000 men by early 1985, and the numbers continue to increase. The composition of these forces was 35,000 men in regular forces and 79,000 in the reserves. Of the reserve army, over 27,000 are on active duty. The Ministry of the Interior has its own infantry brigade, composed of 2,000 elite troops. All Nicaraguan troops are provided with Soviet and East European military equipment.

The few and old armored vehicles from the Somocista army have been rapidly replaced. By late 1984 the Sandinistas had more than 110 T-55 Soviet-made tanks, 30 PT-76 amphibious light tanks, and over 200 armored transport vehicles of the BTR-60 and BTR-152 type for transportation purposes. The army has more than 1,200 East German IFA military trucks.[39]

It is not within the scope of this paper to go into detail about the different branches of the Sandinista military. It is useful, however, to recall that the Sandinista regime has placed 19.3 out of every 1,000 inhabitants in the military. This figure is by far the highest in Central America, where the ratio per 1,000 is 4.1 in Honduras, 4.9 in Guatemala, and 7.8 in El Salvador.[40]

The Sandinistas have not stopped the militarization of society, applying all forms of pressure (from CDS to strict conscription) on the Nicaraguan population. Nor is Sandinista militarization the product of external pressures. It is the visible manifestation of a planned, long-term strategy. "The formidable presence of the Sandinista army," fervently expressed in the FSLN's General Platform, is at last a reality (see Appendix A).

Did actions by the United States and other external factors force the peace-loving Sandinistas to arm themselves? Or was it the ideological nature and political commitments of the FSLN that gave wings to their militarism and hawkish rhetoric? I am afraid that many fundamental facts and documents indicate that the more important cause (although not the only one) was the FSLN's political conception and practice.

I have seen a systematic reluctance by the Sandinistas to discuss openly vital documents such as internal circulars or the Political and Military Platform, where the Marxist–Leninist and militarist nature of the FSLN is

---

39. *CBS News*, interview with Joaquín Cuadra, chief of the Sandinista Army's General Staff, February 1985. Cuadra said that the number of tanks would be increased to more than 150 units. Interview quoted by U.S. Department of State, *El incremento militar Sandinista* [Sandinista Military Buildup], Publicacion 9432, Serie Interamericana 119, May 1985, p. 7.

40. *El incremento militar Sandinista*, p. 37. Figures are for 1984.

explicitly exposed by the National Directorate, long before the 1979 popular victory. This is an objectionable aspect of Francisco López's exposition in this book because there is an intention to deprive us of a basic perspective to understand correctly the FSLN's origins and nature. Furthermore, official accounts of the FSLN's evident failures are explained monocausally: The United States is the source of all evils. A super-scapegoat indeed.

Even though the Sandinista regime has been successful in the militarization of Nicaragua, it has not been successful in the management of Nicaragua's resources and economy. According to CEPAL, the unemployment rate grew from between 5 and 6% in 1982 to 20% later in the same year. Other sources (e.g., INISIEP) calculated unemployment at 25% for 1985.

The GNP was 5.6 million córdobas in 1984 and 5.4 million córdobas in 1985, according to the Ministry of Planning in Nicaragua. These figures are lower than those of 1974 (almost 6 million córdobas). Measured by 1958 prices, the per capita consumption was 1,532 córdobas in 1961 and 1,486 in 1985. The responsibility and influence of the FSLN in the economic area may be seen in the fact that the public-sector share of Nicaragua's GNP exceeds 58%. Additionally, since 1980, public investment has been over 73% of total national investment. Notwithstanding this fact, public investment is today similar in absolute terms to that of 1958, when the state did not have its present hegemonic position.[41]

I do not intend to present detailed account of Nicaragua's economic situation under the FSLN. Nevertheless, the indicators used may well serve as reference points on some aspects of the economic disaster that prevails in the country. These frustrating results are the product of very complex factors. The simplistic thesis that blames the *contra* civil war and the United States for of Nicaragua's woes is unacceptable.

It might seem strange, but the poverty that has increased the suffering of the people has been used to increase FSLN power as the FSLN dominates all channels for distributing goods and services. There is little doubt about the ability of the political and administrative elite to use poverty as another mechanism for dominating popular majorities. The political, military, and legal tendencies of the FSLN clearly reveal the construction of a social model in which the vanguard will have total control unless this process is stopped or reformed by forces that oppose it.

This paper has discussed briefly several related aspects of the Sandinista regime. As has been seen, the legal system is a powerful instrument for the

---

41. A very clear study on Nicaragua's economic evolution is *Nicaragua, Cómo vamos? 1985* [Nicaragua: How Are We Doing? 1985] (Managua: INISIEP, 1985). The analysis is aimed at a wide market but is rigorously backed by statistical data from government and international organisms. The projections of INISIEP [Nicaraguan Institute of Economic and Social Research of Private Enterprise] are clearly indentified in the analysis.

vanguard's goals and has forced a juridical regression by submitting the law to the will of the party and erasing the limits between the law, political morals, and partisan interests. Such regression has not taken place by chance; it obeys a strategic concept based on well-defined ideological foundations. We have seen some practical manifestations of the FSLN's ideology on the Nicaraguan economy and on political and legal matters. Contrary to what is preached, the new Nicaraguan laws have increased insecurity and repression, and have actively aided the rise of a new dominant circle.

From a more global perspective, we can see that in the present century Marxism—Leninism and Nazism—Fascism have both provided, from different perspectives, theoretical bases for the regression of the historical development of law toward greater guarantees, predictability, and freedom. A lack of political creativity and realism, in addition to the historical roots, commitments, and partisan ambitions of the FSLN, have set it on the road to legal regression. It remains to be seen if law will prevail over arbitrary power in Nicaragua. This ideal cannot be achieved without enormous efforts. Here we recall the words of Rudolf Von Ihering in *The Struggle for Law:*

> From the moment in which Law is not ready to struggle it sacrifices itself, and thus we may apply the sentence from the poet: "It is the last word of wisdom / That only he deserves life and freedom / Who every day knows how to conquer them."

• CHAPTER FIVE •

Revolution in Nicaragua

Alfredo César

The first, and now almost exhausted, discussion on the Nicaraguan revolution has been whether it exemplifies a way for Latin American countries to achieve a nationalist, independent solution to their socioeconomic problems or is just another Soviet-backed socialist revolution in the Third World that, like the Cuban revolution, will turn out to be a failure for the people but a successful tool against American "imperialism." Backed by a majority of the Nicaraguan people, the revolution at first was indeed a nationalist, pluralist experience: The three goals stated by the government junta in July 1979 were political pluralism, nonalignment, and a mixed economy. Nevertheless, as the FSLN elite gradually took over, the Nicaraguan revolution became the *Sandinista* revolution, dedicated to building a Marxist–Leninist state.

Even in the most liberal circles in Europe and the United States the discussion is no longer about the character of the Sandinista regime or about its intentions; it is about the legitimacy of their rule and, should it be legitimate, the right that they have, as representatives of a majority of the Nicaraguan people, to build arbitrarily any political system they choose.

The elections held in November 1984 were instrumental in legitimating Sandinista power because, even though they were widely regarded as fraudulent, the same kind of elections many times before in Latin America had produced governments later recognized as legitimate. In Nicaragua, however, the conflict that the regime faces is not only with the majority of the population, who reject totalitarianism, but also with Nicaragua's Central

American neighbors, who feel threatened by the size of the Sandinista army and the growing support that the Frente Sandinista de Liberación Nacional gives to insurgent groups in various of their countries. Moreover, they fear a possible intervention by the United States, who perceives its security interests as being threatened by the Soviet bloc's increasing military presence in the region.

To illustrate only a few of these points:

- In August 1979 General Omar Torrijos, a key supporter of the revolution against Somoza, sent a team of advisers to help organize the Nicaraguan Police; to his disapointment, he was turned down because the Cubans had already been assigned that job.
- During 1980, the Carter administration fought and won a battle with Congress to give an additional $75 million in aid to Nicaragua, even though in March of the same year the FSLN had signed a party-to-party agreement with the Soviet Communist party.
- A plan to aid the ailing Nicaraguan economy, presented by the Central Bank in early 1982, was rejected by the National Directorate of the FSLN because it strengthened the private sector.

Besides the question of legitimacy, the current discussion on Nicaragua also centers on what the options are for terminating the conflict there and, consequently, in Central America. The other four countries of the region have freely elected governments and are advancing toward stable democracies. Presently there exist four sets of democratic actors, each with specific priorities, who are interested in a solution to the Nicaraguan problem:

1. The Nicaraguan democratic opposition, both in Nicaragua and in exile
2. The Latin American countries, including those of Central America
3. The United States
4. The Western European countries

For the Nicaraguan opposition, as well as for some U.S. policymakers, compliance with the original goals of the revolution is the only way to end the conflict. For the Central Americans, a regional peace accord, achieved in such a way that it would guarantee their security, is the first priority, even though they also give a great deal of importance to a national reconciliation process in Nicaragua, mainly because of refugee problems.

Other Latin American countries, geographically more distant from Nicaragua, give highest priority to the avoidance of an all-out war—between the Central American countries or, worse, through military intervention by the United States. They fear that the actual process of democratization in the region would be reversed by military action and they uphold the long-held tenet of nonintervention in the internal affairs of other countries. Most of Latin America would be flexible about full democracy in Nicaragua, forfeiting this if their own peace and security concerns could still be addressed; some policymakers in the United States share this position.

The much more distant Western Europeans would go further in tolerating the internal situation in Nicaragua if war and a clash between the superpowers could be avoided; an additional concern in Western Europe, prompted by the specter of a U.S. military intervention, is that the long-lasting presence of a subtantial American military force in Central America might somehow weaken the U.S. commitment to NATO.

The well-defined project of the Managua–Havana–Moscow axis contrasts sharply with that of the various democratic actors. Their agenda is to gradually put in place a totalitarian state that will coexist with its neighbors and the rest of Latin America, and thus avoid the isolation that has plagued Cuba for so many years (with its very high economic toll); and then spread the revolution to neighboring states, little by little, as the international situation permits.

In a conversation in 1980, in Managua, I heard Fidel Castro say that he had remained in power for 25 years because he obtained a guarantee from the United States that they would not invade Cuba. Castro said that this was the most important condition for staying in power and that the *comandantes* should be looking for the same guarantee.

The key question now is how to prevent the implementation of the totaliarian project without resorting to extreme measures that would produce disarray among the democratic actors, especially between Latin America and the United States. There are three theoretical options for terminating the Nicaraguan conflict:

1. To accept, no matter how unwillingly, another Cuba in the Western Hemisphere—this time on continental soil.
2. The use of military force by the United States.
3. To force a change in FSLN political conduct by applying,on the part of all four democratic actors, appropriate pressure in the political, diplomatic, economic, and military fields. This option implies supporting the democratic opposition of Nicaragua so that a national reconciliation dialogue among all sectors of Nicaraguan political life can be forged.

There appears to be a wide consensus against the first two options, but the debate on how to go about implementing the *third* one is louder than ever among the four democratic players. Several issues form part of this debate.

First, the U.S. government has been backing the Nicaraguan opposition commonly known as the *contras*, who have been plagued with credibility problems: The military arm is headed by some former members of Somoza's army; the question raised is whether they are motivated to fight for democracy or to return to power. Furthermore, the *contras* have been largely ineffective; they have a larger military force than the Salvadoran guerrillas but have been unable to secure portions of liberated territory. Finally, there have been accusations of *contra* corruption (although most of the accusations are not substantiated and/or are related to isolated cases). Second, many Latin Americans and Europeans are critical of the U.S. government's inclination to assign such a high priority to military pressure. Third, internal political pressure in Latin America and Europe, brought about by leftist groups who constantly lobby their respective governments, prevents these governments from taking stronger positions against the Sandinista regíme. And, finally, there is the incapacity, so far, of the Nicaraguan opposition to present to the Nicaraguan people and to public opinion in other countries a coherent, democratic alternative to Sandinista rule.

The only realistic option available to all four democratic actors interested in a solution to the problem in Nicaragua is to *agree* on a combination of measures to be applied to the Sandinista regime. In my opinion that option requires a change in policy in the United States *and* in Latin America and Western Europe, as well as coordinated effort on the part of all sectors of the Nicaraguan democratic opposition.

The United States should back a broader spectrum of the Nicaraguan opposition than the *contras*; it should include rebel organizations that fought against the Somoza regime but have since become disillusioned, as well as the Miskito Indians, who also initially supported the revolution but later turned against the FSLN because of the repressions imposed by Sandinista security forces. The United States should also move toward a bipartisan consensus in Congress and give stronger signals in favor of the political and diplomatic pressures favored by the Contadora countries and by Europe.

The Latin American and European countries should increase political, diplomatic, and economic pressures on the Sandinistas, to force them to accept a national reconciliation process as a requirement for any solution of the conflict. *Isolation* is the biggest bargaining tool that the countries of Latin America have vis-à-vis the Sandinistas.

The democratic opposition should bridge their political differences and construct, in word and deed, a clear and coherent democratic alternative for Nicaragua, with the goal of establishing a democratic system respectful of human rights. This was the overwhelming desire of the people of Nicaragua when they fought against the Somoza dictatorship. Preferably a new system would come about through an internal reconciliation process that would avoid further destruction and bloodshed.

The message from all democratic countries to the Sandinistas should be this: To achieve peace, you must implement the original goals of the Nicaraguan revolution—political pluralism, nonalignment, and a mixed economy. If the Sandinistas do this, the United States should cease all forms of pressure, normalize relations between the two countries, and include Nicaragua as a recipient of economic aid. The opposition should be committed to political solutions, starting with a national reconciliation dialogue, and should be satisfied with the implementation of the promises of the revolution of 1979, which were the cohesive elements in that struggle.

• PART TWO •

Internal Dimensions of the Crisis

• CHAPTER SIX •

Political Legitimacy and Dissent

Margaret E. Crahan

Criteria for determining the legitimacy of governments have been elaborated by Aristotle, St. Augustine, Thomas Aquinas, John Locke, and Joseph de Maistre, among others. Since World War II, a consensus has emerged in international law concerning such criteria that has influenced the charters of the United Nations and the Organization of American States (OAS), as well as numerous laws and treaties. These criteria have been reinforced by the social doctrine of the world's principal religions in their roles as moral legitimators or critics of societal structures. Hence, there is a basis in both law and morality to measure the legitimacy of any government.

While the discussion of parameters for legitimate dissent has not been as detailed, there is consensus in international law concerning the preconditions for insurrection. These suggest that revolt is an absolute last resort against governments whose legitimacy has eroded in the face of long-term gross violations of the full spectrum of human rights (civil, political, economic, social, cultural, and religious). In addition, there must be demonstrable incapacity by the existing government to exercise effective control over the national territory. Without these conditions, legitimate dissent is limited to the utilization of existing channels of popular pressure, as well as such measures as civil disobedience and passive resistance.

This paper measures the present government of Nicaragua against the criteria of political legitimacy commonly accepted by international law.[1]

---

1. These criteria are a synthesis of those cited in international charters, treaties, and law, as well as elucidations of them in standard sources such as Cyril E. Black and Richard A. Falk, *The*

These criteria are (1) widespread diplomatic recognition;[2] (2) effective administrative control over the national territory and its population; (3) meeting of international obligations; and (4) protection and promotion of human rights.[3]

Future of the International Legal Order (Princeton: Princeton University Press, 1971); Charles G. Fenwick, *International Law*, 4th ed. (New York: Appleton-Century-Crofts, 1965); James Fishkin, *Tyranny and Legitimacy: A Critique of Political Theories* (Baltimore: Johns Hopkins University Press, 1979); *International Encyclopedia of the Social Sciences* (New York: Macmillan, 1968); Hersch Lauterpacht, *International Law: Being the Collected Papers of Hersch Lauterpacht*, ed. E. Lauterpacht (Cambridge,England: Cambridge University Press, 1970); idem, *The Development of International Law by the International Court* (London: Stevens & Son, 1958); idem, *Recognition in International Law* (Cambridge, England: Cambridge University Press, 1984); Werner Levi, *Contemporary International Law: A Concise Introduction* (Boulder, Colo.: Westview, 1979); Gary L. Maris, *International Law: An Introduction* (Lanham, Md.: University Press of America, 1984); and L. Oppenheim, *International Law: A Treatise*, 7th ed., ed. H. Lauterpacht (New York: Longmans, Green, 1948).

2. Criteria for diplomatic recognition are at times confused with criteria for political legitimacy, and there is admittedly some overlap. Historically, in some cases de facto control of the state apparatus and at least a portion of the national territory has been considered sufficient for diplomatic recognition. Since 1913, however, during the presidency of Woodrow Wilson, U.S. criteria for recognition have included the ability of the government to fulfill international obligations and the consent of the governed. These criteria were also enunciated by the International Commission of American Jurists in 1927. The prime difference between criteria for recognition and political legitimacy is the emphasis of the latter on a government's obligation to respect and promote human rights. In recent years there has been a growing tendency to use the criteria for political legitimacy to determine the maintenance of diplomatic relations. On May 22, 1986, for example, Argentina broke diplomatic relations with South Africa on the grounds that "a regime of institutionalized racial discrimination [is] totally unacceptable in the framework of the contemporary international community." In addition, it poses "a threat to peace and international security." See "Argentina Breaks Relations with South Africa, Calls It 'Threat.' " *Washington Post*, May 23, 1986, p. A27.

3. The most commonly accepted statement of human rights principles is the Universal Declaration of Human Rights drafted under the auspices of the United Nations in 1948 with strong input from the U.S. delegation headed by Eleanor Roosevelt. Many of the delegates were experienced politicians and diplomats who had survived the rise of fascism and World War II and had come to believe that "disregard and contempt for human rights have resulted in barbarous acts which have outraged the conscience of mankind. . . ." They further stated in the preamble to the declaration that respect for human rights was essential for "freedom, justice and peace in the world." Since 1948, approximately 155 countries have subscribed to the Universal Declaration of Human Rights, thereby demonstrating that the vast majority of the nations of the world accept its criteria. In 1948 the Latin American nations adopted an American Declaration of the Rights and Duties of Man, which included all the rights in the Universal Declaration. These documents include a broad spectrum of civil, political, social, economic, religious, and cultural rights, which are used in this paper to measure the human rights performance of the Nicaraguan government.

Since the greatest area of disagreement concerning the legitimacy of the present government of Nicaragua centers on the fourth criterion, that is the major focus of this paper. As a consequence, the observance or nonobservance of civil and political rights relating to popular participation and pluralism is examined to establish the degree to which the government meets the criterion of representativeness. Even more important is an analysis of the degree to which the Nicaraguan government guarantees the physical integrity of persons (i.e., does not engage in torture, assassinations, disappearances). This is measured not only with respect to protection from abuses by the state but also the capacity of the state to protect its citizens from attacks by others. This essay also evaluates the degree to which the Nicaraguan government has guaranteed socioeconomic rights during its attempt to transform the economy into a socialist one. Respect for religious freedom and liberty of worship is a prime focus, particularly since much of the current political and ideological struggle under way in Nicaragua has centered in and on the churches, particularly the Catholic church, which claims over 85% of the population. Government respect for the rights of ethnic minorities, such as the Miskito, Sumu, and Rama Indians, has also been a prime reason for attacks on the legitimacy of the Nicaraguan government and hence is also treated.

The degree to which the present government of Nicaragua meets accepted criteria for legitimacy is used to determine the parameters of legitimate dissent in Nicaragua. This involves an evaluation of whether or not the armed opposition, know as the *contras*, meet the criteria for insurrection under international law. Other expressions of dissent, including those of political parties, labor unions, business groups such as Consejo Superior de la Empresa Privada [Superior Council of Private Enterprise or COSEP] and sectors within the Catholic and Protestant churches are analyzed to measure the legality of their opposition activities.

The paper concludes with a summary analysis of the legitimacy of the present Nicaraguan government according to generally recognized international legal standards. This serves to determine the scope of legitimate dissent against which both internal and external opponents are measured. Given the limited length of the paper, this analysis, of necessity, has to be more suggestive than exhaustive.

Criteria for Legitimate Government

In international law widespread recognition of a new government is considered persuasive evidence of legitimacy. Within a few days of the taking of power by the insurrectionary forces on July 19, 1979, virtually all the countries with which Nicaragua previously had relations recognized the new government. These included the United States, which in spite of sharp differences with the present government, has continued to accord it recognition. This is a result of the fact that the new government clearly exercised effective control over the national territory and the population inhabiting it. Subsequently, the new government demonstrated capacity to assure public stability and fulfill international obligations, including those incurred by the Somoza government.[4] Recognition of the *contras* as legitimate insurrectionists would require that they control substantial territory within the boundaries of Nicaragua on a long-term basis.[5] Neither the Nicaraguan Democratic Force (FDN), based in Honduras, nor the Democratic Revolutionary Alliance (ARDE), operating out of Costa Rica, succeeded in doing this.

In June 1979 the Catholic bishops of Nicaragua found the popular insurrection against the Somoza government morally and legally justified on the grounds that the Somoza regime had promoted grave and oppressive inequalities among classes. They further charged that Nicaraguans were unable to exercise initiative and responsibility, nor to participate in social and political life in the face of the authoritarianism of the Somoza regime. The episcopacy specifically condemned disappearances, illegal detentions, torture, assassinations, disregard of due process, profaning of cadavers, illegal search and entry, media censorship, and persecution and defamation of church people. The bishops concluded that a peaceful road to democracy was closed, and since constitutional means for change were not available, supported the insurrection.[6]

This pastoral letter reflected the seriousness of the Nicaragua situation in 1979, for Catholic social doctrine traditionally counsels against the use of military force to overturn governments. As recently as April 1986 the Vatican's Congregation for the Doctrine of Faith reaffirmed that armed struggle is a "last resort to put an end to an obvious and prolonged tyranny which is gravely damaging the fundamental rights of individuals and the common good." Furthermore. "because of the continual development of the technology of violence and the increasingly serious dangers implied in its recourse, that which is termed 'passive resistance' shows a way more com-

---

4. Lauterpacht, *Recognition in International Law*, pp. 26–32; Lauterpacht,*International Law*, p. 316; Maris, *International Law*, p. 97.

5. Fenwick, *International Law*, p. 167.

6. Consejo Episcopal de Nicaragua, "Mensaje al Pueblo Nicaragüense," [Nicaraguan Episcopal Council, "Message to the Nicaraguan People"] Managua, Nicaragua, June 2, 1979. Mimeo.

fortable to moral principles and having no less prospects for success."[7] It is notable that while the Nicaraguan bishops have been critical of the Sandinista government, they have not declared it illegitimate nor have they supported the *contras*.

Civil and Political Rights

Government legitimacy is most seriously challenged by allegations of gross violations of human rights. These include not only civil and political rights but also social, economic, religious, and cultural rights. That there have been serious human rights violations in Nicaragua, including assaults on the physical integrity of individuals, is incontrovertible. The Interior Ministry has reported the convictions of Sandinista soldiers involved in the murder, rape, or wounding of 35 persons since 1983.[8] Before that, in late 1983, 13 soldiers and policemen were convicted of murder and rape in the commission of robberies. Accusations of widespread, systematic abuses such as those alleged by a former Interior Ministry official, Alvaro Baldizon, have not been confirmed by independent international human rights organizations.[9]

In particular, the Inter-American Commission on Human Rights of the

7. "Key Sections from Vatican Document on Liberation Theology," *New York Times*, April 6, 1986, p. 14.

8. Nancy Nusser, "Army Abuses Reported in Nicaragua: Sandinistas Pay Victims' Families," *Washington Post*, April 12, 1986, pp. A13, A20.

9. Americas Watch, *Human Rights in Nicaragua: Reagan, Rhetoric and Reality* (New York: Americas Watch, 1985); Amnesty International, *Nicaragua: The Human Rights Record* (London: Amnesty International Publications, 1986); Mary Dutcher, *Nicaragua: Violations of the Laws of War on Both Sides* (Washington, D.C.: Washington Office on Latin America, 1986); Inter-American Commission on Human Rights, *Annual Report, 1984–1985* (Washington, D.C.: Organization of American States, 1985), pp. 161–165. See also the Inter-American Commission on Human Rights, *Report on the Situation of Human Rights of a Segment of the Nicaraguan Population of Miskito Origin* (Washington, D.C.: Organization of American States, 1984); *Report on the Situation of Human Rights in the Republic of Nicaragua* (Washington, D.C.: Organization of American States, 1981); *Annual Report, 1981–1982* (Washington, D.C.: Organization of American States, 1982), pp. 119–122; *Annual Report, 1982–1983* (Washington, D.C.: Organization of American States, 1983), pp. 160–161. The human rights data used in this study are taken from the reports of internationally recognized independent human rights organizations that have conducted extensive on-site investigations in Nicaragua. These are the Inter-American Commission on Human Rights, established by the member nations of the Organization of American States and funded by them; Americas Watch, created as a consequence of the Helsinki Accords; Amnesty International, which over the past 25 years has established itself as the premier human rights organization; the U.S.-based Lawyers Committee on International Human Rights, founded by lawyers specializing in human rights; the Washington Office on Latin America, founded by an ecumenical group of U.S. churches

Organization of American States has not found evidence to sustain allegations of mass violations of the physical integrity of persons. In its *Annual Report* for 1984–1985 it stated that the principal violations were in the area of personal freedom and due process. The commission cited the state of emergency initiated in 1982 as a major cause of this. It did note improvements with respect to the treatment of the Miskito population, which suffered violations of their rights particularly in 1981–1982.[10]

The most serious limitations of political and civil rights in Nicaragua have resulted from the expansion on October 15, 1985, of the 1982 state of emergency. Currently 11 articles of the Nicaraguan Bill of Rights (Decree No. 52, issued August 21, 1979) are suspended or limited. These include some legal rights of criminal suspects, freedom of movement to and from war zones, and freedom of expression on the part of the media. Public meetings and demonstrations require police permits, and the right to strike is suspended. The privacy of communication and freedom of association are also limited. The right to found popular, communal, or other organizations is suspended, as is the right of appeal from governmental administrative decisions to the Supreme Court. The reasons given by Nicaraguan officials for the expansion of the state of emergency are the ongoing *contra* war and the fear of an internal front being opened. A particular preoccupation was the spread of public disorder that would create the impression that the government was incapable of maintaining domestic security.[11]

The expansion of the state of emergency came in the aftermath of the reported foiling of a *contra* sabotage and intelligence operation in Jinotega resulting in the arrest of 129 persons. In addition, the government was preoccupied over increasing criticism of the military draft, particularly that expressed by the cardinal of Managua, Monsignor Miguel Obando y Bravo. In addition, the archdiocese of Managua initiated a new publication entitled *Iglesia*, which alleged that the government had detained seminarians as draft dodgers. While the law of universal military service did not provide for exemptions for seminarians, the government had not been drafting them. This had produced an upsurge of Nicaraguan youths claiming to be seminarians. The result was a crackdown on those the government claimed were not

---

primarily for educational purposes. Amnesty International is notable for having been awarded the Nobel Peace Prize and is funded primarily by individual contributions, benefit concerts, and foundations. The others are financed not only by individual contributions but also by church organizations and foundations such as the Ford Foundation.

  10. IACHR, *Annual Report, 1984–1985, pp. 161–165.*

  11. Foreign Broadcast Information Service (hereinafter cited as *FBIS*), "Borge Interviewed on State of Emergency," *Daily Report: Latin America 6*, no. 221 (November 15, 1985): P7–11; *FBIS*, "Ramírez Mercado Clarifies Emergency Measures," *Daily Report: Latin America 6*, no. 241 (December 16, 1985): P16–17.

formally enrolled in any seminary. The Superior Council of Private Enterprise (COSEP) also organized a series of regional meetings to generate opposition to the government during the summer of 1985.[12] Their leader, Enrique Bolaños, was particularly outspoken in the wake of the expropriation of some of his cotton lands in the Masaya area. The government charged that COSEP and Bolaños had organized a production boycott that resulted in a sharp decline in cotton for export in 1985. Such withdrawal of land from production is a prerequisite of expropriation.[13]

Labor unrest increased in the fall of 1985 as leftist trade unions mounted a campaign for a return of the traditional year-end bonus. It was spearheaded by Alejandro Solórzano of the General Confederation of Labor-Independent (CGT-I), who undertook a hunger strike.[14] The year-end bonus was reinstated but the right to strike suspended. Minister of the Interior Tomás Borge justified the latter by asserting the following:

> In a country full of poverty and beset by economic crisis and aggression, it is very easy to go and seek support to swell one's ranks by urging a section of the workers to demand better living conditions. Instead of boosting support for the attacked revolution, what those allegedly leftwing gentlemen are doing is sabotaging the revolution by identifying themselves objectively with rightwing stances. These elements, which never had the fortitude or the courage to face up resolutely to Somoza, are indeed now challenging us.[15]

Some Sandinista officials pointed out in response to criticism that the right to strike had been suspended in the United States during World War II.

Opponents to the Nicaraguan government have charged that the establishment of Sandinista unions was an attempt to undercut existing unions and control labor. In February 1985 the highest-ranking delegation of U.S. labor leaders to visit Nicaragua for an on-site investigation found that although non-Sandinista unions have been harassed, they do function and are free to meet, organize, and collect dues. There were no allegations that union leaders had been tortured or killed by the government, although some had been detained briefly. While leaders of the independent unions were strongly critical of the Sandinista government, the were also unequivocally opposed to U.S. aid for the *contras*. Their reasons were the damage to the

12. David R. Dye, "The National Emergency in Nicaragua: A Provisional Interpretation," *LASA–NICA Scholar News*, 9 (December, 1985–January, 1986), pp.2–3.

13. Gobierno de Reconstrucción Nacional, *Ley de Reforma Agraria* [Government of National Reconstruction, Law of Agrarian Reform] (Managua: Departamento de Propaganda y Educación Política del FSLN [Department of Propaganda and Political Education of the FSLN], 1981), pp. 6–7.

14. *FBIS*, "Union Leader on Hunger Strike in Demand for 13th Month," *Special Translation: Censored Articles from La Prensa*, October 30, 1985, pp. 10–11.

15. *FBIS*, "Borge Interviewed," p. 10.

economy that the warfare caused and the fact that some union members, who were civilians, had been killed by the *contras*.[16]

From July 1979 to December 1983 union membership in Nicaragua increased from 27,020 to 233,032 and unions from 133 to 1,103. This has caused some to conclude that the present Nicaraguan government is more favorably disposed to labor than Somoza was. Expansion of the unions has, however, increased criticism of government labor policies. Inflation, a decline in real wages, and an expanding black market have preoccupied labor. The Confederation of Labor Unity (CUS), linked to the AFL–CIO's [American Federation of Labor–Congress of Industrial Organizations] American Institute for Free Labor Development (AIFLD), and the Social Democratic party (PSD) have tended to attribute problems to government mismanagement and inadequate policies. The leftist General Confederation of Labor–Independent (CGT–I), Confederation of Action and Labor Union Unification (CAUS), and Workers' Front (FO) blame the problems on U.S. pressures and bourgeois and bureaucratic tendencies within the government. They support a more socialist economy. The Sandinista Confederation of Workers (CST) and Association of Rural Workers (ATC) tend to ascribe them principally to the depredations of the U.S.-supported *contras*.[17] All the unions agree on the desirability of greater worker participation and the need to end the war.

16. *The Search for Peace in Central America: A Special Report by the National Labor Committee in Support of Democracy and Human Rights in El Salvador* (New York, 1985). The National Labor Committee is headed by Douglas Fraser, UAW, Jack Sheinkman, ACTWU, and William Winpifinger, IAM.

17. The following is a list of Nicaraguan trade union federations in 1983:

Federation	Unions	Members	Political Party Affiliation
ATC (Association of Rural Workers)	480	40,000	FSLN
CAUS (Confederation of Action and Labor Union Unification)	15	1,939	PCN
CGT-I (General Labor Confederation—Independent)	19	17,177	PSN
CST (Sandinista Confederation of Workers)	504	111,498	FSLN
CTN (Nicaraguan Workers' Confederation)	21	2,734	PSC
CUS (Confederation of Labor Unity)	17	1,670	PSD
FO (Workers' Front)	—	845	MAP
Other[a]	47[b]	57,299	
Total	1,103	233,162	

[a]This includes ANDEN (teachers' association), FETSALUD (health workers' federation), UNE (public employee association), and UPN (journalists' union), and other affiliated unions.

[b]39 of these are FETSALUD unions. FETSALUD is formally considered a separate federation.

Source: Central American Historical Institute (CAHI), *UPDATE* 3, no 30 (September 6, 1984): 1–3. The CAHI located at Georgetown University in Washington, D.C.. It shares data with the Instituto Histórico Centroamericano (IHCA) based at the Central American University in Managua. Both universities are Catholic institutions.

Before the expansion of the state of emergency, international human rights organizations including Americas Watch, Amnesty International, the Inter-American Commission on Human Rights and the Washington Office on Latin America had criticized Nicaragua for deficiencies in the administration of justice. The Lawyers Committee for International Human Rights, after four on-site visits in 1984 and 1985, concluded that while "the regular judiciary in Nicaragua is generally independent . . . several developments have placed tremendous strains on Nicaragua's fledging court system, undercutting both its independence and the rights it is charged to uphold."[18] According to the Lawyers Committee, a prime impediment to the enjoyment of one's rights was the establishment of Popular Anti-Somocista Tribunals (TPAs) to try those accused of violations of national security. The committee found that the TPAs by their very nature had a bias to convict and sometimes used lower standards of evidence than necessary. There is no right of appeal from the TPAs to the regular courts. The committee also condemned a 1980 law allowing the police to imprison individuals for up to 2 years without trial by an independent court in certain cases and the use of psychological coercion by the Dirección General de Seguridad del Estado [General Directorate of State Security]. Physical coercion was found to be rare. The state of emergency allowed for suspects in national security crimes to be held incommunicado, giving rise to allegations of disappearances.

On the positive side the Lawyers Committee found that the Nicaraguan government did try soldiers and police accused of serious human rights violations including crimes against those suspected of aiding the *contras*. The courts have issued writs of habeas corpus and insisted on examinations by doctors of detainees alleged to have been abused. Prisoners were generally released when their terms were completed, although there have been some exceptions.[19] The Lawyers Committee, like other human rights organizations, concluded that the Nicaraguan government was within its legal rights to impose a state of emergency in order to maintain internal order in the face of the *contra* warfare.

In addition to deficiencies of due process, the Nicaraguan government has been accused of limiting freedom of the press, particularly with respect to the opposition paper *La Prensa*, and the radio station of the Nicaraguan Bishops' Conference and publications of the archdiocese of Managua. In a

---

18. Lawyers Committee on International Human Rights, *Nicaragua: Revolutionary Justice—A Report on Human Rights and the Judicial System* (New York: Lawyers Committee on International Human Rights, 1985), p. 8.
   19. Ibid., pp. 8−12.

statement released in December 1984 on going into self-imposed exile, the co-director of *La Prensa*, Pedro Joaquín Chamorro, stated:

> I feel that our job as an information medium is definitely curtailed by the imagination or the whims and fancies of a censor, who sees in every informative paragraph, in every editorial, or in every opinion expressed by a citizen, an attack against the all-powerful, and ever-present "security of the State."[20]

When questioned as to his response to allegations that *La Prensa* appeared to be serving U.S. and *contra* interests, Chamorro in early 1984 responded that "to demand total objectivity is impossible under present circumstances."[21] The newspaper's partisan stance also led it to refuse to publish information about or run ads by some of the parties participating in the 1984 elections.[22] The revolutionary newspapers *Barricada* and *El Nuevo Diario* experience much less censorship than *La Prensa* and argue that it was not until the beginning of the *contra* war that censorship was imposed.

The other important object of censorship has been Radio Católica, which is closely identified with Cardinal Obando y Bravo and his vicar, Monsignor Bismarck Carballo. On January 1, 1986 Radio Católica was closed for failing to broadcast the New Year's message of President Daniel Ortega, as required by law. The government asserted that this was "an escalation of their actions outside the law."[23] Subsequently, the government issued a lengthy communiqué stating that Radio Católica consistently disregarded prior censorship by altering its programs without notifying the News Media Directorate. It also charged that it had broadcast criticisms of the draft, thereby undercutting national defense.[24]

Before the closure of Radio Católica, the first issue of a new archdiocesan publication, *Iglesia*, was suppressed by the government. The justification offered was that necessary publishing permits had not been obtained. It is also quite clear that the government was irritated by the fact that the issue contained a number of articles criticizing universal military service and

20. Pedro Joaquín Chamorro, "I'll Come Back When There Is Freedom of the Press," Press Release, San José, Costa Rica, December 15, 1984, p. 1.

21. Interview with Pedro Joaquín Chamorro, co-director, *La Prensa*, Managua, Nicaragua, March 16, 1984. The extent of *La Prensa's* links to the United States was suggested when it was learned in 1985 that it had received $100,000 from the U.S. government's National Endowment for Democracy. Americas Watch, *Human Rights in Nicaragua*, p. 33.

22. Interview with Xavier Chamorro, director, *El Nuevo Diario*, Managua, Nicaragua, August 10, 1985.

23. *FBIS*, "Interior Ministry Closes Radio Católica," *Daily Report: Latin America 6*, no. 002, Annex (January 3, 1986): 11.

24. *FBIS*, "New Media Directorate on Radio Católica Closure," *Daily Report: Latin America 6*, no. 003 (January 6, 1986): P 11.

alleging harassment of the church.[25] Although 10,000 copies of *Iglesia* were confiscated, copies did circulate within Nicaragua and abroad, arriving in Washington 2 days after publication.

Media censorship in Nicaragua obviously is encouraged by the military and political struggle currently under way. Since Cardinal Obando y Bravo is widely considered the chief spokesperson of the opposition within the country, Radio Católica and archdiocesan publications have become targets of government action. The government justifies censorship on the basis of national security. Human rights organizations have criticized the restrictions and urged that they be abandoned.[26] They have not concluded that press censorship justifies overthrow of the Sandinista government.

One of the principal issues that has been raised concerning the present government of Nicaragua is its representativeness. Critics of the Sandinistas claim they have abandoned a pledge made at the Organization of American States in June 1979 to establish a pluralistic political system by creating a one-party totalitarian state. The Sandinistas argue that effective popular control over the state is exercised via the creation and maturation of a variety of autonomous social and political organizations and mechanisms, including, but not limited to, political parties. Hence they view the literacy campaign, agrarian reform, the growth of trade unions, creation of the committees for the Defense of Sandinismo, as well as youth, women's, and ethnic organizations, and the establishment of the militia as promoting and

25. Following is a list of headlines from *Iglesia*, October 12, 1985, that indicate its overall content:

Cardinal Carried Message of Peace to the Coast
Cardinal Obando, President of the Nicaraguan Episcopal Conference
Editorial: A New Catholic Newspaper Is Born
Eucharistic Congress Announced
Bishops Denounce Harassing of the Church
Latin America Resists Atheistic Models
The People Know Their Pastors
Catholic Radio Protests to Interior Ministry
Week of the Family
Interior Ministry Muzzles Catholic Radio
Scripture Readings for the Next Two Weeks
Cardinal Obando Acclaimed Throughout the Country
Grenadan Clergy Protests
Seminarians Detained in Río San Juan
Liturgical Reform, 20 Years Later
The Church, Route of Good Hope (by Cardinal Obando)
Communication of the Episcopal Conference
More Seminarians Conscripted

26. IACHR, *Annual Report, 1984–1985*, pp. 162–163; Americas Watch, *Human Rights in Nicaragua*, p. 33.

facilitating popular participation in decision making.[27] Mass organizations
are held to represent majority interests and serve as mediators between the
state and civil society. The Sandinistas would argue that such mechanisms
stimulate greater representation of the views of the whole population than
reliance exclusively on political parties.[28]

Allegations that mass organizations are not autonomous have been denied by supporters of the revolution, who cite the frequency with which such
groups have critiqued government programs and policies. Currently these
organizations, together with political parties, are involved in making recommendations for and critiquing a proposed national constitution.[29] Mass organizations have, themselves, been the object of popular criticism. Both the
Committees for the Defense of Sandinismo (CDSs) and the Luisa Amanda
Espinosa Nicaraguan Women's Association (AMNLAE), for example, have
undergone restructuring and reorientation as a result of pressures to make
them more responsive to local or membership needs. The Sandinista National Liberation Front (FSLN) remains, however, the preeminent actor.

One of the chief bones of contention has been the legitimacy of the
November 1984 national election. Some 240 delegations consisting of more
than 2,000 foreign observers witnessed and reported on this election. Before
the election, the U.S. Department of State categorized it as having "no more
validity than those held by Somoza."[30] It also supported the abstention of
political parties and candidates.[31] In the aftermath of the elections, in which
the Sandinista Liberation Front won 61 seats and opposition parties 35, the

27. *Principios y Políticas del Gobierno de Nicaragua* [Principles and Policies of the Nicaraguan Government] (Managua, 1982), pp. 7–8.

28. José Luis Coraggio and George Irwin, "Revolution and Pluralism in Nicaragua," in
Towards an Alternative for Central America and the Caribbean, ed. George Irwin and Xavier
Gorostiaga (The Hague, Netherlands: Institute of Social Studies, 1984), pp. 278– 279.

29. Asamblea Nacional [National Assembly], "Similiarities, Variations and Reservations
in the Nicaraguan Constitutional Process," *Boletín*, February 1986, pp. 1–5. From April 18 to
20, 1986, 27 Nicaraguans met with some 200 U.S. constitutional specialists at New York
University Law School to solicit criticisms and suggestions for revisions of the draft constitution. The Nicaraguans represented a diversity of perspectives including those of the opposition
political parties. These included the Independent Liberal party, Democratic Conservative
party, Popular Social Christian party, and Socialist party. Also represented were the Law
Faculty of the Central American University, the Bar Association, Evangelical Committee for
Aid and Development (CEPAD), Federation of Professionals, the womens' organization
(AMNLAE), two indigenous representatives, Supreme Court, lower courts, protestant and
Catholic churches, as well as officials from the government, including some members of the
National Assembly.

30. U.S. Department of State, *Resource Book: Sandinista Elections in Nicaragua* (Washington, D.C.: U.S. Department of State, 1984), p. 5.

31. Ibid., p. 17.

Reagan administration charged that the elections were a sham because opposition political parties had been hampered in presenting their platforms by media censorship, the Supreme Electoral Council was pro-Sandinista, and there had been threats against and intimidation of opposition candidates and parties. There was some basis for these charges. It was also asserted that the general population had been unduly pressured by the government to vote for the FSLN and that there was some vote tampering, also in favor of the Sandinistas.

Although admitting defects in the electoral process, most of the observer teams concluded that the election was valid. The delegation of the Latin American States Association (LASA), a U.S.-based organization of professional Latin Americanists, on the basis of an on-site visit by 15 North American scholars of varying political persuasions concluded that the vote was "truly a secret ballot, and was generally perceived as such by voters."[32] They also found no irregularities in voting or vote counting nor evidence of coercion to vote (approximately 75% of registered voters cast ballots). With respect to the charges that certain parties or candidates were "excluded," the LASA delegation concluded that the opposition group, the Coordinadora, had made a policy decision not to participate in an effort to undercut the validity of the elections.[33] The delegation felt that all the opposition parties that participated had reason to complain about the manner in which the FSLN used government resources to promote its candidates. Their

32. Latin American Studies Association, *The Electoral Process in Nicaragua: Domestic and International Influences* (Austin, Tex.: LASA Secretariat, 1984), p. 1. For a critique of the LASA report, see Daniel C. Levy, "Letter to the Editor," *LASA Forum 16*, no. 1 (Spring 1985): 8–10. This critique alleged that the delegation was intent on producing a report discounting or explaining away defects of the Sandinista government, that the delegation was not politically representative and ignored explanations unflattering to the Sandinistas. Similar criticisms have been made by some U.S. officials. In replying to them, Wayne A. Cornelius, president of LASA and a delegation member, offered evidence in support of the absence of any prior agreed upon conclusions or perspective, the diversity of political orientations within the delegation, and lack of any intention to whitewash the Sandinistas. Wayne A. Cornelius, "The 1985 Nicaraguan Elections Revisited," *LASA Forum 16*, no. 4 (Winter 1986): 22–28. (Report hereinafter cited as LASA Report.)

33. A senior U.S. diplomat informed me, in an interview on August 13, 1985, that Arturo Cruz told him that he had not run for the presidency because of pressures from the U.S. government and the Coordinadora. In an interview on August 9, 1986, with Virgilio Godoy, leader of the Independent Liberal party (PLI) and its candidate for the presidency, he denied having withdrawn shorly before the elections as a result of pressure from the U.S. government. Instead, he claimed that the withdrawal occurred because the party, having entered the campaign late, eventually realized that it was not sufficiently organized to carry through. However, since it was too late for the names of the PLI candidates to be dropped from the ballot, nine won seats in the National Assembly.

overall conclusion was that the 1984 election contributed to political pluralism in Nicaragua.[34]

A delegation composed of Ben Stephansky, a former deputy assistant
secretary of state and former ambassador to Bolivia; Charles Whalen, a
former Republican congressman from Ohio, Barbara Blum, the president of
the Womens' National Bank; and William Crotty, a political science professor from Northwestern University, concluded after observing the elections
that the electoral procedures

> provided easy access to the ballot and a secret vote for all Nicaraguans. This is
> impressive when compared to Nicaragua's previous electoral experience and
> that of other countries in the region. The development of fair and easily
> administered procedures builds confidence in the mechanisms of the electoral
> process. The building of this confidence is necessary if the electoral process is
> to play a role in the evaluation of democracy in Nicaragua.
>
> Having set forth the positive aspects of this electoral process, we must also
> express our criticisms and concerns. First, the institutional setting in which this
> election took place is problematic. For the past four years there has been no
> separation of State and party in Nicaragua. This has skewed the political
> climate and affects the fairness of the electoral process.[35]

The delegation also concluded that parties had limited time to organize and
campaign, that they were sometimes harassed, and that their rallies and
meetings were sometimes disrupted. They also heard reports of pressures on
voters by the Committees for the Defense of Sandinismo. The delegation
felt that the creation of a national assembly and the initiation of a national
dialogue were positive contributions to pluralism that would have been
further enhanced if all parties had agreed to participate in the electoral
process.[36]

The majority of observers at the 1984 Nicaraguan elections concluded
that while there were defects, the elections had been valid. Although com-
parisons with the 1984 elections in El Salvador have frequently been made, it
is perhaps more useful to compare them with the July 1985 national elections
in Mexico, which is also a one-party-dominant system. There the Institutional Revolutionary Party (PRI) engaged in extensive vote buying and
ballot stuffing. Opposition parties were at a substantial disadvantage in
campaigning because of lesser resources, particularly for buying media

34. LASA Report, pp. 1–2.
35. *Nicaraguan Elections: Statement of the Observer Team* (Washington, D.C.: International Human Rights Law Group and the Washington Office on Latin America, November 4,
1984), p. 2.
36. Ibid., pp. 2–3.

time. Violence erupted both before and after the election with government police and electoral officials being charged with threats against opposition candidates.[37] Throughout, virtually no foreign observers claimed that the Mexican government was illegitimate. Furthermore, Mexico continues to be widely considered a democracy.

It has also been suggested that the FSLN, as a Marxist–Leninist vanguard party, stifles political pluralism in Nicaragua.[38] Others argue that FSLN does not constitute a Marxist–Leninist vanguard party, in spite of claims made by Sandinistas and others.[39] What appears clear is that, to date, the Sandinistas do not appear to have transformed the FSLN into a Marxist–Leninist vanguard party, irrespective of their intentions. It should be noted that in international law, treaties, and practice, the nature of the dominant party within a government does not determine its legitimacy; rather, it is the actions of the state that do.

Of relevance is the constitutional basis of a government. The Nicaraguan National Assembly, in which 37% of the seats are held by non-Sandinistas, in 1986 drafted a constitution. Its sources are primarily Latin American, European, and North American constitutions and practice, together with Nicaraguan history and current circumstances.[40] Participation for all political organizations, irrespective of ideological orientation, except those that advocate a return to Somocismo, is considered the basis of political pluralism. An economy allowing for state-owned, private, mixed, and cooperative ownership is sanctioned with the welfare of the people being the stated priority. Reasonable profit margins are allowed. Nonalignment is defined as "independence from centers of power and the active peaceful co-existence of all states, through our moral solidarity with the struggles of peoples against imperialism, colonialism, apartheid and racism."[41] Opposition to military blocs and alliances is expressed, as is support for the establishment of a new international economic order and a restructuring of international relations on just principles. Strong support for anti-imperialism, sovereignty, self-determination, nonintervention, and Latin American unity is

37. Vincent Lencioni, data based on field research on the 1985 Mexican elections, Mexico, March–July 1985.
38. Jiri and Virginia Valenta, "Sandinistas in Power," *Problems of Communism* (September–October 1985),1–28.
39. John Weeks, "Las elecciones Nicaragüenses de 1984"[The Nicaraguan Elections of 1984], *Foro Internacional*, 26, No. 1 (July–September, 1985), 88–95.
40. A comparison of the February 1986 draft of the Nicaraguan constitution with other Latin American constitutions and Eastern European constitutions from the 1940s to the present indicates that the proposed Nicaraguan constitution resembles the former more than the latter.
41. *First Draft of the National Constitution of the Republic of Nicaragua* (February 1986), Preamble, Title I, Fundamental Principles, Article 7. (See Appendix C, p. 333.).

expressed. The right of national defense and ownership of natural resources is considered to reside with the people.[42] (See Appendix C.)

An analysis of the constitution as a whole reveals the following strengths and weaknesses.[43] There is strong emphasis on separation of powers, but less so on checks and balances. Reflecting Latin American tradition, the executive is the dominant branch of government. The National Assembly is working on increasing the powers of the legislature, particularly with respect to control over the budget. Criticism has been leveled against judges having terms coterminous with the National Assembly, on the grounds that this would decrease judicial independence. Although this system exists in a number of Western European countries, it has been urged that efforts be made to reinforce the autonomy of the judiciary.

The principal strength of the constitution is the repeated guarantees of civil, political, social, economic, religious, cultural, and ethnic rights. The majority of them cannot be suspended even during states of emergency. While the president may declare a state of emergency, it must be ratified by the National Assembly within 90 days. The president is not similarly limited with respect to declarations of war. The principal weaknesses of the draft constitution are the lack of influence of the legislature over the national budget, specific guarantees of judicial autonomy, and some vagueness in language that creates loopholes. The constitution is a mix primarily of Latin American, Western European, and North American constitutions with a populist–socialist overlay. There are no provisions for a special role for the FSLN. There is considerable potential for concentration of power in the presidency, which is a characteristic of many Latin American constitutions. Overall, the document would have to be described as allowing ample possibilities for democracy, if that is the will of government leaders.

Religious and Ethnic Rights

Allegations of religious persecution by critics of the Nicaraguan government have been frequent. The participation of some priests in the Sandinista government[44] and the leading role Cardinal Obando y Bravo and Bishop

---

42. Ibid., Articles 5–12.

43. This analysis is based on the conclusions of the National Conference on the Nicaraguan Constitutional Process held at New York University Law School, April 18–20, 1986.

44. Miguel D'Escoto, a Maryknoller, serves as foreign minister; the Jesuit Fernando Cardenal is minister of education, his brother Ernesto, a diocesan priest, is minister of culture. Another diocesan priest, Edgard Parrales, served as minister of social welfare and is now Nicaraguan ambassador to the Organization of American States. While the bishops initially agreed to their participation in government, in part in the hopes of influencing its course, in the fall of 1984 the priests were canonically censured for having continued in office. All four claim

Pablo Vega have taken in criticizing the government have tended to make relations between the Catholic Church and the government difficult. The core problem is that leading churchpeople, both clerical and lay, have taken highly partisan positions and have used their identification with the Catholic Church to legitimate their stances. They have also allowed themselves to be used by pro- and antigovernment forces to support their causes. The Catholic Church leadership in Nicaragua is not a neutral actor. This has deeply divided the church and contributed to the further polarization of Nicaraguan society. It also makes it highly unlikely that the Catholic Church could serve as a mediator between the government and its opponents, as proposed by the bishops in April 1984 and encouraged by the Reagan administration.

The roots of the current situation can be found in the tradition of strong anti-Marxism within the Catholic Church. Hence while the bishops in the June 1979 pastoral letter supported the insurrection, that did not mean carte blanche approval for whatever government emerged. In that missive the prelates cautioned that care must be taken to guarantee political pluralism and popular participation.[45]

Subsequently in pastoral letters in July and November 1979 the hierarchy warned against the importation of foreign "imperialisms" and inculcation of state idolatries. Nor was "massification" to be encouraged in the process of attempting to raise political consciousness. Fear was expressed that the projected 1980 literacy campaign would be used to encourage atheism and lead the faithful to abandon the church. This fear made the maintenance of church unity important and encouraged church leaders in 1979 and 1980 to take relatively ambiguous positions in order to accommodate diverse opinions within the church. The hierarchy also insisted on the role of the Catholic Church as the prime moral legitimator and critic of societal structures.[46] The November pastoral, coming as it did at at time of increasing criticism of the government by Nicaraguan conservatives, was interpreted by some as support for the counterrevolutionary position.

Preoccupied with the possibility that the Catholic Church might become a base for the counterrevolution, the Sandinista Directorate issued a com-

---

that they felt their obligation to the welfare of the Nicaraguan people overrode their responsibility to ecclesiastical authority.

45. Conferencia Episcopal de Nicaragua, "Mensaje al Pueblo Nicaragüense" [Episcopal Conference of Nicaragua, "Message to the Nicaraguan People], June 2, 1979, *passim.*

46. Conferencia Episcopal de Nicaragua, "Mensaje de la Conferencia Episcopal al Pueblo Católico y a todos los Nicaragüenses [Message of the Episcopal Conference to the Catholic People and to All Nicaraguans]," Managua, Nicaragua, July 31, 1979; and "Carta Pastoral del Episcopado Nicaragüense: Compromiso Cristiano para una Nicaragua Nueva [Pastoral Letter of the Nicaraguan Episcopate: Christian Commitment to a New Nicaragua]," Managua, Nicaragua, November 17, 1979.

muniqué in October 1980 detailing its position on religion. In it they recognized the contribution of churchpeople to the overthrow of Somoza and their participation in the task of national reconstruction. It also stated:

> For the FSLN, the right to profess a religious faith is an inalienable right of the people that the Revolutionary Government fully guarantees. . . . In addition, no one can be discriminated against in the new Nicaragua for publicly professing or spreading his/her religious beliefs. Those who don't profess any religion have the same rights.[47]

Being a lay activist, cleric, or religious was not to be a barrier to membership in the FSLN, in contrast to the practice of Communist parties in Cuba, Eastern Europe and the Soviet Union, although religious proselytizing within the FSLN was deemed inappropriate. The portion of the communiqué that caused the most controversy was the Sandinistas' assertion of the right to "defend" the public from the utilization of popular religious activities and celebrations for political purposes.[48] This was in view of the fact that some religious processions had turned into antigovernment rallies.

Contrary to the Sandinistas' hopes, the communiqué did not assuage the fears of their critics within the church. Thereafter relations between the hierarchy and the government worsened with a concomitant polarization within the church between pro- and anti-government forces. The majority of Catholics, however, appeared to be uncomfortable with both sides.

A prime issue in the worsening relations between church and state was the allegation that the adoption of a standard curriculum for all primary and secondary schools would result in Marxist indoctrination of students. Approximately 25% of Nicaraguan secondary students attend Catholic schools, most of which receive financial assistance from the government. During his March 1983 visit to Nicaragua Pope John Paul II emphasized the right of the Catholic schools to autonomy.

Another major conflict was precipitated by the hierarchy's accusations in February 1982 that the removal of several Indian communities from the war zone on the northeastern border with Honduras had resulted in grave violations of human rights. The Sandinistas were particularly taken aback by the prelates' failure to use the church–state commission that had been established to discuss such criticisms in order to avoid public conflicts.

Even greater tension was generated during the March 1983 visit of Pope John Paul II. The pope strongly criticized the so-called popular church,

---

47. FSLN, *Communiqué by the FSLN National Directorate on Religion*, New Nicaragua Agency (ANN), Informative Notebooks (Managua: n.p., n.d.), p.2.
48. Ibid, p.3

which was generally pro-Sandinista, on the grounds that it was heavily ideological and radical and espoused ideas, such as class struggle, that were contrary to the salvific plan of Christ.[49] The pope's public mass in Managua on March 4 was the scene of sharp confrontation between pro- and anti-government forces within the audience, and the pope was interrupted a number of times during his homily. In the aftermath, progressive pro-government churchpeople were critical of the pope's language and tone on the grounds that they "seemed admonishing and negative, lacking any connection with the people he addressed. In its religious aspect this language was political. The theological subjects dealt with were beyond the scope of comprehension . . . of the great majority of the people".[50] The political import of the visit for anti-Sandinistas was reflected in a report in the *Washington Post.*

> The Pope has helped us a hell of a lot, said a wealthy business opponent of the government. That's the best thing that could have happened to us.
> His comment reflected a widely held assessment that the church hierarchy increasingly could become the focus of political opposition in this overwhelming Catholic country. Under Obando y Bravo's uncompromising leadership, it is considered more able to attract mass following than the alliance of conservative parties and business groups that constitutes the Sandinistas' tolerated political opposition.[51]

In fact, the pope's visit did appear to encourage antigovernment elements. The bishops subsequently became more publicly critical of the government and more active in attempting to rein in the progressive clergy and laity. Overall, the impression that Christianity and the revolution were antithetical was heightened, and a number of the bishops embarked on campaigns to convince the public of that.

Efforts to defuse church–state tensions have not been particularly successful. Sporadic talks between the bishops and government have not produced any major improvements. In September 1984 a delegation of Sandinista officials visited Rome in an attempt to improve relations. It was unsuccessful. Rome clearly desired major modifications in Sandinista ideology in favor of a liberal reformist political model. To date, however, the

49. John Paul II, "Threats to the Church's Dignity," *Origins: NC Documentary Service* 12, no. 40 (March 17, 1983): 633–636.

50. "Christian Reflection on the Pope's March 4 Visit to Nicaragua by a Theological Reflection Group." Translated from "Imperialismo, Enemigo del Pueblo y la Paz Dicen Intelectuales Cristianos [Imperialism: Enemy of the People and Peace, Say Christian Intellectuals]," *El Nuevo Diario*, March 6, 1983, pp. 1–2.

51. Edward Cody, "Tension Grows in Nicaragua: Sandinistas Take Harder Line," *Washington Post*, March 5, 1983, pp. A1, A10.

Nicaraguan bishops have not categorized the government as illegitimate, as they did Somoza's. Instead, they have been strongly critical of it, and of its supporters within the church. This has apparently resulted in the government's expulsion of more than a dozen clerics and the detention and attempted embarrassing of others. This has been more of a political and ideological struggle than a conflict over freedom of religious belief.

Protestant churches have experienced some of the same difficulties and divisions as the Catholic church. The Moravian church, which is strong among the Atlantic coast population, has within it both pro- and anti-Sandinista elements. Antigovernment sentiment was stimulated by the 1982 removal of Indian villages from the Río Coco region to the interior of Zelaya Province. Before that, some Moravian church activists had joined the *contras* in Honduras; others did after the removal. The leadership of the Moravian church was, however, less critical of the government than the Catholic bishops. The U.S.-based executive director of the Moravian Board of World Mission, Graham H. Rights, held that his church was threatened most by "outside threats to Nicaraguan national security. The Miskito people and the Moravian Church are hostages in an international situation not of their making, which severely hinders their efforts to defend ethnic and religious freedom in their own country." He was also highly critical of U.S. policy on the grounds that "attempts to destabilize Nicaragua are mischievous, and probably self-defeating: more likely to hasten than to halt the erosion of economic pluralism and political freedom in the country as a whole. From the viewpoint of the Miskito, the result has been catastrophic; it has wrought terror and destruction, divided families and left homeless, and brought down on all of them the hostility and suspicion of the authorities."[52] He concluded by urging U.S. Christians to oppose *contra* aid and support a negotiated settlement. To date the Moravian church has maintained a dialogue with the government that has facilitated its efforts to defend the interests of the indigenous people of the Atlantic coast. While some Moravian ministers and lay activists have joined the *contras*, the church as an institution has opposed the warfare and accepted the government as legitimate.

The Inter-American Commission on Human Rights has concluded that hundreds of Miskitos have been arbitrarily detained and some alleged Miskito counterrevolutionaries tortured and abused. In addition, some

52. Graham H. Rights, executive director, Board of World Mission of the Moravian Church, "Memorandum to Moravian Ministers of the Northern and Southern Provinces, Other Christian Clergy and Lay People in North America, U.S. Government Officials and Congressional Representatives re New Fighting in Nicaragua; Reprisals Against the Miskito Indians and the Nicaraguan Moravian Church," Bethlehem, Pennsylvania, August 3, 1982, pp. 1–4.

trials of Miskitos were not in accordance with due process. On September 16, 1983, the Nicaragua Supreme Court overturned 59 of 105 such convictions.[53] The commission found that by 1984 the major problems facing the Miskitos stemmed from their economic dependence on the government as a result of the relocation, their lack of voice in decisions concerning them, and family dislocation. Since then, Misurasata, an umbrella group of Miskitos, Sumus, and Ramas, has engaged in negotiations with the government, achieving some progress in gaining recognition of their rights. For example, the proposed Nicaraguan constitution states:

> Native peoples and communities of the Atlantic coast of Nicaragua have the right: to preserve and develop their cultural traditions, their historical and religious heritage; the right to free use and development of their languages; the right to organize their social and productive activities according to their values and traditions. The culture and traditions of native peoples and communities of the Atlantic coast are part of the national culture.[54]

Political autonomy was not accorded. The claim of Misurasata that ethnic groups have a right of self-determination is not upheld in international law.[55] The problem remains a serious one, but the indigenous people themselves have organized a rights commission and are in the process of opening legal assistance offices in the principal population centers on the Atlantic coast, as well as in Managua. The attitude of these human rights activists is that their work is necessary and possible and that the *contra* activity impedes it.[56]

In the aftermath of the 1985 expansion of the state of emergency a number of fundamentalist Protestants were detained by the government They were accused by the Ministry of the Interior of preaching against universal military service and counseling draft evasion. After warnings not

---

53. Inter-American Commission on Human Rights, Organization of American States, *Report on the Situation of Human Rights of a Segment of the Nicaraguan Population of Miskito Origin* (Washington, D.C.: Organization of American States, 1984), pp. 129–131; Juan Méndez, "La participación de la Comisión Interamericana de Derechos Humanos en los Conflictos entre los Miskitos y el Gobierno de Nicaragua [Participation of the Inter-American Commission on Human Rights in Conflicts Between the Miskitos and the Nicaraguan Government]," *Derechos Humanos en las Américas* [Human Rights in the Americas] (Washington, D.C.: Organization of American States, 1985).

54. Article 210 of the *First Draft of the National Constitution*, p.33. (See Appendix C.)

55. IACHR, *Report*, p. 129.

56. Comisión de Juristas de la Costa Atlántica de Nicaragua, "Proyecto de Bufete Legal para Minorías Étnicas de Nicaragua [Jurist's Commission From the Atlantic Coast of Nicaragua: Project of a Legal Office for Ethnic Minorities in Nicaragua]." Xerox.

to encourage unlawful acts, they were released.[57] According to the Washington-based Institute on Religion and Democracy, some who were detained were forced to "endure several hours of humiliation," including being strip searched.[58] This kind of harassment appears to have been prompted by the strong criticism by some fundamentalist Protestants of the government. The Center for Promotion and Development (CEPAD), an organization of 42 Protestant churches that is prorevolutionary, has maintained good relations with the government.

Charges of anti-Semitism have been leveled against the Nicaraguan government by the U.S.-based Jewish Anti-Defamation League and the Reagan administration. It has been alleged that the Sandinistas have forced most of the Jewish community to leave the country, expropriated the local synagogue as well as the private property of individual Jews, and broken relations with Israel in order to establish them with the PLO. It is estimated that the Jewish community in Nicaragua numbered under 200 before the 1972 earthquake. Most left after that or as a result of the turmoil created by the insurrection in 1978–1979. Only a handful remained when the Sandinistas took power in July 1979. At that time a building used as a synagogue and abandoned months before July 1979 was expropriated by the government under the impression that it was the private property of Abra-ham Gorn. The latter was imprisoned for 2 weeks as a result of charges that he had been a National Guard supplier and had facilitated Israeli arms shipments to Somoza's government as late as June 1979. The government offered to return the synagogue to the Jewish community in 1984, but no one has as yet indicated interest. The cases of 30 individuals who had property expropriated, including that of Abraham Gorn, are currently under review by the Nicaraguan courts. The government broke relations with Israel after its invasion of Lebanon, not in 1979, and has no formal diplomatic relations with the PLO, although there are some PLO operatives in the country. The World Jewish Congress, American Jewish Committee, and the U.S. Em-

57. *FBIS*, "Interior Ministry Official on Religious Activities," *Daily Report: Latin America* 6, no. 235 (December 6, 1985): P9–14.

58. Those detained included the national director of the Nicaraguan Campus Crusade for Christ, the president of the Nicaraguan Bible Society, the pastor of the First Central American Church of Managua, the president and vice-president of the Assemblies of God Youth Organization, and the head of the Alliance for the Evangelization of Children. See Institute on Religion and Democracy, *Action Alert*, November 22, 1985; Roy Howard Beck, "Church Officials in Nicaragua Said Arrested, Harassed," *United Methodist Reporter*, November 15, 1985; and National Association of Evangelicals, "Nicaraguan Evangelicals Subject to Harassment," November 8, 1985.

bassy in Managua have taken issue with the charges of anti-Semitism leveled against the Sandinistas.[59]

Socioeconomic Rights

A prime criterion of government legitimacy is the degree to which it promotes and assists in the fulfillment of basic social and economic rights. These are commonly referred to as basic needs and include food, health care, education, and housing.[60] Beginning in July 1979, the Nicaraguan government placed considerable emphasis on meeting basic needs, and notable progress was made. Since 1983, however, the Nicaraguan economy has suffered some substantial reverses resulting from international economic developments, war losses and defense costs, loss of Nicaragua's historical markets and sources of foreign aid, as well as defects in managing the economy. The impact of international economic developments on a small, export-oriented commodity producer such as Nicaragua has been great. As one analyst noted:

> In the first half of the 1980s the international economy was characterized by low prices and reduced demand for primary products, and generally unfavorable terms of trade between industrial and primary goods. These conditions adversely affected the economies of most underdeveloped countries, including Nicaragua. Economic constraints posed by escalating interest payments on the debt, imports in excess of exports, and fiscal deficit were hardly unique to Nicaragua. Indeed, these conditions have become part of the pattern of economic crisis in nearly all Latin American countries.[61]

War losses from the 1978–1979 insurrection combined with escalating *contra* attacks, particularly after 1980, have imposed additional contraints on the Nicaraguan economy. Statistics from the United Nations Economic

59. Several interviews with U.S. diplomats in Managua, Nicaragua, and Washington, D.C., 1984–1985.

60. For a detailed listing of socioeconomic rights, see the United Nations Covenant on Economic, Social, and Cultural Rights. For a discussion of the concept of basic needs and a comparative study of their fulfillment in pre-1979 Nicaragua, see John F. Weeks and Elizabeth E. Dore, "Basic Needs: Journey of a Concept," and Elizabeth E. Dore and John F. Weeks, "Economic Performance and Basic Needs: The Examples of Brazil, Chile, Mexico, Nicaragua, Peru and Venezuela," in *Human Rights and Basic Needs in the Americas*, ed. Margaret E. Crahan (Washington, D.C.: Georgetown University Press, 1982), pp. 131–187.

61. Elizabeth W. Dore, "Nicaragua: The Experience of a Mixed Economy and Political Pluaralism," in *Latin American Political Economy: Financial Crisis and Political Change*, ed. Jonathan Hartlyn and Samuel A. Morley (forthcoming), pp. 516–517.

	Millions of Dollars
1. Destruction of physical infrastructure during the anti-Somoza insurrection	481
2. Decapitalization and theft in 1978−1979	518
3. Losses due to economic inactivity, 1978−1979	1,246
4. Inherited foreign debt	1,650
5. Service on the foreign debt, 1978−1979	249
6. Total of material losses, decaptialization, and debt inherited from Somoza	4,144

SOURCE: The United Nation's Economic Commission for Latin America (ECLA) and the Central Bank of Nicaragua.[62]

Commission for Latin America (ECLA) and the Nicaraguan Central Bank indicate that in 1979 the total for material losses, decapitalization, and inherited debt amounted to some $4.1 billion.

Losses from *contra* warfare and the U.S. economic embargo are substantially higher. Current estimates of the percentage of the national budget devoted to defense and war-related costs range up to 50%. In 1984 it was approximately one-third the national budget, or 15% of the gross domestic product.[63] Material damage since 1981 has risen from $3.9 million to $24 million in 1984, while production losses have risen from $3.5 million to $159.7 million (see Table 6.1). The impact on primary production has been particularly adverse with respect to forestry, fishing, and mining (see Table 6.2). War-related export losses in coffee, lumber, gold, and fish have reduced foreign exchange at at time of increased pressures to import foodstuffs and capital goods to replace war-related losses (see Table 6.3). The impact on the Nicaraguan balance of payments has been substantial, causing a switch from positive balances in 1981 of $57.7 million and $83.6 million in 1983 to a negative balance of $10 million in 1984 (see Table 6.4). This situation has made it impossible for Nicaragua to meet its foreign debt obligations.

Between 1980 and 1984, Nicaragua paid $234 million in debt service to private banks and $209 million to multilateral banks.[64] By early 1985

62. IHCA, "The Dilemma Confronting the Sandinista Revolution Three Years After the Victory," *Envío* 13 (July 1982): 7.
63. IHCA, "The Economic Costs of the Contra War," *Envío* 4, no. 51 (September 1985): 2b; E. V. K. FitzGerald, "Una Evaluación del Costo Económico de la Agresión del Gobierno Estadounidense contra el Pueblo de Nicaragua [An Evaluation of the Economic Cost of the Aggression of the U.S. Government against the Nicaraguan People]," paper presented at the Latin American Studies Association, Albuquerque, New Mexico, April 1985.
64. Ibid., p. 5b.

TABLE 6.1
Economic Damage and Loss, 1980–1984
(in millions of dollars)

	Material Damage	Production Losses	Total
1980	.5	.9	1.4
1981	3.9	3.5	7.4
1982	10.8	21.1	31.9
1983	57.5	97.4	154.9
1984	24.4	159.7	184.1
Total	97.1	282.6	379.7

TABLE 6.2
Production Losses in Exports and Domestic Production
(in millions of dollars)

	1980	1981	1982	1983	1984	Total
Agricultural export production	.9	3.5	6.1	65.3	102.8	178.6
Coffee	—		—	32.1	37.0	69.1
Tobacco	—	—	—	1.9	1.6	3.5
Livestock	—	.1	.2	1.0	3.3	4.6
Lumber	—	—	—	25.0	52.2	77.2
Fishing	.9	1.2	2.8	4.0	6.6	15.5
Mining	—	2.2	3.1	1.3	2.1	8.7
Production for domestic consumption	—	—	15.0	32.1	56.9	104.0
Basic grains [a]	—	—	—	.4	11.3	11.7
Other crops [b]	—	—	—	1.7	.6	2.3
Construction	—	—	15.0	30.0	45.0	90.0
Total	.9	3.5	21.1	97.4	159.7	282.6
Exports	451.0	499.8	405.8	428.6	381.6	—
Percentage Losses of Exportable Production−Exports		1	2	15	27	

[a]Lost production of basic grains is calculated as a negative effect on the export sector because it must be replaced through imports.

[b]Coconuts, cocoa, cassava, and other root crops.

SOURCE: Instituto Histórico Centroamericáno (here after called IHCA) [Central American Historical Institute], *Envío* 4, no. 51, 1985, 3b.

121

TABLE 6.3
Calculated Direct Losses in External Sector, 1980–1984
(in millions of dollars)

	1980	1981	1982	1983	1984
Increase in commercial deficit due to warfare–embargo	.9	3.4	17.4	100.1	99.0
Loss of capital goods	—	2.2	8.9	66.9	22.6
Total	.9	5.6	26.3	167.0	121.6
Percentage of Exports	—	1	7	39	32

SOURCE: IHCA, *Envío* 4, no. 51, 1985, p.4

TABLE 6.4
Effects on Balance of Payments, 1981–1984
(in millions of dollars)

	1981	1982	1983	1984
Commercial balance				
Actual	−499.6	−369.7	−378.3	−408.6
Without warfare–embargo	−496.8	−368.0	−299.5	−324.8
Exports				
Actual	499.8	405.8	428.6	381.6
Without warfare–embargo	506.0	424.5	557.0	504.6
Imports				
Actual	999.4	775.5	806.9	790.2
Without warfare–embargo	1.002.8	792.5	856.5	829.4
Balance of Services	−85.0	−152.7	−218.6	−226.8
Income	73.4	49.5	40.6	51.6
Outlay	158.4	202.2	259.2	278.4
Donations	70.3	51.5	70.4	117.0
Current Accounts Balance				
Actual	−514.3	−470.9	−526.5	−518.4
Without warfare–embargo	−511.5	−469.2	−447.7	−434.6
Net Capital Movement	572.0	371.4	610.1	507.4
Long-term	599.1	454.3	659.6	512.0
Other	−27.1	−82.9	−49.5	−4.6
Balance of Payments				
Actual	57.7	−99.5	83.6	−10.0
Without warfare–embargo	60.5	−97.8	162.4	73.0

SOURCE: IHCA, *Envío* 4., no. 51, 1985, p. 5b.

Nicaragua had fallen 6 months behind in its loan payments to the World Bank, to which it owed $134.1 million. Total foreign debt by 1985 was approximately $4 billion, a doubling of the debt inherited from the Somoza period.[65] From 1981 to the present, loans to Nicaragua from multilateral financial institutions were generally not forthcoming amid charges that the U.S. government had brought pressure to bear to block new loans and cancel existing ones (see Table 6.5). This seriously affected both the reconstruction and expansion of the economy and hence efforts to meet basic needs.

To date most foreign aid to Nicaragua has come from other Third World countries. Eastern European countries have provided limited assistance in the form of tied loans. The Soviet Union did not provide substantial economic assistance until mid-1985 when it began supplying a portion of Nicaragua's petroleum needs. Such aid does not, however, ameliorate Nicaragua's need for foreign exchange to obtain imports, trading credits, and service its foreign debt.[66]

Compounding these problems have been economic mismanagement and inefficiency. Lack of experience in management and technical expertise on the part of some government officials has caused problems. Intra- and interministerial policy divisions and rivalries have exacerbated the situation.

Evidence suggests that the Sandinistas initially regarded a mixed economy as the most effective manner of obtaining the cooperation of Nicaraguan capitalists and international capital in reconstructing the economy. Such an approach was intended to provide the bourgeoisie with economic benefits within limits, but would not allow them ultimate economic or political control.[67] Such denial undercut private-sector cooperation with the Nicaraguan government. The facts that capital

had lost political power in Nicaragua, lost the ability to manage the economy at the aggregate level, and been denied the mechanisms to reorganize itself, do not in themselves imply that the mixed economy under such circumstances must necessarily result in the degeneration of the productive system and economic warfare. It does imply that such a mixed economy is a volatile mix indeed, representing a transitory arrangement, which must at some point revert to capitalist domination or move on to a form of directly socialized

65. Nicholas D. Kristof, "Nicaragua in Arrears on World Bank Loans," *New York Times*, March 27, 1985, p. 27.

66. Dore, "Nicaragua," p. 516.

67. John Weeks, "The Mixed Economy in Nicaragua: The Economic Battlefield," in *The Political Economy of Nicaragua*, ed. Rose J. Spaulding (New York: Allen & Unwin, forthcoming), p. 9.

TABLE 6.5
Calculation of Foreign Assistance Losses
(in millions of dollars)

	Value of Project	Probable Disbursements				Blocked or Canceled
		1981	1982	1983	1984	
Bilateral U.S.–Nicaragua						
Partial blockage of already approved $75 million loan	15.0		15.0			15.0
Suspension of already approved wheat credits	10.0	5.0	5.0			10.0
Rural development program, education, and health	11.4	2.2	2.3	2.3	4.6	11.4
Bilateral Subtotal	36.4	7.2	22.3	2.3	4.6	36.4
Multilateral						
Inter-American Development Bank (IDB)[a]						
Abisinia–Cua valley (agriculture)	2.2				2.2	2.2
Monte Galán–San Jacinto Tizate Basin (energy)	15.0	1.0	7.0	7.0		15.0
Global Agricultural Program II (agroindustry)	55.0			8.0	11.0	19.0
Livestock Development Program (Boaco–Chontales)	50.0			10.0	15.0	25.0
Agroindustrial Rehabilitation Program	98.0		6.0	23.0	28.0	57.0
Potable water, public service, and sewage program for intermediate cities and rural communities, stage II	21.0		3.0	9.0	9.0	21.0
Preinvestment program	5.3			2.0	3.3	5.3
IDB subtotal	246.5	1.0	16.0	59.0	68.5	144.5
World Bank						
Agricultural Credit Program	50.0				10.0	10.0
Support to food production and export	90.0				9.0	9.0
World Bank subtotal	140.0				19.0	19.0
Multilateral subtotal	386.5	1.0	16.0	59.0	87.5	163.5
Total	422.9	8.2	38.3	61.0	92.1	199.9

[a]Does not include recently blocked U.S. $58 million loan for agricultural development.
SOURCE: IHCA, *Envío* 4, no. 51. 1984, p. 65.

production. But "transitory" here refers to conceptual time; the chronological life of such an unstable mix is indeterminant. Because the mixed economy out of capital's control is inherently unviable does not preclude it from being a more-or-less satisfactory *ad hoc* arrangement for a considerable period of time.[68]

The tensions and conflict inherent in such a situation have dominated discussions of Nicaraguan economic policy. What is evident is that in fact there has not been a consolidation of a socialist economy. What socialist elements do exist differ substantially from the Soviet, Eastern European, Chinese, and Cuban models.[69] Nevertheless, it is clear that the Sandinistas' inclination toward a socialist economy springs from their belief that it is the most effective strategy for meeting basic needs.

The question that arises, as a consequence, is whether the Nicaraguan government has since July 1979 contributed to improved fulfillment of basic needs. A review of per capita consumption of basic foodstuffs reveals overall improvement from 1977 to 1983, except in beef and beans (see Table 6.6). Daily caloric intake in 1984, according to the World Bank, was 99% of that required, which was higher than in Guatemala, Honduras, and El Salvador (see Table 6.7). Shortages of basic foodstuffs such as sugar, rice, corn, beans, oil, and salt occurred in 1985 and 1986, in part the result of production losses caused by war and the diversion of approximately 10% of national production to the armed forces.[70]

Improvements in health care resulted in recognition of Nicaragua in 1982 by the World Health Organization and UNICEF as the country with the greatest health-related achievements in the developing world. In 1979 Nicaragua had 37 hospitals; by 1984, 17 more had been opened. In 1979 there were 150 medical students, and in 1984 there were 550. Hence, in spite of the emigration of some doctors, Nicaragua has 1 physician per 1,800 Nicaraguans (Table 7) and increasingly medical facilities are available in rural areas. Infant mortality has declined from 120–140 per 1,000 live births under Somoza to 72 per 1,000 in 1985.[71]

The warfare has had a substantial impact on health-care delivery. It is

68. Ibid., p. 16.

69. Michael E. Conroy and Gustavo Marquez, "Toward an Evaluation of the Evolution of Nicaraguan 'Socialism': Is It, and Should It Be, a 'Third Road'?" paper presented at conference "The United States and Central America: A Five Year Assessment," University of Southern California, February 20–22, 1986, p. 22.

70. IHCA, *Envío* 4, no. 51 (September 1985): number 11b.

71. David Siegal, "Nicaraguan Health: An Update," *LASA Forum*, XVI, 4 (Winter, 1986), pp. 29–31.

TABLE 6.6
Indices of per Capita Consumption of Basic Goods
(1977=100)

Product	1977	1978	1979	1980	1981	1982	1983
Beef[a]	100	113	69	77	79	90	88
Pork	100	79	86	90	104	160	129
Chicken	100	115	115	176	221	203	244
Milk[a]	100	99	92	86	65	96	115
Eggs	100	115	105	125	120	121	120
Rice	100	111	135	168	143	161	125
Beans	100	199	56	85	168	142	95
Sorghum	100	164	91	163	124	152	111
Corn (maize)	100	154	69	107	105	94	103
Cooking oil	100	96	107	120	118	130	120
Soap	100	101	80	118	144	149	159
Flour	100	80	77	92	117	109	101

[a]Beef consumption was affected by widespread slaughtering of cattle during and immediately after the anti-Somoza insurrection, which reduced the size of the herd by about one-third. Milk production was similarly affected, but imports of powdered milk have compensated for the drop.

SOURCE: "Nicaragua Through Our Eyes." The Committee of U.S. Citizens Living in Nicaragua (CUS-CLIN). *Newsletter* 1.3 [1985], p. 7. Cited from Iván García "Estadísticas básicas en el sector agropecuario," *Revolución y Desarrollo* ["Basic Statistics of the Agriculture and Livestock Sector," *Revolution and Development*] (MIDINRA), No. 1 (April-June 1984).

estimated that 35 health-care workers have been killed by the *contras*, in violation of the Geneva Convention of 1949 relating to the provision of medical care (articles 9 and 11). Eleven others have been wounded and 28 kidnapped. Fifty-one health-care facilities have been damaged by the *contras* and 37 closed because of *contra* activity. The U.S. embargo has contributed to an inability to obtain spare parts for medical equipment.[72]

Education reflects a similar pattern with initial advances being curtailed with the intensification of the war. The 1980 national literacy campaign, according to UNESCO, reduced illiteracy from 40% to 12%. Student enrollment at all levels rose from 501,855 before 1978 to 1,127,428 in 1984 (see Table 6.8). The number of teachers at all levels increased from 12,706 before 1978 to 53,398 in 1984 (see Table 6.9). Tragically, by 1986, 148 teachers had been killed by the war.[73] The war and overall economic situation have curtailed funds available for education. In addition, there are problems resulting from inadequate teacher preparation, weak academic achieve-

72. Ibid. See also Richard Garfield and David Siegal, *Health and the War Against Nicaragua* (New York: Central America Health Rights Network, 1985).
73. IHCA, *UPDATE* 5, no. 2 (January 24, 1986): 2.

TABLE 6.7
Socioeconomic Indicators

Indicator	Guatemala	Honduras	Panama	Costa Rica	El Salvador	Nicaragua
GNP/cap. (1982)[a]	$1,130	$660	$2,120	$1,430	$700	$920
GNP/average percentage annual growth 1960–1982[a]	2.4	1.0	3.4	2.8	.9	.2
Percentage literate[b]	56.4	59.5	88.1	89.8	57.1	87.9
Years of life expectancy at birth[b]	59.0	59.9	71.0	73.1	64.8	59.8
Infant mortality (per 1,000 births)[b]	64.4	17.5	20.4	18.8	43.8	76.4
Mortality (per 1,000 inhabitants)[b]	10.3	4.7	4.1	3.9	6.9	9.7
Child death rates (ages 1–4)[b]	5.0	8.0	2.0	1.0	7.0	9.0
Population per physician[a]	8,610	3,120	980	1,460	3,220	1,800
Daily caloric supply per capita[a]	2,045	2,171	2,271	2,686	2,146	2,184
Percentage of required calories[a]	93	96	103	118	94	99

[a]World Bank, *World Development Report, 1984* (New York: Oxford University Press, 1984).
[b]Inter-American Development Bank, *Economic and Social Progress in Latin America, 1985 Report* (Washington, D.C., Inter-American Development Bank, 1985).

TABLE 6.8
Comparison of Student Enrollment, 1978–1984

Educational Level	Student Attendance					
	1978	*1979–1980*	*1980–1981*	*1982*	*1983*	*1984*
Preschool	9,000	18,292	30,524	38,534	50,163	66,85(
Primary grades	369,640	431,164	503,497	534,996	564,588	635,63˙
Secondary grades	98,874	110,726	139,743	139,957	158,215	186,10˙
Higher education	23,791	29,173	34,710	33,838	39,765	41,23˙
Special education	355	—	1,430	1,591	1,624	2,80˙
Adult education	—	—	167,852	148,369	166,208	194,80˙
Total	501,660	589,355	877,756	897,285	980,563	1,127,42

TABLE 6.9
Number of Schoolteachers, 1978–1984

Educational Level	*1978*	*1980–1981*	*1982*	*1983*	*1984*
Preschool	—	924	1,212	1,310	1,701
Primary grade	9,986	14,113	14,711	16,382	17,969
Secondary grade	2,720	4,221	4,103	5,027	6,014
Higher education	N.A.	N.A.	N.A.	1,413	1,750
Special education	—	131	123	171	204
Adult education	—	18,449	21,607	21,994	25,760
Total	12,706	37,838	42,167	46,407	53,398

SOURCE: IHCA, *Envío* 4, no. 48 (June 1985): 2c.

ment, lack of coordination between primary–secondary schools and the universities, and excessive bureaucracy in the school system.[74]

Housing has been the area of least progress. The economic situation and warfare have substantially limited the resources available for public housing, and the government has placed greater emphasis on health care and education. While some progress was made before 1985, there has been little advance since then.

A review of the World Bank's *Development Reports* from 1977 through 1985 and the Inter-American Development Bank's annual reports on eco-

74. IHCA, "A New Challenge: A People's Education in the Midst of Poverty," *Envío* 48, no. 4 (June 1985): 6c–8c; IHCA, "Nicaragua's Universities in Transition," *Envío* 57, no. 5 (March 1986): 39–40.

nomic and social progress in Latin America reveal that the fulfillment of basic needs has improved in Nicaragua since 1979, largely as a result of government efforts. While there has been some slippage, particularly in 1985 and 1986, this appears primarily attributable to the war. The statistics indicate that the government of Nicaragua has a clear commitment to fulfilling basic socioeconomic rights and providing economic security. Some advances have been made at the same time that the government has had to provide for the physical security of the civilian population because of the war.

Conclusion

On balance, the present government of Nicaragua meets the criteria in international law for political legitimacy. It has demonstrated its capacity to exercise effective control over the national territory and population. In addition, it has demonstrable administrative control over state functions. It should be noted that such control does not require an absence of excessive bureaucracy or inefficiency, all of which afflict the present government of Nicaragua. Further evidence of Nicaragua's having met criteria for political legitimacy is the fact that it has been accorded wide diplomatic recognition, including recognition by the United States. In general, it has fulfilled its international legal obligations. Two exceptions are its interference in the internal affairs of El Salvador and its recent failure to service its foreign debt. The former has not, however, led El Salvador to break relations with Nicaragua, nor is there any indication that the Duarte government regards the present government of Nicaragua as illegitimate. The latter has not caused any foreign governments, multilateral lending institutions, or private banks to regard the present Nicaraguan government as illegitimate.

With respect to civil, political, social, economic, religious, ethnic, and cultural rights, the government of Nicaragua has improved the observance of some, particularly basic needs, and has a spotty record with respect to others, including physical integrity of persons and due process of law. Independent international human rights organizations, have not, however, categorized Nicaragua as a gross violator of human rights.[75] All have noted that the Nicaraguan government has generally been responsive in allowing on-site investigations and responding to specific recommendations, particularly concerning violations affecting the Atlantic coast population. The

---

75. The term *gross* is a technical one used in human rights parlance to indicate a level of violations that substantially undercuts the legitimacy of a government, especially if the violations exist over an extended period of time.

Nicaraguan judiciary has overturned some illegal convictions and detentions of government opponents and the Ministry of the Interior has taken legal action against some government personnel accused of serious violations of the physical integrity of persons. There is no doubt that the government needs to improve its record.

There is discrimination against opponents of the government that affects their enjoyment of rights. Labor leaders, politicians, COSEP members, and *La Prensa* have had their freedom of expression and ability to organize limited, particularly since the state of emergency in October 1985. This obviously responds to the *contra* warfare and the government's conviction that, for national security reasons, it must diminish the possibility of an opening of an internal front. This fear has been exacerbated by the sharp criticism of the draft by some of the Catholic hierarchy and Protestant fundamentalists. Since much of the political and ideological struggle currently under way has been focused in and on churchpeople, a good number of them have come to be considered highly partisan political actors. The bulk of churchpeople seems to be caught uncomfortably in the middle. Most appear to prefer less involvement in politics on the part of church leaders and a reduction in the tension between pro- and anti-Sandinista elements.

Religious freedom and liberty of worship do not appear to have suffered substantial curtailment. Rather, a handful of churchpeople identified as government opponents, particularly those critical of universal military service, have been the objects of detention, expulsion from Nicaragua, and harassment. The complexities of such a situation are revealed by the recent removal of the apostolic nuncio, who reportedly was unsuccessful not only in mediating between the episcopacy and the Sandinistas but also between the various factions within the church. This reflects the degree of polarization not only between church and state but also within the former, and no alternative force has emerged to attempt to mediate between the extremes.

In such a volatile situation the possibilities of opposition forces influencing government policies and actions is somewhat limited. This was reflected in the campaign rhetoric before the 1984 national election, as well as in the government's repeated overreaction to criticism. In this context the Sandinistas' attempts to consolidate their control over the government arouse fears concerning the survival of pluralism, particularly via multiparty competition. It should be noted that revolutionary governments in countries attempting to move from dependent to independent status place high priority on developing primordial loyalties among the citizenry, either to a personalistic leader or to a party. In Nicaragua it is the FSLN. The latter's viability is linked to the survival of the revolution, as well as to the guaranteeing of national sovereignty and autonomy.

Prime mechanisms for building such loyalty are the provision of socioeconomic benefits to those previously denied basic needs. The creation of a state-controlled economy is generally considered to be the most effective way to accomplish this. In Nicaragua dependence on a mixed economy, in the absence of strong capitalist support nationally or internationally, has impeded, to a degree, socioeconomic progress, although it responds to some existential realities. While theoretically the Sandinistas may want to transform the economy into a socialist one, they do not have the possibility to do so under present conditions. Nor is there strong evidence that they have a particular historical model in mind.

Basing an evaluation of the legitimacy of the Nicaraguan government on Sandinista intentions in either the political or economic fields goes against legal practice.Futhermore, the ideology of the dominant political party and the nature of the economic system are not considered criteria for political legitimacy in international law or practice.

Political pluralism expressed via elections is frequently seen as lacking a historical rationale in developing countries emerging out of colonial or authoritarian pasts. Such countries do not have strong traditions of popular participation and where political parties did exist, they were generally an expression of elite sectoral interests rather than majority sentiment. The consequences are a certain lack of credibility for existing political parties and an inclination to search for other mechanisms for the expression of popular interests. Hence, political organization and mobilization may focus more on functional or corporate bodies to be represented in government, or via the revolutionary party, or both. Mass organizations will not, necessarily, be fully autonomous as they will frequently be expected also to serve to generate support for national tasks. They are not, however, totally without input into governmental decision making. Nicaragua today has a mix of traditional representative mechanisms including political parties and labor unions, together with mass organizations. Hence, competition to influence government policy has increased, with those groups identified with the FSLN having an advantage.

Traditional elites have been fragmented along ideological, economic, and generational lines. Some members have been absorbed into government, while others have joined the nonviolent domestic opposition or the *contra* forces. It is notable that 10 of Los Doce continue to participate in government.[76] Support for and opposition to the government seem to derive from a multitude of factors and are not exclusively class based. There is an intense political, ideological, and economic struggle that cuts across classes,

---

76. Los Doce (The Twelve) were selected in the last months of the insurrection in 1979 to represent the principal interest groups supporting the overthrow of Anastasio Somoza and to facilitate the formation of a new government.

geography, and ethnic groups concerning the political and economic direction of Nicaragua. Because of the intensity of this struggle and the defects of the present government, its legitimacy has been repeatedly challenged. These defects, however, do not meet the criteria for illegitimacy in international law. In addition, the *contras* do not meet the internationally accepted criteria for a recognizable insurrectionary force. Such criteria are these:

1. Effective long-term, not transient, control over a substantial portion of the national territory
2. An organized administration to discharge the normal functions of government within that territory
3. Demonstrable commitment to the accepted rules of warfare[77]

Neither the FDN nor ARDE fulfills these requirements. Furthermore, given the fact that funding for the UNO (United Nicaraguan Opposition) comes principally from the United States, under international law it is considered an intervening rather than an insurrectionary force.

If the present Nicaraguan government is legitimate under international law, what are legitimate mechanisms to protest against its abuses of power? Under international law the principal ones are the courts and representative bodies. While the judiciary in Nicaragua does not enjoy full autonomy, it has been instrumental in rectifying some problems, particularly those relating to due process of law. The National Assembly has provided a forum for the expression of opposition views, and opposition parties have succeeded in modifying some government policies, as well as influencing, to a degree, the content of the draft constitution. Their weight is nevertheless circumscribed given their minority status. *La Prensa*, COSEP, and some church leaders have served to present alternative views in spite of the restrictions imposed on them, particularly as a result of the state of emergency. The labor sector has been notably active in expressing dissent in spite of the lifting of the right to strike. Increasingly they have experimented with passive resistance, civil disobedience, and in some cases, economic sabotage. The first two are commonly considered justified forms of dissent, if constitutional mechanisms are not effective, while the third is not, because of its negative impact on the common good.

Under the state of emergency in Nicaragua normal mechanisms for expressing dissent are limited. Recourse to passive resistance or civil disobedience is also difficult, particularly given the fact that the existence of warfare has been offered by the government as justification for the imposition of a state of emergency. Fuller expression of dissent would require,

---

77. Lauterpacht, *International Law*, I: 335.

therefore, a cessation of hostilities so that the state of emergency could be lifted. That, rather than intervention, would appear to be the path suggested by international law, since intervention is prohibited by Article 2, paragraph 4, of the Charter of the United Nations and Article 15 of the Charter of the Organization of American States.

Arguments that to protect democracy and human rights it is necessary to provide military assistance to the *contras* falter in the face of the requirements in international law for legitimate intervention. They are as follows:

That there must be an immediate and extensive threat to fundamental human rights

That all other remedies for the protection of those rights have been exhausted to the extent possible within the time constraints posed by the threat

That an attempt has been made to secure the approval of appropriate authorities in the target state

That there is a minimal effect on the extant structure of authority (e.g., that the intervention not be used to impose or preserve a preferred regime)

That the minimal requisite force be employed and/or that the intervention is not likely to cause greater injury to innocent persons and their property than would result if the threatened violation actually occurred

That the intervention be of limited duration

That a report of the intervention be filed immediately with the United Nations Security Council and, when relevant, regional organizations.[78]

In addition, such intervention should be multilateral.

Such action would also have serious implications for the United States. As the former president of the Inter-American Commission on Human Rights has phrased it, justifying military interventions to create democracies is a dangerous precedent:

In a world where most governments are not democratic, such a norm could never win much support and therefore cannot by its nature be anything more than a challenge to the very existence of a system of law among nations. Moreover, it is doubtful, very doubtful, that we as a people are prepared to act on the basis of the norm except where the non-democratic regime is unfriendly to the U.S. or one of its allies.[79]

Given the political legitimacy of the present government in Nicaragua, other

---

78. Richard B. Lillich, "A United States Policy of Humanitarian Intervention and Intercession," in *Human Rights and American Foreign Policy*, ed. Donald P. Kommers and Gilbert D. Loescher (Notre Dame, Ind.: University of Notre Dame Press, 1979), p. 311.

79. Tom J. Farer, "The U.S. and War in Central America: A Legal Perspective," an address presented at the University of New Mexico School of Law, May 12, 1983, p. 10.

countries are limited in their promotion of human rights to humanitarian intercession. This constitutes diplomatic representations and the withholding or granting of aid. Under international law it does not include the manipulation of tariffs, the imposition of an embargo or a boycott, or military assistance to the *contras*.

The need for the United States as a world power to observe international law is imperative. As former White House counsel Lloyd N. Cutler phrased it:

> It does matter whether our actions comply with international law. It matters precisely because we are a practicing democracy with both philosophical and geopolitical reasons to encourage the democratic aspirations of all peoples. Democracy cannot flourish in a lawless climate; it depends on widely accepted principles of law for its survival. That is obvious with respect to national law. It is equally important with respect to international law, especially our treaty commitments under the charters of the United Nations and the Organization of American States. No democratic nation—least of all a democratic superpower—can afford to act in a manner that admittedly flouts international law. To sustain free-world support of our leadership, our actions must be confined to steps we can justify as consistent with a principled interpretation of the law as we see it.[80]

In addition, Cutler cites the need to have the support of the American people for U.S. foreign policy if its political, legal, moral, and financial costs are to be sustained. Public opinion surveys have repeatedly indicated that such support does not exist. They do, however, indicate a strong preference for a negotiated settlement. That would seem to be the will of the majority.

Acknowledgement

The author wishes to thank the Woodstock Theological Center and Sara Grusky, Eileen Phillips, and Jude Howard for assistance in the preparation of this paper.

---

80. Lloyd N. Cutler, "The Right to Intervene," *Foreign Affairs* 64, no. 1 (Fall 1985): 96–97.

• CHAPTER SEVEN •

Somocismo and the Sandinista Revolution

Arturo J. Cruz Sequeira

The majority of the now vast literature on Central America merely restates the simplistic formulations of the region's problems, reducing its many contradictions to a struggle between an isolated oligarchy and a huge peasant mass. In reality, few authors are capable of recognizing how dynamic these societies really were in the last 30 years of social differentiation and relative modernization, not only in terms of economic development, or the *massive* enlargement (both qualitatively and quantitatively) of the market, but also in terms of the movement of the population from countryside to city.

Having said this, I do not pretend to ignore the inegalitarian and also dependent nature of this growth cycle, or rather, the huge social contradictions that the agroexport model of economic growth engendered, particularly in economies with limited agricultural frontiers. Nonetheless, the problem transcends a growth rate without social distribution, and is in fact related to the emergence of new social forces that demand not merely participation (however restricted) in national decisions but political representation. There is no doubt that the present crisis is linked to what many consider an exhausted economic model and to the larger problems of democracy itself. For this reason we say that today's crisis is much more difficult to resolve than that of the 1930s, when the *social corpus* of these countries was far less complex and permitted "simple" solutions.

To all of this one must add that the Sandinista revolution, which in its first moments represented a paradigm of change for an exhausted regional model, has become part of the Central American problem. This has led to a crisis of alternatives, where the solution to our problems is bound to be *un-*

precedented. Hence the importance of defining the nature of the Central American crisis in accurate terms, and the absolute necessity of not limiting the definition to narrow categories—such as an exhausted growth model, with levels of consumption that are beyond the objective possibilities of the economy, or which result in the maldistribution of national wealth. One must also take into account the objective necessity of a democratic project that will give some space to the multiple expressions that have emerged during these 30 years of growth and social differentiation.

For this reason we say that, in Central America, a revolution plain and simple (*una revolución a secas*) is not sufficient without some means of achieving collaboration. In Brazil, despite the extreme poverty of the northeastern region of that country, few people—including outstanding figures of the left, such as Leonel Brizola or Teotonio Dos Santos—suggest a revolutionary option that does not include a democratic opening. They admit that after more than two decades of "associated dependency" (to borrow the terminology of Ciro Cardozo), the social fabric of Brazil is too advanced to be melded with the Cuban model. Nonetheless, even among the *new* left in Brazil, to which the best of creative Marxism belongs, there has been no real awareness of the changes that have taken place in Central America in the last 30 years. In effect, they continue to recommend to Central America a model that they no longer accept for their own country.

The Economic Crisis and the Lack of Internal Savings

The present crisis in Central America is without historical precedent. In terms of the economy, the agroexport sector has lost the dynamism that characterized its last 30 years; the process of import substitution through the Central American Common Market (MCCA) has stagnated; and the levels of investment are insufficient.[1] The countries of the region lack an economic surplus of their own, and in the 1980s the surplus of outsiders has been converted into a substitute for indigenous funding rather than what it should be, that is, a complement to internal savings. The *degree* of dependence of these countries is such that in the short and middle term, the capacity of their economies for growth is a function almost exclusively of the financial

---

1. *Istmo Centroamericano: el carácter de la crisis, los desafíos que plantea y la solidaridad internacional que demanda* [The Central American Isthmus: The Character of the Crisis, The Challenges It Faces, and the International Solidarity It Requires] (Mexico City:CEPAL, June 4, 1981).

disbursements of foreign sources. For example, whereas in 1977 only 13% of the total savings of the region came from external sources, in 1981 the figure had grown to an average of 45.6% of the total.[2] Quite independently of their professed ideological orientation, the countries of the region began the 1980s with a level of growth based entirely on the acquisition of external resources and circumscribed by enormous financial obligations.

It is true that during the 1960s the countries of Central America were capable of attracting significant amounts of economic aid (in effect, concessionary credits) to complement local savings. Nonetheless, in the 1970s they began to resort regularly to capital markets. This was particularly true of Nicaragua and Costa Rica. Then, toward the end of the decade, the Central American countries began to borrow excessively. By this time these countries had lost the benefits of the coffee bonanza of 1975–1977. To the degree to which the countries saw internal saving decline and foreign assistance decrease, their commercial debt grew. The region's $4 billion foreign debt in 1977 became $9 billion by 1981, the majority of it contracted from private foreign banks.[3] Projections for the next 5 year period indicate $23 billion in economic assistance will be needed to close the resource gap. And even these projections are based on optimistic assumptions—that traditional exports will grow adequately, that imports will be somewhat curtailed, that general levels of consumption will be reduced, and that the countries of the region will be content with unsatisfactory levels of economic growth.

The principal virtue of the Kissinger Commission for Central America was its reevaluation of the financial magnitude of the regional crisis and its placement of Central American necessities within their proper framework. A group of Central American economists (among them, Gabriel Siri, Isaac Cohen, and Gert Rosenthal) has similarly been insisting on the enormous financial difficulties of the region and the necessity of reconsidering with some urgency the *sheer size* of traditional economic assistance.[4]

2. *La crisis Centroamericana: orígenes, alcances y consecuencias* [The Central American Crisis: Its Origins, Scope and Consequences] (Mexico City: CEPAL, May 1, 1983).

3. Banco Interamericano de Desarollo (BID) [Inter-American Development Bank (IDB)] *Progreso económico y social en América Latina,* Informe Anual, 1982 [Economic and Social Progress in Latin America, Annual Report 1982] (Washington, D.C., 1983).

4. For one of the most rigorous treatments of this subject, see Francisco Mayorga, "Crecimiento económico y requirimientos financieros para el desarollo de Centroamérica." [Economic Growth and Financial Requirements for the Development of Central America] in *Centroamérica: más allá de la crisis* [Central America: Beyond the Crisis], ed. Donald Castillo Rivas (Mexico City: Ediciones SIAP, 1983).

Three Decades of Growth and Social Change

What renders the economic crisis more complex is the fact that Central America as a whole managed to achieve truly impressive rates of growth over the last three decades. In the process it experienced significant transformations: in the composition of goods and services, in the labor force, and in the distribution of rural and urban populations. Between 1950 and 1978 the regional gross domestic product (GDP) grew at an annual rate of 5.3%, and between 1970 and 1978 the real growth actually exceeded 5.6% a year. From 1950 to 1980 per capita income doubled, and industrial production grew from 12.3% of the GDP (1960) to 16.8% (1978). Meanwhile, the value of extraregional exports grew from $250 million in 1950 to $3.2 billion in 1975.[5] Further, from the 1950s through the 1960s, the industrial sector grew at an average rate of 8% per year and, according to estimates by Oscar Menjívar, could generate a value-added between $5 and $8 billion. Finally, the structure of exports was greatly diversified, and by the beginning of the 1970s, in addition to coffee, there were many new lines—cotton, sugar, even meat.

In fact, the dynamism of the agroexport sector permitted the countries of the region to overcome their balance-of-payments problems and cover imports of those intermediate goods essential to the growth of industry. It constituted the fundamental motor that impelled all economies of Central America, reflected, among other places, in the numerous studies produced by the United Nations Economic Commission for Latin America (ECLA). These tend to show a direct relationship between the level of exports and the rate of economic expansion, capital accumulation, investment, tax collection, levels of employment, and capacity to import.

Economic development of this sort had strong sociological consequences; in effect, the societies of the region could not—and did not—remain *static*. The period was characterized by what I shall call throughout this essay a radical process of social differentiation. Transformations in the economic base produced corresponding innovations in the class configuration of these societies. With the introduction of cotton and the development of manufacturing activities, not only did new elements emerge within the traditional circles of power, but also there appeared for the first time a rural and urban proletariat. Moreover, with the enlargement of all kinds of services, including those of the informal sector, there appeared a new middle class, within which there was a strong and competent technocracy, especially in Nicaragua.

---

5. *La crisis Centroamericana* [The Central American Crisis].

The Case of Nicaragua

Although the countries of the region all sustained over a 30-year period an accelerated rate of economic growth and experienced relative modernization, differences between countries *were* and *continue to be* of importance. And here we refer very specifically, *not* to political systems (e.g., democracy in Costa Rica versus the Somoza dictatorship in Nicaragua), but to the magnitude of social contradictions that the consolidation of the agroexport model engendered in each country. To take only one example: In El Salvador the expansion of the agroexport model led by the beginning of the 1970s to a situation in which more than 180,000 peasant families were without the least access to land,[6] whereas in Nicaragua the magnitude of the agricultural frontier permitted the coexistence of huge agribusiness operations side by side with small and medium holdings tended by peasants and devoted largely to growing cereals for local consumption. Prior to the fall of Somoza, it was estimated that approximately 300,000 *manzanas* [a land measurement equal to 7026 square meters] of basic grains were sown by small and middle holders, which stands in contrast to the situation since 1979 in which, under the new economic regime, state farms have been converted into the principal producers of corn and other cereals.

In any event, in 1979 more than 87,000 peasant families owned properties averaging 10 *manzanas* in size, rendering them not only self-sufficient for their immediate nutritional needs but also capable of producing a surplus for market and, in so doing, fully participating in the money economy both as *consumers* and *producers.*[7] What is perhaps more interesting is what occurred where peasants were literally despoiled of their ancestral lands, such as occurred in El Viejo, or displaced by the expansion of cotton, as occurred in the Western region—Chinadega and León. Most of these peasants, far from accepting their new role as rural proletarians or semiproletarians, simply opted to become homesteaders in marginal zones such as Rama or Nueva Guinea. The country's agricultural frontier is so large that even in the Pacific region there are zones (such as the estuary of the Gran Lago) that still have not been fully exploited. On the Atlantic Coast, where 10% of the population resides, it is perfectly possible to find peasant families who own upward of 500 *manzanas* of land.

In a certain sense, we could concede that the most "efficient" bourgeois classes have been found historically in El Salvador and Guatemala. It is

6. Eduardo Colindres, *Los fundamentos económicos de la burguesía salvadoreña* [Economic Foundations of the Salvadoran Bourgeoisie] (San Salvador: Editores UCA, 1978).
7. Arturo J. Cruz Sequeira, "Nicaragua: crisis económica, radicalización o moderación?" [Nicaragua: Economic Crisis, Radicalization or Moderation] in Rivas, ed., *Centroamérica.*

likewise true, however, that in those countries we find social tensions most pronounced, partly because the profit margin has been determined by *superexploitation* of the labor force. By this we do not mean to contend that the agroexport bourgeoisie in Nicaragua was not "efficient"—above all the cotton growers of the Western region, who are among the most productive in the world—or that they did not compensate their laborers (a large portion of whom had to be imported seasonally from El Salvador) in an equally niggardly fashion. But the essential point to grasp, specifically in the case of Nicaragua, is that as cotton growers developed a modern, entrepreneurial attitude and learned to live alongside others having small and medium-size holdings, the great ranchers of the southern region, Boaco and Chontales, though also integrated into an export-oriented economy, managed to preserve seigneurial social relations of production. The world view of these great families of the south belonged to the nineteenth century, although the social contradictions that these units of production might normally be expected to produce were somewhat mediated by the paternalistic relationship between patron and retainer.[8]

Socioeconomic differences aside, perhaps the most important characteristic of the region as a whole was the fact that as late as the mid 1970s, the financial indices of El Salvador and, above all, Guatemala were relatively favorable, both with respect to assets and liabilities. The latter, for example, possessed international reserves in 1978 of $790 million, exclusive of gold reserves, against a foreign debt of scarcely $550 million (1977), contracted largely with multilateral lending institutions.[9] This happy situation was partly the result of the coffee boom of 1975–1977, but also due to the fact that in both countries the dominant economic groups did not, historically, bother with social expenditures. They showed little concern with mediating the vast inequalities that the consolidation of the agroexport model necessarily generated.

Costa Rica—characterized by a more or less equitable pattern of land tenure and a large, rural middle class in its central plain—is the outstanding exception. But it has also been the Central American country that historically has maintained the lowest levels of international reserves, the highest public debt, and the largest fiscal deficits.[10] In reality, the economy of Costa Rica has fewer comparative advantages than that of Nicaragua. To main-

---

8. In order to understand fully the relationship between the landed aristocracy and the peasantry one needs to know the stories of Adolfo Calero and Pedro Joaquín Chamorro.

9. Banco Interamericano de Desarollo (BID), *Progreso económico y social en América* [Economic and Social Progress in the Americas] (Washington, D.C., 1977).

10. CEPAL, *Anuario Estadístico de América, Latina 1983* [Statistical Annual of Latin America, 1983], (1984).

tain levels of consumption that exceed the objective possibilities of its economy— including a structure of social overhead more appropriate to a European welfare state—it has had to resort in an excessive and even irresponsible manner to foreign indebtedness, both to finance investment and to subsidize social expenditures and luxury consumption.

In the great paradox that is Central America, Honduras, with the lowest level of development of its productive forces, has been one of the most stable countries in the region. In Honduras, the backwardness of the economic base and political culture has proven highly functional, as both Marx or Huntington might argue, to the preservation of the traditional economic strata and their perpetuation in power.

The Crisis of the 1930s and the Present Crisis

The peculiar challenge posed by the present crisis is that "simple" solutions, such as those employed during the 1930s, are no longer plausible. The complex class configuration of these societies and the *degree* to which the Central American economies are now open to the larger world system preclude a return to the past. (The coefficients of exports and imports as a percentage of GDP went from 18.6% and 16.3% respectively in 1950 to 30.4% and 33.6% in 1976.)[11]

This means, among other things, that the countries of the region are in no position to isolate themselves from the world economy, such as they could have done with relative ease during the 1930s. It is worth recalling that during those years, the cities were still dominated by a rural culture. Artisanal guilds scarcely coexisted with incipient middle sectors, and in the countryside the seigneurial lords of the land confined themselves to perpetuation of their resources rather than expansion. Meanwhile, the peasant masses devoted themselves to subsistence agriculture on their tiny parcels of land. Here we do not pretend to ignore what the majority of Central American authors, among them Edelberto Torres-Rivas, have pointed out: the convergence in the 1930s of personal dictatorship, economic crisis, social upheaval, and popular discontent.[12] It was precisely during this period that the massive slaughter of peasants (*la matanza*) occurred in El Salvador under the dictatorship of General Martínez. According to Thomas Anderson, some 10,000 to 30,000 were murdered. The crisis in Guatemala also pro-

11. Gert Rosenthal, "Economic Trends in Central America," *CEPAL Review*, Second Half, 1978.

12. Edelberto Torres-Rivas, *Interpretación del desarollo social en Centroamérica* [Interpretation of Social Development in Central America] (San José, Costa Rica: EDUCA, 1972).

duced enormous popular unrest following reductions in the day wage imposed on salaried sectors in the fruit companies and on the railroads.[13]

In Nicaragua, nonetheless, the social contradictions produced by the crisis were of far less importance than in the rest of Central America. The only
slaughter comparable to that of El Salvador took place in Wiwili in 1934, in
which some 300 peasants, remnants of General Sandino's guerrilla army,
died. Though there is little concrete data on the subject, the distribution of
land in Nicaragua was as widespread at the time as in Costa Rica. As
Sandino himself noted in an interview in February 1933 with the journalist
Ramón Belausteguigoita:

> In some countries, as in Mexico, many people are under the impression that
> the Sandinista Movement was fundamentally agrarian. I have had occasion to
> note during my stay in Nicaragua that property ownership is widely diffused.
> Latifundia scarcely exist, and what there is, is not of vast extent. The few that
> do not possess land do not, nonetheless, suffer hunger.[14]

In all of this, the important point to bear in mind is that, given the limits of
social differentiation during that period, a military response (through a
"strongman," be it Ubico, Martínez, or Carías) constituted a much more
viable option for purposes of social control than it does today. Even the
more "modern" version of the traditional dictatorship is not viable, since it
lacks the kind of broad social base that present-day conditions require.[15]

The Nature of the Present Crisis

While external factors—excessive financial obligations, an increase in the
price of oil, deterioration in the prices of agroexports, etc.—have seriously
aggravated the regional crisis,[16] simply increasing the volume of traditional

13. Thomas Anderson, *Matanza: El Salvador's Communist Revolt of 1932* (Lincoln: University of Nebraska Press, 1972). See also the unpublished manuscript of Piero Gleijeses on the
Arbenz period and the intervention of the United States, as well as Rut Bunzel, *Chichica-
stenango: A Guatemalan Village, 1930–1932*, American Ethnological Society, Publication 22,
1952.

14. Taken from Sergio Ramírez. *El pensamiento vivo de Sandino* [The Living Thought of
Sandino], 6th ed. (San José, Costa Rica: EDUCA, 1980).

15. In this essay in *Polémica* [Polemic], José Luis Carballo suggested that if the Costa Rican
establishment proved unable to meet the challenge, Costa Rica would be trapped between two
equally undesirable alternatives: neo-fascism or neo-Stalinism. He believed this was true for
the other countries of the region as well.

16. While the price of coffee fell in international markets in 1979, the price of oil rose for the
second time in the decade. The consequent rise in interest rates increased significantly the
burden of the region's foreign debt. See *Cable Centroamericano*, February 1982.

exports or levels of economic aid or even redesigning the functions of the International Monetary Fund would not be sufficient responses. The suggestions of prestigious Central American economists, such as Gabriel Siri, who insist that each country should concentrate on its comparative advantage and rely on traditional exports to solve the crisis,[17] doubtlessly would have been sufficient in the 1960s. During that decade the problems occasioned by the urban explosion were of manageable proportions, international inflation was within reasonable limits, and the levels of luxury consumption were somewhat more modest than they are today. Above all, the Central American countries that possessed a stable political framework could take full advantage of the region's comparative advantage—in some countries abundant agricultural land and in almost all, inexpensive labor. The *present* crisis, is not caused—as the Central American left habitually asserts— simply by economic growth without social progress. It stems from the emergence of new social forces during the process of modernization of agriculture, and the massive incorporation of the rural population into the money economy.[18] The political superstructures, in short, were incapable of adjusting to the changes in the economic base. As a consequence, today we find ourselves before a destructive deadlock between social classes and the ideological incapacity—on the part of both traditional elites and revolutionaries—to offer a solution to the crisis and act either as a true *dominant class* or as true *agents of change*.

A mere increase in traditional exports, huge transfers of financial resources under concessionary conditions, or reforms in the international monetary system will simply act as palliatives to a more profound crisis. Given the magnitude of the external breach and the deadlock between social classes, there is no alternative for these societies but to increase internal savings, forge a new social pact, and overcome the crisis through an innovative project solidly resting on class collaboration. In the final analysis, the Central American crisis is one in which the solution to the problems of the region are bound to be without precedent and to exceed simple definitions of left and right.

Within this context, a group of Central American social scientists, among them Silvio De Franco, José Luis Velásquez, and I, have questioned the

17. On the one hand, studies like the *Interamerican Dialogue* have emphasized the importance of economic aid and the need to alter the mandate of the International Monetary Fund, so as to cushion the social impact of whatever adjustments follow any stabilization program.

18. According to Oscar Menjívar, in Central America and especially in El Savador, following World War II, commercial relations at the village level were supplanted by the national market, and instead of paying rent or salaries in specie, the economy was monetized. Thus was the rural population incorporated into the national economy. See notes for his doctoral thesis, "Capital Accumulation in Agriculture," University of Glasgow.

primary concepts of the dependency theory in favor of a more realistic vision based on the concept of "structural dependency" that is characteristic of all open economies of small size, such as our own. Even more, we have questioned the role of the state as the panacea to our problems and have begun to consider the virtues of fiscal discipline and the possibilities that the market offers to stimulate simultaneously economic growth and a redistribution of resources.

Nicaragua as the New Paradigm

Nonetheless, the reality has been that, faced with the crisis of the 1970s, all reformist schemes in Central America simply failed. This explains why for so many the Sandinista revolution represented, if not the paradigm, at least a point of reference for the entire region. What was particularly irresistible in the Sandinista promise was the notion that an openly revolutionary vanguard—with the support of the society as a whole—could or would adopt on its own what in essence had been the reformist project. In the process a compromise would be struck that would give the model its hybrid quality: The private sector would constitute one of the principal motors of the economy. Meanwhile, the vanguard would guarantee social change through direction of the economic *surpluses* generated by the private sector, rather than through confiscation of the *means of production tout court*.

Inevitably, an entire generation of Central American technocrats of a reformist bent found the youthful vanguard in Nicaragua a far more effective agent for the implementation of their projects than their respective progressive bourgeois classes, the armed forces, or even the political parties of the center and left. The old generation of this group as well as the new—among them, Rafael Glover, Rodolfo Silva, Jorge Sol, Roberto Mayorga, and Gert Rosenthal—had learned that, sooner or later, every attempt at social change initiated by the armed forces—whether in El Salvador under Osorio, Honduras under Oswaldo López Arellano, or Guatemala under Arana—would be frustrated by the resistance of the traditional elites, and especially, by the agroexport bourgeoisie. As one of the most distinguished of these technocrats later remarked, with the revolutionary change in Nicaragua it was easy to see why the Central American Common Market failed. The latter, he said, had been a project of integration responding to the interests of the bourgeoisie, whereas the Sandinista revolution (and future revolutions elsewhere) would be based on the interests of the people. Only then could the promise of the Common Market achieve full realization.

The only difficulty with the Sandinista Front, according to this group of reformist technocrats, was its ideological rigidity. The principal task, then, was to *educate* the new vanguard (the equivalent of our Modern Prince) with regard to the realities of the world economy, the importance of promoting the Common Market and at the same time persuading the *comandantes* to recognize the greater multipolarity of the world and therefore assume a position of equidistance between the United States and the Soviet Union.[19] As things turned out, the difficulty of assimilating or coopting a revolutionary vanguard was no less than that of assimilating progressive military men, for the Sandinistas, no less than their military predecessors, had an agenda of their own. Thus it was very quickly revealed that the crisis of alternatives in Central America afflicted not only reformers but also revolutionaries.

The Crisis of the New Paradigm

The contradictions that confront the Nicaraguan revolutionary process are multiple and complex. It is not sufficient merely to refer to external factors, such as the world recession or the imperial hostility of the United States or even to the remnants of the past, to explain the origins of the present crisis. To understand the contradictions between the revolution and society we need to take into account the contradictions of a unique *strategy* of "transition to socialism," a strategy that, besides being characterized by an alliance with the private sector, is based on wage freezes and a pricing policy designed to discourage agricultural production by the peasantry. It is also a strategy that has not paid sufficient attention to economic reactivation, that has ignored the structural rigidities of the agroexport model, that has operated on unrealistic assumptions concerning Nicaragua's economic dependency, and that has ignored the country's petit bourgeois social fabric, which, like it or not, is an objective reality.[20]

Part of the problem is that, from the beginning, important advisers such as E. V. K. FitzGerald, who belonged to the economic committee charged with advising the National Directorate of the FSLN, held that reactivation of the economy should not be utilized as an excuse to delay the simultaneous

19. This was also the hope of the more moderate advisers to the FSLN. For more detailed explanation, see Arturo J. Cruz Sequeira, "The Origins of Sandinista Foreign Policy," in *Central America: Anatomy of Conflict*, ed. Robert S. Leiken (New York: Pergamon Press, 1984).

20. Arturo J. Cruz Sequeira, "Nicaragua: A Revolution in Crisis," *SAIS Review*, Winter 1984. For a critique of the FSLN's strategy of transition from a Trotskyist perspective, see the manuscript of Oscar René Vargas, "Nicaragua: economía y revolución"[Nicaragua: Economy and Revolution].

transition of what was defined as socialism.[21] In the words of Orlando Núñez, one of the principal theoreticians of the FSLN and the principal architect of the agrarian reform, every socialist project begins with the seizure of political, rather than economic, power. For these theoreticians, the revolutionary challenge consisted of how to confront immediate problems without having to sacrifice intermediate and longer-term goals. Tactical concessions might be desirable or necessary, but they must not be allowed to be converted into permanent realities. Such thinkers also believed in a sharp and definitive break with the agroexport model, since they could not imagine any other way to move toward a different form of society, even though they knew that Nicaragua possessed no other means by which to initiate a new process of capital accumulation.

In contrast, a minority within the new government maintained that the need to obtain external resources and reactivate the productive apparatus through the private sector and the limits imposed by the agroexport model, not only rendered a radical alternative impossible but strongly suggested that the *strategic* goals of the revolution could not go further than what Carlos Coronel defined as a "left-wing social democracy."[22] Included within this minority, in addition to Carlos Coronel, was Arturo J. Cruz, as well as economists and technocrats of a leftish bent. They argued that in order for changes to be effective, they had to be gradual, since a sharp break with the existing system would simply produce the opposite of what the revolution sought to obtain: less economic dependence and a more equitable distribution of resources.[23]

By 1982 all the socioeconomic indicators belied the new regime's revolutionary claims. Income in real terms, measured by the capacity to acquire the most basic consumer goods, had diminished some 18.3%, while the level of unemployment in the second quarter of 1982, according to the Ministry of Industries, reached 20.3% of the economically active urban population (due largely to the closing of state enterprises). For that same year, consumption of essentials by the population had dropped by 12.3% and of nonessentials, by 24.5%.[24] Moreover, in spite of the drop in real income and in the levels

21. E. V. K. FitzGerald, "The Economics of Revolution," in *Nicaragua in Revolution*, ed. Thomas Walker (New York: Praeger, 1982).

22. For one of the most representative works of this minority, see Mario De Franco, *Aspectos del desenvolvimiento económico de Nicaragua* [Aspects of Nicaragua's Economic Development], report prepared for the Friedrich Ebert Foundation, March 1981.

23. For one of the first critiques of the Sandinista strategy for the transformation to socialism, see Jorge Castañeda, *Nicaragua: contradicciones en la revolución* [Nicaragua: Contradictions in the Revolution] (Mexico City: Tiempo Extra Ediciones, 1980).

24. See the documents prepared for internal discussion, Banco Central, *Resultados económicos de 1982 y perspectivas para 1983* [Economic Results of 1982 and Perspectives for 1983] (Managua, 1983).

of consumption, by 1982 the possibilities of capital accumulation were extremely limited. In 1980, and also in 1981, years characterized by a vast inflow of external resources, there simply was no capital formation. Investment in 1981 and 1982 totaled 15.9% and 12% of GDP, significantly below the Central American average of 19.5% in the 1970s. The percentage of resources devoted to investment dropped by 30.8% in 1982, while the country's capacity to import was reduced by 34.3%.[25]

After 2 years (1981–1982) of growth without productive investment, and one year (1982) of austerity without a concrete program to reactivate the economy beyond the grand strategy of a "transition to socialism," the National Directorate of the FSLN decided in 1983 to turn to a standard of growth based *fundamentally* on the promotion of internal savings and in state investments. According to some people, this new model of growth, involving an alliance with monopoly capital, established the bases for a model of state capitalism. Within this new scheme, the order of the day would continue to be labor austerity, characterized by the strict control of wages and levels of consumption. Land reform was "rationalized" in favor of agroindustrial complexes. These complexes alone possessed the capacity to generate growth comparable, in dynamism and in exploitation of the labor force, to the 1950s, when the cultivation of cotton was begun on Nicaragua's Pacific Coast. According to Mario De Franco, a former adviser to the International Fund for Reconstruction (IFR), since 1983 state investments in Nicaragua have had a qualitative importance and have been concentrated in what he calls the three great poles of the "new" economy: energy; the huge stock-raising complexes (Chiltepe); and the sugar mills, such as the mill in Malacatoya, which possesses a fixed investment estimated at somewhat more than $100 million.

This plan for a new cycle of growth is burdened by contradictions between the revolutionary state and society as a whole. In order to "rationalize" the land reform one must face the fact that, among other things, there must be a tradeoff between growth and distribution. Under this system of accumulation, growth can occur only if all consumption, including the most necessary social consumption, is sharply curtailed. That means, among other things, wage freezes. Then, in spite of an increase in imports, and assuming (accord-

25. For the Central American average, see Rosenthal, "Economic Trends in Central America." It is worth noting that the coefficient of gross investment was 21% in 1976 and 28% in 1977; if one takes into account 1970, 1975, 1977, and 1978 to arrive at a representative average, the percentage was equivalent to 19.5 for the entire region. One should also take into account the fact that private investment in the two decades before the revolution fluctuated betwen 68 and 56% of the total of gross investment, but in 1980 it represented only 14% of the total. See Banco Central, *Memoria* (various years), and the statistics assembled by the Department of Overall Accounts of the Planning Ministry. 1981.

ing to official figures) a rhythm of positive growth for 1983, the revolutionary legitimacy of the Sandinista Front is bound to weaken among the masses
of the population. This was and is the case, not because there was no growth
without redistribution, but because this growth was possible only by recourse to a controversial category of analysis, owing to the "superexploitation" of manual labor.[26] It is worth recalling that in 1983 the Nicaraguan
economy was expected to grow in real terms by 4.7% (compared to −2% in
1982) and, more important, that the agropastoral sector was to grow in the
neighborhood of 16%.

Nonetheless, according to the Central Bank, in order to obtain those
rates of growth, imports would have had to increase by $782 million in 1982
and $983 million in 1983 (still a level of imports inferior to 1981). Given the
insufficient volume of exports, it would have been necessary to postpone
service on the foreign debt and receive an additional $300 million in eco-
nomic aid, of which $200 million had been committed by the "socialist"
camp in credit lines to import oil, fertilizers, and medicines.[27]

The political options of the revolutionary elite are limited by a logic of
internal capital accumulation that I have called in this essay a model of
nascent state capitalism. At least in the immediate future, and pending a
limited political opening, such a policy would produce consequences difficult to manage. This, then, is the dilemma of the Sandinista Front: how to
achieve a credible political opening without having to compromise their hold
on power, under circumstances in which the external breach is so enormous,
the levels of foreign aid insufficient, and there remains no other option but
to reduce consumption and vastly increase the social cost of internal savings.

Sandinista Ideology and Nicaraguan Society

The derailment of the "transition to socialism" into *nascent* state capitalism
has produced new contradictions between *revolution* and *society*. It is
precisely the *gap* between the ideological vision of the Sandinista Front and
the objective reality of the country that establishes the origins of the revolutionary crisis and, for that matter, Nicaragua's crisis as a nation.

In effect, we must explain how the FSLN in its different tendencies,
particularly after 1976, understood Nicaraguan reality through its own interpretation of the crisis of *somocismo*. This it saw as inextricably related to the
crisis of accumulation within a peripheral capitalist system; thus the conflict

---

26. Banco Central, *Resultados económicos* [Economic Results].
27. Ibid.

between Somoza and the bourgeoisie could not be, in this view, a serious struggle over political institutions or even political participation, but had to be reduced to a mere matter of competition for the economic spoils of hegemony. As the Front announced shortly after its victory in its first National Assembly of Cadres: "In reality, we are witnessing the fusion of the crisis of the capitalist model with the crisis of the dictatorship, so that the latter is also necessarily the crisis of an economic system, the exhaustion of a system of dependent capitalism, based on the superexploitation of labor, all of which made the military dictatorship a historical necessity."[28]

It follows, according to the *Weltanschauung* of the Sandinista Front, that it was necessary to break cleanly with the agroexport model and economic dependency. As E. V. K. FitzGerald or Núñez suggested, the economy would be reactivated and simultaneously moved in the direction of socialism. In this scheme, the function of the bourgeoisie would be to reactivate the productive apparatus. They would be encouraged by better economic incentives than they had enjoyed in the days of Somoza, such as easier credit and a fuller access to foreign exchange. Meanwhile, the revolutionary state, through its domination of the "controlling heights" of the economy, and the Area of Popular Property (APP), would lay the bases for a new economy, which together with the *political and military monopoly* of the FSLN would guarantee, at the proper time, the qualitative leap—the consummation, really—of the historic project.

In the field of international relations, the leaders of the FSLN thought it possible to implement a peculiar version of the "international division of labor." On the one hand, they expected to receive financial aid from the capitalist countries in order to reactivate the economy; on the other, to establish the bases for a permanent ideological and military integration into the socialist camp. It is important to bear in mind that the majority of the members of the National Directorate could not—within the Central American context—imagine what in other places was known as "socialism in one country." If we take into account the open and dependent nature of the Nicaraguan economy, it is easy to see why the *comandantes* believed that there was no alternative to full integration into the family of "socialist" countries.[29]

From the beginning, this strategy was burdened with tensions and contradictions that time has demonstrated are almost impossible to reconcile. To

28. See *Análisis de la coyuntura y tareas de la Revolución Popular Sandinista* [Analysis of the Conjuncture and Tasks of the Popular Sandinista Revolution], political and military theses presented by the National Assembly of Cadres Rigoberto López Pérez, September 21, 22, and 23, 1979.
29. See Sequeira, "Origins of Sandinista Foreign Policy."

begin with, it was not possible to sustain an alliance with the bourgeoisie in exclusively political terms without making some sort of effective concession in the apportionment of political power. And this was so, not only because the bourgeoisie was not anxious to "buy into" a project of transition to socialism, but also because the bourgeoisie's struggle against the Somozas was in part a class conflict of sorts. The business elite finally acquired (or regained, according to some) a sense of itself as a dominant class and aspired to be not merely entrepreneurs but the principal representatives of the nation.

In truth, what the Sandinista Front offered was precisely what the Somozas had forced on the bourgeoisie for decades, and against which at least a part of the bourgeoisie had already rebelled: participation in the economic sphere and total exclusion from political power. The aggravating factor was that in revolutionary Nicaragua there would no longer be—as there once had been—a guarantee of the *security of capital* and the *right to make a profit*, since, as Orlando Núñez candidly explained, the revolution had virtually expropriated the future of the bourgeoisie.[30] In any case, it was impossible to adopt a short-term reformist model and afterward pretend to move easily toward socialism. The choices were either to embrace a reformist project as a permanent solution, as Carlos Coronel had insisted from the first moment, or to embrace from the beginning what the theoreticians of the FSLN called the "socialist alternative."

This strategy of transition, *formally* coherent, proposed to harmonize tactical moves with strategic objectives. What it really produced, besides indecision and uncertainty, was a profound contradiction between the objective framework of an economy dominated (at least quantitatively) by private property and the ideological discourse of the *comandantes* in favor of socialism. Moreover, the lack of reactivation of the productive apparatus and the necessity to impose economic discipline produced a second contradiction: the need to *punish* the "natural" political clientele of the FSLN—the popular sectors—who in theory were supposed to serve as the constituency and reserve army of the great historic project. In effect, the Sandinistas produced a new and curious version of the dialectic—the worst of both worlds. Economic measures objectively impoverished the popular sectors and *overestimated* the revolutionary vocation and capacity of the working class. The fact that only 19% of the economically active population of the country could properly be considered "workers" in the Marxist sense and that more than 180,000 families, in both city and countryside, were associ-

30. For one of the few works on the origins of the bourgeois rebellion, see Benjamin Crosby, *Panda: alternativas para el desarrollo del sector privado* [Panda: Alternatives for the Development of the Private Sector] (Managua: INCAE, 1980).

ated with private property in one form or another were truths that the theoreticians of the Sandinista Front (with the exception of Orlando Núñez) simply refused to take into account. Núñez not only recognized the small size of the Nicaraguan working class but also conceded its political passivity; he was the first to elevate youth to a universal category, independent of class reference, and to cast it in the role of revolutionary agent par excellence.[31]

As two great Nicaraguan intellectuals, Pablo Antonio Cuadra[32] and José Coronel Urtecho,[33] have maintained, ours is a society of small and medium size merchants, permeated by the distinctive culture of the rural petty bourgeoisie. This is why Pablo Antonio Cuadra's book, dedicated to the study of our national character and our political culture, was the object of the strongest criticisms by the Sandinista Front. In his acid comentary on the book, Jaime Wheelock insisted on a more orthodox vision of the Nicaraguan proletariat—that is to say, a "healthy" working class, free of mere bread-and-butter considerations and waiting on the decisions of the revolutionary vanguard. Obviously, for Wheelock, whose *Imperialismo y Dictadura* [Imperialism and Dictatorship][34] established him as one of the most serious theoreticians of the Sandinista leadership, Cuadra's book represented the complete negation of his revolutionary world outlook.

In reality, the problem with the ideological conception of the Sandinista Front was more fundamental still. It was related to its interpretation of *somocismo* as a mechanical expression of imperial interests, as if it were a static regime without its own social bases of support and whose reproduction in power for 44 years was exclusively due to repression and the support of the United States. This *caricature* of *somocismo*, while lending itself splendidly to certain political agendas, nonetheless does not permit us to analyze with clarity the formation of ideological discourse, which from the first had

31. See Orlando Núñez, "The Third Social Force in National Liberation Movements," *Latin American Perspectives* 29, Spring 1981.

32. Pablo Antonio Cuadra, *El Nicaragüense* [The Nicaraguans] (San José, Costa Rica: EDUCA, 1974).

33. Jose Coronel Urtecho, *Reflexiones sobre la historia de Nicaragua* [Reflections on the History of Nicaragua] (Managua, 1980).

34. In the tiny world of Nicaraguan Marxism of those years, replete with rivalries and neuroses, Wheelock's book was received somewhat ambiguously. Nonetheless, the general opinion could be summed up in the expression of the then Trotskyite militant Julio López, who considered it the "first serious contribution," from a Marxist perspective, to the study of our social development. As such, he compared it (taking into account differences of stature) to an effort similar to the one Lenin undertook at the end of the last century in his study of the origins of Russian capitalism in the nineteenth century. See Jaime Wheelock Román, *Imperialismo y dictadura: crisis de una formacion social* [Imperialism and Dictatorship: Crisis of a Social Formation] (Mexico City, 1975).

alienated the majority of the productive sectors of the country, especially the small and medium-size entrepreneurs.

Jorge Sol, Jr., economic adviser to the IFR in 1980, dramatically disputed the "straitjacket" concepts elaborated by FitzGerald in another, no less celebrated document of the FSLN. Though FitzGerald had been initially optimistic concerning Nicaragua's transition to socialism, as early as 1980 he was alarmed both by the deficits of the public sector—which he wished to reduce from 18.5% of GDP in 1980 to 3.1% in 1981—and the deficit in the current account of the balance of payments. The latter was projected for 1980 to be 10.8% of GDP. He recommended reducing it by 1981 to −2.8%, an achievement that had been possible only in Pinochet's Chile, where the deficit on current account had been shifted from 6.6% of GDP in 1975 to a tiny surplus of 1.1% in 1976. These measures, according to Sol, would have enormous consequences for Nicaragua in terms of possibilities for real growth; unemployment; bankruptcy of enterprises in both public (APP) and private sectors; popular discontent; and the fertile field for counterrevolution. The Sandinista Army would probably have to go out into the streets to repress the working people, who are, after all, the principal subject of the liberation and transformation of Nicaragua.

In any event, the policy of extreme austerity recommended by FitzGerald was postponed, thanks to the economic aid that the revolution received from capitalist countries. But by 1982, with the flood of external resources having diminished to a trickle, there was no alternative but to return to FitzGerald's original recommendations. The social and political consequences were almost exactly what Jorge Sol had predicted.

In its general conception of Nicaraguan society the Sandinista Front *underestimated* the social weight of the petite bourgeoisie, and the Nicaraguan working class and its political predilections, the significance of the *kulaks* in the countryside, and the participation of the bourgeoisie and the middle sectors in the revolutionary process. Ironically, in 1977 the Nicaraguan economy displayed the greatest possibilities for growth in all of Central America. At the same time, it possessed the capacity not only to satisfy internal demand for basic cereals but also to provision the rest of the countries of the region. The crisis of *somocismo* was not, then, a crisis of capital accumulation, a revolutionary crisis where the popular forces, as organic classes, turned to the vanguard of an antidictatorial struggle. Instead, what occurred was that the regime fell victim to its own project of modernization in both economic and social spheres. In sum, it found itself superseded by the new social forces it had summoned into existence.

To put matters as plainly as possible, we cannot understand the Sandinista revolution without understanding the phenomenon of *somocismo* in all its complexity and many dimensions. At this point we simply cannot continue to accept studies that do nothing more than caricature a political phenomenon that marked the history of Nicaragua—so tragically and decisively—for more than a generation. Instead, we must reevaluate the development of the economy, the society, the formation of the state in its different institutional expressions over these last 40 years. Only thus will we be able to differentiate between the *ideological vision* of the leaders of the FSLN and the *objective reality* of the society, shaped and affected even now by the legacy of *somocismo*. We cannot accept the Sandinista slogan so popular with foreigners who scarcely have grasped the first elements of our national experience: "With the [revolutionary] victory, everything begins." This is precisely the opposite of the truth.

Conclusion: Whither Nicaragua?

A mere 10 years ago, no one would have predicted that Nicaragua would become the focus of a comprehensive international debate. This has happened not merely because the United States has chosen to make Nicaragua one of the primary issues of its foreign policy agenda (although this aspect surely is not irrelevant to the sudden efflorescence of Nicaraguan "solidarity" movements around the world, including the United States). Nicaragua has become the crucial battlefield of controversy within Western countries primarily because it embodies the current metaphor against which people can check and revise their notions on the origins of insurgency in the Third World and the potential of revolutionary regimes to remedy backwardness and social injustice there.

Insofar as origins are concerned, Sandinista sympathizers must accomplish two things. First, they must represent the old regime in Nicaragua as more inegalitarian and more static, both economically and socially, than it really was. This requires passing over some very crucial aspects of our national history, including the opposition to Somoza of some of the most socially conservative sectors of Nicaraguan society. Second, they must explain how and why a broad-based, polyclassist democratic revolution against a dynastic dictatorship in 1979 became almost immediately an internecine struggle between various branches of the "revolutionary family," in which the *least numerous* and *least representative* elements ultimately prevailed.

They must also explain the course of social and economic policy since 1979, and in the process account for the widespread disaffection with these policies by distinctly nonprivileged sectors of Nicaraguan society. This can be accomplished only by consigning entire classes, such as small landowners and shopkeepers, an entire petty bourgeoisie, to the "dustheap of history," as if they never existed, and therefore have no claim to our attention, much less our sympathy. Unfortunately, to do this makes it almost impossible to explain the remarkable rise of a counterrevolutionary movement, already several times the size of the one that toppled Somoza.

Accepting these sociological facts does not make resolution of the ideological conflict any easier. For even those who admit the dissonances between state and society are apparently unclear as to what the final resolution will be. Will the Sandinista vanguard finally accept the "facts" of Nicaraguan society and alter their revolutionary project? If that happens, then Nicaragua will indeed follow something of the "Mexican model" of revolutionary development. (This is what many U.S. policymakers under Carter, and now domestic critics of the Reagan policy, still intend.) While the country would still be something less than democratic—not only would it not resemble Costa Rica but would fall somewhat short even of El Salvador or Honduras—it would somehow accommodate the profound differences that exist within Nicaraguan society. There would be a greater measure of political and cultural pluralism, a relative freedom of the press, few or no restrictions on foreign travel, and a truly nonaligned foreign policy. Unfortunately, nothing in the entire history of the regime points in this direction. Whether the United States was a benevolent neighbor attempting to kill the revolution with kindness (and dollars) or a hovering giant threatening to fuel (or, in fact, stoking) the flames of counterrevolution, the *direction* of Nicaraguan society since 1979 has been invariable, inflexible, and unhesitating. At this point the only prop that remains to explain the regime's apparent lack of interest in being another Mexico (or Zimbabwe or Yugoslavia) has been the presence of a counterrevolutionary army and its support by the U.S. government. Should that element disappear from the scenario, through military defeat or the withdrawal of U.S. support or both, this interpretation will be shorn of its last justification; unless, of course, the regime *then* decides—for some reason yet unrevealed—to alter its revolutionary project.

The other possibility is that in the course of time the essentially Leninist nature of the Sandinista ideology will be revealed in Sandinista accomplishments. There still are elements on the Nicaraguan scene that allow one to question this interpretation—the lingering presence of a large private sector, for example—but the recent "state of emergency" and the closing of the independent daily newspaper *La Prensa* are depriving this interpretation of credibility. Exactly what this implies for U.S. policy (or that of Western Europe) is by no means clear, but it suggests that to the degree to which opposition within Nicaragua continues to exist, the nature of the regime will necessarily become more repressive, independent of the wishes or special metaphysical needs of outsiders. While that opposition may not be able to thwart the consolidation of a Marxist–Leninist regime, the facts of Nicaraguan society may ultimately deprive the Sandinista state of its hard-won place in the current pantheon of revolutionary utopias.

PART THREE

Regional Dimensions of the Crisis

• CHAPTER EIGHT •

Nicaragua and Its Neighbors

Mark Falcoff

Whatever one may think of its protagonists, goals, and performance, the Nicaraguan revolution of 1979 must be regarded as one of the two or three most important events in Central American history. It has introduced radically new and different political–military realities to the isthmus, altering forever Nicaragua's relationship with its immediate neighbors. By opting out of the U.S. sphere of influence and entering that of its adversaries, Cuba and the Soviet Union, the new Nicaraguan government has vastly raised the geopolitical stakes of what would otherwise be a purely local affair. In so doing, it has forced the other states of the Caribbean into roles for which they are ill prepared by history, resources, or political will.

The Context

By its very nature, an event of this importance could not be contained within the boundaries of a single state, even were its protagonists to wish it so. Central America is not merely a region but a divided nation, or, as some have suggested, an archipelago of "city-states."[1] The entire isthmus was governed from a single administrative center in Guatemala as early as 1570; it entered and left the independent Mexican Empire of Augustín de Iturbide

---

1. Roland H. Ebel, "The Development and Decline of the Central American City-State," in *Rift and Revolution: The Central American Imbroglio*, ed. Howard J. Wiarda (Washington, D.C.: American Enterprise Institute, 1984), pp. 70–104.

(1821–1823) together. For 14 years thereafter, it figured on world maps as the Central American Federation; and even after the dissolution of a common political authority in 1838, the dream of union persisted.[2]

Paradoxically, Central America's turbulent political history has added an element of regional cohesion of its own. During the nineteenth century, endemic conflict between rival clans, cities, or factions, organized into two contending political parties, made temporary exile a permanent feature of political life. Thus, many "liberals" or "conservatives," momentarily defeated by the fortunes of war, took refuge in neighboring states where their party was in the ascendant. The level of elite interpenetration thus became extremely strong; there were (and to some degree, remain) many binational families, with economic interests that mocked the (at times fictitious) political boundaries. The development of modern transportation and communication since World War II, which makes it possible to monitor each other's radio and television transmissions or travel from one capital to another in a day's time, has replicated the experience for merchants, farmers, small businessmen, political intellectuals, and to an increasing extent, even elements of the rural and urban poor. It is no exaggeration today to speak of a larger Central American community, however imperfectly articulated, in which major events tend to have a significant "spillover" effect.

Moreover, Central America is the site of the only successful effort at economic integration anywhere in the Third World. Counseled by the United Nations Economic Commission for Latin America (ECLA) and financed by the United States and the Inter-American Development Bank, the states[3] of Central America entered into a General Treaty of Economic Integration in 1960. During the ensuing decade, the volume of interregional trade grew from 6% to 24%; manufacturing as a share of gross national product (GNP) rose by 13%;[4] and 150,000 new jobs were created. A common tariff wall acted as an incentive to foreign investment in formerly imported manufactured goods, and in fact during the 1960s more than 1,400 firms, most of them American, were located in the region.[5]

Perhaps as significant was a host of new and specifically Central American institutions created to serve the Common Market community—a Central American Bank of Integration to provide credit to public and private

2. Thomas L. Karnes, *The Failure of Union: Central America, 1824–60* (Chapel Hill, N.C.: University of North Carolina Press, 1961).

3. El Salvador, Honduras, Guatemala, and Nicaragua; Costa Rica subscribed to the document in 1962.

4. In this Nicaragua was the clear leader, with 47% increase (Costa Rica and El Salvador, 30% each).

5. Gary W. Wynia, "Setting the Stage for Rebellion: Economics and Politics in Central America's Past," in Wiarda, *Rift and Revolution*, pp. 53–59.

enterprises and develop a common body of statistics; a think tank, the Center for Central American Economic Research (CIECA), to study macroeconomic trends; a Central American Monetary Council to coordinate different currencies; a Central American Defense Council (CONDECA); even a Central American Court of Human Rights. The insertion of transnational institutions in what had been essentially provincial capitals constituted a sharp break with the past. It undercut the narrowly bureaucratic and political vision of local bureaucracies and created a technocratic vanguard— cosmopolitan in training and outlook—with a broader sense of regional allegiance. These bodies constituted a serious effort at "horizontal" integration, more promising than the "vertical" (i.e., purely political) methods employed, without success, in the nineteenth century.

To be sure, even before the Nicaraguan revolution, the Common Market was experiencing serious difficulties. The unequal distribution of foreign investment produced strains between Honduras, on the one hand, and Nicaragua and Costa Rica, on the other; in 1971 it proved necessary to renegotiate agreements and fix quotas in the export of certain items. A war between El Salvador and Honduras in 1969 interrupted trade relations between those two countries for several years. The first oil shock of 1973 had devastating effects throughout the isthmus, raising energy costs and provoking a worldwide recession that drove down the prices of Central American exports. An earthquake that leveled most of the Nicaraguan capital in December 1972 deprived that country, and the region, of important industrial plants and set in motion events that led to civil war, foreign intervention, and a general climate of instability.

It is also true, as many critics of the Common Market experiment have hastened to point out, that its social and economic benefits were distributed in a highly asymmetrical fashion.[6] Yet, the relationship between this fact and the upheavals in Nicaragua and El Salvador in 1979 has yet to be established.[7] The point is somewhat academic in any event; whatever their cause,

---

6. Richard Feinberg and Robert A. Pastor, "Far from Hopeless: An Economic Program for Post-War Central America," in *Central America: Anatomy of Conflict*, ed. Robert S. Leiken (New York: Pergamon Press, 1984), pp. 193–218. It is perhaps worth noting, however, that in this particular analysis the authors point out that the inequalities were largely rural vs. urban rather than strictly across class lines.

7. Professor Wynia, who is not a conservative, confesses himself unsure whether "political conflict increased primarily because the economic pie did not grow as rapidly as planned, causing discontent leading to protest and conflict, or whether economic conditions were of only marginal importance to those people who had other things on their minds when they expressed themselves through violent protests in the late 1970s" (Wynia, "Setting the Stage," p. 62). I have suggested elsewhere that "Castro's revolution was entirely focused upon the overthrow of a hated dictator, as was the Sandinista revolution in Nicaragua two decades later; other agendas were revealed only later, and economic development, poverty, and social injustice hastily

the effect has been to sunder the fragile consensus on which all efforts toward integration and regional development had been based. The creation of a revolutionary state in the center of the isthmus has broken a crucial institutional link, driven massive amounts of local capital abroad, discouraged foreign investment, and turned the other four states essentially into welfare clients of the industrial states of the democratic world; since 1983, the United States alone has transferred $600 million to El Salvador, Costa Rica, and Honduras, inspired strictly by geopolitical considerations. Whether Washington can continue this policy indefinitely in the context of growing political and budgetary constraints remains to be seen; the harsh fact is, however, that without it, no Central American state will be fully viable in the short run. The ultimate solution must be found on the ground; whatever its failings, the Common Market experience demonstrated the possibility, and even the necessity, of economic integration. Yet it is equally true that any progress in this area requires a minimal degree of political coherence. The Sandinistas understand this as well as the governments of El Salvador, Honduras, and Costa Rica—it is, in fact, probably the only major issue on which they agree. But, evidently, the implications for Managua on the one hand and its neighbors on the other point in radically different directions.

"Revolutionary Internationalism"

Thus, quite apart from ideological considerations, there are imperatives that push the Sandinistas to extend the boundaries of their revolution to the entire Central American isthmus. Not that ideology is a negligible consideration.[8] As long ago as 1969 the Sandinista Front was calling for the "authentic unity" of Central America to "lead the way to coordinating the efforts to achieve national liberation,"[9] and its leaders have repeatedly emphasized

---

summoned to justify them *post hoc*."See my "Marxist–Leninist Regimes in Central America and the Caribbean," in *Third World Marxist–Leninist Regimes: Strengths, Vulnerabilities, and U.S. Policy*, ed.Uri Ra'anan et al. (Washington, D.C.: Institute for Foreign Policy Analysis/ Pergamon-Brassey's, 1985), p.51. For a Marxist "relative depravation" approach, see John Booth, "Toward Explaining Regional Crisis in Central America: Socioeconomic and Political Roots of Rebellion," paper, University of Texas, San Antonio.

8. An indispensable guide is David Nolan, *FSLN: The Ideology of the Sandinistas and the Nicaraguan Revolution* (Coral Gables: Institute of Inter-American Studies, University of Miami, 1984).

9. "Historic Program of the FSLN." (See Appendix B, p. 328.)

the principles of "revolutionary internationalism." Interior Minister Tomás Borge has frankly stated that "this revolution goes beyond our borders,"[10] and his colleague Comandante Bayardo Arce has affirmed that "we cannot cease being internationalists unless we cease being revolutionaries."[11] Are these merely rhetorical flourishes, as some Western journalists, academics, and political figures often suggest? Even the Sandinistas do not fully claim that they are. For example, when asked by a Venezuelan magazine to comment on charges that the Sandinistas had provided arms to the insurgents in El Salvador, Interior Minister Borge coyly remarked,

> They say [this], but they have not offered any real proof. But let us suppose that weapons have reached El Salvador from here. That is possible. More than that, it is possible that Nicaraguan combatants have gone to El Salvador, but this cannot be blamed on any decision of ours.[12]

The matter need not be settled by weighing quotations against one another. By now there is a vast amount of concrete information on Sandinista military, paramilitary, and espionage activities thoughout the region, derived from defectors, aerial photographs, intercepted shipments, the identification of safe houses, and the capture of documents.[13] Although the precise flow is not always easy to establish, the overall patterns themselves are unambiguous. They show, in the first place, that by mid-1980 the Sandinistas had developed an apparatus to sustain regionwide guerrilla operations and give them political as well as military support.

In particular, two new organizations were created in Managua: the International Relations Directorate of the FSLN (DRI), modeled on the Americas Department of the Cuban Communist party, which provides administra tive support for military trainees from other Central American countries; and the Fifth Directorate of Intelligence (DSGE), which provides opera-

10. Foreign Broadcast Information Service (Latin America), July 21, 1981. Hereinafter cited as *FBIS*—LAM.

11. U.S. Department of State, *Comandante Bayardo Arce's Secret Speech before the Nicaraguan Socialist Party (PSN)*, Publication 9422, Inter-American Series 118 (Washington, D.C., March, 1985), p. 4, translated from the text published in *La Vanguardia* (Barcelona), August 23, 1984.

12. *Bohemia* (Caracas), April 20–26, 1981.

13. Much of this is summarized in U.S. Department of State, *Revolution Beyond Our Borders: Sandinista Intervention in Central America*, Special Report 132 (September 1985). Of particular interest is the State Department's White Paper on El Salvador, *Communist Interference in El Salvador*, Special Report 80, with accompanying documentary appendix, not only for the materials it contains, but for the campaign of disinformation that attempted to discredit it. With reference to the latter, see my "The El Salvador White Paper and Its Critics," *AEI Foreign Policy and Defense Review* 4, no. 2 (1982).

tives and the liaison necessary to maintain the clandestine links and support
networks for regional guerrilla activities. The Sandinistas have also taken
over part of the Cuban role in mediating between rival guerrilla groups—in
this case, in Guatemala and Honduras.

The principal target has been El Salvador, whose own political and
military institutions were in a clear state of crisis in 1979–1980.[14] During the
second half of 1980, when the collapse of the Salvadoran civil–military junta
was expected almost momentarily, Managua became the headquarters of
the Salvadoran Unified Revolutionary Directorate (DRU). According to
one captured document, the Nicaraguans promised to provide the directorate with "all measures of security" and were "disposed to contribute in
material terms," assuming "the cause of El Salvador as its own."[15]

Between mid-1980 and January 1981, all guerrilla efforts in El Salvador
(and Nicaraguan support efforts) were aimed at a "general offensive" that
was expected to bring down the government and present the new Reagan
administration in Washington with a fait accompli. As Eastern bloc weaponry poured into Nicaragua, the Sandinistas transferred Western arms to the
Salvadoran guerrillas through a series of clandestine air, land, and sea
routes. By December 1980, guerrillas in El Salvador were using weapons
never before seen in that country, including M-16 rifles and M-79 grenade
launchers. After the failure of the "final offensive," the Salvadoran revolutionaries switched to a tactic of "prolonged war," concentrating on the
destruction of that country's economic infrastructure.

Though the damage has been devastating, the gradual consolidation of an
open political order and the professionalization of the Salvadoran army has
led to a reduction in the number of guerrilla fighters, now estimated at
approximately two-thirds the level of 1983. The Nicaraguan role has shifted
slightly to take into account the changed circumstances on the ground; while
Managua is still a source of arms, its major activities are centered in training
and maintenance, as well as providing a backup system of logistics, radio
communication, and political direction, particularly since the DRU relocated its headquarters in Salvador's Morazán province in 1983.

Honduras has the next-to-the-smallest population and is the poorest and
most backward country of Central America; for these reasons, it is not a
particularly propitious place for the development of an active revolutionary

14. Indeed, some long-time observers of the Salvadoran and Nicaraguan guerrilla move-
ments frankly expected El Salvador to fall before Nicaragua, and so, apparently, did the
Sandinistas. Neither foresaw the peculiar role that the United States would play in the fall of
Somoza, or its reluctance to act forcefully immediately thereafter.

15. "Informe de Eduardo/Viaje de 5 de Mayo al 8 de Junio, 1980," Document D, in U.S.
Department of State, *Communist Interference in El Salvador: Documents Demonstrating
Communist Support of the Salvadoran Insurgency* (February 23, 1981).

movement.[16] Its importance for the Sandinistas lies in its geographical location, since it possesses what Nicaragua clearly lacks—a common border with El Salvador and Guatemala, where insurgent opportunities are deemed to be greater. Thus, in January 1981 a truck bound for Guatemala was intercepted and discovered to be transporting arms originally shipped from Nicaragua (some of whose serial numbers matched those lost by the U.S. Army in Vietnam).[17] There is also a strong presumption that Nicaraguan arms captured several months later in Guatemala City had been trans-shipped through Honduras. For his part, a defector from the Honduran Popular Liberation Force (FPL) told authorities in April, 1985 that his organization had regularly brought military supplies overland from Nicara-gua to Tegucigalpa, and thence to the Chalatenango Department in north-ern El Salvador. He added that the shipments had been notably reduced in size in recent years so as to minimize the chances of discovery.[18]

By its very existence as a Central American social democracy, Costa Rica represents a permanent ideological challenge to the Sandinistas, with whom relations, not surprisingly, have been steadily deteriorating since the latter's assumption of power in 1979. A special investigating commission of the Costa Rican parliament found that immediately after the fall of Somoza (and extending through 1981), weapons originally meant for Nicaragua were abruptly redirected to El Salvador by Cuban and FSLN operatives, in conjunction with corrupt functionaries of the Costa Rican government. The commission also discovered, much to its disquiet, that over 2,000 firearms had disappeared from state arsenals, and in March 1982 Costa Rican secu-rity forces uncovered a safehouse with 175 weapons, including 70 M-16s, half of which correspond to the serial numbers of weapons lost by American forces in Vietnam.

The orthodox Costa Rican Communist party, known as the Party of the Popular Vanguard (PVP), was active in the Nicaraguan civil war to the extent of fielding several hundred combatants. Many remain in Nicaragua and provide paramilitary training for revolutionary compatriots; they also carry on military operations on the so-called southern front, where the followers

16. The Sandinistas have, in fact, been advising Honduran leftist groups, and made serious efforts to unify them after 1980. On the other hand, the available evidence suggests that at present these people are given the task of assisting revolutionary movements in other countries rather than attempting a direct assault against the Honduran government at this time.

17. ACAN-EFE dispatch form Tegucigalpa, January 21, 1981 (*FBIS*—LAM), January 22, 1981. For the issue of matching serial numbers, see "*Revolution Beyond Our Borders*," Appendix 5.

18. "Salvadoran Rebels Change Tactics," *Washington Post*, May 17, 1985; "New Sources Describe Aid to Salvadoran Guerrillas," *Washington Post*, June 8, 1985. Compare "A Former Salvadoran Rebel Chief Tells of Arms from Nicaragua," *New York Times*, July 12, 1984.

of Edén Pastora (Comandante Cero)—mostly former partisans of the FSLN who have become disaffected with its Marxist—Leninist direction—are waging a guerrilla war of their own against the Sandinista regime. Police intelligence has linked the recent outbreak of terrorist incidents in Costa Rica to foreign (i.e., Nicaraguan) sources of support.[19]

There is considerable speculation on the extent of the "internationalist" reach of the Sandinista regime. Several facts are known.[20] Managua has become a haven for revolutionaries from other Latin American countries, including the Chilean MIR and the Argentine ERP, many of whom have moved from Havana to have easier access to Western travel and support groups in Mexico, Western Europe, and the United States. Mario Firmenich, the leader of the Argentine Montoneros, was in residence in Managua before moving to Brazil, whence he was subsequently extradited. A recent incident in Colombia involving the spectacular armed seizure of the Palace of Justice in Bogotá and the murder of that country's minister of justice by the M-19 guerrilla movement has been traced to Sandinista weapons support. This put the Colombian government in a particularly embarrassing situation, particularly vis-à-vis the United States, with whom it had loudly differed on the nature of the Sandinista regime and the danger it represented for the region. Far from attempting to relieve the discomfort of President Belisario Betancur, the Sandinistas all but acknowledged their role in the affair. Interior Minister Borge even fulsomely attended a memorial service in Managua commemorating the "martyrdom" of those insurgents who lost their lives in Bogotá.[21]

Implications for Regional Stability

No single country or cause is responsible for instability in Central America, but it is impossible to discount the profoundly disequilibrating impact that the advent of a new regime in Managua has had on the regional military balance. As early as December 1980, the new Popular Sandinista Army had reached twice the size of Somoza's National Guard at the peak of the 1978-1979 civil war, and it doubled in size again by the end of 1982. By 1984 it

19. República de Costa Rica, Ministerio de Relaciones Exteriores, *Calendario de incidentes entre el gobierno de Costa Rica y el gobierno de Nicaragua* [Calendar of Incidents between the Costa Rican Government and the Government of Nicaragua] (February 1985).

20. Juan O. Tamayo, "Sandinistas Attract a Who's Who of Terrorists" and "From Italy to the PLO, World's Leftists Find Haven in Nicaragua," *Miami Herald*, March 3, 1985.

21. For information on the palace incident, see *Keesings Contemporary Archives*, no. 2 (1986): 34152−34154; and *Facts on File* (1986), p. 948. The funeral service and the Colombian protest are documented in *FBIS*—Latin America, January 6 and 8, 1986.

had reached 61,800, with another 50,000 paramilitary or reserve troops, a force larger than all the other armed forces of the isthmus combined.[22] Though Sandinista spokesmen and their apologists often credit this development to the existence of a counterrevolutionary army supported by the United States, the latter came into existence only in March 1981 and, according to Nicaraguan official sources, did not constitute a serious military threat until late in the following year.[23]

The purpose of this army is not, evidently, to invade neighboring countries but to provide a shield behind which "revolutionary internationalism" can be pursued with impunity.[24] In response, since 1980 the United States has sent vast amounts of economic and military assistance to El Salvador, as well as a training mission of 55 officers and men to improve the professional standards of its armed forces. At the same time, to reassure Honduras (and to provide a psychological and military counterweight to Nicaraguan preponderance), some 900 American soldiers and National Guardsmen (expanded during periods of joint military exercises to as many as 6,000) have been stationed in camps on its Nicaraguan border.

The longer-term impact of both policies may be counterproductive. El Salvador has become addicted to large infusions of U.S. resources and therefore must of necessity have mixed feelings about an expeditious conclusion to its own guerrilla war. Moreover, the qualitative improvements in its defense establishment, made under U.S. auspices, have introduced a whole new series of strains in El Salvador's perennially problematic relationship with Honduras. Meanwhile, any government in Tegucigalpa must necessarily be concerned with the eventual impact of so large a U.S. military presence and the use of its territory by armed opponents of the Nicaraguan government, who operate from Honduran bases.

Costa Rica is in the unenviable position of being caught between its fear and dislike of the Sandinistas and an overpowering urge to remain neutral in the battle between Nicaragua and the United States, a conflict for which—lacking a fortified frontier or an army to defend it—it is singularly ill prepared. On the one hand, all Costa Rican governments historically have been anti-Nicaraguan. Somoza's frequent meddling in Costa Rican politics intensified the feeling and led the government of Rodrigo Carazo to connive actively at the dictator's overthrow. The Costa Rican contribution to the

---

22. These figures from Institute of Strategic Studies, *The Military Balance* (London, 1977, and subsequent editions).

23. *Contrarevolución: desarollo y consecuencias, datos básicos, 1980–1985* [Counterrevolution: Development and Consequences, Basic Data, 1980–1985] (Managua: n.p., 1985).

24. It also provides an excellent instrument for the coercion of the Nicaraguan population and the consolidation of a strongly authoritarian political regime.

Sandinista cause was, in fact, larger than that of the Cubans, since Costa Rica lent the FSLN some 26 kilometers of territory on their Pacific corridor from which to launch raids on their homeland, and, as noted, Costa Rican authorities, some at considerable personal financial advantage, were actively involved in gun-running. The nasty turn of events in Nicaragua—in which those political forces most nearly compatible with the political culture of Costa Rica have been driven underground, into exile,or silenced—has revived the historic antagonism, this time with a sharp ideological and geostrategic cutting edge.

On the other hand, no Costa Rican government can afford the luxury of getting too far out front on the Nicaraguan issue. For one thing, it forfeits a certain legitimacy within the Latin American political community, particularly in nations far from Central America, where the "antiimperialist" dimension of the Nicaraguan–U.S. confrontation is its most salient (at times, its only) feature. For another, it undercuts efforts to obtain diplomatic and economic support in Western Europe, where the parties of the Socialist International have demonstrated a clear fascination with (not to say preference for) the Sandinista experiment, notwithstanding the fact that it is Costa Rica, not Nicaragua, that is ruled by a Social Democratic party and pursues goals fully compatible with its European analogues. Finally, there is a persistent fear of being abandoned by the United States, not illogical in the light of recent history, and intensified by the lack of consensus within the U.S. Congress, press, and public over the importance of Central America and the propriety of the Reagan administration's policies there. The Costa Rican agenda is therefore complicated almost beyond measure—to distance itself from Washington politically and diplomatically as much as possible, yet somehow continue to draw vast resources from the United States by pointing to the Sandinista peril just across the border.[25]

No discussion of threats to the stability of the region would be complete without some consideration of the anti-Sandinista forces known collectively under the name *contras* (though "dissidents" or "insurgents" would do just as well). In the conventional view of Western Europe, Latin America, and the United States, these are ex-functionaries of the Somoza regime, particularly ex-officers of the infamous National Guard, who are fighting to restore their privileges—a "White Army" much like the one that attempted to

25. This game was played masterfully by President Luis Alberto Monge (1982–1986), but his successor, Oscar Arias, seems to have tilted the balance so far in one direction as seriously to endanger its continuance. In effect, by publicly opposing U.S. aid to anti-Sandinista rebels, he has raised the question whether there is really a "problem" in Central America, and if so, whether Costa Rica really needs all the aid it is receiving. For the fact remains that in Central America, as almost everywhere else, U.S. aid policies are basically security-driven.

strangle the Soviet Union at its inception in 1919–1920.[26] The Reagan administration and its supporters prefer to call them "freedom fighters," placing them in the same ideological category as the Afghan guerrillas or the Solidarity movement in Poland. As Robert Leiken has shown,[27] both versions blur some major distinctions.

The anti-Sandinista insurgency unites a number of different political strands, past and present. The FDN (Nicaraguan Democratic Forces), led by Adolfo Calero, is officered by many ex-Guardsmen and has strong ties with some former functionaries and supporters of Somoza, although it is also true that Calero himself and a number of his collaborators have a long history of anti-Somoza activity. Another movement, BOS, formerly led by Edén Pastora, is made up almost entirely of disillusioned ex-Sandinistas; Pastora himself was (and remains) the most popular hero of the war against Somoza. The civilian political directorate, UNO [Nicaraguan Opposition Unity], is a triad in which Calero ostensibly shares power with Alfonso Robelo and Arturo Cruz, two civilians of indisputably democratic antecedents, both of whom participated in the first Sandinista government.

The presence of former Somocistas in the anti-Sandinista coalition is not a particularly devastating fact, since many functionaries of the current Nicaraguan government, including its present foreign minister, share the same disability. The difficulty lies in the fact that there is no genuine power sharing among the big three of UNO: Calero dominates the entire operation because of the apparently unqualified support he enjoys from the Reagan White House and the conservative funding community in the United States and elsewhere, and he seems ill disposed to share control of the movement with those colleagues who could give it greater credibility in democratic circles abroad. But one fact remains indisputable: It is not ex-Guardsmen or millionaire exiles who are doing the fighting and dying, but peasants, small shopkeepers, and Miskito Indians—some 12,000 of them, roughly three to four times the number of insurgents who took up arms against Somoza at the height of the 1978–1979 civil war.

While the insurgency was "created" by the Central Intelligence Agency (CIA) in March 1981, for its first 18 months of existence it was so negligible a factor that the Sandinistas themselves poked fun at it.[28] It has grown in spite of everything the CIA, Calero, and his friends have done to render it a

26. Leonard Schapiro, *The Russian Revolution of 1917: The Origins of Modern Communism* (New York: Basic Books, 1984), demonstrates that the Whites were by no means as reactionary as the liberal and left press in the West suggested at the time. The story has some interesting parallels with the current situation in Nicaragua.

27. "The Battle for Nicaragua," *New York Review of Books*, March 13, 1986.

28. Shirley Christian, *Revolution in the Family* (New York: Random House, 1985), pp. 193–202.

failure: It has overcome poor leadership, mismanagement, lack of a steady funding source, and an indifferent political commitment by the United States to become an undeniable social and political reality. This fact can be explained only as an almost organic reaction to the repressive policies of the Nicaraguan government, particularly its treatment of Indian minorities on the country's Atlantic Coast.

Insurgent activities on Nicaragua's northern and southern borders could hardly be regarded as contributing to regional stability. But their real significance cannot be understood by focusing on them alone. In the larger context of Managua's own activities, they tend to balance things out, compelling the Sandinistas to concentrate their efforts on matters other than the subversion of their neighbors. This explains why, although neither Honduras nor Costa Rica will officially admit that the FDN or BOS, respectively, operate from their territories, they place no insuperable barrier in their way. On the other hand, rebel operations from bases on the border also expose the two—especially Honduras—to Nicaraguan military incursions and underscore the necessity of a permanent U.S. military presence in the area.

Further, to speak of the Nicaraguan insurgents as a purely exogenous phenomenon ignores the fundamental political question. These people are part of the Nicaraguan community and as such have a right to participate in its public life. The Sandinista refusal to regard them as legitimate interlocutors in any negotiation assures that the civil war will continue indefinitely— at least until one side prevails. In this context, suspension of U.S. aid to the rebels will merely eliminate the need for negotiations, or will render them so one-sided as to lose all meaning.

It is nonetheless true that in the present context the Nicaraguan insurgents represent an extension of U.S. power. As such, they necessarily embody the potential for a qualitative escalation of the conflict. As critics in the United States often argue, if the Congress unambiguously lends its prestige, support, and credibility to the *contra* operation, it will have no choice but to send in American troops if the latter fail to obtain their ultimate objective, which most take to be the overthrow of the Sandinista regime. Actually, American foreign policy rarely pursues such linear logic, but even if the statement were literally true, it would amount to nothing more than an acknowledgment that all political–military commitments have costs, some of which cannot be immediately foreseen or, if foreseen, cannot be avoided altogether.[29] Moreover, since the Sandinistas have invited the Cubans, Soviets, and Eastern bloc nations into their country and

29. If most Americans were actually to think through exactly what their membership in NATO *could* involve under certain circumstances, the United States, not Scandinavia, Holland, or Britain, would have the largest unilateralist movement in the West.

accepted from them armaments of a kind never before seen in the region, the countervailing U.S. role can be regarded as essentially "restabilizing," though at a higher level.

The Role of the United States

Though the United States is no longer "hegemonic" in Central America, at least in the sense in which it once was, it remains the most important foreign power in the region. This is certainly not what many Central Americans have wished, but recent history has demonstrated that there are no acceptable alternatives. No other power or combination of powers is able (or at least willing) to offer the same credits, technical assistance, military protection, and cultural innovations—certainly not the European Economic Community or the Socialist International. This leaves the Central Americans with only two options: either ally themselves with the Soviet bloc, as Cuba and Nicaragua have done, at a cost that is prohibitively high in all areas but military and police assistance, or try to widen the margins of autonomy by balancing off U.S. preponderance with economic aid from nontraditional sources (the multilateral lending institutions, other Latin American countries, or the European Economic Community). As Costa Rica demonstrates, this may require some extremely nimble posturing on regional political issues.[30] It remains to be seen whether what are really rather precarious U.S. commitments can endure such serious ideological strains.

The still overwhelming U.S. presence in Central America, particularly in Honduras and El Salvador, masks a fundamental fact about the region: American interest there has been declining steadily for several decades, and there is no consensus on the region's strategic or political importance. Most of the American agribusinesses have withdrawn or drastically cut back their operations, as have multinationals who invested in manufacturing enterprises during the heyday of the Common Market, and no one expects that pattern to reverse for the rest of the century. Paradoxically, at this point, the area's chief value to the United States is its role in the East–West struggle, and those who seek to remove it from that context automatically undercut its only claim to serious attention in Washington.[31]

30. For example, President Vinicio Cerezo of Guatemala, who came to Washington in December 1985 (prior to assuming office) with a request for $130 million aid, nonetheless pointedly refused to support the Reagan administration's position on Nicaragua.

31. Interestingly, the very members of the U.S. Congress who insist that the region's fundamental problem is not communism but poverty nonetheless seem singulary reluctant to address themselves to the purely economic dimensions of the Kissinger Commission report, which recommended an $8 billion aid-and-trade package over a 5-year period.

The domestic debate about Central America in the U.S. Congress is not, of course, about Central America at all, but one more installation in a long-standing and increasingly bitter conflict over the nature (or even existence) of Soviet expansionism, over the significance of Marxist revolutions in the Third World, and over the acceptable costs of U.S. involvement in violent situations overseas.[32] In a sense, the Sandinista regime is perhaps the final beneficiary of what is called the Vietnam syndrome, which while in evident remission, still pervades the majority party, the literary—intellectual community, the universities, the press, the mainstream Protestant denominations, and important segments of the Roman Catholic Church. Though these parties publicly favor a negotiated settlement in Central America, their real purpose is to achieve a dignified withdrawal of the United States from the region altogether, not so much because they favor the Sandinistas (although some of them clearly do), as because they wish to exempt the American people from any responsibility for (or inconvenience from) whatever unfortunate events may occur there in the future. As George Will recently remarked, "Multilateralism is the isolationism which dare not speak its name." It remains true, however, that without the participation of the United States, even a cosmetic solution of this kind is impossible.

The Contadora Phenomenon

The absence of a clear alternative between the policies of the Reagan administration, on the one hand, and the Sandinistas, on the other, has forced the larger subregional powers to create one. Thus, in 1983 Mexico, Venezuela, Colombia, and Panama launched the Contadora initiative, whose purpose is to achieve a negotiated solution to the problems provoked by the Nicaraguan revolution in Central America and the surrounding Caribbean. Some observers have described Contadora as a thinly veiled effort to restrain the United States from invading Nicaragua while other means are found to iron out the differences between Managua and Washington.[33] Contadora could just as easily be regarded either as a device to grant the Nicaraguan government additional time to consolidate a full-blown Marxist—Leninist state (at which point the United States would be powerless to do anything about it) or, conversely, to permit the United States to bleed the Sandinistas to death

---

32. Mark Falcoff, "The Apple of Discord: Central America in U.S. Domestic Politics," in Wiarda, *Rift and Revolution*, pp. 360–378.

33. Tom Farer, "Contadora: The Hidden Agenda," *Foreign Policy*, no. 59 (Summer 1985): 59–72.

while the Latin America governments look on complacently. At a minimum, Contadora has allowed the sponsoring states (and a larger group of Latin American nations who have joined the so-called support group) to distance themselves from Washington without necessarily siding with Managua. And for American politicians who oppose the Reagan administration's policies but do not wish to be seen as favoring communism in Central America, Contadora provides a convenient, apparently painless alternative. The only thing Contadora cannot provide is a definitive solution to *Central America's* problems; it resembles an airplane that can stay in the air indefinitely but that loses its wings and engines the moment it attempts to land.

This is so because Contadora is shot through with acute structural contradictions.[34] The sponsoring parties represent widely different political systems and international orientations. Mexico is a one-party authoritarian state at home, with a social structure that is more inegalitarian than that of any Central American country. Nonetheless, its foreign policy is consistently pro-Cuban and pro-Sandinista and predictably anti-American on everything from UNESCO to arms control, but especially on all matters relating to inter-American security. Venezuela has the strongest democratic political system in the region, and important personal and party ties to many Central American leaders. It has also experienced a Cuban-sponsored guerrilla movement of its own and is genuinely disturbed over the intromission of Eastern bloc forces, advisers, and intelligence agents in Nicaragua. Panama is an unstable political community in which power alternates somewhat unpredictably between the military, the business community, and an unscrupulous political class, in no apparent order, and thus lacks the coherence to project a foreign policy of any sort. Colombia is a highly conservative Latin American society with a stable two-party system that is more democratic in form than content, but that also faces two serious guerrilla movements at home and thus has sought to buy insurance from the Cubans by distancing itself from the United States, much as many believe the Mexicans have done. Thus what would be an acceptable settlement for Mexico quite obviously would not be for Venezuela; nor could the United States share the Colombian appreciation, recently expressed by its foreign minister, that "a bad treaty is better than none at all,"[35] unless, again, the entire purpose of the exercise is to find a graceful way for the United States to withdraw, letting other matters take their "natural" course.

---

34. The analysis here draws upon Susan Kaufmann Purcell, "Demystifying Contadora," *Foreign Affairs*, Fall 1985, pp. 74–95; and Everett A. Bauman, "The Strengths and Weaknesses of Contadora as Regional Diplomacy in the Caribbean Basin," Working Paper 167. Wilson Center, Smithsonian Institution, Latin American Program.

35. *El Tiempo* (Bogotá), February 11, 1986.

The essential documents of the Contadora group do not point in any coherent direction but embrace a wide range of desirable outcomes without specifying how mutually exclusive imperatives can somehow be reconciled.[36] Thus the Cancún document (1983) proposes both national reconciliation and repluralization for Nicaragua, without, however, violating the principle of self-determination and nonintervention. The Sandinistas are fascinated with the withdrawal of foreign military bases in the region (*read*, Honduras), but less so with foreign military advisers (*read*, Nicaragua). Conversely, the United States has no real reason to object to any of the 21 objectives enunciated by Contadora, provided that the Nicaraguan government change its essential nature. Indeed, were the regime in Managua to cut its special ties with the Eastern bloc and respect political pluralism at home—as in fact it promised the Organization of American States at its inception in 1979—there would be no reason for the U.S. military presence in Honduras, and a good argument could be made for drawing down its commitment to El Salvador.

At this point, however, the only conceivable compromise that Contadora might extract from the Sandinistas would be a promise to respect the independence of their neighbors—with or without appropriate alterations in the Cuban, Soviet, East German, and Bulgarian military and intelligence presence; discounting altogether the internal dynamics of any revolutionary Marxist regime that inevitably turn it outward and everything the Sandinistas have done and said about the political order in neighboring states. It also requires one to pass rather lightly over the politically nettlesome problems of verification and control.[37] In effect, this would constitute a Central American Yalta, but with the very important difference that there would be no Central American NATO to make sure that the lines of the treaty stay frozen.

A final obstacle to a Contadora-based solution—one that is often overlooked by commentators—is a serious lack of confidence in its sponsoring powers by the countries most heavily affected, namely, Nicaragua's Central American neighbors. Except for Mexico, whose regional pretensions are heartily resented in Guatemala, none of the Contadora Four have much of a history of involvement in the isthmus. Apart from oil and political advice (some of it no doubt excellent), they have little to offer these republics over

36. Mark Falcoff, "Regional Diplomatic Options in Central America", *AEI Foreign Policy and Defense Review* 5, no. 1 (1983): 54–61.

37. At recent meetings of the Contadora Four and its so-called Support Group of South American nations, some attention has been given to this topic, but the participants are still very far from agreeing on precisely what these mechanisms should be. Of course, even if they could be decided upon, they would be useless in the absence of a firm political will to levy sanctions where necessary.

the longer term and are unlikely to sustain a serious level of interest and commitment once the Untied States (and presumably other extrahemispheric parties) has withdrawn. Put baldly, there are no compelling reasons for the Central Americans to entrust their future to an artificial sovereignty of limited resources and indeterminate political will. This, and not U.S. pressure as such, explains the reticence with which they habitually treat Contadora-based prescriptions.

Conclusions

One of the essential elements of a regional solution to any political problem is a minimal consensus on a desired outcome. This is just what is clearly lacking in Nicaragua. Between the Sandinista regime and its neighbors there are irreconcilable political differences, reflected in (but not wholly due to) their relationship to the United States on the one hand, and Cuba and the Soviet bloc on the other. The notion of Nicaragua as an "ordinary state" that merely happens to prefer Marxism as a form of political and economic organization, an option that need not be relevant to its day-to-day relations with its neighbors, is simply not a possibility. Least of all would the Sandinistas wish an outcome of this sort, however often they say that they would, in an effort to assist their foreign apologists and disarm their foreign critics.

Moreover, outsiders—in this instance, the Contadora nations—cannot assist in a settlement if they do not agree on whether there is a problem or whether the problem is really the United States rather than Nicaragua and *its* allies. While no doubt most members and supporters of the Contadora group sincerely wish the Soviet Union and Cuba to withdraw their military and intelligence presence from Nicaragua, they proceed as if the real problem is the United States. The unspoken presumption is that an American withdrawal would automatically spark a corresponding gesture on the part of the other side, when, in fact, just about the opposite is the case. As long as these illusions persist, what should be a regional problem will continue to function within a much larger geopolitical context.

None of this is intended to suggest that the United States is of one mind on the Nicaraguan question—far from it. Much of the uncertainty and incoherence surrounding American policy, particularly the justifications summoned to support it, are due precisely to a divided public that cannot decide whether Central America is important enough to bother about and, if it is, what price is worth paying. The United States is part of the region whether it wills it or not, however, and whatever decision it finally takes, including that of withdrawal, will have a profound and enduring impact.

• CHAPTER NINE •

Contadora: A Next Phase?

Esperanza Durán

Events in Central America move at a rapid pace and their general trend is unclear, but they seem not to amount to any systematic improvement in the regional situation. The triumph of the Sandinista revolution in Nicaragua introduced into the region what some regarded as the threat of yet another base in the Western Hemisphere for Soviet designs. Furthermore, many fear that increasing instability in Central America might spill over and lead to a major revolutionary upheaval of regional proportions, from which not even the hegemonic power, the United States, would escape. At the same time, the United States has reacted to the Nicaraguan threat with a policy that, in the view of its Latin American neighbors, brings closer the possibility of armed intervention and the escalation of the conflict to wider regional or even global proportions. In order to try to avoid this outcome four Latin American countries—Mexico, Panama, Colombia, and Venezuela—met on the island of Contadora (in the Gulf of Panama) in January 1983 to launch a major peace initiative to find a negotiated solution to the Central American crisis.[1] To this end, the Contadora countries left behind their differences,

1. There is now a relatively large body of literature on the Contadora process, from both the Latin American and U.S. perspectives. See René Herrera Zúñiga and Manuel Chavarria, "México en Contadora: una búsqueda de límites a su compromiso en Centroamérica [Mexico in Contadora: A Search For the Limits of its Commitments in Central America]," *Foro Internacional* 24, no. 4 (April–June 1984): 458–483; Esperanza Durán, "The Contadora Approach to Peace in Central America," *World Today* 40, nos. 8–9 (August–September 1984): 347–354; Fernando Cepeda Ulloa and Rodrigo Pardo García-Peña, eds., *Contadora: Desafío a la diplomacia tradicional* [Contadora: A Challenge to Traditional Diplomacy] (Bogotá: Editorial La Oveja Negra, 1985); Tom Farer, "Contadora, The Hidden Agenda," *Foreign Policy*,

not least in the field of foreign policy and in their relation to their senior partner, the United States, to coalesce in an important diplomatic effort to defuse a potentially explosive situation. And they did so, it should be added, independently of the United States, which was neither consulted on the launching of the initiative nor included in it.

To have left the U.S., a major actor in the region, outside the negotiations appears, particularly with hindsight, to have been naive and unrealistic, if a truly lasting peace was the main objective. Nevertheless it was consistent with, and perhaps a consequence of, the new mood of self-assertion in Latin America and increased political independence from the U.S. Equally important, as was recognized by the Contadora countries themselves, another key actor in the Central American drama was Cuba (and hence the Soviet Union), and a mechanism for consultation with Cuba also was not devised. However, given the low profile that Cuba has maintained since the invasion of Grenada, this chapter will focus on the more prominent of these excluded actors: the United States. Despite these omissions or limitations, the exploration of the means to achieve a regional blueprint that could eventually obtain the support of the Central American countries and the United States, and find accommodation for the Nicaraguan objectives of independent development with social justice, was a legitimate search, which at the outset presented reasonable chances of success.

Today the situation seems to have reached a stalemate. The Contadora process has exhausted itself through negotiations, and after countless deadlines, never met, for the signing of a regional peace treaty. The last one, of June 6, 1986, passed without any major hint at the eventual achievement of a compromise, and the process is moribund. Harsh political realities have eroded well-intentioned aims. What will happen is uncertain. Contadora may dissolve itself, as its member countries have hinted will happen if forward steps are not taken by the parties involved; or the process may be allowed to drag on indefinitely. To be sure, either outcome is just as negative. The termination of the Contadora process would leave a dangerous vacuum and heighten the possibilities for open conflict. The alternative, with negotiations going on and enthusiasm continuing to wane, would be a relatively lesser evil, as a means to contain the intensification of the conflict, but essentially just as disappointing. It must be admitted that the prospects for success within the Contadora formula seem increasingly remote. Instead of solving the crisis, Contadora may end up institutionalizing it.

A major injection of fresh air into the process is badly needed if it is to survive and turn into a useful mechanism for achieving negotiated solutions.

---

no. 59 (Summer 1985): 59–72; and Susan Kaufman Purcell, "Demystifying Contadora," *Foreign Affairs* 64, no. 1 (Fall 1985): 74–95.

Contadora has provided a valuable framework. Some of the central issues have been addressed, and in a sense successfully, attracting a large measure of agreement between the parties involved. And, perhaps most important, the minimum service Contadora is widely credited to have rendered has been to defuse tensions by providing, if not hope for a solution, at least a forum for dialogue. Finally, it has served as a catalyst for furthering the cause of Latin American solidarity.

But, without denying any of the above, our focus at this juncture must be on the very major weakness Contadora has had, which now stands in its way as an inexorably deep obstacle: It has unrealistically attempted to solve *part* of the overall conflict, focusing on relations between the Central American states alone, to the exclusion—aside from lip-service clauses in formal proposals—of the true source of the problem, which is Nicaraguan and Central American relations with the United States and the Eastern bloc. This latter omission is not only central per se but also precludes real progress even on the more limited agenda Contadora has set for itself.

There seem to be a number of specific obstacles that Contadora cannot overcome, all of which can be traced back to the above deficiency. On the part of the Central American countries there is the widespread concern that the FSLN regime is threatening the stability of the area by its display of an increasingly large military apparatus. In this same vein, Nicaragua's relations with El Salvador, Honduras, and Guatemala deteriorated early on in the game because Nicaragua seemed bent on exporting its revolution, a suspicion that has been allayed with time. Managua, on its part, has justified its military buildup as a response to the U.S.-backed *contras*, who are waging a limited war to destabilize the FSLN regime. Nicaragua refuses to disarm itself unless and until the United States withdraws its support for the *contras*. The U.S. position is that it will continue to lend this support unless Nicaragua disarms itself and opens a dialogue with the opposition in exile. In view of this mutual distrust and the intransigence on both sides it is not difficult to see why the Contadora efforts have failed. It is also clear that the way to break the impasse is to widen the reach of Contadora's negotiations. Broadening the base of Contadora seems a *sine qua non* condition if a negotiated solution is to be viable.

The purpose of this essay is to speculate on the possibilities in this direction, seeking to ascertain and identify the main obstacles to real progress as perceived by the various sides to the conflict, particularly Nicaragua and the United States. But first, and to this end, the main areas where progress has occurred and how it was achieved must be examined; then we must ask what impediments there are to a negotiated settlement of the regional problems.

As is clear and often argued, any review of events since Contadora's

inception brings out the manifest contradictions that have never been eliminated between Contadora's aims and expectations on the role and participation of the United States in the process, on the one hand, and the policies
and actions followed by the Reagan administration in Central America, on
the other. Some have blamed these contradictions alone for the failure of
Contadora. No doubt selected evidence accumulated throughout Contadora's
existence would lend support to this contention. But a more important
obstacle in the way of Contadora's fuller success has been its lack of preci-
sion in defining suitable political and military arrangements that would
guarantee regional security. The first section of this essay seeks to highlight
these problems. The second and third sections examine another kind of
obstacle to the success of a negotiated settlement: the relations between the
Central American countries themselves, and the position of the United
States regarding its strategic concern for the region and its response to
security threats. The last section attempts to recapitulate and assess the
whole process of negotiations and speculates on the future of Contadora.

Contadora: A Review of Developments

During its first year in existence the Contadora group sought to establish
a process of mediation that would ease tensions in the area through a process
that sought to incorporate the security concerns of the United States and the
Central American countries. The pacification of the area was regarded as a
precondition for furthering the cause of economic and political development
in each Central American country.

The first obstacle encountered by Contadora was a reluctance on the part
of all parties involved to come to the negotiating table. Nicaragua's position
at the outset was that its problems could be solved through bilateral negotiations with the United States, Honduras, and Costa Rica, rather than through
a multilateral forum.[2] In July 1983, however, Daniel Ortega agreed to
negotiate multilaterally within the Contadora framework.

An indication that the group might advance on the road it had set itself
was the publication in September 1983 of a most important document, which
was to serve as the basis for future negotiations: a 21-point statement of
objectives. The areas covered by the document fell into five broad categories: (1) relations between the states; (2) matters concerning internal stability and peace; (3) national security questions; (4) problems of refugees;

---

2. Nicaragua's preference for bilateralism was to outlive its eventual participation in the
Contadora process, as was demonstrated during the Manzanillo talks between representatives
of the United States and Nicaragua.

and (5) interstate cooperation for social and economic development. [See Appendix D.]

The most important points concerned security questions; the document's key elements in this respect included the commitment to a freeze on arms imports and on the size of armies in Central America, a reduction in the number of foreign military advisers, and a nonaggression pact banning national territories from being used in third-party attacks on other countries. This document was fully endorsed by all five Central American countries.

The 21-point program was meant to form the basis for a peace treaty binding on all five nations of Central America, to be signed in December 1983. But the meeting to sign the treaty had to be postponed because of opposition by Honduras, El Salvador, Guatemala, and Costa Rica to additions to the Contadora blueprint demanded by Nicaragua. These countries feared that if these new Nicaraguan demands were accepted, they would leave Nicaragua's military capability untouched and at the same time force the elimination of the military bases the United States has in other countries.

The Nicaraguan proposal, which had been rejected by Washington, was for the signing of four treaties: two between the United States and Nicaragua, banning the establishment of foreign military bases in Central America and the guaranteeing of free passage for vessels and aircraft of the United States through Nicaraguan waters and airspace; a regional treaty for the five Central American states, prohibiting the traffic of arms as well as overt and covert actions aimed at the overthrow of established governments (including logistic support for the irregular forces in the region); and a treaty on El Salvador, which would involve all the parties and countries in the resolution of the conflict there. The Nicaraguan proposal reflected the way in which Managua perceived the regional problem; it regarded problems in the area as stemming from an organized conspiracy by the United States with the aid of its allies in the region.[3]

The follow-up of the 21-point statement of objectives came in early 1984 when a document on the "norms of implementation" of the 21 points was issued, following a meeting of the Central American and Contadora foreign ministers in Panama City January 8, 1984. Three commissions were set up to develop a series of recommendations on security and political and socioeconomic matters.[4] These were later integrated into the Act of Contadora on Peace and Cooperation in Central America, which was presented to the

---

3. This interpretation can be found not only in circles close to the Reagan administration but also in Latin America, for instance in Herrera Zúñiga and Chavarría, "Mexico en Contadora," pp. 476–477.

4. Summary report, *Regional Cooperation in Peace and Security in Central America and the Caribbean* (New York, International Peace Academy, 1984), pp. 25–27.

Central American countries for comments in June 1984. This peace plan, drafted in the form of a treaty, would be binding on its five Central American signatories and would include an additional protocol to be signed and adhered to by other countries interested in supporting peace in the area.

The reference to "other countries" is a reflection of the major flaw in the peacemaking efforts of the Contadora group referred to above. To a large extent, events in Central America have been influenced by two countries that have become part and parcel of the area's problems and that would inevitably play a role in any possible solution: the United States and Cuba. For historical and security reasons, the former has a much larger stake in the area than the latter. The fact that it was left out of the Contadora negotiations may have served the purpose of regional unity, but it was unrealistic if the aim was to seek a genuine negotiated settlement to the region's conflicts. Put differently, Contadora did not represent a dialogue between the two sides of the conflict (Nicaragua and the United States) but between one side and many witnesses.

This weakness was realized, and a significant attempt to remedy it was put in place in mid 1984. Bilateral talks started taking place outside the Contadora framework between the U.S. special envoy for Central America, Harry Shlaudeman, and the Nicaraguan vice-minister of foreign affairs, Victor Hugo Tinoco, in Manzanillo (Mexico), through Mexican mediation. Simultaneous to these bilateral talks, the Contadora process continued to advance.

The Act of Contadora of June 1984 represented the first effort to harmonize the various proposals that had emerged since the process started, trying to accommodate the different interests of the would-be signatories. The tone was to stress the need for détente in Central America and the importance of confidence-building measures. It sought to lay down rules for the conduct of military maneuvers; ban the establishment of foreign military bases or training establishments; end arms sales, support for "irregular forces," and the arms race in the area; and set up a mechanism for control and verification.

To facilitate the task of coordination, the act envisaged the creation of rapid communication channels between governments and military authorities. Similarly, joint bilateral commissions were to be set up, particularly between Honduras and Nicaragua, and El Salvador and Nicaragua; existing ones, such as the Costa Rica—Nicaragua commission, which had been reestablished in May 1984 under Contadora auspices, were to be strengthened.

On the political side, the Act of Contadora upheld the principles of pluralist democracy with full freedom for different currents of opinion and called for measures conducive to national reconciliation and dialogue, including an amnesty for political opponents and guarantees for its beneficiaries (but being less than specific as to the nature and scale of the amnesty). In particular, a political commission would be set up to receive and assess information about the implementation of political, electoral, and human rights obligations undertaken by the parties to the agreement.

During the summer of 1984, after the submission of comments on the Act of Contadora by the Central American countries, a revision was effected and a second draft presented on September 7, 1984 (hereafter called Revised Act). The most sensitive points contained in the Act, and those that were to provide the major stumbling block to the signature of the treaty by the Central American countries, concerned questions of security.

Under the Revised Act, signatories would commit themselves to regulate national or joint military exercises and prohibit the holding of international military maneuvers in their respective territories. Exercises currently under way would have to be suspended within 30 days after signature. The Act would prohibit support for irregular forces advocating the overthrow or destablization of governments. Signatories would also pledge to refuse installation of foreign military bases in their countries and dismantle existing ones within 6 months of signature. With regard to armaments, there would be an effective freeze and a commitment not to introduce new weapons systems. Inventories of arms, installations, and troop levels would have to be submitted to a Verification and Control Commission not later than 30 days after signature, and their reduction would take place in stages negotiated after signature. On completion of negotiations and final agreement on the calendar, all foreign military advisers engaged in operations and training would be withdrawn immediately, while the number of those involved in the running of installations and maintenance would be limited. Verification of these agreements was left to the Verification and Control Commission, which was to be established 30 days after the signing of the agreement. This commission would have responsibility for continuing negotiations and arbitration of possible disputes among the signatories.

The Revised Act of Contadora was presented to the five Central American countries for consideration, and an October 15 deadline was set for them to respond to the initiative. It was evident that some major flaws and sticking points would make it difficult for all parties to agree to it, although several Central American officials expressed their countries' willingness to subscribe to the act. To everybody's surprise, however, not least that of the United States, Nicaraguan President Daniel Ortega beat the deadline and on September 21, 1984, announced he would sign the Revised Act without modification, calling on the United States to sign and ratify the additional protocol. This political coup on the part of the Nicaraguan government was interpreted as aimed at creating the impression that Nicaragua was not standing in the way of Contadora, knowing that no one else would sign the treaty. As could have been expected, the response of the rest of the Central

American countries to Managua's unqualified decision to sign the act was to voice reservations on several of the act's provisions.

Indeed, the governments of Honduras, El Salvador, and Costa Rica met in Tegucigalpa after the October deadline to consider their reservations to the act and propose modifications. Guatemala was also present during the discussions, but distanced itself from the results. Nicaragua, which had been invited to the meeting but had refused to attend, blamed the U.S. government for putting pressure on the "Tegucigalpa group" and forcing its Central American allies to draw back from their initial acceptance and support for the draft treaty.

The modifications to the Act of Contadora proposed by the Central American countries are contained in what became known as the Tegucigalpa draft agreement. Its text, basically the same as that of the revised act, called for specific changes regarding security issues seen as affecting the United States and its Central American allies directly. The Tegucigalpa group's reservations concerned mainly the demilitarization process and the control and verification procedures. It sought simultaneity between the signing of the treaty and the enforcement of the main provisions on arms freezes and ceilings (to be negotiated before signature) and the elimination of foreign military bases and training establishments. It also called for the regulation, rather than prohibition, of international military exercises. The Tegucigalpa draft proposed that commitments undertaken under the treaty should come into force after ratification by the five Central American countries, whereas, under the text of the revised act, some provisions and commitments were to be negotiated after the signing of the treaty.

The Tegucigalpa group also modified the Contadora proposal on the subjects of enforcement and verification. The act provided that the Commission on Verification and Control make recommendations on charges of noncompliance with security provisions and that disputes arising on security or political and economic issues be considered by the 5 foreign ministers of the Central American countries, who would arrive at a unanimous decision. In the event of failure to reach unanimity, disputes would be referred to the Contadora foreign ministers, who would mediate or recommend solutions in accordance with United Nations and OAS charters. The Tegucigalpa group proposed that the provision for "unanimity" in disputes be modified to the reaching of decisions by consensus. Appeals would be referred to the five Central American foreign minister in addition to the Contadora four (instead of exclusively to the latter).

Regarding indigenous irregular forces, the Act of Contadora had what can probably be fairly described as a serious omission. It referred to these forces only in the abstract, as general situations not to be permitted. It shied away from being specific as to the groups in question, their composition and location, and their sources of support and relations to the host countries.

Furthermore, it did not address the question of the logistics of the solution: How would these groups be disarmed and disbanded? And where would they be relocated? The Tegucigalpa group's proposal, still imprecise in its reference to irregular forces, proposed that on their disarmament, they be relocated outside the region.

Managua rejected the Tegucigalpa draft. The Nicaraguan leaders insisting that they would abide only by the Revised Act (summer 1984) submitted to them, without further modifications. The FSLN also insisted that any regional peace treaty would be effective only if it was supported by a formal and binding assurance the the United States. The U.S. public reaction was to state that, although in principle it favored the Contadora peace efforts, it objected to the act because negotiations on troop levels and arms reductions would take place after, rather than before, signature and because the process of verification and enforcement was not adequate. It was pointed out that the revised act established the body in charge of verification and enforcement but did not specify standards and procedures. Another point on which American opposition existed concerned the prohibition of support for irregular forces. Abiding by the act meant the cessation of both the supervision of support for the *contras* by the United States and the continued toleration of these forces by the governments of Honduras and El Salvador.

The end of 1984 did not augur well for Contadora's future. The fragile situation became aggravated by the U.S. announcement, in October 1984, that Nicaragua was expected to receive a cargo of offensive weapons—MIGs in particular—from the Soviet Union. Managua denied the allegations, stating that the expected Soviet delivery was limited to helicopters. It was difficult for the Contadora countries, which had kept insisting on the need to isolate Central American from East—West considerations, to view Nicaragua's close military trade with the Soviet Union without growing concern.

The Nicaraguan elections that took place in November 1984 produced a mixed reaction on the part of international opinion. Some observers, favorable to the FSLN government, saw these elections as proof that the Sandinista government was fulfilling its pledge to democracy and pluralism. Washington and large sectors of public opinion in the United States and elsewhere described the Nicaraguan elections as a travesty. The harassment of Arturo Cruz and the Coordinadora Democrática by Nicaraguan official forces were pointed to as proof that the elections were not valid.[5]

---

5. These different interpretations of the electoral process in Nicaragua were patent in the different newspapers that covered it. Reports in the European press tended to stress that the process itself was fair. See, for instance, David Gardner, "Sandinistas Seek National Consensus after Poll Victory," *Financial Times*, November 7, 1984; and Jonathan Steele, "The Revolution that Proved Itself at the Poll," *Guardian*, November 7, 1984. There were, however, other opinions, both in the United States and Europe, which saw the elections as a sham. For

Further progress in negotiations was marred by a bilateral dispute between Nicaragua and Costa Rica in December 1984.[6] Costa Rica claimed that Nicaragua had violated its right to grant political asylum to a Nicaraguan citizen. In view of this, Costa Rica refused to attend the meeting schedules by Contadora to take place in Panama in February 1985, to discuss questions of verification and control. On taking this stand, Costa Rica found support from El Salvador and Honduras. The three countries issued a joint communiqué reiterating their decision not to participate in the meeting proposed by Contadora; they stated the need to delay further meetings until "general conditions were more favourable." Essentially, this meant that Nicaragua should recognize Costa Rica's right to offer political asylum, to its neighbor's citizens.

On another front—the bilateral channel established at Manzanillo between Nicaraguan and U.S. representatives—things also were not improving. By the end of 1984 there had been nine rounds of talks (plus an initial one that took place in Managua in June 1984), but the differences between the two sides remained. In fact, by the end of the year the Nicaraguan position had become more flexible on security questions, and it was willing to compromise in this area on a bilateral basis. But the U.S. position was that it had agreed to engage in these talks in order to facilitate a successful outcome of the Contadora process and that Nicaragua's preference for bilateral agreements undermined the multilateral forum. On these grounds, the United States decided to put an end to the negotiations in early 1985. The Nicaraguan side claimed that the reason for the suspension of the talks was that good progress was being make toward the completion of an acceptable agreement, which was contrary to U.S. wishes.[7]

Nicaragua's setbacks in the regional peacemaking forum and bilateral talks with the United States left Managua isolated on all negotiating fronts concerned with the regional crisis. This situation must in fact have greatly upset the FSLN government, or this is the impression one gets from a series of moves by Managua. In late February 1985, at a meeting with U.S. bishops visiting Nicaragua to learn about the problems between the FSLN en government and the Catholic church, President Daniel Ortega announced a

---

instance: "A Charade in Nicaragua," *Baltimore Sun*, reproduced in *International Herald Tribune*, November 7, 1984; Marcel Niedergang, "Le Front est Partout," *Le Monde*, November 3, 1984; and George Black, "U.S. Pressure, Sandinist Quarrels Make Nicaragua's Vote a Travesty," *International Herald Tribune*, November 3–4, 1984.

6. This was an incident over a Nicaraguan draft dodger who took refuge in the Costa Rican Embassy in Managua. The Nicaraguan security forces, according to Costa Rica authorities, had violated diplomatic immunity by entering the embassy, while Managua claimed that the draft dodger had left the embassy before being arrested.

7. Purcell, "Demystifying Contadora," pp. 78, 93.

peace proposal he had sent to U.S. congressional leaders, aimed at the renewal of negotiations with the United States and the resumption of Nicaragua's participation in the Contadora process. The latter point had in turn been facilitated by the fact that the Sandinistas released the Nicaraguan who had sought asylum in the Costa Rica Embassy in Managua. Another gesture was the pledge to send home 100 of the Cuban military advisers in Nicaragua. These actions were aimed at creating a good impression in the U.S. Congress, which would persuade it to refuse to sanction financial aid to the *contras*.

The Contadora process was revived after the inauguration of the new Brazilian president in March 1985, when the resumption of further meetings between the five Central American foreign ministers and their Contadora counterparts was announced. The occasion in Brasilia was used to reiterate the commitments made until then and enunciate future proceedings to restore continuity to the process.

The subsequent Contadora meeting, in Panama in mid-May, concentrated on commitments aimed at halting the arms race in the region, the arms traffic problem, and the establishment of direct communication system and mixed commissions. On the topic of military advisers there was consensus on withdrawing them gradually rather than immediately. Most important, the relocation of irregular forces were discussed, with Honduras recognizing for the first time the presence of Nicaraguan guerrillas on its territory and agreeing to the inclusion of a clause to remove "all irregular insurgent forces" from national territories. But a new draft to which all parties could agree was a long way off.

During the summer of 1985 an important development occurred. At the inauguration of Peru's new president, Alan García, which took place in Lima in late July 1985, the Contadora process received the formal backing of a further four Latin American countries, which became known as the Lima, or Support, Group: Argentina, Brazil, Peru, and Uruguay. At a time when the Contadora process was faltering, this Latin American endorsement lent valuable moral weight to the initiative. In a sense this development had no direct significance in itself, for the countries in question were not parties to the conflict nor did they have direct, or even geopolitical, interests in Central America. Nevertheless, it was evident that countries that had earlier faced the destabilizing effects of guerrilla activities (e.g., Argentina and Uruguay) or were still waging a war against them (Peru) could not remain indifferent regarding Contadora's efforts to solve these problems. Apart from this regional unity against the destabilizing effects of political violence, the Support Group gave Contadora a major symbolic significance by putting essentially the whole of democratic Latin America firmly behind a regional effort to solve the crisis.

The creation of the Support Group, however, turned out to be not quite enough for concrete advances to be achieved in the ensuing negotiations. In September 1985 yet another draft treaty was presented to the Central American countries by Contadora. It stipulated the gradual elimination of foreign military advisers and allowed for a "reasonable balance of forces." It also included a proposal for the establishment of an international corps of inspectors drawn from neutral countries to monitor arms levels and military activities. Regarding political and refugee questions and social and economic matters, the Central American countries were required to form two committees to cover these issues.

The idea of the creation of a corps of inspectors was included at the insistence of the Tegucigalpa group. Nicaragua objected to it, as well as to the rest of the new draft, claiming that it was totally made to suit and defend the interests of the United States in the region. According to the initial timetable set by the Contadora group, a meeting was to be held in early October, with a limit of 45 days for a permanent agreement to be reached. If this did not take place, Contadora would wind up. Contadora was spared having to take such drastic action, however. At the request of Nicaragua, the group suspended all negotiations for 5 months on the grounds that new governments were taking office in the forthcoming months (Guatemala and Honduras in January and Costa Rica in April) and that this could change policies toward negotiations.

With the January 1986 inauguration of Christian Democratic President Vinicio Cerezo, the return to democracy in Guatemala after 15 years of military dictatorship offered a most favorable climate for relaunching the regional peacemaking effort. The event provided the opportunity for a Central American "summit," attended by all the Central American presidents (including Daniel Ortega of Nicaragua) and the ministers of foreign affairs of the Contadora and Lima groups.

The occasion was used by President Cerezo to express his full support for the Contadora process and to insist on an idea he had frequently voiced during his election campaign: the creation of a Central American parliament as a forum for regional discussions and the easing of tensions. The idea of a formal regional forum was not only novel but pointed to a possible "in-house" alternative to "external" mediating efforts such as those of Contadora, by focusing on and stressing the need for consultation with and among Central Americans. A meeting between Central American heads of state was scheduled to take place in May to talk about the project.

The outcome of the discussions held in Guatemala City on the occasion of Cerezo's inauguraton was the so-called Declaration of Guatemala. This document, which contained some of the peace proposals from the Contadora plan, proposed an end to foreign military involvement in Central America, including an end to U.S. support to El Salvador and the *contras* on the one hand and an end to Cuban support for the FSLN government on the other.

The Contadora process continued in its own right. Another attempt to reinvigorate it took place in mid January 1986 with a meeting held by the foreign ministers of the Contadora and Support groups at the Venezuelan resort of Caraballeda. The document that came out of this meeting, known as the Caraballeda declaration, included a number of points that, although not new, were given greater significance through this concerted effort to strengthen the peacemaking process. The document called for the signing of a nonaggression pact between the five Central American countries. Other recommendations included the end of foreign support for irregular forces and insurgent movements in the region, a freeze in arms purchases, the reduction in levels of foreign military advisers, and the suspension of international military maneuvers. It also urged the United States and Nicaragua to resume bilateral talks. In a veiled reference to the Nicaraguan political situation it stated that "pluralist government" in the region was an indispensable condition for the establishment of a permanent basis for peace. In short, Caraballeda repeated some of the well-known points, but by directly addressing the most sensitive issues, the weak flank of the pacification process was exposed. For instance, the reference to pluralist government made Contadora vulnerable to a charge of meddling in the internal affairs of other countries. On its call for the suspension of international military exercises, it opened the way to criticisms of lack of realism.

A test of the new spirit of Caraballeda came soon, with a meeting in Panama City in April 1986 to agree on a deadline for signing the regional peace treaty. This meeting, with the foreign ministers of the Central American five, the Contadora four, and the Support Group, was a stormy one and perhaps the least satisfactory meeting in the entire Contadora process. No agreement was reached. Differences between the Tegucigalpa group and Nicaragua seemed insurmountable, particularly regarding two military provisions of the draft treaty. One concerned the foreign military presence in the area. The Tegucigalpa group wanted to "regulate" it; Nicaragua wanted it out altogether. On the question of scaling down military installations and armaments, Nicaragua refused any curbs on this unless the United States agreed to become a party to the treaty. Nicaragua also made it clear that it would not sign any agreement until the United States ceased its support for the *contras*. The meeting ended in disarray, and although members of the group refused to admit failure, it was clear that the process was in a deep state of crisis. As the vice-president of El Salvador declared after the meeting: "Nicaragua rejected everything that was presented to it . . . there was nothing left to talk about.'"[8] A new "final deadline" was set for June 6, but it had become obvious that there could be no illusions about the possible success of the process. (For the final draft of the Revised Act, see Appendix D.)

If the Contadora process was not advancing, the Central American states were moving, slowly and gradually, in their exploration of concrete ways to improve relations among themselves. The meeting of Central American leaders called by President Cerezo on his inauguration took place in the mountain town of Esquipulas, Guatemala, in late May 1986. It was the first time that the five Central American presidents had met to discuss common problems since the FSLN took power in 1979. The general tone of the discussions was frank and open. Although the presidents expressed a willingness to sign the regional peace treaty proposed by Contadora, they recognized that outstanding points remained that needed to be resolved regarding arms control, regional military exercises, and ratification and compliance. The final joint declaration was described as "thin" by official observers. This was not surprising because there were various difficulties among the Central American leaders, not the least of which was achieving a consensus on the wording of the joint final declaration. For instance, the final communiqué omitted a phrase that appeared in its first draft and called the five presidents "freely elected by the will of the majority." Apparently, Costa Rica's newly inaugurated president, Oscar Arias, had insisted on its omission from the final document, no doubt wishing to distance himself from his Nicaraguan counterpart. Nevertheless, the Esquipulas meeting did produce one concrete achievement: agreement on the creation of a Central American parliament whose members would be freely elected by universal suffrage.

On the Contadora front, things did not look too bright. As could have been expected, the "final deadline" of June 6, 1986, passed without producing a signed regional peace treaty. The Contadora group tried to play down repeated suggestions that their initiative had suffered a major blow, and the Contadora representatives met once more in Buenos Aires to try to work out a new and more flexible timetable. The future of Contadora is still open, but its chances of success in bringing about a peacefully negotiated, long-lasting solution to the Central American conflict are liable to grow slimmer if no major change takes place in its outlook and organization.

The Stumbling Blocks in Contadora's Way

There are serious obstacles in the way of Contadora's success as a regional peacemaking initiative. The first and most important obstacle is

8. "Contadora Peace Talks Break Down," *International Herald Tribune*, April, 8, 1986.

inherent in the structure of the process. It lacks the participation of the United States, the most important actor in the process. Washington has the power to alter the military balance in Central America and exert decisive influence in the economic and political situation there. A clear illustration of this is that U.S. actions have had destabilizing effects on Nicaragua, whereas in El Salvador they have helped stabilize the situation. The United States is the most influential actor in the region, and it is unrealistic to search for a solution that ignores this fact. President Daniel Ortega of Nicaragua realized this by calling for U.S. participation in the negotiations on several occasions.

But leaving the United States outside the regional peacemaking effort was the main *raison d'être* for the Contadora process, since it sought to provide a regional alternative to U.S. unilateral actions in the region. Indeed, as has been stated repeatedly, one of the main values of Contadora is that it provides a regional forum for the discussion and eventual solution of the region's problems, independently of Washington. Contadora was created "to resist the interference of the hegemonic power . . .—or of other external forces—in Latin America."[9]

Another possible obstacle to Contadora's effective action also is structural. It is well known that the Contadora group members have profound differences regarding their internal political structures and foreign policy traditions. There are also great divergences between them about what they perceive to be at stake in Central America and their interests there.[10] Mexico, for instance, is less worried than, say, Colombia and Venezuela, about the one-party nature of the Sandinista state or its Marxist–Leninist credentials. These different perceptions may make it more difficult for the Contadora countries to draft a peace treaty acceptable even to the group, not to mention its eventual signatories.

Another source of conflict pointed out as a possible obstacle to the success of the Contadora initiative is regional tensions that stem from territorial conflicts between the actors involved. For instance, there is a dispute between Colombia and Venezuela regarding limits to territorial waters and submarine areas; a territorial dispute between Colombia and

9. Mario Ojeda Gómez, "Contadora: la política exterior de México [Contadora: Mexico's Foreign Policy]," in Cepeda Ulloa and Pardo García-Peña, *Contadora*, p. 47.

10. It was in fact a series of ad hoc circumstances that led these countries with so many marked differences to converge in the formation of the Contadora group. Some of these circumstances had to do with the 1982 financial crisis, the Falklands/Malvinas war and the U.S. indirect participation in it, and change of governments and ideologies in power in Central America and the Contadora countries. For the antecedents on the formation of the Contadora group, see Durán, "The Contadora Approach to Peace in Central America." An analysis of the differences between the Contadora countries is found in Purcell. "Demystifying Contadora."

Nicaragua over the archipelago of San Andrés and Providencia, which the Sandinista government revived soon after taking power; and a long-standing territorial dispute between El Salvador and Honduras, which led to the so-called soccer war in 1969. No doubt these frictions between parties involved in consultation to negotiate a regional peace agreement have had some influence in retarding the process at specific stages, but concrete evidence on this is lacking.

More important perhaps as a concrete obstacle for the conclusion of a lasting peace agreement is the impossibility of striking the right balance in the treaty between Central American and, by extension, U.S. security interests. That Contadora's drafts have not been able to propose commitments acceptable to all regarding security and military questions, and verification and control, points to two major obstacles to the process. One concerns the deeply ingrained distrust between the Central American countries. The second refers to the U.S. perception about how its national security is affected by events in Central America.

The Changing Pattern of Central American Relations

The role of the Central American countries is, of course, crucial for the success of any lasting peace agreement. Relations between them a and the Sandinistas turned tense soon after the latter came to power in July 1979. The main elements of concern among the Central American countries has been, and remains, the vicious spiral of Nicaragua's military buildup and the U.S. response of pouring considerable military aid to its allies in the region, particularly Honduras and El Salvador. Shortly after the Contadora process started, Nicaragua's growing military strength was used by Honduras, El Salvador, and Guatemala as justification for reviving the 1963 regional military pact CONDECA (Central American Defence Council) in 1983. This signaled a lack of confidence by these countries in the ability of the fledgling Contadora initiative to promote an acceptable negotiated solution to the region's problems. Costa Rica, whose neutrality and lack of an army ruled out its joining CONDECA, nonetheless shared the sentiment. This was evidenced by its participation in the San José meeting of October 1982, which established the Forum for Peace and Democracy.[11]

One of the main tasks of Contadora was therefore to try to harmonize

---

11. This meeting, with full U.S. backing, issued its own peace initiative for the region, which included the same basic ends as Contadora—an end to arms trafficking and the export of subversion in Central America, as well as withdrawal of all military advisers. But it was aimed at different actors.

relations between the Central American countries and promote confidence-building measures in the area. Despite the major problems that persist on the way to an overall settlement, this is perhaps an area where much (albeit subtle) progress has been achieved. Indeed, since the Contadora process started in January 1983, mutual perceptions in Central America have undergone noticeable changes.

More generally, the unease in Central American countries about Nicaragua under the Sandinistas has been and remains strong, and so has their distrust for experiments with any solutions not centered in the approval and active support of the United States. But Contadora has left its mark. Continuous meetings between the Central American countries under the aegis of Contadora have created a feeling of regional self-confidence. Bilateral relations between the Central American countries and Nicaragua may not have improved directly, but the former have come to realize that accommodation is possible. They have been able to talk with Nicaragua through the Contadora framework. Some measure of progress in negotiations has been achieved; and, at any rate, things have not got out of hand. But is is precisely in this respect—the strengthening of self-reliance and increased dialogue among the Central American countries—that Contadora faces a new challenge. Its peacemaking efforts are being overtaken by the Central American countries, no doubt in close but discreet consultation with the United States. The first sign of this was the unanimous decision taken at Esquipulas to establish a Central American parliament.

At this stage of the game the possible gradual substitution of Contadora for Central American collective action would exhibit a number of possible characteristics. It would probably have a greater degree of independence from the United States than the joint efforts that emerged in the past (the Central American Democratic Community or the Forum for Peace and Democracy), mainly because the inspiration for them came from within Central America. Also, to judge from the recent Central American summits in Guatemala City and Esquipulas, Nicaragua would join in and not be isolated, as in the past. There is a danger, however, that either because of a further radicalization of the FSLN government or through increased pressure by the United States, the old pattern will reemerge. The consequent lack of dialogue would probably lead to the recrudescence of tensions and violence.

A new trend is emerging in Central America countries. They are starting to take an active interest in steering relations among themselves, independently and outside the Contadora framework. It is too early to assess any long-term results of this process, but a basis for it has been established. In walking this route the Central American countries are aided by the fact that, at present, relatively free and democratic regimes have replaced military dictatorships. Another element that would facilitate this development has to do with the relations between Contadora and the Central American countries. It is well known that some currents of opinion in Central America view Contadora (and some of its individual members) with suspicion and not much sympathy. This would make it easier to relinquish, albeit discreetly, the "tutelage" exercised by Contadora. There are instances of serious misgivings about the true intentions of certain Contadora states. The feeling in some quarters of Central America is that they are utilizing the unstable situation there to further their own political ends. Internally, so goes this argument, belonging to the Contadora group and putting on a "Good Samaritan" face aids a government in winning popularity with its electorate, and may appease reformist elements, who now have a viable outlet. Externally, acting within Contadora may increase a country's bargaining power in bilateral negotiations (related to trade or finance) with the hegemonic power.[12]

East–West—and North

The U.S. policy toward Central America has not been of one piece. On the one hand, the United States has consistently expressed support for the Contadora process, particularly when it was first launched. President Reagan welcomed the adoption of the 21-point statement of objectives, and several voices in the administration have stated their "willingness to support its comprehensive and verifiable implementation."[13] On the other hand, the U.S. antipathy for the Sandinista regime in Nicaragua has led it to engage in active destabilizing actions, either directly through economic pressures or indirectly through support of the *contras*, who seek a violent overthrow of the FSLN administration, which not only is the de facto government of Nicaragua but has been recognized as the legitimate government by the international community. The justification offered by the Reagan administration for the pressure it has applied on Nicaragua, particularly for supplying "humanitarian" and military aid to opponents of the

12. These points are made with specific reference to Mexico by the ex-minister of foreign affairs of Costa Rica, Gonzalo S. Facio, in "La Paz de Centroamérica y la Acción del grupo de Contadora" [Central American Peace and the Contadora Group Action], *Relaciones Internacionales* (Heredia, Costa Rica), nos. 8–9 (Second and Third Quarters 1984): 23–35. Facio adds to these arguments the point that the logic behind Mexico's support for the "Marxist–Leninist regimes of Cuba and Nicaragua" is that Mexico expects to avoid being chosen as a target for the infiltration of Marxist–Leninist revolutionaries. In other words, by supporting these regimes, Mexico guarantees its own stability.

13. U.S. Department of State, *The Contadora Resource Book* (Washington, D.C: GPO, January 1985), p. 1.

Sandinista regime, rests on several points. The national interest and security of the United States has been invoked, as has the defense of human rights in the region and the promotion of liberal democratic values.

The security argument has been used to persuade Congress to support the administration's strategy of destabilization and support for the *contras* as the best means to halt the arms supply to the Salvadoran guerrillas and thus the "export of revolution" by the Sandinistas. But the matter is not confined to regional proportions. The United States has perceived the conflicts in Central America as part of the East–West confrontation. The U.S. administration often has contended that Nicaragua represents a genuine security threat to the United States because the Sandinista regime's relations with Moscow open the possibility of the Soviet Union's establishing new bases in the Western Hemisphere.[14] Some have stated that this argument is not altogether valid. It is pointed out that the U.S. administration has never indicated why the Soviets would want to establish new bases, apart from those they already have in Cuba. Furthermore, some contend that, for the Soviets, the cost of maintenance and defense of these bases in the event of open conflict would far exceed the U.S. cost in neutralizing them. This misses the fact that Nicaragua provides an outlet for the Soviet Union to the Pacific Ocean in the Western Hemisphere, and this would be a significant addition to Soviet global strategic interests. At any rate, having two military allies in the region would strengthen and render more flexible the Soviet position in the area. But despite these qualifications, many Latin Americans would subscribe to the general feeling among commentators that the argument about Soviet threats to the United States with Nicaragua as the springboard is more political than military.[15]

The other argument often raised to justify the Reagan administration's policy on Nicaragua is the defense of human rights and democratic values. This seems not to hold water at all. Despite a general shared sense of frustration, with the limitations to free and fair political play obviously in place in Nicaragua, it seems far-fetched to claim that the situation is so bad as to justify the kind and scale of intervention the Reagan administration has effected and advocated. As far as the human rights issue is concerned, reports by Amnesty International, for example, are not particularly damning of the Nicaraguan situation. Problems do exist (e.g., among the Miskito population or in political harassment of the opposition), but these are not

14. The U.S. concern over the Soviet and Cuban military penetration of the region is illustrated in a pamphlet published by the U.S. Department of State, *The Soviet and Cuban Connection in Central America and the Caribbean* (Washington, D.C.: GPO, March 1985).

15. See, for instance, Richard H. Ullman, "At War with Nicaragua," *Foreign Affairs*, Fall 1983, p. 53.

the rule. Limitations to democratic principles and practice are a truer and more serious argument. The FSLN leadership has gradually established a monolithic control of most aspects of political life, as well as the media.

The human rights situation generally does not seem critically bad, not any worse than the situation in the average Latin American country. How can this issue justify mining Nicaraguan ports, with CIA direct involvement, or the appalling and widespread violations of human rights by some *contra* factions that have terrorized the Nicaraguan civilian population? This external threat has in turn prompted and justified tighter internal control by the Sandinista leadership on the political life of the country. Also, the FSLN leadership insists that it stands by the original pledge of maintaining political pluralism, a mixed economy, and nonalignment in foreign policy. Any delays or departures from this program are explained as the result of the external threat.

The lack of respect Washington seems to be showing to its senior Latin American partners, by insisting on a military solution through the *contras*, cannot be constructive and may backfire. With all the obstacles in its path, the Contadora process is widely agreed on as the best venue for a negotiated solution, with perhaps a Central American parallel initiative. The Central American countries (including Nicaragua), plus Contadora, plus the Support Group, although still in disagreement as to form and content, favor a negotiated settlement over a military alternative (which in any event would not guarantee to solve the region's problems). The number and importance of the countries that make up these regional groupings cannot be dismissed lightly; they almost amount to the OAS minus the United States. American isolation on this issue is without precedent. (One must recall the extent of support that White House policies secured in isolating Fidel Castro 25 years ago.) The outstanding level of consensus among the Latin American countries on this major issue should be read more carefully by U.S. and Latin American policymakers, and grasped as a perfect opportunity to help its neighbors to a new political maturity and restore balance and trust in them.

Contadora II?

This essay began by stating that current inertia points at two directions for Contadora: (1) dissolution and confrontation; or (2) continuation of the status quo—and latent confrontation all the same. A third way out may yet be found. As I have argued, looking back at the Contadora process with the benefit of hindsight, it seems self-evident that a political solution to the crisis can be found only if the main parties involved in the conflict form part of the negotiating process. As far as the manner of negotiation is concerned, it would perhaps be best to stick to the Contadora formula: a small but significant group of countries, related to and aware of the different sides of the dispute, playing the role of mediators and active negotiators. But two basic elements would need to be incorporated in a revamped version of the current negotiating framework: First and foremost, it is essential that the United States not be excluded from the negotiating process. If the United States values a political solution, it must be in a position to influence directly the detailed content of negotiations and hence the spirit and specifics of any document to be agreed upon.

Second, and relatedly, is the problem of the *contras*, that central (and varied) group of actors who have managed to go entirely unnoticed (except for veiled references) in all official Contadora documents on the problem. Again, it is essential to hear what the *contras* have to say as part of the negotiating process and to face directly the problem of their orderly disbandment as well as their absorption as part of the solution.

To be sure, a distinction needs to be drawn between different *contra* leaders and groups—between those (especially of Somocista origin) bent on force, often the most brutal use of force, and those whose origin and vocation are more truly political. It is sad that, at least in public pronouncements, neither the Reagan administration nor the indirect references to the *contras* by the Contadora group seem to be interested in drawing any distinction among the *contras*. This can only result in the quite natural refusal by the Sandinistas to open up any kind of place for *contra* participation in informal negotiations or more generally in Nicaraguan political or public life.

The oldest and most important *contra* group is the Nicaraguan Democratic Forces (FDN), which was founded in 1981 in Honduras. Its commander-in-chief is Adolfo Calero, a former businessman, and its military commander is Enrique Bermúdez, a former National Guard officer under Somoza. The Democratic Revolutionary Alliance (ARDE) is another important *contra* group, whose first military commander, Edén Pastora, was a hero of the Sandinista revolution who later defected from the FSLN. After some months of negotiations, the FDN and ARDE formed an alliance in July 1984, which offered a cease-fire if several conditions were met by the FSLN government. These included amnesty, the lifting of the state of emergency, and a "national dialogue" that would include the *contra* forces. They also demanded the acceptance of a presidential candidate from the Coordinadora Democrática Nicaragüense Ramiro Sacasa, better known as Coordinadora Democrática (CDN). Discussions on these demands broke before the elections. [See FDN and ARDE in Glossary.]

The CDN was set up as an alliance of the main internal opposition parties, which boycotted the 1984 elections because its prospective presidential candidate, Arturo Cruz, did not receive adequate guarantees from the FSLN government to run in fair elections. Other concessions demanded by the CDN were the same as those demanded by ARDE plus an end to government control of the media, an independent judiciary, and the separation of the FSLN from the government apparatus. In June 1985 the CDN joined the main *contra* groups in the United Nicaraguan Opposition (UNO) opposition alliance. [See Glossary.]

Shortly after the founding of UNO, the Southern Opposition Bloc (BOS) was formed by members with previous associations with CDN and FDN opposition movements, such as Alfredo César and Edén Pastora. According to BOS, conditions for the coordination of all *contra* activities would have to include a common political program and equal status for member parties. [See BOS in Glossary.]

Of these groups, which have now the umbrella organization United Nicaraguan Opposition (UNO), the one that inspires the least sympathy is the FDN. This is so because of its well-known ties with the CIA and because of the large presence of ex-Somocista guards within it. In fact, a couple of months after the formation of the FDN/ARDE alliance (accomplished under heavy pressure by the United States) this presence of ex-Guardsmen in the FDN was the cause of a split within ARDE. Another element that contributed to discrediting the FDN was a number of reports, made public in early 1985, of human rights violations (including the execution of prisoners) by FDN forces. In view of the FDN record it would be too much to ask the negotiators of Contadora or the FSLN leadership to bring these FDN forces into a dialogue with the aim of their possible incorporation into a legalized opposition bloc. The FDN does not have the democratic credentials of the other groups and leaders (although some members of the FDN may not have been associated with Somoza's National Guard), despite having joined forces with them.

On the other hand, it is clear that any element of *contra* political partici-pa-tion in negotiations would have to be ad hoc and informal, for the *contras* cannot have a place at the negotiating table on a par with the recognized government of Managua. But not for that reason should their voices be heard through the press and the bullet only. Informal but organized and systematic consultations by the Contadora countries with the representatives of the more democratic *contra* factions (particularly those stemming from political organizations, such as CDN) would be possible and are indispensable. Perhaps a more imaginative and indeed flexible approach to this issue, with the Contadora countries providing the lead, would be the only way to avoid a bloodbath in Central America.

Nicaraguan President Daniel Ortega has called for the United States to join the the Contadora negotiations. For its part, the United States has on several occasions expressed its support for the Contadora process. President Reagan agreed that the 21-point statement of objectives of Contadora was the best basis for a lasting regional peace settlement in Central America. A convergence of the two positions seems almost at hand. It only requires a measure of greater flexibility and courage than has been granted so far by the two ultimate opponents in the conflict, with their common friends and neighbors serving as catalysts in the long process of normalization.

Two questions remain open. Will the United States find itself able to coexist with a Marxist regime in Nicaragua, even if the latter pledged not to export revolution and to sever ties with Moscow? Conversely, will Nicaragua agree to strive for peaceful regional coexistence under these conditions and to democratize its regime? If the answer to either question is in the negative, no Contadora process, nor any other negotiating means, will bring peace to the region.

PART FOUR

International Dimensions of the Crisis

• CHAPTER TEN •

Nicaragua between East and West:
The Soviet Perspective

Vernon V. Aspaturian

General Context

The crisis in Central America, manifesting itself primarily in Nicaragua and to a lesser degree in El Salvador, is the latest installment of Soviet–American rivalry in the Western Hemisphere. The Arbenz regime in Guatemala, the Castro revolution in Cuba, the Allende government in Chile, and the Bishop regime in Grenada are all perceived by both the United States and the Soviet Union as important milestones in this competition. During the course of this rivalry, the position and power of the United States and the West generally has eroded in a relative dimension and that of the Soviet Union has been enhanced. From the standpoint of Moscow, its existing clients, and movements and regimes in various parts of the world aspiring to become Soviet clients, the overall "correlation of forces" between capitalism and socialism has steadily, if not always uninterruptedly, shifted in favor of the Soviet Union.

This was particularly evident during the 1970s when Soviet power and influence spread throughout the Third World, and pro-Soviet "socialist-oriented" regimes and their precursor "national liberation movements" mushroomed across three continents: Africa, Asia, and Latin America. It generated a spirit of optimism in Moscow and throughout pro-Soviet movements and regimes in the Third World. Viewed as a process set into motion by the successful establishment of a communist system in Cuba and accelerated by the revolutions in Grenada and Nicaragua, Soviet observers anticipated a general upsurge of more pro-Soviet "socialist-oriented" regimes in the Western Hemisphere. According to one Soviet analyst, writing in 1979,

> The strengthening of the Socialist setup in Cuba and the recognition of its international influence, the victory of the people's democratic anti-Imperialist revolution in Nicaragua and the overthrow of the pro-American regime in Grenada could not fail to give mighty impetus to the revolutionary liberation movement.[1]

By the same token, the overthrow of the pro-Soviet Grenada regime, the containment of the El Salvador insurrection, and the possible ouster of the Sandinistas in Nicaragua could not fail to discourage similar movements and regimes and dampen the revolutionary momentum. Soviet optimism engendered during the 1970s concerning the favorable general trends in the international system and the "correlation of forces" in particular even impelled Leonid Brezhnev boldly to incorporate for the first time purely ideological themes in foreign policy in the new Soviet constitution. Among the goals of Soviet foreign policy, as outlined in the new chapter on foreign policy in the 1977 constitution, are "consolidating the positions of world socialism, supporting the struggle of peoples for national liberation and social progress."[2]

With the advent of the Reagan administration and its assertive, if sometimes belligerent and threatening, rhetoric during its early years, coupled with the disorientation of the Soviet leadership as three aging and ailing top leaders died in rapid succession, the favorable trends in the international environment were arrested, and a new assertiveness in U.S. foreign and military policy took shape. Forceful U.S. intervention to overthrow the Soviet client regime in Grenada (1983), assistance in the arrest of the insurrection in El Salvador, and escalating pressure on the Sandinista regime appeared to resurrect an earlier tendency in U.S. foreign policy, as reflected in the successful overthrow of the Arbenz regime in Guatemala (1954), the military intervention in the Dominican Republic (1965) and the ouster of the Allende government in Chile (1973). Announced intentions of support for Jonas Savimbi in Angola and increased assistance to the Afghan guerrillas were perceived by Moscow as part of a general trend in which Washington sought not only to arrest the wheels of history but to reverse them to a substantial degree. Correspondingly, the U.S. President's Strategic Defense

---

1. Alexander Bavyshev, Moscow Domestic Service, March 3, 1983, in Foreign Broadcast Information Service FBIS—USSR March 4, 1983 p. K/1.
2. *Constitution of the Union of Soviet Socialist Republics* (Moscow: Novosti, 1977), PP. 31—32.

Initiative (SDI) is also viewed as part and parcel of an overall, integrated U.S. strategy to alter the correlation of forces in its favor in order to arrest and roll back socialist gains, first in marginal areas and then closer to the Soviet center.

There is considerable controversy over whether the overall "correlation of forces" has any direct influence on revolutionary and other social processes in the Third World. Without entering into a contentious debate on this point, what is indisputable—whether the linkage can be proven or not—is that the Soviet leadership and its client regimes and movements believe that such a linkage exists, and they act on it. This is supported not only by repeated Soviet pronouncements on this point but also by the Grenada Documents, which reveal that both the Soviet and the Grenadian leaderships acted on this linkage. Thus, one of the most elaborate Grenadian documents boasts:

> One of the main characteristics of the present international conjuncture is the changing balance of forces. Previously imperialism, led by the USA, held unchallenged sway over mankind. Now the Socialist community is strong and growing still. . . . The point is that U.S. imperialism no longer holds sway over mankind [and] . . . is on the decline. . . . Grenada's foreign policy *must* be cognizant of and reflect this change in the balance of forces.[3]

There is strong evidence to suggest that Moscow and its clients have been misled by their analyses and that they misjudged the possible range of U.S. behavior as a consequence, believing that the change in the "correlation of forces" had effectively blocked the possibility of armed U.S. intervention in the Caribbean and Central America and the Third World generally. Open Soviet literature explicitly links the failure of the United States to intervene and prevent the collapse of the shah in Iran to "a shift in the balance of forces of the two socioeconomic systems in favor of socialism."[4] With specific reference to the failure of the United States to prevent the Sandinista revolution in Nicaragua, no less an authority than Karen Brutents, a deputy director of the International Department of the CPSU Central Committee, maintained:

> Another eloquent example is the popular revolution in Nicaragua. Since the time the Monroe Doctrine was proclaimed, U.S. imperialism had looked on Latin America, and especially the Caribbean, as its own private domain. It has repeatedly resorted to armed intervention in the region. . . . The fact that U.S. imperialism did not dare to drown the Nicaraguan revolution in blood

---

3. *Foreign Relations Report, Grenada Documents*, Log. 105757, undated.
4. Karen Brutents, *The Newly Freed Countries in the Seventies* (Moscow: Progress Publications, 1983), pp. 273–274.

proves that the world situation has changed and that the Socialist countries' solidarity with the liberation movement is of paramount importance.[5]

Even the Soviet chief of staff, Marshal Ogarkov, in attempting to reassure an anxious Grenadian colleague, stated that no matter what the United States attempted to do, it could not roll back the wheels of history in the face of the changing correlation of forces. Specifically linking Cuba, Nicaragua, Grenada, and the El Salvador insurrection as part of a single continuous process unleashed by these shifts in the world balance, Major Louison reported to his government:

> About the situation in the world, Marshal Ogarkov pointed out that the United States would try now and in the future to make things difficult for progressive changes in all regions and continents. The Marshal said that over two decades ago, there was only Cuba in Latin America. Today there are Nicaragua, Grenada, and a serious battle is going on in El Salvador. The Marshal of the Soviet Union then stressed that United States imperialism would try to prevent progress, but there were no prospects for imperialism to turn back history.[6]

As Hegel intimated in his enigmatic reference to the "Owl of Minerva," history has a perverse tendency to mislead political leaders where timing is concerned. Just as the Soviet leaders were persuaded that U.S. behavior in the face of Soviet expansion during the 1970s reflected a secular, irreversible decline of American will and power to shape, much less control, world events, the Reagan administration appeared on the scene to undermine that judgment. It was not always true that Moscow expected the United States to be unable to frustrate and block unacceptable revolutions in the Western Hemisphere. The almost simultaneous collapse of the shah in Iran and Somoza in Nicaragua, coupled with the seizure of the American Embassy in Teheran, however, appeared to convince Moscow that the long-awaited decisive threshold in the changing "correlation of forces" had finally arrived.[7]

Only a few years earlier, Soviet writers were warning that, under American protection, the regime in Iran had been stabilized and that the shah's

5. Ibid., p. 275.

6. Memorandum of Meeting Between Chiefs of General Staff of Soviet Armed Forces and People's Revolutionary Forces of Grenada [Marshal N.V. Ogarkov and Major Einstein Louison], *Grenada Documents*, Log. 100008, March 10, 1983.

7. See V. V. Aspaturian, "Soviet Global Power and the Correlation of Forces," *Problems of Communism*, May–June, 1980, pp. 1–18.

modernization program was progressing successfully.[8] And given the lone success of Cuba—which was viewed by many Soviet leaders as a fortuitous windfall rather than a product of the changing "correlation of forces"—in the face of successful U.S. direct and indirect interventions in Chile and the Dominican Republic, the Soviet leaders were not very sanguine about the imminent possibilities of successful Marxist–Leninist revolutions in Latin America. Indeed, the official Soviet counsel to Latin American revolutionaries was one of caution and prudence. The lesson of Chile was to refrain from pushing the revolution too fast, lest it stimulate American intervention. Indeed, there was reason to believe that Moscow expected the United States, unlike its inaction in the Persian Gulf, not to allow another Marxist-Leninist regime to be established on its doorstep in Central America. It fully expected U.S. intervention to forestall it, either through cooptation or military means, and while Moscow was prepared to encourage revolutions in Latin America, it was not prepared to commit itself directly to their success in the face of strong American reaction. Accordingly, it viewed the Carter administration's abandonment of Somoza as a policy of "damage limitation" or "cutting one's losses," and its initial expressions of support for the Sandinista revolution as an attempt to shape and alter its direction. The offer of U.S. financial aid and economic assistance was further viewed as an attempt by Washington to "buy off" the Sandinistas, and if this failed, it would surely be followed by more forceful measures, including military. According to one Soviet interpretation of these developments:

> Present events bring back memories of 1965 when the United States, using the banner of the OAS as a cover, transferred 25,000 marines to the Dominican Republic to suppress the people's uprising. But today, . . . it is not easy to implement such plans. However, the idea of direct military interference in Nicaragua's internal affairs is not giving higher ranking officials in Washington any peace.[9]

Once it was apparent that the Carter administration was not prepared to

8. Thus, one Soviet specialist described the situation in Iran in 1976 as follows: "Iran is one of the few Third World countries that have experienced a marked change in their economic and social indices over the past ten years or so. Her success is due to very diverse factors, not least the effective use made of natural resources, the obvious adaptation of ruling circles to the country's new internal situation, a realistic foreign policy that recognizes the importance of good-neighborly relations with adjacent states, and lastly, her relative demographic stability. Her achievements have attracted the attention of the governments of a number of Asian countries, who are now trying to adopt some of the methods being used in Iran." O. Dreyer, *Culture Changes in Developing Countries* (Moscow: Progress Publishers, 1976), p. 9.

9. Moscow Domestic Service, June 12, 1979, *FBIS—USSR*, June 15, 1979, p. A2.

use military force to quash the Sandinista revolution and had failed to "buy off" the new regime, the perception was that it would pursue a policy of containing the Sandinista revolution to Nicaragua and attempt to manipulate internal anti-Sandinista social forces against it. The United States would set "pro-imperialist forces in motion, to create political tension and to complicate the situation so as ultimately to remove from power any government which does not wish to subordinate itself to the dictate of its northern neighbors."[10]

Soviet leaders have a persistent habit of confusing transitory U.S. policies with irreversible organic defectiveness. Interpreting the Carter administration's unwillingness to act forcefully as an organic U.S. incapacity, determined by larger events beyond its control, Moscow abandoned its initial cautious and prudent approach to the Sandinista revolution in favor of a deeper commitment just as the Carter administration was being replaced by the Reagan administration. The Soviet initial analysis that the United States would not tolerate another Marxist–Leninist regime on its doorstep was correct, but its timing was off. Surely, if Carter was reelected—and Moscow fully expected him to be—the existing policy of inaction would probably continue; even in the event Reagan won, his belligerent election rhetoric would be insufficient to alter the situation. Moscow now thought that the Nicaraguan revolution was "home free." Thus, in the years before Grenada, Moscow was convinced that the "correlation of forces" would deter the United States from direct military intervention but that Reagan might nevertheless attempt to use indirect means to overthrow the Sandinista regime. As Maurice Bishop assured a Soviet journalist only a few short weeks before the invasion of Grenada, "Reagan prefers to use a cat's paw and would not dare to attack Grenada."[11] Correspondingly, Moscow perceived Reagan's chosen cat's paw in Central America to be Honduras and exiled Somoza followers:

> The idea is to create favorable conditions for military actions against Nicaragua and even for an intervention. It is true that things have changed and a U.S. intervention is bound to lead to consequences unpleasant for Washington which is why the role of invaders has been reserved for the neighboring military regime [Honduras] and for pro-Somoza counterrevolutionaries entrenched in Honduras.[12]

10. R. Tuchin in *Izvestia*, June 18, 1980.

11. Y. Alexandrov, ed., *Grenada: U.S. Terrorism in Action* (Moscow: Novosti Press, 1983), p. 13.

12. Nikolay Morev, "Nicaragua Besieged by U.S. 'Aggressiveness,' " Moscow Radio Service in Spanish, October 7, 1982, FBIS–USSR, October 19, 1982, p. K/3.

Soviet assessments of a possible military intervention have changed since Grenada, but the implications of these reassessments have been reserved for discussion below.

It is, of course, somewhat perverse to be examining Soviet–American rivalry in Central America, given the asymmetrical geostrategic context of the confrontation. The heavy Soviet investment and escalated commitment to the Sandinista regime reflects not Soviet security or even economic interests but rather its interests as a global, revolutionary power. Under no definition can it be said that the Soviet involvement in Nicaragua is an act of self-defense, as opposed to an act designed to render more secure its global and imperial conquests. Nicaragua is not a vital interest of the Soviet Union as a state; even Cuba is not such an interest. A successful stabilization of a Marxist–Leninist regime in Nicaragua, as in Cuba, enhances the power, prestige, and influence of the Soviet Union and, more important, correspondingly debases those of the United States. From the Soviet perspective, Nicaragua becomes another pebble in the overall "correlation of forces," but a rolling revolutionary pebble that, while gathering no moss, serves to aggregate neighboring pebbles into a larger mass. We, of course, do not have access to a Nicaraguan version of the Grenadian Documents, but if we did, it might demonstrate more conclusively that Nicaragua is playing a larger role for Moscow in Central America than simply that of an isolated mini-dependency. It is not entirely unreasonable to assume that Nicaragua, like Grenada, might seek to deepen Soviet commitments to its survival if it could increase its value as an instrument of Soviet ambitions. One key Grenadian Document, with but minor changes in words, could well apply to the Nicaraguan situation:

> By itself, Grenada's distance from the USSR, and its small size, would mean that we would figure in a very minute way in the USSR's global relationships. Our revolution has to be viewed as a worldwide process with its original roots in the Great October Revolution. For Grenada to assume a position of increasingly greater importance, we have to be seen as influencing at least regional events. We have to establish ourselves as the authority on events in at least the English-speaking Caribbean, and be the sponsor of revolutionary activity and progressive developments in this region, at least.[13]

If the "domino effect" of the Nicaraguan revolution reflects a Reagan

---

13. *Confidential Report on Grenada's Relations with the USSR*, from Grenadian Ambassador to Moscow W. Richard Jacobs to Foreign Minister Unison Whiteman, Prime Minister Bishop, et al., *Grenada Documents*, Log. W, July 11, 1983.

administration nightmare, it is clear that Moscow and its clients visualize it as a delightful dream, prophesying things to come. Only recently, the preeminent Soviet foreign affairs analyst, Alexander Bovin, eloquently expressed Soviet anticipations by casting them in the form of the Reagan Administration's nightmares:

> They are taking very aggressive action because they fear Nicaragua. They fear exactly the same way that they feared Chile during the time of Allende and Grenada under Bishop. They fear it just as they do Cuba. But it's not the fear that a weak country feels of a strong one. The U.S., we surmise, is somewhat stronger than Grenada or even Cuba. The U.S. is afraid in a different way. . . . In the way that the world's bourgeoisie has feared and still fears all those who have decided to live without capitalists and landowners. It fears Nicaragua because the revolutionary regime in that country marks the beginning of the end of U.S. hegemony in Central America.[14]

Thus, Soviet analysts, if not always American and European critics of U.S. policy, clearly appreciate how a small, weak country can threaten the broad geostrategic and ideopolitical interests of a large, powerful state.

Clearly, if for both Washington and Moscow, El Salvador was nominated as the first of the dominoes destined to fall because of the Nicaraguan revolution, Mexico is perceived as the most substantial domino in the region. Furthermore, it is rather clear that what Nicaragua was doing in neighboring El Salvador was only what Grenada was dreaming about doing in Surinam and Belize, to mention the two most likely candidates for Grenadian recruitment to the Soviet fold named in the Grenadian Documents.[15]

Nicaragua, like Grenada, is even more important to Cuba in a direct dimension than it is to the Soviet Union. For Cuba, Nicaragua is not a randomly located, interchangeable Third World country to be manipulated and bargained in the interests of global ambitions, but a more prosaic and parochial quantity—a close neighbor, where a successful, kindred, revolutionary regime would not only enhance Cuba's prestige and legitimize its ideological underpinnings, but would serve to increase Cuban security as well. It would end Cuban isolation in the hemisphere and create the possibility of additional ideological playmates. The stakes for Cuba are higher than they are for Moscow, although the overall yield might be greater for the Soviet Union because it would affect the balance between two giants. Should the Nicaraguan regime be crushed, it would serve to deflate Soviet prestige, damage its self-confidence, and set back its imperial ambitions, but

---

14. Alexander Bovin, "The Heart of the Matter," *Izvestia*, May 5, 1985.
15. See Jacobs, *Confidential Report*.

it would threaten neither the existence of the Soviet state nor its regime. For Cuba, the overthrow of the Sandinista regime could spell disaster for the Castro regime, by enhancing the self-confidence of the United States and encouraging it in making another effort to overthrow Castro as well. There is great fear in Havana that if Nicaragua follows Grenada, then as night follows day, Cuba will follow Nicaragua.[16]

Given the geostrategic asymmetries in the situation, it is likely that neither Nicaragua or Cuba can rely on the Soviet Union to risk its own destruction by going to the mat with the United States over issues that are of vital interest to the United States and of peripheral interest to the USSR. To be sure, Soviet failure to risk destruction in order to protect Nicaragua or Cuba, in particular, will severely damage Soviet prestige and self-confidence. The damage, as mentioned, would be to its imperial incarnation rather than its existence as a state or social system. States have survived the losses of their imperial dependencies throughout history—most notably in recent decades—and the Soviet Union is equally capable of surviving the loss of a few remote appendages to its empire. The reassertiveness of U.S. foreign and military policy serves to delineate these asymmetries in stark and graphic terms.[17]

Soviet Perceptions of the Sandinista Revolutionary Process: The Seizure of Power

In examining the course of the Sandinista revolution, one is immediately struck by its syncretic character—a curious amalgam of the Cuban process of revolutionary seizure of power by armed insurrection and the East European process of consolidating power in incremental transitional phases, masquerading at each point as an idiosyncratic, terminal, ideological hybrid, shaped and conditioned by national and local peculiarities. Jiri and Virginia Valenta have lucidly shown that the revolutionary seizure of power in Nicaragua was modeled on that of the Castro revolution. It would be an exaggeration to state that it was a clone of the Cuban revolution, but it drew its inspiration from Cuba, whether it be from the Castro or Guevara spirit or a combination of both. Its connections with Moscow during its existence as a movement seeking power were somewhat tenuous, although

16. For a fuller development of this analysis, see V.V. Aspaturian, "The Impact of the Grenada Events on the Soviet Alliance System, " in *Grenada and Soviet/Cuban Policy*, ed. J. Valenta and H. Ellison (Boulder, Colo.: Westview Press, 1986), pp. 41–62.

17. Jiri and Virginia Valenta, "Sandinistas in Power," *Problems of Communism*, September–October 1985, pp. 1–28.

major Sandinista figures were instructed and trained in the Soviet Union as well as Cuba, but principally the latter, for a variety of reasons, mainly geographical propinquity and ethnocultural kinship. Marxism–Leninism was more a pragmatic manual for the seizure of power, eminently malleable and adaptable to a variety of local conditions, rather than a belief system. As was true in Cuba, Marxism–Leninism was grafted onto a prior nationalistic anti-Yankee sentiment, and served to draw in the Soviet Union as a potential supporter and protector of the revolution against possible U.S. counteraction.

Although similar to the Cuban seizure of power, three factors serve to distinguish the Sandinista revolutionary process from the Cuban. The first was the prior existence of Cuba to serve as a model and local crutch. Cuba had no model to emulate, nor did it have a local supporter; instead, the Cuban revolution was to survive confrontation with the United States in isolation and without external support. The second factor was the existence of the Soviet Union as a reservoir of indirect support, initially via Cuba, then more directly. Thus Nicaragua's confrontation with the United States during the seizure period was neither isolated nor without external support. Furthermore, the Sandinistas converted to Marxism–Leninism before the seizure of power rather than after, as in the Cuban case. The third distinguishing factor is that Nicaragua is on the mainland, contiguous to other states, most of them hostile; Cuba is an island state without adjacent hostile neighbors.

This third factor created a more inhospitable local environment for prolonged armed insurrection because of the continuous possibility of outside intervention. The opposite side of the coin was that the geographical situation enabled the Sandinistas to use neighboring states as a refuge or hideout and enhanced opportunities to foster kindred and supportive revolutions, as they attempted to do in El Salvador. By the same token, adjacent territories could be used by the United States to support anti-Sandinista guerrillas or local forces, or as staging bases for its own military preparations for an invasion.

During the early stages of the genesis of the Sandinista movement and revolution, Moscow observed it mainly from afar, through field glasses as it were. The genealogy of the Sandinista Front is relatively recent. It was a spin-off from the Nicaraguan Socialist party, founded in 1944 and essentially Stalinesque in nature. The predecessor had followed Moscow's prudent and cautious line of not challenging the United States in its own hemisphere.[18] Modeled on the communist-impregnated anti-fascist fronts of World War

18. The Nicaraguan Socialist party (PSN) survived the split and still exists today as a member of the National Assembly controlled by the FSLN.

II, it was ordered to support Somoza, just as the Indian Communist party was enjoined to support British rule, the Cuban communists to cooperate with Fulgencio Batista, and the Chinese communists to coordinate their activities with the Kuomintang—all in the service of the allied war effort, irrespective of the credibility problems this created locally. Fonseca and Borge were early leaders who became increasingly disenchanted with Moscow's line of revolutionary inaction; it was the Castro revolution in 1959 that lit a fire under Fonseca, Borge and others and impelled them to peel off and form a National Liberation Front in 1961, soon to be renamed the Sandinista National Liberation Front (FSLN).[19]

The new organization retained its "front" character and attracted a wide spectrum of recruits, who were anti-Somoza, anti-American, or both. Although the leadership was made up of recent recruits to Marxism−Leninism, its followers were by no means all communists or even Marxists. During the early 1960s it attracted mainly idealistic students, who were animated more by their zeal to rid the country of Somoza and his American backers than by communist ideology. It was during this period that the Ortega brothers (Daniel and Humberto) joined the front. By the late 1960s, it adopted a more definitive Marxist−Leninist line and developed the concept of protracted or prolonged guerrilla insurgency, based on a "revolutionary worker−peasant alliance," a concept that goes all the way back to Lenin on the eve of the Bolshevik Revolution. In operational terms, however, it was modeled more on Maoist and Vietnamese notions of prolonged rural insurgency, sprinkled with a dash of Guevarista ideas.

In 1969 a National Directorate was established to guide the front and instill revolutionary and ideological discipline among its followers. The leadership was monopolized by Marxist−Leninists. Subsequently the movement assumed the character of a "front," a broad coalition open to a wide spectrum of groups ranging from Marxist−Leninists to anti-Somocistas, but who were not necessarily anti-American. The struggle against Somoza assumed greater priority and indeed was a prerequisite for the movement toward anti-Americanism.

Indeed, the East European flavor of the Sandinista Front became rather evident when the first slice of salami, the non-anti-American anti-Somocistas, were lopped off and the group was converted from an anti-Somoza front into an anti-imperialist (i.e., anti-American) front. Since many of the early supporters of the front were also prominent business people, it also as-

19. See David Nolan, *The Ideology of the Sandinistas and the Nicaraguan Revolution* (Miami: Institute of Interamerican Studies, 1984), pp. 22−24. See also Roy Wells, "The Soviet Union and Nicaragua: Perceptions and Policies," Masters thesis in Political Science, Pennsylvania State University, 1986.

sumed the character of being an anti-big capitalist front, much in the manner of East European "fronts" before 1948, (i.e., during the first phase of the "people's democracies").

The Soviet line on struggle in Latin America did not change until the late 1970s. It remained one of caution, especially after the overthrow of the Allende government, which Moscow attributed to its excessive and flagrant revolutionary zeal. This was a period of ideological tension between Havana and Moscow, as Cuba advocated and sponsored a more active revolutionary line patterned after its own experience. Thus, the Soviet view of the Sandinista movement before its advent to power was that of an exotic bloom in Castro's strange revolutionary garden in which flowers were not clearly distinguishable from weeds in the eyes of Moscow.

Spontaneously spawned, volunteer "do-it-yourself," self-designated Marxist–Leninists have always been viewed with some suspicion and wariness by Soviet leaders since the days of Stalin. The history of the communist movement has demonstrated rather conclusively that leaders of such Marxist–Leninst revolutions tend to retain their habit of autonomy and reserve for themselves the ultimate decision whether to follow or not follow the Soviet line. Mao, Tito, Hoxha, Castro, and Ho Chi Minh were all indigenous communist leaders cast in this mold and, largely because of geographic factors, were beyond the disciplinary reach of Soviet power. Other communist leaders of similar tendencies in Eastern Europe were not so fortunate and were successfully purged. Since these communist leaders originally volunteered to associate themselves with the Soviet Union, they retained the right to disassociate themselves from Moscow as well—a process that Moscow seeks to prevent or at least to minimize. In cases of communist states beyond the reach of Soviet power, the only alternatives for Moscow are refusal to recognize such Marxist–Leninist credentials as bona fide, to excommunicate them from the communist fold and declare them anathema, or to accommodate and adjust to their autonomous tendencies.

Stalin's practice was to reject the Marxist–Leninist credentials of those who refused to accept rigid Soviet dictates and expel them from the Comintern before the advent of new communist states, or later to expel them from the communist fold, if they were in power, and call for their overthrow. Stalin's successors rejected the practice of strict orthodoxy in the examination of volunteer recruits (like Castro) and the practice of excommunication. Krushchev, for example, attempted to retrieve Yugoslavia by accommodating Tito, and attempted to prevent China's defection from Moscow, but failed. In any event, China was never formally excommunicated, as was Tito during the Stalin years, and the divorce has been more of Beijing's making than of Moscow's.

New, exotic Marxist–Leninist flowers in the Third World, in particular, have caused no end of ideological anguish for Moscow in dealing with them. Because of Cuba's exotic genesis, it took Soviet leaders many years and nearly a decade of internal ideological disputation before Cuba was finally recognized and accepted as a bona fide Marxist–Leninist state. Various and successive rubrics were coined and discarded in attempting to define Cuba ideologically for many years before it was finally accepted as "socialist." In recent years, Soviet writers have settled on the elastic concept of "socialist-oriented" regimes, countries, and movements to describe self-designated Marxist–Leninists and other self-appointed Soviet client states in the Third World.[20] This amorphous concept of "socialist orientation," in turn, has been further broken down into two types, of which the "vanguard party" type most closely approximates a bona fide Marxist–Leninist socialist system. Most of the "vanguard party," "socialist-oriented" regimes or movements are led by leaders who call themselves Marxist–Leninists, and the Marxist–Leninist core exercises hegemonic control over non Marxist–Leninist elements in the coalition or front that exercises formal authority.[21] From the Soviet standpoint, "socialist orientation" designates a regime or country whose "political will" is Marxist–Leninist, but whose country is at a stage of development that "objectively" precludes the translation of these political goals into social and economic reality. It reflects in many ways a variant of "utopian socialism;" whereas the leaders are imbued with Marxist–Leninist ideology and would like to transform their countries into socialist systems, neither the social development nor economic capabilities of the countries are sufficient for such a transformation. As a consequence, in many instances, "socialist-oriented" countries are woefully underdeveloped countries in the Third World, whose leadership constitutes the "advanced detachment" of a working class that does not exist but at some point in the future will presumably materialize out of the historical process.

The main translateable aspects of Marxist–Leninist ideology in most instances are political: strategies and tactics of organizing revolutionary seizures of power; consolidation of social and political control of the country by a small, dedicated elite; and imposition of its will on a larger, uninitiated mass. In Third World countries, Marxism–Leninism becomes essentially a process of seizing and maintaining power, and this is its most attractive characteristic to ambitious political personalities. Furthermore, the adoption of Marxism–Leninism as a guiding ideology links them to a global

20. For a lucid survey and analysis of the spectrum of Soviet specialist literature dealing with regimes and social systems in the Third World, see Elizabeth K. Valkenier, "Revolutionary Change in the Third World: Recent Soviet Reassessments," *World Politics* 38, no. 3 (April 1986): 415–434.

21. For a fuller discussion and analysis of "vanguard" parties and "socialist-oriented" countries, see Aspaturian, "Impact of Grenada Events."

power, whose authority and capabilities they seek to manipulate for their own purposes. Correspondingly, however, this means that they also incur the disfavor and hostility of the United States, whose capabilities many of them ironically need for developmental requirements.

These geostrategic consequences of ideological alignments were fully evident to the Sandinista leaders and were entered into freely and voluntarily. The world, according to a statement by Humberto Ortega in August 1981, is

> polarized into two great camps: on the one side the imperialist camp headed by the United States and the rest of the capitalist countries of Europe and the world, and on the other side the socialist camp, composed of different countries of Europe, Asia and Latin America, with the Soviet Union in the vanguard.[22]

It is noteworthy at this point to mention that although the Sandinista movement originated as a dissident fragment of a Moscow-line party, in its criticism of the parent party, unlike dissident Marxist–Leninists in other Central American countries, it scrupulously refrained from criticizing the Soviet Union, its policies, or its system as a revolutionary model. Instead, as subsequent events demonstrated, the Sandinistas were convinced that their more pragmatic, practical approach to revolution would in the long run be acceptable to Moscow, even though they may have violated abstract ideological imperatives in the process. After all, this was true of other indigenous revolutionary leaders from Mao to Castro.

The Consolidation of Power: Lessons from the East European and Cuban Experience

As noted, in the process of seizing power, the Sandinistas modeled themselves after Cuba, but in the consolidation of power, the process resembled more that of Eastern Europe in terms of form, strategy, and tactics, with many specific modifications and adjustments dictated by different spatial, temporal, and power contexts. The elements of deceit and duplicity in the consolidation of Sandinista power are more evident and perhaps necessary for success than in Cuba, where Castro's ultimate destination was neither preprogrammed nor even known by Castro himself. Historical analogies and models are always tricky, and history never repeats itself precisely.

22. Cited in Nolan, *Ideology of the Sandinistas*, p. 116. See also p. 128 note 26, in that volume.

Historical models rarely clone perfectly and using the Cuban and East European experiences as reference points in examining the Sandinista consolidation of power is no exception. With these caveats in order, we can proceed with a limited comparative analysis.

The Sandinista consolidation of power is distinguishable from the Cuban in a number of respects. Cuba's consolidation and transformation into a Marxist–Leninist state was and is likely to remain unique. Unlike the Cuban case, in Nicaragua preprogrammed sequential phases in the consolidation of power were largely absent, and the principal obstacle to consolidation was external—the United States. Given its island character, once it became evident that the United States had abandoned serious attempts to overthrow Castro, the consolidation process was one of dealing primarily with domestic obstacles, and thus deceit and concealment in the transition process were unnecessary and perhaps even undesirable.

The consolidation of Castro's power was complicated by an important feature that is absent in Nicaragua: the presence of an orthodox Cuban Communist party. This meant that Cuba had two "vanguard" parties in competition with one another to a certain degree, and this dichotomy had to be settled to the satisfaction of Moscow, among other matters. Once Castro self-converted to Marxism–Leninism and similarly converted his movement into a Marxist–Leninist vanguard, it was necessary to resolve the anomaly of two ruling Marxist–Leninist parties. Integration was necessary, but who would swallow whom in the process became the supreme conundrum. As it turned out, Castro swallowed the orthodox Communist party and subordinated it to his movement that assumed the identity of the Cuban Communist party. This pattern was necessary because, for a brief period, Castro's movement was non-Marxist–Leninist and coexisted with an established communist party, which had been tainted to some degree because it followed Moscow's advice to cooperate with the ousted Batista.

In Nicaragua, in contrast, the Sandinista Front before the seizure of power had already established itself as a surrogate for a Communist party, as did the East European fronts from 1945 to 1947. The leadership of the Front was Marxist–Leninist before the seizure of power, and no competing Marxist–Leninist party existed—only non-Marxist–Leninist partners in the coalition.[23] The Marxist–Leninist core leads the front and defines and

---

23. In a technical sense this is not precisely correct, since not only does the Nicaraguan Socialist Party exist as a separate entity, but a Communist party of Nicaragua (PCdeN), which is neo-Stalinist and critical of the FSLN, also exists. Neither constitutes a real or political threat to the Sandinistas, and they were not competitors with the Sandinistas during the revolutionary process since they were, by and large, pessimistic about the outcome. Both parties, however, have representatives in the National Assembly.

redefines its composition in accordance with the stages or phases of transition toward socialism. Thus, whereas in Cuba the process of consolidation involved the integration and assimilation of the Cuban Communist party into the Castro movement, in Nicaragua, as in Eastern Europe, the process of consolidation involves the integration, assimilation, or purging of non-Marxist–Leninist elements in the coalition.

As it progresses from one phase to another, conflict erupts between the Marxist–Leninist core and the partners slated for expulsion from the front. This occurs as the Sandinista regime assaults political, social, or economic interests of constituencies represented by non-Marxist–Leninist elements in the front, who resist these efforts. Conflict between factions and personalities within the Marxist–Leninist core itself may erupt as differences over strategy, tactics, and timing arise to intersect with personal ambitions and rivalries that exist within the leadership.

Even more important, the process in Nicaragua differs from both Cuba and Eastern Europe in a significant dimension: the existence of a hostile territorial environment within which the Nicaraguan process takes place. In Cuba, the process of consolidation was taken within the context of relative isolation without the presence of either an external threat or an interventionist Soviet Union. In Eastern Europe, the process of consolidation took place under the protective umbrella of Soviet power and in a substantial number of instances under Soviet military occupation or intervention in one degree or another. But Nicaragua has neither a friendly protective umbrella nor an interventionist USSR that inevitably accompanies it, and is surrounded by unfriendly or hostile neighboring states that give refuge to anti-Sandinista guerrillas and constitute potential staging areas for a possible direct U.S. intervention, the threat of which the Sandinista's find real, especially after Grenada and now Libya. From the Sandinista perspective, the recent behavior of the United States can only suggest that President Reagan means business.

Since the Sandinista consolidation of power takes place in territorial proximity to its enemies and distant from its major protector, the process of consolidation must move more cautiously, relying to a considerable extent on deception and dissimulation, to deceive the outside world into thinking they are something that they are not in order to minimize the pretext for a full-fledged U.S. military intervention. At the same time, the Sandinistas must make sufficient progress in accordance with Soviet prescriptions to retain their credentials as a Marxist–Leninist, socialist-oriented regime. Simultaneously, they must move with sufficient caution so as, first, not to alert groups slated for "purging" in order to fulfill Soviet ideological imperatives and, second, not to stimulate a strong American response. The Sandinista nightmare is the eruption of a serious domestic social conflict in which dissident elements "invite" U.S. intervention to save the revolution from itself. Hence the Sandinista strategy will resemble East European strategy in that at any particular stage in their development, the Sandinistas will continue to emphasize residual pluralistic and mixed elements in the system. This will not always be an easy matter.

From the Soviet standpoint, two indicators of authentic "socialist orientation" are an anti-imperialist, pro-Soviet foreign policy and a domestic policy of "progressive" social and economic transformation and development. This entails adopting what Soviet ideologists call a "noncapitalist" path of development, relying on the socialist world for direction, assistance, and advice. Since Soviet assistance capabilities are limited and since the possible implementation of internal socialist measures also may be limited, Soviet advice often includes the suggestion of a limited allowance for a petty-capitalist sector and restricted commercial and economic transactions with the capitalist world, but both policies executed in such a manner as to prevent capitalist ideological penetration that might derail their socialist orientation.[24] After prolonged ideological disquisition concerning the category of "socialist orientation," a definitive definition, which is still current, was finally arrived at and formulated by Leonid Brezhnev at the 26th Party Congress:

> These include gradual elimination of the positions of imperialist monopolies of the local big bourgeoisie and feudal elements, and restriction of foreign capital. They include the securing by the people's state of commanding heights in the economy and transition to planned development of the productive forces, and encouragement of the cooperative movement in the countryside. They include enhancing the role of the working masses in social life, and gradually reenforcing the state apparatus with national personnel faithful to the people. They include anti-imperialist foreign policy, revolutionary parties, expressing the interests of the broad mass of working people which are growing stronger there.[25]

A more specific and pointed linkage of the domestic and foreign policy aspects of "socialist orientation" is found in the formulation by Karen Brutents, deputy director of the International Department in charge of Third World countries:

> The cornerstone of socialist orientation is naturally the direction of domestic development. But experience has shown that a progressive anti-imperialist foreign policy is also an essential component. These two aspects are organi-

24. See Valkenier, "Revolutionary Change in the Third World."
25. Cited in Brutents, *Newly Freed Countries*.

cally linked. . . . Socialist orientation is impossible without close friendship and cooperation with the socialist world; it is even less possible on the basis of hostility towards it.[26]

The Soviet wariness of the Sandinistas before their accession to power carried over to a brief period after the seizure of power, particularly during the last years of the Carter administration when Moscow considered it still possible that the "socialist-oriented" direction of the Sandinistas in power might either be "bought off" or that domestic non-Marxist–Leninist forces might seize the upper hand with U.S. support. Once it became evident that the Marxist–Leninist core of the Sandinista leadership was firmly entrenched against internal displacement and the Carter administration demonstrated little predisposition to use force, Moscow took a more positive and optimistic attitude toward its chances and formally extended its offer of support in response to requests from Managua. It might be noted here that Castro's acceptance of the Sandinistas and his more optimistic evaluation of their survival possibilities also played a key role in persuading the Soviet Union to increase its stake in the Sandinista future.

Currently, the Sandinista regime is considered to be "socialist-oriented," of the "vanguard party" type, but Soviet strategy is to downplay this feature and encourage the Sandinistas to emphasize the mixed nature of the economy and the residual pluralistic character of its political system in order not unduly to arouse U.S. hostility. One lesson of Grenada is that the Grenadian leaders talked too much in public about their ultimate intentions, in violation of a crucial Soviet tactical rule that communists should not prematurely display their flag or show their cards. This was a strategy successfully implemented in Eastern Europe and unsuccessfully urged on Allende in Chile and apparently accomplished with limited success in Nicaragua. Particularly during periods of external danger, a successful consolidation and stabilization of power requires that Marxist–Leninists conceal their true intentions and convey the impression that a current, temporary transitional phase marked by residual pluralism and capitalism is a new, permanent hybrid of socialism and capitalism, a characterization that never fails to find broad acceptance domestically and among liberals and socialists in capitalist democratic countries.

Thus between 1945 and 1948, in Eastern Europe, during the first stages of the "people's democracies," emphasis was on the novelty of these new

26. Ibid., pp. 79–80.

systems, which were distinguished by an admixture of capitalism and socialism. A typical Soviet authoritative view of the period was as follows:

> Democracy of a special type [i.e., the "people's democracies" in Eastern Europe] corresponds to new production relationships which are being formed and which do not belong to capitalism, such as those in the lands of the old-type democracy, but neither are they socialist. By virtue of their building-up process, arising from specific historical developments in various countries, this special type of democracy yields a new historical pattern of both political and economic development which is sharply differentiated from common bourgeois economic development.[27]

Similarly, the political organizations, typically organized as "people's fronts" of one kind or another, were described as broad coalitions of political parties in which the Communist party did not occupy a predetermined dominating role. Thus, another Soviet ideologist characterized these "fronts" as follows:

> To represent the workers as the sole leaders in the countries of the new democracies is a vicious misrepresentation of the facts. The political foundation of state authority in countries of new democracy . . . rests on an alliance of all sections of the population except a narrow clique of big capitalists and landowners, and on a bloc of all democratic organizations and parties. . . . The prominent role of workers' parties in these governments, the leading role of the Communists in some of them, are determined by the democratically expressed will of the people.[28]

Beginning in 1947 and by 1948, these views were disavowed as ideologically incorrect and abandoned in favor of the immediate transformation of the "people's democracies" into "dictatorships of the proletariat" politically and "socialist countries" economically. The subsequent story of Eastern Europe is well known, but what is not equally well known is the cynical and crude manner in which some communist leaders revealed the cruel but successful deception and duplicity that was involved. Soon after the communist seizure and consolidation of monopolistic power in Hungary in 1947, an important Hungarian theoretician, J. Revai, revealed the consummate utility of ideological and political deceit.

---

27. I. P. Trainin, "Democracy of a Special Type," *Sovetskoye Gosudartsvo i Pravo*, no. 3 (March 1947): p. 3.

28. I. Konstantinovsky, "Progressive Role of the Working Class in the Countries of Eastern Europe," *New Times*, July 11, 1947, p. 28.

It was correct at that time [i.e., 1945–1947] to stress that the issue was not a choice between socialism or bourgeois private property. . . . It was correct that in the fight against big capital, we did not stress that this was a transition into the struggle for socialism. . . . *It was correct not to show our cards.*[29]

We currently find similar echoes of this strategy in Nicaragua, where the pluralistic character of the political order and the mixed nature of the economy are stressed and find a welcome acceptance in liberal, democratic, and socialist circles abroad. Even Arturo Cruz at one time was persuaded that although the Sandinista hard core was Marxist–Leninist, they would nevertheless be persuaded to institute a social democratic social order:

It was no secret that the hard core of the Sandinistas was Marxist. However, the non-Marxists in this alliance of political parties, labor unions, business-men, students and professionals were comforted by the pluralistic spirit which then prevailed. Nearly everyone felt confident that the Marxist vanguard was going to promote a social democracy.[30]

At about the same time, however, Humberto Ortega, in a letter to Francisco Rivera (Rubén) dated January 7, 1979, and subsequently cap-tured and published, specifically ruled out the establishment of a social democratic order simply because the immediate possibilities for establishing a socialist system were absent in Nicaragua, and made it quite clear that what was to be established would be a temporary way station on the road to socialism:

The fact that we [cannot] establish socialism immediately after overthrowing Somoza does not mean that we are planning a capitalist type Social Demo-cratic or similar development policy. What we propose is a broad, democratic and popular government, which although the bourgeoisie has participation, is a means and not an end, so that in time it can make the advance towards a more genuinely popular form of government, which guarantees the movement to-ward socialism.[31]

What Ortega had in mind was evidently a Sandinista equivalent of a first-

29. Josef Revai, "The Character of a People's Democracy," *Foreign Affairs*, October 1949, pp. 47–48.

30. Arturo Cruz, "Nicaragua's Imperiled Revolution," *Foreign Affairs*, Summer 1983, p. 1033. For illustrations of U.S. liberal perceptions of the Sandinista regime, see Alan Riding, "The Central American Quagmire," *Foreign Affairs* (America and the World) (1983); and Richard Ullman, "At War with Nicaragua," *Foreign Affairs*, Fall 1983.

31. As cited in Nolan, *Ideology of the Sandinistas*, p. 67., See also p. 80, note 18, for provenance of the letter.

stage "people's democracy," which would lead to the second stage, preparatory to the establishment of socialism, similar to what transpired in Eastern Europe between 1945 and 1948. (See also Appendix A.)

The Sandinistas have also apparently learned well from the East European experience the tactical importance of ideological deception during the process of seizing and consolidating power. In the same letter from Humberto Ortega to Francisco Rivera (Rubén), Ortega shrewdly outlines the tactical necessity of temporarily downplaying or even discarding overt Marxist–Leninist slogans, in order to broaden the appeal of the Sandinista Front. He also makes it clear that this does not mean disavowing Marxism–Leninism:

> Without slogans of "Marxist orthodoxy," without ultra-leftist phrases such as "power only to the workers," "toward the dictatorship of the proletariat," etc., we have been able – without losing at any time our revolutionary Marxist–Leninist Sandinista identity—to rally all our people around the FSLN.[32]

Thus it appears evident that the "socialist-oriented" regime is the Third World equivalent of the "new" or "people's democracy" of Eastern Europe in 1945–1948, in Soviet ideological formulations. Since "socialist-oriented" Third World countries are much less developed than Eastern Europe in the postwar period, the "model" of choice by Soviet writers for these countries is the People's Republic of Mongolia, which has been on the path of noncapitalist development toward socialism (retrospectively determined) for over six decades, and another 60 years is likely to ensue before the journey has been completed, if ever.[33]

With specific reference to the Sandinista Front, Soviet writers note that fronts of this character can become surrogates for the Communist party, which may no longer be absolutely necessary to carry out a program of socialist orientation.

> The military-political fronts of the sort of the "July 26 Movement" in Cuba and the Sandinista National Liberation Front in Nicaragua have shown (and now, it can be considered, proven) that under certain conditions they are capable of

32. Ibid., p. 69.

33. Soviet writers, however, have been suggesting in recent analyses that the Mongolian and Central Asian models may not be appropriate for Third World countries, mainly for two reasons, one covert and the other overt. The overt reason is that geographical adjacency to Russia was a decisive factor in their development and thus cannot be replicated in Latin America and Africa. The covert reason is that since Central Asia wound up as part of the USSR and Mongolia virtually an incorporated part of the Soviet Union, this might suggest a similar fate for other Third World countries.

taking *power* over the political parties of the proletariat as a revolutionary vanguard.[34]

Soviet writers have praised recent reorganizations of the Sandinista Front as evidence that the FSLN is successfully consolidating its power as it transforms itself into an authentic "vanguard type" party:

> The Sandinista revolution has disclosed additional and in many respects specific features of formation of the political vanguard in countries of a similar type. The experience of Nicaragua has shown that the formation of the political vanguard . . . determines the beginning of a new stage in historical development, which is institutionally manifested in the formation of a revolutionary democratic regime.[35]

And what, precisely, is a vanguard party in the Soviet view?

> Vanguard parties have a number of classical features in common with Marxist–Leninist parties. They acknowledge Marxism–Leninism as their ideological basis, build their activity on the basis of democratic centralism, and add to their ranks by individually selecting the best representatives of the working class, the peasantry and other working strata of the population. The above features determine the vanguard nature of these parties, which in a way are prototypes of Marxist–Leninist parties.[36]

And if vanguard parties, of which the Sandinista Front is one, are prototypes of Marxist–Leninist parties, then it means that countries of "socialist orientation," of which Nicaragua is an example, are prototypes of "socialist states."

Soviet descriptions of the consolidation process in Nicaragua are remarkably similar to those that characterized East European countries from 1945 to 1947. Thus, one Soviet observer waxes ecstatic over the "novel" aspects of the Nicaraguan revolution, which bear a striking resemblance to the historical novelties earlier alluded to:

> The implementation of the program of the Junta of the Government of National Reconstruction of Nicaragua started immediately after the victory of

---

34. S. A. Mikoyan, "On the Particular Features of the Revolution in Nicaragua," *Latinskaya Amerika,* no. 3 (March 1980): 34–44.

35. Yu. N. Korolev, "Historical Experience of the Transitional Period," *Latinskaya Amerika,* no. 6 (June 1984): 9-22.

36. Yu. V. Irkhin, "Vanguard Revolutionary Parties of the Working People in Newly Independent Countries," *Voprosy Istorii,* April 1982, pp. 55–67

the revolution. . . . The economic policy of the Sandinista leadership during the stage of reconstruction was aimed at creating a mixed economy, and primary attention was given to strengthening the state and public sector or the public ownership sphere.[37]

Another Soviet analyst was even more emphatic in describing the Nicaraguan experiment as "new" or even "unique" because of its mixed character:

> An experiment is being set up of an exceptionally interesting and possibly still unique variation of a people's democratic revolution. A model of the transitional period is being worked out in which the economic position of neither the national nor the foreign bourgeoisie will be seriously infringed upon.[38]

To obfuscate further the ultimate destination of the Sandinista revolution, a Soviet writer, in direct response to President Reagan's charge that Nicaragua was headed for the same goal that Castro took two decades earlier, maintained that Nicaragua was following "its own national path," in which a mixed economy and a multiparty political system were characteristic features:

> The Sandinistas are following their own national path. Nicaragua has a mixed economy—a state and private sector. There are opposition bourgeois parties. All these are features of the development of the Nicaraguan revolutionary processes. It is substantially different from the Cuban process.[39]

The above description could literally apply to what was being said about Poland, Czechoslovakia, and Hungary from 1945 to 1947, with the obligitory final passage at the time being that their path "is substantially different from the *Soviet* process."

Of course the process is different from the Cuban process; the point is, where does the process lead? In Marxist–Leninist ideology, a transitional stage in the revolutionary process is precisely that—a temporary phase of development—and must not be confused with a terminal or normative goal except by the uninitiated. Indeed, the essential purpose of the "transitional stage" is to dispatch two directly opposite messages to two different audiences. One message, dispatched to Marxists–Leninists, is that the revolution is temporarily parked in an interim stage, which will be superseded by another, depending on circumstances and conditions, on its way to socialism.

37. M. L. Chumakova, "On the Difficult Path of National Rebirth," *Latinskaya Amerika*, no. 7 (July 1980): 38–56.

38. Mikoyan, "Particular Features of the Revolution," p. 34.

39. V. Volski, "A White Paper of Black Deeds," *Sovietskaia Rossiya*, June 26, 1983.

The other message, sent essentially to non-Marxist–Leninists, conveys the impression that what is, in fact, an interim station is a definitive and terminal sociopolitical order.

The Sandinista leaders are even more circumspect in their ideological pronouncements, being careful never to refer to the FSLN as a Marxist–Leninist organization. Although they maintain relations with the Soviet Communist party through the Central Committee of the CPSU, only on rare occasions do Sandinista leaders like Ortega or Borge allude to their Marxist–Leninist connections. On one occasion, Borge did manage to mutter that "I believe that it would be frivolous, and even dishonest to say that no one here talks of Marxism. . . . I believe we are Marxists."[40]

One interesting peculiarity of the Nicaraguan situation is that their true credentials are betrayed more by their behavior and actual contacts with Moscow and the Soviet bloc and the descriptions appearing in Soviet writings than in their own utterances, which are more cautious and often elliptical to the point of dissembling. To repeat, we do not have the Nicaraguan equivalent of the Grenadian Documents and hence no access to internal, confidential discussions concerning the ideological character of the Sandinista movement and its organizational links with the Communist Party of the Soviet Union (CPSU). We do know that Sandinista leaders meet often with Soviet leaders in their party capacity and that party relations are conducted through Boris Ponomarev's International Department. Unfortunately, we do not have access to information or documents concerning party-to-party relations, which under these conditions are often more important and revealing than state-to-state relations, and for that reason are concealed from the outside world. Unlike the Grenadian leaders, however, the Sandinista leadership apparently found little difficulty in establishing regular contact with the highest levels of Soviet state and party leadership.

Thus Daniel Ortega successfully managed to meet with all four Soviet general secretaries since the Sandinista advent to power. Although Yuri Andropov was in office for about 18 months and accessible for less than a year because of illness, Daniel Ortega managed to meet him in March 1983. Similarly, although Konstantin Chernenko was in office for barely a year, Ortega managed to meet with him and a high-level Soviet delegation in June 1984. And finally, as if to make sure that Mikhail Gorbachev did not leave the scene before he could make contact, Ortega was in Moscow in May 1985, meeting with Gorbachev, this time with a high-level Nicaraguan party and state delegation, only 2 months after Gorbachev assumed office.

These high-level meetings invariably included Ponomarev and his top assistants in the International Department and their Nicaraguan counter-

40. Cited in Valenta and Valenta, "Sandinistas in Power," p. 8.

parts in the Sandinista Front, most notably Julio López (Campos), chief of the FSLN International Relations Department. These frequent high-level meetings between Moscow and Managua are more than symbolic and signify that Nicaragua has managed to find a place on the Soviet scale of priorities that is relatively high for a "socialist-oriented" country (i.e., at a level close to that of Ethiopia and Angola).

The Soviet and East European Connections: Political, Economic, and Military Relations

As stated, Nicaraguan behavior is a better guide to the nature of the Sandinista system than its pronouncements. Before the fall of Somoza, Moscow and Eastern Europe had virtually no contact with Nicaragua. The Soviet Union had little operational contact even with the Sandinistas as they were seizing power, but they moved with remarkable alacrity once the Government Junta of National Reconstruction was established. Soviet recognition of the new regime came one day after the fall of Somoza, and by March 1980 the top Sandinista leaders were already being feted in Moscow. This contrasts sharply with the relative delay the Soviets took before establishing relations with Castro.

During the years of Sandinista rule, Managua has oriented its political, economic, and military relations almost totally toward the East. Not only the Soviet Union, but all the countries of the Warsaw Pact have a presence of some sort in Nicaragua. Generally speaking, the presence of the East European countries follows a pattern similar to that found elsewhere in friendly Third World countries, especially "socialist-oriented" states. The East German (GDR),Czech, and Bulgarian presence is most conspicuous after that of Moscow, whereas Hungary and Poland bring up the rear, with Poland's Third World activity being nearly nil. Romania also has a presence, but whereas the activity of the other Warsaw Pact states appears to be closely intertwined and coordinated with that of Moscow, Romania tends to follow a more individualistic path, reflecting more its associate membership in the nonaligned group than its membership in the Soviet bloc. A peculiarity of the Romanian connection is that whereas it was one of the first countries to recognize the Sandinista government, by the beginning of 1985 Romania was the only Warsaw Pact country that had not exchanged ambassadors with Nicaragua. This was so even though a high-ranking Romanian official attended Daniel Ortega's installation as president in January 1985 and a Ceausescu–Ortega meeting had taken place in Bucharest in June 1984. In contrast, Albania established diplomatic relations as early as November 1979, Yugoslavia in March 1980, and Poland in August 1980.

On January 19, 1980, a delegation of Soviet planning officials arrived in Managua for a familiarization visit, which was a prelude to the first Soviet–Nicaraguan economic agreements, and, what was more important, probably laid the groundwork for the first high-level Nicaraguan political delegation to visit Moscow. On March 18, 1980, ministers of the interior (Tomás Borge), economic planning (Henry Ruiz), defense (H. Ortega), and junta member Moisés Hassan met with Soviet leaders Andrei P. Kirilenko, Boris Ponomarev, Ivan P. Arkhipov, and Georgi Korniyenko, a mixed party–state delegation. Ponomarev repesented the International Department of the Central Committee, Korniyenko the American Section of the Foreign Ministry, Arkhipov the Council of Ministers, and Kirilenko the Politburo. It was a high-level Soviet delegation, but not the *highest* level. Various political, economic, trade, party, and possibly military agreements were signed at this time, as Andrei Gromyko, Dimitriy Ustinov, and Pyotr Demichev also joined the Soviet group.

Particularly significant was the agreement signed between Ponomarev and Ruíz establishing relations between the Soviet Communist party and the FSLN. This signaled that the FSLN was being recognized and accepted by Moscow as a "fraternal" party. The presence of defense ministers Ustinov and H. Ortega suggests very strongly that initial military agreements also were signed, but no public mention was made of this.

As noted, Daniel Ortega has since managed to visit and confer with Leonid Brezhnev, Yuri Andropov, Konstantin Chernenko, and Mikhail Gorbachev, and high-level Nicaraguan leaders are no longer strangers to Moscow. Extensive and intensive party relationships also have been established, and the Sandinistas are clearly accepted as a "fraternal party."

Although Nicaragua's trade is still mainly with the noncommunist world, its commercial transactions with the Soviet Union and Eastern Europe have increased substantially since the advent of Sandinista rule (see Table 10.1). Soviet and East European economic assistance was very modest in 1980–1981, most of it free donations, including medical supplies. Educational exchange agreements also were signed, resulting in an initial contingent of several hundred Nicaraguan students being sent to the Eastern bloc for higher education.

The GDR and Bulgaria were the first East European countries to extend relatively extensive economic and financial assistance to Nicaragua, beginning in March 1980. In 1981 additional agreements were signed with Hungary and Czechoslovakia. Romania also entered into economic agreements at this time. Since then, Warsaw Pact countries have carried on a wide spectrum of political, economic, and military relations with Nicaragua, of which only the economic agreements are for the most part on the public record. Political and military agreements generally remain secret and confidential, particularly as to details.

TABLE 10.1

Nicaragua: Foreign Trade Structure by Economic Region, 1980–1983 (in percentages)

	Exports				Imports			
	1980	*1981*	*1982*	*1983*	*1980*	*1981*	*1982*	*1983*
eveloping Countries	19.4	28.7	25.5	24.4	57.9	50.6	46.9	44.1
CACM[a]	16.7	13.9	12.8	7.8	33.9	21.1	15.1	15.3
ALADI[b]	.1	2.2	3.6	2.1	20.2	26.0	27.2	23.5
Others	2.6	12.6	9.1	14.5	3.8	3.5	4.6	5.3
Caribbean	1.7	1.9	2.2	1.2	3.0	2.5	1.7	3.4
Asia	.6	10.7	6.9	13.3	.8	1.0	2.9	1.9
Europe	.3	—	—	—	—	—	—	—
ECD[c]	77.9	64.0	67.1	62.9	41.9	46.1	41.3	39.1
USA	36.0	25.8	22.2	18.1	27.5	26.3	19.0	19.4
EEC	28.8	19.4	23.5	25.7	7.9	11.5	14.1	9.7
Other OECD	13.1	18.8	21.4	19.1	6.5	8.3	8.2	10.0
MEA[d]	2.7	7.3	7.4	12.7	.2	3.3	11.5	16.6
Eastern Europe	2.7	4.9	7.1	8.5	.2	2.5	7.5	11.4
Others	—	2.4	.3	4.2	—	.8	4.0	5.2
thers	—	—	—	—	—	—	.3	.2
Total [Rows I, II, III, IV only]	100	100	100	100	100	100	100	100

[a]CACM=Central American Common Market
[b]ALADI=Latin American Association for Integration
[c]OECD=Organization for Economic Cooperation and Development
[d]CMEA=Council for Mutual Economic Assistance
SOURCE: Rubén Barrios, *Relations between Nicaragua and the Socialist Countries*, paper (Washington, D.C.: Woodrow ■lson International Center for Scholars, September 1984).

According to one source, promised economic assistance to Nicaragua by 11 communist countries during 1979–1983 totaled nearly $1.25 billion, broken down as follows: economic assistance, $450 million; trade credits, $424 million; $194 million in donations; $81 million in non-trade-related aid; and $66 million in technical assistance. From the Soviet bloc countries, the USSR leads in assistance with $443 million, followed by Bulgaria with $232 million, the GDR with $103 million, Czechoslovakia with $75 million, and Hungary with $5 million. The total for Eastern Europe and the Soviet Union amounted to $859.45 million.

Arms transfers from the Soviet bloc show even more dramatic increases, having steadily increased since mid-1980, soon after the first arms agreement was signed. Between 1979 and 1982, arms shipments to Nicaragua amounted to about $125 million, which was relatively modest, but after mid-1982, arms shipments from the Soviet bloc were speeded up; in 1983 alone, Nicaragua received more than $120 million worth of arms. It soon became evident that Nicaragua was embarked on a military buildup of a magnitude never before seen in this region. Military equipment came not only from the Soviet bloc but from other countries as well, although the USSR supplied the bulk. By 1983 the Nicaraguan military machine had been enlarged substantially, and Soviet bloc military deliveries were estimated at approximately 20,000 tons per year, compared to 10,000 tons in 1981–1982. By 1985 it was also estimated that the Soviet bloc was subsidizing Nicaragua to the tune of $300 million per year and that about 400 East European and Cuban ships were docking every year at the port of Corinto. In a country with a population of fewer than 3 million, Nicaragua's armed forces now total over 35,000 with an additional ready reserve of 27,000, a substantial burden for a small, impoverished country.

All this economic and particularly military assistance from the Eastern bloc was justified in terms of the U.S. threat, which in turn was a response to the Nicaraguan "export of revolution" to El Salvador. Daniel Ortega, in explaining the Soviet-East European connection, maintained:

> At a time when U.S. imperialism is causing us tremendous economic damage by denying us supplies of essential raw material for our industry, the Soviet Union is displaying fraternal solidarity, giving us all-round assistance to develop our economy, and providing raw materials and food, and this is helping us to overcome the difficulties created by imperialism.[41]

Needless to say, the reasons for the large Nicaraguan military force are subject to serious controversy and debate. Is it there for legitimate self-defense or for the purpose of exporting and/or supporting anti-American revolutionary movements? Given the escalating hostility between Nicaragua and the United States, the Nicaraguan military buildup can support either explanation or even both simultaneously. What is not disputable is that anti-U.S. animosity was structured into the Sandinista movement, and even after the Carter administration pulled the rug out from under Somoza and welcomed the Nicaraguan regime with a hefty offer of financial and economic assistance, the Sandinistas showed little interest in ameliorating relations with Washington and quickly established connections with Moscow and the East European states. Furthermore, the Sandinistas, fresh and smug after their victory, increased support to guerrillas in neighboring El Salvador, aimed at creating another center of anti-Yankee sentiment in Central America.

Although the advent of the Reagan administration resulted in the escalation of tensions between Washington and Managua, the Sandinistas had clearly set off on their pro-Soviet, anti-American path well before the

---

41. Interview with Daniel Ortega, *Pravda*, January 11, 1984.

Reagan administration was installed. It should be reiterated that high-level Sandinista leadership visits to Moscow had already taken place during the Carter administration.

Periodic Soviet support for the Nicaraguan military buildup, usually couched in self-righteous, legalistic, but politically insensitive language does little to reduce U.S. suspicions of Nicaraguan intent. Thus, in connection with a meeting between Sandinista Defense Minister Humberto Ortega and Marshals Ustinov and Ogarkov and Admiral Gorshkov in April 1984, an *Izvestia* commentator rebuked President Reagan because he warned that the delivery of MIG fighters to Nicaragua could be a provocation justifying intervention:

> And what if modern fighter interceptions suddenly did appear in Nicaragua? What of it? Every country has the right to acquire the weapons that it needs to ensure the inviolability of its borders. . . . D. Ortega stated firmly that Nicaragua is fully entitled to acquire any types of weapons necessary for its self defense.[42]

On February 15, 1984, at Andropov's funeral, Daniel Ortega met with Foreign Minister Andrei Gromyko, the new general secretary, Chernenko, and with the CPSU Central Committee in full session. Economic and military relations of an "urgent and long-term" nature were discussed, as Nicaragua's economy was integrated more intimately with that of the Soviet Union. Exchanges of high-level political, economic, and military delegations between the two countries had become routine by this time, as Nicaragua was practically incorporated into the Soviet bloc when it joined the Council of Economic Mutual Assistance (CEMA) as an observer in September 1984. There is little question that by the beginning of 1985, the Soviet investment in Nicaragua was substantial and was designed, first, to deter an American invasion of Nicaragua and, second, to make the cost of a U.S. military intervention extremely dear if deterrence failed. Accordingly, Gorbachev in his meetings with Daniel Ortega in April 1985, pledged:

> The USSR will continue to give friendly Nicaragua assistance in resolving urgent problems of economic development, and also political and diplomatic support in its efforts to uphold its sovereignty. The Soviet leadership proceeds from the assumption that in the present-day situation, broad international solidarity with Nicaragua is an inalienable part of its common struggle for peace and for the right of all peoples to freedom and independence.[43]

42. "Behind a Scene of Trumped Up Pretexts," *Izvestia*, November 20, 1984.
43. "Meeting with Nicaraguan Delegation," *Pravda*, April 30, 1985.

Conclusions

In spite of the progressive integration of Nicaragua, politically and economically, into the Soviet bloc, and the relatively large material investment made by Moscow and its allies in a remote and small country, the Soviet material stake is not matched by any qualitative change in the nature of its commitment to the survival of the Sandinista regime. Nicaragua is not classified as a socialist country but a "socialist-oriented" one, which means that the Soviet Union is not committed to its defense either by formal treaty obligations or self-assumed ideological obligations (i.e., the Brezhnev Doctrine).

Futhermore, given Nicaragua's vulnerability to U.S. pressure and possible assault, Moscow calculates that the United States could at any time unilaterally choose to destroy the Sandinista regime, given the isolation of Nicaragua and the disparate capabilities of the two countries. From Moscow's perspective, Nicaragua is simply a larger Grenada, and this image is probably shared by Managua and Cuba as well. What restrains the Reagan administration, in Moscow's view, is neither Soviet military power nor the costs that Nicaragua might inflict on the United States in its defense, but the lack of societal and political consensus in the United States and the opposition of the world at large, including America's principal allies. Nevertheless, Moscow has publicly conceded that "socialist-oriented" countries such as Nicaragua, unlike socialist countries, are subject to historical reversibility as a result of imperialist aggression. Thus, according to Soviet calculations:

> Imperialism is aware of historical experience, which has shown that the ultimate choice of direction . . . may be a long time in the making . . . which may zigzag, and that socialist orientation in itself does not guarantee the victory of socialism and does not rule out backtracking and returning to capitalism.[44]

And while the socialist world, including the USSR, is not committed to preserve the survival of such regimes, Moscow recognizes that the overthrow of "socialist-oriented" regimes does undermine Soviet prestige and the credibility of its protective capability:

> The socialist-oriented countries are subjected to imperialism's mounting pressure. . . . In its effort to defeat the trend of social development represented by these countries, imperialism hopes to minimize the prestige of socialism . . . [and] to undermine or to weaken in this way the alliance and cooperation of these countries and the socialist world.[45]

44. Brutents, *Newly Freed Countries*, pp. 105–106.
45. Ibid., pp. 104–105.

Soon after the invasion of Grenada, fear akin to paranoia gripped both Nicaragua and Cuba, since the action increased the credibility that Reagan's belligerent rhetoric might be translated into actual behavior. Both Cuba and Nicaragua dampened their anti-American rhetoric, and Sandinista leaders slowed down the pace of their revolution and internal transformation. The Soviet connection was deepened, however, and military assistance was escalated in both quantity and quality.

Consequently, a U.S.-sponsored or direct invasion of Nicaragua would come as no great surprise to Moscow, although it would send shock waves through the Kremlin halls. Whereas, before Grenada, the Moscow position was that the United States was effectively deterred from resorting to military force to impose its will on Third World countries, after Grenada, the perception changed dramatically. Soviet writings are now replete with charges and accusations that the Reagan administration is about to unleash a military adventure in Central America. All the talk about a "favorable shift in the correlation of forces" has vanished from Soviet writings. In its place, ominous observations such as the following have taken their place:

> Everything is being done to get Americans and world opinion accustomed to acts of lawlessness towards Nicaragua and in doing so to give the White House a free hand for any kind of action against that country. The desire is to get the people to put up psychologically with an aggression that is being prepared.[46]

Both the Sandinistas and Moscow are by now persuaded that President Reagan's only acceptable solution to the issue is the overthrow of the Sandinista regime, and while the President's rhetoric seems to support this view, his position may not be cast in concrete and may be adopted primarily for hard bargaining. Nevertheless, the Soviet perception appears to be that the Reagan administration is determined to crush the Sandinista regime:

> The U.S. President publicly announced his intention to overthrow Nicaragua's democratic government, which was legally elected by its people. All attempts at hiding this have been abandoned. The *New York Times* notes that the Washington administration is no longer trying to justify its hostile actions with arguments to the effect that Nicaragua should cease buying weapons abroad and get rid of its foreign military advisers, or trying to term Nicaragua's aid to the Salvadoran guerrillas its "greatest sin." Now the White House is saying that it simply "will not tolerate" the government that is not to its liking.[47]

46. "To Thwart U.S. Criminal Plans in Central America," *Pravda*, April 8, 1984.
47. V. Ovchinnikov, "Hostility Intensifies," *Pravda*, March 5, 1985.

It appears that Moscow's perception of the situation is that the Reagan administration and the Sandinista regime are on a collision course, which suits neither Moscow nor Nicaragua, and the leaders of both countries have been expecting an American military intervention since the Grenada action. Apparently, this is a view shared by European and American critics of U.S. policy and even by many within the Reagan administration. Since Soviet press commentary repeatedly cites leading U.S. newspapers (*The New York Times* and *The Washington Post* mainly) and statements of congressional and other U.S. political critics as charging the administration with deception and duplicity insofar as its aims and intentions with respect to Nicaragua are concerned, it is difficult to determine whether this type of U.S. commentary is viewed in Moscow as confirmation of Soviet perceptions or whether it is adopted by Soviet writers because it will receive a favorable reception by the critics and be cited as confirmation of their own ominous perceptions of the Reagan administration's policies and intentions.[48]

Much of American journalism, especially critical journalism, is marked by hyperbole, exaggeration, sensationalism, and speculation, as is the case with domestic political debate, and it is not always clear that the outside world—friends or enemies—is sufficiently attuned to the American public debating style to make the appropriate allowances and distinguish reality from its various rhetorical ornamentations. This applies, of course, not only to Nicaragua but to a wide spectrum of international, social, and political issues. If the outside world takes seriously some of these exaggerations and speculations, a seriously distorted image of Washington and its policies is likely to be the consequence. After all, outsiders are likely to say, if prominent American critics believe that the Reagan administration is out to overthrow the Sandinista regime, then it must be true.

It is, of course, commonplace that exaggerated and speculative accusations are made as a deterrent or preventive mechanism. This is particularly true of Soviet rhetorical behavior. Thus, much of the Soviet accusation of imminent U.S. armed intervention in Nicaragua (repeated incessantly since

48. Some liberal critics of administration policy may agree that the Sandinistas are hard-core Marxist–Leninists and even allied with Moscow, but even this acknowledgement is insufficient to justify American intervention. One critic even insists that a Soviet missile base in Nicaragua would be no cause for alarm. Thus, Richard Ullman writes: "Even in the worst (and least possible) case—the establishment of Soviet bases on its territory—Nicaragua could not seriously harm the United States. . . . If they were ever to set up a base in Central America . . . the cost to the United States of neutralizing it would be slight. Moreover, in an era of intercontinental missiles, firing nuclear weapons from nearby bases conveys no benefit." *Foreign Affairs*, Fall 1983, p. 52. If it is Ullman's conviction that "nearby" missile bases convey no threat, he might find it enlightening to ask Moscow why it was so concerned about U.S. Pershing II and Cruise missiles in Europe.

Grenada) is aimed at deterring and preventing such an event rather than predicting it. It becomes part of an overall Soviet strategy to preserve the Sandinista regime and avoid conflict and confrontation with the United States. Continued and even escalating military and economic assistance from the Soviet bloc can be anticipated, together with Soviet words of caution and prudence to the Sandinistas not to yield to provocation or engage in rash actions.

It is the apparent Soviet intent, on this issue as well as others, to wait out the Reagan administration, since up to this point it has been unwilling to pay the price (in terms of modifying its behavior and policies) necessary to engage in serious businesss with the current administration. Nicaragua seems to be following the same course. Hence the Soviet leaders will continue to pay lip service to the Contadora process, since it is viewed as a delaying mechanism, and to echo and reinforce European and domestic American critics of the Reagan administration.

Nicaragua, for its part, will reluctantly follow Soviet advice and refrain from provocation or excessive activity, although past experience has shown that the Sandinista leaders are notoriously imprudent in their political behavior. Expansion of the public sector of the economy will be kept at a slow pace, the residual pluralistic character of the Sandinista system will be stretched out, but Managua will resist entering into negotiations with the *contras*, much less share power with them.

Broad sectors of European opinion and substantial American domestic constituencies are also opposed to armed U.S. intervention, whose costs will steadily escalate as the Sandinistas consolidate their control and continue the military buildup for "defensive purposes." Soviet and Nicaraguan strategy will attempt to manipulate, support, and reinforce these sentiments. Support for revolutions in neighboring countries will also probably taper off, since it would be viewed as a provocation by the administration.

And if deterrence or prevention fails, Soviet military assistance will serve to raise the costs of a successful (or even unsuccessful) U.S. military intervention in terms of human and material losses, to say nothing of the incalculable domestic and international political damage that will ensue. In a sense, the Soviets stand to gain something whether the Sandinista regime survives the Reagan administration or whether it succumbs to armed intervention. Moscow, of course, would prefer that the Sandinista regime survive, since its survival, from the Soviet perspective, as pointed out by Alexander Bovin, will undermine and erode the U.S. position in Central America. And if serious socioeconomic problems continue or increase in Mexico, this can result in ominous consequences of incalculable proportions.

Both the United States and Nicaragua have defined their respective positions toward one another in such a manner that no rational compromise between the Reagan administration and the Sandinista regime seems possible. Instead, the administration earlier could have framed its dispute with Nicaragua purely in terms of the Soviet connection, irrespective of Nicaragua's internal social and economic order, which might have laid down a foundation for a tradeoff: severance of the Soviet connection by Managua in return for U.S. acceptance of a purely Nicaraguan internal socialist order. But in the Reagan administration's calculations, the Sandinista regime's foreign and domestic policies were inseparably linked. To a certain extent, the Sandinista leadership shared this ideologically inspired notion of the inseparability of domestic and foreign policy. The Sandinista concept of full independence includes choosing its external friends and allies without American interference and with a disturbing unconcern for U.S. security interests that would be affected by Managua's choice of friends.

The issue is no longer whether the Sandinista regime is Marxist–Leninist or not. This has, by and large, been settled; even critics of the administration no longer dispute this, except in marginal terms. The issue is what to do about another Marxist–Leninist regime in the Western Hemisphere or the Central American isthmus: to undermine and destroy it one way or another, or to seek an accommodation. Since the United States has learned to live and cooperate with Marxist–Leninist systems not under Soviet direction or influence, it is a distortion to maintain, as critics do, that the administration's principal objection to the Sandinistas is the internal order and that no accommodation is possible unless that order is changed.

To be sure, the Reagan administration is not delighted with Marxist–Leninist regimes anywhere, but they are not all treated and viewed interchangeably either. The chief objection to the Sandinistas is the Soviet connection; this is also true of Cuba. Were Castro and Ortega successfully to reorient their foreign policies away from the Soviet Union, most of the objections to normalization would evaporate. After all, the United States welcomed China with open arms in the 1970s, although serious domestic excesses continued to take place; the welcome to Marshal Tito did not require a fundamental domestic change in the Yugoslav social order, although one transpired in any event. Romania, which is one of the worst residual Stalinesque communist states in the world, finds that its domestic order plays only a marginal role in its relations with the United States.

The common factor that shapes U.S. relations with non-Soviet influences or dominated Marxist–Leninist states is severance or diminution of the Soviet connection, not internal reform or transformation, although insistence on the latter plays both a secondary and bargaining role. There is little reason to believe that the administration does not consider the Sandinista–Soviet connection to be the main obstacle to normalization of relations. Nicaragua's connection with the Soviet Union ineluctably threatens the security of the United States; its internal social order does not, although it may be unpalatable to American political tastes.

The United States, however, in the case of Nicaragua, cannot afford the luxury of waiting for "Titoization" to take its normal path of a period of intense Soviet embrace followed by disillusionment, conflict, and disassociation. Given Nicaragua's geostrategic importance to American security and hemispheric interests, the process of "Titoization" itself, especially if protracted, constitutes a danger because it would include an indefinite period of intense Soviet–Nicaraguan involvement, which appears inevitable unless something drastic intervenes. To borrow a page from Soviet ideostrategic notions, the United States must insist on the elimination of several stages of development and insist that Nicaragua sever its Soviet connection immediately, in return for U.S. acceptance of Nicaragua's choice of an internal social order, which in the absence of a Soviet connection is bound to move away from "socialist" positions in any event.

Such a tradeoff has never been explicitly articulated by the Reagan administration, and whether such a tradeoff is possible or was ever possible has never been tested. In any event, given the fact that many critics of U.S. policy believe that the administration's intolerance of the internal Sandinista social order constitutes the main obstacle to normalization and that the Soviet connection is merely a fig leaf, an explicit U.S. articulation of such a tradeoff, which is at once serious and credible, would confront the Sandinista regime with a choice between survival without the Soviet connection or more draconian measures. At the same time, domestic and external critics of administration policy would be deprived of their most important objection to administration policy and be forced to acknowledge their indifference to American security interests unless they support such a tradeoff. Should the Sandinistas refuse to negotiate such a tradeoff, which admittedly will be very difficult for them, the central issue of the U.S. – Sandinista controversy would clearly emerge as being U.S. security and not administration ideology.

Neither this administration nor any other can tolerate a Sandinista autonomy that includes the right to endanger the security of the United States. This has always been the central nexus of the Monroe Doctrine and U.S. hemispheric policy, and this conditioned U.S. opposition to Argentine and other sporadic Latin American attempts to establish close connections with Nazi Germany, and will continue to shape U.S. policy toward any hemispheric country that aligns itself with nonhemispheric great powers that endanger U.S. security.

• CHAPTER ELEVEN •

Western Europe and Central America
Ottfried Hennig

Although Western Europe does not have vital interests in geographically distant Central America, the political turmoil in this area has captured Europe's attention. Is it "arrogance" on the part of the European Economic Community (EEC) to state that it is prepared to offer the Central American states its assistance in solving the latter's problems? What form could a common European policy on Latin America, or at least on Central America, take? Can it be coordinated successfully with U.S. policy? Finding answers to these questions is of paramount importance not only for Euro–Latin American relations but, perhaps more important, for relations between Europe and the senior Atlantic alliance partner.

As Federal Foreign Minister Hans-Dietrich Genscher stated on December 17, 1985, before the Simón Bolívar Society in Wolfenbüettel,[1] Europe's relations with Latin America are currently experiencing a revival, the scope of which is impossible to gauge today but the thrust of which is clear: "Over and above the emphasis placed on links that have their roots in history and tradition, we [Europeans] wish to arrive at a new form of political, economic and cultural cooperation [with Central America and] we are prepared to lend substance and meaning to this new cooperation."

Interest in Latin America, however, was almost nonexistent during the previous Social Democratic government of the Federal Republic of Germany. In those days, the German government devoted little attention to Latin America in general and Central America in particular. In the percep-

1. See *Bulletin der Bundesregierung* (Bonn), no. 145 (December 20, 1985).

237

tion of Europeans (with the exception of Spain and Portugal), this region was not only geographically far away but apparently of little relative importance. Only after a revolutionary government acceded to power in Nicaragua, the military in El Salvador were replaced, and the danger of a new Vietnam loomed in Central America did the Europeans commit themselves more strongly to this area. Because of a lack of correct information, however, they often aligned themselves with the wrong side.[2]

Important steps have been taken by European governments to ensure that greater attention is given to Central America, where political instability threatens to spark a major international confrontation. The indirect effects that such a conflict would likely have on Europe have prompted the European Community in general and its individual members in particular to take action with respect to the region. In this endeavor, the government of the Federal Republic of Germany has played a major role. On the latter's initiative, the European Community launched an intraregional dialogue and cooperation program at a major conference held in San José, Costa Rica, in September 1984. This was an unprecedented step. The meeting was attended by the ministers of foreign affairs of the 10 members of the EEC as well as the EEC president, the ministers of foreign affairs of Spain and Portugal (as prospective members of the EEC), and their counterparts in the five Central American countries and the four Contadora group countries. A follow-up to this conference took place in Luxemburg in November 1985, when the EC signed a cooperation agreement with Central America and issued a political declaration.

The Luxemburg conference furnished political proof of the strength and viability of what became known as the "San José process" whose objectives were the promotion of peace, freedom, and social justice on the basis of complete equality. The principle of equality was of prime importance in that the cooperation agreement did not discriminate against any country; Nicaragua was also part and parcel of the San José process and its outcome.

---

2. One example: The official credit guarantee department in Germany, Hermes, offers guarantees in cases where an excessively high political risk would otherwise prevent deals by German businessmen and investors. During the dictatorship of Romero y Galdámez in El Salvador, the Federal government gave unlimited Hermes guarantees, subsequently introduced a ceiling of DM 100.000 under the first Salvadoran junta, and stopped giving guarantees in 1980. The reverse procedure would have made some sense. Today, under the new democratically elected government in El Salvador, the federal government is giving unlimited Hermes guarantees to that country. After October 1, 1982, the day on which the new government came to power in the Federal Republic of Germany, things began to change for the better. While the catastrophic budgetary situation that the new government found on taking office also limited the possibilities of providing assistance in the field of development policy, a number of signals were soon given.

The signing of the cooperation accord and the political declaration in Luxemburg marked the beginning of what has been conceived as a long-term process of European cooperation with Central America. For the Latin American countries involved, it meant that the "Europe of Twelve" had become an important source of support and that its individual members could be considered partners (1) capable of understanding the Latin Americans' political and economic concerns and (2) prepared to make tangible contributions toward solving their problems. In the case of the Federal Republic of Germany, the aims are neither to overshadow nor to play down the existing political, economic, and strategic interests of other actors in the region.

On May 15, 1985, the European Parliament adopted a resolution welcoming the Luxemburg cooperation agreement. The program laid down there envisaged aid totaling 40 million ECU for Costa Rica, El Salvador, Guatemala, Honduras, and Nicaragua. The resolution of the European Parliament called for this sum to be doubled, to a total of 80 million ECU per annum, for the duration of the accord. At the same time, the resolution criticized the Council of Ministers for excluding from the accord the political cooperation suggested by the European Commission.[3]

At the bilateral level, calls for greater cooperation with Central America also bore fruits. For instance, the Federal Republic of Germany has stepped up the amount of developmental aid to the Caribbean and Central America to such an extent that this region is becoming a fulcrum in the context of official developmental assistance. Since 1980, German developmental aid for the Caribbean and Central America has increased from DM 138.3 million to DM 151.5 million. The Federal Republic's aim is to contribute to the political and economic stabilization of the region, particularly by helping to alleviate the population's economic and social hardships, which constitute one of the major causes of internal and external strife.

Central America's and the Caribbean nations' difficult economic situations have made it necessary for them to reschedule their debts, which remain one of the region's worst economic problems. In 1985 the Federal government concluded rescheduling agreements with Jamaica, Costa Rica, and the Dominican Republic. Haiti's debt to Germany, amounting to DM 25.9 million, has been cancelled. Not all cases have been resolved successfully, however. For example, Nicaragua owes the Federal Republic approximately DM 40 million, and that debt has not been rescheduled. The Federal government continues to fulfill its outstanding commitment to Nicaragua but no new aid is forthcoming because of the dissatisfaction with Nicaragua's nonfulfillment of the goals of the revolution—nonalignment, a mixed economy, and political pluralism. German aid to Nicaragua will not be resumed

3. See *Das Parlament* (Bonn), no. 24/25 (June 14 and 21, 1986): 10.

until Nicaragua's Leninist leadership reinstates the original principles of the revolution.

It is possible for West Germany to pursue a very specific policy toward Central America, just as it has been possible for France to do so. France's policy is governed mostly by tactical considerations. The French socialist government has often closed its eyes to the Central American reality and has concentrated more on aspects that seemed to be politically opportune for domestic and foreign policy purposes. Germany, or even Britain, could conceive a similar policy, but in official circles this is not deemed desirable.

A preferable policy, at least from the West German point of view, would be one agreed on within a European context, at EC level, and coordinated with the United States. Only a very comprehensive, coherent policy would be taken seriously and would exert a corrective influence on the policies of important Latin American countries geographically close to the United States. The conference held in San José in September 1985 is the most significant success achieved thus far in this direction. For the first time, the Europeans acted as a political unit and spoke with one voice, presenting a jointly prepared and coordinated stance.

The European Community has offered to make assistance available to the Central American states with a view to solving the region's current problems. This assistance includes (1) a political dialogue aimed at safeguarding peace through negotiations; (2) a revival of the Central American organizations of integration; and (3) regional development projects. Even though all EC member states were willing to engage in a lasting and meaningful cooperative process between the two regions, evidenced by the cooperation agreement with Central America, this effort was not universally welcomed in Europe. Some pointed out that Europe already has overextended itself. Others argued that the decision to increase developmental aid was reached without consulting the will of the people. On this point, the Europeans do not speak with one voice.

The lack of European consensus on the question of increased attention to Central and Latin America has to do with a variety of political, economic, social, military, and strategic considerations concerning the Latin American region. Is it possible to draw general conclusions from the total of these considerations? Do these countries have enough in common, or is the situation too different from one case to the next? Are there any common features that are valid for the whole of Latin America? One thing which these countries seem to have in common and which is encountered in the same form everywhere is a virulent and militant anti-Americanism at worst or, at best, a very ambivalent attitude toward the United States. But yankeephobia, apart from its historical bases, is a scapegoat for other kinds of resentment, some of them cultivated not least of all for domestic reasons.

Many negative aspects of this most difficult relationship have their roots in purely individual psychology: On the one hand, Latin Americans reject the life style of the United States, and its way of conducting politics; they perceive the United States as an overpowering neighbor and therefore respond with excessive sensitivity to any sign of hegemonic presumption. On the other hand, Latin Americans admire American prosperity and the orderly functioning of U.S. society and institutions. No doubt, Latin Americans would like to emulate this efficiency of organization and enjoy similar material benefits and high living standards. But historical differences, an altogether different political culture, and a relative lack of organizational skills have accounted for Latin America's failure in this respect. This in turn has created new animosities.

Some European politicians think that because Latin America is far from Europe, it is of comparatively little importance for them. They can leave it to leftist ideologues, as a playground where they can "let off steam" and be diverted from domestic policy issues. For a long time, this was a dangerous trend in European politics, with all the expected consequences.

Among the European governments, the Federal Republic is one of those which attaches great importance to Latin America. It knows that this region is of vital importance to the United States strategically, and if only for this reason, it is therefore important to Europe. Coherent policies should be formulated toward this region, where politics must be more than the preserve of ideologues. The importance of the region becomes clearer when one contemplates the current Nicaraguan situation or tries to imagine a recrudescence of the conflict in El Salvador. Is American military intervention a distinct possibility? Could the United States tolerate a second Cuba in the Western Hemisphere? Does a second Cuba not already exist in Nicaragua?

For Europeans, it is not a matter of making America's interests their own, as is often claimed. It is a matter of paying due attention to the necessarily global interests of the United States as a world power and as the leading power in the West. This does not mean that Europe has no interests of its own in Latin America. There are valid European interests, some of them stemming from the influence of nations, big and small, in the international community. Indeed, regardless of size, economic weight, or ideology, all countries have equal weight in organizations such as the United Nations, and in an era of world revolution this consideration takes on vital importance.

In this respect, Latin America can exert a significant influence on European interests. And, equally important, Europeans cannot be indifferent to a stronger political and military involvement of the United States in Central America. Because the totality of military forces is limited, Western defense can be affected by such an involvement. Ultimately, the Central American trouble spot is almost as important for Europe as is the geographically closer Middle East.

The Soviet factor has indeed made a difference. The days are gone when minor conflicts are of no importance internationally; when two small states of relatively minor importance, such as Honduras and El Salvador, can wage a "soccer war" and there is no involvement by the superpowers. Today, the fact that extraregional powers are becoming deeply involved in Central America poses an incomparably greater danger than in the past. At present and under current conditions, it would be impossible to limit such conflict to two states. The prestige of both world powers and the strategic interests of the United States would necessarily be affected. Equally, the potentially explosive social and political situation in which El Salvador, Guatemala, Nicaragua, Honduras, and, in certain respects, even Mexico find themselves makes highly possible a conflagration that could spread throughout the region.

An inexplicable shortcoming of the current analyses of the Central American situation is their failure to take Mexico into account. This is even true of analyses emanating from Mexico. The Soviet Union obviously has an interest in unrest and conflict in the region which, because of the Panama Canal and Mexico's oil, just to mention two factors, is of evident strategic importance to the United States. Moreover, Castro's Cuba gives considerable aid to left-wing radicals in the region, with consequent destabilizing effects. Considering Cuba's commitment to revolution east of Venezuela, a pincer movement in the direction of this country's energy resources is also conceivable.

In Havana, people speak openly of the *revolución latinoamericana*. The areas to be liberated include not only Puerto Rico but also Texas and California. Although this is certainly not realistic, the long border between Mexico and the United States, which is already giving Washington considerable trouble in terms of illegal immigration and drug trafficking, makes the United States especially vulnerable.

All this has to be considered when defining Soviet perceptions about the region's potential for instability and Soviet interests in the area. An obvious interest would be to tie down U.S. forces in a conflict in the Western Hemisphere or, more likely, to provoke U.S. reactions that would impair its ability to act and dent its prestige in the eyes of its Western allies. An extra bonus would be that bellicose American attitudes would distract attention from events that are embarrassing to Moscow (Poland and Afghanistan). Moscow would then find considerable and articulate Western opinion on its side.

Still, this scenario is rather unlikely. It is irresponsible scaremongering on the part of the chairman of the Socialist International to behave as though the danger of a U.S. intervention in Central America is imminent. The United States cannot want such an escalation to take place; it would rather not face the possibility of direct military intervention. Washington knows very well that such an action domestically would be politically divisive. And in view of the prevailing public opinion in Central America, American servicemen would not exactly be welcomed as liberators, as was the case in Grenada. From the vantage point of the United States, such regional conflict is to be shied away from. The exercises conducted in Honduras do not mean that the United States is drifting into a new Vietnam; among other things, these exercises are meant to show the "world revolutionaries" that Washington is prepared to take action and is responding flexibly, in line with the requirements of each situation. It is not allowing itself to be lured into a Soviet trap.

The feeling exists in the Federal Republic of Germany that in view of this situation and a possible escalation of the regional conflict to global proportions, Germany has an opportunity and a responsibility vis-à-vis Central America, within the recent European context of rapprochement to the area. Because of colonial or ex-colonial commitments, Germany's EEC partners have been largely absent from the region. For instance, the United Kingdom and France have had their attention concentrated on such parts of the Third World as Asia or Africa. Germany, however, since Alexander von Humboldt, has shown more interest in Latin America and has enjoyed a good reputation there. Intellectually, German thinkers—Hegel and Marx and, more recently, Max Weber—have had an important influence in Latin America. In economic terms, Germany has a substantial economic potential at its disposal, as, for example, in the field of developmental policy. Although mistakes may have been made in the past, facts speak louder than words, and Germany's efforts to achieve a rapprochement with Latin and Central America have been very real.

The possibilities for Europe to exert a salubrious influence on Latin America are considerable. Many Latin Americans, including those in leading positions, are of European descent, and Europe's political currents have their equivalents in Latin America. The two regions share similar cultural and even religious roots. Despite these elements, which could augur a closer relationship between Europe and Latin America, the latter has been disappointed by the former's lack of real commitment, on a long-term basis, and is beginning to turn away. It is important to halt this trend.

In reappraising these interrelationships, one must begin by analyzing past mistakes. In the course of the past 100 years, the United States has committed many mistakes vis-à-vis Latin America. The traditional U.S. policy of demonstrating economic and military strength has often antagonized its smaller and weaker neighbors; another kind of policy would have been more appropriate. Equally, the U.S. pursuit of economic strength, without political controls, has been detrimental to harmonious relations. On other occasions, U.S. support for military regimes was the result of the conviction, in the long run perhaps misconceived, that peace and quiet in a country were beneficial for the United States and its interests. All these actions have, over time, strained U.S. relations with Latin American countries.

It is obviously not possible to undo past errors. But it is important that American policymakers realize their mistakes and at the same time engage in a deliberate policy of improving their image among Latin Americans. A world power such as the United States should make clear that it is on the side of freedom, democracy, and social justice—not just in the abstract but, by taking active steps, within a framework of respect for national sovereignties.

Is it possible for Europeans to define a common policy on Latin America— a common policy on Central America and the Caribbean—together with the United States? Many people doubt that this is possible. Yet the experiences of the recent past prove that a partly common, partly parallel policy on Latin America that has been coordinated with the United States, is both possible and practical. It may well be in the best interest of all concerned to proceed on the basis of a division of labor.

Who should be supported in Latin America? With the limited resources available, aid should go primarily to the democracies which now have a real chance in Latin America. Latin American democrats are engaged in successful activities from Kingston to Bogotá and São Paulo, from Caracas to San José, in Buenos Aires and Montevideo, and one hopes that in the future democracy will return to Santiago de Chile and Asunción. There is widespread agreement, both in the United States and Europe, that the Latin American democracies need all the support they can rally.

Military leaders of all political persuasions—from the rightist Pinochet to the leftist military of Peruvian, Bolivian, and Nicaraguan origins—have failed to solve economic, social, and political problems, even when for a limited time they appeared to be successful. Aid to the military is no real alternative. The assistance granted to the democracies should therefore be so concentrated as to make a military alternative improbable.

Unfortunately, the Socialist International has in some instances befriended and assisted the wrong parties. The fateful role played by the Socialist International in influencing public opinion in Europe and the indirect influence it has exerted on political decisions in Latin America have often complicated problems rather than contributed to their solution.

In decisions about what form of assistance to offer, military aid must not take priority. Currently this is not the case, although military aid or cooperation often has been the cornerstone of European countries' commercial policy toward the Third World. It should be noted that arms trading not only boosts export earnings; it also resolves "economies of scale" problems in a country's military industries. Furthermore, it alleviates some problems of unemployment and balance of payments. There are signs of a change in attitudes, however. Thus, in June 1983 the European Council adopted the following resolution:

> The Heads of State and Government confirmed their close interest in develop-ments in Central America. They are deeply concerned at the economic and social conditions in many parts of the region, at the tensions which these create and at the widespread misery and bloodshed.
>
> They are convinced that the problems of Central America cannot be solved by military means, but only by political solutions springing from the region itself and respecting the principles of noninterference and nonviolability of frontiers. They, therefore, fully support the current initiative of the Contadora Group. They underline the need for the establishment of democratic condi-tions and for the strict observance of human rights throughout the region. They are ready to continue contributing to the further development in the area, in order to promote progress to stability.[4]

So much for the heads of state and government of the 10 EC members. Suffice it to say that, on this basis, it is undoubtedly possible to develop a common policy with the United States.

In November 1982 Secretary of State George Shultz appealed to the Central American states to dispense with foreign military advisers, not to import any more offensive weapons, and to concentrate all their strength in furthering economic development. An indication that the American side is not merely paying lip service to theoretical principles, but is actually practic-ing a policy to that effect, is exemplified by the priorities of U.S. aid. In 1983 approximately 77 cents of each dollar spent by the United States in Central America were spent on food, fertilizers, and other essentials for economic growth and development. Testifying before a subcommittee of the House of Representatives on March 18, 1986, Elliott Abrams, Assistant Secretary of State for Inter–American Affairs of the U.S. State Department, explained in detail for what purpose the Reagan administration intends to use the funds it has asked for in the 1987 budget for Latin America and the Carib-bean. Of the more than $2 billion requested, $1.6 billion is to be used for economic aid and $357 million for military aid. These figures reflect an appropriate political course. The root of the evil in Latin America, the main cause of the conflict, lies in social injustices. All other matters, particularly all military matters, are less important by comparison. Nevertheless, it is important to endeavor to defuse the military situation. As early as 1983,

---

4. See *Bulletin der Bundesregierung (Bonn)*, no. 65/1983 (June 21, 1983)

President Reagan stated that the United States was prepared to extend these four assurances:

1. To support any agreement among the Central American countries for the withdrawal, under fully verifiable and reciprocal conditions, of all foreign military and security advisers and troops
2. To help opposition groups to join the political process in all countries and compete by ballots instead of bullets
3. To support any verifiable, reciprocal agreement among Central American countries on the renunciation of support for insurgencies on the territory of neighboring states
4. To help Central America end its costly arms race and to support any verifiable reciprocal agreement on the nonimportation of offensive arms

These comprehensive assurances should be fully supported. They express an unwillingness to send combat troops to Central America, although the backing of other forces of insurgency in the region by the United States points to the complexity of the situation. However, principles espoused by Europe and the United States, and which have a long tradition in both regions, should receive more than vocal support: elections and negotiations, peace and democracy, and pluralist participation.

Nevertheless, there are clear signs that certain elements that have acquired significant influence in countries of the region do not espouse any of these principles. My own experience clearly illustrates this: When, in early 1982, I proposed to one of the most powerful men in Havana, Carlos Rafael Rodríguez, that Cuba completely renounce the dispatch of soldiers, military advisers, and weapons, if the United States agreed to do the same, he rejected the proposal.

Despite setbacks, however, it is important that the Western countries continue to make such proposals and consistently back them with appropriate actions wherever possible. These principles are in line with the European people's longing for peace. This kind of public relations cannot be expected to emanate from Afghanistan or Nicaragua, where the leaders practice the opposite. However, neither are these basic principles commonly disseminated in the Western media. For instance, the above-mentioned four assurances given by President Reagan were not disseminated by the mass media in Europe.

To sum up: A coordinated policy with the United States that does justice to our shared responsibility is both possible and desirable. It may be that such a policy already exists to a greater degree than many Europeans would like to admit. What is important is that solidarity exist between the two regions and that common policies be attempted because they have a better chance of success than isolated or opposing stands.

Sometimes it is helpful to imagine similar situations in which contrary polices have been applied. Would the democrats who suffered under Hitler and the Soviet blockade of Berlin have considered America's aid and commitment to be adequate and sufficient if they had been made available to the extent they are now being offered to Central America by the West in a situation that can be considered comparable? One should bear in mind that democrats in Latin America—from Cuba to Haiti, and from Chile to Nicaragua—often find themselves in situations in which their lives are endangered. They rightly expect assistance, not merely understanding, from the West. Understanding, however, presupposes knowledge of the facts. Those who refuse to grant assistance to forces seeking to build democracy because they are not yet "ideal democrats," as we understand the term, make it too easy for themselves and further the objectives of the antidemocrats.

A common policy on Latin America must be conceived on a long-term basis. The task to be solved is too difficult to be achieved in two years or five years. It would also be a historic mistake to change our strategy after a short time.

In the future, the Europeans will have to attach special and continuing importance to the problems of Central America, informing themselves as accurately as possible and making contributions to peace in the region. The maintenance of peace there is by no means ensured, nor is it an automatic process, as many people hope.

In El Salvador, progress is slowly being made. But a final solution to the conflict is possible only through basic social changes that will take at least 10 years to realize. In Costa Rica, democratic stabilization could be promoted by European democrats. The same applies to Honduras, Panama, Belize, and Guatemala, where the democratic path is by no means assured. The greatest problem is Nicaragua. Despite all the skillful camouflage, we are basically concerned with a Marxist—Leninist system that will not disappear overnight. The "elections" of November 2, 1984, offered no real choice. Furthermore, the numerous rounds of negotiations between Nicaragua and the United States have not yet led to any major progress.

Latin American countries will for many years to come remain trouble spots bearing on international politics. Stamina and consistent policymaking are required from both sides of the Atlantic. A common strategy, prepared on the basis of a correct analysis of the starting conditions, must be pursued for at least 10 years. This is especially significant in Nicaragua.

Responsible Europeans should understand that the Sandinista dictatorship in the end threatens their own liberty.

• CHAPTER TWELVE •

The United States: The Search for a Negotiated Solution

Raymond Burghardt

When I was asked by Jiri Valenta to discuss U.S. policy toward Nicaragua, I noted that we do not view our policy toward Nicaragua in isolation from our overall Central American policy. American foreign policy toward Nicaragua is inextricably wound with our policies toward its neighbors. I focus my remarks on the current diplomatic situation because there has been considerable interest in the Contadora negotiations and the prospects for a negotiated solution ever since the Contadora countries set June 6, 1986, as a deadline for completion of negotiations and the signing of a treaty. But first I would like to outline briefly the four points of the U.S. overall regional policy:

1. We support democracy and political reform in each country.
2. We seek the renewal of economic development and growth in the democratic countries.
3. We will help the democratic countries defend themselves against subversion and aggression.
4. We seek a verifiable and comprehensive diplomatic settlement of the region's problems.

All these objectives are closely related, and as the Kissinger Commission concluded, we cannot definitively achieve one without the others.

Our Central American policy involves a great variety of activities and programs designed to achieve all four objectives. I should stress that over 70% of our time and money is devoted to *economic* assistance. Military and security assistance is vital too. Aid to the Nicaraguan resistance is an important element of our policy; we view it as essential to providing incentives and pressure on Nicaragua to achieve a diplomatic agreement that will be acceptable to the other four countries of Central America, as well as ourselves. But this is only one element of our policy. We are also helping to train labor union leaders in collective bargaining, providing computers for speedy and accurate election tabulation, helping the Salvadoran government defend itself against a violent guerrilla minority, providing crop-development programs, and running (in Honduras) the largest Peace Corps program in the world.

These programs have had a great deal of success. As some others in this volume have noted, there has been much progress toward meeting the first three of the four mentioned objectives. Democratic governments prevail in four of the five countries, the economies of all except Nicaragua are expected to grow (or, in Guatemala, to remain stable) and El Salvador's guerrillas have been reduced by more than a third. We do not take the credit for all this, but we have played a major role. All this progress in strengthening democratically elected governments in Costa Rica, Honduras, El Salvador, and Guatemala is still fragile. President José Azcona expressed it best in an April 4, 1986, television address:

> As long as there is a totalitarian regime in Central America with expansionist ambitions, supported by an enormous military apparatus, the social, economic, and political stability of all the countries of the region, especially the neighboring countries that have common borders with that country, which is the source of the problem, will be under constant threat.

Our efforts in the diplomatic field are designed to support the Contadora group in seeking a settlement that could make possible a stable achievement of our political, economic, and security objectives.

On Manzanillo

Although the Manzanillo talks ended many months ago, it is worth reviewing what happened. The U.S. government has never really explained publicly how the talks broke down and why the renewal of these talks would be of much less transcendental importance than the Sandinistas profess to believe.

Sandinista views during those talks tell us a great deal about the current behavior of the Nicaraguan government in the Contadora negotiations. When the Contadora process began, the Contadora countries decided they wanted a Latin process, without U.S. participation. We respected that decision. Then, at Contadora's request, Secretary of State George Shultz visited Managua and met with Daniel Ortega in June 1984. During the next 5 months we held nine rounds of meetings. We entered the talks prepared to reach bilateral understandings, which could then be channeled into the Contadora process to facilitate achieving a comprehensive, regional agreement. The Contadora group repeatedly told us that this is what they wanted to do. From the start, however, the Sandinistas' aims were entirely different: They wanted to negotiate bilateral accords dealing exclusively with our own security concerns. Much of the first seven rounds were hobbled by this basic disagreement over the purpose of the talks.

Then, in September 1984, Nicaragua declared it would sign the September 7, 1984, draft Contadora agreement. On October 20, Honduras, El Salvador, and Costa Rica, with Guatemalan participation, issued their own redraft, with modifications they deemed essential. These modifications amplified verification mechanisms in security and political spheres and provided protection for other parties in the event that Nicaragua failed to negotiate in good faith on key security issues, particularly on restoring the military balance. The Contadora mediators accepted the validity of the Core Four's concerns.

We therefore reasoned that there was an opportunity for Manzanillo to become more useful. In a new approach to the discussions, we proposed to the Sandinistas that we reach some specific bilateral understandings that would make it possible for Nicaragua to agree to modifications in the act proposed by other Central American countries. We proposed, for example, that in exchange for Nicaraguan agreement to the continuation of international military exercises, the United States would limit such exercises to levels worked out with Nicaragua. We had proposals on issues of advisers and bases as well. This approach appeared to interest our Nicaraguan interlocutors, and we engaged in serious negotiations during the eighth round.

Then, at the ninth round in December 1984, Nicaraguan Vice Foreign Minister Víctor Hugo Tinoco arrived with new instructions. Our new approach was unacceptable to the Sandinistas, he declared, because they would not accept any changes in the September 7 draft Contadora act. Instead, Tinoco suggested that the United States and Nicaragua work out a bilateral agreement on security issues, along the lines of our discussions. Ambassador Harry Shlaudeman asked how such an agreement could possibly be consistent with the September 7 draft act if Nicaragua would not agree to any changes in that document. At that point, Tinoco said perhaps we could arrange a secret bilateral agreement. We responded that making it secret would not eliminate the inconsistency with the multilateral treaty, and, at any rate, that Nicaraguans knew that there were no secrets in the United States. Tinoco then fell back to stating that he was only suggesting some personal ideas. On hearing this, I passed a note to Shlaudeman noting that if he were his friend, Henry Kissinger, he would get up from the table, telling Tinoco that he was not there to listen to his personal ideas.

What Shlaudeman did tell Tinoco was that the only logical interpretation of what Tinoco said was that Nicaragua did not want a comprehensive, regional Contadora agreement. What they really wanted was a bilateral agreement, dealing exclusively with Nicaragua's concerns. Shlaudeman said he would welcome hearing anything Nicaragua could say to refute that interpretation. We are still waiting for a response—more than two years later.

Of course, we know what Nicaragua's position is. Tinoco put it quite inelegantly at one of the more memorable moments in Manzanillo. When we were pressing the Sandinistas to negotiate seriously with their neighboring countries, his response was that Nicaragua "preferred to talk with the master rather than with the dogs." I still can remember former Costa Rican President Monge's reaction when we related that remark to him.

Present Status of the U.S.–Nicaraguan Bilateral Dialogue

Despite this disappointing experience, the door is still open for a negotiated solution to Central America's problems. We have maintained diplomatic relations with Nicaragua. The contrast in how the two countries use those relations is quite informative. In Managua, our ambassador has taken the initiative to maintain an informal dialogue with the Sandinista leadership, particularly with Interior Minister Tomás Borge, but also with others. In Washington, Nicaraguan Ambassador Carlos Tunnerman's job description begins and ends with promoting the Sandinista point of view to the U.S. Congress, press, and public. Only once in the past two years has Tunnerman sought meetings with U.S. policymakers—and then only because we had embarrassed him by pointing out the inconsistency of the Sandinistas' behavior with their professed interest in a bilateral dialogue.

Obviously, Managua is not interested in a conventional diplomatic dialogue. Instead, it has devised a major propaganda campaign to press for formal diplomatic talks, which are more effective in undermining the pursuit of a multilateral treaty, more effective for avoiding the only real solution: serious negotiations with neighboring countries and with fellow Nicaraguans in the armed and unarmed opposition.

Our position on resuming the bilateral talks is that we would only do so if the Sandinistas initiate simultaneous talks with the internal and external opposition. These are the only circumstances under which such talks might be useful.

Contadora: The Present Situation

The present status of the Contadora talks is generally known. At the April 5–7, 1986, meeting of the foreign ministers from countries in Central America, Contadora, and the Support Group, the Nicaraguans stood alone. They took the position that they would neither negotiate nor sign an agreement on June 6, as called for by the other Central Americans, unless the United States, as a precondition, stopped all aid to the Nicaraguan resistance forces. This position was not accepted by any of the other parties, including the Central Americans and the eight mediators.

Two facts make the Sandinista position absurd: First, this precondition was never part of the Sandinista position before 1986. During almost 3 years of negotiations in Contadora and Manzanillo, the Sandinistas never raised this as a prerequisite. The inevitable conclusion is that it was an excuse to block further negotiations and stymie an agreement. Second, no other parties are setting preconditions, although they would have at least as much right do do so. For instance, Honduras is not demanding restoration of the previous military balance as a precondition. El Salvador is not demanding that Nicaragua stop aiding the Salvadoran guerrillas.

These are very important considerations for these countries, but they are not demanding these preconditions because they know that they cannot be credibly implemented without elaborate verification mechanisms, which could not go into effect until a treaty is signed and ratified. The Sandinistas do not have this problem, since their adversaries are open, democratic societies. Their great advantage is that any precondition would be self-enforcing for democratic countries. If the United States agreed to stop aid to the resistance forces, the American Congress and public would ensure that this commitment was carried out.

The latest word on Contadora is that in response to pressure from the Contadora and support group countries, Nicaragua has agreed to resume talks on remaining issues. The seriousness of that agreement is not clear. Since November 1985, Nicaragua has been periodically dragged to the table, but only to argue points extraneous to the Contadora negotiations.

Nicaragua appears to acknowledge that the remaining issues are setting arms and troop levels to restore the regional balance and the regulation of military exercises. Other Central Americans point to a third important issue: the treaty annex, or Statute on Execution and Verification of the Act. They have proposed a precise schedule for negotiations to resolve all these issues. The Contadora group still has not convened negotiating sessions. Recent statements by the democratic Central American leaders indicate that they will continue to insist that, in addition to dealing with security issues, the Contadora accord must provide concrete mechanisms for ensuring compliance with political commitments to democratization and national reconciliation.

During a visit to Montevideo, President Oscar Arias of Costa Rica said there was no possibility for success in the negotiations as long as Nicaragua adopted positions such as those of Tomás Borge, to wit, "The seas of the world will dry up and the stars will fall from the heavens before the Sandinista government will negotiate with its adversaries." Arias said that both the Sandinista government and the opposition needed to sit down and negotiate. In Honduras, President José Azcona, in an April 4, 1986, television address, said: "National reconciliation in Nicaragua resulting from respect of citizens' rights is the key to peace in Central America and restoration of trust among our governments." And this sentiment is not limited to the Central Americans. Argentine Foreign Minister Dante Caputo stated: "It is indispensable that Nicaragua be Latin American and enjoy a full democracy."

In a recent trip by the President's special envoy for Central America, Philip Habib, we made clear to the Contadora and Support Group countries that the United States backs the insistence by Central American democracies on the need to resume the Contadora negotiations, without delay or sensitivity to Nicaraguan preconditions. We hope that Contadora will quickly convene negotiations so that the five countries can work on the remaining issues.

During the Habib trip, much interest was shown in the U.S. position, expressed in the April 11, 1986, letter from Philip Habib to three U.S. congressmen. The letter stated that the United States would support and abide by a comprehensive, verifiable, and simultaneous implementation of a treaty, based on the Contadora document of objectives of September 1983, as long as such an agreement was fully respected by other parties. As required by the provisions of the Act of Contadora, this would include ending support to the Nicaraguan resistance forces. The draft act itself notes that financing for the purposes of relocation or return of the insurgent forces to their country would be permitted. This letter is not new U.S. policy. We have consistently taken this position. We made this very clear to the Nicaraguans at the Manzanillo talks. We also stated to them that anyone who studies the U.S. political system as carefully as they do must know that our Congress and public would not permit U.S. government actions counter to what the Central Americans agreed on in a Contadora treaty.

Final Point

We attach great importance to negotiating and concluding a treaty with strong mechanisms for implementation and verification. The Contadora group took on the responsibility of obtaining such a treaty, which would implement all 21 Contadora objectives. It should be clear to all that Central America's problems will not be solved by yet another romantic treaty or high-sounding statement of general principles. They already have one: In 1923, the five Central American countries signed a Treaty of Peace and Amity in which they agreed not to recognize governments that came to power through coups d'etat or revolution unless they were subsequently legitimized by free elections. The treaty provided that governments would not assist exiles or contending parties anywhere in Central America, nor interfere in one another's internal affairs. By 1934 the agreement was denounced by four of the five because there were no mechanisms for verification. The Central American democracies do not want to repeat that experience.

PART FIVE

Conclusion and Appendixes

Synthesis of Viewpoints: Concluding Remarks

Jiri Valenta

Roots of the Conflict in Nicaragua

At the national level, the Nicaraguan conflict is primarily a struggle between the Sandinista Front of National Liberation (FSLN), on the one hand, and its two antagonists: the Nicaraguan political opposition (both inside and outside the country) and the military resistance popularly known as the *contras*. There is widespread consensus that this domestic conflict has the potential to take on regional dimensions and even become internationalized as the military involvements of Cuba, backed by the Soviet Union, and the United States continue to grow. Both superpowers have committed an array of resources to the conflict: The Soviets and their allies have provided a large amount of military–security aid, hundreds of advisers, and considerable economic aid; the United States has extended humanitarian aid and limited military assistance to the resistance, considerable economic and some military aid to Nicaragua's neighbor Honduras, and economic aid to Costa Rica. By late 1986, both superpowers had stepped up their military commitment to the feuding parties, as the U.S. Congress approved the long-debated $100 million aid package for the rebel fighters and the Soviets increased the Nicaraguan stock of Soviet-made transport helicopters, air defense equipment, and logistic vehicles.

There are various schools of thought regarding the roots of the Nicaraguan conflict. Leaders of the FSLN and analysts such as Francisco López, who writes in this volume, view the traditional geopolitical designs of the United States and its allegedly exploitative international capitalist system as

259

key antecendents. According to this hypothesis, the anti-FSLN posture of the United States in the 1980s is a logical continuation of the U.S. disposition toward political and economic hegemony over the Central American isthmus. Specifically, the FSLN perceives the regional problems of Central America, including the present conflict in Nicaragua, as products of an organized, U.S.-led conspiracy.

This interpretation is challenged by the leaders of the democratic Nicaraguan opposition—senior members of the FSLN government turned defectors, such as Arturo Cruz, Sr., and Alfredo César. While recognizing that the Somoza dynasty and the United States, which supported the Somoza dictatorship, share initial responsibility for the crisis, these leaders argue that the dynamics of internal change and the system's inability to adapt were equally important as external factors. It is often forgotten that the present conflict was preceded by 30 years of accelerated economic growth and relative modernization that resulted in improved living standards for many Nicaraguans. Ironically, as Arturo Cruz Sequeira points out in this volume, in 1977, just as the political struggle against the Somoza leadership was about to intensify, Central America was the site of the only successful effort at regional economic integration in the Third World, and the Nicaraguan economy displayed the most impressive economic growth in the region. Thus the conflict was caused neither by U.S. exploitation nor economic growth without social progress, as argued by the FSLN, but by the inability of an oppressive, authoritarian political structure to adjust to the changes brought about by modernization. The Somoza regime, as I demonstrate in Chapter One, fell victim not only to its political errors but also, as explained by Arturo Cruz Sequeira, to the country's rapid modernization. Ultimately these factors proved to be more instrumental in Somoza's downfall than was the FSLN vanguard's revolutionary class struggle.

This school of thought argues further that a large share of the responsibility for the second stage of the conflict, in the 1980s, lies with the FSLN's policies for building a one-party, Leninist-oriented system. Instead of working to achieve the democratic, nationalist changes expected by those who engaged in the anti-Somoza revolution, including many Sandinistas, the FSLN National Directorate concentrated on consolidating its power, using "salami tactics" to slice away at the opposition and clever forms of concealment, strategies employed by Leninist-oriented parties in Eastern Europe (particularly Hungary and Czechoslovakia) in 1945–1948 during the so-called "people's democracy" stage of the transition toward socialism. These tactics are clearly advocated in the 1977 FSLN Platform (see Appendix A).

On balance, as I show in Chapter 1, past U.S. interventionism has been a conditioning factor in the Nicaraguan conflicts of the 1970s and 1980s. This and the ill-advised U.S. support for the Somoza family rule gave rise to a degree of "Yankeephobia" still prevalent in certain strata of Nicaraguan society. This has been recognized not only by most North American and West European political analysts but also by U.S. policymakers, the latter more recently.

To insist (as the FSLN does) that the present Nicaraguan conflict was caused only by an organized U.S. conspiracy, however, is simplistic. This interpretation ignores President Carter's decisions to pull the rug out from under Somoza in 1979 and thereafter not to intervene militarily to prevent the FSLN victory. It also neglects the Carter administration's policy of providing economic assistance to the FSLN in 1979–1981, aid that was terminated when FSLN involvement in the Salvadoran conflict was uncovered. Finally, this school of thought overlooks the internal source of the conflict in the 1980s; that is, the FSLN's Leninization of Nicaragua, which started long before the United States seriously began to support the resistance in 1982.

Internal Dimensions of the Conflict

Four elements fuel the internal crisis in Nicaragua: (1) a breakdown of the national anti-Somocista unity that existed at the outset of the FSLN victory in June 1979; (2) the legalization and institutionalization of coercive instruments of FSLN power; (3) a large FSLN military buildup; and (4) the profound deterioration of the economy. There is a growing consensus about the undemocratic, authoritarian nature of the FSLN regime; the focus of the debate has now shifted to the issue of FSLN legitimacy and, above all, to possible solutions to the conflict.

Even those who criticize the policies of the present U.S. administration rarely dispute the undemocratic, oppressive nature of the FSLN regime. What is still debated is the legitimacy of the regime. One school of thought, represented by Margaret Crahan in this volume and promoted by such West European social democratic leaders as Spain's Felipe González, contends that whether or not the FSLN rulers are authoritarian or Leninist is their own prerogative. What matters to the outside world is that they are legitimate rulers in their own country. The advocates of this school do not defend the FSLN's human rights record or its treatment of dissent; if anything, they are critical of the authoritarian nature of the FSLN regime, concluding that its human rights record has to be much improved. They are equally critical of FSLN interference in the internal affairs of El Salvador in the early 1980s. The main point of this argument is that, irrespective of ideology and the fact that the crisis was in part caused by FSLN internal policies, the present government in Managua meets the basic criteria for political legitimacy established by international law. As to its bearing on a resolution of the crisis, this position clearly favors a negotiated settlement, as opposed to externally sponsored direct or indirect intervention.

Concerning the actual causes of the domestic conflict in Nicaragua, the school of thought represented here by Cruz Sequeira, insists that the main determinant is the systemic failure of FSLN internal policies. The FSLN "vanguard," its "exhausted economic model," and the political–ideological program for institutionalizing the revolution have failed to deliver on the early, seductive promise of national reformist development. Ideological rigidity and FSLN failure to heed the country's traditional structures have led to a breakup of the broad anti-Somoza national unity, institutionaliza- tion of coercive instruments of power, an enormous military buildup, and seriously deteriorating economic conditions.

The Breakdown in National Unity

The authoritarianism and arbitrariness of the FSLN National Directorate have alienated diverse segments of the Nicaraguan population, including original revolutionary leaders and dozens of other members of the FSLN government. (As but one example, within the ranks of the Southern Opposi- tion Bloc (BOS)—one of the two main branches of Nicaragua's democratic political opposition in exile—there are 14 former members of the FSLN government.) With the exception of their treatment of the Miskito Indians in 1981–1982, the FSLN had managed until June 1986 to avoid the radical excesses of socialist transformation of the Soviet type (including concentra- tion camps and official use of anti-Semitism) common to some Leninist and Leninist-oriented regimes. They also tolerated longer than most a token opposition and an opposition newspaper, *La Prensa*. The FSLN even man- aged to gain the blessing of a small but active segment of the Church, skillfully using radical elements of the so-called popular church to gain a legitimacy withheld by Rome.

Equally astute was the FSLN's manipulation of the electoral process during general elections in November 1984. The FSLN decision to proceed with elections was tactically very shrewd: It permitted the opposition's much restricted but not entirely controlled participation while ensuring —through discreet application of the state's coercive instruments before and during the elections—that the FSLN would not be voted out of power. The elections thus created the impression, both at home and abroad, that the FSLN regime was becoming, or at least *could* become, more democratic and legitimate. As intended, some Western policymakers and analysts who had already been supporting FSLN legitimacy often cited the 1984 elections as convincing evidence. Because of this impression, Arturo Cruz, Sr., the presidential candidate of four opposition parties in the 1984 elections, pointed out that it was a bad tactical move on his part to withdraw his candidacy. The opposition should have continued to participate, if only to demonstrate to those who believed in FSLN fair play and the regime's legitimacy what the elections really meant.

These and other clever tactics, aimed at concealing the FSLN's real objectives and confusing democratic supporters at home and abroad, had the distinction of being easily reversible or producing easily reversed results. Indeed, any subsequent hardening of the FSLN's tactical flexibility could be easily carried out provided that the real power base—the FSLN vanguard leadership, the state security, and the army—remained unaltered. Regarding these power sources, which are the heart of any Leninist system, the Sandinistas have indicated that they are very unlikely to make concessions. The fact that the army is "the instrument" of the FSLN is confirmed in the draft of the new Nicaraguan constitution (see Appendix C, Article 177). The easy reversibility of FSLN tactical concessions was demonstrated in June 1986 when the Sandinistas closed *La Prensa*, barred two prominent Roman Catholic clerics (Bishop Pablo Antonio Vega and Father Bismarck Carballo) from returning to Nicaragua from abroad, and restricted the activities of the political parties allowed to run in the 1984 elections.

The Sandinista pledge to continue with the basically irreversible institutionalization of a revolutionary, "popular-democratic system," envisaged in the FSLN platform of 1977 (see Appendix A), was unambiguously restated by Nicaraguan President Daniel Ortega in 1985:

> Six years after the great popular victory, we are institutionalizing the revolutionary process. . . . For six years the FSLN has been defending the implementation of the original program. [See Appendix B.] In October 1977 this program was prepared and presented as a government platform . . . . [defining] a new order. . . . We have [in it] an institutional framework that encompasses the revolutionary system . . . "the popular-democratic system." The institutional framework must be respected . . . . the revolution is not under discussion. It is irreversible.[1]

The Legalization—Institutionalization of FSLN Coercive Instruments

Many analysts who are familiar with the Nicaraguan context would agree that the Nicaraguan revolution is unlike the revolution in Mexico several decades ago, contrary to the comparison between the two that Daniel Ortega likes to make in his public relations campaign abroad. Nor is the FSLN leadership evolving into a semireformist, nationalist political force patterned after Mexico's ruling Revolutionary Institutional Party (PRI). Adopting many features of the Leninist-Castroite model of communism, the FSLN has become an authentic vanguard party, structured vertically and functioning according to the Leninist doctrine of "democratic centralism"

---

1. Radio Managua, September 5, 1985, as reported in *Foreign Broadcast Information Service—Latin America*, cited hereinafter as *FBIS—LAM*, September 6, 1985, P7, P8.

(see Appendix A). In this transformation it has been necessary to construct coercive instruments for maintaining the FSLN in power. Cuban and East European advisers have helped the Sandinistas erect the necessary coercive structures—the Sandinista Army, Ministry of the Interior, People's Militia, Sandinista Defense Committees, special revolutionary tribunals, *turbas divinas* (divine mobs), etc.

The FSLN legal system, as former Nicaraguan Ambassador to Ecuador Alvaro Taboada shows in this volume, is based on an antijuridical ideology devoted almost entirely to the rationalization of FSLN power. Thus the key legal decrees issued by the FSLN National Directorate through the government junta in the initial stage of the revolution (1979–1981) helped create permanent instruments of coercive power and made possible majority FSLN representation in the executive and legislative branches of the government. It is noteworthy that the introduction of most of these laws occurred when the Carter administration, sensitive to past errors in U.S. policy toward Nicaragua, was displaying a very conciliatory attitude toward Managua.

The repressive capacity of the coercive instruments of power has been further refined and institutionalized in the last several years. A thorough and comprehensive system of militant education, spearheaded by Cuban advisers, and a generous scholarship program for study in Warsaw Pact countries are helping to indoctrinate thousands of Nicaraguan youth. The FSLN repression in Nicaragua is not as conspicuous as that in some other Leninist-oriented countries (e.g., Kampuchea, Afghanistan) or as right-wing dictatorships in Latin America (e.g., Chile), but it is more selective and insidious.

A Massive Military Buildup

The FSLN military buildup was neither a simple response to aggressive U.S. policies (as FSLN analysts argue) nor the manifestation of a clear desire to conquer neighboring Central American nations (as some critics of the FSLN postulate); but it did have defensive and offensive rationales in that it served as an internal instrument of coercion and a deterrent to outside intervention as well as an effective shield for regional subversion. The FSLN initiated the buildup in 1979 at the signing of a secret military agreement with Cuba. This was a time when the United States was displaying a very supportive posture vis-à-vis the Sandinistas and when other Central American leaders, such as Panama's Omar Torrijos, were eager to help rebuild Nicaragua's armed forces.

In 1979 the FSLN had only 10,000 combatants, an inadequate supply of arms to sustain a long conflict, and a very inferior knowledge of the military arts. In 1986 the FSLN's armed forces constitute a well-equipped, well-trained body of 62,000 (35,000 regular army and 27,000 reservists in active service), which can be augmented by an additional 79,000 from the militia, the reserves, and the elite security forces of the Ministry of the Interior.

The Profound Deterioration of Economic Conditions

In their analyses of the Nicaraguan case Cruz Sequeira and others explain that the main causes of the economic deterioration in Nicaragua are systemic, as they are in other Leninist-oriented states. In spite of the FSLN's cautious approach toward nationalization and collectivization, mismanagement and erratic policies (e.g., the creation of inefficient, bankrupt collective farms) have contributed significantly to the current economic difficulties. The largest producer of grain in Central America in 1978, Nicaragua is now plagued by some of the same problems that face most other Leninist and Leninist-oriented countries (e.g., shortages and rationing). The economic difficulties have been compounded by the U.S. embargo and the civil war.

In the wake of these problems, the social base of the FSLN has eroded, particularly among peasants, heads of family, and young men. The prestige and popularity of the FSLN have also suffered abroad. At this juncture, the Sandinista revolution appears to have entered its second phase, experienced by the Bolshevik Revolution after 1925 and by the Eastern European revolutions after 1949. This phase, described by Isaac Deutscher as the "revolution betrayed," is characterized by increasing bureaucratization, disillusionment of the more dedicated revolutionaries, loss of the regime's popularity among former supporters, alienation of broad masses of the population, and the formation of what Milovan Djilas called the "new class." Revolutions tend to deviate from their objectives and consume their best men; the Nicaraguan revolution is no exception.

Militarization, war, poor economic conditions, and the insidious suppression of human rights have produced signs of popular discontent; for example, a rise in the number of *escondidos* (the hidden), young men who, in spite of the indoctrination and forced military recruitment for the ongoing war, escape military service and leave the country, assisted by a vast network of relatives and friends. The numbers of legal and illegal Nicaraguan emigrants (whose ranks include many *escondidos*) in Central America, the United States, and other nations is at least 250,000.

The Regional Dimension of the Crisis

The Nicaraguan conflict has acquired an alarming regional dimension, underwritten by the admitted messianic content of the FSLN program. That program prompts the Sandinistas to "revolutionary internationalism" in the region, which they see as necessary to the survival of the Nicaraguan revolution. To curb FSLN ambitions to play the role of revolutionary "bridge" in Central America, the effects of which were witnessed particularly in El Salvador in 1979–1981, the United States has encouraged the growth of the Nicaraguan opposition and its military arm in border areas of neighboring Costa Rica and Honduras. The resistance ranks have swelled to include thousands of Nicaraguan peasants as well as disenchanted Sandinistas.

To curb expansion and escalation of the Nicaraguan conflict, several Caribbean Basin nations, the so-called Contadora group (Mexico, Venezuela, Colombia and Panama)—supported since 1985 by the Lima group (Argentina, Brazil, Uruguay and Peru)—conducted a series of multilateral negotiations with the Sandinistas between 1983 and 1986 (see Appendix D). Beginning in 1984, there has also been a lengthy process toward bilateral negotiations between the United States and Nicaragua. Neither of these negotiating attempts has been successful as of late 1986. Irreconcilable differences among the negotiators became clear when the FSLN rejected a mutually verifiable agreement on curbing the arms race in Central America and insisted on preconditions, although no preconditions had been stipulated by the other negotiating partners.

The FSLN commitment to revolution in one region, as opposed to one country, Nicaragua, is suggested in the FSLN program of 1969 (see Appendix B). The FSLN believes that support for revolution beyond the Nicaraguan borders is a vital imperative. The results of this belief became visible from 1979 to 1981 when the FSLN developed an apparatus to support the guerrilla operations of its sister organization, the Farabundo Marti National Liberation Front (FMLN) in El Salvador. On this point—the FSLN interference in El Salvador from 1979 to 1981—there has been wide consensus among analysts, including Mark Falcoff, Esperanza Durán, and Margaret Crahan.

The FSLN aid to the FMLN has declined since 1982, however, demonstrating that the National Directorate is apparently prepared to follow the example of the Bolshevik Revolution—promoting socialism mainly in one country until circumstances permit otherwise. The FSLN does continue to back various revolutionary groups, though more discreetly until conditions permit the resumption of large-scale support.

Contrary to some supposition, the FSLN threat to regional stability does not necessarily stem from the possibility that the Sandinistas will invade a neighboring country. Rather, as Mark Falcoff shows, the threat lies in the FSLN's willingness and ability to provide (through their military buildup) an effective shield, selective covert support, arms supplies, and sanctuaries necessary for revolutionary struggles to be pursued indigenously, not only in Central America but also in South American nations such as Colombia. Both Esperanza Durán and Mark Falcoff agree that there is widespread concern in Central America about the FSLN's militarization. The consensus is broadened by opinion polls in various countries, showing that most citizens of those countries regard Nicaragua as a threat. Likewise, many Central American leaders and observers fear that Nicaragua's Leninist system will prevent it from playing a viable role in the Central American economic system. Nevertheless, some analysts, such as Francisco Villagrán Kramer, though convinced that the Central American leaders share to a degree U.S. security concerns about Nicaragua, also believe that some FSLN leaders have indicated their willingness to abide by a common set of rules reached by consensus among the Central American leaders.

The domestic and regional dimensions of the Nicaraguan conflict are influenced by the geographic imperatives flowing from Nicaragua's location at the heart of the Central American isthmus. This is an asset as well as a liability, since it gives the FSLN easy access to its neighbors, for the support of revolution, while increasing its vulnerability to penetration by the armed opposition. The United States, ever aware of Nicaragua's meddling in El Salvador from 1979 to 1981, has tried since 1982 to forestall the FSLN's regional ambitions by aiding Nicaraguan opposition forces operating in border areas of Honduras and Costa Rica. A case can be made that the resistance activities have helped to occupy the FSLN at home and curb larger FSLN support for the FMLN. But they have also prompted FSLN retaliatory attacks on sanctuaries in both nations, increasing concern about a widening of the conflict.

Since 1983, the four regional actors of the Contadora group have tried to find a negotiated solution to the national and regional dimensions of the Nicaraguan conflict. Since 1985, their efforts have been backed by the Lima support group. Analysts disagree as to what exactly has motivated the various actors—whether it is a desire to negotiate peace, to restrain the United States from military intervention in Nicaragua, to play a larger regional role, and/or to provide the FSLN regime with breathing space to consolidate its power. What analysts do agree on is the futility thus far, not only of this process but of the process of bilateral negotiations between the United States and Nicaragua. As Esperanza Durán aptly describes it, "Instead of solving the crisis, Contadora may end up institutionalizing it."

Ambassador Harry Shlaudeman and Raymond Burghardt, both of whom were engaged in U.S. bilateral negotiations with the FSLN, show in this volume that the Contadora negotiations have been unsuccessful in part because of (1) the FSLN's refusal to submit to control and verification procedures; (2) Managua's insistence on a bilateral agreement with the

United States, which would have worked to undermine the multilateral negotiations process and therefore was unacceptable to the other partners; and (3) FSLN insistence on preconditions to further negotiations, e.g., that the United States cease all support for the resistance. In contrast to Shlaudeman and Burghardt, Francisco Villagrán argues in this volume that the United States should display even more flexibility in dealing with the Sandinistas.

What is undeniable is that, except for veiled references, the Contadora negotiations and documents have until now lacked sufficient focus on U.S. regional interests and participation in the conflict, and have almost completely ignored the resistance groups. As Esperanza Durán insists, the negotiations process cannot succeed as long as the United States does not form part of it and the views of the democratic elements of the Nicaraguan resistance are not voiced. Broadening the base of Contadora is an essential condition to its revival.

Some analysts believe that the Contadora process thus far has benefited primarily the FSLN leaders, not as a serious negotiating forum as much as a convenient delaying mechanism, allowing them time to consolidate their power. Other analysts believe that the main objective of the Contadora group has been to keep the United States from invading Nicaragua.

International Dimensions of the Conflict

Beyond the national and regional contexts, there is a distinct international dimension to the Nicaraguan conflict. The FSLN program and desire to develop close ties with such strategic allies as the Soviet Union, Cuba, and other pro-Soviet communist countries and radical forces, has helped internationalize and accentuate the East–West nature of the crisis. On the one hand Nicaragua assists and supports revolutionary groups in its own geographic area. On the other hand, Nicaragua is the recipient of Soviet security aid and substantial multilateral communist economic aid, with Cuba playing a pivotal role in this process.

The alarming trend toward internationalization of the Nicaraguan conflict has become increasingly worrisome to the NATO allies of the United States. Their differences notwithstanding, the West European allies are primarily concerned that a widening Nicarguan conflict may eventually lead to a large-scale U.S. military involvement in Central America, with detrimental political and perhaps even military consequences for NATO cohesion. This fear has been accentuated by the failures of the Contadora process and U.S. diplomacy to reach a negotiated solution with Nicaragua from 1983 to 1986.

The Soviet Union and Cuba

On the international level, the FSLN strategic objective is to pursue the goals implied in the doctrine of "proletarian internationalism"; that is, to carry on close ties with the Soviet Union, Cuba, and other Leninist and Leninist-oriented regimes. Accordingly, the FSLN program of 1977 (see Appendix A) depicts the Sandinista revolution as an integral part of the worldwide revolutionary process. In this volume, Alvaro Taboada confirms that, by 1979, the FSLN had concluded a secret agreement with the Cuban army and was conducting diplomatic relations with the Soviet Union and Cuba, not through the usual channels of the Ministry of Foreign Affairs, but (as in other Leninist and Leninist-oriented regimes) through party channels institutionalized in the Department of International Relations. This demonstrates the importance the FSLN attaches to its relations with strategic allies as well as its intention to behave as a Leninist-oriented party.

The FSLN's basic adherence to what it sees as a "large socialist camp," led by the Soviet Union, became obvious during the Falkland Islands War in 1982. According to Taboada's testimony, Managua, like Havana and Moscow, despite their vocal public support for Argentina, viewed Argentina's defeat by U.S. ally Great Britain as a desirable outcome that would enable the Soviet Union to demonstrate to Latin American nations that the USSR, not the United States, is their natural ally.

For the Soviets, Nicaragua is one of various pawns in the global game with the United States. But the Cubans see Nicaragua as the only faithful ally in the Caribbean Basin (after the New Jewel Movement was defeated in Grenada in October 1983). From the Soviet perspective, Nicaragua is neither vital nor negligible to Soviet national security. As Vernon Aspaturian explains, the Soviet Union stands to gain something from the Nicaraguan conflict whether the FSLN regime survives the Reagan administration or whether it succumbs to armed intervention. The Soviets do not have a great deal to lose if the FSLN is overthrown. For the Cuban regime, however, any action against the FSLN can be seen as a possible prelude to similar action against Cuba.

Moscow's presence looms heavily in the background, but Havana is the more active and visible player in Nicaragua. Although the Soviets have been engaged in an arms transfer to Nicaragua, similar to their arms transfers to Cuba in the 1960s, the role that several thousand Soviet advisers played in Cuba in the 1960s is being carried out in Nicaragua (as in Grenada before October 1983) by the Cubans, who are present in much greater numbers than the Soviets.

Neither the Soviets nor the Cubans have been very helpful in trying to defuse the crisis in Nicaragua. True, both advised Managua to refrain from imprudent moves (e.g., massive incursions into neighboring countries and deployment of advanced aircraft in Nicaragua), which would openly provoke the United States. Nevertheless, Soviet support of the massive military buildup in Nicaragua goes on unabated, while the Cubans continue their military advisory program. As reported in this volume by West German Minister Ottfried Hennig, Cuban Vice-President Carlos Rafael Rodríquez as early as 1982 refused to contemplate withdrawing Cuba's military advisers from Nicaragua, even if the United States agreed to withdraw its advisers from the region. In this light, the well-publicized withdrawal of 100 Cuban military advisers in 1985 must be considered only a maneuver designed to enhance the FSLN's negotiating position during the Contadora talks at that time.[2]

Western Europe

The West European leaders are clearly concerned about an internationalization of the Nicaraguan conflict. Among them is a growing consensus, shared by members of the social democratic parties who were early supporters of the FSLN, about the undemocratic, Leninist nature of that regime and its destabilizing regional ambitions. (The Grenada Documents illuminate Leninist tactics of the New Jewel Movement and the FSLN in dealings with the Socialist International. See Appendix E.)[3] However, the West European leaders still look upon Central America with a rather "distant eye," and they differ as to how the crisis should be resolved.

Most West European leaders agree that a protracted military conflict in Central America is in the interests of the Soviets and contrary to NATO interests, since such a conflict could occupy the United States at its periphery and thereby detract from U.S. ability to fulfill its NATO obligations. For these reasons, Minister Hennig argues, West European leaders cannot afford to be indifferent about the internationalization of the conflict in Nicaragua. Considering the negative consequences of a protracted U.S. military involvement in Central America for the whole Western defense system, the Central American imbroglio has become as important to NATO as is the Middle East. The West European governments have a clear stake in helping the United States resolve the Nicaraguan conflict, and this could best be done by increasing economic assistance to democratic forces in the

---

2. The Cuban first vice-minister of revolutionary armed forces, Casas Regueiro, described this move as indicating readiness by the Cuban government to support the Contadora process. *Notimex* (Mexico City), September 15, 1985, as reported in *FBIS—LAM*, September 17, 1985, Q1.

3. See Jiri Valenta and Herbert Ellison, eds., *Grenada and Soviet/Cuban Policy: Internal Crisis and US/OECS Intervention* (Boulder, Colo.: Westview Press, 1986), p. 479.

region. At a minimum, Hennig believes America's European partners should refrain from undermining U.S. policies in the region.

Toward Conflict Resolution: Possible Alternatives

The United States and its allies have basically three alternatives in efforts to resolve the Nicaraguan crisis: (1) to seek political accommodation with the FSLN regime and accept its present policies; (2) to overthrow the regime by military means; and (3) to pressure the FSLN by a variety of coordinated instruments, including support for the resistance, so as to force FSLN accommodation with the opposition, both within and outside Nicaragua, and FSLN abandonment of a revolutionary regional strategy.

Political Accommodation with the FSLN

A U.S. policy of coexistence with the present FSLN regime would mean to tolerate, no matter how unwillingly, another Leninist-modeled regime in the hemisphere, similar to that of Cuba. In practical terms, such a policy alternative would mean signing a vague Contadora and/or bilateral agreement with the FSLN, with implicit or explicit guarantees against U.S. invasion with the intent to overthrow the regime in Nicaragua. That is exactly what the Sandinistas, following the advice of Fidel Castro, are seeking. Alfredo César, whose comments appear in this volume, was present when Castro assured FSLN leaders in 1980 that such a guarantee was the single most important reason he was still in power. The Cuban experience suggests that this alternative would lead to further consolidation of power by the Sandinistas. The eventual consequence for the United States could be a growing military commitment to Nicaragua's Central American neighbors and possibly, in the long term, neglect of other U.S. global commitments.

The statements of the FSLN leaders reported in this volume by U.S. negotiators Shlaudeman and Burghardt—specifically the Sandinistas' reference to other Central American leaders as "dogs" of the U.S. "master"— reveal a lot about FSLN attitudes toward their Central American neighbors and unfortunately cast a dim light on the possibility of fruitful negotiations. Although ostensibly negotiating, under pressure from the United States, the FSLN leadership has been unwilling to conclude a comprehensive, verifiable, and simultaneously implemented agreement with its Central American neighbors or with the United States.[4] Also, the FSLN, unlike the other

---

4. The National Directorate's position on verification was expressed publicly by one of the nine commanders, the president of the National Assembly, Carlos Nuñez: "The method

negotiating partners, insists on certain preconditions before agreeing to further negotiations, principally the cessation of all U.S. aid to the resistance. The Sandinistas are aware of the advantage this would give them, for any preconditions would be self-enforcing in the democratic environment of the United States. Meanwhile, there would be no constraints or pressure on the Sandinistas to force them to reach a negotiated solution.

The FSLN leaders also reject symmetrical solutions to the Nicaraguan and Salvadoran conflicts, called for by the other negotiators. While demanding a negotiated settlement in El Salvador between President Duarte and the FMLN guerrillas, the FSLN refuses to negotiate with the resistance guerrillas in Nicaragua. Finally, the FSLN leaders have refused to agree to a substantial reduction in the number of Cuban, Soviet, and East European advisers, which would, in their view, "insult" their strategic allies and not be "gracious."[5]

Under severe economic strain, popular disillusionment, and external pressure, the FSLN leaders' search for bilateral negotiations with the United States could induce them to offer the opposition a share in the administrative apparatus, even at the highest level, if such a move would mean the termination of U.S. aid to the rebel groups and a nonaggression pact. The Sandinista regime might also agree to a reduction in the size of its army and to the withdrawal of foreign military advisers, ostensibly freezing its militarization and regional ambitions. None of these measures, however, would change the intimate nature of the Sandinista regime, for the administrative apparatus is not the real power structure. Power, in the case of the FSLN, as in any other Leninist or Leninist-oriented regime, lies mainly in the party, and in its armed and security forces.

For these reasons, some analysts believe that any meaningful negotiation between the FSLN and the opposition or the United States would have to include the thorny subject of the nature and control of the military and security forces which could no longer be organs of the FSLN or under its exclusive control. A mere reduction in any of these forces would only be a tactical move easily reversible at a time when internal and international conditions would permit.

As of fall 1986 there are signs in Nicaragua that the Sandinistas are approaching political leaders from the civic opposition (Conservative party,

---

adopted to verify the weapons capacity of the Central American countries, and I would say specifically in Nicaragua's case, is actually superfluous, because any army, regardless of how small its intelligence service may be, knows quite well its neighbors' potential." An interview with Carlos Núñez, *El Día* (Mexico City), December 5, 1985, p. 5.

5. An interview with Humberto Ortega, *Barricada* (Managua), October 10, 1985, pp. 1–14.

Christian Socialist party, Independent Liberal party) in order to offer them participation in the public administration while leaving untouched the real basis of Sandinista power. If they are able to implement this political move, the Sandinistas could convey an image of democratization which could lure many foreign observers and build pressure on the United States for a formal promise of nonaggression to the Sandinista regime. The outcome of these budding developments remains to be seen.

The FSLN program and policies suggest that the *comandantes* consider the agreements and alliances with their "bourgeois" partners, nationally and regionally, only temporary tactics. Meanwhile, they believe that time is working in their favor, allowing them to continue consolidating a Leninist system in Nicaragua. Their short-term goal is to survive Ronald Reagan's presidency. As to the messianic content of the FSLN program, the National Directorate appears to be united in the belief that the revolution eventually will become regionalized or die. Although democracies have at times allowed themselves the luxury of self-destruction, Leninist or Leninist-oriented regimes have rarely been known to do so. Grenada may be the only exception. Thus the signing of an unverifiable bilateral or multilateral agreement may constitute what Mark Falcoff aptly calls an "American Yalta" without a Central American NATO to reinforce it and ensure an effective policy of containment.

This first policy alternative—political accommodation with the FSLN—would require, at a minimum, that the United States permanently station U.S. forces in countries neighboring Nicaragua and, at a maximum, that it create a new military alliance system in the region (e.g., with Honduras and perhaps also Costa Rica) to contain what will certainly be the FSLN's eventual efforts to implement their regional ambitions. Moreover, it is not entirely certain that the United States would be able, effectively or indefinitely, to maintain a military and political containment zone in Central America. Can Honduras really be turned into another South Korea, a permanent U.S. military staging area in the event of Nicaraguan aggression? The acceptance of a Leninist-oriented regime in the region could represent a heavy price for the United States in another sense. Policymakers in the United States fear that such a policy would be perceived as a strategic retreat, causing anti-Sandinista forces and governments friendly to the United States to become disillusioned while encouraging radical forces not only in Latin America but elsewhere.

In contrast to the Soviet Union, the United States has vital national security interests in Nicaragua stemming from its proximity to U.S. logistical supply lines in the Caribbean. The evolution of Soviet–Nicaraguan security ties could complement Soviet–Cuban security and military ties and in the long run further constrain the U.S. ability to resupply NATO countries in any large-scale West European conflict. Thus, in the view of U.S. policy-makers, the United States cannot afford to wait and see if the Nicaraguan regime continues its strategic alignment with the Soviets or if it develops into a national communist regime "a la Yugoslavia" under Tito or "a la China" under Mao Zedong. What was feasible at the Soviet periphery may not be practical so close to the United States. First, history does not repeat itself easily or exactly, and the often predicted rift between Managua and Moscow may never materialize, regardless of what the United States does. If it does materialize, such a rift could still have a detrimental impact on U.S. security. All things considered, a U.S. policy of accepting present FSLN policies could eventually imperil the U.S. regional role and, in the long run, add further constraints on U.S. fulfillment of global responsibilities.

Military Intervention

A second alternative available to the United States for resolving the Nicara-guan conflict is direct military intervention. Like political accommodation, military intervention is very costly. It is impossible to estimate the material and political costs of such action, although there has been speculation. To forestall any kind of intervention, the FSLN leaders and diplomats and their Soviet and Cuban allies have tried to heighten U.S. concern about another Vietnam-style involvement. Moreover, their continuous speculation about a U.S invasion has kept the Nicaraguan military on alert so as to preempt any possible surprise intervention.

The material costs of a large U.S. military intervention have been esti-mated by an American scholar and repeated by Soviet analysts. This esti-mate concludes that an outright invasion of Nicaragua would require a task force of 61,000 men; 216 combat aircraft; 730 helicopters, tanks, and ar-mored transports. To overthrow the FSLN would require a 5-year occupa-tion and cost the United States 5,000 dead, 20,000 wounded and $10.5 billion.[6]

Obviously, an estimate of this kind depends on a number of variables and circumstances and can only be highly speculative. An actual U.S. interven-tion could be more or less costly in lives and material, depending on the mode of conflict and the degree of resistance by the Nicaraguan armed forces. The FSLN leadership is on record as asserting that if the U.S. invades, it intends to take the following measures: to defend the capital city of Managua in a war of attrition "from house to house"; to mobilize the population; to deploy tanks in strategic positions around the city and draw

6. See a Soviet report on Ted Morgan's estimate: M. Beliat, "The Facts Show: Civil War, US Style," *Krasnaya zvezda*, August 29, 1984, p. 3.

from depots of ammunition and weapons in secret, predetermined sites in the capital; and, utilizing the *turbas divinas* ("divine mobs"), to arrest and make hostages of the political opposition and bourgeois elements. Should the National Directorate not succeed in defending the capital, some of its leaders would depart from secret destinations to Cuba, while others would engage in a lengthy insurgency.[7]

At the regional level, in the event of a U.S. invasion, the FSLN professes that it will spread the conflict "all over,"[8] turning Central America into another Vietnam, but above all *incendiar* ("to set fire") to Costa Rica. It is seriously to be doubted that a U.S. military intervention would provide the FSLN with an opportunity to invade neighboring countries. What one could anticipate, however, is a series of terrorist attacks organized by the FSLN in the immediate region (above all, in Costa Rica and Honduras), and even in the United States.

The FSLN leaders have tried to intensify the concern of the United States and its allies about another prolonged Vietnam-style military conflict in the Third World. The notion that Nicaragua would become another Vietnam in the event of a U.S. invasion has been repeated by FSLN leaders and officials at every opportunity. In 1984 one of two prominent displays facing visitors in the waiting room of the Nicaraguan Ministry of Defense was a poster with the caption *No Vietnam in Central America*. The same can be said about Nicaraguan diplomats in Washington, D.C. Indeed, the job of Nicaraguan Ambassador to the United States Carlos Tunnerman appears to be not the traditional art of diplomacy but public relations to promote the FSLN point of view and promulgate fear of another Vietnam among the media, the U.S. Congress, and U.S. decision makers. Burghardt reports in this volume that only once from 1984 to 1986 did Tunnerman seek a meeting with U.S. policy makers, and this only because the U.S. government had recently pointed out the inconsistency in the behavior of the FSLN, professing an interest in bilateral negotiations while completely avoiding diplomatic contact with U.S. officials. In the same period, Harold Bergold, U.S. ambassador to Managua, seized every initiative in maintaining an informal dialogue with the FSLN leaders.

The FSLN's well-advertised speculations concerning an imminent U.S. invasion have intensified since the Grenada operation in October 1983. Grenada was perceived as a signal that the United States might be recovering from the so-called Vietnam syndrome, which inhibited the direct use of

7. See speech of Commander Luís Carrión at the plenary session of the FSLN regional assembly (region 3), reported by *La Nación* (San José), October 19, 1985.

8. Humberto Ortega interview, *Barricada*; and Jiri and Virginia Valenta's interviews in Managua, December 1984.

military force in defending U.S. interests in the Third World. Although originally the FSLN leaders sincerely thought that the Grenada invasion might be a prelude to U.S. intervention in Nicaragua, by the following year they had concluded that this was not very likely. Yet they, along with the Soviets and Cubans, continued the rhetoric about an imminent U.S. armed intervention. As pointed out by Vernon Aspaturian in this volume, these tactics kept the Nicaraguan military vigilant and further discouraged such an occurrence.

The second policy option, military intervention, would inevitably have considerable political repercussions for the United States vis-à-vis its NATO partners and also in the Third World, especially Latin America. True, in Latin America there has been much disillusionment and doubt about the Sandinistas' objectives, and certainly Nicaragua's immediate neighbors would probably be relieved at any outcome that would remove the Sandinista threat to their own nations. But many South Americans tend to be indulgent and supportive of the Sandinistas as a matter of principle, particularly after the Falklands War. Thus one could anticipate, in the event of an invasion, a great rise in anti-U.S. sentiment, as additional volunteers from Latin American communist parties, some of whom are being recruited today, would rally to the cause of the FSLN.

But there would be no substantial military support for the FSLN from any of these countries, Cuba included. The Cuban military now in Nicaragua would probable put up a symbolic resistance in an invasion, as they did in Grenada in 1983. At that time, the futility of trying to bring reinforcements from Cuba, given U.S. military might, was clearly recognized by Fidel Castro. The Soviets have made it clear to Managua that they will support the FSLN primarily by political means. When asked about this, a Soviet official pointedly explained that in the event of an invasion, "We are going to make a very categorical protest."[9]

The most significant impediment to U.S. intervention, as Margaret Crahan reasons, may be the legal and moral argument. According to this view, the United States should adhere to higher standards than those displayed by Germany, Italy, and Japan during World War II and the Soviet Union more recently. When the United States adopts a policy that leads it to reject the jurisdiction of the International Court of Justice, it is clearly on the "wrong track." Somehow, the United States, as a democratic world power, needs to see the imperative in observing the tenets of international law. Like John Kennedy during the 1962 Cuban missile crisis, U.S. policymakers have to deal with the key question whether a democratic republic can morally and

---

9. An interview with Deputy Chairman of the USSR Supreme Soviet Presidium Antanas Barkauskas, *Clarín* (Buenos Aires), December 10, 1983. p. 16.

politically afford to intervene militarily in another country, regardless of the official oppression exercised in the latter or the legitimate security concerns of the former.

Multiple Pressures

The option of further pressuring the FSLN to change Nicaragua's national and regional conduct would require a policy to coordinate and sustain, over the long term, the various diplomatic, economic, and military pressures available. The United States has tried to exercise this option over the last few years. And while the FSLN has indeed become more isolated and its economic performance has deteriorated considerably, the pressures have not yet been effective enough to force a change in FSLN behavior. The main problem appears to have been the absence of the effective use of military pressure by what was then a divided and inadequately supplied Nicaraguan resistance. The U.S. congressional vote in the summer of 1986 in favor of military aid for the resistance and the simultaneous coordination agreement between the northern and southern branches of the resistance were considered by some to be turning points in the struggle.

As we have seen, U.S. diplomacy has failed in its quest for a negotiated solution to the Nicaraguan conflict, surely in part because of FSLN obstinacy. Ironically aiding U.S. diplomatic efforts to isolate the FSLN regime in the international community, FSLN conduct itself is the factor that has most worked to the regime's detriment, even antagonizing former supporters in Latin America and Western Europe. Indeed, by late 1986 the view expressed in the National Directorate was that "Latin America has abandoned" the FSLN regime.[10]

The United States has also used economic pressure. At first it cut off economic aid to Nicaragua in the wake of the latter's support for the FMLN guerrillas in El Salvador. Related to this, subsequently, were the negative incentives imposed on the FSLN via the international credit system, and finally, in May 1985, the U.S.-imposed economic embargo. Typically, the economic pressures served primarily as important psychological signals of U.S. displeasure with FSLN conduct. Undoubtedly they further burdened the already strained Nicaraguan economy. However, the FSLN was able to deflect some of the intended losses by increasing trade with the Soviet Union and its allies, and before the embargo, by founding a number of dummy corporations in various parts of the world. So far, the economic pressure has not led to a perceptible change in FSLN conduct.

The most effective pressure has been the U.S.-backed Nicaraguan armed

10. Report of a speech by commander Víctor Tirado López, Managua Radio, December 1, 1985, *FBIS— LAM*, December 3, 1985, p. 20.

resistance, whose activity between 1982 and 1986 did indeed contribute to deteriorating economic conditions and increasing FSLN casualties—10,000 by August 1985, according to FSLN claims.[11] Like the other instruments of pressure, however, the resistance war has not been able to achieve the U.S. objective in Nicaragua. Up to June 1986 the resistance has lacked a unified leadership, effective coordination of its military activities, a coherent democratic program to offer as an alternative to the FSLN agenda, and U.S. military aid. As recognized by Humberto Ortega, the resistance could have advanced significantly in 1984 and perhaps, as the National Directorate feared, could have divided the northern and southern parts of the country. At that time there were propitious conditions for the rebel struggle in neighboring Honduras and Costa Rica; the Sandinistas, on the other hand, had serious military problems.[12]

From 1984 to 1986 the resistance struggle became more difficult because of a considerable strengthening of Sandinista military capabilities (building of special counterinsurgency forces in the army and in the Ministry of the Interior, consolidating the reserves and the territorial militia) on the one hand, and the absence of U.S. military support for the rebels on the other. The struggle of the resistance changed decisively in 1985 when apparently it suffered severe losses and the FSLN increased its control over the communication system and the rural areas, which were a former preserve of the resistance.

The most serious impediments to the rebels' success have been the lack of a unified, cohesive leadership (in contrast with a strong FLSN leadership), squabbling and serious strategic differences among leaders of various opposition groups, lack of credibility of some leaders, and stories about mismanagement of U.S. humanitarian aid by others. Edén Pastora, military commander of the BOS, was not able to work with the military leaders of the northern United Nicaraguan Opposition (UNO) front, particularly Enrique Bermúdez, a former member of the National Guard.[13] Until June 1986 the resistance struggle was also constrained by a lack of U.S. congressional consensus about military aid. President Reagan's initial failure to convince the U.S. Congress to provide military aid to the resistance was interpreted

11. An interview with Deputy Interior Minister Commander Omar Cabezas, *Uno más uno* (Mexico City), August 21, 1985, p. 1.

12. Humberto Ortega interview, *Barricada*.

13. Humberto Ortega described Pastora in the fall of 1985 as "totally neutralized . . . practically alone . . . [and with] great demoralization of his forces." Ibid. Ortega's prediction proved to be correct. For an excellent analysis of differences among the Nicaraguan opposition, see *La Nación* (San José), July 28, 1985, p. 6.

by FSLN leaders and their Soviet allies as evidence of discord between the will of the American people and that of the U.S. government.[14]

Some of these conditions changed in June 1986. First, a cooperation agreement was reached between UNO and BOS.[15] Abandoned by most of his military commanders in May 1986, Pastora has, at least for the moment, given up the military struggle against the Sandinistas. The resignation of the brave, romantic, yet undisciplined Pastora opened prospects for better cooperation, if not military coordination of the resistance movement in the north and south. In June also, the U.S. Congress approved the long-debated $100 million in military aid to the resistance. However, at the time of this writing (late 1986), it remains to be seen whether the unification pact and the military aid will make a significant difference. The key question is whether the resistance can become a viable military force capable of pressuring the FSLN inside Nicaragua to undertake the serious bilateral and multilateral negotiations urged in this volume by Francisco Vallagrán and Esperanza Durán. (Neither Durán nor Villagrán, however, supports this policy of pressure.) Moreover, the "Irangate" scandal of November 1986 could seriously imperil support for the resistance and hamper the U.S. policy of putting military pressure on Nicaragua.

Other Measures

According to many analysts, a vigorous pursuit of the third option, which avoids the extremes of doing nothing or invading Nicaragua outright, appears to be the best choice facing U.S. policymakers, although all are imperfect. While carrying out this course, policymakers must also (1) encourage far-reaching democratization of the resistance movement and program; (2) pursue a more agile diplomacy throughout Central America; and (3) consider additional measures that would render prohibitive FSLN security ties with the Soviet Union and Cuba.

Democratization of the resistance. The United States should encourage the Nicaraguan opposition, including the resistance, to provide a truly democratic alternative to the Sandinistas' Leninist program. The war of the resistance will never be won militarily alone. In spite of recent attempts at coordination and greater ideological maturity, expressed in the June 1986 agreement between BOS and UNO, the opposition both within Nicaragua and abroad needs to refine and elaborate further its democratic—reformist

14. See an interview with the Soviet ambassador to Mexico, Rostislav Sergeiev, *Notimex* (Mexico City), March 21, 1986.

15. See the document "*Acuerdo Democrático de la Resistencia Nicaragüense* (Democratic Agreement of the Nicaraguan Resistance)," June 18, 1986.

political program. Guarantees must be provided that would both prevent restoration of the Somocista political structures and ensure respect for the positive social and economic changes (including some aspects of the agrarian reform) introduced by the revolution and later betrayed by the FSLN. Meanwhile, the United States should insist that democratic elements in the Nicaraguan opposition be involved in any future negotiations process, for their participation is essential to any negotiated settlement that might be reached. The United States should not and cannot support some of the more notorious figures of the Somoza era, many of whom made possible the triumph of the FSLN and who are seeking now to regain lost privileges.

More consistent U.S. policy and public diplomacy. The United States should seek to change the existing perceptions not only of many Nicaraguans but also of other Central Americans about the lack of continuity in U.S. policy toward Central America. It is naive to think that Central American nations such as Honduras and Costa Rica will vigorously contain Managua's ambitions without a clear perception of U.S. willingness to do the same, unhesitatingly and without the probability of later reversals. The lack of continuity in U.S. policymaking feeds insecurity and hesitation on the part of Honduras and Costa Rica and deepens the isolation of Guatemala from the Nicaraguan problem.

A U.S. policy should be made for the long haul so as to break the vicious cycle of indecision fed by the lack of continuity, resolve, and energy in the United States. Such inconsistency promotes inaction both in the United States and in friendly Central American nations. The United States should also indicate clearly to the right-wing forces in Central America that pressure on the FSLN does not mean a return to the status quo before 1979. As to the West European allies of the United States, they need to be convinced about U.S. democratic objectives in the region, and about the continuity and better coordination of U.S. policies. Western Europe's economic, political, and moral aid can make a difference in the region.

The United States needs to combine the ongoing pressures on the FSLN with effective public diplomacy in Latin America and Western Europe. U.S. policymakers should not concede the debate over Leninism in Central America to members of the radical left, leaving them to define the parameters of the discussion. Efforts to increase awareness, in a sophisticated and convincing fashion, about the dual threats of Leninism and right-wing dictatorships in Central America would enhance implementation of U.S. policy in the area.

Making FSLN and Soviet–Cuban security ties prohibitive. Above all, the United States must address seriously the question of Soviet and Cuban security ties with Nicaragua. Arms control negotiations with the Soviets should not lure policymakers into compliance with evolving security ties between the Soviet Union and Nicaragua which appear to be an inherent part of Soviet calculations regarding Central America. Indeed, Mikhail Gorbachev was said to have told the FSLN leadership that the forthcoming arms talks between the superpowers could lead to a "little détente." The FSLN leaders, for their part, believe that in future U.S./Soviet talks Gorbachev will try to induce Reagan to establish negotiations with Nicaragua.[16] The administration should indicate to the Soviets that the ongoing arms control talks will not inhibit the United States from pursuing drastic measures in Nicaragua, if need be—an indication that might increase the stakes for Soviet and Cuban security ties with that country.

Above all, the U.S. government should insist on the elimination of Soviet–Nicaraguan security ties, even if this were to mean a U.S. acceptance of Nicaragua's internal order. Such an explicit tradeoff, as Vernon Aspaturian points out, although not yet articulated by U.S. officials, would confront the FSLN with the choice between survival and more draconian measures (e.g., a naval blockade). If the FSLN refuses such a tradeoff, the central issue in the Nicaraguan crisis will become U.S. security concerns. The eruption of these concerns would enable U.S. policymakers to articulate a policy of even greater pressure, and, if necessary, more extreme measures. However, in the absence of U.S. determination, the attitude of the FSLN is likely to remain as presently epitomized in a slogan of the Sandinista youth: "To learn from the Soviet Union is to learn how to conquer. To learn from the United States is to learn how to retreat."

16. An interview with Commander Tómas Borge, *Excélsior* (Mexico City), March 17, 1985.

• APPENDIXES •

(Each Appendix Is Preceded by a
Short Explanatory Introduction)

APPENDIX A: General Political–Military Platform of the FSLN
for the Triumph of the Popular Sandinista Revo-
lution (May 1977)
APPENDIX B: Historic Program of the FSLN (1969)
APPENDIX C: First Draft of the National Constitution of the
Republic of Nicaragua (February 1986)
APPENDIX D: Contadora Act on Peace and Cooperation in
Central America (April 1986)
APPENDIX E: Report on Meeting of Secret Regional Caucus,
Managua (January 1983)

General Political–Military Platform of the FSLN for the Triumph of the Popular Sandinista Revolution (May 1977)

Perhaps no other document among those written by the Frente Sandinista de Liberación Nacional (FSLN), since its creation to the present day, has defined that political organization with greater clarity than has the *General Political–Military Platform of the FSLN for the Triumph of the Popular Sandinista Revolution*. It includes a great deal of crucial information: the origins of the Sandinista Leninist vanguard and its perceptions about Nicaragua's historical development and orientation; tactical maneuvers to be used in the struggle for power; descriptions of the stages of development that the FSLN has already passed through and those that still must be traversed; the political, military and ideological bases of the regime; and the fundamental Leninist goals of the FSLN.

The Platform reputedly was published "someplace" in Nicaragua on May 4, 1977, more than two years before the downfall of the Somoza regime. The National Directorate intended it as a manual for militant members of the Front. Evidence seems to indicate, however, that the Platform was really written in Costa Rica, a peaceful, democratic country where the principal members of the FSLN found refuge, support, and rest throughout the struggle against Somocismo. The style and content of an important part of the document show a striking similarity to the book *Cincuenta Años de Lucha Sandinista* (Fifty Years of Sandinista Struggle) written by Humberto Ortega in San José, Costa Rica, and published in Tegucigalpa, Honduras in 1978, with the full support of Víctor Meza (a prominent Honduran Sandinista who severed his ties with the FSLN after it took power). Whether or not the Platform is attributable to Commander Ortega, it was certainly inspired by the philosophy of the Tercerista group to which he belonged and whose members would have revised and approved the manuscript. In any case, the Platform undoubtedly codified Sandinista ideology prevailing since the formation of the Front, and set down in an indubitable and clear fashion the official strategic line of the FSLN.

The original Spanish version of the Platform contains minor but numerous typographical and linguistic errors. To facilitate smoother reading, the present editor has corrected some of these errors in translation. (Capitalization, verb tenses and italics have been left as in the original.) The importance of the document has not been matched by its circulation for obvious reasons; it was intended for FSLN militants. However, now a wider audience has access to the complete text of the Platform—a document that provides penetrating insights into the FSLN and its revolutionary process.

CONTENTS

The spirit of the working classes will be embodied in a future and implacable avenger. The nether wave will topple the upper class . . . all tyrannies shall come crashing to the ground: political tyranny, economic tyranny, religious tyranny . . . because the omens of the cata-

*clysm are already within sight but still humanity cannot see. What
humanity will see are the swamp and the horror of the day of wrath.
There will be no force able to contain the torrent of that fatal vengeance.
A new Marseillaise will have to be sung, which, like the trumpets of
Jericho, will destroy the dwellings of the infamous. The fire will en-
lighten the ruins. The popular knife will sever hated necks and bel-
lies; the women of the populace will tear out the blond locks of the
proud virgins; the foot of the shoeless will trample the carpets of the
wealthy; the statues of the bandits who oppressed the poor shall be
broken; and the sky will witness with frightened joy, amid the thunder
of the redeeming catastrophe, the punishment of the haughty sinners,
the supreme and terrible vengeance of those drunk with misery.*

RUBÉN DARÍO*
(Nicaraguan poet)

PREFACE

This political–strategic document has been elaborated and approved by our National Directorate. It is the product of the type of theoretical efforts that the
Sandinista Front endorses in order to interpret justly and more correctly our extensive revolutionary practices. This modest political work synthesizes the inquietudes
and the political-ideological, schematic, organizational, and strategic-military reserves of all of our Sandinista insurgency, which, in the mountains, countryside and
city maintains the armed revolutionary struggle with firmness and conviction.

The National Directorate of the F.S.L.N. (Sandinista National Liberation Front)
is sure that this document will strengthen even more our unwavering revolutionary
march. At the same time, it will facilitate consolidation of the Sandinista Monolithic
Unity that has been maintained exemplarily and traditionally in our vanguard
organization, the Sandinista Front.

This document will also facilitate definitive eradication of pseudo-revolutionary
currents who, masquerading as Marxists, hope to divide the FSLN and postpone the
armed revolutionary struggle until the creation of what they call a "Communist
Party," which would replace the F.S.L.N. We say definitive eradication because
fundamentally said micro-faction, also known as the *replegada* (retreaters), formed
by a ridiculous minority of dissidents and renouncers of the F.S.L.N. and its Armed
Struggle, does not represent anything more than a passing peril for the popular
Sandinista revolution. We reassure our militants that no member of the National
Directorate nor any relevant F.S.L.N. cell supports this retreating micro-fraction.
Likewise, all of the F.S.L.N., from the wilderness [of Nicaragua] to the world
outside, stick together in their common attachment to the revolutionary principles

---

*These segments of prose, attributed to Rubén Darío, appear on the outer back cover
of the original Spanish document.

synthesized within both the higher and infrastructural organizations of the F.S.L.N., principally the National Directorate, the Guerrilla's General Staff and the Regional Committees.

It is the duty of the entire Sandinista militancy to enrich this political document. This document should be discussed within each organism or structure of the Sandinista Front, not only to increase our understanding of it, but also to encourage its sound, just and constructive criticism.

Through appropriate channels, the National Directorate shall dutifully attend to all the queries, anxieties, suggestions, etc., that the Sandinista militants might express, either orally or in writing, to their superior organisms.

The Popular Sandinista Revolution Shall Triumph!
A Free Homeland or Death.

BRIEF INTRODUCTION

The present struggle of the Nicaraguan people, directed and synthesized by their historic vanguard, the Sandinista Front of National Liberation, is the highest and most revolutionary expression of the vigorous struggle that the Nicaraguan people have pursued throughout their history. This struggle draws on the traditions of the patriotic independence struggles against Yankee expansionism during the past century and the imperialist domination of the present century.

Immediately after obtaining its independence from the Spanish colonial yoke in 1821, our country is transformed into the favorite target, for various political and strategic ends leading to the control of the continent, of the expansionist North American capitalism of that time. In reference to this, the Sandinista leader Carlos Fonseca pointed out, "Nicaragua is a country that has suffered foreign aggression and oppression for more than four centuries. Nicaragua, along with other Latin American nations, had to face subjugation by the Iberian Peninsula. It also suffered British domination of part of its Atlantic coast that lasted for 150 years, until 1893. At the same time, Nicaragua finds itself among the first victims of aggressive U.S. policies."

The banners of freedom were passed from hand to hand, at the cost of sweat and blood, starting with the National War against the slave-driving Yankee invaders in 1856 and continuing today.

To the slogans of "War to the Thieving Yankees," in 1856, "Long-live Sandino," in the 1930s, and, "A Free Homeland or Death" in the present, our nation has hammered out a certain and strong foundation for its total and final liberation from the yoke of both local and foreign exploitation.

Starting with a historical analysis of the roots and general line followed by our Popular Sandinista Revolution, this document establishes the general platform pertaining to the present struggle of our revolutionary movement. By starting with an understanding of the development of our process, we can better grasp the strategy and tactics that currently impel the revolutionary vanguard of the Nicaraguan people, the Sandinista National Liberation Front.

This document is born of the results of the consistent revolutionary practice of the Sandinista Front since 1960. It stems from the vast political, military and organizational experience gathered throughout these years and attempts to orient and guide our journey toward the national and social liberation of our people.

CHAPTER I

BRIEF HISTORICAL ANALYSIS OF THE POPULAR SANDINISTA REVOLUTION

The armed Yankee aggression of 1909 violently demolishes Zelaya's bourgeois, liberal-reformist process initiated in 1893 because of the obvious danger that such policies represented for absolute U.S. control of the Central American isthmus. The conservative oligarchy regains political hegemony of the country at the expense of converting it into a republic dominated by Yankee imperialism.

From 1909 to 1926, the conservative oligarchy maintains fundamental control of the State. This power is then sought by the agrarian bourgeoisie, the dominant and more progressive sector, from the economic point of view; but it is not until after 1926 that they manage to obtain power, thereby becoming the most pliable social vehicle for the multiple schemes of Yankee imperialism in Nicaragua.

The liberal bourgeoisie that clashes with the conservative oligarchy in 1926, in what is called the Constitutional War, nevertheless has lost by this time its progressive content of Zelayist liberalism and shows itself completely in accord with the political and strategic interests maintained by the Yankees in Nicaragua.

After losing to the liberals in 1926, the conservative oligarchy is eliminated as a relevant factor in the country's political correlation; and after Sandino's assassination it accepts the tutelage of the liberal bourgeois faction and yields to the capitalist option of development, strengthened by Yankee support and the newly created National Guard.

The war of 1926, despite its vast anti-Yankee and anti-oligarchic popular base, has a counter-revolutionary outcome because of the treachery perpetrated by Moncada and Sacasa—both symbols of the castrated bourgeoisie—against the true liberal cause embraced and defended with blood by our people from 1909 until that cruel Constitutional War of 1926. More than thirteen armed uprisings—among which the 1912 uprising of the patriot Benjamín Zeledón is the most notable—help to synthesize the spirit of anti-imperialist and anti-oligarchic struggle among our people during this period.

At that time, the popular revolutionary movement could not expect a degree of evolution sufficient to allow it to assume the leadership role in the struggle against Yankee intervention and the conservative oligarchy. This limitation was caused in part by the youth of our organization and the lack of awareness among our workers, especially the peasant proletariat—an important pillar in the cultivation of coffee and the export of timber and other products—who were horribly exploited and oppressed by the three-sided reactionary force represented by armed Yankee intervention, the oligarchy and the bourgeoisie.

But not everything had a counter-revolutionary denouement in 1926. Our people, besides their own stock of anti-imperialist feelings, also integrated, via Augusto César Sandino, the revolutionary and proletarian ideas which circulated vigorously in Mexico at that time. It was precisely the popular proletarian army led by Sandino in the Constitutional War that determined at Bejuco, Las Mercedes, and Boaco the triumph of the liberals over the conservatives. Out of this War of 1926 came the first political—military revolutionary detachment, led by Sandino and having a firm, fundamental, anti-imperialist, and class base.

The general political—military situation at the end of the Constitutional War on May 4, 1927 presents, on the one hand, the local liberal-conservative reactionary forces in the position of having completely sold out to Yankee imperialism, and, on the other hand, the popular-revolutionary forces armed and ready to fight a national, anti-imperialist, anti-class war of liberation against the Yankees and their Nicaraguan lackeys. This budding of a political-military revolutionary organization, a-chieved in the war of 1926, developed tremendously during the anti-interventionist war of 1927—1934, until all the fundamental, anti-imperialist revolutionary foundations of our present struggle for final and total liberation from the yoke of exploitation and oppression were attained. The heroic struggle that our hard-working and patriotic people sustained with sacrifices and incredible efforts under Sandino's able and firm leadership, from 1926 to 1934, represents the synthesis of our people's entire moral and revolutionary reserves and, at the same time, the fundamental *startlng* point for the present struggle of our people for their final liberation.

The *first* great phase of our Sandinista Revolution is constituted by the 1926—1934 struggle of our nation. In this vital historical phase, our process of liberation is comprised, on the one hand, of a profound and clear understanding of the imperialist and class phenomenon, and on the other, of a proper and just armed revolutionary strategy for confronting armed Yankee intervention, as well as for fighting local reactionary forces. At the end of the Constitutional War, two alternatives are presented to the incipient revolutionary vanguard detachment led by Sandino:

1. To confront the reactionary liberal—conservative forces through a process of revolutionary civil war (different from the recently ended civil war that, because of its direction, was not revolutionary), or

2. To confront Yankee military intervention in order to resolve the nation versus intervention contradiction.

The vanguard detachment correctly decides first to resolve the fundamental contradiction at that time, represented by armed Yankee intervention. The contradiction people versus reactionary local forces thus recedes and gives way to the fundamental contradiction.

The colossal liberation crusade that manages to expel the Yankee interventionists from the native soil deeply moved our nation and the whole world. The Yankees' superior material resources clashed shamefully with our nation's moral and revolutionary superiority. In an eminently irregular and predominantly guerrilla war of more than a thousand skirmishes, it was possible to defeat such a gigantic adversary due to the combination of guerrilla troops and quasi-regular Sandinista troops; with the participation of the whole country, laborers, peasants, students, Indians, blacks and mestizos; and the firm participation of internationalist Latin American patriots. This was our Holy War, as the Soviets described their war against the Hitlerian hordes [sic].

Having resolved the nation versus intervention contradiction with the expulsion of the Yankee invaders in 1933, the center of the struggle shifts from the *armed political* stage to the *unarmed political* stage. The incipient process of revolutionary civil war that began in 1926 reemerges in 1933 after the expulsion of the Yankee troops from our native soil.

The revolutionary movement led by Sandino, by means of political struggle, aims at the *Accumulation of Material and Human Forces* that will allow military victory to be complemented by political and economic victory over the local reactionary forces backed by North American imperialism.

Sandino led the way to a *revolutionary civil war* through the constant *accumulation of* political, human, material, and other *forces*. This task is cut short by the counterrevolutionary maneuvers of imperialist and local reactionary forces who, in February 1934, assassinate General Augusto César Sandino, and manage to behead the political–military leadership of the movement, also cutting off the principal guerrilla base located at Wiwilli, and engaging the remaining rebel forces in a three-year war of attrition, ending with the fall of General Pedro Altamirano in 1937 and the forced exile of the remaining Sandinistas.

The February 21, 1934 fall of Sandino, while he was dutifully accumulating the forces needed for the revolutionary process, marked the *beginning* of a *second great phase* of the Popular Sandinista Revolution, characterized by a profound decrease in revolutionary activity. It must be emphasized that this decline does *not* mean the disappearance of the revolutionary movement begun in the first phase, from 1926 to 1934.

Among some of the local and international conditions that objectively blocked the fruition of the revolutionary tasks established by the Sandinista movement after 1933, the most notable are: the weak development of our labor class, especially the incipient Nicaraguan proletariat, due as much to the backward economic development of the country as to this group's limited level of organization and class consciousness. Even though our people knew fundamentally how to organize themselves militarily, it was almost impossible at that time also to conjugate the political and economic forms of struggle; the masses could not really understand that military control alone was not sufficient and, as Sandino pointed out, they were not able to see the political and economic domination that our country was still subjected to. The subjective direction of the struggle basically rested in one man: Sandino. This situation—the lack of a collective leadership, which is the product of our complex historical process—had a negative effect on the continuation of our project once Sandino was assassinated.

On the international scene, let us highlight the incipient quality of the worldwide revolutionary movement, which, at the same time, was under the terrible siege of fascism. The glorious October Revolution in Russia was still in the process of consolidation, faced, as it was, with the necessity of having to combat the terror of counterrevolution in the very heart of the country. The socialist camp at that time was thus reduced to Revolutionary Russia. World attention was focused on the danger of the German—Italian—Japanese fascist axis. The Yankees themselves, who had killed so many of our nation's sons, recovered prestige in having to confront the fascist peril alongside the allied forces.

Such internal and external conditions determined in great part the revolutionary decline that the Popular Sandinista Revolution undergoes from 1934 to 1956.

Over the next 22 years that characterize the phase of revolutionary decline, the initiative and thrust of strategic withdrawal (*repliegue*), which had been outlined by the Sandinista movement in 1933 in its search for the accumulation of materials, are lost. The revolutionary movement is reduced to a prolonged passivity wherein the dispersion and atomization of the Sandinista bloc are evident.

Even though the organized Sandinista struggle is reduced to an almost total paralysis, the same was not to occur with the spontaneous popular class struggle which, in spite of lacking an organized vanguard leadership, inexorably reacts to the exploitation and oppression of the reactionary classes led by the bourgeois military dictatorship. It is precisely this impetus of pressure and social reaction which permits the revolutionary movement to gradually and slowly RESTORE ITSELF (*RE-INTEGRARSE*) until the moment of the leap *forward* (salto *ascendente*) starting with the various social upheavals in the 1950s and 1960s and synthesized in the heroic action of Rigoberto López Pérez in 1956, when he put the tyrant to death.

Various examples, among many, of those popular struggles are: the demonstration quelled by the National Guard on May 1, 1935; the popular strike against an increase in fuel prices in 1936; armed protests by rubber workers on the southern border in 1944, and at La Mina La India and Muelle de los Bueyes in 1948; labor strikes in the Chichigalpa plantations; peasant uprisings against the large absentee landowners at Boaco in 1954; anti-Somoza student demonstrations in 1944; the armed movement of 1954, in which the Sandinista Optaciano Morazán participates; and, in 1957, the National Guard conspiracy in which several officials are assassinated.

There were very many land-related problems faced by our peasantry in this very difficult stage of descent. Abroad, the exiled Nicaraguans always continued their denunciation of the dictatorship and their willingness to return to the homeland with the liberating rifle in hand.

The most relevant characteristics of the period of revolutionary decline are, among others:

1. Lack of revolutionary leadership.
2. Absence of a vanguard revolutionary organization. (Even though the Nicaraguan Socialist Party was created in 1944, the complexity of this stage of development and the subjective character of the leadership prevented it from fulfilling this role).
3. Incipient armed spontaneous revolt of the masses.
4. Popular leftist organization, weak and in the gestation stage.

5. Unorganized, heterogeneous student struggle.
6. Disorganized activities abroad by exiled Nicaraguans, consisting mostly of periodic denunciations.
7. Uninterrupted bloody repression of the people.
8. Political hegemony in the anti-Somocista struggle will be in the hands of the conservative bourgeoisie, dragging the people behind pseudo-popular leaders.
9. The masses will be "conservative" because they are fundamentally anti-Somocista and because they lack a revolutionary vanguard.
10. Yankee imperialism's unconditional economic, political, diplomatic, and ideological support, and unrestricted military support of the dictatorship by way of advising and equipping the National Guard.

The decade between 1950 and 1960 marks a series of historical events that are determinants in the development of the Sandinista Popular Revolution. On the one hand, the Somoza García dictatorship met with moderate success stemming from the power struggles among the bourgeoisie, through the 1950 liberal-conservative pact, and by the creation of important business enterprises which, along with the rise in the importance of cotton, contributed to the economic consolidation of the dynasty. On the other hand, these achievements would not accrue to their favor before the eyes of the masses, who each day were becoming more agitated against the cruel Somocista domination in the economic, social, political, and cultural realms.

Cotton production, which intensifies in the 1950s, lent a degree of economic stability to the system, but at the same time, accentuated popular dissatisfaction, especially among the large group of middle to poor peasants who were violently dispossessed of their land by the great cotton landowners in the occidental zones of the country. This important mass of discontented peasants, which overnight was transformed into salaried agricultural laborers overwhelmed by poverty, constituted a proletarian army which, although only incipient, was imbued with the irreversible ideal of class consciousness.

Domination by the Somocista clique and its protector, Yankee imperialism, which, through the dictatorship, multiplied its commercial, political, financial and strategic hold over Nicaragua, provokes widespread popular anger that serves to reestablish the Sandinista struggle and prompt the crisis of the Somocista dictatorship and of the accompanying system of exploitation and repression.

The revolutionary feat of Rigoberto López Pérez—supported by his small group of patriots, composed of heroes like Cornelio Silva, Ausberto Narváez and Edwin Castro—which culminated in Somoza García's execution, synthesizes the ideals of the 1950s struggle. Rigoberto López's deeds mark a *new beginning* for the Sandinista movement and illustrate for the masses the armed revolutionary strategy willed to us by Sandino. With this historic step, that difficult stage of revolutionary decline is forever transcended. With this justiciary act a strong foundation is forged for the great phase of REVOLUTIONARY ASCENT, propelled today by our nation under the leadership of the Sandinista Front.

The political crisis of the Somocista clique, that begins with the execution of the tyrant in 1956, and with the armed and unarmed popular uprisings that take place uninterruptedly until 1960, is sharpened by the economic crisis following the decline in coffee and cotton prices at that time.

Railway workers, shoemakers, stone cutters, teachers, miners, farm workers, health workers, students and peasants spontaneously organized and mobilized in the struggle against the dictatorship. Construction workers, electricians, stevedores and others form 18 labor unions. The masses generally flowed into the streets to protest the high cost of living and inflation, and the lack of adequate housing, health care, and social security, and to voice other social complaints.

Deriving impetus from the generation of July 23, 1959, the student movement openly confronts the imperialists, raising Sandino's banner against the dictators, at the cost of being imprisoned or shedding blood. The most notable of these confrontations is the León massacre, perpetrated by the National Guard in 1959, against peaceful protesters decrying the crimes committed against Sandinista patriots at Chaparral that same year.

In 1956, a Marxist cell is formed at the University [of León]. The majority of the students who joined this group become a part of the Sandinista front in the 1960s. Among them were the heroes Carlos Fonseca and Francisco Buitrago, along with other leaders of our organization who are now members of the National Directorate.

With the formation of the July 23 revolutionary student movement, in which Silvio Mayorga and Jorge Alberto Navarro are the most notable participants, fraternal ties are strengthened with the international community. Marxism already inspires the thinking of many of these student leaders and with the help of the National Student Congress of 1962, they found the Revolutionary Student Front, the vanguard organization of the Nicaraguan student movement.

In 1960, the most aware members of the student movement organized important revolutionary sectors—composed of laborers, students, wage earners and craftsmen—into the Nicaraguan Patriotic Youth Group (JPN). Because of the great anti-Communist influence of the imperialists and reactionaries over our people, this group was forced to adopt as its motto, "Neither left nor right, but forward." Activitists on the left attempt to join forces within the National Front of Revolutionary Youth but that same year both youth organizations disintegrate.

The highest expression of popular struggle during 1956—1960 is found in the more than 20 armed attacks against the dictatorship. The most notable are those led by the Sandinista veterans Ramon Raudales and Heriberto Reyes, as well as the armed movement of Chaparral, where Carlos Fonseca Amador, later a leading figure in the Sandinista Front, is seriously injured.

At this time, the Liberal Independent Party (PLI) founded in the 1940s was very weak due to a large number of its members having joined the Somocistas in 1947 and thereafter. This party has survived and today consists of a small group of petit bourgeois elements, apparently radical and anti-Somocista.

The Nicaraguan Socialist party, due to the political line followed by its leadership and because it was still trying to organize as a political group among various popular sectors, was left at the tail end of the popular struggles during the years of the Sandinista movement's restoration.

The opposition [anti-Somoza] bourgeoisie resorted to various maneuvers in an attempt to take over the leadership of the mass movements that were slowly slipping out of their control. Thus it feigned armed resistance in order to pressure the Yankee embassy to bring about the fall of Somoza and their own rise to power. When these maneuvers—those of Olama and Mollejones [two Nicaraguan plains where the armed revolutionary movement led by the upper classes was defeated] and those at the military posts of Jinotepe and Diriamba in the 1960s—met with failure, they resort to electoral schemes mounted by Somoza in 1963 and 1967.

Yankee imperialism—in support of the Somoza clique, which, in spite of its weaknesses, represented in the 1960s the most convenient sector for securing Yankee interests—sends the Seventh Fleet to Nicaragua's coast to confront the rising strength of the popular struggle against the Somoza tyranny.

In brief, this situation is a repeat of the popular struggles of 1956–1960. The activities that mark the *beginning* of the great phase of REVOLUTIONARY ASCENT are carried out by the mobilization of laborers, peasants, students, intellectuals, and other sectors of society in the realm of political recovery as well as in the military arena.

Some of the characteristics of this initial ascendent phase of the Popular Sandinista Revolution of 1956–1960 are the following:

1. Generalized unrest on the part of the masses in anticipation of the struggle against the tyranny.
2. Lack of a political and military organization able to assume the vanguard of the struggle.
3. Reaffirmation of the popular decision to find a solution to the problem of tyranny through force of arms.
4. A variety of armed groups trained for invasion through neighboring states.
5. Revolutionary leadership in the nascent stage, with plans to converge in a revolutionary vanguard detachment.
6. The revolutionary movement, even though it raises Sandino's banner and disseminates some Marxist doctrine, does not succeed in completely understanding Sandino's political thought concerning class consciousness and anti-imperialism, nor the scientific doctrine of the proletariat.

This phase of 1956–1960 is distinguished by the forging of conditions necessary for the creation of a revolutionary vanguard capable of leading the struggle. The Popular Sandinista Revolution, after the creation in 1960–1961 of its political-military vanguard detachment, enters a more advanced stage of development that enables it to extend and consolidate the stage of Revolutionary ascent initiated in 1956.

The forgers of such a vital historical step were, among others, Sandinista Colonel Santos López, Jorge Navarro, Carlos Fonseca, Silvio Mayorga and other leaders of our organization, presently residing in the wilderness or in the urban underground. The creation of the Sandinista National Liberation Front represents the most important historical milestone of these early years of the reintegration of the revolutionary movement.

The progress made thus far traverses more than 15 difficult and bloody years. The immense anti-revolutionary campaign conducted by Yankee imperialism and the reactionary classes led by Somoza, the demagogic development plans of the Alliance for Progress, the anti-militarist schemes of the liberal—conservative reactionaries, the brutal repression continuously exercised by the National Guard and other repressive organisms of the government clique, the intervention by reactionary CONDECA [Central American Council of Defense] forces, the Yankee army's shameless advisory role concerning counterinsurgency, and the abundant and daily anti-Sandinista propaganda have not been able to halt the irreversible progress of the Popular Sandinista Revolution, synthesized in its political—military vanguard, the Sandinista Front. The Sandinista struggle has accelerated the dissolution of the Somocista clique and its system of exploitation and oppression.

The impetuous advance of the Popular Sandinista Revolution would not be possible if the vanguard were not in alliance with the masses.

The firm, revolutionary participation of laborers, peasants, students, professionals, white collar workers, patriotic ex-soldiers, and other sectors have made it possible to confront the bestial enemy and move forward the heavy wheels of history.

We will now briefly recount the activities of the vanguard, from its inception to the present, in order to better understand the accomplishments of the ascendant stage of the Popular Sandinista Revolution and to identify the difficulties that we have to overcome in order to attain our final revolutionary goal.

1. Ideological Development

In 1967 our organization, because of the Historical Expedition at Pancasán, made considerable gains with respect to the control of our historical process, the ideology of the proletariat and the lessons to be gotten from the struggles of fraternal nations. Our people, in spite of the ignorance imposed by the system, little by little will assimilate the revolutionary ideology propagated in those years by the vanguard among various working class sectors of the countryside and the city and among the students.

Between 1960 and 1967, neither the rebel forces nor the reactionaries will provide the masses with an ideological apparatus capable of sustaining them with systematic and continuous guidance. On the one hand, this problem occurred because the vanguard was deeply involved in the necessary work of strengthening clandestine political-military structures to be used later to propel the organization and mobilization of the masses. On the other hand, the opposition bourgeoisie, due to the clearly electoral character of its position and its lack of a well-structured ideological party, did not provide a revolutionary alternative to the masses (although it would not have been able to do so even if such a party had existed).

Between 1967 and 1969 the FSLN is able to produce several vital documents that had been slowly outlined over a number of years. These documents embodied, among other components, the vindicatory and popular program and statutes of our organization, some documents about ideological line and strategy, and some studies concerning the state of the nation. Casimiro Sotelo, Julio Builtrago, Roberto

Amaya, Oscar Turcios, Silvio Mayorga, Carlos Fonseca, Fernando Gordillo are, among others, the Sandinista brothers who contributed to these efforts.

In the last 6 years, in spite of the great difficulties of the struggle, there has been a notable improvement in the understanding of revolutionary theory within the organization. Simultaneously, there has been a deepening of the analysis of our historical process and a greater understanding of the socio-economic and political reality of the country. Ricardo Morales, Leonel Rugama, Patricio Argüello, Oscar Turcios, Edgard Munguía, Mauricio Duarte are, among other Sandinista militants, those who synthesize the achievements of our vanguard.

"Red and Black," "The Trench," and "The Sandinista" have been the propaganda organs of the vanguard in its political-ideological work. The organization of study circles even in the most difficult conditions of repression, such as in prison and on rest stops during guerrilla campaigns, has been a constant preoccupation, as have been the printing and distributing of flyers, circulars, and newspaper reports about revolutionary activities. These undertakings, as well as anything else that contributes to the general dissemination of revolutionary ideology have been the constant occupation of our vanguard. Today our task is to redouble the efforts to organize and adequately systematize the constant political-ideological work which guides the movement.

Revolutionary ideology has created a profound impact among our oppressed and exploited masses, principally through the vanguard's organizational work among the people, and through their various political-military operations in the mountains and in the cities. To develop and to systematize this task among the masses, and especially among the labor and peasant classes, are urgent imperatives for the advancement of the struggle.

One of the ideological achievements of this ascendant stage was to rupture the deep cultural and ideological encirclement imposed on our labor class since 1934 by imperialism and its local expression, the Somoza dictatorship. This accomplishment puts the political-military ideals of Sandino, linked closely and dialectically with proletarian scientific thought, within ever greater reach of the masses. It also helps determine the conformation of the Sandinista Front as a political organization with a clear revolutionary ideology capable of absorbing the programmatic legacy of Sandino and giving a true class content to the popular struggles.

2. Political and Military Development

Until now the most important historical leap taken during the stage of revolutionary ascent consists of the ability of the revolution, led by the FSLN, to take a position of military and political strength outside the traditional liberal-conservative political authority.

Thus our people once again count on the independent and organized *REVOLUTIONARY POLITICAL IDEOLOGY* realized by Sandino in the 1930s.

Our vanguard trod a difficult path between its creation in the 1960s and the heroic events of Pancasán in 1967 when political and moral success were manifested at a national level. The efforts at Boca and Río Coco in 1963, the efforts at organizing proletarian sectors in 1964—1967, the creation of the urban resistance during these years, and the armed propaganda efforts in the mountains and the cities are, among others, vital tasks that contributed decisively to the great political gains achieved at Pancasán.

With respect to Pancasán, the hero Ricardo Morales pointed out: "Pancasán opened the horizon to the people's war and closed it for the bourgeoisie and for the pseudo-revolutionary reformists. Pancasán unleashes the people's initiative so that they can begin a vigorous attack on the oligarchy and imperialism, fomenting revolutionary firmness and rejecting servility. . . ."

The hero Silvio Mayorga, a leader of our organization, said in 1964, "I believe that in Nicaragua, the fundamental strength of the revolution lies in the coalition of laborers, farmers, students, and all other sectors that are not allied to the dictatorship and its hounds. Against the back drop of political, moral, economic and cultural repression that our country suffers, there is no recourse but the daily, incessant, arduous struggle of all patriots. Only in this manner can a combatant coalition be forged among the laboring masses and honest intellectuals."

Silvio Mayorga's thoughts found application in the FSLN's work among the Yaosca and Ulse Unions, in the infiltration of the production centers of Gadala María and Aceitera Corona and in the neighborhoods of our nation's capital. The popular civic committees created by the vanguard participated in these tasks, wherein some of the most notable work was done by the brothers Enrique Lorente and Carlos Reyna, Francisco Moreno and other workers who currently form part of the National Directorate of our organization.

Among the most important accomplishments of the vanguard in 1960—1967 are:

1. Overcoming the dispersion of revolutionary forces that characterized the 1956—1960 phase.
2. Continuity of revolutionary tasks in spite of the military setback suffered by the vanguard in 1963.
3. Gradual strengthening of the movement's leadership (our National Directorate), which, even though reduced, advanced the revolutionary work of the moment and planned for the future.
4. Overcoming the short-term mentality, which [achievement] can be appraised in the various programmatic and ideological documents that the vanguard creates during this phase.
5. Maintaining the continuity of the Sandinista revolutionary struggle, which, because of the continuous defeats of 1956—1960, seemed to have been permanently halted.

The Pancasán guerrilla campaign was the result of organizational work among the masses that the hero Rigoberto Cruz had been directing for several years. This campaign decisively overcomes the invasionist mentality (with preparations at border points) that previously had characterized the guerrilla movement.

By 1969 the previous achievements are notably confirmed in our national and international political reality by the vigorous presence of our organization in the mountains, the countryside and the city.

The Zinica guerrilla campaign in 1969–1970; the popular mobilizations of 1970; the massive undertakings in 1971 that rescued 13 Sandinistas from Somoza's jails; and the popular street uprisings in 1975 protesting the Sauce massacre are some of the mass movements that constitute decisive impulses in the development of the struggle.

Today's guerrilla movement in the wilderness, which is the Vertebral Column of the Revolution, developed uninterruptedly since the 1970s through ample contacts with the masses and patient paramilitary work. In the rest of the country, through a difficult stage of accumulation of forces in the political, organizational, logistical, military and conspiratory fields, the bases have been laid for the political–military and organizational leap that will permit the overthrow of the Somocista clique and the seizure of power leading us to a total and definitive national and social liberation.

Paralleling the accomplishments taking place in our country there has been a formidable international campaign created by the direct efforts of our Sandinista militants. It has been possible to break down the international isolation that limited our struggle during the period of revolutionary descent. Presently, the struggles of our vanguard are widely disseminated and respected, while each day the lack of legitimacy and isolation of the Somoza dictatorship becomes more evident.

The revolutionary act of December 27, 1974, commanded by the hero and leader of our vanguard, Eduardo Contreras Escobar, synthesizes all the past efforts of our organization. This action marks the beginning of a superior phase of the struggle in the political and military areas. If the revolutionary action accomplished by Rigoberto López Pérez signified "the beginning of the end of tyranny," the feat of December 27 means the deepening of its agony and the beginning of the end of its attendant bourgeois system of exploitation and political oppression.

This action clearly demonstrated the political and military capacity acquired by the vanguard throughout all these years, and the masses' support and recognition of the political supremacy of the Sandinista Front as the only organization capable of leading them to the realization of their freedom.

Today, with a more favorable national and international situation than the one faced by Sandino in the 1930s, the Popular Sandinista Revolution has entered a superior phase and the final one of the ascendant revolutionary stage. In this phase the people, duly organized and supported by virtue of the indestructible base constituted by the alliance between the workers and the peasants, will be mobilized under the direction of their vanguard, the Sandinista Front. They will be organized like an enormous army to topple the Somocista clique and establish a popular-democratic, revolutionary government that will allow us, guided by the ideology of the proletariat and the Sandinista historical legacy, to direct this triumph toward the achievement of socialism and the society of free men that Augusto César Sandino dreamed of.

CHAPTER II

CONCERNING THE GENERAL CAUSE OF THE POPULAR SANDINISTA REVOLUTION

1. Our Cause Is That of National Liberation, Democracy and Socialism

The dialectical development of human society entails the progress from capitalism to socialism. Capitalism developed the means of production to a colossal degree, by means of production for profit and the appropriation of surplus value. However, today it has become the major obstacle to social progress. Capital's supremacy over labor, through the machinations of the bourgeois state, subjects the majority of the people—from laborers and semiproletarians, to farmers and other sectors of the population—to the cruelest oppression and exploitation. The hard work of the common man, and especially that of the laboring and peasant classes, is the source of the riches and income of the dominant classes.

Capitalism—which in the beginning of the twentieth century entered its last phase by destroying free competition through the process of concentration and centralization of capital, finally becoming monopolistic capitalism or imperialism—today constitutes the antechamber of the oncoming social revolution of the proletariat.

With the establishment of the first socialist state in Bolshevist Russia in 1917, world capitalism was profoundly shaken and from that moment its historical agony and death commenced. Today, most of humanity fights for democracy and socialism. The cause of the proletariat has triumphed in various parts of Europe, Asia, Africa, and in America, with revolutionary Cuba.

The first great stage of the Sandinista revolution in 1926–1934, aside from having integrated the fundamental political and military tenets of our revolutionary movement, managed to resolve in favor of our struggle the contradiction of nation versus North American military intervention. Such a historical accomplishment enormously strengthened the position of the Nicaraguan revolutionary movement in the struggle against the imperialist domination of our country. The expulsion of the invading Yankee forces meant a *backward step* for imperialism in terms of its total control over our nation since the beginning of the century. Imperialism *was forced* to modify its tactics for dominating our nation and maneuvered in such a way that its military defeat was counterbalanced by political, economic, diplomatic, and indirect military successes whereby it exercised control through local reactionary classes from 1934 until today.

More than 40 years of Somocista dictatorial rule have allowed, on the one hand, the subjugation of our nation by North American imperialism and, on the other, the exploitation and oppression of our masses by the backward dependent-capitalist, agro-exporting system of Nicaragua.

To break the chains that bind our country to the yoke of foreign imperialism is the determining factor in our struggle for *national liberation*. Breaking the yoke of exploitation and oppression imposed by the dominant reactionary forces over our masses determines our process of *social liberation*. Both historical enterprises will advance together, indissolubly, if there exists a Marxist-Leninist cause and a solid vanguard to direct the process.

The present struggle against tyranny should lead us to a true democracy of the people (not a bourgeois democracy) that will form an integral part of the struggle for socialism. Our struggle should never be left midway, even if conciliatory, bourgeois forces should strive for such a goal. The popular-democratic phase should be, for the Sandinista cause, a means used for consolidating its revolutionary position and organizing the masses, so that the process moves unequivocally toward socialism. The necessary *popular-democratic revolutionary phase*, to be fulfilled once the tyranny is toppled, should not lead us to capitalism, reformism, nationalism, or any other development [other than socialism].

The hero Ricardo Morales pointed out in the 1970s, "What is happening here is a class struggle and a struggle against imperialism. On one side, in the foreground, is the bourgeoisie, the faction in power, which is allied with Yankee imperialism; on the other side, are the revolutionary laborers, peasants, students and intellectuals, united in their struggle with the rest of the world's common people, with revolutionary forces throughout the world. Our destination is socialism, a historically concrete mode of production, and not a utopian society, such as the 'kingdom of man' or the 'kingdom of the angels.'

The Sandinsita leader Silvio Mayorga said in 1964, "I hope that those who will come after me will understand what a treasure it is to be a combatant for the future of our nation, to struggle for its *definitive emancipation,* and to achieve the aspirations of all of our heroes and martyrs." The part of the thought that we have underlined reflects the profound revolutionary cause that even then propelled our militants toward the conquest of the future.

Our cause lives and evolves within our patriotic, working people. It is the sacred and historical cause of Marx, Engels, Lenin and Sandino.

CHAPTER III

VARIOUS FUNDAMENTAL TENETS OF THE POPULAR SANDINISTA REVOLUTION

1. The Revolutionary Popular-Democratic Government

The vanguard organization, the Sandinista Front, guided by the ideology of the proletariat and Sandinista political thought, should depend heavily on its base—our labor and peasant classes—thus ensuring the *revolutionary toppling* of the Somocista clique and the reaffirmation of the historical process of struggle.

The foreign imperialist enemy and the local reactionary classes, directed by the financial sector of the bourgeoisie and the Somocista dictatorship, will try by all means to destroy the revolutionary passage to *national* and *social liberation* that enlightens our cause. The bourgeoisie in general, including the faction that presently opposes the Somoza Regime, along with the country's large liberal-conservative landowners, also constitute part of the reactionary forces that will block to the maximum our general socialist cause.

The motor forces of the Sandinista Revolution, composed of the *worker—peasant* class allied to the petite bourgeoisie (especially the students and intellectuals), during this phase of struggle to unseat the Somocista dictatorship, must primarily fight for the establishment of a *Revolutionary Popular-Democratic Government* that will guarantee national independence, and full democracy that will carry the anti-imperialist, anti-oligarchic, and democratic revolution to its completion.

The guarantee that the democratic process will lead, sooner or later, to socialism, will be the degree of political, moral, and military strength wielded by the Popular Sandinista Revolution at the time that it unseats the tyranny and begins the *revolutionary democratic* process, aided principally by the participation of the working class and other *non*-proletarian progressive sectors. This revolutionary position will allow the seizure (*conquista*) of *real political power* by the Sandinista forces.

The backward and dependent-capitalist system of our country objectively necessitates completion of the popular-democratic, revolutionary phase wherein will be developed the structural and superstructural bases enabling the revolutionary process to culminate in socialism. Nicaraguan capitalism, unlike that of Europe and other highly developed and industrialized nations, does not facilitate the immediate establishment of socialism. At the same time, strategic and tactical factors do not permit (because of national and international constraints) the open establishment of socialism in this phase.

The fact that we do not immediately establish socialism in this phase does *not* mean that we support a *democratic-bourgeois revolution*. Once our revolutionary process resolves the contradictions *stemming from the backward capitalism* of our country, it is clearly indicated that our process *is not resolving* the anti-feudal contradictions that would determine the democratic-bourgeois revolution. In another vein, our country's bourgeoisie— which liquidated and castrated itself as a progressive political force by clearly surrendering to the interests of Yankee imperialism and by cooperating with the most reactionary Nicaraguan forces on May 4, 1927—is not and will never be a vanguard in the struggle against tyranny and in the democratic-revolutionary process.

The present *character* of the Popular Sandinista Revolution is that of a revolutionary-democratic process, directed by a *profoundly* popular government. It is a *popular government* because it will represent all the sectors of the people and the nation (not exclusively the proletariat) that fight against tyranny and imperialist Yankee domination. It will be a revolutionary popular-democratic government (not a bourgeois democracy) because, even though bourgeois forces may still be participating in the revolutionary struggle, the democratic accomplishments achieved by humanity since 1789, but unknown to our people due to reactionary domination, will be applied; not for developing or reforming the present system of capitalist exploitation, but to ENSURE the ground work that will enable our people to be liberated in a revolutionary manner from the foreign yoke, and from the domination of bourgeois and oligarchic reactionaries, if they are still around once the tyrants have been toppled. It [the government] is revolutionary-democratic because it will guide us to socialism, total and definitive liberation from the yoke of exploitation and oppression.

Toppling the Somocista regime and establishing a revolutionary popular-democratic government is the *immediate objective* of the Popular Sandinista Revolution. Such a revolutionary government will immediately affect the large monopolies and general fortune of Somoza and his clique, as well as the capital of the financial monopoly, and the traditional agrarian production of the large landholders. This revolutionary government will fight for national sovereignty, confronting imperialism's political and economic domination. It will develop national industry simultaneously with the radical transformation of the agrarian sector, aided by the peasants, and in their interest. It will bring about a profound social and cultural revolution, both urban as well as rural, favoring mainly the great majorities of the helpless masses. It will follow an independent foreign policy and one that will aid the progressive and revolutionary causes of humanity. It will ensure the organization and mobilization of the masses and especially the worker-peasant class, in order to truly strengthen the democratic process. It will establish a Sandinista army, composed of laborers and peasants, that will replace the National Guard (G.N.) and defend the interests of the Revolution. Among other tasks of the democratic-revolutionary phase are supervision and control over financial affairs, reducing unemployment both in the countryside and in the city, halting the high cost of living, improving the workers' wages, nationalization of foreign monopolistic enterprises, and the acquisition of land for the peasants who work the land.

Laborers, peasants, the petite bourgeoisie, intellectuals, Christians, patriotic soldiers, professionals, small to medium proprietors in the countryside and in the city, opposition bourgeoisie, progressive and patriotic people of the middle and upper classes, students, women, children, the elderly, indigenous peoples, blacks, whites and mestizos comprise the formidable force that will topple Somocismo and establish a revolutionary, popular-democratic government. The revolutionary laborers, peasants, students and intellectuals will be its *basic elements*. The working class, synthesized and guided by the Sandinista vanguard, the F.S.L.N., will be the leaders of the revolution.

Under the leadership of the Popular Sandinista Revolution, the popular-democratic process will march firmly toward the true liberties and spiritual and material conditions that socialism offers. Then, having swept away the bourgeois obstacle, we shall have marched the path that will allow us to stamp our banners with the central motto of socialism, "From each according to his capacity, to each according to his work."

2. The Revolutionary Civil War (To Overthrow the Dictatorship and Establish a Revolutionary, Popular-Democratic Government)

The Popular Sandinista Revolution in its third great phase of REVOLUTIONARY ASCENT has demonstrated and completely ripened the process of ACCUMULA-

TION of political, human, moral and material forces. This was the central task left to us by the Sandinista movement of 1933. Now the movement can proceed to the *revolutionary civil war* that will allow us to succeed and to achieve economic as well as political and social independence from the yoke of foreign and local oppression and exploitation. After a *prolonged struggle* against imperialism and the local reactionary classes, that encompasses more than 50 years of struggle since 1926, the Popular Sandinista Revolution gets ready to complete the military victory achieved against Yankee intervention during the 1930s, with the economic and political as well as social victory of the revolution over the Somocista dictatorship and other reactionary classes that represent direct Yankee domination in Nicaragua.

We are speaking of a *civil war* because its protagonists are fundamentally the local reactionary classes versus the local revolutionary classes. It is a revolutionary war because the worker—peasant alliance, guided by its Marxist-Leninist vanguard, does not only seek to topple the Somocista clique, but also to prepare the conditions that will allow the Sandinista process to advance from the [popular] democratic stage to socialism.

To fight a revolutionary civil war does not mean we forget about the war against imperialism. On the contrary, in this great stage of Revolutionary Ascent, the struggle against imperialism *demands* that we resolve the contradiction *people versus Somocista clique* in order to yank away from the Yankee empire its present instrument for ruling [in Nicaragua]: Somoza and his shield, the National Guard.

It was Sandino's place to favorably resolve, in our process of struggle, the contradiction *people versus armed Yankee intervention*. It is the place of the present revolutionary movement, headed by the FSLN, to resolve the contradiction people versus dictatorship, and at the same time to *prevent* to the maximum a new wave of foreign intervention that would make our liberation process bloodier and longer.

If a new armed Yankee intervention should occur, our process surely will be prolonged for an indefinite time. In such a case, the present strategy and tactics, generated as they are by objective and subjective conditions, internal as well as external, will vary. Should the inexorable victory over the interventionists occur, the conditions of the struggle would be so different that surely we would decide to resolve the democratic propositions of the revolution from an *openly socialist* position, supported by the socialist camp and the rest of the progressive and revolutionary forces of the world.

3. The Nicaraguan Working Class: Forgers of the Popular Sandinista Revolution

Since 1956, the year in which the period of Revolutionary Ascent begins, our working people, in the fields and in the city, have been generating the political, military and organizational conditions necessary for the development of the revolutionary struggle as a whole, despite the multiple difficulties imposed by the terror of the dictatorship.

The struggles that the various popular sectors have taken part in, under the leadership of the vanguard, have created political-military conditions that allow a real liberating alternative outside the traditional liberal-conservative rule.

To think that our people should have proceeded between 1960 and 1970 like in other countries—where concrete conditions allowed the adaptation of organizational forms to the classic, orthodox norms of the Marxist-Leninist party—would be tantamount to ignoring the concrete conditions of our process of struggle. Our movement acted exactly in accordance with the concrete historical conditions of the moment; first it created its vanguard, the FSLN, conquering, through its struggle, the moral and political position that at the national and international level *now prepares the way* for a political and organizational leap needed for the maximum development of the dialectical interrelationship between *the masses and the vanguard*.

The fact that our process has not generated such a historical leap until now does not mean that in the past our vanguard has not been able to put into practice the correct relationship with our working masses. Palpable proof of this situation is the presence of a vigorous and firm guerrilla movement in the mountains. That has only been possible due to the wide base of popular support that the vanguard's guerrilla detachments have been able to elicit uninterruptedly for more than 6 years.

The policy toward the masses that our vanguard has been developing since the 1960s enables us now to count on the *minimum basic* conditions necessary so that our masses can organize in a more solid and partisan manner. The extensive experience that our vanguard has accumulated, especially over the last 5 years, in its direct interaction with the people, in its efforts to organize the peasants, workers, students, indigenous peoples, christians, intellectuals, slums, communities, etc., MAKES IT POSSIBLE today for us to leap toward superior forms of organization.

Our mass movement has an eminently class character. Because of this we consider that the fundamental weight of our work among the masses should fall back upon the unification, organization, and mobilization of the most *combative* sectors of the proletariat, the *peasants* and the *petite bouregoisie*. Heeding the historical character of the proletariat as the most *revolutionary* and *fundamental* class for the maximum development of our liberating process, we consider that our organizational efforts among the proletariat, both urban and rural, should be the central axis of all of our work among the masses. The ideology and interests of the most revolutionary class, the Nicaraguan proletariat, will be the cause around which, in one form or another and according to each juncture of the struggle, all the other exploited and oppressed sectors should coalesce.

The working class, involved in manufacturing in the cities and in agricultural production in the country, is *the fundamental* and determinative class for bringing about profound revolutionary changes in the present capitalist system of exploitation and oppression. Its force, development and organization will be the guarantees of achieving the much desired socialist society.

The working class, because of its direct links with capitalist production, has acquired collective habits, work discipline, mental and manual ability and dexterity, and other traits that place it at the vanguard in terms of organizing and directing the masses. And what is fundamental is that the working class, because of its daily close and direct ties with bourgeois exploitation, is the most aware and interested in toppling all forms of exploitation and oppression, pre-capitalist and otherwise.

In this sense, the working class, with its liberation over capital, not only thinks about liberation but assumes a position at the front of the struggle for the liberation of all the other oppressed and exploited sectors of our society.

Even though the working class is the *fundamental* force in the present and future revolutionary process, it will not be able to achieve the revolutionary goals unless it has the tight support of all other popular sectors, especially the *peasants and the petite bourgeoisie*, composed of *intellectuals and students*.

In order to topple the dictatorship and construct a new society, the Sandinista vanguard must guarantee, by creative means and by following our objective [national] conditions, the solid conformation of the worker-peasant alliance. This alliance will be the central *axis* of the entire popular struggle; it will be the vital support of the revolution. Without this historic alliance, there [can be] no real liberation of the remaining nonproletarian sectors of our working class.

By way of summary, we point out that the working class is the *fundamental* force of the revolutionary process and that we always should depend on it above all else. The peasants represent the *principal* force of the revolution because of their militancy and their anti-Somocista as well as anti-Yankee sentiment.

The active struggle that for long years has been waged by the peasants against the large landowners and the money lenders (*agiotistas*), as well as directly against the repressive mechanisms of the regime (local judges, National Guard, etc.) who serve the land monopolizers, especially in the Sandinista war zones, make the peasants a *vital* force for the accomplishment of the various revolutionary tasks and especially the struggle against tyranny.

The students and intellectuals represent the most important sector of the petite bourgeoisie in terms of the revolutionary process. They are an indispensable complement of the struggle directed by the workers and the peasants of the vanguard.

The bloc consisting of the labor force, the peasantry and the petite bourgeoisie represent the motor force of the revolution.

Of the total population of our country —more than 2 million inhabitants, according to statistics of official entities—there is an economically active population of more than 650,000 workers dedicated to agriculture; hunting; fishing; mining and quarry excavation; manufacturing; housing construction; electrical, water and sanitary services; commerce; transportation; warehousing and communications; servicing communal, social and personal enterprises; and other unspecified activities.

This economically active population occupies more than 300,000 workers in agriculture and fishing; about 4,000 workers in mining and stone cutting; more than 60,000 workers in industrial manufacturing; close to 50,000 men in construction work; some 4,000 in electrical, water and sanitary services; more than 60,000 people in commerce; about 23,000 in transportation, warehousing and communication; about 100,000 in financial establishments, insurance, real estate, services, etc., etc.

The manufacturing, construction, and mining industries, together with capitalistic agrarian and livestock production, are propelled fundamentally by some 150,000 permanent and seasonal workers. This number of workers constitutes the urban and rural proletariat of our country. The branches concerned with the manufacture of chemicals, petroleum derivatives, seed oils, textiles, milk products, soft drinks, fishing, sugar, metals, shoes, highway and other general construction, loading and unloading of ships, transportation, electrical energy, banana production, mining, tobacco, livestock, beef, poultry and pig farms, cotton cultivation, sugarcane, pea-nuts, coffee, etc., are fundamentally the productive branches that hold together (*aglutinan*) the Nicaraguan proletariat.

The proletariat engaged in manufaturing and construction is concentrated pri-marily in the cities of Managua, Granada, and Chinandega, and, to a lesser extent, in Estelí and Rivas.

The seasonal agricultural proletariat—affiliated primarily with the export prod-ucts of Chinandega and León (cotton, sugarcane, etc.) and with coffee production in Jinotepe and Matagalpa in the north-central zone and in Managua and Carazo in the Pacific—is the most numerous. The permanent agricultural workers toil in the more modernized operations having to do with bananas, tobacco, livestock, and poultry and pig farms, located primarily in Chinandega, Estelí, León, Rivas, Boaco and Managua.

Our work among the masses should be directed toward the 650,000 workers that make up, in one form or another, the economically active population. The funda-mental work should be implemented among the urban and rural proletariat com-posed of 150,000 wage earners, especially in the industrial and agro-capitalistic zones of Managua, León and Chinandega. Our principal work among the masses should be directed to the large population of about 300,000 peasants in the northern, central and Pacific regions of the country, especially the poor peasants, the semi-proletarian peons and the small entrepreneurs. Our work among the masses should also focus special attention on the petite bourgeoisie consisting of over 150,000 people, among them artisans, professionals, merchants, and those dedicated to other services, and the bureaucracy in general.

The revolutionary students and intellectuals, even though they do not represent an active economic force, constitute sectors of the petite bourgeoisie that are basic complements to the revolution.

Guided by the proletarian Sandinista vanguard, the FSLN, that large working mass, and all those who in one way or another suffer in their own flesh the conse-quences of this system of exploitation and capitalist oppression—even though they may not be directly linked to the economic means of production—constitute the central nerve of the struggle of the entire country; they comprise the social base of the Popular Sandinista Revolution that will inexorably crush the agricultural, com-mercial and industrial forces of the bourgeois reactionaries, and their vanguard—the financial faction of the large monopolies and the large landowners of the traditional, exploitative latifundium. With this revolutionary social base, we shall eliminate political—economic domination and the indirect military domination of Yankee imperialism, the fundamental support for exploitation in general and for the Somo-cista clique in particular.

4. The Sandinista Front:
Vanguard of the Revolution

Our revolutionary vanguard detachment has been forged gradually over 17 years of struggle, beginning with its creation in the 1960s. The difficult, just and inevitably bloody revolutionary experience has slowly consolidated it as the conscious vanguard force of our exploited and oppressed people, especially the working class and its indispensable historical ally, the peasantry.

Gradually overcoming the mistakes and difficult limitations imposed on our [national] reality by Yankee imperialism and the local reactionary classes; armed with the revolutionary theories of the proletariat and the Sandinista historical legacy; and acquiring each day an even greater understanding of the laws of social progress, class struggle and politics, our organization has come to fulfill its historical function as the militant vanguard of the most revolutionary class and of exploited people in general.

Our numerically small revolutionary vanguard detachment is the advance nucleus of the great majority of our people who express through their vanguard what Che described as the will to conquest, even though they themselves may not fight directly with arms.

Our current revolutionary vanguard organization, the FSLN, represents the central axis of all the other popular and revolutionary forces that in one way or another confront the Somocista dictatorship and imperialist Yankee domination. Our Sandinista vanguard welds solidly together in one selective, advanced fistfull the best representatives of the working class in Nicaragua.

With the development of the Popular Sandinista Revolution, with the triumph over the dictatorship and the establishment of a revolutionary popular-democratic government, our present Marxist-Leninist vanguard organization will be able to develop to the maximum its organic structure until it becomes an iron-hard Leninist party, created and strengthened by the process itself and with the capacity for developing to the maximum the organization and mobilization of the masses.

The Sandinista vanguard, in assuming its historical role, should correctly assign (*delimitar*) duties among the masses and intermediate or immediate peripheral sectors or those that have its trust. We are trying to create a *mass* struggle without *enlarging* (*masificar*) the FSLN. We should not inflate (*engordar*) the organization nor reduce it to a nucleus unattached to the masses. The FSLN, the vanguard, should be the political and military General Staff of a militant people. The FSLN should be composed of the best and most conscious members of the most combative sectors of our working class. The organic political structures that form the vanguard should allow iron-like bonds with the intermediate organizations and the general masses.

Due to the enormous prestige of our vanguard, the people that in one or another way are aligned with this vanguard feel themselves immediately to be *militants* of the FSLN. This aspect is of enormous importance in terms of morale and should not be curtailed. What is important is to ensure that those elements that are not truly members of vanguard structure—even though they may *feel* a part of the same—not be allowed to assume the responsibilities, duties, rights, etc., of the vanguard's true militants. In time, the people will understand the difference between the vanguard and the masses, the vanguard and co-operants, the vanguard and activists, the vanguard and support networks, etc.

In the fundamental organizations of the Sandinista vanguard, the exigencies of revolutionary life, in terms of partisanship and discipline, should be maintained at the maximum level under the axis of proletarian ideology and the Sandinista political legacy. In the guiding organizations, having to do with ideology, propaganda and organization, as well as in the intermediate, regional, zonal, and base organizations, application of Sandinista, Marxist-Leninist norms of party life should also be a constant goal.

Our organization promotes the revolutionary war and by the glow of this liberating war, it should develop the norms of revolutionary life, creatively and without following preexisting patterns. It is not a matter of creating the Russian Bolshevist Party in Nicaragua; it rather entails stengthening to the maximum the conditions that reaffirm and solidify our position as the vanguard of the Sandinista Popular Revolution.

Some aspects to which we should give special consideration in the life and development of the vanguard are:

1. Selective recruitment and growth, keeping within the ranks the best of the exploited and oppressed people.
2. Constant political-ideological instruction imbued with Marxist-Leninist guidelines and the wealth of Sandinista political assets.
3. Constant tactical-technical preparation in the arts of conspiracy and war.
4. Assignment of responsibilities under iron-hard party criteria, valuing above all COMBATIVE MILITANCY, HONESTY AND PROOF OF SANDINISTA FIRMNESS, REVOLUTIONARY CREDIT acquired through consistent and prolonged battle practice, POLITICAL-MILITARY APTITUDE AND REVOLUTIONARY EXPERIENCE. Having all these minimum prerequisites, each candidate will occupy posts according to his capacity and the actual possibilities of accomplishing the assigned mission. An ample command of Marxism, WITHOUT PROLONGED MILITANCY AND PROOF OF REVOLUTIONARY FIRMNESS, is no guarantee of occupying such posts. [The same applies to] a prolonged militancy riddled with defects in performance or of a personal or other nature that were allowed in the past, but that by now should have been overcome.
5. Strengthening of conscious political discipline, of the application of democratic centralism, of the rational division of labor and collegial responsibility, of the unitary and fraternal application of revolutionary criticism and self-criticism. To develop to the maximum the objective scientific analysis of reality and to plan prudently all tasks while systematically evaluating these.
6. To strengthen to the maximum collective (*colegiada*) leadership as a guarantee against unilateralism, subjectivism and arbitrariness in the conduct of the struggle.
7. To maintain always exemplary unity within Sandinista ranks, who should stick to the vanguard concerning positions of principle; to maintain internal unity based on respect and obedience to the superior organs of the vanguard, in spite of the logical differences that arise during the struggle; and to reject energetically any factional or divisive manifestation in our movement.

The F.S.L.N., historical vanguard of the Nicaraguan revolution, will know how to accomplish its revolutionary mission of leading and organizing the masses, providing them with ideological instruction, and in the political realm, unleashing their political initiative by mobilizing them to act in the Popular Sandinista Revolution for the accomplishment of its historical tasks.

CHAPTER IV

VARIOUS ASPECTS OF OUR GENERAL STRATEGY FOR STRUGGLE

1. Concerning the Periods and Phases of the Sandinista Popular Revolution

In the first part of this work we looked at the different periods and phases that our Sandinista Revolution has already traversed.

In way of a brief summary, we can say that our movement is divided into three historical periods:

1. Period of Historical Integration of the Revolutionary Movement (1926– 1934).
2. Period of Descent of the Revolutionary Movement (1934–1956).
3. Period of Ascent of the Revolutionary Movement (1956 to the present).

Synthesizing the development of each one of these periods, we can say that:

In the first historical period of armed struggle against Yankee intervention and its liberal–conservative lackeys, there is forged a profound sense of anti-imperialism and the need for social emancipation from the yoke of exploitation and oppression, local as well as foreign. At the same time, the movement acquires an appropriate military and political strategy for the achievement of the struggle's various objectives.

The Sandinista movement successfully developed the armed strategy of PROLONGED RESISTANCE in order to confront an enemy a thousand times more powerful in terms of resources and material. Such a strategy of prolonged resistance relied on the military technique of continuous and uninterrupted attrition of the enemy through a predominantly IRREGULAR and fundamentally GUERRILLA-TYPE war. The Sandinista guerrilla war, in confronting the interventionist, was always based on OFFENSIVE tactics and on the ACTIVE DEFENSE of the SANDINISTA WAR ZONES. By means of this offensive modality, the Sandinista movement was able to form, in a relatively short time, REGULAR FORCES that it was able to integrate creatively in the strategy of GUERRILLA war (*Guerra de movimientos*). It was through Guerrilla Warfare that Sandinismo managed to defeat and expel the Yankee invader from our country. Guerrilla warfare was made possible by the fact that the Sandinistas could count on large and voluminous columns that never proceeded to FRONTAL COMBAT against the Yankees, but fought rather according to the laws of IRREGULAR war, never presenting a stable and definite line to the adversary. The tactics of the OFFENSIVE and ACTIVE DEFENSE were based fundamentally on attack and continuous attrition, and the partial and total annihilation of the enemy forces.

As much as possible, the Sandinista movement utilized the successes in the battlefield for political and propagandistic ends, so as to reinforce local as well as international moral and material support for the patriotic, anti-imperialist struggle.

Through the successful Sandinista war, it was possible to resolve, in favor of our liberating process, the contradiction NICARAGUAN PEOPLE VERSUS ARMED YANKEE INTERVENTION. Once having resolved this, in 1933 the Sandinista movement immediately applies itself to the complex revolutionary task of creating the conditions necessary for resolving the contradiction EXPLOITED PEOPLE VERSUS REACTIONARY, LIBERAL–CONSERVATIVE FORCES.

The Sandinista movement envisioned a political–military strategy of PRO-LONGED ACCUMULATION of political, human and material SUPPORT, both national and international, once the Yankees were expelled in 1933, their goal being to prepare conditions that would permit the toppling of the local reactionary government and the takeover of power so as to achieve the total realization of the process of NATIONAL AND SOCIAL LIBERATION for our people. Such a strategy is weakened and interrupted by the blows received by the Sandinista movement in February 1934 and by the adverse local and international situation that impeded the accomplishment of the tasks required by the revolutionary process at that time.

By resolving the contradiction PEOPLE VERSUS LOCAL REACTIONARY FORCES, the Sandinista movement attempted to sever profoundly the ties of authority that still bound our country to the imperialist yoke, even though the latter had been defeated in the recently finalized anti-interventionist war in 1927–1933.

The strategy of ACCUMULATION OF FORCES and the liberating trajectory traced by Sandino undergo difficulties in the period 1934 to 1956, defined clearly as a period of Revolutionary Descent. In spite of the adversities of this period, our people were slowly and gradually led forward to conditions wherein the REINTEGRATION of the revolutionary movement was possible.

The actual period of REVOLUTIONARY ASCENT that begins immediately after the heroic revolutionary action of Rigoberto López Pérez in 1956, has traversed various phases: The INITIAL phase was that of revolutionary reintegration from 1956 to 1960 in which our people lay the necessary bases for the formation of the revolutionary vanguard detachment. The Second Phase starts with the creation of the vanguard, the FSLN, in 1960–1961 and continues until 1967. In this second phase the Sandinista movement was born, grew and developed, and achieved national recognition, in the moral and political sense, with the Pancasán campaign. The Third Phase stretches from 1967 to the successful events of December 27, 1974. In this phase, the vanguard is strengthened politically and ideologically and the process of ACCUMULATION OF political and military FORCES is developed throughout the country. At the same time, political, moral, military and organizational influence are gained among the people, and work in the mountains, our principal bastion for struggle, is strengthened.

From 1956 to the present, our Sandinista struggle has achieved the historical REINTEGRATION of the revolutionary movement. It also has managed to fulfill, in a fundamental sense, the exigencies of the long-term strategy of ACCUMULATION OF FORCES, inherited from the Sandinista movement of the 1930s. Presently, our liberation movement synthesizes in the Sandinista Front of National Liberation, our historical vanguard, the development of our revolutionary process, placing us ever closer to the favorable resolution of the antagonistic historical contradiction: PEOPLE VERSUS LOCAL AND FOREIGN REACTIONARIES.

Our general strategy in the struggle for national and social liberation, ongoing now for 50 years, today sets as a priority the development and completion of the REVOLUTIONARY CIVIL WAR in order to resolve the principal contradiction of today: PEOPLE VERSUS SOMOCISTA CLIQUE. Today, when the revolutionary situation, both nationally and internationally, is more favorable than in the past, our movement prepares to resolve successfully this principal contradiction, and at the same time create conditions that will allow us to favorably confront imperialist domination and a new potential North American intervention, either directly or disguised under the auspices of Latin American Forces such as CONDECA.

In spite of the limitations and difficulties of the struggle, the Somocista clique has been gravely weakened, at the same time that there has been a strengthening of the revolutionary work that will allow, at the appropriate time, an unchaining of the political–military GENERAL OFFENSIVE that will topple the Somocista clique and establish the Revolutionary, Popular-Democratic Government.

The present phase includes the stern preparations of the minimum basic conditions for leading the people to INSURRECTION by means of a process of REVOLUTIONARY CIVIL WAR. This vital and strategic phase is product of the GENERAL STRATEGY followed in the three preceding stages of the Sandinista struggle which began in the 1930s. What we call within our ranks, SANDINISTA POPULAR REVOLUTION or PROLONGED POPULAR WAR, is the strategy that encompasses the entire process of struggle, including the present phase, the democratic-revolutionary stage, that will take place once the dictatorship is toppled and will be followed by the phase in which the democratic revolution gives way to socialism.

In synthesis, we have:

1. Our most general strategy is that of the POPULAR SANDINISTA REVOLUTION OR PROLONGED POPULAR WAR, which will lead us to national and social liberation, and toward socialism.

2. The revolutionary civil war comprises the strategic mode of struggle that is directly derived from the contradiction PEOPLE VERSUS SOMOCISTA DICTATORSHIP. This strategy will make POPULAR INSURRECTION possible in a shorter time, supported by the central axis: the wilderness (*montaña*) and other war fronts in the rural areas and cities, and in the exterior. The Revolutionary Civil War will facilitate the advancement of the struggle against imperialist domination in that, by toppling the Somocista tyranny, the principal instrument for present Yankee domination in our country will be destroyed.

3. The strategic modality of PROLONGED RESISTANCE for coming to power will be placed into practice in the case that armed foreign intervention prolongs the

duration of the struggle. This strategy of PROLONGED RESISTANCE was first put into practice in the 1930s, when the Sandinista movement confronted the Yankee intervention.

4. For both the INSURRECTIONAL and PROLONGED RESISTANCE modalities, the WILDERNESS plays a determinant, vital role in political and military as well as moral aspects. Without its genuine and active presence in the wilderness, our movement would not be able to lead the masses to accomplish the various political, military, organizational, and other tasks of the revolution.

2. The Strategy and Tactics To Be Followed for the Defeat of the Somocista Clique and the Establishment of the Revolutionary Popular-Democratic Government

Knowing clearly that the Somocista clique is the principal obstacle to revolutionary advancement, and knowing the power needed to overthrow the dictatorship, the Sandinista movement has outlined various ways of successfully resolving the tasks that lay before us.

Among other important strategic and tactical aspects for the accomplishment of these present revolutionary tasks are:

A. To properly develop and equip our Popular Program for Social Redress (basic program) according to the present needs of the patriotic, anti-Somocista struggle. Such a program should reflect the bases for the establishment of a Revolutionary Popular-Democratic Government. It should be the center around which the functions of agitation, mobilization, and organization of the struggle against Somocista tyranny should be conducted. It should be the base for the *slogans* (*consignas*) that are launched in this phase. It must be identified with the interests of the largest sectors of the Nicaraguan masses, from the most exploited and oppressed, including the sectors that do not directly suffer from exploitation and oppression but which are affected by Somocista tyranny. At the same time, such a program should encourage the major part of the world's progressive forces (not only socialists) to support a Sandinista, patriotic, anti-Somocista struggle.

B. To urge our revolutionary work among the masses, especially among the sectors of laborers, peasants and the petite bourgeoisie, the most *militant and strategic* components for conducting the insurrectional process against tyranny.

C. To strengthen our Intermediate Mass Organizations, redoubling the creation of clandestine mechanisms that will allow a systematic and favorable interlocking between the vanguard and the masses. Through these intermediate mass organizations, the vanguard should encourage daily struggles for social benefits, related to the problems faced by the laborers, peasants, neighborhoods, communities, schools, service workers, and other sectors. The vanguard should maintain, in this fashion, constant popular agitation. The struggles for redress in each sector will inflame the masses, enabling them to take the qualitative leap towards the violent political struggle against tyranny.

D. The FSLN should by all means foment the organization of the masses in fronts for struggling against the dictatorship. It should be the leader and advisor in the insurrections undertaken by these sectors. At the same time that it promotes and organizes these uprisings according to the demands of the Popular Program of Redress, the FSLN should support these groups militarily and with its propaganda and agitation organizations. The allied labor and peasant sectors should be emphasized in this work because they represent the most revolutionary class.

E. To urge likewise, in practice, the creation of an ample Anti-Somocista Front that will cluster in one way or another, all the anti-Somocista sectors, parties and mass organizations throughout the country, including the opposition bourgeoisie. In such an Anti-Somocista Front the FSLN would work actively through the mass organizations that respond to the FSLN's partisan orientation. The FSLN would militarily and politically support the actions of the masses, both those promoted by intermediate organizations as well as those promoted by the Ample Anti-Somocista Front. Political hegemony in this Front will be obtained and maintained by the FSLN to the extent that the demands that the Front states and the agitation that it unfurls, revolve around the Popular Redress Program and the military insurrectional tasks (*consignas*) promoted by the FSLN through the mass movements of said Front. The opposing bourgeoisie thereby will not be allowed the *political leadership* of the Anti-Somocista Front; the struggle will be planned and conducted according to the guidelines (*consignas*) set forth by the FSLN, based as much on the Minimum Program as on the military considerations that will lead to the unleashing of the Insurrection. This does not mean that our mass organisms will have to form political groups like UDEL [Unión Democrática de Liberación (Democratic Union of Liberation)] but rather that our mass organizations, along with UDEL and other forces, will compose the Broad Anti-Somocista Front, always striving, as was indicated earlier, so that our forces maintain political hegemony in this *tactical* and *temporary* alliance.

F. In view of the fact that the *political objective* of this phase is to unleash the insurrection *through armed struggle*, our political and recovery (*reivindicativo*) mass movement efforts should be directed toward the organization and mobilization of the entire population to promote *armed insurrection* as deemed necessary by our *political objectives*. Presently, agitation of the masses, given the limitations imposed by Somocista repression, does not allow the Front to place priority on the political and unionist struggle. The rationale for the mass movements (*trabajo de masas*) at this moment stems from their capacity to strengthen the revolutionary struggle and prepare the people at the appropriate moment to unchain all of their political and military VIOLENCE. It will be precisely by destroying the repressive Somocista obstacle that we will be able to accomplish the organization and mobilization of the masses in all of their revolutionary magnitude. In this way we will be fulfilling the *military* requirements for our general political strategy.

G. Our work among the masses, both among the intermediate mass organizations and other organizations of influence among the people, will be complemented and supported by the formidable presence of the SANDINISTA ARMY in the wilderness, the countryside and the cities, as well as the sure and unwavering guidance of the vanguard, the FSLN. Three strategic pillars will guarantee the success and consolidation of the Popular Sandinista Revolution:

1. The existence of the Revolutionary Vanguard of the FSLN.
2. The mass movements organized and based on the historical and revolutionary alliance of the working class and the peasantry.
3. The formidable presence of the Sandinista Army in the mountains, country-side and cities of Nicaragua.

H. In order to strengthen our organizational and mobilization work among the masses, our vanguard, the FSLN, should support joint actions among the various organizations which, in one way or another, project their influence on the masses, espccially the leftist organizations of the country.

I. To develop maximally the various methods of overt and clandestine struggle (political, guild (*gremiales*), reparative (*reivindicativos*), paramilitary, and mili-tary), having as political objective and central axis the promotion of armed struggle.

J. To organize in order to unfurl a continuous and creative campaign of San-dinista agitation and propaganda. To allow the maximum development of the various political goals contained within our Minimum Program and the necessary military goals for leading the people toward INSURRECTION. Not just to depend on modern means of propaganda but to utilize profusely rumors, posters, watch-words on treasury notes, plus hand-written, mimeographed or printed flyers. To make use of the strategic posting of red and black banners or Sandinista emblems everywhere: roads, trees, churches, buses, etc. To make each propaganda item (*consigna*) coincide with the reparations (*reivindicaciones*) that our Minimum Pro-gram contemplates for each sector or at the appropriate juncture in time. To foment uprisings among the broadest sectors of the popular masses, making them aware of the necessity of a difficult, bloody and perilous struggle, especially in the phase immediately preceding the general offensive.

K. To maximally strengthen our Sandinista Army in the wilderness, the country-side and the city. To combine tactically and strategically the various armed San-dinista forces so as to strike simultaneously, in coordinated fashion, at specific times and in specific directions. To strengthen our mobile strategic forces in the wilderness and all the other small armed units, commandos or special platoons throughout the country. To accelerate the formation of nuclei of two or three men in the various production centers, neighborhoods, communication arteries, schools, etc., who will coordinate their activities through the corresponding Regional Militia Centers. To know how to creatively combine the central military force of the FSLN with the various groups, small units, individual combatants, etc., that make up the principal paramilitary force of the Sandinista Army.

L. To develop to the maximum a war infrastructure that will permit the mobiliza-tion, organization and preparation of various military and paramilitary tasks such as: the formation of commando units; training; smuggling of weapons and supplies; production of bombs and incendiary devices; maintaining espionage; procuring underground shelters; conducting meetings; and keeping direct and indirect clandes-tine communication.

N. To develop to the maximum a practical and theoretical understanding of OFFENSIVE TACTICS, having in mind that in terms of Insurrection, a PROFOUND, SOLID and SIMULTANEOUS OFFENSIVE against the enemy plays a decisive role. The principal mission of the OFFENSIVE is the *rupture* and *total control* of the *defensive* positions that the enemy erects for strategic purposes. The OFFENSIVE requires *constant and uninterrupted* attack without ever having recourse to a defensive position. The offensive is only used to *consolidate* victory and when the enemy is fundamentally conquered. Parallel to this OFFENSIVE, the Sandinista movement should prepare the conditions for an ORGANIZED RETREAT, without disbanding or succumbing to anarchy should a retreat become necessary.

Ñ. To foment among our masses, through our propagandists and activists, violent, active and secret struggle. Starting now the masses should begin neutralizing the informants and enemies of the revolution. Let the masses fight with the weapons that are within their reach, even though they might be very rudimentary, against the local ruffians and informants. With shrewdness, may the latter be surprised and eliminated. This should be done everywhere, and in each place these punishments should be publicized. In this manner, little by little, the masses will be inflamed and slowly the process of moral decomposition of Somoza's lackeys will begin, at the same time that their ability to maneuver (*su capacidad táctica operativa*) will be weakened. To all those who, as "perfectionists," oppose this type of initiative, Lenin pointed out, "We must begin to act now (*aprender en la práctica*): do not fear these trial attacks. They can, naturally, degenerate into extremism. but this is a future tragedy, today the tragedy lies in our routine, in our doctrinairism, in the inherent immobility of intellectualism, in the senile fear of all initiative."

O. To maintain in a constant process of decomposition the ranks of the National Guard and other Somocista sectors in the bureaucracy and the goverment. To fully win the good will of low ranking soldiers and the support of various officials in the army. To reinforce the contradictions existing, for reasons of power, in the National Guard and other repressive sectors. To constantly write letters directed toward the families of low ranking soldiers and officers, placing emphasis on our patriotic, democratic, Anti-Somocista character, leaving open the door for social reparations if they cooperate by one means or another with the Sandinista movement. This type of work reinforces the military blows that the movement inflicts on the National Guard. This does not mean that the National Guard should join the revolution; the purpose here is to disband and demoralize it to the maximum in order to better attack it as an institution and destroy it.

P. To strengthen the traditional unity of the Sandinista movement, knowing how to be consistent in dealing with our large popular masses that conglomerate and mobilize around the revolutionary struggle unleashed by the FSLN. In the same firm and sure manner that our people unite and cluster around the central axis of the struggle, which is its party, the FSLN, all of our militants should stick together and severely discipline themselves in accordance with the revolutionary principles that are synthesized by the superior organisms of our vanguard, especially the National Directorate. Whoever weakens, even in a small amount, the stern Sandinista discipline that our actual phase of revolutionary war demands, contributes to the counterrevolution and should be implacably rejected and sanctioned by our Sandinista movement.

The profound political and moral weakness of the regime, the favorable international situation that has constrained the imperialist interventionist supporters of tyrannical regimes like Somoza's, the regimes's lack of prestige among all sectors of the country, Somoza's own great lack of prestige, especially in Latin America, present us with a favorable panorama for shrewdly achieving the immediate objectives of the Popular Sandinista Revolution.

Our strength is political and moral; it is an invincible force that multiplies by the hundreds the potential of the gun that we point toward our enemies.

Our revolutionary movement holds high the colors hoisted by Augusto César Sandino, Rigoberto López Pérez, Carlos Fonseca and so many other Nicaraguan revolutionaries that symbolize the sacrifice of thousands of Sandinista patriots who lost their lives in our liberation struggle since the 1930s. Standing before them and before our banners, we repeat our oath:

With my thoughts and heart focused on the immortal patriotic example of Augusto César Sandino and Ernesto Che Guevara, in memory of all the heroes and martyrs in the liberation of Nicaragua, Latin America and humanity as a whole, with history as witness, I place my hand on the red and black flag that signifies "A Free Homeland or Death (Patria Libre O Morir)." With weapon in hand, I promise to defend the national decorum and fight for the redemption of the oppressed and the exploited of Nicaragua and the world. If I fulfill this oath, the liberation of Nicaragua will be my reward. If I betray this vow, opprobrious death and ignominy will be my punishment.

LONG LIVE THE LATIN AMERICAN HERO AUGUSTO CÉSAR SANDINO!!!
LONG LIVE OUR REVOLUTIONARY HEROES AND MARTYRS!!!
THE POPULAR SANDINISTA REVOLUTION WILL TRIUMPH!!!
A FREE HOMELAND OR DEATH!!!
(*Patria Libre o Morir*)

NATIONAL DIRECTORATE OF THE SANDINISTA FRONT
FOR NATIONAL LIBERATION (FSLN)

May 4, 1977, "Day of National Dignity,"
Someplace in Nicaragua

The Historic Program of the FSLN (1969)*

The 1969 "Historic Program" was important in that it lent ideological and pragmatic cohesiveness to the small and battered FSLN during several difficult years and because the fundamental principles of this program were incorporated into the larger and more explicit statement of Leninist ideology found in the 1977 Platform of the FSLN.

By 1969, the FSLN had traversed several stages of its development but had not yet acquired substantial political weight in Nicaragua. Between 1962, when it was founded, and 1969, the FSLN had to overcome several setbacks or defeats. These included (1) the failure of its guerrilla strategy at Río Coco and Bocay (1963), (2) the setback in open political work in 1964–1965 while allied with *Movilización Republicana* (Republican Mobilization) under the presidency of Dr. René Shick Gutiérrez, and (3) the demise of its *foquista* strategy following the defeat at Pancasán in 1967.

Thus the Sandinista Front was forced into a period of retreat and reflection that has been described by such Sandinista leaders as Commander Henry Ruíz. Until 1968 FSLN progress was practically nil. Despite these frustrating experiences, the FSLN continued its efforts, with the the knowledge that the existence of the Somoza dictatorship provided it with the possibility, however remote, for future growth and victory. This was recognized by Carlos Fonseca, founding father of the FSLN, who called Somoza a

*Reprinted from *Sandinistas Speak*, Pathfinder Press (New York City), 1982, pp. 13–22.

precious stone in whom all historical and social contradictions converged and who would make possible the anti-imperialist revolution in Nicaragua.

During 1969, the FSLN consolidated the role of its National Directorate (DN) under the leadership of Secretary General Fonseca and issued the "Historic Program." Both developments were very important. Strengthening of the DN improved FSLN structure and function; the "Historic Program" provided coherence, within a general political program, to the FSLN's Leninist ideological foundations.

Although the 1969 Program is less comprehensive than the Platform of 1977, it foreshadows some of the Leninist elements contained in the later document. For instance, the Program presents the FSLN as a "vanguard organization" dependent on a "new people's army," the key element for retaining power in Leninist states. Sections IX and XI of this document contain the FSLN commitments to struggle against the "common enemy" of "Yankee imperialism" in the Third World and to pursue a regionwide, revolutionary, "national-liberation" struggle in Central America.

Historic Program

The Sandinista National Liberation Front (FSLN) arose out of the Nicaraguan people's need to have a "vanguard organization" capable of taking political power through direct struggle against its enemies and establishing a social system that wipes out the exploitation and poverty that our people have been subjected to in past history.

The FSLN is a politico-military organization whose strategic objective is to take political power by destroying the military and bureaucratic apparatus of the dictatorship and to establish a revolutionary government based on the worker-peasant alliance and the convergence of all the patriotic anti-imperialist and anti-oligarchic forces, in the country.

The people of Nicaragua suffer under subjugation to a reactionary and fascist clique imposed by Yankee imperialism in 1932, the year Anastasio Somoza García was named commander in chief of the so-called National Guard (GN).

The Somozaist clique has reduced Nicaragua to the status of a neocolony exploited by the Yankee monopolies and the country's oligarchic groups.

The present regime is politically unpopular and juridically illegal. The recognition and aid it gets from the North Americans is irrefutable proof of foreign interference in the affairs of Nicaragua.

The FSLN has seriously and with great responsibility analyzed the national reality and has resolved to confront the dictatorship with arms in hand. We have concluded that the triumph of the Sandinista people's revolution and the overthrow of the regime that is an enemy of the people will take place through the development of a hard-fought and prolonged people's war.

Whatever maneuvers and resources Yankee imperialism deploys, the Somozaist dictatorship is condemned to total failure in the face of the rapid advance and development of the people's forces, headed by the Sandinista National Liberation Front.

Given this historic conjuncture, the FSLN has worked out this political program with an eye to strengthening and developing our organization, inspiring and stimulating the people of Nicaragua to march forward with the resolve to fight until the dictatorship is overthrown and to resist the intervention of Yankee imperialism, in order to forge a free, prosperous, and revolutionary homeland.

I. A Revolutionary Government

The Sandinista people's revolution will establish a revolutionary government that will eliminate the reactionary structure that arose from rigged elections and military coups, and the people's power will a create a Nicaragua that is free of exploitation, oppression, backwardness; a free, progressive, and independent country.

The revolutionary government will apply the following measures of a political character:

A. It will endow revolutionary power with a structure that allows the full participation of the entire people, on the national level as well as the local level (departmental, municipal, neighborhood).
B. It will guarantee that all citizens can fully exercise all individual freedoms and it will respect human rights.
C. It will guarantee the free exchange of ideas, which above all leads to vigorously broadening the people's rights and national rights.
D. It will guarantee freedom for the worker union movement to organize in the city and the countryside; and freedom to organize peasant, youth, student, women's, cultural, sporting, and similar groups.
E. It will guarantee the right of immigrant and exiled Nicaraguans to return to their native soil.
F. It will guarantee the right to asylum for citizens of other countries which are persecuted for participation in the revolutionary struggle.
G. It will severely punish the gangsters who are guilty of persecuting, informing on, abusing, torturing, or murdering revolutionaries and the people.
H. Those individuals who occupy high political posts as a result of rigged elections and military coups will be stripped of their politicial rights.

The revolutionary government will apply the following measures of an economic character:

A. It will expropriate the landed estates, factories, companies, buildings, means of transportation, and other wealth usurped by the Somoza family and accumulated through the misappropriation and plunder of the nation's wealth.
B. It will expropriate the landed estates, factories, companies, and means of transportation, and other wealth usurped by the politicians and military officers, and all other accomplices, who have taken advantage of the present regime's administrative corruption.

C. It will nationalize the wealth of all foreign companies that exploit the mineral, forest, maritime, and other kinds of resources.
D. It will establish workers' control over the administrative management of the factories and other wealth that are expropriated and nationalized.
E. It will centralize the mass transit service.
F. It will nationalize the banking system, which will be placed at the exclusive service of the country's economic development.
G. It will establish an independent currency.
H. It will refuse to honor the loans imposed on the country by the Yankee monopolists or those of any other power.
I. It will establish commercial relations with all countries, whatever their system, to benefit the country's economic development.
J. It will establish a suitable taxation policy, which will be applied with strict justice.
K. It will prohibit usury. This prohibition will apply to Nicaraguan nationals as well as foreigners.
L. It will protect small to medium-size owners (producers, merchants) while restricting the excesses that lead to the exploitation of the workers.
M. It will establish state control over foreign trade, with an eye to diversifying it and making it independent.
N. It will rigorously restrict the importation of luxury items.
O. It will plan the national economy, putting an end to the anarchy characteristic of the capitalist system of production. An important part of this planning will focus on industrialization and electrification of the country.

II. The Agrarian Revolution

The Sandinista people's revolution will work out an agrarian policy that achieves authentic agrarian reform; a reform that will in the immediate term, carry out a massive distribution of the land, eliminating the land grabs by the large landlords in favor of the workers (small producers) who labor on the land.

A. It will expropriate and eliminate the capitalist and feudal estates.
B. It will turn over the land to the peasants, free of charge, in accordance with the principle that the land should belong to those who work it.
C. It will carry out a development plan for livestock raising aimed at diversifying and increasing the productivity of that sector.
D. It will guarantee the peasants the following rights:
   1. Timely and adequate agricultural credit.
   2. Marketability (a guaranteed market for their production).
   3. Technical assistance.
E. It will protect the patriotic landowners who collaborate with the guerrilla struggle by paying them for their landholdings that exceed the limit established by the revolutionary government.
F. It will stimulate and encourage the peasants to organize themselves in cooperatives so that they can take their destiny into their own hands and directly participate in the development of the country.

G. It will abolish the debts the peasantry incurred to the landlord and any type of usurer.

H. It will eliminate the forced idleness that exists for most of the year in the countryside, and it will be attentive to creating sources of jobs for the peasant population.

III. Revolution in Culture and Education

The Sandinistas people's revolution will establish the bases for the development of the national culture, the people's education, and university reform.

A. It will push forward a massive campaign to immediately wipe out "illiteracy."

B. It will develop the national culture and will root out the neocolonial penetration of our culture.

C. It will rescue the progressive intellectuals, and their works that have arisen throughout history, from the neglect in which they have been maintained by the anti-people's regime.

D. It will give attention to the development and progress of education at the various levels (primary, intermediate, technical, university, etc.) and education will be free at all levels and obligatory at some.

E. It will grant scholarships at various levels of education to students who have limited economic resources. The scholarship will include housing, food, clothing, books, and transportation.

F. It will train more and better teachers who have the scientific knowledge that the present era requires, to satisfy the needs of our entire student population.

G. It will nationalize the centers of private education that have been immorally turned into industries by merchants who hypocritically invoke religious principles.

H. It will adapt the teaching programs to the needs of the country; it will apply teaching methods to the scientific and research needs of the country.

I. It will carry out a university reform that will include, among other things, the following measures:

1. It will rescue the university from the domination of exploiting classes, so it can serve the real creators and shapers of our culture: the people. University instruction must be oriented around man, around the people. The university must stop being a breeding ground for bureaucratic egotists.

2. Eliminate the discrimination in access to university classes suffered by youth from the working class and the peasantry.

3. Increase the state budget for the university so there are the economic resources to solve the various problems confronting it.

4. Majority student representation on the boards of the faculties keeping in mind that the student body is the main segment of the university population.

5. Eliminate the neocolonial penetration of the university, especially the penetration by North American monopolies through the charity donations of the pseudophilanthropic foundations.

6. Promotion of free, experimental, scientific investigation that must contribute to dealing with national and universal questions.

7. Strengthen the unity of students, faculty and investigators with the whole people, by perpetuating the selfless example of the students and intellectuals who have offered their lives for the sake of the patriotic ideal.

IV. Labor Legislation and Social Security

The Sandinista people's revolution will eliminate the injustices of the living and working conditions suffered by the working class under the brutal exploitation, and will institute labor legislation and social assistance.

A. It will enact a labor code that will regulate, among other things, the following rights:
   1. It will adopt the principle that "those who don't work don't eat," of course making exceptions for those who are unable to participate in the process of production due to age (children, old people), medical condition, or other reasons beyond their control.
   2. Strict enforcement of the eight-hour workday.
   3. The income of the workers (wages and other benefits) must be sufficient to satisfy their daily needs.
   4. Respect for the dignity of the worker, prohibiting and punishing unjust treatment of the workers in the course of their labor.
   5. Abolition of unjustified firings.
   6. Obligation to pay wages in the period required by law.
   7. Right of all workers to periodic vacations.
B. It will eliminate the scourge of unemployment.
C. It will extend the scope of the social security system to all the workers and public employees in the country. The scope will include coverage for illness, physical incapacity, and retirement.
D. It will provide free medical assistance to the entire population. It will set up clinics and hospitals throughout the national territory.
E. It will undertake massive campaigns to eradicate endemic illnesses and prevent epidemics.
F. It will carry out urban reforms, which will provide each family with adequate shelter. It will put an end to profiteering speculation in urban land (subdivisions, urban construction, rental housing) that exploits the need that working families in the cities have for an adequate roof over their heads in order to live.
G. It will initiate and expand the construction of adequate housing for the peasant population.
H. It will reduce the charges for water, light, sewers, urban beautification; it will apply programs to extend all these services to the entire urban and rural populations.
I. It will encourage participation in sports of all types and categories.
J. It will eliminate the humiliation of begging by putting the above mentioned measures into practice.

V. Administrative Honesty

The Sandinista people's revolution will root out administrative governmental corruption, and will establish strict administrative honesty.

A. It will abolish the criminal vice industry (prostitution, gambling, drug use, etc.) which the privileged sector of the National Guard and the foreign parasites exploit.
B. It will establish strict control over the collection of taxes to prevent government functionaries from profitting, putting an end to the normal practice of the present regime's official agencies.
C. It will end arbitrary actions of the members of the GN, who plunder the population through the subterfuge of local taxes.
D. It will put an end to the situation wherein military commanders appropriate the budget that is supposed to go to take care of common prisoners, and it will establish centers designed to rehabilitate these wrongdoers.
E. It will abolish the smuggling that is practiced on a large scale by the gang of politicians, officers, and foreigners who are the regimes's accomplices.
F. It will severely punish persons who engage in crimes against administrative honesty (embezzlement, smuggling, trafficking in vices, etc.), using greatest severity when it involves elements active in the revolutionary movement.

VI. Reincorporation of the Atlantic Coast

The Sandinista people's revolution will put into practice a special plan for the Atlantic Coast, which has been abandoned to total neglect, in order to incorporate this area into the nation's life.

A. It will end the unjust exploitation the Atlantic Coast has suffered thoughout history from the foreign monopolies, especially Yankee imperialism.
B. It will prepare suitable lands in the zone for the development of agriculture and ranching.
C. It will establish conditions that encourage the development of the fishing and forest industries.
D. It will encourage the flourishing of this region's local and cultural values which flow from the specific aspects of its historic tradition.
E. It will wipe out the odious discrimination to which the indigenous Miskitos, Sumos, Zambos, and Blacks of this region are subjected.

VII. Emancipation of Women

The Sandinista people's revolution will abolish the odious discrimination that women have been subjected to compared to men; it will establish the economic, political, and cultural equality between woman and man.

A. It will pay special attention to the mother and child.
B. It will eliminate prostitution and other social vices, through which the dignity of women will be raised.
C. It will put an end to the system of servitude that women suffer, which is reflected in the tragedy of the abandoned working mother.
D. It will establish for children born out of wedlock the right of equal protection by the revolutionary institutions.
E. It will establish daycare centers for the care and attention of the children of working women.
F. It will establish a two-month maternity leave before and after birth for women who work.
G. It will raise the women's political, cultural, and vocational levels through their participation in the revolutionary process.

VIII. Respect for Religious Beliefs

The Sandinista people's revolution will guarantee the population of believers in freedom to profess any religion

A. It will respect the rights of citizens to profess and practice any religious belief.
B. It will support the work of priests and other religious figures who defend the working people.

IX. Independent Foreign Policy

The Sandinista people's revolution will eliminate the foreign policy of submission to Yankee imperialism and will establish a patriotic foreign policy of absolute national independence and one that is for authentic universal peace.

A. It will put an end to the Yankee interference in the internal problems of Nicaragua and will practice a policy of mutual respect with other countries and fraternal collaboration between peoples.
B. It will expel the Yankee military mission, the so-called Peace Corps (spies in the guise of technicians), and military and similar political elements who constitute a barefaced intervention in the country
C. It will accept economic and technical aid from any country, but always and only when this does not involve political compromises.
D. Together with other peoples of the world it will promote a campaign in favor of authentic universal peace.
E. It will abrogate all treaties, signed with any foreign power, that damage national sovereignty.

X. Central American Peoples' Unity

The Sandinista people's revolution is for the true union of the Central American peoples in a single country.

A. It will support authentic unity with the fraternal peoples of Central America. This unity will lead the way to coordinating the efforts to achieve national liberation and establish a new system without imperialist domination or national betrayal.
B. It will eliminate the so-called integration, whose aim is to increase Central America's submission to the North American monopolies and the local reactionary forces.

XI. Solidarity Among Peoples

The Sandinista people's revolution will put an end to the use of the national territory as a base for Yankee aggression against other fraternal peoples and will put into practice militant solidarity with fraternal peoples fighting for their liberation.

A. It will actively support the struggle of the peoples of Asia, Africa and Latin America against the new and old colonialism and against the common enemy: Yankee imperialism.
B. It will support the struggle for the Black people and all the people of the United States for an authentic democracy and equal rights.
C. It will support the struggle of all peoples against the establishment of Yankee military bases in foreign countries.

XII. People's Patriotic Army

The Sandinista people's revolution will abolish the armed force called the National Guard, which is an enemy of the people, and will create a patriotic, revolutionary, and people's army.

A. It will abolish the National Guard, a force that is an enemy of the people, created by North American occupation forces in 1927 to pursue, torture and murder the Sandinista patriots.
B. In the new people's army professional soldiers who are members of the old army will able to play a role providing they have observed the following conduct:
    1. They have supported the guerrilla struggle.
    2. They have not participated in murder, plunder, torture, and persecution of the people and the revolutionary activists.
    3. They have rebelled against the despotic and dynastic regime of the Somozas.
C. It will strengthen the new people's army raising its fighting ability and its tactical and technical level.

D. It will inculcate in the consciousness of the members of the people's army the principle of basing themselves on their own forces in the fulfillment of their duties and the development of all their creative activity.
E. It will deepen the revolutionary ideals of the members of the people's army with an eye toward strengthening their patriotic spirit and their firm conviction to fight until victory is achieved, overcoming obstacles and correcting errors.
F. It will forge a conscious discipline in the ranks of the people's army and will encourage the close ties that must exist between the combatants and the people.
G. It will establish obligatory military service and will arm the students, workers and farmers, who—organized into people's militias—will defend the rights won against the inevitable attack by the reactionary forces of the country and Yankee imperialism.

XIII. Veneration of Our Martyrs

The Sandinistas people's revolution will maintain eternal gratitude to and veneration of our homeland's martyrs and will continue the shining example of heroism and selflessness they have bequeathed to us.

A. It will educate the new generations in eternal gratitude and veneration toward those who have fallen in the struggle to make Nicaragua a free homeland.
B. It will establish a secondary school to educate the children of our people's martyrs.
C. It will inculcate in the entire people the imperishable example of our martyrs, defending the revolutionary ideal: Ever onward to victory!!!

First Draft of the National Constitution of the Republic of Nicaragua (February 1986)*

Despite its long-standing authoritarian political tradition, Nicaragua has had liberal democratic constitutions since 1893. For example, the 1950 constitution recognized individual rights and political freedom and emphasized that private property must be subject to the common good and have a social function. Article 54 of that constitution established the right to political asylum without political bias. (However, the 1986 draft imposes one-way political qualifications for granting asylum [see Article 85].) In general terms, the spirit of the 1986 constitution and the guarantees it offers make it similar to previous Nicaraguan constitutions. Moreover, the 1986 draft constitution offers guarantees similar to those stated in the revolutionary statutes that are mandatory to this day in Nicaragua. Unfortunately, in the past as in the present, the constitutional rights of Nicaraguans have been violated by those in power. For this reason, the content of Nicaraguan constitutions do not provide reliable criteria for analyzing Nicaraguan political life. Comparing law and political praxis will surely be a rewarding experience for the analyst of Nicaragua's past and present.

*This English translation of the National Constitution was provided by the Embassy of Nicaragua in Washington, D.C. It has not been edited.

The draft of 1986 has at least two novelties in Nicaragua's constitutional history:

1. The definition and explicit acceptance of a mixed economy (Articles 30–37), although there are no limits or proportions set for each sector. A mixed economy was only implicit in previous constitutions.

2. The establishment, at the constitutional level, of partisan armed forces (Articles 177–181). Critics of the FSLN would argue that this provision reflects the FSLN's Leninist orientation. Surely this provision is a notable departure from the anti-Somoza national alliance's original goal of having a non-partisan army.

An earlier constitutional draft, made of 21 points, was prepared by the FSLN in 1985. It established as an immediate goal the construction of a "popular democracy" in the sense that this concept was used in the 1940s to describe the political systems evolving at that time in the East European countries. External and internal factors, however, seem to have forced the Sandinista-dominated National Assembly to change this original draft into a more traditional constitution, notwithstanding the fact that it preserves some crucial sections (the articles 177–181 already mentioned) which are in line with the basic thrust of the 21 points contained in the 1985 draft constitution.

PREAMBLE

TITLE I
SOLE CHAPTER
FUNDAMENTAL PRINCIPLES

Article 1. The principles enumerated in this chapter constitute the interpretive spirit of the national Constitution of the Republic of Nicaragua.

NICARAGUA AND NICARAGUANS VENERATE
THE HEROES AND MARTYRS

Article 2. Nicaragua and its people will remember with gratitude, veneration and respect the Heroes and Martyrs of our country. Present and future generations will be educated by their exemplary legacy of heroism and generosity.

*Editors' note: Some articles of the Nicaraguan Constitution were modified further as this volume went to press. Thus, according to the final draft, "The Sandinista Popular Army has a national character" (Article 95). This formula, however, does not appear to change the partisan nature of that body, according to many analysts.

THE FORCES UPON WHICH REVOLUTIONARY POWER RESTS

Article 3. Revolutionary power lies in the people: city and rural workers, women, youth, patriotic agricultural and industrial producers, artisans, professionals, technicians, intellectuals, artists and members of religious orders, all of whom together constitute the majority of the nation's (social) forces and who are the guarantors of the irreversible character of the National and Democratic Revolution in Nicaragua.

DEMOCRACY

Article 4. Democracy is understood to be a combination of the concepts of liberty and equality, just as Sandino dreamt it: "Effective Democracy and Social Justice." In other words, the construction of a society with the real participation of the people where the right to elect and to be elected is affirmed; the right to expression, the right to organize, the right to demonstrate; the right to decent shelter; the right to education, to health, to work. In sum, the right to live with dignity.

A democracy where all the political, economic and social sectors of the country may participate toward concrete goals and objectives and where those sectors propose to re-establish and develop the country's economy in order to protect it from destruction and war, to make possible the people's happiness, to eradicate misery, hunger, destruction, unemployment; and to promote the social development of Nicaragua.

POLITICAL PLURALISM

Article 5. Political pluralism means the existence and participation of all political organizations without ideological restrictions except for those that seek a return to Somocismo or advocate the establishment of a political system similar to that of Somocismo.

MIXED ECONOMY

Article 6. A mixed economy means an economic model where diverse types of property may exist and associate: state-owned, private, mixed and cooperative ownership, where all have as their principal objective, the benefit of the people, together with the establishment of reasonable profit margins.

NON-ALIGNMENT

Article 7. Non-alignment seems to be the principle that guarantees independence from centers of power and the active peaceful coexistence of all states, through our moral solidarity with the struggles of peoples against imperialism, colonialism, apartheid and racism.

As Nicaraguans we also express our opposition to the existence of military blocks and alliances and recognize the urgent need through the establishment of a new international economic order, for a restructuring of international relations based on just principles.

ANTI-IMPERIALISM

Article 8. The basis of our anti-Imperialism is our country's historic struggle for independence and sovereignty. For this reason we reaffirm our right to self determination and we reject unjust commercial trade relations that function against developing countries, we reject consideration of Latin American countries as geo-political reserves and the military, political, and economic intervention against the legitimate sovereign rights of peoples.

LATINAMERICANISM

Article 9. We understand Latinamericanism to be the ideal of Bolívar and Sandino of achieving the unity of Latin American countries to strengthen and fortify our peoples.

ANTI-INTERVENTIONISM

Article 10. Nicaragua subscribes to the principle of non-intervention in the internal affairs of other states.

DEFENSE OF THE NATION

Article 11. We understand the defense of the nation as the participation of all the people in this defense and in the struggle to preserve the peace as indispensable to the social and economic development of the country.

SOVEREIGNITY AND NATIONAL INDEPENDENCE

Article 12. Sovereignty resides in the People, the legitimate owners of the nation, of its territory and of its natural resources, all to be used towards the progress of the nation and the social well-being of all Nicaraguans.

TITLE II
SOLE CHAPTER
GENERAL PROVISIONS

ON THE STATE

Article 13. Nicaragua is a free sovereign, independent and unitary state.

FORM OF GOVERNMENT

Article 14. Nicaragua is a democratic participatory, representative and nonaligned republic. The organs of the government are the Legislative, Executive, Judicial and Electoral Powers.

SOVEREIGNTY

Article 15. The nation's sovereignty is one, indivisible and inalienable: it belongs to the people, who will exercise their sovereignity according to the norms provided by this Constitution.

NATIONAL TERRITORY

Article 16. Nicaragua is the territory delimited by the Republics of Honduras and Costa Rica and the Atlantic and Pacific Oceans. The soil, the subsoil, the continental platform, the territorial sea, the underwater insular shelves, the airspace, the stratosphere, the adjacent islands and keys are all part of the national territory. Treaties and the law will determine the parts of the territory that are not delimited.

SUPREMACY OF THE CONSTITUTION

Article 17. This National Constitution is the fundamental law of the Republic: all other laws are subordinated to the Constitution. Acts of government bodies as well as laws, decrees and regulations, orders, provisions or treaties that explicitly or implicitly oppose the Constitution or alter its provisions will be void.

NATIONALITY

Article 18. All those so considered by law or treaty are nationals.

LANGUAGE

Article 19. Spanish is the official language of the State. The diverse ethnic groups have a right to the free use and development of their languages, since they belong to the national culture.

CAPITAL AND SEAT OF GOVERNMENT

Article 20. The city of Managua is the Capital of the Republic of Nicaragua and the seat of the State's Powers: they can be re-established in another part of the national territory if required by exceptional circumstances.

NATIONAL SYMBOLS

Article 21. The National Symbols are: the Flag, the Coat of Arms and the National Anthem established by law. The law determines their characteristics and their use.
Article 22. The state has no official religion.

TITLE III
SOLE CHAPTER
THE RIGHTS OF THE NICARAGUAN PEOPLE
AS OF PEACE AND SOCIAL ORDER

DEFENSE OF THE COUNTRY AND PEACE

Article 23. It is the right of all Nicaraguans to fight for the defense of the Nation and for Peace for the integral development of the nation.

RIGHT OF THE NICARAGUAN PEOPLE TO FREE DETERMINATION

Article 24. The Nicaraguan people have the right to self-determination in the political, economic, social, cultural and all other spheres of life.

RIGHT OF THE PEOPLE TO DISPOSE OF THEIR NATURAL RESOURCES

Article 25. The Nicaraguan people have the right to freely dispose of their wealth and natural resources, without prejudice to the obligations derived from international cooperation based on the principles of reciprocal benefit, solidarity and international law. In no case may the Nicaraguan people be deprived of their own means of substance.

THE REMOVAL OF THE OBSTACLES THAT HINDER
CITIZEN EQUALITY

Article 26. It is the obligation of the State to remove, by all the means within its reach, the obstacles that effectively hinder the equality of Nicaraguans and their participation in the political, economic and social life of the country.

THE RIGHT OF THE PEOPLE TO ORGANIZE

Article 27. In Nicaragua, the urban and rural labor, women, youth and patriotic agricultural and industrial producers, artisans, professionals, technicians, intellectuals, artists and members of religious orders have the right to form organizations to participate in the building of the new society.

RIGHT OF THE PEOPLE TO PARTICIPATE IN STATE AFFAIRS

Article 28. All citizens have the right to participate in the management of the country's public matters and in the fundamental affairs of the State at all levels.

LEGAL EFFECTS OF HUMAN RIGHTS

Article 29. The State guarantees all unqualified respect, promotion and protection of Human Rights, as well as the full effect of the Human Rights law subscribed to in the Universal Declaration of Human Rights, the International Agreement on Economic, Social and Cultural Rights; the International Agreement on Civil and Political Rights of the United Nations; the American Declaration on the Rights and Duties of Man; and in the American Convention on Human Rights of the Organization of American States, all of which are wholly incorporated into this Constitution.

TITLE IV
NATIONAL ECONOMY

CHAPTER I
GENERAL PRINCIPLES

STRATEGIC NATURE

Article 30. The economy is a strategic element of the nation's development. Its propelling force is derived from labor as the main source for production of wealth.

SATISFACTION OF MATERIAL AND SPIRITUAL NEEDS

Article 31. The economy of the Nicaraguan republic is a strengthening factor for National Sovereignty and for consolidating Democracy. It is directed at the material and spiritual needs of Nicaraguans.

POLICYMAKING AFFAIRS OF THE STATE

Article 32. The direction of the economy corresponds to the State, which plans, and gives orientation to economic activity in order to guarantee national development.

CHAPTER II
FORMS OF PROPERTY

THE FUNCTION OF PROPERTY

Article 33. Property, be it individually or collectively owned, fulfills a social function by virtue of which it can be subject to limitations on its title, enjoyment, use and alienability whether for reasons of security, public interest or utility, social interest for reasons relating to the national economy, national emergencies or disasters or for the purpose of agrarian reform.

PEOPLE'S PROPERTY

Article 34. People's property is constituted by all these goods and means of production that have been entrusted to the State for their administration.

PRIVATE PROPERTY

Article 35. Private property consists of all those goods and means of production that belong to one or more persons, to the exclusion of others. No one may be deprived of their property unless they are indemnified in accordance with the law.

MIXED PROPERTY

Article 36. The goods and units of production utilized by the State with the participation of other persons, natural or legal, are mixed property.

COOPERATIVE PROPERTY

Article 37. Cooperative property is the voluntary organization of workers for the joint utilization of goods and units of production according to the law.

CHAPTER III
AGRARIAN REFORM

OBJECTIVE

Article 38. Agrarian reform is a fundamental instrument of the economy and of revolutionary transformation. By means of agrarian reform the active participation of farm workers in the economic and social development of the country will be guaranteed.

LATIFUNDIA

Article 39. The State will secure, according to the terms established by the Agrarian Reform Law, the transfer of both the land and the means of production used in its development to the person or persons working that land, through the appropriation of latifundia.

GUARANTEES TO REAL PROPERTY

Article 40. The agrarian reform law will guarantee proprietary rights to the land to those efficient farmers who use it as an instrument of their work as established by law.

AGRICULTURAL COOPERATIVES

Article 41. The State will promote the voluntary formation of cooperatives for the development of the land.

FINANCING

Article 42. The State will furnish financial and technical assistance to agricultural and cattle raising production in the People's Property Areas, and in private, mixed and cooperative or other forms of property.

FARM LABORERS PARTICIPATION

Article 43. In the application of Agrarian Reform and in the organs created by the State to that effect, the participation of the agricultural laborers and producers through their organizations is established.

CHAPTER IV
COMMERCE

DOMESTIC TRADE

Article 44. The State has the obligation to regulate and oversee domestic trade in order to guarantee consumer defense. The law will establish the scope of State action.

FOREIGN TRADE

Article 45. The State formulates, carries out, promotes and oversees Foreign Trade Policy in order to secure the country's development and the diversification of markets to promote economic independence.
Article 46. The State will promote active participation in international organizations associated with foreign trade, especially with Central and Latin American countries.

CHAPTER V
FOREIGN INVESTMENT

Article 47. Foreign investment complements domestic investment. Likewise, it shall contribute to the country's development, conform to the law and not damage National Sovereignty.

Article 48. The State will ensure that technical knowledge derived from foreign investment will be transferred to it or to its subjects and that the State or its subjects adequately participate in the ownership and administration of the enterprises.

CHAPTER VI
REGARDING THE BUDGET OF THE REPUBLIC

OBJECTIVE

Article 49. The nation's Federal Budget will monitor all income and its declared sources; expenditures will be structured in such a way as to agree with the production of goods and services in order to determine the expenditure limits of the State Bodies.

FISCAL YEAR

Article 50. The Public Sector Budget year begins on January 1st and ends on Dec. 31st. The Budget will be drafted and then approved by the President of the Republic by means of the Annual Budget Law.

ITS CONSIDERATION

Article 51. The budget will be considered by the National Assembly.

CHAPTER VI
TAX SYSTEM

SYSTEM OF TAXATION

Article 52. The Law will determine the system of taxation which shall take into account the distribution of wealth and income as well as the needs of the State.

TAX

Article 53. Taxes shall be created by the law that will establish the incidence of taxation, the type of taxation and the taxpayer guarantees.

TAX EVASION: A CRIME

Article 54. The non-payment of taxes due and tax evasion are crimes.

PROHIBITION

Article 55. The State will not demand payment of taxes that have not previously been established by law.

TITLE V
NATIONAL DEFENSE
SOLE CHAPTER

NATURE

Article 56. The nature of national defense is defined by the Nicaraguan's people's dedication to peace and their unyielding will to permanently and integrally defend the vital interests of the Nation and the triumph of the Revolution.

SOCIAL BASIS OF DEFENSE

Article 57. The social basis of the integral defense of the Nation are all levels and social sectors that make up the Nicaraguan society.

POPULAR PARTICIPATION

Article 58. National defense against military, political, or economic aggression, either external or internal, is guaranteed by means of popular organized participation.

TITLE VI
RIGHTS, DUTIES AND GUARANTEES OF THE NICARAGUAN PEOPLE

CHAPTER I
INDIVIDUAL AND CIVIL RIGHTS

INVIOLABILITY OF THE RIGHT TO LIVE

Article 59. The right to live is inviolable and inherent to the human being. In Nicaragua there is no death penalty.

PERSONAL LIBERTY

Article 60. All persons have the right to individual liberty and security. No one may be subjected to arbitrary detention or imprisonment, nor deprived of their freedom, except for causes determined by the law and in keeping with legal procedures.

PROTECTION OF AND RESPECT FOR PRIVATE LIVES

Article 61. All persons shall have the right to private and family lives, to the inviolability of their residences, their correspondence or communications, to their honor and reputation.

EQUALITY BEFORE THE LAW

Article 62. All persons are equal before the law and have a right to equal protection.

FREEDOM OF EXPRESSION

Article 63. All Nicaraguans have the right to express their thoughts.

FREEDOM OF MOVEMENT

Article 64. Anyone on national territory shall have the right to move freely and to select a place of residence. The Nicaraguan people shall have the right to enter and leave the country freely.

FREEDOM OF CONSCIENCE, THOUGHT AND RELIGION

Article 65. All persons have the right to freedom of conscience, of thought and of professing a religion or not. No one may be the object of coercive measures that might impair the right to hold or adopt the beliefs of his or her choosing.

RETROACTIVITY OF THE PENAL LAW TO BENEFIT THE OFFENDER

Article 66. The Penal Laws retroactive effect in favor of the offender.

PRINCIPLE OF LEGALITY

Article 67. No functionary has more authority than that established by the Constitution and the laws. No one is obliged to do that which is not required by Law, nor is hindered from doing what the law does not forbid.

RIGHT TO CRIMINAL PROCEDURE GUARANTEES

Article 68. All persons have the right of individual freedom and personal security. No one may be subjected to arbitrary detention or imprisonment, nor be deprived of freedom except for causes determined by law and in keeping with legal procedure. Consequently:
   1. Detention can only occur by virtue of the written order of a competent judge or of the authorities expressly designated by law, except in the case of a flagrant crime.
   2. All persons detained shall have the right:
      a. To be informed without delay and in detail in a language or tongue they understand, of the nature and causes of the accusation made against them.
      b. To be brought, within the same established by Law, before the competent authority or to be freed.
      c. To obtain reparations in case of illegal detention.

Article 69. Everything else being equal, all defendants shall have the following minimal guarantees:
   a. They are presumed innocent until their guilt is proven in conformity with the law.
   b. They are guaranteed participation and defense from the beginning of the process.
   c. They are not obliged to testify against themselves or their relatives, nor to make confession of guilt.
   d. They may not be tried for a crime for which they have already been condemned or acquitted by a definitive sentence.
   e. They may not be tried and condemned for an act or an omission which at the time of its commission had not previously been expressly and inequivocally

designated by law as a punishable offense, or be sanctioned with penalties not foreseen in the law.

Article 70. Minors may not be subjects or objects of judgement, nor be subjected to any judicial proceeding. The law shall regulate this area.

PROHIBITION OF DEGRADING PUNISHMENT

Article 71. No one shall be subjected to torture or to penalties or treatment that is cruel, inhuman or degrading. No punishment may be imposed for more than thirty years.

RESPECT FOR PHYSICAL, PSYCHOLOGICAL AND MORAL INTEGRITY

Article 72. All persons have the right to respect their physical, psychological and moral integrity. *The penalty shall only affect the defendant's person.*

HABEAS CORPUS APPEAL

Article 73. The Remedy of Habeas Corpus shall be presented before a competent Court in accordance with the law by the persons designated under that law.

WRIT OF PROHIBITION (RECURSO DE AMPARO)*

Article 74. The Writ of Prohibition is established whereby all citizens whose rights and liberties are recognized under the present Constitution shall have been affected, may present an appeal for a writ of prohibition in accordance with the Law.

PROHIBITION OF SLAVERY, SERVITUDE AND TRAFFICKING IN PERSONS

Article 75. No one shall be subjected to slavery and servitude. Any kind of slavery or trafficking in persons is prohibited in all its forms.

NO IMPRISONMENT FOR DEBT

Article 76. No one shall be imprisoned solely for failure to comply with financial obligations, whatever its origins.

RIGHT TO ENJOY CONSTITUTIONAL GUARANTEES

Article 77. The State respects and guarantees the rights and guarantees established in this Constitution to all persons who are in its territory and are subject to its jurisdiction.

*Note: a constitutional provision peculiar to Mexico, which resembles United States writs of prohibition, certiorari, injunction and habeas corpus.

CHAPTER II
POLITICAL RIGHTS

CITIZENSHIP

Article 78. All native or naturalized Nicaraguans having reached the age of 16 are citizens. Citizens enjoy the political rights suscribed to by the laws in force.

RIGHT TO PETITION

Article 79. All native or naturalized Nicaraguans have the right to petition the State or any authority and to obtain a prompt answer and resolution.

RIGHT TO ASSEMBLE

Article 80. The right to peacefully assemble on private property does not require prior permission.

RIGHT TO PUBLIC MEETING OR DEMONSTRATION

Article 81. The right to a public meeting or demonstration shall be regulated by the respective Law.

RIGHT TO ELECT AND TO BE ELECTED

Article 82. All citizens have the right to elect and to be elected.

RIGHT TO BE A CANDIDATE FOR PUBLIC OFFICE

Article 83. All citizens shall have the right to be candidates for public office.

RIGHT TO ORGANIZE POLITICAL PARTIES

Article 84. All citizens shall have the right to organize political parties with the object, among others, of aspiring to obtain political power to carry out a program that responds to the needs of national development.
Political parties are institutions of public law. They shall be regulated in accordance with public Law.

RIGHT TO ASYLUM

Article 85. In Nicaragua, the right to asylum is guaranteed to those who are persecuted for struggling for peace, justice and the recognition or extension of human, civil, political, social, economic and cultural rights.
The Law shall define who is a political exile or refugee.

PROHIBITION OF EXTRADITION

Article 86. In Nicaragua there is no extradition for political offenses or common offenses connected with them according to Nicaraguan definition. No Nicaraguan may be the object of extradition from the National territory.
If for some reason the expulsion of a person who has been granted asylum is agreed to s/he shall never be sent to the country in which s/he was persecuted.
Extradiction shall be regulated by Law and by International Treaties.

SUSPENSION OF POLITICAL RIGHTS

Article 87. Political rights are suspended or lost on the grounds established by the respective laws.

CHAPTER III
SOCIAL RIGHTS

RIGHT TO RELIGIOUS WORSHIP

Article 88. All persons both individually and collectively have the right to express their religious beliefs in public or in private, through worship, the celebration of rites, practices and teachings, all in conformity with the laws.
No one may invoke religious beliefs or disciplines in order to elude compliance with the laws or to impede others from exercising their rights.

RIGHT TO INFORMATION

Article 89. The right to information is a social responsibility and shall be exercised without impairing the right of those informed nor the values of the Nicaraguan people.

SOCIAL SECURITY AND WELFARE

Article 90. All persons have the right to social security and welfare in accordance with the law in that area.

PROTECTION OF COMBATANTS

Article 91. The State guarantees attention through all its programs to the Nation's Combatants and to the families of those who have fallen in the defense of the nation, in accordance with the laws.

RIGHT TO NOURISHMENT

Article 92. The Nicaraguans have the right to be protected from hunger. The State shall promote programs that will assure an adequate availability and an equitable distribution of food.

RIGHT TO HEALTH

Article 93. All Nicaraguans have the right to health. The health of the Nicaraguans constitutes a public good.
The State shall provide free health care to Nicaraguans and has the obligation to adopt measures so that Nicaraguans enjoy optimal conditions of physical and mental health.

HEALTH SERVICES (*JORNADAS DE SALUD*)

Article 94. The State shall promote community health services through the corresponding organization with the participation of the people.

RIGHT TO HOUSING

Article 95. The Nicaraguans have the right to decent housing, in conditions of hygiene, comfort and security that guarantee family privacy.

PROTECTION, RECOVERING AND CONSERVATION OF THE ENVIRONMENT

Article 97*. All persons have the right to freely meet and associate with others for licit ends.
Nicaraguans have the right to establish and promote popular, community, neighborhood and rural organizations.

RIGHT TO RECREATION AND RELAXATION

Article 98. The Nicaraguans have the right to recreation and relaxation. The State guarantees these rights through specific programs and projects.

CHAPTER IV
RIGHTS OF THE FAMILY

PROTECTION OF THE FAMILY

Article 99. The family is the natural and fundamental nucleus of society and has the right to be protected by the society and the state.

RIGHT TO FORM A HOME

Article 100. The right of the Nicaraguans to constitute a family is recognized. It can be constituted through marriage or a de facto union.

*Editors' note: Article 96 is missing from the original document.

EQUALITY OF THE COUPLE

Article 101. Family relations rest on the absolute equality of rights and responsibilities between men and women.

PATRIA POTESTAS

Article 102. Patria Postestas shall be exercised in accordance with the law of relation between Mother, Father and Children. Parents must maintain their home and the formation of the children through their common effort.
In turn, children are obligated to respect and help their parents.

PROTECTION OF MATERNITY

Article 103. The state shall give special protection to mothers during pregnancy. During the pre-and postnatal periods working mothers must be given paid leaves and adequate benefits of social security. Parents have the right to expect the State to care for their minor children while they are at their work places.

EQUALITY OF CHILDREN

Article 104. All children have equal rights. No discriminatory designations shall be used with regard to parent-child relationships.

PROTECTION OF MINORS

Article 105. All minors have the right to protection measures required by their age, or the part of their families as well as society and the State.

ON PATERNITY

Article 106. The State protects responsible paternity. The right to investigate paternity in accordance with the Law is established.

RIGHT TO ADOPTION

Article 107. All legally capable Nicaraguans have the right to adopt minors, exclusively in the interest of the minor's integral development in accordance with what has been established by Law.

FAMILY

Article 108. The State guarantees the establishment of family patrimony, inalienable, unattachable and exempt from all public encumbrances; the law shall determine its function.

CHAPTER V
ECONOMIC RIGHTS

Article 109. All workers have the right to participate in the elaboration, oversight and execution of all the major economic and social measures that the State may promote.

DUTY OF THE STATE TO REMOVE OBSTACLES THAT HINDER ECONOMIC EQUALITY

Article 110. The State shall promote the economic well-being of the Nicaraguans to eliminate the obstacles that impede economic equality.

EQUITABLE DISTRIBUTION OF WEALTH

Article 111. The State shall set forth the necessary corrective measures in order to achieve an equitable distribution of wealth and income among all citizens.

DECENT MATERIAL LIFE

Article 112. The State shall try to guarantee the harmonious development of all productive forces and the just distribution of the national product in order to guarantee a decent material life to the Nicaraguan people.

TITLE VII
LABOR RIGHTS

RIGHT TO WORK

Article 113. Work is a right and a social responsibility of all persons. It is the obligation of the State to procure full and productive work for all Nicaraguans under the conditions that guarantee fundamental rights of human beings.

PARTICIPATION OF WORKERS IN THEIR PLACES OF WORK

Article 114. All laborers through their organizations have the right to make use of diverse forms of participation in their places of work in comformity with the law.

WORKERS' RIGHTS

Article 115. All workers have the right to enjoy equitable and satisfactory working conditions that especially quarantee them,

a. Equal wages for equal work.
Equal wages for equal work in identical conditions of efficiency and adequate to their

social responsibility with no discrimination by reason of sex that will assure a well being compatible with human dignity.

b. Payment in legal tender.
To receive wages in legal tender

c. Unattachable minimum wage.
An unattachable minimum wage, except for attachments toward the protection of the laborer's family in accordance with the law.

d. Workday, weekly rest, vacations
A limited workday a weekly rest and vacations regulated by the law.

e. Work stability
Workers have the right to stability in their work in comformity with the law.

RIGHT TO STRIKE

Article 116. The right to strike is recognized, and is to be exercised in the manner established by law.

RIGHT TO SOCIAL SECURITY

Article 117. The State guarantees the right of workers to Social Security with all the benefits and protection contemplated by the law; and which can be added to. The law shall also regulate the progressive integration of all levels of society.

WORK FOR MINORS

Article 118. Work by minors is prohibited when incompatible with their physical capabilities or dangerous to their moral development.

RIGHT TO TRAINING

Article 119. Laborers have the right to cultural and technical skills training. The State shall facilitate this through special programs.

RIGHT TO FREELY ASSOCIATE IN UNIONS

Article 120. Laborers are guaranteed the freedom to associate in unions; in exercise of this freedom they may establish unions at all levels. No laborer shall be forced to belong to a specific union.

AUTONOMY OF UNIONS

Article 121. Laborers are guaranteed autonomy to establish those organizations they may deem necessary.

INDIVIDUAL CONTRACT AND COLLECTIVE AGREEMENT

Article 122. Laborers are able to execute contracts and collective agreements with their employers, subject to the provisions of the law.

TITLE VIII
EDUCATION AND CULTURE

EDUCATION

Article 123. Education has as a goal, the development in Nicaraguans of critical and liberating consciousness under the principles established in the Constitution. It must also be scientific, based on a knowledge of history and the national reality, on the domain of science, on participation in the development of the revolution, on social justice and on human solidarity.

EDUCATIONAL POLICY.

Article 124. The State in directing education shall promote the democratization of education and its conditions, so that through the means available to it, it may contribute to the development of the personality and the establishment of a democratic society with social justice.

RIGHT TO CULTURE

Article 125. It is the State's role to stimulate all expressions of literary, artistic, craft and folkloric production, so that a truly popular Nicaraguan culture may be built.

ACADEMIC FREEDOM

Article 126. The State guarantees academic freedom in comformity with the plans and programs approved by the State and in accordance with the law and public order. Primary education shall be obligatory.

SECULAR EDUCATION IN STATE SCHOOLS

Article 127. In public schools, education shall be secular.

RELIGIOUS EDUCATION IN PRIVATE SCHOOLS

Article 128. Non-obligatory religious teaching is authorized in private schools.

OBLIGATIONS OF PARENTS

Article 129. Parents have the obligation to contribute along with the schools to the educational process of their children.

FREE EDUCATION

Article 130. Education shall be free at all levels. University education shall be regulated in accordance with the law.

LITERACY

Article 131. A permanent literacy and adult education campaign shall be maintained with the goal of raising the educational and cultural levels of the Nicaraguans.

ACADEMIC AUTONOMY AND LIBERTY

Article 132. Education, administrative and economic autonomy of the universities is guaranteed, in order that they respond to the country's need for transformation within the national plans for development. The State will provide the necessary economic support so that they may develop a creative curriculum and scientific research appropriate to the national reality. Academic and research freedoms are guaranteed as essential principles of education at all levels.

COORDINATION OF HIGHER EDUCATION

Article 133. In order to coordinate higher education there will be a National Council for Higher Education. The law shall determine its composition and attributes.

COPYRIGHT

Article 134. The State guarantees authors' copyright and that of inventors and artists. The law shall regulate in this area.

CULTURAL AND HISTORIC PATRIMONY

Article 135. The State shall have the obligation of preserving, maintaining and conserving all monuments, paleontological, archaeological, historical, cultural and artistic objects of the country, situated in the territory of the Republic, whoever their owner may be. The law shall determine the provisions for their conservation, restoration, maintenance and restitution.

RIGHT TO SPORTS

Article 136. The practice of physical education and sports shall be stimulated by all means as a part of the integral development of the person.

TITLE IX
CITIZEN'S DUTIES

Article 137. All persons have duties with regard to family, community, the nation and Humanity. The rights of all persons are limited by the rights of others, by security and by the just demands of the common good.

SERVICE TO AND DEFENSE OF THE NATION

Article 138. It is the duty of all Nicaraguan citizens to fight for the defense of the Nation and for the maintenance of Peace.

MILITARY SERVICE

Article 139. All Nicaraguans have the duty to serve in the military in accordance with the law.

OBSERVANCE OF THE CONSTITUTION

Article 140. It is the duty of all citizens to respect and obey the provisions contained in the Constitution and in the laws in force.

CONTRIBUTION TO PUBLIC EXPENDITURES

Article 141. All Nicaraguans have the duty to contribute to public expenditures through the payment of taxes created by the law.

EFFICIENT AND HONEST PERFORMANCE IN PUBLIC OFFICE

Article 142. All citizens who hold public office in the government or in the State institutions are obligated efficiently and honestly, to fulfill their duties.

TITLE X
ON THE ORGANIZATION OF THE STATE

CHAPTER I
GENERAL PRINCIPLES

ON THE POWERS OF THE STATE

Article 143. The Powers of the State are: the Legislative, the Executive, the Judicial and the Electoral. The functions of the State powers are determined in this Constitution.

INDEPENDENCE AND INTERRELATION

Article 144. In the exercise of their functions, each one of the State powers shall have its own activities, but they shall collaborate among themselves in accomplishing the State's goals.

CHAPTER II
LEGISLATIVE POWER

EXERCISE

Article 145. The legislative function is exercised by the National Assembly.

COMPOSITION

Article 146. The National Assembly shall be composed of ninety representatives of the Nation with their respectives alternatives. In addition, candidates for the President and Vice-President of the Republic shall be part of the National Assembly as seatholder and alternative respectively, as long as they have obtained in the national territory a number of votes equal or superior to the average of the regional quotients.

QUALIFICATIONS

Article 147. In order to be a representative in the National Assembly, the following qualifications are required:
a. To be a native of Nicaragua and in full enjoyment of his or her rights.
b. To be over 21 years of age.

TERMS OF OFFICE

Article 148. The representatives of the National Assembly shall be elected for a term of six years.

ATTRIBUTIONS

Article 149. The responsibilities of the National Assembly are.

1. To elaborate and approve laws and decrees as well as to reform and repeal the existing ones. It shall also have the authentic interpretation of the law.
2. To decree amnesty and pardons of penal sanctions, as well as commutations or reduction of sentences in comformity with the Law of Pardon.
3. To solicit reports and examine the Ministers or vice Ministers of State, Presidents of Autonomous Entities and Directors of Governmental Entities as well as summon them to appear.
4. To grant and cancel the legal personality of civil or religious entities.
5. To consider the General budget of the Republic in comformity with the procedure established in the present Constitution.
7. To enact laws regulating inversions by foreigners.
8. To ratify or not ratify international agreements, treaties or negotiations.
9. To regulate everything relating to the national symbols (The Flag, the Coat of Arms, The National Anthem).
10. To create honors and distinctions of National Character.

11. To receive solemn session of the annual report of the President of the Republic.
12. To delegate legislative powers to the President of the Republic, except for those powers which relate to the laws of the Republic.
13. To create permanent and special commissions.
14. To appoint research commissions for any matter of public interest or to delegate that work to the appropriate permanent commissions.

   Their conclusions will not be binding for the courts, nor will they affect judicial resolutions; the result of the research will be communicated to the Minister of Justice for proper action if necessary.

   The National* has power to issue subpoenas; the law will regulate what actions can be taken to deal with non-compliance
15. To grant pensions and honors to individuals for outstanding services to the Nation and to humanity.
16. To reform the political and administrative division of the Nation.
17. To fill Presidential and Vice-Presidential vacancies, if both are definitive vacancies.
18. To authorize the President of the Republic to leave the national territory if his absence should last more than two months.
19. To acknowledge and resolve complaints presented against public officials who enjoy immunity.
20. To appoint the Magistrates of the Supreme Court of Justice and the Members of the Supreme Electoral Councils selected from slates of three candidates proposed by the President of the Republic.
21. To determine its own statute and internal rules.

ELECTION

Article 150. Representatives shall be elected by means of a popular, secret, and direct ballot according to the system of proportional representation in judicial districts determined by law.

IMMUNITY

Article 151. Representatives will be free from responsibility for their opinions and votes in the National Assembly and will have immunity in accordance with the law.

EXECUTIVE COMMITTEE

Article 152. The National Assembly will be presided by an executive committee formed by one president, three vice-presidents and three secretaries.

Editors' note: The word "Assembly" appears to have been omitted in translation.

COMMISSIONS

Article 153. There will be two types of commissions: permanent and special. Permanent commissions shall be responsible for studying and ruling on drafts of legislation submitted to the National Assembly for consideration. Special commission shall perform occasional functions, which will be determined by the National Assembly upon their proposal by the Presidency. Both types of commissions shall be approved by the President of the National Assembly, after consultation with the Executive Committee.

INTRODUCTION OF BILLS

Article 154. The representatives of the National Assembly and the President of the Republic may introduce bills. The Supreme Court of Justice and the Supreme Electoral Council may also do so in matters of their competence.

Article 155. Bills presented by the President of the Republic, the Supreme Court of Justice and the Supreme Electoral Council in agreement with the preceding article will be sent directly to the commission.

In case of emergency concerning bills from the executive, the President of the National Assembly will submit them immediately to the whole assembly for discussion if the bill had been given to the representatives 48 hours in advance.

PROCEDURE AND DEBATE

Article 156. The regulations and the General Statute of the National Assembly shall determine the procedure in regard to Bills and the method of conducting debates in the sessions.

SANCTION, PROMULGATION AND PUBLICATION

Article 157. Once a bill is approved by the National Assembly, the final text, after discussion and revision, shall be written in three original documents. All three shall be signed by the President and the Secretary of the National Assembly, with the date of the Bill's approval. One of the documents shall be filed in the National Assembly Archives, the other two shall be sent to the President of the Republic for sanction, promulgation and publication. The President will return one of them to the National Assembly to be filed. The length of time allotted for the sanction shall be fifteen days.

VETO

Article 158. The President of the Republic shall have the right to veto any bill, rejecting it totally or partially within fifteen days of the date of receipt.

Article 159. If the President does not exercise the right to veto in the established period of time and does not promulgate the law, the President of the National Assembly shall promulgate the law and order its publication.

Article 160. A bill totally vetoed by the President of the Republic shall be brought back by the Secretary to the National Assembly to be debated in the plenary session. The President of the Republic at the same time shall state the reasons for his veto.

If the veto of the President is rejected by vote of 60% of the attending representatives, the National Assembly shall sanction, promulgate and publish the law.

Article 161. If the President of the Republic partially vetoes a bill and proposes reforms, suppressions or additions to it, the bill shall be returned to the National Assembly by the Secretary with an explanation of the reasons for such proposed changes. In all cases, the bill shall be sent to the President of the Republic for its sanction, promulgation and publication. If this is not done in fifteen days, the process established here shall be followed.

CHAPTER III
EXECUTIVE POWER

EXERCISE

Article 162. The executive power shall belong to the President of the Republic of Nicaragua. The President of the Republic is the Head of the State and the Commander in Chief of the Armed Forces.

THE VICE-PRESIDENT OF THE REPUBLIC

Article 163. The Vice-President of the Republic shall perform the functions delegated to him by the President and shall replace the President if a temporary or definitive vacancy occurs in the Presidency.

ELECTION

Article 164. The President and Vice-President shall be elected by relative majority votes obtained by popular, direct and secret ballots.

QUALIFICATIONS

Article 165. To be elected President or Vice-President the following qualifications are required.
   a. A Nicaraguan national in full possession of all his rights
   b. To be over 25 years of age
   c. Not to be a member of a religious order.

TERM

Article 166. The presidential term will last six years, from the date of inauguration by oath or affirmation before the National Assembly.

SUBSTITUTION FOR TEMPORARY ABSENCE

Article 167. If a temporary or simultaneous absence of the President and Vice-President should occur, the President shall appoint one of the Ministers, according to regulations, to act in his place.

SUBSTITUTION FOR DEFINITIVE ABSENCE

Article 168. If a definitive absence of both the President and Vice-President of the Republic should occur, the National Assembly shall determine how to proceed.

PREROGATIVES OF THE PRESIDENT

Article 169. The President of the Republic has the following attributions:
1. To enforce the Political Constitution and the laws.
2. To exercise the power of introduction of bills as established in this Constitution.
3. To formulate executive orders considered as laws when they are:
    a. Of fiscal and administrative nature.
    b. Related to international, economic or political agreements including those related to foreign debt.
    c. For developing and approving the General Budget of the Republic.
4. To appoint ministers as delegates of the government in all geographical jurisdictions included in the national territory.
5. To appoint the mayor of the capital of the Nation.
6. To assume the legislative power that the National Assembly shall delegate during its period of recess.
7. To conduct the foreign relations of the Republic and sign international treaties and agreements.
8. To declare a state of emergency on occasions foreseen by this Political Constitution. The state of emergency shall be ratified by the National Assembly within ninety days. In case of war such ratification is not necessary.
9. To appoint or to remove from office Ministers and Vice-Ministers of the State, Presidents of Autonomous Entities and other officials whose appointments or dismissal is not otherwise determined by the Constitution or by law.
10. To appoint the heads of the diplomatic missions.
11. To totally or partially regulate the laws according to their context or purpose.
12. To sign agreements of national interest.
13. To declare war.
14. To establish by decree additional credits to the budget and send it to the National Assembly for acceptance.
15. To award national honors and decorations.
16. To direct the public administration.
17. To propose slates of the three candidates to the National Assembly for the election of Magistrates of the Supreme Court of Justice and of members of the Supreme Electoral Council.

18. To present information or special reports to the National Assembly either personally or through the Vice-President.
19. All other attributions noted in the Constitution or regulated by law.

SECTION I
MINISTERS OF STATE

FUNCTION

Article 170. In the exercise of his duties, the President of the Republic shall be advised by Ministers, Vice-Ministers, Presidents of Autonomous Entities and other officials considered appropriate for the welfare of the Public Administration.

QUALIFICATIONS

Article 171. To be a Minister a Vice-Minister, or a President of an Autonomous Entity, the following qualifications are required.
   a. To be a Nicaraguan
   b. To be over 21 years old
   c. To have the full exercise of political and civil rights.

RESPONSIBILITY

Article 172. Ministers are responsible for their actions, as stated in this Constitution and in the laws.

NUMBER AND ORGANIZATION OF MINISTRIES

Article 173. The law shall determine the number and organizations of ministries of state and autonomous entities, as well as their respective competences.

DUTIES OF THE CIVIL SERVANTS

Article 174. Public and Civil Servants in the exercise of their functions must strictly fulfill their duties to the State. The use of State resources for purposes other than public functions is forbidden. All activities related to any political party cannot be carried out during working hours.

SECTION II

GENERAL CONTROLLER OF THE REPUBLIC

Article 175. The duties of the Public Controller of the Republic are to audit, control and supervise the income, expenditures and national or connected goods, as well as all operations related to all the above.

ORGANIZATION AND OPERATION

Article 176. The law shall determine the organization of the office of the General Controller of the Republic.

SECTION III
THE SANDINISTA ARMED FORCES

NATURE

Article 177. Because of its highly popular and democratic nature, the Sandinista Armed Forces are the strategic instrument of national defense and revolutionary gains, of public security and for the preservation of inner stability. The people in arms as basis of the Sandinista Armed Forces guarantee the sovereignity and territorial integrity of the nation.

Article 178. The Sandinista armed forces are strictly governed by this Constitution, by its constitutional laws and by all other military laws and regulations.

Article 179. The Sandinista Armed Forces are the only armed body of the nation. The organization of any other operation of any armed group is forbidden and shall be penalized by the laws of the Republic.

STRUCTURE, COMMAND AND OPERATION

Article 180. The Sandinista armed forces have a national, patriotic and popular nature. The law shall regulate its structure, command and operation.

The Sandinista armed forces are organized according to the principle of a single and vertical command that shall be exercised in accordance with the established hierarchical structure.

CIVIL DEFENSE

Article 181. The civil defense shall be organized by the Sandinista armed forces with the active participation of the people. The law shall regulate its actions and operations. Its main objective shall be to serve the population in case of war or natural disaster.

SECTION IV
STATE OF EMERGENCY

STATE OF EMERGENCY

Article 182. The President of the Republic may declare a state of emergency for a limited or extended period of time in all or in part of the national territory. The decree must be ratified by the National Assembly within ninety days. In case of war, such ratification is not necessary.

REASONS FOR A STATE OF EMERGENCY

Article 183. The state of emergency may be declared:
1. If the nation were engaged in international war or in imminent danger of a foreign invasion.
2. If natural disasters occur, such as earthquakes, flooding epidemics or any other public calamity.
3. If maintenance of peace or national security are in danger for any reason.

GUARANTEES THAT CANNOT BE SUSPENDED

Article 184. The President of the Republic shall not have the power to suspend the Rights, Duties and Guarantees established in the following articles of this Constitution; 59, 62, 63, 65, 67, 69, 70, 71, 72, 75, 76, 82, 83, 85, 86, 88, 90, 91, 92, 93, 94, 95, 96, 97, 98, 99, 100, 101, 102, 103, 104, 105, 106, 107, 108, 109, 110, 111, 112, 113, 114, 115, 117, 118, 119, 120, 121, 122, 123, 124, 125, 126, 127, 128, 129, 130, 131, 132, 133, 134, 135, 136, 137, 138, 139, 140, 141, and 142.

CHAPTER IV
JUDICIAL POWER

THE PEOPLE, SOURCE OF JUSTICE

Article 185. Justice emanates from the people and shall be enforced in their name and as their delegates by the Courts of Justice determined by law.

LEGALITY AND HUMAN RIGHTS GUARANTEE

Article 186. The administration of justice guarantees the principle of legality and protects and guards all human rights through the enforcement of the Law in matters of its competence.

JUDICIAL POWER

Article 187. The judicial power is represented by the Supreme Court of Justice and other agencies established by law.

SUPREME COURT OF JUSTICE

Article 188. The Supreme Court of Justice is the highest court of the Republic and holds the representation of the judicial power.

POPULAR PARTICIPATION

Article 189. The administration of justice shall be organized and shall operate with popular participation. Appropriate laws should determine such participation.

CHARACTERISITICS OF THE COURTS OF JUSTICE

Article 190. The Courts of Justice shall be formed by three or more members in accordance with the law which shall also determine the qualification of their members.

TERM OF SERVICE

Article 191. The term of service for the Magistrates of the Supreme Court of Justice shall be the same period of time determined for the members of the National Assembly. The law shall decide the length of term of service for members of all other courts.

DISMISSAL

Article 192. The Members of the Supreme Court of Justice may only be dismissed during their term of service by a just cause duly proven.

ELECTIONS OF MAGISTRATES

Article 193. The National Assembly shall elect the members of the Supreme Court of Justice from slates of three candidates presented by the President of the Republic.

SPECIAL LAWS

Article 194. The organic law of the Courts of Justice shall rule in any matter not included in this Constitution and pertaining to the judicial power.

PRINCIPLE OF INDEPENDENCE

Article 195. The judicial power is independent from any other power of the State.

UNITY AND EXCLUSIVENESS

Article 196. The Courts of Justice form a unitary system where the Supreme Court of Justice is the highest organism. The exercise of jurisdiction belongs exclusively to the courts, excepting what the laws regulate in military and agricultural matters and in matters related to maintaining the security of the State. The Supreme Court of Justice shall be notified by means determined by law of any official appeal against a decision of the court.

JUDICIAL PROFESSION

Article 197. The judicial profession is established according to the law of the matter.

SPECIAL SECTION
CONSTITUTIONAL CONTROL

APPEAL BECAUSE OF UNCONSTITUTIONALITY

Article 198. The appeal because of unconstitutionality is established against any law, act or regulation that is contrary to what is prescribed by the Constitution.

COMPETENT BODY

Article 199. The Supreme Court of Justice is the competent body to deal with appeals because of unconstitutionality.
A corresponding law will determine how to proceed.

PERSONS WHO CAN LEGALLY FILE AN APPEAL

Article 200. An appeal because of unconstitutionality may be legally filed by:
  a. The President of the Republic
  b. The President of the Supreme Electoral Council in matters of his competence.
  c. Forty nine representatives in the National Assembly
  d. The signatures of thirty thousand citizens duly verified according to law.

INDIVIDUAL APPEAL

Article 201. The individual appeal is established against any disposition action or resolution and in general against any action or omission of any official authority or any of their agents that violates or shows intent to violate the rights and guarantees asserted in the Constitution. The corresponding law will determine how to proceed.

CHAPTER V
ELECTORAL POWER

Article 202. The organization, management and control of all actions related to voting are the exclusive competence of the Supreme Electoral Council.

COMPOSITION

Article 203. The Supreme Electoral Council shall be formed by five members and their respective substitutes elected by the National Assembly from slates of three candidates proposed by the President of the Republic.

QUALIFICATIONS

Article 204. To be a member of the Electoral Council the following qualifications are required:
a. To be a native of Nicaragua
b. To be over 25 years old
c. Not to be a member of a religious order
d. To have full exercise of political and citizen rights

ATTRIBUTIONS

Article 205. The attributions of the Supreme Electoral Council are:
a. To initiate the electoral process
b. To appoint the members of all the electoral bodies according to electoral law.
c. To enforce the constitutional and legal dispositions related to the electoral law.
d. To know the outcome of the resolutions adopted by the subordinate electoral bodies.
e. To institute the necessary measures so that, according to law, the electoral process be developed with full guarantees.
f. To be in charge of the final count of votes in the presidential and vice presidential elections and in the elections of representatives to the National Assembly and other authorities.
g. To give the final result of the elections of the President and Vice-President of the Republic and of the Representatives to the National Assembly and other authorities in the period of time determined by law.
h. To issue its own by-laws.
i. All other functions indicated by law.

TERM OF SERVICE

Article 206. The members of the Electoral Council shall serve for a term of six years.

TITLE VIII
POLITICAL ADMINISTRATIVE DIVISION OF THE NATION

CHAPTER I

CRITERIA OF TERRITORIAL DIVISION

Article 207. For administrative purposes, the national territory shall be divided into several geographic circumscriptions. The following criteria will be adopted:
a. Strategic location from the point of view of national defense and economy
b. dedication to culture and production
c. population density

d. historical tradition

e. special circumstances

The law of the matter shall determine the number of circumscriptions and their organization, structure and operation.

MUNICIPALITY

Article 208. The municipality, considered as the basic unit of political administrative division of the nation, shall be organized according to what is established by law. The government and administration of municipalities shall be the responsibility of local authority with autonomy but in cooperation with the central government. The law shall regulate how the election of local authority must proceed.

INTEGRAL DEVELOPMENT

Article 209. The State guarantees the establishment of the integral development among the different areas of the Nicaraguan territory.

CHAPTER II

AUTONOMY OF NATIVE PEOPLES AND COMMUNITIES IN THE ATLANTIC COAST

Article 210. Native peoples and communities of the Atlantic coast of Nicaragua have the right to preserve and develop their cultural tradition and their historical and religious heritage; the right to free use and development of their languages; the right to organize their social and productive activities according to their values, culture and tradition. The culture and traditions of native peoples and communities of the Atlantic coast are part of the national culture.

TITLE IX
SOLE CHAPTER
CONSTITUTIONAL REFORM

TO INITIATE REFORM

Article 211. The National Assembly may partially reform this Constitution at the request of the President of the Republic or at the request of forty representatives to the National Assembly or by a petition with forty thousand signatures duly verified.

PROCEEDINGS

Article 212. The proceedings shall be the following:
   a. The reform proposal must contain the text of the articles to be reformed and a rationale of the motives in which the proposal is based.

b. The proposal shall be sent to a special commission appointed by the President of the National Assembly.
c. The Commission shall adopt a resolution within sixty days.
d. After presenting the resolution, discussion of the same will be held following the established procedures for the adoption of laws. A constitutional reform must be approved by 60% of the whole membership of the National Assembly.

VETO

Article 213. The President of the Republic may use the right to veto as established in the Constitution.

ARTICLE THAT MAY BE CONSIDERED FOR REFORM

Article 214. No constitutional reform may be considered in matters related to the popular nature of the revolution, to democracy, to the national defense, to anti-imperialism, to nonalignment, to anti-interventionism and to Latinamericanism.

TITLE X
SOLE CHAPTER
FINAL AND TRANSITORY DISPOSITIONS

VALIDITY

Article 215. The Fundamental Statute and the Statute of Right and Guarantees shall be in effect until this Constitution is adopted and promulgated. Then where it says "State Council" it shall read "National Assembly" and where it says "Commission for National Reconstruction" it shall read "President of the Republic" in all the laws of the Republic.

EXECUTIVE ORDER

Article 216. All executive orders issued by the Commission for National Reconstruction and by the Government of the Republic since July 19, 1979 are recognized as valid and effective.

PUBLICATION OF THE CONSTITUTION

Article 217. This Constitution shall be published and widely distributed in the official language. It will also be translated in the ethnic languages of the Atlantic coast for its distribution there.

BODY OF LAWS

Article 218. Pending the modification or repeal the existing body of laws shall be maintained as long as it is not contrary to the Constitution.

ORGANIZATION OF THE JUDICIAL POWER

Article 219. The present structure and organization of the judicial power shall be maintained so long as the law for a new organization is not enacted.

PRESENT POLITICAL AND ADMINISTRATIVE DIVISION OF THE NATION

Article 220. The existing political and administrative division of the National Territory shall remain until a law of the matter be enacted.

MANUSCRIPTS

Article 221. Four manuscripts of this Constitution shall be signed by the President of the National Assembly, by the Representatives of the National Assembly, by the President of the Republic, and by a Nicaraguan mother on behalf of the heroes and martyrs of the Nation. Each one of the four manuscripts shall be respectively kept in: the Presidency of the National Assembly, the Presidency of the Republic, the Presidency of the Supreme Court, and the Presidency of the Electoral Council. Each manuscript shall be considered to be the original text of the Political Constitution of Nicaragua. The President of the Republic shall have it published in "La Gaceta", the official newspaper. This draft of the Political Constitution has been presented by the Special Constitutional Commission to the Plenary Session of the National Assembly on February 21, 1986.

SPECIAL CONSTITUTIONAL COMMISSION

• APPENDIX D •

Contadora Act on Peace and Cooperation in Central America

The Contadora Act for Peace and Cooperation in Central America, submitted for approval to the Central American countries with June 1986 as the final deadline, is the most recent of the documents created by the Contadora mediator group. Formed in January 1983, and composed of Mexico, Panama, Colombia, and Venezuela, the Contadora Group since July 1985 has received the active support of Argentina, Brazil, Uruguay and Peru, the so-called Lima Group.

The search for a strictly Latin American solution to the problems of Central America has been one of the basic goals of Contadora. Achieving this goal, however, has been extremely difficult. In September 1983, the five Central American countries approved Contadora's "Document of Objectives," known as the "21 Points." These were of a general character and did not constitute a treaty. Nevertheless, that document was a step forward for Contadora because it represented a multilateral consensus on major issues by the signers.

On January 8, 1984, a joint meeting between the Contadora Group and the Central American countries approved the "Norms for the Execution of the Document of Objectives." Work commissions were created for the analysis of specific matters contained in the two previous Contadora documents (September 1983 and January 1984). The commissions reported the results of their work in April 1984, and in June of that year Contadora presented to the Central American governments the first draft of an Act for Peace and Cooperation. After studying it, the Central American parties sent the document back to Contadora for revision.

Contadora then presented a "Revised Contadora Act" to the parties on September 7, 1984. However, this Act was not entirely acceptable to Costa Rica, Honduras, and El Salvador, who explained their objections in the Document of Tegucigalpa" on October 20, 1984. The Revised Act lacked sufficient mechanisms for verification and control, but aside from specific objections, the "Tegucigalpa group" (Costa Rica, Honduras, and El Salvador) continued backing the fundamental purposes of the Act. The FSLN government, which had been willing to sign the first Revised Act, strongly protested the Tegucigalpa Document. Nicaragua had stated on numerous occasions that verification and control would be detrimental to its sovereignty.

The year 1985 started ominously for Contadora. Costa Rica accused the FSLN government of violating the extraterritoriality of the Costa Rican Embassy in Managua and its right to grant diplomatic asylum. This was in response to the events of December 24, 1984, when the Nicaraguan José Manuel Urbina was arrested and wounded during his arrest by the Sandinista police on the embassy's premises, according to Costa Rican claims. As a result of this incident, Costa Rica withdrew from the Contadora meetings, returning only after her protests were acknowledged, and Urbina was released. Border clashes and other incidents, however, further complicated this situation.

Despite these many obstacles, Contadora, in September 1985, presented a new version of the Act. The 1985 Revised Act dealt with essential matters of internal politics, such as democratization and national reconciliation. The Act also dealt with basic issues of international security, such as control of the military buildup in the area and mechanisms for verification and control, and proposed the creation of a corps of inspectors to monitor the agreements. The FSLN government, nevertheless, refused to sign it unless the United States signed a bilateral treaty guaranteeing that it would not invade Nicaragua. The 1985 Contadora Act was certainly the most comprehensive of all the documents produced by the Contadora group to the present day. When presenting the new document, the members of the group stated that if no agreement was concluded by November, they would cease their efforts to mediate.

After the September 1985 setback, the Contadora Group tried to revive the spirit of mediation and, together with the Lima Group, it issued the Declaration of Caraballeda (January 1986) which, although basically a reiteration of the main ideas contained in the Contadora Act, obtained renewed international support for the Contadora objectives.

In April 1986, a new Contadora meeting took place in Panama. Its purpose was to iron out the differences among the potential signatories and to agree on a deadline for signing the Act. The text presented for signature is the one reproduced here as Appendix D. The Panama meeting, however, ended up in disarray; and since no agreement on a deadline for the signature of the treaty could be agreed upon, the Contadora countries proposed June

6 and requested that the Central American governments indicate their willingness to meet that deadline.

June 6 came and no signs of agreement could be seen. Nicaragua declined to sign since it objected to the modification of the Act which referred to regulating rather than banning foreign military exercises. As to the Act's provision on the scaling down of regional military establishments, Nicaragua refused to accept it unless the United States became a party to the agreement. Lastly, the FSLN government made its approval of the treaty conditional on the American government halting the planned $100 million aid program for the Nicaraguan resistance. The other Central American countries also objected to some of the points of the new Act, which, except for some short but fundamental modifications, was basically the same as the Act which had been rejected in September 1985. These modifications referred to the commitments on security questions, particularly the regulation of foreign military exercises, the limitation of arms and military troops and the gradual elimination of foreign military bases. An important addition to the new version of the Act was the establishment of a corps of inspectors which would help the Verification and Control Commisison fulfill its duties. After the June deadline passed, the Contadora Group decided to leave the entire matter of negotiations in the hands of the Central American governments, and to mediate only if requested to do so by them.

The most recent version of the Act has important limitations, not least because it cannot accommodate the security interests of the Central American states, which are perceived differently by different states. Notwithstanding its limitations, the Act still represents a bold attempt in the field of international law by virtue of its efforts to submit vital issues concerning the soverign negotiating parties to supranational arbitration and regulation.

PREAMBLE*

The Governments of the Republics of Costa Rica, El Salvador, Guatemala, Honduras and Nicaragua:

1. AWARE of the urgent need to strengthen peace, cooperation, trust, democracy, and the economic and social development of the nations in the region through the enforcement of principles and measures to promote greater understanding among the Central American Governments;

2. CONCERNED over the situation prevailing in Central America, which is characterized by a serious deterioration in political confidence; a deep economic and social crisis; the serious situation faced by refugees and displaced people; border

*The text of this document is a reproduction of the English translation provided by FBIS—LAM in its Daily Report of June 19, 1986, pp. A1–A30.

incidents; the arms buildup; arms smuggling; the presence of foreign military advisers; the holding of international military maneuvers in the territory of States in the region; the existence of military bases, schools, and installations; and other forms of foreign military presence as well as the use of the territory of some States by unconventional forces in order to carry out destabilizing actions against other States in the region;

CONVINCED:

3. The tensions and current conflicts may grow worse and lead to a widespread military conflagration;

4. The objective of restoring peace and confidence in the area may only be attained through unlimited respect for the principles of international law, particularly the one referring to the right of peoples to freely select, without foreign interference, the model of political, economic, and social organization that best suits their interests through institutions representing their freely expressed will;

5. It is important to create, promote, and bolster representative, participatory, and pluralistic democratic systems in all countries in the region;

6. It is necessary to establish political conditions aimed at guaranteeing the security, integrity, and sovereignty of the States in the region;

7. The attainment of genuine regional stability lies in the adoption of agreements on matters of security and disarmament;

8. In order to adopt measures aimed at stopping the arms race in all of its modes, account must be taken of the national security interests of the States in the region with a view toward establishing a reasonable balance of forces;

9. The establishment of ceilings of military development, troop strength, and military installations in keeping with the stability and security needs in the area would be highly advisable for the establishment of the reasonable balance of forces;

10. Military superiority as an objective of the States in the region; the presence of foreign military advisers; the holding of international military maneuvers in the territory of States in the region; the existence of military bases, schools, and installations and other forms of foreign military presence as well as unconventional forces; and the arms smuggling endanger regional security and constitute destabilizing elements in the region;

11. That the regional security agreements should be subject to an effective verification and control system;

12. That the destabilization of the Governments in the area by advocating or supporting activities by irregular groups or forces, terrorist actions, subversion, or sabotage, and the use of a State's territory for actions that affect the security of another State is contrary to the basic rules of international law and of peaceful coexistence among States.

13. That the creation of documents that will allow the application of a policy of detente should be based upon the existence of trust between the States that will effectively diminish political and military tensions among them;

14. RECALLING the United Nations' decisions regarding the definition of aggression, and other actions prohibited by international law, particularly in resolutions 3314 (XXIX), 2625 (XXV) and 2131 (XX) of the General Assembly.

15. TAKING INTO ACCOUNT the declaration regarding the strengthening of international security adopted by the UN General Assembly in its resolution 2734 (XXV), as well as the Inter-American system's respective juridical instruments.

16. REAFFIRMING the need to promote national reconciliation actions in those cases where there have been deep schisms within society, which will allow popular participation in accordance with the law, in authentic political processes of a democratic nature;

WHEREAS:

17. Beginning with the UN Charter in 1945 and the Universal Human Rights Declaration in 1948, different international organizations and conferences have prepared and adopted declarations, pacts, protocols, conventions, and laws that tend to provide effective protection of human rights in general, or of some specific human rights;

18. That not all of the Central American States have accepted all of the international instruments that exist in regard to human instruments in order to have an integrated system that would make respect possible and guarantee human, political, civilian, economic, social, religious, and cultural rights;

19. That in many cases, inadequate internal legislation interferes with the effective implementation of human rights as defined in statements and other international instruments;

20. That each State should be concerned over modernizing its legislation so that it will guarantee the effective enjoyment of human rights;

21. That one of the most effective ways of achieving the implementation of the human rights stated in the international instruments, political constitutions, and laws of different States consists in having the judicial branch enjoy enough authority and autonomy to end the violations those laws are subject to;

22. That in order to do this, the judicial branch's total independence must be guaranteed;

23. That that guarantee will only be achieved if judicial officials enjoy stability in their posts, and the judicial branch has economic autonomy, so that its independence from other branches can be total and indisputable;

CONVINCED ALSO:

24. The need to improve just economic social structures that consolidate a genuinely democratic system that allows its peoples full access to the right to employment, education, health, and culture;

25. The high level of interdependence among the Central American countries as well as of the potential which the process of economic integration offers;

26. The dimensions of the social and economic crisis affecting the region which become evident in the need to implement structural, economic, and social changes that would allow a decrease in dependency and promote the Central American countries' self-sufficiency as they reaffirm their own identity;

27. The need to cooperate in the efforts each country is making to accelerate its social and economic development through mutual active assistance compatible with the development needs and objectives of each country;

28. The need to consolidate the process of Central American integration into an effective instrument for economic and social development based on justice, solidarity, and mutual benefits;

29. The need to reactivate, upgrade, and restructure the process of Central America's economic integration through the active and institutional participation of the States of the region;

30. The key role Central American institutions and authorities must play in reforming the current economic and social structures and in reinforcing the process of regional integration;

31. The need and advisability of jointly undertaking economic and social development programs to contribute to the process of economic integration in Central America within the framework of development plans and priorities which are adopted by our countries as sovereign nations;

32. The indispensable need of expanding and reinforcing the programs by international, regional and subregional financial institutions for Central America in view of the essential need of investments for Central America's development and economic recovery, as well as the joint efforts to obtain financing for specific priority projects;

33. The need to provide urgent attention to the massive flow of refugees and displaced people caused by the regional crisis;

34. CONCERNED by the constant deterioration of the social conditions, including employment, education, health, and housing, in the Central American countries;

35. REAFFIRMING, without excluding the right to appeal to other competent international forums, the commitment to resolve their controversies within the framework of the current document.

36. RECALLING the support conveyed to the Contadora Group through resolutions 530 and 562, of the UN Security Council and resolutions 38-10 and 39-4 of the UN General Assembly, as well as resolutions Ag-Res 675 (XIII-0-83) and Ag-Res (XIV-84) of the OAS General Assembly; and

37. PREPARED to fully comply with the Document of Objectives and guidelines to implement the commitments acquired in the document, which were signed by the Ministers of Foreign Relations in Panama on 9 September 1983 and on 8 January 1984 respectively, under the aegis of the Governments of Colombia, Mexico, Panama, and Venezuela, which comprise the Contadora Group.

Have agreed as follows:

CONTADORA ACT ON PEACE AND COOPERATION IN CENTRAL AMERICA

PART I
COMMITMENTS

CHAPTER I
GENERAL COMMITMENTS

Single Section. PRINCIPLES

THE PARTIES pledge, in accordance with the obligations stemming from international law which they have undertaken:

1. To respect the following principles:
   a) Renouncement of threats or use of force against the territorial integrity or political independence of the States;
   b) Peaceful settlement of controversies;
   c) Non-meddling in the internal affairs of other States;
   d) Cooperation among States for the resolution of international problems;
   e) Juridical equality of the States, respect for sovereignty and self-determination of peoples, and promotion of respect for human rights;
   f) Right to freely engage in international trade;
   g) Abstention from engaging in discriminatory practices in economic relations among States, respecting their systems of political, economic and social organization;
   h) Compliance in good faith obligations assumed in accordance with international laws.
2. Pursuant to these principles:
   a) They will abstain from engaging in any action that is not consistent with the objectives and principles of the UN Charter and the OAS Charter; that violates the territorial integrity, political independence, or unity of any State; and particularly any similar action that may constitute a threat or use of force;
   b) They will settle their controversies through peaceful means set forth in the UN Charter and the OAS Charter;
   c) They will respect the rules embodied in the treaties and other international agreements with regard to diplomatic and territorial asylum;
   d) They will respect the existing international borders among States;
   e) They will abstain from militarily occupying the territory of any of the other States in the region;
   f) They will abstain from any act of coercion of a military, political, economic, or any other nature aimed at subordinating to their own interests the exercise by other States of the rights inherent in their sovereignty;
   g) They will take all actions necessary to guarantee the inviolability of their borders by irregular groups or forces seeking to destabilize from their own territory the Governments of other States;
   h) They will not allow their territory to be used to carry out acts in violation of the sovereign rights of other States, and will see to it that conditions prevailing therein will not pose a threat to international peace and security;
   i) They will respect the principle that no State or group of States has the right to intervene directly or indirectly by force of arms or any other type of meddling in the international or external affairs of another State;
   j) They will respect the right of self-determination of peoples, free of foreign intervention or coercion, avoiding the direct or covert use of force to break up the national unity and the territorial integrity of any other State.

CHAPTER II
COMMITMENTS ON POLITICAL MATTERS

Section I: COMMITMENTS REGARDING REGIONAL DETENTE AND FOSTERING OF TRUST

THE PARTIES pledge to:

3. Promote mutual trust through all means available to them, and to avoid any action which may break peace and security in the Central American area.
4. Refrain from issuing or promoting propaganda endorsing violence or war or propaganda hostile to any Central American Government, and to comply with and spread the principles of peaceful coexistence and friendly cooperation.
5. Towards that goal, their respective government agencies will:
   a) Avoid any verbal or written declaration that may aggravate the current conflict-ridden situation in the area;
   b) Urge the mass media to contribute to the understanding and cooperation among the peoples of the region;
   c) Promote greater contact and information among the peoples through cooperation in all fields related to education, sciences, technology and culture;
   d) Jointly study future actions and mechanisms that will contribute to achieving and reinforcing a climate of stable and lasting peace.
6. Jointly seek a regional solution to eliminate the causes of tension in Central America, protecting the inalienable right of the peoples in the face of outside pressures and interests.

Section 2: COMMITMENTS REGARDING NATIONAL RECONCILIATION

Each one of the Parties acknowledges before the other Central American States the commitment it has made with its own people to guarantee that internal peace is preserved as a contribution to peace in the region, and therefore resolves to:

7. Adopt measures towards the establishment or, as the case may be, to improve democratic, representative, and pluralistic systems that guarantee the effective participation of the people politically organized in the decision-making process and that ensure free access of the diverse currents of opinions to honest and periodic electoral processes based on full compliance with the rights of the citizens.
8. Urgently promote, in those cases where there are deep divisions within society, actions towards a national reconciliation so as to allow the people to participate with full guarantees in genuinely democratic processes based on justice, liberty and democracy; and to create the mechanisms to allow talks with the opposition groups, in accordance with the law, in order to achieve that goal.
9. To issue or, as the case may be, to endorse, broaden and improve legal guidelines to offer a genuine amnesty that would allow citizens to fully resume their political, economic and social activities. Likewise, it agrees to guarantee the sanctity of the lives, liberty and personal safety of the people who have received amnesty.

Section 3: COMMITMENTS REGARDING HUMAN RIGHTS

In accordance with their respective internal laws and with the obligations they have acquired based on international law, THE PARTIES pledge to:

10. Guarantee full respect of human rights, and to abide by the obligations con-

tained in international legal instruments as well as constitutional rulings on the matter in order to achieve this goal.

11. Initiate their respective constitutional proceedings so as to adhere to the following international instruments:
    a) International Agreement on Economic, Social and Cultural Rights of 1966;
    b) International Agreement on Civil and Political Rights of 1966;
    c) Enabling Protocol of the International Agreement on Civil and Political Rights of 1966;
    d) International Convention of the Elimination of All Forms of Racial Discrimination of 1965;
    e) Convention on the Status of Refugees of 1951;
    f) Protocol on the Status of Refugees of 1967;
    g) Convention on the Political Rights of Women of 1952;
    h) Convention on the Elimination of All Forms of Discrimination Against Women of 1979;
    i) Protocol to Modify the Convention on Slavery of 1926 (1053);
    j) Supplementary Convention on the Abolition of Slavery, the Slave Trade, and Institutions and Practices Similar to Slavery of 1956;
    k) International Agreement on the Civil and Political Rights of Women of 1953;
    l) American Convention on Human Rights of 1969;
    m) International Convention Banning Torture and Other Cruel, Inhuman, or Degrading Treatment or Punishment of 1985.

12. Draft and present at their competent internal organs the necessary legislative initiatives with the purpose of speeding up the modernization and updating of their regulations to make them more suitable to foster and guarantee due respect for human rights.

13. Draft and present at their competent internal organs the necessary legislative initiatives to:
    a) Guarantee the independence and stability of those in charge of the judicial branch so that they can operate without political pressure, and also guarantee the stability of the other judicial branch officials;
    b) Guarantee the judicial branch's autonomy and sufficiency regarding its budget in order to preserve its independence from the other branches.

Section 4: COMMITMENTS REGARDING ELECTORAL PROCESSES AND PARLIAMENTARIAN COOPERATION

Each of the Parties acknowledges, before the other Central American States, the commitment made in the eyes of its own people to guarantee the preservation of domestic peace as its contribution toward regional peace. To this end, each Party resolves to:

14. Adopt the measures to guarantee, under equal conditions, political parties' participation in electoral processes and ensure these Parties' access to mass media. Each Party will also ensure freedom of meeting and freedom of expression for the Parties;

15. Implement these measures:
    1) To promulgate or revise the electoral regulations so that they can guarantee an effective participation by the people;
    2) To set up independent electoral organs that will draft a reliable electoral listing and ensure the process' impartiality and democratic nature;
    3) To dictate or update, as necessary, the provisions to guarantee the existence and participation of political parties that represent the various trends of opinion;
    4) To establish an electoral schedule and take the measures to make sure that the political parties will participate under equal conditions.

The parties also pledge to propose the following to their respective legislative organs:
    1) To meet regularly in alternate sites to exchange experiences, contribute to detente, and foster better communication for a rapprochement among the area countries;
    2) To take measures to maintain relations with the Latin American Parliament and its working commissions;
    3) To exchange information and experiences in matters of their competence and collect, for a comparative study, electoral regulations from each country, as well as related provisions;
    4) To attend, as observers, the various stages of the electoral processes in the region. For this, the express invitation of the State holding the elections will be indispensable;
    5) To hold technical meetings on a fixed schedule at the place and according to the agenda agreed upon by consensus during each preceding meeting.

CHAPTER III
COMMITMENTS ON SECURITY MATTERS

In accordance with their duties under international law and in order to establish the foundations for an effective and lasting peace, the Parties make commitments in security matters related to banning international military exercises; stopping the arms race; dismantling bases, schools, or other foreign military facilities; withdrawing foreign military advisers and other foreign people who participate in military or security activities; banning arms trafficking; suspending support for unconventional forces; refraining from fostering or supporting acts of terrorism, subversion, and sabotage; and, finally, establishing a regional system of direct communication.

For such purposes, the Parties pledge to execute the following specific actions:

Section 1: COMMITMENTS IN MATTERS OF MILITARY EXERCISES

16. Regarding the execution of national military exercises, to heed the following provisions, effective as of the date on which this Act comes into force:
    A) In the case that national military exercises are held less than 30 kilometres

from the territory of another State, the proper prior notification to the other member States and the Verification and Control Commission should be made 30 days in advance, as provided for by Part II of this Act.

B) The notification should include the following information:
   1. Name;
   2. Purpose;
   3. Number of men, units, and forces that participate;
   4. Areas where the exercise is planned to be held;
   5. Program and schedule;
   6. Equipment and armament to be used.

C) An invitation should be extended to observers from the bordering member States.

17. To abide by the following provisions regarding the carrying out of international maneuvers:

   1) For a period of 90 days from the moment the Act goes into effect, international military maneuvers implying the presence of armed forces from States other than those of the Central American area will be suspended;

   2) After 90 days, with basis on mutual agreements and taking into consideration the recommendations of the Verification and Control Commission, the Parties can extend that suspension until the top arms and military troops limit is reached according to what is established in paragraph 19 of this chapter. In the event there is no agreement on extending the suspension, international military maneuvers will be subjected, during that period, to the following regulations:

      a) It must be assured that they will not have an intimidatory purpose against any Central American State or any other State;

      b) Any such maneuver must be reported to the Central American States and to the Verification and Control Commission at least 30 days in advance, as Part II of this Act establishes. The notification must contain the following information:
         1. Name;
         2. Purpose;
         3. Participating States;
         4. Troops, units, and forces participating;
         5. Area where the maneuver will take place;
         6. Program and program schedule;
         7. Equipment and arms to be used.

      c) The maneuvers will not take place less than 50 kilometres from the territory of a State not participating in them, unless there is expressed consent from that State;

      d) The maneuvers must be limited to one per year and their duration must not be over 15 days;

      e) The total number of troops participating in the maneuvers must be limited to 3,000. Under no circumstances can the number of troops from other States be larger than that of national troops participating in the maneuvers;

      f) Observers from the Central American States should be invited;

g) If a Central American State considers that any of the above dispositions has been violated, it can appeal to the Verification and Control Commission.

3) Once the top arms and military troops limit, established in paragraph 19 of this chapter, is reached, military maneuvers implying the participation of States from outside the Central American region are prohibited;

4) International maneuvers carried out with the exclusive participation of Central American States in their respective territories will abide by the following provisions the moment this Act goes into effect:

a) The participant States must notify the Central American States and the Verification and Control Commission about the maneuvers, in line with what is established in Part II of this Act, at least 45 days in advance. The notification must contain the following information:

1) Name;
2) Purpose;
3) Participating States;
4) Troops, units, and forces participating;
5) Area where the maneuver will take place;
6) Schedule of program;
7) Equipment and arms to be used.

b) The maneuvers will not take place less than 40 kilometres from the territory of a State not participating in them, unless there is expressed consent from that State;

c) Maneuvers can last a total of 30 days a year. In the event that several maneuvers are to take place in one year, the duration of each maneuver will not be greater than 15 days;

d) The total number of troops participating in the maneuvers must be limited to 4,000;

e) Observers from the Central American States should be invited;

f) If a Central American State considers that any of the above stipulations has been violated, it can appeal to the Verification and Control Commission.

5) International military maneuver commitments will be regulated by what is established in paragraph 19 of this chapter.

Section 2: COMMITMENTS ON THE SUBJECT OF ARMS AND MILITARY TROOPS

18. To stop the arms race in all its manifestations and to initiate, immediately, negotiations aimed at establishing limits on arms and on armed troops; and at their control and reduction in order to establish a reasonable balance of power in the area.

19. On the basis of this, THE PARTIES agree on the following implementation stages.

FIRST STAGE

a) THE PARTIES agree to suspend, from the date the Act goes into effect, all purchases of military equipment, except replacements, ammunition, and spare parts needed to keep already existing equipment functional. They also agree not to increase the number of their military troops until military development limits are established within the deadline set for the second stage.

b) THE PARTIES agree to simultaneously deliver to the Verification and Control Commission their respective current inventories on arms, military installations, and armed troops, 15 days after this Act goes into effect.

The inventories will be prepared in line with the basic concepts listed in the Annex of this Act and with the definitions that appear there.

c) Within 60 days after the Act goes into effect, the Verification and Control Commission will conclude its technical study and will suggest to the Central American States, without detriment to negotiations that could have been initiated, what could be the top limit of their military development on the basis of the basic concepts established on paragraph 20 of this section, as well as what could be the schedules for the respective reductions and dismantlings.

SECOND STAGE

Sixty days after this document is implemented, the Parties will establish within the following 30 days:

a) The maximum limits on the different types of weapons classified in the Appendix of this document, and the dates of their reduction.

b) The maximum limits on the number of troops and military installations that each Party can have, and the dates for their reduction or dismantling.

c) If within this period of time the Parties do not reach an agreement regarding the maximum limits and dates in question, the maximum limits and dates suggested by the Verification and Control Commission in their technical studies will be temporarily implemented with the prior consent of the Parties. The Parties will mutually agree on a new deadline for the negotiation and establishment of the limits in question.

If an agreement on the maximum limits is not reached, the execution of the agreements regarding international military maneuvers, foreign bases and military installations, and foreign military advisers—for which deadlines have been established in the document—will be suspended except in cases in which the Parties decide against suspension.

The maximum limits referred to in Sections a), b) and c), as well as the dates, will be considered part of this document and will have the same obligatory juridical effects of this document, as of the day after the expiration of the 30 days established for the second stage, or the day after being established through an agreement between the Parties.

The maximum limits agreed upon must be achieved within 180 days after the implementation of the present document, or within the deadline established by the Parties, unless the Parties establish an agreement to the contrary based upon Section c).

20. In order to satisfy the need for peace, stability, security, and social and economic development in the countries of the region, and in order to establish the maxi-

mum limits of military development in the Central American States, and military control and reduction, the sides will agree on a factorization table that will consider the following basic criteria, in which all weapons will be controlled or reduced:

1) Each Central American country's security needs and defense capabilities;
2) Territorial extension and population;
3) Extension and characteristics of their borders;
4) Military expenditures in relation to the Gross Domestic Product (GDP);
5) Military budget in regard to public expenditures and a comparison with other social indicators;
6) Military technology, relative combat capability, military troops, quality and quantity of the installations and military resources;
7) Weapons subject to control; weapons subject to reduction;
8) The military presence and the presence of foreign advisers in each Central American State.

21. Not to introduce new weapons systems that would qualitatively and quantitatively modify the current war material inventories.
22. Not to introduce, possess, or use lethal chemical, biological, radiological, or other weapons that could be considered excessively damaging or of indiscriminate effects.
23. Not to allow the transit, stationing, mobilization or any other form of use of territories by foreign armed forces whose actions could be a threat to the independence, sovereignty, and territorial integrity of any Central American State.
24. To initiate the constitutional processes so that in case it has not been done already, the Parties can sign, ratify, or adhere to treaties and other international agreements regarding disarmament.

Section 3. COMMITMENTS REGARDING FOREIGN MILITARY BASES

25. To eliminate the foreign military bases, schools, or installations in their respective territories, as established in points 11, 12, and 13 of the Appendix within 180 days as of the signing of this document. For this purpose, the Parties are obliged to simultaneously turn over to the Verification and Control Commission lists of these foreign bases, schools, or installations within 15 days of the signing of this document, which will be prepared in accordance with the criteria established in the Appendix numerals in question.
26. Not to authorize in their respective territories, the establishment of foreign military bases, schools, or other installations.

Section 4. COMMITMENTS REGARDING FOREIGN MILITARY ADVISERS

27. To give the Verification and Control Commission a list of the foreign military advisers and other foreign individuals participating in a military, paramilitary and security activities in their territory within a period no greater than 15 days as of the signing of the present document. In preparing the list, the definitions stated in point 14 of the Appendix will be taken into account.

28. To have the foreign military advisers and other foreign elements capable of participating in military, paramilitary, and security activities withdraw within a period no greater than 180 days as of the signing of the present document, and in accordance with the studies and recommendations made by the Verification and Control Commission.

29. Regarding the advisers who are performing technical functions installing or providing maintenance to military equipment, a roster (*registro de control*) will be maintained based on the terms established in the respective agreements or pacts. Based on this roster, the Verification and Control Commission will propose to THE PARTIES a reasonable number for this sort of adviser, within the deadline established above in point 27. The limits agreed on will be an integral part of this document.

Section 5. COMMITMENTS REGARDING ARMS TRAFFICKING

30. To eliminate the illegal trafficking of arms, as defined in point 15 of the Annex, destined for persons, organizations, unconventional forces, or armed groups that seek to destabilize the Government of the signing States.

31. To establish toward that goal mechanisms of control at airports, landing strips, ports, terminals, border points, land, air, sea, or river routes, or at any other point or area that may be used for drug trafficking.

32. To present to the Verification and Control Commission charges of violations on this aspect based on suppositions or on proven facts which provide sufficient elements of judgement so as to allow the Commission to conduct the necessary investigations and present the conclusions and recommendations it may deem appropriate.

Section 6: COMMITMENTS REGARDING BANNING SUPPORT TO UNCONVENTIONAL FORCES

33. To refrain from providing political, military, financial, or any other kind of support to individuals, groups, unconventional forces, or armed groups that advocate the ousting or destabilization of other governments. Likewise, to prevent through all available means the use of their territory to attack or organize attacks, acts of sabotage, kidnappings, or other criminal actions in another State.

34. To maintain a strict watch on their respective borders to prevent their territories from being used to conduct any armed action against a neighboring State.

35. To deny the use of or dismantle installations, means, and facilities for logistical and operational support in their territories, whenever these are used for actions against neighboring governments.

36. To disarm and to remove from the border zone any unconventional group or force that may have been held responsible for actions against a neighboring State. Once these unconventional forces have been disbanded, to proceed to relocate or return them to their respective countries, in accordance with the terms which the governments involved may establish. This will be achieved with

the financial and logistical support of international organizations and governments interested in peace in Central America.

37. To present to the Verification and Control Commission charges of violations on
    this aspect based on suppositions or on proven facts which provide sufficient
    elements of judgement so as to allow the Commission to conduct the necessary
    investigations and present the conclusions and recommendations it may deem
    appropriate.

Section 7: COMMITMENTS REGARDING TERRORISM, SUBVERSION, OR SABOTAGE

38. To refrain from lending political, military, financial, or any other kind of support
    for subversive, terrorist, or sabotage activities aimed at destabilizing or ousting
    governments in the region.
39. To refrain from organizing, promoting, or participating in acts of terrorism,
    subversion, or sabotage in another State, or from allowing actions aimed at
    perpetrating these criminal actions to be organized within their territories.
40. To abide by the following international treaties and conventions:
    a) The 1980 Convention for the Suppression of Unlawful Seizure of Aircraft of
       1970;
    b) The 1971 Convention to prevent and sanction acts of terrorism in the form of
       crimes against persons and extortion or related crimes when these crimes are
       of international significance;
    c) The 1971 Convention for the Suppression of Unlawful Acts Against the
       Safety of Civil Aviation, 1971;
    d) The 1970 International Convention Against the Taking of Hostages.
41. To take the constitutional steps so that, in the event that they have not done so
    already, they can sign, ratify, or abide by the international treaties and agree-
    ments mentioned in the previous paragraph.
42. To prevent terrorist groups or organizations from planning and implementing
    criminal acts against other States or nationals of those States in their respective
    territories. With this purpose in mind, they will increase the cooperation among
    police and immigration agencies, as well as the pertinent civilian authorities.
43. To report any violations related to this matter based on presumptions or proven
    facts to the Verification and Control Commission with sufficient detail to carry
    out the necessary investigation and present the conclusions and recommenda-
    tions that are deemed advisable.

Section 8: COMMITMENTS CONCERNING DIRECT COMMUNICATIONS SYSTEMS

44. To establish a regional communications system that would guarantee a quick
    link between the pertinent governmental, civilian and immigration authorities
    and the Verification and Control Commission in order to prevent incidents.
45. To establish joint security commissions to prevent incidents and solve controver-
    sies among neighboring States.

CHAPTER IV
COMMITMENTS ON ECONOMIC AND SOCIAL MATTERS

Section 1: COMMITMENTS ON ECONOMIC AND SOCIAL MATTERS

In order to strengthen the Central American economic integration process and the institutions that constitute and support it, THE PARTIES promise:

46. To reactivate, improve, and reorganize the process for economic integration in Central America in order to bring it in line with the various forms of political, economic, and social organizations of the countries in the area.
47. To back resolution 1−84 of the 30th meeting of ministers in charge of the Central American economic integration of 27 July 1984 aimed at restoring the institutionality of the Central American integration process.
48. To support and promote the implementation of agreements aimed at strengthening trade among Central American countries within the law and the spirit of integration.
49. Not to adopt or support coercive or discriminating measures that would hurt the economy of any of the Central American countries.
50. To adopt measures aimed at strengthening the area's financial organizations including the Central American Bank of Economic Integration, by supporting its negotiations to obtain resources and accomplish the diversification of its operations preserving the decision-making power and the interests of all the Central American countries.
51. To strengthen multilateral payment mechanisms within the Central American Common Market fund and to reactivate those that exist within the Central American Clearing House. To support these organizations, the Central American nations can resort to available international assistance.
52. To begin sectorial cooperation projects in areas such as energy production and distribution systems, a regional system to guarantee food, a plan to supply the urgent health needs of Central America and Panama, and other systems that contribute to the Central American economic integration.
53. To jointly study the Central American foreign debt problem based on an evaluation that takes into consideration the internal causes of each country, its payment capacity, the critical economic situation in the area, and the flow of additional resources needed to take care of economic and social development.
54. To support the process to draft and subsequently implement a new Central American tariff and customs system.
55. To adopt joint measures to defend and promote their exports, implementing, as much as possible, the processes to transform the market, and transport their products.
56. To adopt the necessary measures to give legal status to the Central American Monetary Council.
57. To support the efforts that CADESCA, in coordination with subregional organizations, may make to obtain additional financial resources from the international community for the economic reactivation of Central America.
58. To apply international labor regulations and improve their internal labor regula-

tions with ILO help, especially those regulations that help in the reconstruction of the Central American societies and economies. In addition, to implement, with ILO help, programs for the creation of jobs; the training of workers; and the application of the right technology that will result in a greater use of the labor and natural resources of each country.

59. To call for the support of the Pan American Health Organization and UNICEF, as well as that of other development agencies and the international financial community in order to finance the plan of urgent health needs of Central America and Panama approved by the Central American Health Ministers in San Jose on 16 March 1984.

Section 2: COMMITMENTS ON THE SUBJECT OF REFUGEES

THE PARTIES commit themselves to conduct the necessary efforts in order to:

60. Proceed with, if not already done, the constitutional procedures to adhere to the 1951 Convention on the Status of Refugees and the 1967 Protocol.
61. Adopt the terminology established in the Convention and Protocol mentioned in the above paragraph, in order to make a difference between refugees and other types of immigrants.
62. Establish, with the adherence to documents, the necessary domestic mechanisms in order to apply the regulations outlined in the Convention and Protocol mentioned in 57.
63. Establish a mechanism for consultations among the Central American countries with representatives of the government offices responsible for handling the refugee problems in each State.
64. Support the work carried out by the UN High Commissioner for Refugees (UNHCR) in Central America, and to establish direct mechanisms for coordination to facilitate compliance with its mandate.
65. Ensure that the repatriation of refugees is carried out on a voluntary basis, upon individual request, and with the collaboration of the UNHCR.
66. Establish three-party commissions made up of representatives from the country of origin, the receiving country, and the UNHCR in order to facilitate the repatriation of refugees.
67. Strengthen the programs for the protection and assistance to refugees, particularly in the areas of health, education, work and security.
68. Establish programs and projects to make the refugees self-sufficient.
69. Train the government officials who are responsible in each State for the protection of and assistance to refugees, with the collaboration of the UNHCR or other international organizations.
70. Request from the international community immediate aid for the Central American refugees, both directly, through bilateral and multilateral agreements, as well as through the UNHCR and other organizations and agencies.
71. Detect, with the UNHCR's collaboration, other countries that could possibly receive Central American refugees. In no case will a refugee be transferred to a third country against his will.

72. Encourage the countries in the area to conduct the necessary efforts in order to eradicate the causes of the refugee problem.
73. Guarantee that once the basis for the voluntary and individual repatriation is agreed on with full guarantees for the refugees, the receiving countries will allow official delegations from the countries of origin to visit the refugee camps accompanied by representatives of the UNHCR and of the receiving country.
74. Facilitate the procedures at the receiving countries for the departure of the refugees in cases of voluntary and individual repatriation, in coordination with the UNHCR.
75. Establish the pertinent measures at the receiving countries in order to prevent the participation of refugees in activities against their country of origin, respecting at all times the refugees' human rights.
76. To consider as displaced persons all those who have been forced to leave their usual residence, their belongings and working means as a result of the prevailing conflicts, and have had to move to another place in their own country seeking protection and personal security, as well as help in order to satisfy their basic needs.
77. Act in a coordinated manner before the international community, upon request from an interested party, in order to obtain the necessary cooperation for the programs carried out by each Central American country on the subject of refugees.

PART II
IMPLEMENTATION AND FOLLOW-UP COMMITMENTS

1. The Foreign Ministers of the Central American States will adopt instructions, reports, and recommendations as outlined in the mechanisms for the implementation and follow-up described in this Part II and will make the pertinent decisions by consensus and without delay in order to ensure full compliance with the commitments acquired through the Act. As applied to this Act, consensus means the absence of any expressed opposition that may constitute an obstacle for the adoption of a decision under consideration in which all the parties involved participate. Any controversy will be subject to the procedures outlined in this Act.
2. In order to ensure the implementation and follow-up of the commitments included in this Act, THE PARTIES agree to create the following mechanisms:
   A. Ad Hoc Committee for the Evaluation and Follow-up of the Commitments Concerning Policy, Refugees and Displaced People;
   B. Verification and Control Commission on the Subject of Security; and
   C. Ad Hoc Committee for the Evaluation and Follow-up of the Economic and Social Commitments.
3. The mechanisms established in the Act will have the following makeup, structures, and functions:
   A. Ad Hoc Committee for the Evaluation and Follow-up of Commitments Concerning Policy, Refugees, and Displaced People.

a) *Integration*

The Committee will be made up of five persons of well-known competence and impartiality, proposed by the Contadora Group and accepted by common agreement by the Parties involved. The members of the Committee must not be citizens from the countries involved. The Committee will have a Technical and Administrative Secretary, which will guarantee its permanent operation.

b) *Functions*

The Committee will analyze the annual reports to be submitted by THE PARTIES involved concerning the way in which they will implement the commitments on the subjects of national reconciliation, human rights, electoral processes, and refugees.

In addition, the Committee will receive reports from organizations or individuals who wish to contribute with useful information to ensure compliance with its mandates.

The Committee will gather the information it considers pertinent; to that effect, the Party mentioned in the report will allow members of the Committee to enter in its territory and will give them all the necessary facilities.

The Committee will prepare an annual report and as many special reports as it considers necessary on the compliance of the commitments, including the pertinent conclusions and recommendations, as warranted.

The Committee will submit its reports to the Parties involved and to the Contadora Group Governments. At the conclusion of the deadline established in the regulations for the Committee to receive observations from the countries involved, the Committee will prepare the final reports which will be made public, unless the Committee itself decides the contrary.

c) *Internal Regulations*

The Committee will draft its own internal regulations which will be made known to the Parties involved.

d) *Installation*

The Committee will be installed with the implementation of the Act.

B. Verification and Control Commission on Security Matters

a) *Membership*

The Commission will be made up of four members, representatives from four States with well-known reputations for being unbiased and with a genuine interest to help solve the Central American crisis. They will be proposed by the Contadora Group and accepted by all the Parties.

A Latin American Executive Secretary with technical and administrative duties, proposed by the Contadora Group and accepted by the common agreement of all the Parties, will guarantee the permanent operation of the Commission.

b) *Operation*

To fulfill its duties, the Commission will have an international team of inspectors, supplied by the States that make up the Commission and coordinated by an Operations Director.

The international team of inspectors will fulfill duties established by the Commission, with any changes it may indicate or establish in its internal regulations.

The international team of inspectors will have all the human and material resources that the Commission may decide to assign to it in order to guarantee that the security commitments are strictly fulfilled. Its actions will be expeditious and thorough.

THE PARTIES promise to fully cooperate with the Commission so that it can fulfill its duty.

The Commission will have a Consultative Committee to help the Commission do its job better. This Committee will include a representative from each Central American State and their duties will be the following:

1. To serve as a link between the Verification and Control Commission and the Parties.
2. To help in the fulfillment of the duties assigned to the Verification and Control Commission.
3. To help, at the request of the Commission, resolve incidents and controversies quickly.

— The Commission may invite one representative from the UN Secretary General and one from the OAS, as observers, to its meetings.
— The Commission can establish auxiliary organizations and seek the help of any existing Joint Security Commissions.

c) *Duties of the Commission*

The Commission will guarantee that security commitments are fulfilled. To this end, it will:

— Verify the compliance of commitments regarding military maneuvers mentioned in this Act.
— Confirm that war material purchases are suspended and that military troops are not increased in line with what is established in point a) of the first stage of 19 of Chapter III of Part I of this Act.
— Simultaneously receive from all the Parties the respective inventories on their current weapons, military installations, and armed troops in line with point b) of the first stage of 19 of Chapter III of Part I of this Act.
— Conduct technical studies in line with what is stated in point c) of the first stage of 19 of Chapter III of Part I of this Act.
— Check that all the Parties are staying within the maximum limits that were agreed upon or that are temporarily in effect in regard to the various categories of weapons, military installations, and armed troops. It will also verify that the weapons reduction schedules that were agreed upon or that are temporarily in effect will be kept.
— Verify that the purchases of replacements, ammunitions, spare parts,

and equipment replacements will be compatible with the inventories and registries delivered by the Parties in advance and with the limits and deadlines that were agreed upon or that are temporarily in effect.
— To verify that no new weapons systems capable of qualitatively and quantitatively modifying the current inventories of war material are introduced and no weapons banned in the present document are introduced, held, or used.
— To set up a record of all transactions in weapons by the Parties, including donations or transfers of weapons.
— To verify compliance with the commitment undertaken by the Parties of initiating and finalizing constitutional arrangements to sign, ratify, or adhere to treaties or other international agreements in matters of disarmament and to follow-up on actions aimed at achieving such purpose.
— To receive simultaneously from the Parties the listing of foreign bases, schools, and installations of a military nature and to verify that they are dismantled in accordance with the provisions of this document.
— To receive the census of foreign military advisers and other foreign personnel who participate in military and security activities and to make certain that they are withdrawn in accordance with the recommendations of the Verification and Control Commission.
— To verify compliance with this document in matters of arms smuggling and to review all charges in that regard. To do so, the following criteria must be borne in mind:
  1. Origin of the arms smuggling; port or airport of shipment of the weapons, ammunition, equipment or other types of military supplies bound for the Central American region.
  2. Personnel involved: persons, groups, and organizations that took part in the arrangements for or accomplishment of the arms smuggling, including the participation of governments, their representatives, or intermediaries.
  3. Type of armament, ammunition, equipment, and other types of military supplies; type and caliber of weapons; country of manufacture; country of origin; and the quantities of each type of weapon, ammunition, equipment, and other types of military supplies.
  4. Extraregional means of transportation: land, maritime, or air means, including nationality.
  5. Extraregional transport routes: to define routes used, including stops, or intermediate destination points.
  6. Places of storage of weapons, ammunition, equipment, and other types of military supplies.
  7. Intraregional traffic areas and routes: description of areas and routes; participation or consent by government or other sectors in the accomplishment of the arms smuggling; frequency of use of these areas or routes.

8. Intraregional means of transportation: determination of means of transportation used, owners of such means, facilities granted by governments, government sectors, and others, and other modes of delivery.

9. Receiving entity or consignee: determination of persons, groups, and organizations to which the smuggled weapons are consigned.

— To verify compliance with the present document with regard to irregular forces and the non-use of a country's own territory to carry out destabilization actions against another State as well as to review all charges in that regard. To do so, the following criteria must be borne in mind:

1. Installations, means, bases, camps, or facilities for logistical and operational support to irregular forces, including command centers, radio communications centers, and radio stations.

2. Determination of propaganda activities or political, material, economic, or military support of actions against any State in the region.

3. Identification of persons, groups, and government sectors involved in such actions.

— To verify compliance with commitments in matters of terrorism, subversion, and sabotage stipulated in this document. The Commission and the States-Parties may ask, whenever they deem it advisable, the Red Cross International Committee for its assistance in resolving the problems of a humanitarian nature that are plaguing the Central American countries.

d) *Norms and Procedures*

— The Commission will receive all properly filed accusations regarding violations of security agreements reached in the present plan; it will report to the Parties involved and will begin the investigations of the case.

It will also have the power to carry out, of its own account, the investigations deemed necessary.

— The Commission will carry out its investigations by *in situ* inspection, the gathering of reports, and any other procedure deemed necessary to carry out its functions.

— Without interfering with its special quarterly reports, the Commission will file, in the case of a reported violation or the unfulfillment of the agreements of the present plan in matters of security, a report with the recommendations to the Parties involved.

— The Commission will receive from the Parties all facilities and their prompt and full cooperation to achieve an adequate fulfillment of its functions. It will also make sure that all information gathered and received during the investigations is kept confidential.

— The Commission will send confidential reports and recommendations to the Party states and to the Contadora Group Governments. It can make them public when it considers that this will contribute to the fulfillment of the agreements established in the Plan.

    e) *Internal Regulation*
      — Once appointed, the Commission will draft its own internal regulations in consultation with the Party States.
    f) *Duration of the Commission Members' Mandate*
      — The representatives of the member-states of the Commission will be initially appointed for a two-year period, which can be extended by common agreement among the participant Parties and States.
    g) *Installation*
      — The Commission will be installed at the moment that the Plan is signed.
C. Ad Hoc Committee for the Evaluation and Follow-up of the Economic and Social Commitments
    a) *Integration*
      — Regarding the present plan, the Central American economy ministers meeting will become the Ad Hoc Committee for the evaluation and follow-up of the economic and social commitments.
      — The Committee will have a Technical and Administrative Secretariat, which will ensure its permanent operation, and whose work will be carried out by the Secretariat of Central American Economic Integration, SIECA.
    b) *Functions*
      — The Committee will receive annual reports from the Parties regarding progress in complying with the agreements on economic and social matters.
      — The Committee will make a periodic evaluation of the progress made in carrying out the agreements on economic and social matters, making use of the information provided by the Parties as well as competent international and regional organizations.
      — The Committee will submit in its periodic reports, proposals for strengthening regional cooperation and promoting development plans, placing special emphasis on the aspects established in the agreements of the Plan.
4. Financing of Implementation and Continuation Mechanisms
    a) The implementation and continuation mechanisms referred to in Part II of the Plan will be financed by a fund for peace in Central America.
    b) The resources for this fund will be obtained from equal contributions from the Party-States, and from additional contributions obtained from other States, international organizations, and other sources, which can be sought by the Central American countries with the cooperation of the Contadora Group.

PART III
FINAL PROVISIONS

1. The obligations agreed upon by all Parties in this Act and its Annex are legally binding. Therefore, they are commitments.

2. This Act shall be ratified according to constitutional procedures established by all Central American Governments. Every Government that signs shall present its ratification procedure to the Foreign Ministry of the Republic of Panama.

3. This Act shall be in effect eight days after the date in which the fifth procedure is presented.

4. From the date the Act is signed until the date it goes into effect, all Parties shall refrain from carrying out actions that could frustrate the object and the purpose of the Act, and in addition they shall try in good faith, according to their internal laws, to adopt individual measures that can facilitate the functioning of the mechanisms referred to in Part II.

5. Any dispute regarding the interpretation or the implementation of this Act that could not have been settled through the mechanisms established in Part II shall be submitted to the Foreign Ministers of the Parties involved for their consideration and decision, by unanimity.

6. In case the dispute persists, the Foreign Ministers of the Contadora Group, upon request by any of the Parties involved, shall intervene so that they may resolve the dispute. If this option does not work the Foreign Ministers of the Contadora Group may suggest another means for the peaceful resolution of the dispute in accordance with Article 33 of the UN Charter and Article 24 of the OAS Charter.
   If after 30 days there has been no agreement between the sides regarding the implementation of the suggested procedure, any of them may release the considerations, reports, or recommendations of the implementation and follow-up mechanisms established in Part II of this Act regarding the dispute.

7. This Act does not allow reservations.

8. The Annex and the additional entries I through IV are integral parts of this Act.

9. This Act shall be in effect for five years, and may be extended for five-year periods except if any of the Parties announces six months before the five-year period ends its decision against extension. Six months before the expiration date of each period, the Governments of each Party and the Contadora Group shall meet at the request of any of the Parties to evaluate it and adopt the provisions they consider necessary.

10. This Act shall be registered by all Parties at the UN Secretary General's Office according to Article 102 of the UN Charter.

The Foreign Ministers of the Central American Governments hereby have signed this Act in the Spanish language in six originals, one of which shall remain at the Foreign Ministry of the Republic of Panama.

ANNEX

THE PARTIES agree on the following definitions of military terms:

1. Registry: Numerical or graphic information on military, paramilitary, and security troops, as well as on military installations.

2. Inventory: A detailed report on nationally or foreign owned arms and military equipment with as many specifications as possible.
3. Census: Numerical information on foreign military or civilian personnel who function as advisers on defense and/or security issues.
4. Military Installation: An establishment or infrastructure that includes airports, garrisons, bases, camps, air and naval installations, or similar installations under military jurisdiction, including their geographical location.
5. Organization and Equipment Table (TOE): A document that contains the mission, organization, equipment, capabilities, and limitations of a typical military unit at its different levels.
6. Military Equipment: National or foreign-owned individual or joint materials used by a military force for subsistence and operations. Weapons are not included.
7. Weapons classification:
    a) By their type:
        i) Conventional;
        ii) Chemical;
        iii) Biological;
        iv) Radiological.
    b) By their range:
        i) Short: Portable weapons operated by individuals or teams;
        ii) Medium: Non-portable support weapons (mortars, shells and cannons);
        iii) Long: Rockets and guided missiles, which are broken down as follows:
            a) Short-range rockets: Their maximum range is less than twenty (20) kilometres;
            b) Long-range rockets: Their range is of twenty (20) kilometres;
            c) Short-range guided missile: Its maximum range is up to one hundred (100) kilometres;
            d) Medium-range guided missile: Its range is greater than one hundred (100) kilometres, but less than five hundred (500) kilometres;
            e) Long-range guided missile: Its range is from five hundred (500) kilometres up.
    c) By their caliber and weight:
        i) Light: One hundred and twenty (120) millimetres or less;
        ii) Medium: More than one hundred and twenty (120) millimetres and less than one hundred and sixty (160) millimetres;
        iii) Heavy: More than one hundred and sixty (160) millimetres and less than two hundred and ten (210) millimetres;
        iv) Very heavy: More than two hundred and ten (210) millimetres.
    d) By their trajectory:
        i) Weapons with flat trajectory fire:
        ii) Weapons with a curved trajectory:
            a) Mortars;
            b) Shells;
            c) Cannons;
            d) Rockets.

e) By their mode of transportation:
   i) On foot;
   ii) Horse-drawn;
   iii) Towed or track equipped;
   iv) Self-propelled;
   v) All of the weapons that can be transported by highway, railrod, ship, or air;
   vi) Those transported by air are classified as follows:
      a) Transported by helicopter;
      b) Transported by airplane.
8. Characteristics of the different types of airplanes and helicopters that should be considered:
   a) Model;
   b) Quantity;
   c) Crew;
   d) Manufacturer;
   e) Speed;
   f) Capacity;
   g) Propulsion system;
   h) Armored or not armored;
   i) Type of weapons;
   j) Radius of action;
   k) Navigation system;
   l) Communications system;
   m) Type of mission it fulfills.
9. Characteristics to be considered in the different types of ships:
   a) Type of ship;
   b) Shipyard and year of manufacture;
   c) Tonnage;
   d) Displacement capacity;
   e) Draught;
   f) Length;
   g) Propulsion system;
   h) Type of weaponry and firing system;
   i) Crew.
10. Services: Logistical and administrative organizations that provide overall support to the military, paramilitary, and security forces.
11. Military Education Centers: Installations used for the education, instruction, and training of military personnel at the various levels and fields of specialization.
12. Military Base: Surface, maritime, or air space that houses military installations, personnel, and equipment under a military command. The definition of foreign military base must take into consideration the following factors:
   a) Its administration and control;
   b) Sources of financing;
   c) The percentile ratio of local and foreign personnel;
   d) Bilateral agreements;
   e) Its location and geographical area;

f) Transfer of part of the territory to another State;

g) Number of troops.

13. Foreign Military Installations: those which have been built for use by foreign units in maneuvers, training, or other military purposes, in accordance with bilateral treaties or agreements. Said installations may be of a temporary or permanent nature.

14. Foreign Military Advisers: the terms military and security adviser will be understood as foreign military or civilian personnel who carry out technical, training, or advisory functions in the following operational areas: tactical, logistical, organizational and security, in the ground, sea, air, or security forces in the Central American States under agreements with one or several Governments.

15. Arms Traffic: arms traffic will be understood as all kinds of transfers by governments, individuals, or regional or extraregional groups of arms for use by irregular forces or armed bands seeking to destabilize governments in the region. This also includes the passage of said traffic through the territory of a third State with or without consent, for said groups in another State.

16. Domestic Military Maneuvers: Are combat or war exercises or games conducted in times of peace by troops for training purposes. The armed forces of the country participate in these on their own territory and they can include the use of ground, sea and air units for the purpose of increasing their operational capacity.

17. International Military Maneuvers: Are all those operations conducted by the armed forces of two or more countries in the territory of one of these countries or in international zones, including ground, sea, and air units, with the purpose of increasing their operational capacity and developing measures of joint coordination.

18. The inventories prepared in each State and separately by each of its service branches, taking into account the troops, arms and ammunition, equipment and installations of the forces that are enumerated below, in accordance with their peculiar modes of organization.

a) Security Forces:

   1. Border guards;

   2. Urban and rural guards;

   3. Military forces assigned to other ministries;

   4. Public security forces;

   5. Education and training centers;

   6. Others.

b) Naval Forces:

   1. Localization;

   2. Kind of base;

   3. Number and characteristics of the naval fleet. All kinds of armaments;

   4. Defense systems. Kinds of armaments;

   5. Communication systems;

   6. War services and materiel;

   7. Air or ground transportation services;

   8. Health services;

   9. Maintenance services;

     10. Quartermaster services;
     11. Recruitment and time in service;
     12. Education and training center;
     13. Others.
c) Air Forces:
     1. Localization;
     2. Airstrip capacity;
     3. Number of characteristics of the air fleet. Kind of armaments;
     4. Defense systems. Kinds of armaments;
     5. Communication systems;
     6. War materiel services;
     7. Sanitation services;
     8. Land transportation services;
     9. Training centers;
     10. Maintenance services;
     11. Quartermaster services;
     12. Recruitment and time in service;
     13. Others.
d) Army Forces:
     1. Infantry;
     2. Mechanized infantry;
     3. Airborne infantry;
     4. Cavalry;
     5. Artillery;
     6. Armored;
     7. Communications;
     8. Engineers;
     9. Special troops;
     10. Reconnaissance troops;
     11. Sanitation services;
     12. Transportation services;
     13. War materiel services;
     14. Maintenance services;
     15. Quartermaster services;
     16. Military police;
     17. Training center;
     18. Accurate information regarding the system of recruitment and time in service should be included in this document;
     19. Others.
e) Paramilitary forces.
f) Information requirements for airports; existing airfields:
     1. Details on location and category;
     2. Location of installations;
     3. Dimension of the take-off, taxiing, and maintenance strips;
     4. Facilities: buildings, maintenance installations, fuel supply, navigation aids, communications systems.

g) Information requirements for terminals and ports:
   1. Location and general characteristics;
   2. Main and accessory channels;
   3. Breakwaters;
   4. Capacity of the terminal.
h) Personnel: in regard to personnel, numerical information on troops on active duty, in the reserves, and in the security forces and paramilitary organizations is required. Likewise, immigration status, specialty, nationality, and time spent in the country, as well as agreements and contracts, depending on the case.
i) Regarding weapons, all types of ammunition, explosives, ammunition for portable weapons, artillery, bombs and torpedoes, rockets, hand and rifle grenades, depth charges, land and sea mines, fuses, mortar grenades and shells, etc., must be included.
j) Regarding national and foreign military installations, hospitals and military first aid centers, naval bases, airports, and landing strips must be included.
19. Reasonable balance of forces: A reasonable balance of forces is the balance that results from summing up the States' military forces, taking into account their needs in order to preserve their sovereignty, political independence, security, and territorial integrity.

ANNEX I
ADDITIONAL PROTOCOL I TO THE CONTADORA ACT ON PEACE AND COOPERATION IN CENTRAL AMERICA

THE GOVERNMENTS of Colombia, Mexico, Panama, and Venezuela, desiring to continue contributing to the achievement of the goals of peace and cooperation in Central America contained in the Contadora Act for Peace and Cooperation in Central America,

Have agreed:

1. To cooperate with the Central American States in the achievement of the objectives and goals of the document.
2. To lend their support for the establishment and implementation of the mechanisms of execution and follow-up stated in the document.
3. To contribute to the peaceful resolution of controversies that might stem from the application or interpretation of the Act, in accordance with the provisions of Part III of the Act.
4. No reservations may be made to this Protocol.
5. This Protocol shall enter into force for each signatory State on the date of deposit of its respective instrument of ratification, which must be done simultaneously in the General Secretariats of the United Nations and the OAS.
6. This Protocol will be registered in the UN General Secretariat pursuant to Article 102 of the UN Charter.

In witness thereof the undersigned plenipotentiaries, being duly authorized by their respective Governments, have signed this Protocol: The Government of the Republic of Colombia; the Government of the Republic of Panama; the Government of the United Mexican States; and the Government of the Republic of Venezuela.

ANNEX II
ADDITIONAL PROTOCOL II TO THE CONTADORA ACT ON PEACE AND COOPERATION IN CENTRAL AMERICA

THE UNDERSIGNED PLENIPOTENTIARIES, representatives of States of the American continent, duly authorized by their respective Governments,

CONVINCED that the effective cooperation of the States of the continent is necessary to guarantee the implementation, effectiveness, and viability of the Contadora Act for Peace and Cooperation in Central America,

Have agreed:

1. To refrain from actions that would frustrate the aim and objective of the Act.
2. To cooperate with the Central American States in the attainment of the aim and objective of the Act.
3. To give all their support to the fulfillment of the functions of the implementation and follow-up mechanisms established in the Act, whenever the Parties so demand.
4. No reservations can be made to this Protocol.
5. This Protocol shall be open for signature of all the States of the American continent.
6. This Protocol shall enter into force for each signatory State on the date of deposit of its respective instrument of ratification in the General Secretariat of the United Nations in accordance with Article 102 of the UN Charter.

This Protocol, whose Spanish, English, French, and Portuguese texts are equally authentic, shall be open for signature in the UN General Secretariat.

ANNEX III
ADDITIONAL PROTOCOL III TO THE CONTADORA ACT ON PEACE AND COOPERATION IN CENTRAL AMERICA

THE UNDERSIGNED PLENIPOTENTIARIES, representatives of States of the American continent, duly authorized by their respective governments,

CONVINCED that the effective cooperation of the international community is necessary to guarantee the implementation, effectiveness, and viability of the Contadora Act for Peace and Cooperation in Central America,

Have agreed:

1. To respect the commitments adopted by the Central American Governments.

2. To refrain from actions that would frustrate the aim and objective of the Act.
3. To cooperate to the extent possible with the Central American States in the economic and social development of the region.
4. No reservations can be made to this Protocol.
5. This Protocol shall be open for signature of all the States that wish to contribute to peace and cooperation in Central America.
6. This Protocol shall enter into force for each signatory State on the date of deposit of the respective instrument of ratification in the UN General Secretariat.
7. This Protocol shall be registered in the UN General Secretariat pursuant to Article 102 of the UN Charter.

This Protocol, the copies of which in the official languages of the United Nations are all genuine, will be placed for signing at the UN Secretariat General in New York City.

ADDITIONAL ANNEX IV
ADDITIONAL PROTOCOL IV TO THE CONTADORA ACT ON PEACE AND COOPERATION IN CENTRAL AMERICA

THE PLENIPOTENTIARIES who sign this document invested with full powers from their respective Governments,

CONVINCED that it is necessary to guarantee the fulfillment of the commitments made by the Contadora Document for Peace and Cooperation in Central America,

Have agreed:

1. To accept the invitation to participate in and cooperate with the establishment and implementation of the mechanisms of execution and follow-up as stated in the document in the terms agreed upon by THE PARTIES through agreements that will be annexed to this Protocol.
2. To be fully impartial in implementing the mechanisms of execution and follow-up.
3. This Protocol will be placed for the signature of the States proposed by the Contadora Group and agreed upon by all Parties.
4. This Protocol will be in effect for each State on the date that the State ratifies this Protocol at the UN Secretariat General.
5. This Protocol does not allow any exceptions.
6. This Protocol will be registered at the UN Secretariat General, in accordance with Article 102 of the Charter of the Organization.

This Protocol, the copies of which in the official languages of the United Nations are all genuine, will be placed for signature at the UN Secretariat General in New York City.

Report on the Meeting of a Secret Regional Caucus, Managua (January 1983)

Despite their deep-rooted conviction that social democracy is a reformist bourgeois doctrine, Leninist parties have seen in the social democratic parties and in their international organization (the Socialist International) useful tactical allies. This utilitarian perception was illustrated by several of the secret documents of the New Jewel Movement (NJM) captured in Grenada in October 1983. It is noteworthy that the regional caucus organized by the Grenadian NJM and the Nicaraguan FSLN on January 6–7, 1983, was secret.

The report of this meeting clearly illustrates how the FSLN and the NJM, both Leninist-oriented ruling parties, were dividing the membership of the Socialist International into parties "that are against us" and friendly, "progressive parties." The latter were considered useful tactical allies, the most progressive among them being those within a "Marxist–Leninist trend," that is, the FSLN and the NJM. The FSLN representative to the secret caucus was Dr. Antonio Jarquín, erroneously named Harguin and Marguin in the report. This document, which was written in Grenada, was published earlier by Jiri Valenta and Herbert J. Ellison (eds.), in *Grenada and Soviet/ Cuban Policy: Internal Crisis and U.S./OECS. Intervention* (Boulder, Colorado: Westview Press, 1986).

The following organizations were represented:

FSLN	Nicaragua	Antonio Marquin
MNR	El Salvador	Hector Oqueli
RP	Chile	Freda
PNP	Jamaica	Paul Miller
PCC	Cuba	Silva
NJM	Grenada	Chris DeRiggs

The following items constituted the agenda.

1. An analysis of the balance of forces within the Socialist International (SI)
   —The regional situation
   —The international situation
2. Initiatives to be taken to strengthen the position of progressive forces of Latin America and the Caribbean within the organization
3. Initiatives to neutralize forces within the SI that are against us.
4. Upcoming activities of SI—regionally and internationally.
5. Activities of Copaal—combining SI work with Copaal work
6. Conference on non-intervention and peace in Central America
7. Political character of projected growth of SI—conference of African SI.
8. Structure of SI
   —Chairmanship of regional committee
   —Proposed regional executive secretary
9. Proposed Institute of Economic and Political Studies
10. ALDHO (Latin American Human Rights Organization)
11. Work of social democracy in the region

The meeting was organized for the purpose of deepening the process of coordination among the most progressive SI forces in Latin America and the Caribbean with a view towards expanding the influence of the Region as a whole in the organization and outlining a number of concrete initiatives related to the upcoming Congress of SI in Sydney, Australia.

The meeting was chaired by Antonio Harguin of the International Relations department of the FSLN.

I. ANALYSIS

1. *Regional situation:* The progressive forces are in control.
   a. There are fourteen members of the SI Committee for Latin America and the Caribbean. Of these fourteen, there are seven parties that are generally progressive and some within a Marxist–Leninist trend.

b. There are three new parties that have recently gained consultative observer status in SI. They are:

   i) Puerto Rico,
   ii) WPA—Guyana,
   iii) PLP—St. Lucia.

The presence of these parties will help to strengthen the influence of the progressive forces within the Regional Committee. These parties can, in effect, function like full members of the organization. We must always consult with them and keep them informed.

2. *Europe in relation to Latin America*
   a. There are sharp divisions among the European parties in their outlook on Latin America.
   b. Our friends in this area are prepared to accept the Latin American revolutionary process as being palatable if restricted to the Latin American context.
   c. There is a great amount of misunderstanding about Latin America, both among our friends and our enemies—some amount of fear and uncertainty.
   d. Many of the European SI parties expect us to understand the concept of "the Soviet Menace."
   e. Some European parties are concerned that by the Latin American presence in SI, they have let in a
   f. Many European parties are willing to hold discussions with us at levels that indicate the contradictions among themselves—the difference between Kryski of Austria and Braudl of Germany on the PLO question.
   g. Our strongest allies in Europe are the Nordic SI parties and that of Holland. There is also good potential with the UDP of Canada.
   h. Our principal enemies are to be found among the parties of Soares and Horgo in Portugal and Italy respectively—the Social Democrats of the USA are also our sworn enemies.
   i. The reason why the European parties did not allow WPA and PLP to get beyond the consultative membership status is because of their fear of the growth of membership with parties that they do not control.
   j. A Mission to Europe comprising of our most trusted forces in Latin America and the Caribbean can be strategically valuable before the Sydney Congress. It can help assure our friends and confuse our enemies.

II. DECISIONS

1. The next meeting of the Broad Latin American Region SI Committee will be in any one of the following places:

   La Paz, Bolivia
   Mexico

Caracas
Canada

Michael Manley of PNP and Auselmo Sule of PR will coordinate with B. Carlson of the SI Secretariat on this matter. Member parties will be informed accordingly.

2. A broad resolution on the Latin American and Caribbean situation will be passed at the meeting of the Regional Committee.

   Agenda for this meeting will include:
   a. Analysis of current political situation
   b. Attitudes to SI in Latin America
   c. Issues for Sydney:
      i) New situation
      ii) Expansion of SI
   d. SI Latin American Committee:
      i) Structure
      ii) Staff
      iii) Officers
   e. Christian Democracy in Latin America
   f. Actions to strengthen ALDHU
   g. Sydney Resolutions

3. Hector Oquel of MNR of El Salvador will draft a resolution on Latin America and the Caribbean by January 31, 1983. This Resolution will be specifically for the Sydney Congress and will address only the most major issues.

   The following guidelines will be the basis for the resolution:

   a. The Basle Resolution—including such themes as Peace and non-intervention, antimilitarisation, in the Region, Anti-Dictatorship, the settlement of disputes, etc.
   b. Solidarity with Nicaragua, Grenada and the FDR, FMLN, and MNR of El Salvador.
   c. A limited number of all key issues in the region.
   d. The creation of a platform and frame of reference in SI for the approach on the Latin American and Caribbean region until the next Congress in Belgium (in the subsequent 2 years).

4. Subject to the approval of NJM, the next meeting of the Secret Regional Caucus of Progressive SI parties will be in Grenada around March 13 and 14. This meeting will have strategic value in that it will provide the opportunity to:
   i. Assess the result of the tour of Europe by the selected parties, and
   ii. Conduct a final assessment on issues relating to the Sydney Congress— questions on tactics and levels of coordination can also be discussed.

[No Item 5 in original document]

6. Grenada should consider inviting a few key SI personalities to March 13 celebrations.
7. Bilaterals will be held with new regional SI forces before Congress—Grenada will speak with WPA and PLP.

8. In the meeting in Grenada, we are going to consider what initiatives can be taken to support Surinam. If the Surinam government wishes, an unofficial familiarization visit can be organized subsequent to proposed Grenada meeting.

This, it is felt, may have value in preparing members of the Regional Caucus to be able to speak with authority if the question of Surinam is raised in Sydney. If a decision is made to go ahead with this, the team can comprise Radical Part of Chile, FSLN, PNP, NDP.

NJM will establish contact with Surinam and guide the Regional Secret Caucus accordingly.

At the meeting of the SI Resolution Committee and Finance Committee in Madrid and Italy respectively during the middle of February, Regional parties should try to have the possible presence. Subsequent to the Madrid and Italy meetings, a tour of Europe should be organized to hold bilaterals with all European parties who belong to SI.

The participants of this mission should include:
Ungo of MNR
Oquel of MNR
Sule of PR
Manley of PNP
Miller of PNP
A senior representative of NJM

This mission will seek to counter the forces of Portugal, Italy, and the U.S.

Seek to spread discussion within hostile European parties.

Work of the expulsion of the (CIA) U.S. Social Democratic party.

9. Progressive SI forces in the Region should seek to attend Copaal meeting scheduled for Brazil in March and secure reinforcement of the Sydney SILA Resolution.

10. To push ahead and implement the proposal for the establishment of a Regional Institute for Political and Economic Research.

—Paul Miller of Jamaica as director
—Open bank account in the Bahamas with signatures of Miller and Hector Oquel.

Maintain the Secret Regional Caucus with periodic and special meetings.

Review membership in the future.

Submitted by
CDE, Chris De Riggs

(Chris De Riggs was a NJM leader involved in the conspiracy against Prime Minister Maurice Bishop in October, 1983.)

Bibliography

Books and Monographs

A Revolution Beyond Our Borders: Sandinista Intervention in Central America. Washington, D.C.: U.S. Department of State, September 1985.

Aguilera, Gabriel. *La Integración Militar en Centroaméica* [Military Integration in Central America]. Guatemala: Instituto Centroamericano de Estudios Políticos (INCEP) (n.d.).

Alaniz Pinell, Jorge. *Nicaragua, La Revolución Reaccionaria [Nicaragua, the Reactionary Revolution]*. Panama: Editorial Kosmos, 1985.

Alexander, Robert J. *Communism in Latin America*. New Brunswick, NJ: Rutgers University Press, 1957.

Análisis de la Coyuntura y Tareas de la Revolución Popular Sandinista [Analysis of the Conjuncture and Tasks of the Sandinista Popular Revolution]. Managua: Meeting of the FSLN's National Directorate, September 21–23, 1979.

Apuntes: Curso Sobre la Problemática Actual [Notes: A Course on the Current Problems]. Managua: Department of Social Sciences, History Section, Universidad Nacional Autónoma de Nicaragua (n.d.).

Apuntes de Historia de Nicaragua [Notes on the History of Nicaragua] (2 vols). Managua: Department of Social Sciences, History Section, Universidad Nacional Autónoma de Nicaragua, 1982.

Arce, Bayardo. *Las Fuerzas Motrices antes y después de la Revolución*. [The Driving Forces before and after the Revolution]. Managua: Sección de Propaganda y Educación Política del FSLN, 1980.

Arellano, Jorge Eduardo. *Lecciones de Sandinismo: Doce Ensayos* [Lessons of Sandinism: Twelve Essays]. Ministerio de Educación Pública. Talleres del Instituto La Salle (León: August, 1981).

Argüello, Álvaro (Ed.) *Fe Cristiana y Revolución Sandinista en Nicaragua* [Christian Faith and Sandinista Revolution in Nicaragua]. Managua: Instituto Histórico Centroamericano, 1980.

Baez, Gladys, Omar Cabezas, Ana Julia Guido, *et al. Testimonios sobre la Reforma Agraria* [Testimonies on the Agrarian Reform]. Managua: Centro de Investigaciones y Estudios de la Reforma Agraria (CIERA), 1985.

Barahona, Amaru. *Estudio sobre la Historia Contemporánea de Nicaragua* [Study on the Contemporary History of Nicaragua]. Managua: Primer Congreso de Científicos Sociales Nicaragüenses, September 1976.

Belli, Humberto. *Una Iglesia en Peligro* [An Endangered Church]. San José, Costa Rica: Comité Ecuménico Para Defensa de Religión y Culto en Nicaragua (CEDRENIC), 1983.

Black, George. *Triumph of the People: The Sandinista Revolution*. London: Zed Press, 1981.

Borge, Tomás. *El Axioma de la Esperanza* [The Axiom of Hope]. Bilbāo: Editorial Desclee de Brouwer, 1984.

Borge, Tomás. *Los Primeros Pasos: La Revolución Popular Sandinista* [The First Steps: The Sandinista Popular Revolution]. Mexico: Siglo Veintiuno, 1981.

Borge, Tomás. *Historia Político–Militar del FSLN* [Political–Military History of FSLN]. Managua: Editorial Universidad Centroamericana (UCA), 1980.

Brutents, Karen. *The Newly Freed Countries in the Seventies*. Moscow: Progress Publications, 1983.

Cabezas, Omar. *La Montaña Es Algo más que Una Estepa Verde* [The Wilderness Is Something More Than a Green Steppe]. Mexico: Siglo XXI, 1985.

Calendario de Incidentes entre el Gobierno de Costa Rica y el Gobierno de Nicaragua [Calendar of Incidents between the Government of Costa Rica and the Government of Nicaragua]. San José, Costa Rica: Ministry of Foreign Relations, 1985.

Cannabrava Filho, Paulo. *Tras los Pasos de Sandino: Nicaragua, 1978* [In the Footsteps of Sandino: Nicaragua, 1978]. Madrid: Ediciones Encuentro, 1978.

Carácter y Perspectivas de la Revolución en Nicaragua [Characteristics and Perspectives of the Revolution in Nicaragua]. Managua: Centro de Investigación de la Realidad Nacional, Universidad Centroamericana (UCA), September 1984.

Cardenal, Ernesto. *En Cuba* [In Cuba]. Mexico: Serie Popular ERA, 1977.

Cardenal, Ernesto. *Antología* [Anthology]. Managua: Editorial Nueva Nicaragua, 1983.

de Castilla, Miguel. *Educación y Lucha de Clases en Nicaragua* [Education and Class Struggle in Nicaragua]. Managua: Editorial Universitaria, Universidad Centroamericana (UCA), 1980.

Castillo, Donald. *Acumulación de Capital y Empresas Transnacionales en Centroamérica* [Accumulation of Capital and Transnational Corporations in Central America]. Mexico: Editorial Siglo XXI, 1980.

Castillo, Donald (Ed.). *Centroamérica más Allá de la Crisis* [Central America Beyond the Crisis]. Mexico: Ediciones SIAP, June 1983.

Cepeda Ulloa, Fernando and Rodrigo Pardo García (Eds.). *Contadora: Desafío a la Diplomacia Tradicional* [Contadora: A Challenge to Traditional Diplomacy]. Bogotá, Colombia: Editorial la Oveja Negra, 1985.

Chamorro Cardenal, Pedro Joaquín. *La Patria de Pedro: El Pensamiento Nicaragüense de Pedro Joaquín Chamorro* [The Fatherland of Pedro: The Nicaraguan Thought of Pedro Joaquín Chamorro]. Managua: La Prensa, 1981.

Christian, Shirley. *Nicaragua. Revolution in the Family*. New York: Random House, 1985.

Cole Chamorro, Alejandro. *145 Años de Historia Política de Nicaragua* [145 Years of Nicaraguan Political History]. Managua: Editora Nicaragüense, January, 1967.

Collins, Joseph. *What Difference Could a Revolution Make*. San Francisco: Food First Editors, 1981.

Communist Interference in El Salvador. Washington, D.C.: U.S. Department of State, Special Report, No. 80., February 1981.

Conflict in Nicaragua: National, Regional and International Dimensions. A Conference Report.

University of Miami and the Royal Institute of International Affairs at Chatham House, London, United Kingdom (28–30 April 1986).

Coraggio, José Luís and George Irwin. "Revolution and Pluralism in Nicaragua." In George Erwin and Xavier Gorostiaga (Eds.), *Towards an Alternative for Central America and the Caribbean*. The Hague: Institute of Social Studies, 1984.

Country Reports on Human Rights Practices for 1983. Washington, D.C.: Government Printing Office, February 1984, p. 636.

Country Reports on Human Rights Practices, 1984. Washington, D.C.: Government Printing Office, pp. 608–624.

Czarkowski, Robert. *De Polonia a Nicaragua* [From Poland to Nicaragua]. San José, Costa Rica: Talleres Gráficos Hermanos Trejos, 1984.

Diederich, Bernard. *Somoza and the Legacy of U.S. Involvement in Central America*. New York: Dutton, 1981.

The Dilemma Confronting the Sandinista Revolution: Three Years After the Victory. Managua: Instituto Histórico Centroamericano (IHCA), July 1982.

La Dirección Nacional en el primer Encuentro Internacional de Solidaridad con Nicaragua [The National Directorate in the First International Meeting of Solidarity with Nicaragua]. Managua: Secretaría Nacional de Educación y Propaganda Política del FSLN, Colección Juan de Dios Muñoz, 1981.

Escobar, José Benito. *Rigoberto López Pérez: El Principio Del Fin* [Rigoberto López Pérez: The Beginning of the End]. Managua: Secretaría Nacional de Educación y Propaganda Política del FSLN, Colección Juan de Dios Muñoz, 1980.

Estado y Clases Sociales en Nicaragua (State and Social Classes in Nicaragua). Managua: Segundo Congreso de la Asociación Nicaragüense de Cientistas Sociales, Colección Blas Real Espinales, 1982.

Evers, Tilman. *El Estado y la Periferia Capitalista* [The State and the Capitalist Periphery]. Mexico: Editorial Siglo XXI, 1979.

Farer, Tom J. *The U.S. and the War in Central America: A Legal Perspective*. Paper presented at the University of New Mexico School of Law, May 12, 1983.

Feinberg, Richard E. (Ed.). *Central America: The International Dimensions of the Crisis*. New York: Holmes and Meier, 1982.

Fonseca, Carlos. *Bajo la Bandera del Sandinismo: Textos Políticos* [Under the Banner of Sandinismo: Political Writings]. Managua: Editorial Nueva Nicaragua, 1981.

Fonseca, Carlos. "Nicaragua: Zero Hour." *The Sandinistas Speak*. New York: Pathfinder Press, November, 1982.

Fonseca, Carlos. *Un Nicaragüense en Moscú* [A Nicaraguan in Moscow]. Managua: Publicaciones de Unidad, 1958.

Fonseca, Carlos. *Sandino Guerrillero Proletario* [Sandino Proletarian Guerrilla]. Managua: Secretaría Nacional de Propaganda y Educación Política del FSLN, Colección Juan de Dios Muñoz, 1980.

de Franco, Mario. *Aspectos del Desenvolvimiento Económico de Nicaragua* [Aspects of Nicaragua's Economic Development]. Essay prepared for the Friedrich Ebert foundation (n.p.), March 1981.

FSLN. Notas Sobre la Montaña y Algunos Otros Temas [FSLN. Notes on the Wilderness and Some Other Topics]. Ediciones Frente Estudiantil Revolucionario (FER), Managua (n.d.).

FSLN Proletario. *Documentos Básicos* [Basic Documents]. I.M.P.: 1978.

Fundación del FSLN. Por la Senda de Sandino [The Inception of the FSLN: Following the Path of Sandino]. Movimiento de Izquierda Revolucionaria (Mir). Ecuador: Editorial René Pinto, 1981.

García Caracas, Carlos, *et al. Alianzas Políticas de la Oposición en Centro América* [Political

Alliances of the Opposition in Central America]. Guatemala: Ediciones Incep., November 1975.

García Márquez, Gabriel, Gregorio Selser, and Daniel Warsman Shinca. *La Batalla de Nicaragua* [The Battle of Nicaragua]. Mexico: Bruguera Mexicana de Ediciones, 1979.

Gilly, A. *La Nueva Nicaragua: Anti-Imperialismo y Lucha de Clases* [The New Nicaragua: Anti-Imperialism and Class Struggle]. Mexico: Editorial Nueva Imagen, 1980.

Guido, Lea. *Movimiento y Organización Políticas* [Politics: Organization and Movement]. Managua: Centro Editorial, Universidad Centroamericana (UCA), 1980.

Habla la Dirección de la Vanguardia [The Directorate of the Vanguard Speaks]. Selected speeches by members of the FSLN's National Directorate, July 1979–May 1981. Managua: Departamento de Propaganda y Educación Política del FSLN, July 1981.

Hernández, Plutarco. *El FSLN por Dentro* [The FSLN from Within]. San José, Costa Rica: Published by author, 1982.

Hurtado González, Armando. *Sandino Desconocido* [The Unknown Sandino]. San José, Costa Rica: Ediciones Populares Nicaragüenses, 1984.

Indicadores Socio-Económicos—1979–1980 [Socioeconomic Indicators—1970–1980]. Managua: Instituto Nacional de Estadística y Censos, July 1981.

Introducción al Pensamiento Sandinista [Introduction to Sandinista Thought]. Managua: Secretaría de Propaganda y Educación Política del FSLN, Colección "El Chipote," 1981.

Irwin, George and Xavier Gorostiaga (Eds.) *Towards an Alternative for Central America*. The Hague: Institute for Social Studies, 1984.

El Istmo Centroamericano: El Carácter de la Crisis, los Desafíos que Plantea, y la Solidaridad Internacional que Demanda [Central American Isthmus: The Character of the Crisis, the Challenges It Poses and the International Solidarity It Requires]. Mexico: Comisión Económica Para América Latina (CEPAL), June 1981.

Lanuza, Barahona and Serres, Chamorro. *Economía y Sociedad en la Construcción del Estado en Nicaragua*. [Economy and Society in the Construction of the State in Nicaragua]. San José, Costa Rica: Editorial Unviersitaria Centroamericana (EDUCA), 1980.

Macauley, Neill. *The Sandino Affair*. Chicago: Quadrangle Books, 1967.

Macías, Edgard, Álvaro Taboada, and Luís H. Guzmán. *Perfil de una Revolución* [Profile of a Revolution]. Managua: Ediciones Instituto Nicaragüense de Capacitación y Estudios Sociopolíticos (INCEP), September 1978.

Mantilla, Fabio Gadea. *Nicaragua Ayer y Hoy* [Nicaragua Yesterday and Today]. Transcription of Selected Editorials Broadcast by the Author, San José, Costa Rica, 1977–1981.

Maurice Bishop Speaks: The Grenada Revolution, 1979–83. New York: Pathfinder Press, 1985.

Mirandi, N. Pedro (Ed.). *El Pueblo que Asombra al Mundo* [The People That Astound the World]. Panama: Ediciones Punto Rojo, 1979.

Morales Avilés, Ricardo. *La Dominación Imperialista en Nicaragua* [The Imperialist Domination of Nicaragua] [an interview]. Managua: Secretaría Nacional de Propaganda y Educación Política del FSLN, Colección Juan de Dios Muñoz-Serie Pensamiento Sandinista, 1980.

Morales Avilés, Ricardo. *Prosa Política y Poemas (Political Writing and Poems)*. Managua: Editorial Nueva Nicaragua, 1981.

Nicaragua: Estudio de la Situación del Empleo, la Absorción de la Mano de Obra y Otros Aspectos en Fincas y Productores de Café y Algodón [Nicaragua: Study of the Employment Situation, the Absorption of Labor and Other Aspects Concerning the Farms and the Producers of Coffee and Cotton]. Managua: Instituto Centroamericano de Administración de Empresas (INCAE), 1981.

Nicaragua: Revolutionary Justice—A Report on Human Rights and The Judicial System. New York: Lawyers' Committee on International Human Rights, 1985.

Nicaragua: The Sandinista People's Revolution. Speeches by Sandinista Leaders. New York: Pathfinder Press, 1985.

Nolan, David. *The Ideology of the Sandinistas and the Nicaraguan Revolution.* Coral Gables, FL: Institute of Interamerican Studies, University of Miami, 1984.

Núñez, Orlando. *La Ideología como Fuerza Material y la Juventud como Fuerza Ideológica* [Ideology as a Material Force and Youth as an Ideological Force]. Managua: Centro de Investigaciones y Estudios de la Reforma Agraria (Ciera), 1981.

Núñez, Carlos. *Un Pueblo en Armas: Informe del Frente Interno* [A People in Arms: Report from the Internal Front]. Managua: Departamento de Propaganda y Educación Política del FSLN, 1980.

Ortega Saavedra, Daniel. *Documento de Estudio* [Document for Study]. Managua: Dirección de Divulgación y Prensa de la Junta de Gobierno de Reconstrucción Nacional y Casa de Gobierno, September 1981.

Ortega Saavedra, Humberto. *Sobre la Insurrección* [On the Insurrection]. La Habana, Cuba: Editorial de Ciencias Sociales, 1981.

Ortega Saavedra, Humberto. *Cincuenta Años de Lucha Sandinista* [Fifty Years of Sandinista Struggle]. México: Editorial Diógenes, 1979.

Ortega Saavedra, Humberto. *Un Solo Ejército* [One Single Army]. Managua: Dirección de Prensa de la Junta de Gobierno, 1981.

Pastora, Hector Darío. *Calavario de la Iglesia Nicaragüense* [The Calvary of the Nicaraguan Church]. Comité Ecuménico Para Defensa de Religión y Culto en Nicaragua (CEDRENIC), San José, Costa Rica, (n.d.).

Programa de Reactivación Económica en Beneficio del Pueblo [Program of Economic Reactivation for Benefit of the People]. Managua: Ministerio de Planificación Económica, 1981.

Programa Económico de Austeridad y Eficiencia 81 [Economic Program for Austerity and Efficiency 81]. Managua: Centro de Publicaciones Silvio Mayorga, February 1981.

Ramírez, Sergio (Ed.). *El Pensamiento Vivo de Sandino* [The Living Thought of Sandino] (6th ed.). San José, Costa Rica: Editorial Universitaria Centroamericana (EDUCA), 1974.

Ramírez, Sergio. *Sandinismo, Hegemonía y Revolución* [Sandinismo, Hegemony and Revolution]. Mexico: Cuadernos Políticos Ediciones ERA, September 1980.

Randall, Margaret. *Sandino's Daughters: Testimonies of Nicaraguan Women in Struggle.* Vancouver, B. C.: New Star Books, 1981.

Regional Cooperation in Peace and Security in Central America and the Caribbean. New York: International Peace Academy, 1984.

Report of the National Bipartisan Commission on Central America. [The Chairman of this Commission was Dr. Henry Kissinger. The report was prepared for the President of the United States.] Washington, D.C.: Government Printing Office, January 1984.

Report on the Situation of Human Rights of a Segment of the Nicaraguan Population of Miskito Origin. Washington, D.C.: Inter-American Commission on the Situation of Human Rights, Organization of American States, 1984.

Resource Book: Sandinista Elections in Nicaragua. Washington, D.C.: U.S. Government Printing Office, 1984.

La Revolución a través de Nuestra Dirección Nacional. [The Revolution through Our National Directorate]. Managua: Secretaría National de Propaganda y Educación Política del FSLN, June 1980.

Rudolph, James D. (Ed.). *Nicaragua: A Country Study.* Washington, D.C.: U.S. Government Printing Office, 1982.

Los Sandinistas y los Extremistas del Oriente Medio [The Sandinistas and the Middle East Extremists]. Washington, D.C.: U.S. Department of State, August 1985.

Sarti, C. *Nicaragua, Aproximación al Estudio del Carácter de la Revolución y la Naturaleza del Estado, 1979–1981* [Nicaragua, Approach to the Study of the Character of the Revolution and the Nature of the State, 1978–1981]. San Juan, Puerto Rico: Lecture to the XIVth Latin American Congress of Sociology, 1981.

Sequeira, Carlos Guillermo. *State and Private Marketing Arrangements in the Agricultural Export Industries: The Case of Nicaragua's Coffee and Cotton*. Doctoral dissertation. Cambridge: Harvard University 1981.

Somoza, Anastasio. *Nicaragua Betrayed* [Somoza's Account to Jack Cox]. Boston: Western Islands, 1980.

The Soviet–Cuban Connection in Central America and in the Caribbean. Washington, D.C.: Department of Defense and U.S. Department of State, 1985.

Spadafora, Hugo. *La Derrota Comunista en Nicaragua* [The Communist Defeat in Nicaragua]. Writings of the former vice-minister of health of Panama who fought with the FSLN in 1978–1979 and fought against the FSLN after 1982.

Talavera, J. L. *Nicaragua: Crisis de la Dictadura Militar* [Nicaragua, Crisis of the Military Dictatorship]. San José, Costa Rica: Estudios Sociales Centroamericanos, 1979.

Tefel, Reinaldo Antonio. *La Revolución Sandinista* [The Sandinista Revolution]. Managua: Instituto Nicaragüense de Seguridad Social, October 1979.

Torres Rivas, Edelberto. *Ocho Claves Para Comprender la Crisis Centroamericana* [Eight Basic Insights for Understanding the Central American Crisis]. San José, Costa Rica: Editorial Universitaria Centroamericana (EDUCA), 1981.

Valenta, Jiri and Herbert J. Ellison (Eds.). *Grenada and Soviet/Cuban Policy: Internal Crisis and the U.S./OECS Intervention*. Boulder, CO: Westview, 1985.

Valle, Marcos A. *Desarrollo Económico y Político de Nicaragua, 1912–1947* [Economic and Political Development of Nicaragua, 1912–1947]. Thesis for licentiate degree in sociology, Universidad de Costa Rica, San José, 1978.

Vanderlaan, Mary B. *Revolution and Foreign Policy in Nicaragua*. Boulder, CO: Westview, 1986.

Von Appun, Detlef and Joachim Roder. *Nicaragua*. San José, Costa Rica: Deha Press, 1983.

Walker, Thomas W. *Nicaragua: The Land of Sandino*. Boulder, CO: Westview, 1982.

Walker, Thomas W. (Ed.). *Nicaragua in Revolution*. New York: Praeger, 1982.

Wesson, Robert (Ed.). *Communism in Central America and the Caribbean*. Stanford, CA: Hoover Institution Press, 1981.

Wheelock, Jaime and Luís Carrión. *Apuntes Sobre el Desarrollo Económico y Social de Nicaragua* [Notes on the Economic and Social Development of Nicaragua]. Managua: Secretaría Nacional de Propaganda y Educación Política del FSLN, 1980.

Wheelock, Jaime. *Frente Sandinista: Diciembre Victorioso* [Sandinista Front: Victorious December]. Managua: Secretaría de Propaganda y Educación Política del FSLN (n.d.).

Wheelock, Jaime. *Vanguardia, Hegemonía Popular y Unidad Nacional* [Vanguard, Popular Hegemony and Popular Unity]. Mexico: Cuadernos Políticos-Ediciones ERA, September 1980.

Wheelock, Jaime. *Imperialismo y Dictadura: Crisis de Una Formación Social (Imperialism and Dictatorship: Crisis of a Social Formation)*. Mexico: Siglo Veintuino. 1975.

Wiarda, Howard J. (Ed.). *Rift and Revolution: The Central American Imbroglio*. Washington, D.C.: American Enterprise Institute, 1984.

Zavala, Xavier; Pablo Antonio Cuadra, Franco Cerutti, Rodrigo Madrigal, *et al. 1984 Nicaragua*. San José, Costa Rica: Asociación Libro Libre, 1986.

Articles

Ameringer, Charles C. "The Thirty Years War between Figueres and the Somozas," *Caribbean Review*, Vol. 8 (Fall 1979): pp. 4—7, 40—41.

Arce, Bayardo. "El Difícil Terreno de Lucha: El Ideológico" [The Difficult Field of Struggle: The Ideological One"]. *Nicarauac*, No. 1 (May-June 1980): pp. 152—57.

Basu, R. "The Road Warriors," *Nation*, Vol. 236 (June 4, 1983): p. 690.

Belli, Pedro. "Prolegómeno Para Una Historia Económica de Nicaragua, 1905—1966" ["Prolegomenons for an Economic History of Nicaragua, 1905—1966"], *Revista del Pensamiento Centroamericano*, Vol. 146 (January-March, 1975).

Berríos, Rubén. "Economic Relations between Nicaragua and the Socialist Countries," *Journal of Interamerican Studies and World Affairs*, Vol. 27, No. 3 (Fall 1985): pp. 111—140.

Black, George. "Central America: Crisis in the Backyard," *New Left Review*, No. 135 (September-October 1982): pp. 5—34.

Burke, Charles E. "The Impact of Censorship on Nicaraguan Newspapers: A Before and After Comparison of 'Superpower' Coverage," *Gazette*, No. 3 (1985): pp. 173—181.

Cardenal, Fernando. "Como Cristiano Revolucionario Encontré un Nuevo Camino" [As a Revolutionary Christian I Found a New Path] [Interview], *Nicarauac*, No. 5 (April-June 1981): pp. 99—108.

"Central America Watch," *Nation*, Vol. 233 (October 31, 1981): pp. 429.

Christian, Shirley, "Nicaraguan Nemesis: Resurfacing of Commander Zero, E. Pastora," *New Republic*, Vol. 186 (May 26, 1982): pp. 16—19.

Chumakova, M. "On the Difficult Path of National Rebirth," *Latinskaya Amerika*, Vol. 7 (July 1980): pp. 38—56.

Clement, Peter. "Moscow and Nicaragua: Two Sides of Soviet Policy," *Comparative Strategy*, Vol. 5, No. 1 (1985): pp. 75—91.

Clerc, Jean Paul. "Nicaragua: Triumph of Moderation? The Fragile Foothold of a 'Free Socialism,' " *World Press Review*, (January 1980): pp. 27—29. (From *Le Monde*, Vol. 10 [12 October 1979]).

Colburn, Forrest D. "Nicaragua Under Siege," *Current History* (March 1985): pp. 105—108,

Cornelius, Wayne A. "The 1985 Nicaraguan Elections Revisited," *LASA Forum*, Vol. 16, No. 4 (Winter 1986): pp. 22—28.

Corradi, Juan E. "Nicaragua: Can It Find Its Own Way?" *Dissent*, Vol. 31, No. 3 (Summer 1984): pp. 275—284.

Crawley, Eduardo. "Nicaragua: The Key to Regional Peace," *Conflict Studies*, Vol. 166 (1984): pp. 1—23.

Cruz, Arturo Sr. "Managua's Game: 1986 Strategy," *New Republic*, (March 10, 1986): p. 17.

Cruz, Arturo Sr. "Nicaragua's Imperiled Revolution," *Foreign Affairs*, Vol. 61 (Summer 1983): pp. 1031—1047.

Cruz, Arturo Sr. "The Sandinista Regime at Watershed," *Strategic Review*, Vol. 12 No. 2 (Spring 1984): pp. 55—70.

Cruz, Arturo Jr. "Nicaragua: A Revolution in Crisis," *SAIS Review*, Vol. 4 (Winter 1984).

"Department Releases Report on Sandinista Intervention in Central America," *Department of State Bulletin* (November 1985): p. 68.

D'Escoto, Miguel. "Nicaragua and the World" [Interview], *Christianity and Crisis*, Vol. 40 (May 1980): pp. 141—148.

Domínguez Reyes, Edme. "Soviet Relations with Central America, the Caribbean, and Members of the Contadora Group," *Annals of the American Academy*, Vol. 481 (September 1985): pp. 147—158.

Dye, David R. "The National Emergency in Nicaragua: A Provisional Interpretation," *LASA—NICA Scholar News*, Vol. 91 (December 1985–January 1986): pp. 2–3.

Enders, T.O. "Nicaragua: Threat to Peace in Central America," *Department of State Bulletin*, Vol. 83 (June 1983): pp. 76–80.

Fagen, Richard R. "The Nicaraguan Crisis," *Monthly Review*, Vol. 34 (November 1982): pp. 1–16.

Farer, Tom. "Contadora: The Hidden Agenda," *Foreign Policy*, No. 59 (Summer 1985): pp. 59–72.

Farnsworth, E. "Un año libre" ["One Free Year"], *Nation*, Vol. 231 (July 19–26, 1980): pp. 69–70.

Feinberg, Richard E. "Central America: No Easy Answers," *Foreign Affairs*, Vol. 59 (Summer 1981): pp. 1121–1146.

Feinberg, Richard E. "Central America: The View from Moscow," *Washington Quarterly*, Vol. 5 (Spring 1982): pp. 171–175.

Fox, G. "The Lone Ranger," *Nation*, Vol. 237 (November 26, 1983): p. 525.

Frieden, F. "Revolution under the Guns," *Nation*, Vol. 237 (December 17, 1983): pp. 630–633.

FSLN. "Sandinista Front: People's War in Central America." *Tricontinental*, No. 17 (March–April 1970): pp. 61–68.

Gleijeses, P. "Nicaragua: Resist Romanticism," *Foreign Policy*, Vol. 54 (Spring 1984): pp. 122–138.

González, Edward. "The Cuban and Soviet Challenge in the Caribbean Basin," *Orbis*, Vol. 29 (Spring 1985): pp. 5–71.

Gorman, Stephen M. "Power and Consolidation in the Nicaraguan Revolution," *Journal of Latin American Studies*, Vol. 13 No. 1 (May 1981): pp. 133–149.

Gutman, Roy. "Nicaragua: America's Diplomatic Charade," *Foreign Policy*, Vol. 56 (Fall 1984): pp. 3–23.

Harris, Hermoine. "Nicaragua: Two Years of Revolution," *Race and Class*, Vol. 23 (Summer 1981): pp. 1–23.

Hitchens, C. "The Selling of Military Intervention," *Nation*, Vol. 236 (April 9, 1983): p. 418.

Hoffmann, Stanley, W. Hardy Callcott, Caniel W. Gentges, Abraham Brumberg, Robert Coles, Henry Fairlie, Hendrik Hertzberg, Vint Lawrence, R.W.B. Lewis, Mark Crispin Millee, Robert B. Reich, Ronald Steel, Richard L. Strout, Anne Tyler, Michael Walzer, C. Vann Woodward, Anthony J. Barbera and Jerry E. Rosenthal. "The Contra-versy (vs. *New Republic* pro-aid editorial)," *New Republic* (April 14, 1986): pp. 4–6.

Horowitz, Irving Louis. "Fresh Havana Breezes? (Changes in Cuban Foreign Policy Relating to Nicaragua, El Salvador, Grenada, and Angola)," *Freedom at Issue* (November/ December 1984): pp 16–18.

Irvin, G. "Nicaragua: Establishing the State as the Centre of Accumulation," *Cambridge Journal of Economics*, Vol. 7 (June 1983): pp. 125–139.

"La Revolución de Nicaragua" ("The Nicaraguan Revolution"), *Cuadernos Universitarios*, No. 26, January, 1980.

"Permanent Dictatorship in Nicaragua?" *Department of State Bulletin* (April 1986): p. 83.

Rabkin, Rhoda Pearl. "U.S.–Soviet Rivalry in Central America and the Caribbean," *Journal of International Affairs*, Vol. 34 (Fall–Winter 1980–81): pp. 329–351.

Radosh, R. "Darkening Nicaragua," *New Republic*, Vol. 189 (October 24 1983): pp. 7–12.

Ramírez, Sergio. "Nuestra Forma Sandinista de Democracia" [Our Sandinista Way of Democracy"], *Nicarauac*, No. 5 (April–June 1981): pp. 5–16.

"Review of Nicaragua's Commitments to the OAS," *Department of State Bulletin* (May 1985): pp. 22–24.

Riding, Alan. "The Central American Quagmire," *Foreign Affairs*, Vol. 61, No. 3 (1983): pp. 641–659.

Rothenberg, Morris. "Latin America in Soviet Eyes," *Problems of Communism*, Vol. 22 (September/October 1983): pp. 1–8.

Ruíz, Henry. "La Montaña Era como un Crisol donde se Forjaban los Mejores Cuadros" ("The Wilderness Was Like a Furnace Where the Best Cadres Were Forged") [interview], *Nicarauac*, No. 1 (May–June 1980): pp. 2–25.

Sánchez, Néstor D. "Revolutionary Change and the Nicaraguan People," *Strategic Review*, Vol. 12, No. 3 (Summer 1984): pp. 17–22.

Schwab, Theodore and Harold Sims. "Revolutionary Nicaragua's Relations with the European Communist States," *Conflict Quarterly*, Vol. 5 (Winter 1985): pp. 5–14.

Shultz, Donald E. "The Strategy of Conflict and the Politics of Counterproductivity," *Orbis*, Vol. 25 (Fall 1981): pp. 679–713.

Solís, Rafael. "The Future of Nicaragua," *Vital Speeches*, Vol 46 (15 February 1980): pp. 273–277.

Sotelo, Casimiro. "In Sandino's Footsteps," *Tricontinental*, No. 3 (November–December 1967): pp. 113–122.

Ullman, R. H. "At War with Nicaragua," *Foreign Affairs*, Vol. 62 (Fall 1983): pp. 39–58.

Valenta, Jiri. "Nicaragua: Soviet Pawn or Non-Aligned Country," *Journal of Interamerican Studies and World Affairs*, Vol. 271, No. 3 (Fall 1985): pp. 163–175.

Valenta, Jiri. "The USSR, Cuba, and the Crisis in Central America," *Orbis*, Vol. 25 (Fall 1981): pp. 715–46.

Valenta, Jiri and Virginia Valenta. "Sandinistas in Power," *Problems of Communism* (September/October 1985). (Translated in *Problemas Internacionales* [September/October 1985]): pp. 1–28.

Valenta, Jiri and Virginia Valenta. "Leninism in Grenada," *Problems of Communism*, Vol. 33 (July/August, 1984). [Translated in *Problemas Internacionales (July/August 1984)*]: pp. 1–23.

Vanden, Harry E. and Waltraud Queiser Morales. "Nicaraguan Relations with the Nonaligned Movement," *Journal of Interamerican Studies and World Affairs*, Vol. 27, No. 3 (Fall 1985): pp. 141–161.

Walker, Thomas W. "The Sandinista Victory in Nicaragua," *Current History*, Vol 78 (February 1980): pp. 57–61.

Wheeler, Jack. "Fighting the Soviet Imperialists: The Contras in Nicaragua," *Reason* (16 June/July 1984): pp. 28–36.

Contributors

Jiri Valenta was educated at the Prague School of Economics and Johns Hopkins University. Former coordinator of Soviet and East European studies at the U.S. Naval Postgraduate School in Monterey, California, Professor Valenta was also a fellow at the Brookings Institution, the Council on Foreign Relations, and the Woodrow Wilson International Center for Scholars among other appointments. He is the author of *Soviet Intervention in Czechoslovakia, 1968: Anatomy of a Decision*; coauthor of *The Soviet Invasion of Afghanistan: Three Perspectives*; coeditor and contributor to *Eurocommunism between East and West; Soviet Decisionmaking for National Security; Grenada and Soviet/Cuban Policy: Internal Crisis and U.S./ OECS Intervention* and *Conflict in Nicaragua*. Dr. Valenta testified before the Kissinger Bipartisan Commission on Central America and at hearings of the U.S. House of Representatives and the Senate. He is a member of the Council on Foreign Relations in New York City.

Esperanza Durán, a Mexican national, is a Research Fellow at the Royal Institute of International Affairs (Chatham House), where she has directed the Latin American program since 1983. Formerly she was Professor of International Studies at El Colegio de Mexico and the editor of *Foro Internacional*. Dr. Durán has also taught at the University of Warwick, the London School of Economics and the University of Southern California's School of International Relations in London. Her publications include *Latin America and the World Recession* (editor and contributor, 1985), *Guerra y revolución. Las grandes potencias y México 1914–1918* (1985), and *European Interests in Latin America* (1985) as well as numerous articles published on both sides of the Atlantic.

415

Vernon V. Aspaturian received his B.A. and Ph.D. from the University of California, Los Angeles. He is Evan Pugh Professor of Political Science and director of the Slavic and Soviet Language Area Center at Pennsylvania State University. He has authored and coedited several books on Soviet foreign policy and comparative communism including, among others, *The Soviet Union in the World Communist System; Process and Power in Soviet Foreign Policy; Eurocommunism between East and West;* and *The Union Republics in Soviet Diplomacy.*

Raymond F. Burghardt is a career foreign service officer who in July 1985 was appointed by President Reagan as special assistant for national security affairs. Since March 1984 he served on the National Security Council staff as director for Latin American affairs, with responsibility for Central America and the Caribbean. He participated in all the talks with the FSLN government in Manzanillo, Mexico, and accompanied Ambassador Phillip Habib in consultations with the Central American, Contadora and Support Group countries. Prior to his presidential appointment Mr. Burghardt served as chief of the political section of the American Embassy in Honduras (1982 to 1984). Mr. Burghardt received a B.A. from Columbia College in New York in 1967 and attended Columbia's School of International Affairs in 1967–1968.

Alfredo César was born in Nicaragua in 1951. He holds a masters degree in finance from Stanford University where he was awarded an assistant professorship during his last year of study (1975). Mr. César participated actively in the struggle against the Somoza regime and subsequently served in several important posts under the Sandinista revolutionary government: minister–secretary of the government board of junta (1979); minister of national reconstruction (1980); president of the National Banking System and president of the Central Bank of Nicaragua (1979–1982). During the 1979–1982 period, Mr. César was the chief negotiator of Nicaragua's external debt. After resigning from the FSLN government, Mr. César became the coordinator-general of the National Rescue and Reconciliation Movement (MRCN). Since July 1985 he has served as a member of the Executive Committee of the Democratic Opposition Bloc of the South (BOS).

Margaret Crahan received her Ph.D. in Latin American History from Columbia University. She is currently Henry R. Luce Professor of Religion, Power, and the Political Process at Occidental College in Los Angeles. Dr. Crahan is editor and coauthor of *Human Rights and Basic Needs in the Americas.* Currently Dr. Crahan is working on a book about religion and politics in Nicaragua.

Arturo J. Cruz, Sr. received his bachelor's and masters degrees from the School of Foreign Service of Georgetown University. He served as chief of operations of the Central-American Bank for economic Integration and as Associate Treasurer of the Inter-American Development Bank. Mr. Cruz was a member of the Conservative Party of Nicaragua, opposed for years to the Somoza government. During the initial years of the FSLN government, he was a member of the government junta, and later, ambassador to Washington. After his resignation from Sandinista government service Mr. Cruz was nominated as presidential candidate for the 1984 Nicaraguan elections by an opposition alliance. Currently Mr. Cruz is a member of the three-man directorate of the Unity of Nicaraguan Opposition (UNO).

Arturo Cruz Sequeira was an official in the Sandinista government. He resigned his government post to protest to FSLN's failure to comply with the original principles of the revolution. Cruz Sequeira is a doctoral candidate at the Johns Hopkins University's School of Advanced International Studies. He writes frequently for the *Christian Science Monitor*, *The New York Times*, and *The Los Angeles Times*; he contributed to and coedited (with J.E. Velázquez) the book *Nicaragua, Regresión en la Revolución* [Nicaragua, Regression in the Revolution].

Mark Falcoff received his M.A. and Ph.D. from Princeton Unviersity. Until very recently he was a resident fellow at the American Enterprise Institute for Public Policy Research, Washington, D.C. Prior to that (1979–1980) he was a fellow at the Hoover Institution on War, Revolution, and Peace, Stanford University. Dr. Falcoff served as a senior consultant to the National Bipartisan Commission on Central America, chaired by former Secretary of State Henry Kissinger. Dr. Falcoff's books include (with Ronald H. Dolkart) *Prologue to Peron: Argentina in Depression and War, 1930–43* (1975); (with Federick B. Pike) *The Spanish Civil War, 1936–39*; *American Hemispheric Perspectives* (1982); and (with Robert Royal) *Crisis and Opportunity: U.S. Policy in Central America and the Caribbean.*

Ottfried Hennig is a prominent member of the German Christian Democratic Party (CDU). He is currently Parliamentary Minister of State for Intra-German Affairs, Federal Republic of Germany.

Francisco López studied at the Law School of the Universidad Centroamericana (UCA) in Managua. He is currently director of the Instituto Nicaragüense de Investigaciones Económicas y Sociales (Nicaraguan Institute of Economic and Social Research—INIES) located at Managua, Nicaragua. INIES is one of a number of institutions that carry on research for the FSLN government in the fields of economics and sociology.

Ambler H. Moss is dean of the Graduate School of International Studies and director of the North/South Center of the University of Miami, Coral Gables, Florida. Between 1978 and 1982 he was U.S. Ambassador to Panama at the appointment of both President Carter and President Reagan. Prior to that time Moss was deputy assistant secretary of state for congressional relations and a member of the negotiating team for the Panama Canal treaties of 1977, for which work he was awarded the Harold Weill Medal by New York University. He is a graduate of Yale and the George Washington University School of Law. He is a member of numerous international law societies and is a member of the Council on Foreign Relations of New York City.

Harry Shlaudeman received a B.A. from Stanford University in 1953. A career Foreign Service officer, Ambassador Shlaudeman has served in the following capacities: special assistant to Secretary of State Rusk (1967–1968); deputy chief of mission, Santiago, Chile (1969–1973); deputy assistant secretary for inter-American affairs (1973–1975); ambassador to Venezuela (1975–1976); assistant secretary of state for Inter-american affairs (1976–1977); ambassador to Peru (1977–1980); ambassador to Argentina (1980–1983); executive director, National Bipartisan Commission on Central America (1983–1984); ambassador at large and President Reagan's special envoy for Central America (1984–1986) (replaced by Phillip Habib in February 1986).

Álvaro Taboada Terán was educated at the Universidad Nacional Autónoma of Nicaragua and Tulane University. He is a lawyer who was actively involved in the political activities that helped to bring down the Somoza government. A former president of the Socialist-Christian Party of Nicaragua (1976–1978), he also served as an ambassador of the Nicaraguan Sandinista government in 1980–1982. He is the author of several monographs on Latin American politics, and of the book *Mesoamerica: de Su Origin al Modo de Produccion Asiatico* [Mesoamerica: From Its Origins to the Asiatic Mode of Production].

Virginia Valenta received a masters degree in romance languages from the University of Missouri, Columbia. She has written several articles on Soviet and Cuban policies in Latin America, and is coauthor of *Soviet Strategy in the Caribbean Basin* (Wiarda and Valenta, forthcoming) and the articles "Sandinistas in Power" (*Problems of Communism*, Oct.–Nov., 1985) and "Leninism in Grenada" (*Problems of Communism*, May–June, 1984).

Francisco Villagrán Kramer is a Guatemalan citizen who holds a doctoral degree in international law from the University of Geneva. Dr. Villagrán Kramer was vicepresident of Guatemala during the initial year of General Lucas Garcia's government (1978). He later resigned to protest the government's noncompliance with the promises of social reform made by García to the Guatemalan people. Villagrán Kramer is an expert in the field of Central American economic integration and he has written books and monographs on this subject.

Glossary

APP: Area Propiedad del Pueblo (People's Property Area)—Comprises all the means of production, industrial and agricultural, urban and rural, that have been confiscated by the state since 1979, as well as property owned by the state prior to the revolution, including extensive areas of Nicaraguan territory. Presently, at least 60% of Nicaragua's GNP is APP generated.

ARDE: Alianza Revolucionaria Democrática (Revolutionary Democratic Alliance)— An organization opposed to the FSLN, formed by the coming together in 1982 of the *FRS, Frente Revolucionario Sandino* (Sandino Revolutionary Front), led by Edén Pastora; the *MDN, Movimiento Democrático Nicaragüense* (Nicaraguan Democratic Movement), led by Alfonso Robelo; the *MISURASATA (Sandinista Miskitos, Sumos,* and *Ramas),* led by Brooklyn Rivera; and the *FARN, Fuerzas Armadas Revolucionarias de Nicaragua* (Armed Revolutionary Forces of Nicaragua), led by Fernando Chamorro. Later, in 1983, ARDE was joined by *FSDC, Frente de Solidaridad Demócrata-Cristiana* (Front of Democratic-Christian Solidarity), led by José Dávila.

Since its inception, ARDE has undergone several crises owing to rivalries among its component organizations and leaders, and different perceptions regarding how to carry on relations with other rebel groups outside the alliance. At its peak, ARDE embodied the strongest of the center-left rebel forces consisting of supporters of the Nicaraguan revolution, who later opposed the FSLN political project. ARDE was the embodiment of the political position known as "the South," which is now represented by BOS, *Bloque Opositor del Sur* (Southern Opposition Bloc). Following its disintegration and its ideological and military replacement by BOS, ARDE's present role is minimal, at best.

Bluefields—A port on the Caribbean Coast of Nicaragua. Bluefields is the main city and capital of the eastern department of Zelaya, the largest yet least populated department in the country. Particularly since 1982, fighting between the Sandinista Army and the rebel forces of UNO, ARDE and other organizations such as the Misura has been frequent in Zelaya, including the area surrounding Bluefields.

419

Boaco—An administrative division or department, similar to a province in other countries, located in the middle-eastern part of Nicaragua. Boaco is fundamentally rural. Its population played a small part in the anti-Somoza war. Presently, Boaco is the theater of armed clashes between the Sandinista army and rebel forces of UNO and BOS.

BOS: Bloque Opositor del Sur (Southern Opposition Bloc)—An anti-FSLN political alliance born in July 1985. BOS was formed by the amalgamation of *MCRN*, *Movimiento de Rescate y Conciliación Nacional* (Movement of National Rescue and Reconciliation), led by Alfredo César, former president of the Nicaraguan Central Bank under the Sandinistas; the *CSOCANE*, *Comité Sindical de Obreros y Campesinos Nicaragüenses en el Exilio* (Syndical Committee of Nicaraguan Workers and Peasants in Exile), led by the trade union leader Bayardo López; and the *CPNE*, *Confederación de Profesionales Nicaragüenses en el Exilio* (Confederation of Nicaraguan Professionals in Exile), led by Dr. Álvaro Jerez. Another opposition organization that joined BOS, but later separated from the organization, was ARDE. Presently, BOS has been reinforced by MSOE, the *Movimiento Social Cristiano Organizado en el Exterior* (Christian Socialist Movement organized abroad), led by the Former vice-minister of labor of the FSLN regime, Edgard Macías.

BOS is a center-left democratic alliance representing the political orientation known as "the South." To most Nicaraguans, "the South" connotes those organizations that sustain a belief in deep social and economic reforms within a political structure of representative democracy. BOS has received political support from important sectors of the Socialist International. Despite Sandinista protests, the June 1986 regional congress of this worldwide organization (held in Lima, Peru) admitted BOS as an observer with the same standing as the FSLN (also present in observer status). In June 1986, BOS and UNO (Unión Nacional Opositora [National Opposition Unity]) signed a national agreement, committing themselves to form and abide by a democratic platform for Nicaragua. They also agreed to coordinate efforts while retaining their separate managements, an arrangement as yet unrealized.

Cancún—A resort in the Yucatán Peninsula of Mexico where, on July 16 and 17, 1983, the presidents of Mexico, Panama, Colombia, and Venezuela (the Contadora countries) met and issued a declaration bearing the name of the resort. This declaration underlined the need to withdraw from Central America all foreign bases and soldiers. However, some analysts have considered its verification methods too general and its provisions less favorable to the rest of the Central American countries and to the United States than to Nicaragua and her allies.

Caraballeda—Resort close to Caracas, Venezuela where the "Lima Group" or "Support Group" to Contadora (Argentina, Uruguay, Brazil, and Peru) met in January 1986 to try to give new life to the Contadora process after it had suffered a severe setback in November 1985, when the FSLN government refused to sign the Contadora Act for Peace and Cooperation in Central America. The Support Group's "Message of Caraballeda for Peace, Security and Democracy in Central America," also known simply as "Caraballeda," repeats the basic concepts of the Contadora Act but is not as complete. For some months, the FSLN government, with Mexico's support, insisted that the Caraballeda Document be signed prior to the Contadora Act. However, the other Central American countries would not accept this proposition and the Contadora Group then developed a revised act in June 1986, which, at this writing, also remains unsigned.

Comités de Defensa Civil (Civil Defense Committes)—These committees were originally created as small civil unities that would provide medicines, water, etc. during the war against Somoza. The

FSLN attempted to transform the CDCs into political organizations but it failed because the people understood the CDCs only as emergency organizations. Later, almost at the end of the war, the FSLN replaced the CDC with the *CDS, Comités de Defensa Sandinista* (Sandinista Defense Committees), which clearly had a party nature. Once in power, the FSLN used the CDS for a block−by−block control of the population's movements, rationing cards, etc. Although backed by the state and the FSLN party, the CDS's activities are not defined by any law, and they have been seen by some analysts as an example of the repressive nature of the Sandinista regime.

CDN: Coordinadora Democrática Nicaragüense (Nicaraguan Democratic Coordinator)—This political organization was formed in Nicaragua in 1980 by the *PSC, Partido Social-Cristiano* (Social-Christian Party); *PSD*, the *Partido Social-Demócrata* (Social Democratic Party); *COSEP*, the *Consejo Superior de la Empresa Privada* (Higher Council of Private Enterprise); *MCL*, the *Movimiento Liberal Constitucionalista* (Liberal Constitutionalist Movement); *MDN*, the *Movimiento Democrático Nicaragüense* (Nicaraguan Democratic Movement); *CTN*, the *Central de Trabajadores de Nicaragua* (Nicaraguan Workers' Confederation); and *CUS*, the *Central de Unidad Sindical* (Confederation for Syndical Unity). The leadership of the MDN went into exile in 1982. At the same time, however, the *PCN*, the *Partido Conservador de Nicaragua* (Conservative Party of Nicaragua) became a member of the CDN. As the largest of all the civil organizations opposed to the FSLN, the CDN was harassed by the Sandinistas, and its members decided not to participate in the 1984 presidential elections. The CDN's candidate was Mr. Arturo Cruz, who later went into exile. Although the CDN still exists within Nicaragua, its activities are restricted by the FSLN government.

CEPAD—Comité Evangélico para Ayuda al Desarrollo (Evangelical Committee for Aid to Development)—Consisting of 38 protestant groups, this organization was born in December 1972 to help victims of the 1972 earthquake in Managua. CEPAD became a permanent institution and is now involved in several assistance programs in Nicaragua such as children's health, housing, women's assistance, etc.

Chinandega—A province located in the northwestern part of Nicaragua. The capital and principal city of this department is also named Chinandega. This department is agriculturally very rich (cotton, sugar cane, banana cultivation, and cattle breeding). During the war against Somoza in September 1978, Chinandega suffered heavily from both sides in the fighting.

Chontales—A department located south of Boaco and west of Zelaya whose main economic activity is cattle raising. In the war against Somoza, Chontales participated minimally, but today anti-FSLN rebels are operating in Chontales' extensive rural zones.

CIECA: Consejo de Integración Económica Centroamericana (Council for Central American Economic Integration)—The most important of the organizations devoted to Central American economic integration. Its headquarters are in Guatemala.

CONDECA—Consejo de Defensa Centroamericano (Central American Defense Council)—CONDECA was formed in December 1963 by Guatemala, Honduras, and Nicaragua. El Salvador signed the treaty on CONDECA in 1965. Costa Rica, a country without an army, signed the treaty in 1966. Panama signed in 1974. The 1969 war between El Salvador and Honduras, after which Honduras withdrew from the Council, was a serious setback for CONDECA. After the FSLN takeover, Nicaragua also withdrew (although not officially) because it considered CONDECA an "instrument of imperialism," especially since the Council had conducted some anti-insurgency military exercises in the 1970s when the FSLN was a small guerrilla organization. Today, under pressure from the FSLN's own strong military presence, some efforts are being made, particularly by Honduras and El Salvador, to revive military cooperation under CONDECA auspices.

Contadora—Resort island located in the Gulf of Panama. In January 1983, representatives of the governments of Mexico, Panama, Colombia, and Venezuela met in Contadora to try to devise some type of Latin American solution to what those governments have called the Central American crisis, focusing on Nicaragua and El Salvador. The meeting concluded with the establishment of the "Contadora Group," whose efforts have been analyzed in this book by Dr. Esperanza Durán. Contadora's role suffered what may have been a fatal setback in June 1986 when a second Revised Act was not signed by the Central American countries. After a long process that included the fruitless presentation of acts and revised acts, the Contadora Group and the Support Group (Argentina, Peru, Brazil, and Uruguay) decided to postpone further negotiations until the Central American states themselves requested them.

COSEP: Consejo Superior de la Empresa Privada (Higher Council of Private Enterprise)—An organization composed of the chambers of construction, industry, and commerce; *UPANIC, Unión de Productores Agrícolas de Nicaragua* (Union of Agricultural Producers of Nicaragua); by *INDE, Instituto Nicaragüense de Desarrollo* (The Nicaraguan Institute for Development); *CONAPRO Confederación de Profesionales de Nicaragua* (Confederation of Nicaraguan Professionals), composed of university graduates grouped according to profession; and the Asociación Bancaria Nicaragüense (Nicaraguan Banking Association). When all Nicaraguan financial institutions were nationalized, the Banking Association left COSEP. Despite COSEP's contribution to the anti-Somoza struggle (it actively participated in the strikes against Somoza in 1978–1979), it has suffered restrictions and harassment at the hands of the Sandinista government.

CPDH: Comisión Permanente de Derechos Humanos (Permanent Human Rights Commission)—Independent organization founded in 1977 under the direction of José Esteban González, with support from the Christian Socialist party and the World Council of Churches. CPDH played an important role protecting people during the Somoza regime and has played the same role under the FSLN regime although it is subject to harassment. José Esteban González went into exile in 1981 and was replaced by Martha Patricia Baltodano, who in turn was forced into exile in 1985. CPDH has the merit of having constantly worked within Nicaragua, facing two different regimes. Its reports on human rights violations by the Somoza and the FSLN governments are very ample.

CST: Central Sandinista de Trabajadores (Sandinista Worker's Confederation)—Trade Union controlled by the FSLN, the aim of which is to achieve the so called *"Central Única"* or Unified Worker's Confederation. CST is the largest organization of its kind in Sandinista Nicaragua and enjoys support from the party and the state, including the political police.

CTN: Central de Trabajadores de Nicaragua (Worker's Central or Worker's Confederation of Nicaragua)—Christian labor organization affiliated with the Confederation of Latin American Workers or CLAT. The CTN, founded in 1962, has participated in different coalitions against the Somoza regime, but it has been subjected to harassment from the FSLN government.

DGSE: Dirección General de Seguridad del Estado (General Directorate of State Security)—The chief organization under the ministry of the interior. The DGSE is in charge of the political police and espionage. (See organizational chart, page 23.)

DN: Dirección Nacional (National Directorate)—Highest decision-making organism within the FSLN. The DN contains nine members, three from each of the tendencies dividing the FSLN between 1975 and 1979. The members of DN are: Daniel

Ortega, Humberto Ortega and Victor Tirado (of the Tercerista Tendency); Tomás Borge, Bayardo Arce and Henry Ruíz (of the Prolonged Popular War Tendency; and Jaime Wheelock, Luís Carrión and Carlos Núñez (of the Proletarian Tendency).

DRI: Dirección de Relaciones Internacionales (International Relations Directorate) —High-level FSLN organization in charge of relations with foreign communist and revolutionary parties. Since 1979 the DRI has taken over some key activities of the Ministry of Foreign Relations. Thus it conducts all diplomatic relations (with the exception of protocol) with Cuba and the USSR, both considered by the FSLN to be strategic allies.

ECLA: Economic Commission for Latin America—Founded by the United Nations in 1948, ECLA has become very active since 1950, developing a current of economic thought in which the ideas of the Argentine economist Raúl Prebich figure prominently. ECLA has always stressed the necessity of structural social change in Latin America, enhancing the role of the state without destroying the market-economy system.

El Viejo—Agricultural town in the department of Chinandega, located within a very fertile area dedicated to cotton growing and cattle ranching.

EPS: Ejército Popular Sandinista (Sandinista Popular Army)—Officially created by decree in September 1979, EPS is an organ of the FSLN whose nature, critics say, is contrary to the basic legal and political agreements that made possible the national unity against Somocismo. EPS is the largest army in Central America— 35,000 men, not counting the militias, which comprise some 79,000 men.

Esquipulas—Old colonial town populated primarily by Indian people, located in the eastern part of Guatemala. In May 1986, all the Central American presidents met at Esquipulas at the invitation of Guatemala's president, Vinicio Cerezo Arévalo. Presidents José Azcona (Honduras), Na-

poleón Duarte (El Salvador), Oscar Arias (Costa Rica), and Daniel Ortrega (Nicaragua) were in attendance. No agreements were reached at Esquipulas with the exception of the decision to form a Central American parliament composed of representatives from each Central American country. President Cerezo was behind the idea of the Central American parliament. However it had already been contemplated by the Contadora Act (Chapter 2, Section 4, No. 15) of 1986.

Estelí—Capital and main town of the department of the same name, located in the northwestern part of Nicaragua. Estelí is mainly an agricultural and cattle-ranching town. It suffered heavily from bombardments by Somoza's forces in September 1978. Surrounding areas of Estelí have witnessed new armed confrontations in the present civil war between the FSLN and the rebel forces.

FAO: Frente Amplio Opositor (Ample Opposition Front)—An anti-Somoza organization composed of political parties of very diverse ideological orientation: conservative, liberal, socialist, social-democratic, Christian-democratic, etc. The FSLN participated indirectly in FAO through the "Group of Twelve." By June 1978, the recently instituted FAO had already gathered strength in the anti-Somoza struggle. When the struggle became more radicalized, FAO split into two organizations, one of which was the *FPN*, or Frente Patriótico Nacional (National Patriotic Front). Officially instituted on February 2, 1979, the FPN was formed of some Democratic-leftist organizations that separated from the FAO, plus a number of smaller groups that were peripheral to the FSLN. With its remaining forces, the FAO functioned for all practical purposes until the beginning of 1980. It was formally included as a part of the legislative body of revolutionary Nicaragua ("Program for the Government of the National Board of Reconstruction," July 1979). Many FAO members went into exile in 1981–1982 and thereafter.

FDN: Fuerza Democrática Nicaragüense (Nicaraguan Democratic Force)—A political and military organization opposed to the FSLN, founded on August 3, 1981. The FDN has had two successive political directorates. Presently, besides the political directorate, the FDN has a political and military commander in chief, Adolfo Calero. A member of the Conservative Party and an executive in the Nicaraguan private sector, Calero was opposed to Somoza in the 1970s. In addition to the Directorate, the FDN has a Council of Regional Commanders. To date, the FDN has neither a government platform nor a well-defined ideological basis, although its conservative orientation is clear. The FDN has been criticized for the make-up of its membership, which includes former *Somocista* national guards, among them Colonel Enrique Bermúdez who in fact is the highest FDN military authority. Bermúdez was military attaché of the Somoza government in Washington when that government was overthrown. However, some other officers of the FDN are even more controversial. The FDN's military leadership is composed of 27% former *Somocistas*, 20% former Sandinista soldiers, and 53% peasants, students, etc. The FDN operates in the northern and central regions as well as in the deep south of Nicaragua. Within the Nicaraguan opposition, it represents "the North" or conservative tendency, as opposed to "the South" or center-left tendency. Presently, the FDN is a member of *UNO*, the *Unión Nacional Opositora* (National Opposition Unity) and has around 15,000 troops, according to spokesmen of UNO. Officially those troops are known as FDN–UNO.

FSLN: Frente Sandinista de Liberación Nacional (Sandinista National Liberation Front)—Guerrilla organization founded in 1962, presently in power in Nicaragua. The historical evolution of this organization is explained in the present book in the chapter by Jiri Valenta and Virginia Valenta.

GPP: Guerra Popular Prolongada (Prolonged Popular War)—A guerrilla strategy that consists in promoting a guerrilla war of attrition against a given government and its allies. The FSLN officially ascribed to the GPP strategy in its 1969 Program. When the FSLN suffered divisions about what strategy to follow in the struggle for power after 1975, the oldest sector of the FSLN remained committed to traditional GPP tactics, despite the meager success it yielded. In 1979 this sector was headed by Tomás Borge, Henry Ruíz, and Bayardo Arce. Despite such divisions, the goal of constructing a Leninist state remained common to all three tendencies of the FSLN (GPP, TP or *Tendencia Proletaria* [Proletarian Tendency], and TT or *Tendencia Tercerista* [Third Way Tendency]).

Kisan—Indian guerrilla organization born in September 1985 under the leadership of Wilcliff Diego, Roger Herman, and Adán Artola. Kisan integrates Miskito, Sumo, and Rama Indians, and is one of the three Indian organizations (the others being Misura and Misurasata) that are involved in the guerrilla struggle against the FSLN government. Kisan is a member of UNO and coordinates its activities with the FDN.

La Rosita—Mining town located in the northern part of the department of Zelaya. La Rosita's mining activities declined many years ago. The Sandinistas have military installations near La Rosita and the area is a focus of military clashes between Sandinista troops and FDN rebel troops.

León—Old colonial city, principal city of the department of the same name, and former capital of Nicaragua until the middle of the nineteenth century. León has had an intellectual tradition since Spanish Colonial times. Despite its conservative tradition, León bred the liberal Nicaraguan revolutionaries of the nineteenth century and the Marxist cells of the 1950s that helped to create the FSLN. During the 1978–1979 insurrection, León suffered heavily from the fighting forces of both sides. León is mainly agricultural. Cotton agriculture and industry reached high levels of modernization and efficiency during the period between 1950 and 1978.

Lima Group—Also known as the Contadora Support Group, the Lima Group is composed of Peru, Uruguay, Argentina, and Brazil, whose leaders met in Lima in July 1985 to give new life to the Contadora process. (*See also* **Caraballeda**.)

Los Doce ("The Twelve")—A group of 12 intellectuals and businessmen who acted as the civic arm of the FSLN between 1977 and 1979. The original 12 were Ernesto Cardenal, Fernando Cardenal, Miguel D'Escoto, Carlos Gutiérrez, Arturo Cruz, Felipe Mántica, Ernesto Castillo, Ricardo Coronel, Carlos Tunnermann, Sergio Ramírez, Emilio Baltodano, and Joaquín Cuadra. Of these, Mántica, Gutiérrez, and Cruz separated themselves at different moments from the group when they disagreed with the FSLN's strategic objectives. Cruz is author of Chapter 2 in this volume.

Manzanillo—Resort on the Pacific Coast of Mexico, where, on the suggestion of the Contadora group, the United States and Nicaragua started bilateral talks. Nine rounds of negotiations were held at Manzanillo from July to November 1984. The United States was represented by Ambassador Harry Shlaudeman (author of the Introduction to this volume) and Nicaragua, by Vice-Minister of Foreign Affairs Víctor Hugo Tinoco. Very little progress, if any, was achieved by the talks, and the United States decided to suspend them. The United States has proposed reviving bilateral talks if the FSLN government initiates talks with all the Nicaraguan opposition as a first step toward democracy and national reconciliation.

MCCA: Mercado Común Centroamericano (Central American Common Market)—An economic integration project instituted by the Treaty of Managua (1960) and involving the five Central American republics (Guatemala, El Salvador, Honduras, Nicaragua, and Costa Rica). The MCCA multiplied inter-Central American trade and was initially successful. However, an imbalance in MCCA benefits created difficulties. Other problems concerned foreign investment in Central America which, although necessary, encountered practically no legal restrictions. Additionally, demographic and migratory problems led to a short war between Honduras and El Salvador (1969). Honduras subsequently withdrew from the project.

MDN: Movimiento Democrático Nicaragüense (Democratic Nicaraguan Movement)—A political party formed in 1978 when the struggle against *Somocismo* was approaching its most intensive stage. The MDN basically included anti-Somocista members of private enterprise in Nicaragua. Its leader is Alfonso Robelo, who became a member of the first junta or government board that replaced Somoza. In 1980 Robelo resigned because of the FSLN's control over Nicaraguan political life through the use of Leninist tactics and mechanisms. Robelo and his organization were subjected to systematic repressions and went into exile in 1982. The MDN became an important component of ARDE from 1982 to 1984. Today the MDN is a member of the National Opposition Unity (UNO). It has kept its social-democratic orientation since its appearance in 1978.

Miskito—Indian people ethnically mixed with the blacks who inhabit the Caribbean Coast of Honduras and Nicaragua and the northeastern coast of Costa Rica. The Miskito are descended from the Macro-Chibcha family of pre-colonial Colombia. The Miskito language has been heavily penetrated by English words and some Spanish words. Forgotten in Somoza's time, the Miskito Indians have had serious confrontations with the FSLN government, which has forced massive relocations for military and political purposes. Some 15,000 Miskitos sought refuge in Honduras. Many others have taken up arms against the FSLN. The Miskito's traditional habitat has been the mouth of rivers and the coastal zone of Nicaragua's East Coast, where they have lived on a very simple economy based on fishing, hunting, and agriculture. According to a census made by the Indian organization in 1979 there were some 100,000 Miskito Indians, although the numbers might be inflated. The census was made by the chief of each Miskito community and reported to Misurasata, which in turn reported it to the FSLN at the very start of the revolutionary government when there existed friendly relations between the FSLN and the Miskito communities.

Misura (Miskitos, Sumos, and Ramas)—This Indian organization was established by Stedman Fagoth in 1982. Misura was closely allied to FDN, but later distanced itself. There is rivalry between Misurasata, Misura, and Kisan for the leadership of the Indians from Nicaragua's Atlantic region, despite the fact that all three are FSLN enemies. There have been efforts to unite among the three organizations. Among those efforts a very important one was launched in June 1985, with the project ASLA ("unity" in Miskito) which included the group SIC (Southern Indigenous Creole Community) formed by blacks, known as creoles on the Atlantic Coast. The SIC is headed by Jenny Lee Hodgson. Despite the fact the ASLA has had no tangible results, the efforts at unification or coordination among Misurasata, Misura, Kisan and SIC have not been discarded. Misura, however, is in the process of rapid decline.

Misurasata: (Miskitos, Sumos, and Ramas) —This organization was founded in September 1979 to renew and even substitute more broadly the former *ALPROMISU* (Alliance for the Advancement of the Miskito and Sumu) from Somoza's times. In August 1980 friction arose between the FSLN and Misurasata owing to the latter's dissatisfaction with the government's political/literacy campaign which Misurasata felt was deeply pro-Sandinista in its content and lacking an emphasis on Indian languages in its focus. Misurasata finally denounced what it considered to be repressive FSLN policies and broke with the government in February 1981, joining the military struggle within ARDE in May

1983. Misurasata's highest authority lies with its Assembly and Council of Elders. The most well known Misurasata leader is Brooklyn Rivera. Misurasata suffered a split in 1985, resulting in the formation of Kisan, which now has strong ties with FDN–UNO. Misurasata carries on close relations with the Southern Opposition BLOC (BOS).

Nueva Guinea—Extensive grain-producing agricultural zone located in the southern part of the department of Zelaya. Nueva Guinea was started as a project within the rather weak agrarian reform program in Somoza's time. Since the 1960s many landless peasant families from the Pacific Coast have been sent to Nueva Guinea. Some fighting by FSLN squads took place in this region during the struggle against Somoza in the 1970s. Today Nueva Guinea is a zone of active armed struggle against the FSLN government.

Puerto Cabezas—Second most important port on Nicaragua's Caribbean Coast and today a war zone between FSLN troops and rebel forces.

Punta Huete—Facing Lake Managua (Xolotlan) and located north of the capital, Punta Huete is the site of construction of an airport for military purposes started in 1980. Punta Huete's landing strip is over 3000 meters long. It is capable of receiving even the most modern military planes. From the beginning, the U.S. government has been concerned with Punta Huete, fearing that it would provide Soviet and Cuban planes with facilities for spy flights over the West Coast of the United States.

Rama—Small fluvial port located in the department of Zelaya on the Escondido River which is wide and navigable. It links Rama with Bluefields, on the Caribbean Coast. Rama and the Escondido River are strategically important because they are the gateway to the center and western parts of Nicaragua from the Caribbean, a location made especially significant by the existing links between Cuba and Nicaragua.

Rama—Indian tribe related to the Sumo and,

to a lesser degree, the Miskito. All these tribes originated with the Macro-Chibcha family of Colombia. The Rama inhabit jungle zones of Nicaragua's Atlantic region. Unlike the Miskitos, the Ramas have not accepted commingling with other ethnic groups, whether white, black, or mestizo. The Ramas today number only about 1200 persons.

Sumo—Indian people that inhabit Nicaragua's Atlantic zone. Like the Miskitos and Ramas, the Sumos have their origins in South America. In Nicaragua, they established themselves along the course of rivers where their economic activities are fishing, hunting, and agriculture. Some of them used to work in the mining industry of the region. Presently the Sumos number some 25,000 persons. Some have suffered persecution by the FSLN government.

TP: Tendencia Proletaria (Proletarian Tendency)—One of three factions that became the FSLN in 1979. The insignificant progress of the FSLN during its adherence to the "Prolonged Popular War" strategy forced some members of the FSLN to reflect on alternative strategies. Thus in 1975 Jaime Wheelock, followed by a small sector of the FSLN, proclaimed that a long period of ideological indoctrination and political organization among the Nicaraguan proletariat would necessarily precede any direct action against the dictatorial regime. Wheelock was expelled from the FSLN for this unorthodox approach and was termed a coward and a traitor for advocating what became known as the "Proletarian Tendency." This tendency had the fewest followers among the three FSLN tendencies but it did some useful work for the FSLN among certain "barrios" or sectors of Managua, León, and other towns. At the time of reunification of all FSLN tendencies in March 1979, the three leaders of the "Proletarian Tendency" were Jaime Wheelock, Luís Carrión, and Carlos Núñez.

TT: Tendencia Tercerista (Third Way Tendency)—After following the "Prolonged Popular War" strategy for many years

with very little progress, the FSLN fell subject to severe internal tensions. Somocismo was crumbling faster than the FSLN was growing, making it unlikely that the FSLN would be a force of importance at the moment of Somoza's downfall. After the "Proletarios" (adherents of the "proletarian tendency") had broken away from the FSLN in 1975, another sector of the FSLN proposed a strategy of tactical alliances with the bourgeosie and the commencement of urban activities aimed at provoking, in the short to medium term, a popular insurrection against Somoza that would give the FSLN the chance to become the small vanguard organization of a widespread national revolution. While recognizing the correctness of the "Prolonged Popular War" strategy, of which they considered themselves followers, the "Terceristas" argued that the political conditions then prevailing in Nicaragua forced a new tactical approach. Attacked as revisionists by those adhering to the "Prolonged Popular War" and "Proletarian Tendencies" of the FSLN, the "Terceristas" nevertheless proved to be correct. By March 1979 all three FSLN tendencies had reunited, backing the "Tercerista" strategy but still keeping some internal differences influenced by personal outlooks and ambitions. It seems that Fidel Castro was a very important factor in the FSLN's reunification. The "Tercerista" leaders are Daniel Ortega, Humberto Ortega, and Víctor Tirado.

UDN-FARN: Unión Democrática Nicaragüense-Fuerzas Armadas Revolucionarias de Nicaragua. (Democratic Nicaraguan Union-Nicaraguan Armed Revolutionary Forces)—Born in 1960, FARN has had a long record of anti-Somoza military and political activities, including the takeover of the towns of Jinotepe and Diriamba in November 1960 and an attack against the headquarters of Somoza's elite troops in Managua in August 1978, which was wrongly attributed to the FSLN. Led by Fernando Chamorro, FARN adopted an anti-Sandinista stance almost immediately after the ouster of Somoza. The UDN was founded in Honduras in October 1980 as an anti-FSLN group which shortly afterwards established an alliance under FARN direction. Initially UDN−FARN was associated with groups from "the North," but in 1982, UDN−FARN made an alliance with ARDE. After it separated from ARDE, it became associated with the FDN in 1983. It finally retreated from that association and joined UNO with the political backing of MDN, headed by Alfonso Robelo, a member of the UNO Directorate and former member of the first National Board of the revolutionary government of Nicaragua (1979−1980). UDN was ultimately absorbed by FARN. Today, officially known as UNO−FARN, this organization operates in Southern Nicaragua.

UNO: Unión Nacional Opositora (National Opposition Unity)—Instituted in 1985, UNO is composed of the FDN led by Adolfo Calero, the MDN (and their associated organizations led by Alfonso Robelo), and by Arturo Cruz's new group *AD, Acción Democrática* (Democratic Action). Arturo Cruz and Alfonso Robelo were both members of the revolutionary National Board for the Reconstruction of Nicaragua. Cruz's group and the MDN are considered to be of social-democratic orientation. UNO represents an attempt to integrate forces from "the South" and "the North." However, there have been internal tensions, with Robelo and Cruz usually siding together against the more conservative FDN, which still has some former Somocistas in its ranks. UNO's directorate is formed by Robelo, Cruz, and Calero. UNO professes to have around 15,000 men under arms.

Wiwillí—Small Nicaraguan town located near the border between the Nueva Segovia and Jinotega departments. In the early 1930s, the famous guerrilla leader Augusto César Sandino gathered hundreds of his followers in Wiwillí. After his assassination on February 22, 1934, the National Guard attacked Wiwillí, killing most of its Sandinista militants. Today Wilwillí is a war zone between the FSLN army and the Nicaraguan rebels.

Index

429

Publications of the
Institute for Soviet and East European Studies
of the Graduate School of International Studies,
University of Miami, Coral Gables, Florida

Books

Jiri Valenta and William Potter (Eds.), *Soviet Decisionmaking for National Security* (London: Allen and Unwin, 1984). Sponsored in conjunction with the Center for Strategic and International Studies, University of California, Los Angeles.

Jiri Valenta and Herbert Ellison (Eds.), *Grenada and Soviet/Cuban Policy: Internal Crisis and U.S./OECS Intervention* (Boulder, Co: Westview Press, 1986). Sponsored in conjunction with the Kennan Institute for Advanced Russian Studies.

ISEES Occasional Papers Series

No. 1 (January 1985)—F. Stephen Larrabee, Peter Hardi, Zoran Zic, and Jiri Valenta, *The Geneva Summit: Implications for East—West Relations* (in conjunction with the Institute of East—West Security Studies).

No. 2 (March 1986)—Richard Pipes, Jerry Hough and Jiri Valenta (moderator), *Gorbachev's Party Congress: How Significant for the United States?*

No. 3 (April 1986)—Norman Podhoretz, William Maynes and Jiri Valenta (moderator), *Terrorism: Reagan's Response.*

No. 4 (September 1986)—*Conflict in Nicaragua: National, Regional and International Dimensions* (conference report published in conjuction with the Royal Institute of International Affairs, London, featuring Admiral Sir James Eberle, Ambassador Ambler H. Moss, Arturo Cruz, Jr., Alfredo Cesar, Ambassador Harry Shlaudeman, Ray Burghardt, Francisco Lopez, and many others.

No. 5 (January, 1987)—Zbigniew Brzezinski, *U.S./Soviet Rivalry: Game Plan.*

No. 6 (February, 1987)—Congressman Dante Fascell, *How to Deal with the Soviet Union.*